CONSUMER GUIDE

1975 Consumer Buying Guide

CONTENTS

GUIDE TO FIGHTING INFLATION:
Hints for Saving Money as Prices Soar 6
AUTOS 1975 10
  Auto Best Buys 21
  How to Buy an Auto 24
  Auto Prices 26
HI-FI COMPONENTS 1975 108
  Hi-Fi Components Best Buys 116
TAPE RECORDERS 1975 120
  Tape Recorders Best Buys 127
  Hi-Fi Components and Tape Recorders Prices 130
TELEVISIONS 1975 158
  Televisions Best Buys 165
  Televisions Prices 168
RADIOS 1975 180
  Radios Best Buys 185
  Radios Prices 188
PERSONAL CARE APPLIANCES 1975 195
  Personal Care Appliances Best Buys 204
  Personal Care Appliances Prices 208
TRASH COMPACTORS 1975 217
FOOD PREPARATION APPLIANCES 1975 218
  Food Preparation Appliances Best Buys 233
  Food Preparation Appliances Prices 240
FLOOR CARE APPLIANCES 1975 255
  Floor Care Appliances Best Buys 259
  Floor Care Appliances Prices 264
WASHERS/DRYERS 1975 268
  Washers/Dryers Best Buys 277
  Washers/Dryers Prices 280
DISHWASHERS 1975 286
  Dishwashers Best Buys 292
  Dishwashers Prices 294
REFRIGERATORS 1975 296
  Refrigerators Best Buys 303
  Refrigerators Prices 306
FREEZERS 1975 310
  Freezers Best Buys 314
  Freezers Prices 316

CONTENTS

AIR CONDITIONERS 1975 318
  Air Conditioners Best Buys 322
RANGES 1975 325
  Ranges Best Buys 331
MICROWAVE OVENS 1975 333
  Microwave Ovens Best Buys 338
CALCULATORS 1975 340
  Calculators Best Buys 343
GARBAGE DISPOSERS 1975 344
  Garbage Disposers Best Buys 345
PHOTO EQUIPMENT 1975 346
  Photo Equipment Best Buys 354
  Photo Equipment Prices 362
INDEX 382

STAFF

LAWRENCE TEEMAN
Editor & Publisher

LOUIS WEBER
President

STAFF: Assistant to President: Estelle Weber; Managing Editor: Susan Berger Green; Assistant to Publisher: Marilee J. Wood; Editors: Stuart Grossgold, Jerold Kellman; Assistant Editors: Kay Conlon, Stephen G. Irmo, Helen Parker; Editorial Assistants: Linda Bishop, Leslee Fivelson, Marian Mirsky; Art Director: Frank E. Peiler; Art Assistant: Geraldine Rush; Graphic Design: Gregory Thornton; Production Consultant: Jack Lynn; Circulation Director: Ira Briskman; Business Manager: Jack Lowell; Public Information Director: Steven Feinberg

EDITORIAL & SUBSCRIPTION OFFICES: 3323 W. Main St., Skokie, Illinois 60076. All rights reserved under International and Pan-American copyright conventions. Copyright©1975 Publications International, Ltd. This book may not be reproduced or quoted in whole or in part by mimeograph or any other means or for presentation on radio or television without written permission from Louis Weber, President of Publications International, Ltd. Permission is never granted for commercial purposes.

Printed in U.S.A. CONSUMER GUIDE Magazine 1975 Consumer Buying Guide. Compiled by the editors of CONSUMER GUIDE Magazine and published in this edition by New American Library, New York, N.Y.

Cover Picture Credit: Automobile, Dodge Charger

INTRODUCTION

Guide to Fighting Inflation

Hints for Saving Money as Prices Soar

THE WORDS on everyones lips today are "inflation" "recession" "the state of the economy." With the concern for our country's current economic woes comes concern for how we spend our hard-earned dollars. There is more emphasis than ever before on spending wisely and getting value for money spent.

President Ford recently suggested that what we need now are more good old-fashioned Yankee traders, people able to drive a hard bargain and get the most for their money. Sylvia Porter, head of the nonpartisan Citizen's Action Committee to Fight Inflation, suggested buying, "when possible, only those products and services priced at or below present levels."

CONSUMER GUIDE Magazine's *1975 Best Buys & Discount Prices* is designed to help you fight inflation. The products listed here combine reliable performance, good design, and fair price to make these the best values available. CONSUMER GUIDE Magazine works with experts in each product field who test or examine each item to see that it does what it should do efficiently and economically. But because our experts cannot possibly test all of the thousands of products that are available, we also give you the tools for examining and choosing products on your own. We tell you what to look for in a quality product and what to be wary of. We suggest what personal considerations you should keep in mind when shopping. Many large stores sell appliances under their own private labels. Often these appliances are made by major manufacturers for the stores. It is sometimes possible to buy an

INTRODUCTION

appliance with a private label at a considerably lower price than if you bought a similar one sold under the manufacturer's name. With the shopping suggestions CONSUMER GUIDE Magazine gives you, you can examine a particular private-label appliance intelligently and determine if it is a quality machine at a bargain price or not.

In addition to the buying guidelines, we also list the low price available on each product. This is your special tool to help you be an old-fashioned Yankee trader. Unfortunately, prices are changing rapidly these days—and the change is mostly up. So you may be able to use these prices only as a guide, not as a hard-and-fast rule.

Although buying the best product for the best price is an important part of fighting inflation, there are other things you can do to make yourself a wise shopper.

Throughout this guide we stress the fact that you should not buy a product that you do not need. If your present appliance is serviceable, keep it, repair it if necessary, but do not buy a new one. If you discard a serviceable appliance just because a new one has more attractive features, you will be paying a lot of money for those features. Not only will you be paying the price for the new item, but you will be losing the cost of the serviceable time left in the old item. Some appliance dealers claim to deduct a trade-in value off your old appliance when you buy a new one. Do not believe it. If you shop around, you will find another store that will meet the first one's price—without figuring in a trade-in. The truth is: Appliances have little or no trade-in value, certainly not enough to make it worthwhile to trade in a serviceable unit.

Buying an Automobile or Appliance

OF COURSE, that is not true of automobiles. They do have a trade-in value. When shopping for a car, do not tell the salesperson that you have a car to trade in. Strike the best deal you can on the new car, then mention your trade-in. A common practice of auto salespeople is to shuffle the cost of the new car and the value of the trade-in to make it appear as if they are offering you a great low price on the new car and a generously high trade-in value. By keeping the fact that you have a trade-in secret, you can get a truer picture of what you are really spending. Auto dealers normally offer a trade-in allowance equal to the wholesale value of your old car. You can usually get more for you old car if you sell it yourself to a private individual.

Once you have determined that you need a particular appliance or want it enough to be willing to buy it, check carefully the features you are buying. Usually the difference between a low-priced unit and a high-priced unit is the number of features it offers. Basically both units work just as well. For example, a 17-foot frost-free refrigerator sells for $371.85. The exact same refrigerator with an automatic icemaker costs $417.75. The icemaker feature costs $45.90. So if you do not have a real need for the extra feature, if you do not think you will get enough use out of it to justify its cost, then do not buy that feature. Buy the basic unit that does a basic, good job.

INTRODUCTION

Another consideration when you are purchasing an appliance or car is its efficiency. The cost of an item does not end with its purchase. After that, comes the constant cost of running the item. With an automobile that cost is reflected in the cost of fuel not to mention the cost of insurance and maintenance, all of which increases with the size of the car. With an electrical appliance it is the cost of electricity. When buying a car, check the miles-per-gallon ratings. Remember a car that gets only 10 miles to a gallon is going to cost you twice as much fuel to run as a car that gets 20 miles to the gallon. And in light of the cost of gasoline today, that is a serious consideration. On an appliance, check the wattage necessary to run the unit. If two models are almost alike except one uses less wattage, buy that one; it will be less expensive to operate. Air conditioners list their energy efficiency ratio (EER), so when buying a room air conditioner it is easy to choose one that gives the most power for the least amount of energy spent. Similar labeling will soon be appearing on refrigerators and freezers. Also check the amount of energy a specific extra feature will use. The self-defrosting feature on a freezer, for example, uses an inordinate amount of energy. This feature may make defrosting an easy chore, but it will be an expensive chore. Before you buy an energy-consuming feature, ask yourself if you are willing to pay the extra money the feature will cost in the purchase price as well as the extra money it will cost to use it.

Shop Wisely

ANOTHER WAY to buy wisely and fight inflation is to pay cash. Most store charge accounts and all bank charge accounts charge 1½ percent interest per month on unpaid balances. Over a year's time this comes to 18 percent interest. If you buy an appliance using either of these credit means, you will be adding substantially to the cost of the item. Banks will issue small loans, and their interest rates are more favorable than the "handy" charge card. At the moment, the effective annual interest on a small loan is approximately 12½ percent. This means that borrowing from a bank is more economical than using a store's charge account or using your bank charge card, but it still is an expensive way to buy.

The wisest way to buy is to pay cash and to save the interest charges. If you know in advance that you want a certain item (the washing machine is getting old and will probably have to be replaced in a year, or this is the year that you are going to treat the family to a dishwasher), save for it. Pretend you are paying those monthly installments you would have to make to a store or bank if you bought it now, and put the money in the bank. When you have saved enough money, withdraw it and pay for the item with cash. You will not only have saved yourself the interest you would have had to pay if you had borrowed the money or bought on credit, but you will have earned money—the interest paid by the bank on the money you saved. Even if the washing machine breaks down before you thought it would and you have to buy a new machine

INTRODUCTION

earlier than planned, you will already have saved some of the money towards the purchase and, therefore, will have to borrow less.

But sometimes you cannot plan your expenditures so nicely. All too often the unexpected happens and you are forced to buy an appliance that you have not saved for. If the money is not already available in your savings account, you will have to borrow. You will probably also have to borrow if you plan to purchase an automobile. Few people can afford to buy a car with cash out of pocket. The important thing to do in these cases is to shop for credit. Determine how much money you must borrow and how long you intend to take to pay it back. For an appliance, you will probably pay back the loan in less than a year.

An auto loan may take you two or three years to pay back. Shop for the loan at several banks, as well as at the store or dealership where you are buying the item. Do not only ask how much interest you will be charged; this can sound deceptively low (like 1½ percent per month). Ask specifically how much, in dollars and cents, it will cost you to borrow the given amount of money for the determined period of time. Because of Federal truth-in-lending legislation, all lenders must give you this information. Then borrow the money from the one who will be charging you the least. Another place to shop for a low-cost loan is your insurance company. If you have a life insurance policy, you may be able to borrow against it. The effective interest rate on such loan is usually lower than the rate charged by banks.

If the law of supply and demand holds up, this should be the year of the consumer. As prices have skyrocketed, people have started limiting their purchases. As the demand for products decreases, the prices should decrease also. You can help bring about this decrease by buying only what you need or really want and have use for and by using CONSUMER GUIDE Magazine's *1975 Best Buys and Discount Prices* to help you be a wise, bargain-conscious shopper.

AUTOMOBILES

FOR THE AUTOMOBILE buyer in 1975, there is a lesson to be learned from the drastic shift from large, to mini, and back to not-too-small cars during the 1974 model year. Many small-car buyers last year realized that mini-autos may well be the vehicles of the future, but more often than not, those who traded down found the shock of plunging from a full-size model to a subcompact a little traumatic. They discovered that no matter how well-designed, a subcompact did not handle, ride, or offer comfort like a standard size machine. By the end of 1974, and the easing of the gas shortage, many Americans began looking enviously back to the full-size automobiles.

The big question for 1975, therefore, seems to be what will happen to the small car? The answer has come loud and clear from Detroit. Automakers have geared up 1975 production to churn out greater quantities of smaller economy models. In fact, several new models have been introduced—the Ford Granada, Mercury Monarch, Chevrolet Monza, Oldsmobile Starfire, and Buick Skyhawk. Eventually, the carmakers predict, a slower economy may force Americans into total small car immersion, but for the next few years, the compact and smaller intermediate size will probably be the compromise decision for many buyers.

In the final analysis, only the buyer can decide if 1975 is the year to trade down, or go on as if nothing had happened to the economy and buy a big car. It depends on where you are sitting, and how large a wallet you are sitting on. The decision must be based on how the buyer evaluates the 1975 models, for it is a year of dramatic change that

AUTOMOBILES

promises definite advantages and disadvantages over 1974 offerings.

In the wake of dramatically lower car sales, plant shutdowns, assembly line layoffs, and a shaky economy, car buyers in 1975 should ask themselves not which size car to buy, but if they should purchase a new car at all. There has been a colossal jump in new car prices, with many standard-size models upped in price as much as $1000 and subcompacts soaring $500 to $700 more than comparable 1974 machines. This has been accomplished both with hardly-noticeable markups (Chrysler, for example, has posted nine small price increases) while General Motors and Ford have increased their cars a whopping eight and nine percent at a crack. Imported cars, which lost their price advantage with a shift in Federal regulations and monetary revaluations, will also have equally outlandish price jumps on their 1975 line.

The price increases, in combination with warnings of even more to come, has resulted in a consumer buying cutback early in the 1975 model year, and new car sales fell better than 20 per cent behind the 1974 sales levels, which also were depressed. It is unfortunate because 1975 automobiles have a lot to offer the consumer.

Catalytic Converters

THE MOST controversial new item on the automotive scene for 1975 is the catalytic converter, the muffler-like device that brought platinum and palladium out of the jewelry stores and into the car's belly in order to lower exhaust pollutants both from our highways and our lungs. Although adding roughly $150 to $300 to the price tag of the car, the converter allowed Detroit engineers to retune engines back to some semblance of pre-emission days because now the converter, not the engine, has the task of cleaning up the exhaust fumes. Another benefit to the consumer is better starts in all types of weather.

But catalytic converters also have some problems connected with them. Because lead in gasoline ruins the effectiveness of the converters, the 1975 model cars sold in the United States, which are equipped with these devices, must be operated exclusively on lead-free gas. After two or three tanks of leaded gas, the converter will not operate. This will not affect the car's performance, but it will eliminate the much-needed emission controls. In short, you must use unleaded gas.

Unleaded gas, in turn, has two strikes against it—availability and higher prices. Surveys indicate that there should be a sufficient supply of unleaded gas in the cities, but if you live in a less populated area, you might have some difficulty getting enough for your car. In addition, unleaded gas costs more than regular. Although the government requires that it not be sold at prices above premium, the rules on the books do not always show up on the pumps, and unleaded gas has been found selling anywhere from one cent to ten cents above the cost of regular fuel.

Catalytic converters have been put on a vast majority of the new 1975's, but certain small engines and some V8's can meet the emission standards set forth by the Environmental Protection Agency without the

AUTOMOBILES

expensive device. Consequently, some auto companies (Ford, Chrysler and AMC) are leaving them off. General Motors, however, has all its 1975 models fitted with converters. Unfortunately, there is no price advantage to buying a car without the converter. The automakers, for the most part, are averaging out the cost of the converter and assigning equal costs to all cars, so you will pay the same whether the converter is installed or not.

Other 1975 Factors

ELECTRONIC IGNITIONS, pioneered by Chrysler in 1972, continue to spread throughout the auto industry, and nearly all cars from the four major American companies will have them. This means faster, surer starts and less maintenance for almost every 1975 machine. Essentially, the system eliminates contact parts, such as breaker points entirely, replacing them with friction-free electronics. The electronic ignition is virtually maintenance-free, which means tune-ups are simpler and cheaper, whether you do them yourself or have them done at a service station. Because of surer starts, spark plugs do not foul as quickly, less fuel is consumed in the startup process, so better fuel economy results.

Also promising for 1975 is the extended usage of steel belted radial ply tires which provide greater traction, surer stops; and because of less resistance to the road, better fuel economy. The longer wear and fuel economy gains mean more dollars in the consumer's pocket, instead of in the hands of the neighborhood tire and gasoline retailers.

A new carburetor which adjusts automatically to changes in altitude and temperature for improved air to fuel ratio, and thus better performance under all conditions and subsequently better fuel economy, has been included on new General Motors' models for 1975. And throughout the industry, axle ratios were lowered, and smaller, more economical engines replaced the bigger gas-guzzling ones. Models associated with performance, but not economy, were dropped. Among these were AMC's Javelin, the Dodge Challenger, and Plymouth's Barracuda.

But perhaps the most controversial item of all met its death early in the 1975 model year when the government decided to abolish the seat belt interlock and buzzer system designed to force motorists to buckle up their belts before starting the car. All that is left now is a warning light to remind motorists to fasten the belts. Unfortunately, while the interlock and buzzer passed away, there was no subsequent reduction in the price of the car, so the consumer may have saved himself some aggravation, but no money.

Not only are a host of engineering improvements in store for consumers in 1975, so are a host of new cars, vehicles that are supposed to portend the wave of the future, small in size but with all the comforts of today's big models. And they are to be economical, too. As mentioned, the Ford Granada and Mercury Monarch promote the luxury image in compacts; the Chevrolet Monza, Olds Starfire, and Buick Skyhawk put

AUTOMOBILES

new sportiness in the subcompact market; the Chrysler Cordoba and Dodge Charger Special Edition add a new mark of distinction to the personal and intermediate luxury category.

Even more new models are in the works for mid-1975, such as the Mercury Bobcat, a Pinto with luxury trim; the AMC Pacer, an all-new subcompact luxury car; the Capri II from Lincoln-Mercury, first styling overhaul for the successful sexy European; and the Rabbit and Scirocco from Volkswagen, the former Beetle-sized and the much-talked of successor to the Bug, the latter the replacement for the Karmann Ghia. Both claim fuel economy in the 30-miles-per-gallon range.

Mini-Compacts for '75

THE MINI-COMPACTS, which appeared most attractive during the fuel shortage, are now battling for existence again. The problem, of course, is price. Less than five years ago, you could buy any one of the mini-compacts for less than $2000. Today, the prices have shot up to $3000 or more. But the prices of bigger cars have gone up just as quickly and their increases have been even larger. Nonetheless, the American shopper is conditioned to getting a standard model in the $3000 to $4000 range, and this has made it quite disappointing when all that is available at that price is a car that is almost one-third the size.

Where the mini-compacts have the edge is in fuel economy. Fuel economy throughout the mini-compact class is outstanding, as indicated by the Environmental Protection Agency reports, and CONSUMER GUIDE Magazine road tests. Each of the small models in this class will deliver 25 mpg in most driving situations, and get far above 30 mpg when cruising on the highways.

The Datsun B210 again topped the EPA list as the most economical in terms of fuel economy, with a rating of 27 mpg in city driving and 39 mpg on the highway. The Fiat 128 offers a choice of performance and efficiency in a small car, but the car demands frequent attention to keep it in top running condition. In the past, Fiat has had some service problems, but this has been corrected with a new marketing plan which includes the building of a solid base of dealerships to handle the additional servicing.

The Toyota Corolla is one of the lowest priced cars sold in the United States, carrying a sticker price lower than either the Gremlin or Vega. Both General Motors and Ford are working on mini-compacts, and this should give a shot of credibility to the market. Ford's small car will first be built in Spain. The new small car from GM could be out sooner than Ford's. Its design is based on an existing car, the Brazilian Chevette. With a tiny OHC 4-cylinder engine, similar in size and power to the Fiat, it is now being built in Brazil.

In light of the shaky economy, there is still a big need for the mini-compact models which offer high fuel economy. Car prices are zooming, fuel costs are rising, and the prospect of fuel rationing makes the small car an inevitable choice for many new car buyers, even in face of their many shortcomings.

AUTOMOBILES

Subcompacts

DURING THE 1974 FUEL shortage, the subcompacts, both new and used, commanded top dollar. That situation has reversed itself, and you can expect some discounting on the 1975 models, while used car values have fallen off. Fuel economy, as can be expected, is good in this classification, with the Chevrolet Vega topping the list of American-made subcompacts. A Vega, with 140 cubic-inch engine, scored 22 miles-per-gallon in city driving, and 29 mpg on the highways during the EPA tests. Pontiac's new Astre (as-tra), a Vega with a Pontiac grille and Pontiac price tag, ranked right under the Vega. The Ford Pinto brought up the rear in fuel economy with 18 mpg and 26 mpg for city and highway driving respectively.

Among the foreign subcompacts, the Datsun 710 and VW Beetle rated higher than the Vega in the EPA test, while the Toyota Corona scored better than the Pinto at 19 mpg and 28 mpg. The Opel and Fiat 124 were not tested during the last EPA survey.

Domestic subcompacts for 1975 continue to go with 2-door models, while the imports offer some 4-doors which provide more ease of entry and exit. While the small cars, both U.S. models and those made overseas, were originally billed as economy cars (with low price tags), the consumer demanded, and got, a host of luxury options put on the 1975 offerings. The options make the trip more pleasant, but they also raise the price considerably. Subcompacts of just a few years ago were advertised as under $2000. Inflation, currency revaluations, etc., now mean that in 1975 you will be hard pressed to find one under $3000—and these are only a handful at best.

The subcompact class will be further expanded in the spring of 1975 when Mercury will spring its Bobcat into the market. This is an offshoot of the Pinto which will be offered in sedan, 3-door Runabout, and wagon versions. Chrysler is still relying on Japan for its subcompact, the Colt.

Compacts for '75

THE COMPACT cars, born to combat the invasion of imports into the U.S. market back in the beginning of 1960, have been the domain of American manufacturers. It is one model classification that Detroit builds best, and over the years it has become much larger, more luxurious, and more powerful. The 1975 models are perhaps the most luxurious of all, with restyled offerings from General Motors—the Chevrolet Nova, Oldsmobile Omega, Pontiac Ventura, and Buick Apollo; the plain-Jane Maverick and Comet from Ford, along with the dressed-up luxury cars that were supposed to replace them, but now complement them, the Granada and Mercury Monarch; the Hornet from AMC; the Dodge Dart and Plymouth Valiant from Chrysler; and the Mazda from Toyo Kogyo in Japan.

One good thing that has happened in the compact class for 1975 is the all-new Ford Granada. It has the most frugal design that has come out of Detroit since the introduction of the Plymouth Valiant eight years

AUTOMOBILES

ago. The Granada is tailored on the European concept of thrift. Instead of wasting space and weight on a long hood, rakish roofline, and puffed sides in the American tradition of opulent styling, the Granada places the space where it is needed, in the interior.

Although compacts were synonymous with economy in the past, the appeal is somewhat different today, and the Granada and Monarch point the way with luxury appointments in a compact car. In the much smaller compact, the consumers are now getting what they previously wanted in full-size models. Prices, however, are not so small and $5000 or more price stickers are found on the compacts for 1975, even though they have just a few of the more common options. Like the bigger cars, you will also find steel belted radials, electronic ignitions, et al, on the compacts—features which provide some returns for the added costs.

For the most part, fuel economy has been improved considerably in the compact division over the 1974 figures. For example, a 1975 Hornet with 232 cubic-inch engine (which leads the compact class) scored 18 mpg in city driving EPA tests (24 mpg on the road), while a comparable model was rated only at 14.7 mpg in city driving in 1974. The lowest rated compact in 1974, the Comet, however, remained about the same at 16 mpg in city driving tests. A new Monarch and Granada with 250 cubic-inch powerplants, scored even less than the Comet with 15 mpg and 20 mpg in city and highway driving tests respectively.

Sporty Compacts for '75

IN THE sporty compact category, it is not what is offered for 1975, but what is left. The Plymouth Barracuda and Dodge Challenger have gone the way of the Chevrolet Corvair and Edsel, along with the Javelin AMX. This leaves the field to the Chevrolet Camaro and Pontiac Firebird. Mustang, the originator of the genre, is now considered in the subcompact sporty car division and as such is not competitive to the Camaro and Firebird.

The muscle car image has gone flat, and the crunch of the fuel crisis has helped the gradual demise of this car category. In an effort to salvage some sales, however, Chevrolet and Pontiac are promoting good looks and economy of operation in the Camaro and Firebird offerings for 1975, rather than speed off the line. Understandably, these are hardly family cars, and with the General Motors sports subcompacts borrowing much of the styling from the Camaro/Firebird, there is the annual speculation as to their longevity. Sporty cars do well when consumers are optimistic—and this is not the case in 1975.

One saving factor is the improved fuel economy of the 1975 Camaro and Firebird. In the 1975 EPA test, they ranked along with the compact cars. Equipped with 250 cubic-inch engines, they both recorded 16 mpg in city test and 21 mpg on the highway. In CONSUMER GUIDE Magazine's fuel economy tests in 1974, a Camaro with 350 cubic-inch power-plant was rated at 13.5 mpg, while the 1974 Firebird with 400 cubic inch engine tested out at 11 mpg.

AUTOMOBILES

Intermediates for '75

ARE THE intermediates of 1975 the full-size cars of tomorrow? This could well be the case. Detroit is determined to cut down on the size of the bigger cars, and it seems to be just a matter of time before the present intermediates become the full-size sedans and coupes of the late 1970's. The intermediate group is where consumers have to turn when they need room to carry five or six passengers, when they need adequate comfort and weight for long distance traveling, when they do not want to be loaded down with all the cosmetic luxuries of bigger cars, when they want some of the economy of the subcompacts and compacts combined with the room and safety of a larger car, and when they want a lower purchase price.

There is really nothing new in the intermediate lineup for 1975. Chrysler is claiming that the all-new Cordoba and revised Dodge Charger Special Edition fall into the intermediate classification, but in reality, they compete with the Monte Carlo and Grand Prix, which are classified in the personal luxury group. Chrysler, however, has restyled its regular intermediate line, the Dodge Coronet and Plymouth Fury (Satellite in 1974). General Motors' lineup includes the Chevrolet Chevelle, Pontiac LeMans, Oldsmobile Cutlass and Buick Century; Ford is offering the Torino and luxury Elite; and American Motors lists the Matador 2- and 4-door models and wagon. AMC is banking so much on big cars getting smaller that the Matador is the largest car it is rolling off its assembly lines in 1975.

As all automakers trim weight off of their big car line to save raw materials and boost fuel economy, the intermediates look even more promising for the future. As expected, the intermediates show some improvement in the 1975 EPA fuel economy test. All models, with the exception of the Ford Torino, showed an improvement over 1974 figures. The Chevelle and LeMans lead the fuel economy pack in 1975. With 250 cubic-inch engines, they recorded 16 mpg in city tests and 21 mpg on the highways. The Torino, symptomatic of the fuel economy disaster throughout the Ford line in 1975, brought up the rear in the intermediate class with only 11 mpg and 16 mpg in city and highway tests respectively.

Standards for '75

THE AUTOMOBILES classified as standards for 1975 are a far cry from the traditional "low-priced three" of the Thirties and Forties. Today, they are big cars, no longer low priced, although they still carry the same names—Ford, Plymouth, and Chevrolet. The AMC Ambassador, which was included in this group for the past few years, has been dropped as American Motors concentrates all its efforts in the small car field. The Ambassador name will not be lost, however. AMC plans to switch the name to the 4-door intermediate line it produces in 1975.

The rising cost and shortage of materials; fears over a renewed fuel crisis, and the realization that gas prices probably will go even higher,

AUTOMOBILES

has done little to bolster the sagging standard car market. There was some recovery after the Arab oil embargo was lifted and people once again sought the comfort and room of the big cars, but as compacts and intermediates began offering comparable interior dimensions, the appeal of the standard started to ebb.

Detroit is still claiming that many people need a big car. It has found, however, based on current new-car sales, that some people may need a big car, but they are not demanding one. High initial costs and lowering trade-in values are starting to turn some people away from the standard. In 1974, the base Chevrolet Impala 8-cylinder 4-door sedan retailed at $3870. A comparable 1975 model carries a $4561 price tag.

The cars in the standard group — Chevrolet Impala and Caprice, Ford LTD, and Plymouth Gran Fury, are roomy and comfortable, but recent studies point out that the average passenger load in a car is 1½ people which applies 5000 pounds of material to move one person to the store and back. Based on this revelation, it would seem wasteful and expensive to have a standard car.

It is even more wasteful when you consider the fuel economy of the standard cars. Even though figures are up in the Chevrolet and Plymouth models in the 1975 EPA report, they are still nothing to brag about. A Chevrolet with 350 cubic-inch engine recorded only 12 mpg in city runs, and 18 on the highway. The Plymouth Gran Fury, with 318 cubic-inch powerplant, was rated at 12 mpg and 17 mpg. The Ford LTD, like most Ford products, was a complete bust in the EPA economy runs. It ranked fourth from the last in all the cars rated, with a calamitous 10 mpg score in city driving, and only 14 on the highways.

Medium Standards for '75

THE YEAR 1974 was one of the blackest in the history of the medium standard cars, and 1975 does not look any brighter. One factor against the models in this group—Buick, Oldsmobile, Pontiac, Chrysler, Dodge, and Mercury—is that buyer motivation in this class is rarely product-oriented, or even based on considerations of real value. Exterior styling and prestige seem to sway buyers. Cost is secondary, reputation of primary importance. Comfort and dependability are taken for granted. Lineups are being simplified in realization of what is ahead. The medium standards are loaded with luxury items, fancy trim, and other cosmetic features, causing purchase prices to run high. And as demand slackens, resale value has leveled off.

With high gas consumption, skyrocketing initial cost, the medium standards have taken the brunt of changing consumer preferences, even more so than the luxury cars or the lower-priced standards. The reasons are easy to grasp. Luxury cars always have the attraction of prestige, the buyers of these models are more interested in the impression they make, than the tangible value offered. The low-price standards, on the other hand, are simply lower priced, and the buyer does not lose much in the way of comfort and performance.

Today, the medium standards provide little more in fuel economy

AUTOMOBILES

than the luxury cars, so the inclination to step down from a Cadillac or Lincoln to save gas is not a motivating force for buyers. The Buick LeSabre headed the list in the 1975 EPA test, with a 12 mpg rating in city driving and 15 mpg on the road. Bringing up the rear, as usual, was a Ford product—the Mercury with 10 mpg and 14 mpg respectively.

Personal Luxury Models for '75

TYPIFIED by such elegant, higher-priced cars as the Buick Riviera, Oldsmobile Toronado, Cadillac Eldorado, Ford Thunderbird, Continental Mark IV, Pontiac Grand Prix, and Chevrolet Monte Carlo, the personal luxury cars for 1975 should continue with their percentage of the industry sales. Sales, for the most part, are going well, and the 5.7 share of the total auto market which personal luxury cars enjoyed in 1974 should hold up in 1975.

There is, however, a little confusion as to what now justifies a personal luxury car classification. Nearly all automakers have intermediate offerings filled with all the luxury items that the more expensive models contain. The Ford Elite (Torino) and Mercury Cougar give the Thunderbird a run for its money while the Olds Cutlass, Buick Regal, and Pontiac Grand Am come extremely close to the Grand Prix and Monte Carlo concept, and for far less money. The Riviera, Toronado, and Eldorado are built on full-size frames, but all the rest of the personal luxury models have intermediate frames.

What could hurt the personal luxury sales in 1975 is the fact that the same elegance is now being found in compacts and even subcompacts; for example, the Mustang II Ghia, Granada/Monarch, and Nova LN.

Included in the personal luxury group for 1975 is Chrysler's all-new Cordoba. It offers appealing styling, more than ample room (except for the trunk which is dominated by the spare tire), and adequate fuel economy. In the 1975 EPA fuel economy tests, a Cordoba with 360 cubic-inch V8, recorded 13 mpg in the city and 22 mpg on the highway. This is slightly better than the Monte Carlo's 13 mpg and 18 mpg rating and much superior to the Mark IV's low score of 10 mpg and 15 mpg. Due to the use of large-displacement, high-powered engines, however, the personal luxury cars are not noted for significant fuel economy. People who buy them, in any case, are more interested in good looks, better-than-average performance, and prestige.

Luxury Models for '75

THE BUYERS of luxury cars have always turned their backs on a bull market, soaring interest rates, double digit inflation, and just about any economic hardship that comes along. The question is not whether they could afford a Cadillac, Mercedes, Imperial, or Lincoln Continental, but rather how soon could they get their hands on one. The luxury cars flame the prestige image, indicating the man who has become a success in

AUTOMOBILES

life. The high cost of gas also is not a roadblock to the person who has worked years to get behind the wheel of his or her own Cadillac, Continental, et al.

The gas shortage of the winter of 1974 did cause some difficulty for the luxury car owners, who do not like to wait in line for anything, much less a tankful of gas. Reports were circulated during the height of the shortage that some of the luxury models were sold for the price of an Impala just to get them off the showroom floor. But those rumors were more fiction than fact. Their fuel economy, as you might suspect, is nothing to write home about, but it has been improved throughout the luxury class since 1974. A Cadillac, with 500 cubic-inch engine, for example, was rated at 8.9 mpg in the 1974 EPA tests. A comparable model hit 11 mpg in city driving and 16 mpg on the road in 1975.

Cadillac still holds a lion's share of the market, with Mercedes running number two. In this case, everyone is trying hard to emulate number two. Ford even advertises its Granada/Monarch as "Mercedes-like." Look at the grilles of most American cars in 1975, and you will instantly see a resemblance to the Mercedes. Ironically, Mercedes has been trying to do away with its grille design since 1950, and has totally abandoned it on its sports models.

Although readily copying exterior styling, the safety structure, pin-type door locks, and superior space utilization of the Mercedes has not as yet been instituted on any Detroit model. The upcoming Cadillac LaSalle hopefully will change that. Cadillac has already taken a step in the right direction—instead of being a Mercedes imitator, the LaSalle will look more like the Rolls Royce.

In the final analysis, the luxury models offer effortless performance, well-muffled sound, but high gas consumption. They truly can be considered a home away from home since the items you find optional in other cars, such as air conditioning, automatic transmission, radio, and clock are usually standard equipment. When the 1975 price increases were announced, the luxury cars were given hefty increases, but ones that the buyers will typically absorb.

Low Price Sports Cars for '75

PRIMARILY 2-door coupes with four seat capacities, built on wheelbases of 90 to 96.5 inches, the low price sports car group includes such marques as the Mercury Capri, Ford Mustang II, Audi Fox, Fiat 124 sports coupe, Toyota Celica, and Opel Manta Rallye. Newest entries for 1975 are the Chevrolet Monza 2+2, Olds Starfire, and Buick Skyhawk. Later in 1975, the Volkswagen Scirocco, a boxy successor to the Karmann Ghia, will be added, as will a hatchback version of the Monza.

The Mustang II took the public by storm in 1974, but 1975 should be the year of the Monza—at least in the low price sports car group. Not only is the Monza attractive looking, with rectangular headlamps highlighting the sleekness of the design, they also get creditable gas mileage. In the 1975 EPA tests, a Monza with 262 cubic-inch V8 re-

AUTOMOBILES

corded 15 mpg in city driving and 23 on the highway. A Ford Mustang II, with 140 (2.3L) engine, surprisingly recorded 18 mpg and 26 mpg.

Mustang II was supposed to be the car to counteract by one year the advent of the rotary engine in the Monza at General Motors. Now that the rotary engine in the Monza at General Motors has been scrapped at GM, Ford's move to offer the Mustang II both as a small sporty fastback and a little luxury notchback with a bit more roominess than the Monza seems to be a wise move. Rear seat room in the Monza fastback is nearly non-existent.

General Motors decided to share the Monza subcompact sporty car with Oldsmobile and Buick, both big car divisions stung by the fuel crisis. As a result, the styling of the Monza, Skyhawk, and Starfire is virtually the same, except for the grille work. Individuality will return in 1976 when designers have more time to put new touches on the original Monza. A styling gem and an economical car to boot, the Monza also has guts on the road. The base 4-cylinder engine on the Monza is under-powered, just like it was in the original Mustang II in 1974. Ford came up with a peppy V-8 for 1975, and Monza is offering one as an option as well. The Starfire and Skyhawk both offer V6's that are nearly as peppy as Monza V8.

There are two hardships buyers will have to face if they purchase any one of the low price GM sports cars. One is lack of room from the intruding powerplant housing extending from the fire wall to the rear cargo area. The same will happen with the AMC Pacer which is planned for distribution in the spring of 1975. The second hardship is a high price tag. Each of the low price (a misnomer at best) sports cars will carry a $4000 base price which could reach $5000 easily with the common options.

High Price Sports Cars for '75

POWER, speed, and good looks typify the high price sports models. Fuel economy is never a consideration in this car grouping although the Corvette recorded a creditable 13 mpg in city driving and 20 mpg in highway driving during the 1975 EPA tests. High prices, as well, hardly constitute a concern among the sports car buyers since the prices range anywhere from $5000 to $25,000 and up for a Ferrari or Maserati. What high price sports car enthusiasts look for, and get, in their choices are superior road holding, steering, braking, and esthetically pleasing styling that is also aerodynamically designed for better performance. The two-seat coupes or convertibles (roadsters) are low slung models with wide stances and low centers of gravity. Some of the more popular models are the Chevrolet Corvette, Porsche 911, and Datsun 260Z.

AUTOMOBILES

BEST BUYS

CONSUMER GUIDE Magazine's automotive experts have given the 1975 offerings from Detroit and abroad a critical going over. They were most concerned with safety, visibility, brakes, steering, handling ease, comfort, roominess, ease of entry and exit, instrumentation, and control location.

SUBCOMPACT

Chevrolet vega has continued to be upgraded while most of its competition has stood still. Many convenience features demanded in bigger models can be found in Vega; power steering, automatic transmission, low sound levels, factory air conditioning, extended maintenance intervals, smooth ride, and the look and feel of a finely finished automobile. Vega provides the money-saving value small car customers are demanding. The Pontiac Astre, identical to the Vega except for some standard equipment that is optional on the Chevy, has the same merits. Both the Vega and Astre rate high in fuel economy. The Vega lead the subcompact group in the 1975 EPA test, scoring 22 mpg in city driving and 29 mpg on the highway. It was the highest rated U.S. made auto.

COMPACT

Chevrolet Nova looks like an all-new car for '75, with new outer sheet metal that adds to the practicality, safety, and overall quality of the car. There is newfound quietness from standardization of radial ply tires and a new body mount system. The Nova is tops in roadholding and maneuverability since it now has the Camaro front suspension. It also has superior directional stability from installation of a torsion spring in the steering gear. Standard engine is Chevy's 250 cubic-inch six, which is a quiet, understressed engine with long life potential. For those who normally would buy a larger Chevy on the basis of luxury fittings, CONSUMER GUIDE Magazine recommends the Nova LN with its deluxe interior. Fuel consumption rating is better than most in its class. In EPA tests, a Nova with 250 cubic-inch engine recorded 16 mpg and 21 mpg in city and highway evaluations respectively. The AMC Hornet topped the compact list with 18 and 24 mpg.

INTERMEDIATE

Oldsmobile Cutlass is almost as big inside as the much larger Olds

AUTOMOBILES

Delta 88, so you can think of it as a big car. The Cutlass comes with Olds engines, an area where Olds seems to have assumed absolute leadership within General Motors ranks. The Olds V8's are more fuel economical than most of the other models in its class and have higher power output. An Olds Cutlass with 250 cubic-inch powerplant ranked first in its group in fuel mileage, as judged by the EPA. It was rated at 16 mpg in city driving and 21 mpg on the road, the same rating as the smaller Pontiac LeMans. The Olds Cutlass has special provisions for long life and heavy duty operations, such as valve rotators on both intake and exhaust valves. Olds also makes its own axles and final drive gear units and offers its own exclusive limited slip differential.

SPORTS CAR

Chevrolet Monza 2 plus 2 *could be sold on looks alone. Soft curvacious lines combine to give an overall appearance of sleekness. When put up against its chief competitor, the Mustang II, the Monza comes out the sportier looking. The optional 260 cubic-inch V8 gives it pep, but the base four-cylinder powerplant that is also found in the Vega cannot handle the load. The Monza scored much higher in the '75 EPA gas mileage runs than the Mustang II — 25 mpg in the city and 29 on the highway as opposed to the Mustang's 18 mpg and 26 mpg. Both, however, were beat by models from Volkswagen. High steering and handling precision with immediate response and slight initial understeer are easily noticeable.*

STANDARD

Plymouth *now calls its standard size car Gran Fury; its intermediate model had been designated simply Fury. The name may be only slightly different but the Gran Fury for 1975 is quieter and more solid feeling than before. The Gran Fury can boast of first rate seating comfort and top driver visibility from increased glass area. The motorist can readily notice the difference between a Plymouth and any other standard make. The Plymouth offers faster steering response and greater handling precision without overreacting to abrupt steering wheel inputs. Not as quiet on a good road as the Ford, it makes up for it with more comfort on bad surfaces. As a rule, Gran Fury usually undersells its competition on a model for model basis. In fuel ratings, the Plymouth Gran Fury scored only 12 mpg in city tests, the same as the Chevrolet Impala. But then, the Ford LTD only received a 10 mpg rating.*

UPPER STANDARD

Chrysler Newport *gets the nod as the "Best Buy" over all its competitors. The principal reasons are superior space utilization and fuel efficiency, engine driveability and response, maneuverability and steering precision. Add to this ride comfort, noise and vibration control, and trouble free life expectancy, and you have an exceptional machine.*

AUTOMOBILES

Engineering improvements initiated in the 1974 model year show no signs of trouble, such as a revised cooling system with wider radiators, addition of a coolant reserve tank, and 20-inch diameter flexible blade fan. Steel belted radials are standard, a self leveling rear suspension system for hauling trailers or boats is optional. Fuel economy is about average for the medium standard group — Chrysler recorded 11 mpg in EPA city driving tests and 18 mpg on the highways.

PERSONAL LUXURY

Chrysler Cordoba *was designed with Chevrolet Monte Carlo handling precision and ride comfort and Ford Thunderbird quietness and refinement in mind. The result, however, is strictly Chrysler using some familiar construction principles — unit body, torsion bar front suspension, etc. The Cordoba is a better balanced car than Monte Carlo, and a more practical vehicle than the T-Bird, and it is priced somewhere in between. Power brakes and power steering are standard. One convenience feature not to be overlooked is the fact that back seat passenger entry is easier because the doors have been widened by five inches more than found on former Chrysler 2-door intermediates. The Cordoba's score in the 1975 EPA fuel run was surprisingly creditable — 13 mpg in city driving and 22 mpg on the highway.*

LUXURY

Mercedes-Benz 450 Sel *(long wheelbase — 116 inches versus 112 inches in the 450 SE) is intermediate in size and weight, but luxurious in interior space dimensions. Truly a luxury car, it offers performance levels beyond anything the U.S. competitors can reach. Standard equipment includes air conditioning, power windows, electrically heated rear window, central door lock system, and Becker stereo radio with automatic antenna that retracts when the radio is turned off. Traveling comfort has no equal. The ride is well-cushioned, and sound absorbing materials shield the passenger compartment from outside noise. A Mercedes 450 SL/SLC, with 276 cubic-inch engine, rated at the top of the luxury class in the EPA gas mileage tests with 11 mpg and 17 mpg in city and highway driving respectively.*

IMPORTED SPORTS CAR

Datsun's 260/Z *is the original 240/Z moved up from 2.4 liters to 2.6 liters as a result of increasingly stringent emission control standards which made it necessary to provide greater displacement if existing performance levels were to be maintained. So while displacement went up, power output remained the same. The 2 plus 2 offers an extra dimension of value for this already excellently packaged model. Slightly heavier (220 pounds) and built on a 103-inch wheelbase rather than the 91-inch wheelbase, it therefore provides leg room for the back seat passengers.*

AUTOMOBILES

How to Buy an Auto

THE BIGGEST news about the 1975 automobiles is their prices. The price of small cars has risen $300 to $400 over 1974 models. Intermediate cars are up $400 to $500, and full-size and luxury models are up from $600 to $800. Part of the reason for the rise is the addition of the catalytic converters in 1975 models, but most of the reason is inflation. With the tremendous increase in prices, the most important question the auto buyer will face in 1975 is: How can I get a good deal on the car I want?

When shopping for a 1975 auto the first thing you must do is decide the kind of car you really need. Analyze your driving habits and transportation requirements. Is a large trunk a necessity? Do you need a station wagon? Can a small, economical car serve for your type of transportation? Remember, whatever car you buy now will continue to cost you day after day—in the form of fuel operating costs, maintenance, and taxes. It is foolish to buy more car than you really need.

The volatile state of the general economy, and particularly of the automotive industry, complicates the problems of getting the right car at the right price. But one way you can get the "best deal in town" is to take advantage of CONSUMER GUIDE Magazine's exclusive price listing for 1975 cars. Using this listing, follow these three simple steps:

1. Learn as much as possible about the cars you think suit your needs (and your pocketbook) by reading the descriptions of each category listed in the automobile section of this book. Be sure to check CONSUMER GUIDE Magazine's "best buy" selections.

2. Once you have determined the type of car you require and perhaps the brand and model you want, list the equipment you desire. Remember options add to the price of the car, and the price of accessories has skyrocketed with everything else. When you know exactly which features you need, check your list against the new car window sticker to see which equipment is standard and which is optional.

3. Next check the price listings in CONSUMER GUIDE Magazine for the car of your choice. Add together the low prices for the auto and all the options you desire. To that add the freight costs (listed as the F.O.B. cost on the sticker), the dealer preparation costs (which range from $30 to $50), and state and local sales taxes. The total is the best deal you can make on the car.

4. Now, with your low-price goal, you are ready to bargain. But stop arguing when the dealer asks a figure within $50 of your aimed-at price. At that price, he is offering you a good deal.

Buying Foreign Cars

UNFORTUNATELY you will not find foreign car prices listed in this issue of CONSUMER GUIDE Magazine. The new model foreign cars are not introduced until several months after the American cars. Consequently,

AUTOMOBILES

at press time, the foreign car prices had not as yet been determined by the foreign manufacturers. The foreign car dealers still have plenty of 1974 cars to sell, and the manufacturers want to wait and see where the American prices settle so they can bring their prices as high as possible and still be competitive.

In the past, there have been few discounts available on foreign cars. That made foreign car shopping pretty simple; whatever the price was on the price sticker, that was the price you paid. But foreign car dealers have been hit by inflation also. The high cost of commercial borrowing has made the cost of holding inventory soar. That coupled with the increased competition from American dealers in the small car market has changed the foreign dealers' practices. The foreign car shopper can expect to deal for a 5- to 7 1/2-percent discount on the sticker price of a foreign car. CONSUMER GUIDE Magazine would suggest you first try for a 10-percent discount. If the dealer will split the difference with you so you come up with a 5-percent discount, you have made a good deal. If you are an even sharper shopper you may be able to manage a 7 1/2-percent discount.

Other Ways to Save

IF YOU HAVE a car that you will be replacing with your 1975 purchase, try selling it yourself instead of trading it in. Auto dealers offer only the wholesale value of a used car, which they turn around and sell for several hundred dollars more. That profit belongs in your pocket. Just as the prices of new cars have risen sharply, so have the values of used cars. You should have little difficulty in selling the car for several hundred dollars more than a dealer would offer on a trade-in. Just be sure to give yourself plenty of time to sell, so you do not feel pressured by the first offer that comes along.

Another way to save money is by shopping for credit. Determine how much money you will need to borrow to buy the car and how much time you need to pay the loan back. Then visit several banks to find the one that will charge you the least interest for the period you need the money. Be sure to ask what the actual cost of the loan will be (the total interest you will have to pay) since this is an easier figure to understand and compare than a percentage figure.

If you work at a company that has a credit union, inquire about interest rates there also. Credit unions often offer less expensive loans than banks do. One of the least expensive ways to borrow money is to borrow against your life insurance policy. The reason this is so inexpensive is that you will continue to earn dividends on the total policy even though some of the money has been borrowed out of it.

It is true that 1975 auto prices have risen almost out of sight. Today, buyers are faced with paying the same price for a new compact that they once paid for a full-size luxury car. But the wise shopper—the one who knows what price he or she ought to be able to pay for a car, and the one who knows how to shop for the least expensive credit—can still make a good deal.

AUTOMOBILES

1975 Automobile Prices

AMC

	Retail Price	Dealer Cost	Low Price
GREMLIN			
2 Door Sedan, 4 Passenger	$2798	$2478	$2678
HORNET			
2 Dr. Hatchback	3174	2742	2942
2 Dr. Sedan	3074	2667	2867
4 Dr. Sedan	3124	2705	2905
4 Dr. Sportabout, Wagon—2 Seat	3374	2915	3115
MATADOR			
2 Dr. Coupe	3526	2904	3104
4 Dr. Sedan	3551	2945	3145
4 Dr. Wagon	3943	3260	3460

GREMLIN ACCESSORIES

	Retail Price	Dealer Cost	Low Price
"Levi's"® Fabric Seats	$60	$50	$51
258 CID, Six 1 BBL Engine	69	57	58
304 CID V8, 2 BBL Engine	154	131	133
Torque-Command, Column Shift			
6-Cylinder	240	199	201
V-8	249	207	210
Torque-Command, Floor Shift			
6-Cylinder	260	216	219
V-8	269	223	226
Fuel Economy Gauge	25	21	22
Light Group	25	21	22
Custom Steering Wheel	14	12	13
Sports Steering Wheel	33	27	28
Leather Wrapped Sports Steering Wheel	46	38	39
W/Gremlin "X" Package	13	11	12
Wheel Discs (4)	30	25	26

HORNET ACCESSORIES

	Retail Price	Dealer Cost	Low Price
Vinyl Roof	88	73	74
Wood-Grain Side Panels	95	78	79
Optional Axle Ratio	12	10	11
Vinyl Bench Cushion			
Sedan & Hatchback	20	17	18
Individual Reclining Seat			
"Seville" Custom Fabric	99	82	83
Vinyl, Sedan	79	65	66
Vinyl, Sportabout	60	49	50
Bucket Seats			
Vinyl, Hatchback	49	41	42
"Seville" Custom Fabric, Hatchback	99	82	83
"Seville" Custom Fabric w/Hatchback "X"			

Option				
3-Speed Manual, Floor Shift w/Overdrive (6-Cylinder Only)	149	149		
Twin-Grip Differential	46	46		
Gremlin "X" Package	280	280		
Interior Appointment Package	20	20		
Decor Package	20	20		
Rally Package	133	133		
W/Gremlin "X" Package	100	100		
Power Steering	119	119		
Power Brakes	56	56		
Power Disc Brakes	79	79		
W/Rally Package	32	32		
Manual Disc Brakes	47	47		
AM Push-Button Radio	69	69		
AM/FM Push-Button Multi-Plex Stereo Radio	179	179		
Rear Speaker	19	19		
All-Season Air Conditioning System	400	400		
Air Conditioning Package	500	500		
Tinted Glass, All Windows	42	42		
Tinted Windshield Only	34	34		
Electric Rear Window Defogger	60	60		
Tailgate Air Deflector	21	21		
Roof Rack	50	50		
Rear Quarter Vent Windows	30	30		
Cruise-Command Automatic Speed Control	65	65		
Adjust-O-Tilt Steering Wheel	49	49		
Visibility Group	60	60		
W/Rally Package or "Econo-Miser" Package	44	44		
Inside Hood Release	13	13		
Deluxe Electric Wipers	25	25		

Option				
Package	126	124		
258 CID 6, 1 BBL Engine	39	38		
304 CID, V-8, 2 BBL Engine	241	238		
Torque-Command, Column Shift	18	17		
6 Cylinder	18	17		
304	112	110		
Torque-Command, Floor Shift, Hatchback & Sportabout	84	83		
6 Cylinder	100	99		
304	48	47		
3-Speed Manual, Column Shift w/Overdrive	67	66		
Twin-Grip Differential	28	27		
Hatchback "X" Package	40	39		
Sportabout "X" Package	58	57		
Sportabout D/L Package	151	149		
W/"Seville" Custom Fabric	17	16		
W/Vinyl	336	332		
Rally Package	420	415		
W/"X" Packages & Touring Trim Package	36	35		
Power Steering	29	28		
Power Brakes	51	50		
Front Power Disc Brakes	18	17		
W/Rally Package	43	42		
Front Manual Disc Brakes	26	25		
AM Push-Button Radio	55	54		
AM/FM Push-Button Multi-Plex Stereo Radio	42	41		
Rear Speaker	51	50		
Hidden Compartment				
All-Season Air Conditioning System	37	36		
Air Conditioning Package	12	11		
Tinted Glass, All Windows	22	21		

50	42	43
69	57	58
138	115	117
240	199	201
249	207	210
260	216	219
269	223	226
149	124	126
46	38	39
227	188	190
139	115	117
333	277	280
294	244	247
119	99	100
100	83	84
119	99	100
57	47	48
79	66	67
32	27	28
47	39	40
69	57	58
179	149	151
19	16	17
39	32	33
400	332	336
500	415	420
45	37	38

AUTOMOBILES

Option	Retail Price	Dealer Cost	Low Price
Tinted Windshield Only	34	28	29
Rear Window Defogger	—	—	—
Sedan, Blower-Type	39	32	33
Hatchback & Sportabout, Electric-Type	60	50	51
Roof Rack	75	62	63
Rear Quarter Vent Windows	30	25	26
Cruise-Command Automatic Speed Control	65	54	55
Adjust-O-Tilt Steering Wheel	49	41	42
Visibility Group	60	50	51
W/Rally Pkg. or "Econo-Miser" Pkg.	44	36	37
Inside Hood Release	13	11	12
Deluxe Electric Wipers	25	21	22
Fuel Economy Gauge	25	21	22
Light Group	29	24	25
Space-Saver Spare Tire	15	13	14
Sports Steering Wheel	19	16	17
Leather Wrapped Sports Steering Wheel	32	27	28
W/"X" Package	13	11	12
Wheel Discs (4)	30	25	26
Custom Wheel Covers (4)	50	42	43
Styled Road Wheels (4)	115	45	46
W/"X" Package	50	41	42
W/D/L Package	65	44	45
W/Touring or Sedan D/L Package	85	71	72
Extra-Quiet Insulation Package	30	25	26
Protection Group	55	46	47
W/Touring or Sedan D/L Package	19	16	17
Trailer Towing Package No. 1	—	—	—
W/o Air Conditioning	47	39	40
AM/FM Push-Button Multi-Plex Stereo Radio	230	182	184
Rear Speaker	20	16	17
Entertainment Center	300	237	240
Center Armrest & Cushion	39	31	32
All-Season Air Conditioning System	450	356	360
Tinted Glass, All Windows	49	39	40
Tinted Glass, Windshield	40	31	32
Electric Rear Window Defogger	70	55	56
Cruise-Command Automatic Speed Control	69	55	56
Visibility Group	60	47	48
Inside Hood Release	14	11	12
Deluxe Electric Wipers, Intermittent-Action	26	21	22
Light Group	34	27	28
Remote Control Right Outside Mirror	26	21	22
Fuel Economy Gauge	26	21	22
Sports Steering Wheel, 3-Spokes, 15"	20	16	17
Leather Wrapped Sports Steering Wheel	34	27	28
W/"X" Package	14	11	12
Wheel Discs (4)	32	25	26
Custom Wheel Covers (4)	53	42	43
W/Brougham Package	21	16	17
Styled Road Wheels (4) 14" x 6"	121	95	96
W/Brougham Package	89	70	71
W/"X" Package or "Cassini" Package	52	41	42
Appearance Protection Group	54	43	44
Protection Group	20	16	17
Heavy Duty Cooling	17	13	14
Trailer Towing Package No. 2	—	—	—
W/o Air Conditioning	110	87	88

28   CONSUMER GUIDE

AUTOMOBILES

W/Air Conditioning	31	26	27	93	74	75
Heavy Duty Engine Cooling System	16	13	14	16	12	13
Heavy-Duty Battery	14	12	13	30	24	25
Handling Package	23	19	20	15	12	13
Engine Block Heater	16	13	14	17	13	14

MATADOR COUPE ACCESSORIES

Two-Tone Color	$40	$32	$33
Special Non-Standard Color	60	47	48
Vinyl Roof	100	79	80
Optional Axle Ratio	14	11	12
Vinyl Bench Cushion	29	23	24
Vinyl Individual Reclining Seat	29	23	24
Vinyl Bucket Seats	91	72	73
"Oleg Cassini" Trim Package	299	236	239
304 CID, V-8, 2 BBL Engines	99	78	79
360 CID, V-8, 2 BBL Engines	143	113	115
360 CID, V-8 4 BBL W/Dual Exhaust	253	200	202
Torque-Command, Column Shift, 6 Cylinder	249	199	201
304 CID	255	204	207
360 CID	268	214	217
Torque-Command, Floor Shift & Console			
304 CID	314	251	254
360 CID	327	261	264
Twin-Grip Differential	50	40	41
Matador "X" Package	199	157	159
Brougham Package	219	173	175
Power Steering	130	103	105
Front Power Disc Brakes	57	45	46
AM Push-Button Radio	73	57	58

MATADOR SEDAN/WAGON ACCESSORIES

Two-Tone Color			
Sedan	$40	$32	$33
Wagon	75	60	61
Special Non-Standard Paint	60	47	48
Sedan Vinyl Roof	100	79	80
Wood-Grain Panels	112	89	90
Optional Axle Ratio	14	11	12
Vinyl Bench Cushion	29	23	24
Individual Reclining Seat			
Fabric	29	23	24
Vinyl	29	23	24
304 CID, V-8 2 BBL Engine	99	78	79
360 CID, V-8 2 BBL Engine	143	113	114
360 CID, V-8 4 BBL w/Dual Exhaust	253	200	202
Torque-Command, Column Shift, 6 Cylinder	249	199	201
304 CID	255	204	207
360 CID	268	214	217
Twin-Grip Differential	50	40	41
Brougham Package			
Sedan	179	141	143
Wagon	259	205	207
Power Steering	130	103	105
Front Power Disc Brakes	57	45	46

AUTOMOBILES

	Retail Price	Dealer Cost	Low Price
Power Lift Window	35	27	28
Side Power Lift Windows	131	104	106
Side & Tailgate Power Lift Windows	170	134	136
AM Push-Button Radio	73	57	58
AM/FM Push-Button Multi-Plex Stereo Radio	230	182	184
Rear Speaker	20	16	17
Entertainment Center	300	237	240
All-Season Air Conditioning System	450	355	360
Tinted Glass, All Windows	49	39	40
Tinted Glass, Windshield	40	31	32
Third Seat	121	96	97
Electric Rear Window Defogger	70	55	56
Tailgate Air Deflector	23	18	19
Luggage Rack	59	47	48
Cruise-Command Automatic Speed Control	69	55	56
Adjust-O-Tilt Steering Wheel	52	41	42
Visibility Group	60	47	48
Inside Hood Release	14	11	12
Deluxe Electric Wipers	26	21	22
Light Group	34	27	28
Remote Control Right Outside Mirror	26	21	22
Fuel Economy Gauge	26	21	22
Sports Steering Wheel	20	16	17
Leather Wrapped Sports Steering Wheel	34	27	28
Wheel Discs (4)	32	25	26
Custom Wheel Covers (4)	53	42	43
W/Brougham Package	21	16	17
Styled Road Wheels (4) 14" x 6"	121	95	96
W/Brougham Package	89	70	71

	Retail Price	Dealer Cost	Low Price
4 Dr. 3 Seat Wagon	4764	3888	4088
CENTURY CUSTOM			
4 Dr. Colonnade Hardtop Sedan	4224	3461	3661
2 Dr. Colonnade Hardtop Coupe	4167	3410	3610
4 Dr. 2 Seat Wagon	4815	3929	4129
4 Dr. 3 Seat Wagon	4930	4123	4323
REGAL			
4 Dr. Colonnade Hardtop Sedan	4324	3538	3838
2 Dr. Colonnade Hardtop Coupe	4270	3494	3794
LE SABRE			
4 Dr. Sedan	4784	3715	4015
4 Dr. Hardtop	4911	3814	4114
2 Dr. Sport Coupe	4853	3769	4069
LE SABRE CUSTOM			
4 Dr. Sedan	4949	3845	4145
4 Dr. Hardtop	5074	3941	4241
2 Dr. Sport Coupe	5020	3899	4199
2 Dr. Convertible	5146	3998	4298
ESTATE WAGON			
4 Dr. 2 Seat, Clamshell Gate	5460	4239	4539
4 Dr. 3 Seat, Clamshell Gate	5604	4350	4650
ELECTRA 225 CUSTOM			
4 Dr. Hardtop	6214	4827	5177
2 Dr. Sport Coupe	6054	4702	5052
ELECTRA LIMITED			
4 Dr. Hardtop	6529	5069	5469
2 Dr. Sport Coupe	6365	4942	5342
RIVIERA			
2 Dr. Sport Coupe	6433	5022	5422

30 CONSUMER GUIDE

AUTOMOBILES

Heavy Duty Cooling	17	13	14
Trailer Towing Package No. 2			
W/o Air Conditioning	110	87	88
W/Air Conditioning	93	74	75
Heavy-Duty Battery	16	12	13
Handling Package	30	24	25
Rear Sway Bar	15	12	13
Engine Block Heater	17	13	14

BUICK

SKYHAWK
2 Dr. Hatchback Coupe	$4186	$3567	$3767

APOLLO
4 Dr. Sedan	3449	2959	3159

SKYLARK
2 Dr. Coupe	3476	2982	3182
2 Dr. Hatchback Coupe	3599	3090	3290

APOLLO SR
4 Dr. Sedan	4105	3517	3717

SKYLARK SR
2 Dr. Coupe	4149	3554	3754
2 Dr. Hatchback Coupe	4266	3657	3857

CENTURY SPECIAL
2 Dr. Colonnade Hardtop Coupe	3828	3126	3326

CENTURY
4 Dr. Colonnade Hardtop Sedan	3957	3235	3435
2 Dr. Colonnade Hardtop Coupe	3907	3188	3388
4 Dr. 2 Seat Wagon	4649	3794	3994

SKYHAWK ACCESSORIES

Turbo Hydra Matic 350 Transmission	$237	$201	$204
Power Steering	111	94	95
Radio			
AM	63	54	55
AM/FM Stereo w/Single Front & Rear	214	182	184
Spkrs. AM/FM	129	110	112
Single Rear Speaker	18	15	16
Calif. Emission Equipment & Testing	45	38	39
Positige Traction Differential	45	38	39
Manual Controls Air Conditioner	398	338	342
Custom Shoulder Belts & Seat Belts	12	10	11
Soft Ray Tinted Glass	42	36	37
Soft Ray Tinted Windshield	29	25	26
Electric Rear Window Defogger	60	51	52
Door Guards	7	6	7
Right Hand Manual Sport Mirror	11	9	10
Front & Rear Floor Mats	13	11	12
Adjustable Driver's Seat Back	16	14	15
Heavy Duty Energizer	14	12	13
Tilt Steering Wheel	45	38	39
Convenience Group	17	14	15
Deluxe Wheel Covers	36	31	32
Protective Body Side Moldings	21	18	19
Custom Leather Trim	198	168	170

APOLLO AND SKYLARK ACCESSORIES

V8 350 Cu. in. w/2 BBL. Carb.			
Skylark	$78	$61	$62
Apollo	130	101	103

CONSUMER GUIDE

AUTOMOBILES

	Retail Price	Dealer Cost	Low Price
V8 260 Cu. In. w/2 BBL. Carb.			
Skylark	26	20	21
Apollo	78	61	62
V8 350 Cu. In. w/4 BBL. Carb.			
Skylark	129	101	103
Apollo	181	141	143
Full Length Console	68	53	54
Turbo Hydra-Matic 350 Transmission	237	194	196
Convenience Center	27	21	22
Power Front Disc Brakes	55	43	44
Power Steering	129	101	103
Radios			
AM	69	54	55
AM & Stereo Tape Player w/Single F & R Spkrs.	203	158	160
AM/FM & Stereo Tape Player w/Single F & R Spkrs.	363	283	286
AM/FM Stereo w/Single F & R Spkrs.	233	182	184
AM/FM	135	105	107
Single Rear Speaker	19	15	16
Fuel Usage Indicator	15	12	13
Calif. Emission Equipment & Testing	45	35	36
Positive Traction Differential	49	38	39
Firm Ride & Handling Suspension	16	13	14
Rallye Firm Ride & Handling Suspension	32	25	26
Heavy Duty Radiator	17	13	14
Heavy Duty Cooling w/Air Cond.	22	17	18
W/o Air Cond.	44	34	35
Manual Controls Air Conditioner	435	339	343

	Retail Price	Dealer Cost	Low Price
Convenience Group	25	19	20
Hatchbacks	23	18	19
Electric Clock	17	13	14
Deluxe Wire Wheel Covers	106	83	84
Deluxe Wheel Covers	30	23	24
Wide Rocker Appearance Group	30	23	24
Custom Door & Window Frame Moldings			
Skylark	22	17	18
Apollo	27	21	22
Rocker Panel Molding	14	11	12
Protective Body Side Moldings	35	27	28
Body Side Accent Stripe	22	17	18
Rallye Steering Wheel	33	26	27
Carpeted Door Trim w/Map Pocket, Reflector	19	15	16
Luggage Rack	60	47	48
5 Wire Trailer Tow Flasher & Harness	15	12	13
Special Order Paint, Current Color	102	80	81
Two Tone Paint	33	26	27
Custom Vinyl Roof			
Apollo Sedan & Skylark	92	72	73
Apollo SR & Skylark SR	87	68	69
Custom Trim Bench Seats & Custom Interior	45	35	36
Vinyl Bucket Seats	75	58	59

CENTURY, CENTURY SPECIAL, CENTURY CUSTOM AND REGAL ACCESSORIES

	Retail Price	Dealer Cost	Low Price
V8 350 Cu. Inc. w/2 BBL. Carb.	$78	$61	$62

AUTOMOBILES

Custom F Shoulder Bwts & R & R Seat Belts	13	8	9	V8 350 Cu. Inc. w/4 BBL. Carb.	129	101	103
W/Bucket Seats	14	11	12	Gran Sport Package	171	133	135
W/Bench Seats				Full Length Console	68	53	54
Three Speed Windshield Wiper w/Low Speed Delay Feature	26	20	21	Turbo Hydra-matic 350 Transmission	237	194	196
Soft Ray Tinted Glass	45	35	36	Short Non-Shift Floor Console	39	30	31
Headlamp On Indicator	6	5	6	Convenience Center	27	21	22
Engine Block Heater	11	9	10	Power Front Disc Brakes	55	43	44
Blower Rear Window Defogger	41	32	33	Radios			
Heavy Duty Air Cleaner	10	8	9	AM.	73	57	58
Front & Rear Bumper Strips	27	21	22	AM & Stereo Tape Player w/F & R			
Front Only Bumper Guards	32	25	26	Dual Spkrs.			
Door Guards	16	13	14	AM/FM Stereo & Stereo Tape Player	203	158	160
Remote Control O/S Rear View Mirror, Left	11	9	10	w/F & R Dual Spkrs.			
O/S Rear View Sport Mirrors, Remote, Man.	13	10	11	AM/FM Stereo w/F & R Dual Spkrs			
Remote Control R & L Sport Mirrors	25	19	20	AM/FM.			
Carpet Savers & Handy Mats	38	30	31	Rear Speaker	363	283	286
Carpet Savers	13	10	11	Front & Rear Dual Speakers	233	182	184
Power Windows	7	5	6	Fuel Usage Gauge	135	105	107
2 Door				Calif. Emission Equipment & Testing	19	15	16
4 Door				Positive Traction Differential	39	30	31
Swing Out Rear Quarter Vent Window	91	71	72	Firm Ride & Handling Suspension	23	18	19
Heavy Duty Energizer	132	103	105	Automatic Level Control	45	35	36
Cruise Master	44	34	35	Hvy. Duty Cooling w/Extra Hvy. Duty Radiator	49	38	39
Tilt Steering Wheel	16	13	14	Hvy. Duty Cooling w/Fan Drive Thermo Cont.	16	13	14
Electric Trunk Release	69	54	55	Automatic Climate Control Air Cond.	84	65	66
Electric Door Locks	49	38	39	Manual Control Air Conditioner	22	17	18
	16	13	14	Custom Front Shoulder Belts	44	34	35
2 Door				w/F & R Seat Belts	534	416	421
4 Door				W/Bucket Seats	453	353	357
	56	44	45	W/Century Custom, 3 Seat	12	9	10
	82	64	65		15	12	13

CONSUMER GUIDE

AUTOMOBILES

	Retail Price	Dealer Cost	Low Price
W/Other Front Seat Styles	16	13	14
W/Century Custom & Century 3 Seat	19	15	16
Speed Alert	13	10	11
Three Speed Windshield Wiper w/Low Speed Delay	26	20	21
Soft Ray Tinted Glass	48	38	39
Soft Ray Tinted Windshield	32	25	26
80 AMP Delcotron w/Air Cond. Cooling	33	26	27
W/o Air Cond. or Heavy Duty Cooling	37	29	30
Electric Rear Window Defogger	73	57	58
Blower Rear Window Defogger	41	32	33
Heavy Duty Air Cleaner	10	8	9
Front & Rear Bumper Strips	27	21	22
Front & Rear Bumper Guards	33	26	27
Rear Bumper Guards	16	13	14
Door Guards, 2 Dr.	7	5	6
4 Dr.	11	9	10
Remote Control Outside View Mirror	13	10	11
Outside Rear View Sport Mirrors, L Remote & R Manual	25	19	20
Carpet Savers & Handy Mats	15	12	13
Carpet Savers	8	6	7
Six Way Power Seat	117	91	92
Combination Dome & Reading Lamp	14	11	12
Power Windows, 2 Front Drs.	91	71	72
4 Drs.	132	103	105
Swing Out Rear Quarter Vent Window	44	34	35
Heavy Duty Energizer	16	13	14

	Retail Price	Dealer Cost	Low Price
Custom Vinyl Roof Covering & Stand Up Hood Ornament	108	84	85
Custom Vinyl Roof Covering	103	80	81
Short Custom Vinyl Roof Covering & Stand Up Hood Ornament	93	73	74
Landau Custom Top, Regal 2 Dr. Coupe	105	82	83
Custom Trim w/Notchback Front Seat, 2 Dr.	119	93	94
4 Dr.	144	112	114
Custom Trim w/60/40 Notchback Front Seat 2 Dr.	200	175	177
4 Dr.	225	175	177
60/40 Notchback Front Seat Cloth & Vinyl	106	83	84
Vinyl Seat	81	63	64
Custom Trim w/Vinyl Bucket Seats	126	98	99
Century Colonnade Hardtop Sedan	151	118	120

LE SABRE, ESTATE WAGON, ELECTRA & RIVIERA ACCESSORIES

	Retail Price	Dealer Cost	Low Price
V8 400 Cu. In. w/4 BBL. Car. (Deduct)	(63)	(49)	(50)
V8 400 Cu. In. w/4 BBL. Carb. &THM 400 Transmission	72	55	56
V8 455 Cu. In. w/4 BBL. Carb. & THM 400 Transmission	135	104	106
Riviera GS Ride & Handling Package	73	56	57
Full Length Console	68	52	53
Convenience Center	27	21	22
AM Radio	86	66	67

AUTOMOBILES

Cruise Master	69	54	55	
Tilt Steering Wheel	49	38	39	216	166	168
Electric Trunk Release	16	13	14			
Electric Door Locks, 2 Dr.	56	44	45			
4 Dr.	82	64	65	363	280	283
w/Front & Rear Dual Speakers						
AM/FM Stereo Radio & Stereo Tape Player						
Comb. w/Front & Rear Dual Speakers						
AM/FM Stereo Radio w/Front & Rear Dual Speakers						
AM/FM Radio	16	13	14	233	179	181
Remote Tailgate Lock				145	112	114
Single Rear Speaker	19	15	16	19	15	16
Power Antenna	40	31	32	34	26	27
Electric Clock				39	30	31
Instrument Gauges & Clock	10	8	9	39	30	31
Front & Rear Dual Speakers	30	23	24	23	18	19
Sunshade Map Light & Trunk Light						
Fuel Usage Gauge	59	46	47	45	35	36
Deluxe Wheel Covers						
Super Deluxe Wheel Covers, Colonnade	87	68	69	51	39	40
Deluxe Wire Wheel Covers, Colonnade	117	91	92	16	12	13
Calif. Emission Equipment & Testing						
Positive Traction Differential						
Firm Ride & Handling Suspension						
Other Models	15	12	13	84	65	66
Custom Rear Quarter Lower Molding	17	13	14	22	17	18
Front & Rear Wheel Opening Moldings	25	19	20	44	34	35
Protective Body Side & Front Fender Mldg.	31	24	25	568	437	442
Body Side Accent Stripe						
Automatic Level Control						
Heavy Duty Cooling w/Air Cond.						
Heavy Duty Cooling						
Automatic Climate Control Air Cond.						
Wood Grain Applique, Century	173	135	137	487	380	384
Wood Grain Applique, Century Custom	139	108	110	13	10	11
Custom Steering Wheel	15	12	13			
Rallye Steering Wheel	33	26	27			
Custom Front & Rear Seat Belts						
Custom Front Shoulder Belts & Front & Rear Seat Belts						
Lower Body Molding & Custom Rear Quarter Lower Molding	32	25	26	39	30	31
Front & Rear Carpeting	22	17	18	19	15	16
Load Floor Carpet	21	16	17	16	12	13
2 Dr. Convertible						
Estate 3 Seat Wagon						
Other Models						
Air Restraint System						
Luggage Rack	68	53	54	251	193	195
Riviera				300	231	234
Luggage Locker w/Lock	13	10	11	38	29	30
Other Models				18	14	15
Air Deflector	23	18	19			
Cornering Lights						
Electric Sun Roof	350	273	276			
Speed Alert & Trip Odometer						
5 Wire Trailer Tow Flasher & Harness	15	12	13	26	20	21
Three Speed Windshield Wiper w/Low Speed Delay Feature						
7 Wire Trailer Tow Flasher & Harness	25	19	20			

CONSUMER GUIDE

AUTOMOBILES

	Retail Price	Dealer Cost	Low Price
Soft Ray Tinted Glass	60	47	48
Soft Ray Tinted Windshield	37	29	30
80 AMP Delcotron Battery W/Air Cond.	33	25	26
W/o Air Conditioning	35	27	28
Electric Rear Window Defogger	73	56	57
Blower Rear Window Defogger	41	32	33
Four Note Horn	16	12	13
Heavy Duty Air Cleaner	10	8	9
Bumper Guards, Front & Rear	33	24	26
Bumper Guards, Rear	16	12	13
Front Bumper Reinforcement	13	10	11
Rear Bumper Reinforcement	6	5	6
Chrome Air Cleaner	16	12	13
Door Guards, 2 Doors	7	5	6
4 Doors	11	9	10
Left Remote Control Outside RV Mirror	13	10	11
Right Remote Control Outside RV Mirror			
Estate Wagon	22	17	18
Other Models	27	21	22
Right & Left Remote Control Sports Mirrors			
Riviera	34	26	27
Other Models	47	36	37
Carpet Savers & Handy Mats	16	12	13
Carpet Savers	9	7	8
6 Way Bench Power Seat	117	90	91
6 Way Power Seat, Left Side	117	90	91
6 Way Power Seat, Both Sides	230	117	119
LeSabre Custom	87	67	68
All Other Models	66	51	52
Heavy Duty Wheels	11	9	10
Protective Body Side Moldings, Body Side			
Front Fender Moldings			
LeSabre, LeSabre Custom & Estate Wagon	35	27	28
Electras, Park Ave. Limited & Riviera	49	38	39
Custom Door Window Frame Moldings	28	22	23
Custom Moldings	43	33	34
Body Side Accent Stripes	31	24	25
Wood Grain Applique	182	140	142
Tailgate Moldings	17	13	14
Custom Steering Wheel	15	12	13
Belt Reveal Moldings	28	22	33
Wide Rocker Panel Moldings	30	23	24
Wide Rocker Panel Molding Group	73	56	57
Load Floor Area Carpet	56	43	44
Luggage Rack	89	69	70
Luggage Locker w/Lock	13	10	11
Power Tailgate Door	49	38	39
Deluxe Trunk Trim	35	27	28
Trunk Trim Carpet	44	34	35
Customline Boot Cover	45	35	36
Electric Sun Roof	644	496	501
5 Wire Trailer Tow Flasher & Harness	15	12	13
7 Wire Trailer Tow Flasher & Harness	25	19	20
Rear Stabilizer Bar	16	12	13
Special Car Order Paint, Current Color	119	92	93

36   CONSUMER GUIDE

AUTOMOBILES

Door Courtesy & Warning Lamps				
2 Dr.	22	17		
4 Dr.	38	29		
Dome and Reading Lamp	14	11		
Power Windows	149	115		
Front Lamp Monitors	22	17		
Front & Rear Lamp Monitors	48	37		
Heavy Duty Energizer	16	12		
Maintenance Free Energizer	27	21		
Cruise Master	74	57		
Tilt Steering Wheel	49	38		
Tilt & Telescoping Steering Column	89	69		
Riviera	40	31		
Electric Trunk Release	16	12		
2 Door Electric Door Locks	56	43		
4 Door Electric Door Locks	82	63		
Electric Door & Seat Back Locks	82	63		
2 Door Automatic Door Locks	68	52		
4 Door Automatic Electric Door Locks	94	72		
Automatic Electric Door & Seat Back Lock	94	72		
Low Fuel Indicator	10	8		
Accessory Group				
LeSabre Convertible	50	38		
Estate Wagons w/Air	54	42		
Other Models w/Air	53	41		
Estate Wagons w/o Air	61	47		
Other Models w/o Air	60	46		
Lighted Sun Shade Vanity Mirror	37	29		
Deluxe Wheel Covers	30	23		
Super Deluxe Wheel Covers	38	29		
Deluxe Wire Wheel Covers				
LeSabre & Estate Wagon	117	90		
Custom Vinyl Roof & Molding				
Electra Sedans, Park Avenue Limited & Estate Wagon	142	109	111
LeSabre	132	102	104
Custom Vinyl Roof w/Halo Molding	154	119	121
Custom Vinyl Roof, Hvy Padded w/Halo Mldg.	58	45	46
Heavily Padded Custom Rinyl Roof	389	300	303
Landau Custom Vinyl Roof			
LeSabre & LeSabre Custom Coupe	132	102	104
Electra Custom & Electra Limited Coupe	154	119	121
Riviera Coupe	389	300	303
60-40 Notchback Front Seat	81	62	63
Custom Trim w/60-40 Notchback Front Seat	286	220	223
Custom Trim w/Notchback Front Seat	205	158	160
Leather Upholstery	302	233	236
Park Avenue Limited, Small Group	495	381	385
Park Avenue Limited, Large Group			
W/o Air Restraint System	1,718	1,323	1,338
W/Air Restraint System	1,629	1,254	1,268
Riviera Leather Upholstery Group	393	303	307
Custom Trim w/60-40 Notchback Front Seat			
Cloth & Vinyl	116	89	90
Vinyl	91	70	71
Riviera Custom Trim w/40-60 Front Seat	55	42	43

CADILLAC

Calais Coupe	$8197	$6300	$7100
Calais Sedan	8390	6448	7248
Coupe de Ville	8613	6618	7418

AUTOMOBILES

	Retail Price	Dealer Cost	Low Price
Sedan de Ville	8814	6773	7573
Fleetwood Eldorado Coupe	9948	7642	8642
Fleetwood Eldorado Convertible	10,367	7962	8962
Fleetwood Sixty Special Brougham	10,427	8004	9004
Fleetwood Seventy-Five Sedan	14,231	10,914	12,414
Fleetwood Seventy-Five Limousine	14,570	11,171	12,671

CADILLAC ACCESSORIES

	Retail Price	Dealer Cost	Low Price
Air Cushion Restraint System	$300	$231	$234
Astroroof	843	649	656
Astroroof, Painted	913	703	711
Automatic Level Control	84	65	66
Brougham d'Elegance	784	604	611
California Emission Equipment & Testing	45	35	36
Controlled Cycle Wiper System	26	20	21
Controlled Differential	60	46	47
Cruise Control	100	77	78
De-Fogger, Grid Type Rear Window	73	56	57
Deluxe Robe & Pillow	85	65	66
Coupe De Ville Cabriolet	236	182	184
Coupe De Ville Cabriolet Astroroof	1149	884	893
Coupe De Ville Cabriolet Sunroof	974	750	758
Coupe De Ville d'Elegance	323	249	252
Sedan	380	293	296
2 doors Door Edge Guards	7	5	6
4 doors Door Edge Guards	11	8	9
Dual Comfort Seat 60/40	113	87	88
AM/FM Stereo Signal Seeking	141	109	111
AM/FM Stereo Rear Control Signal Seeking	250	192	194
6 Way Seat Passenger's Seat Adjuster			
Recliner	188	145	147
Dual Comfort	125	96	97
6 Way Front Bench Seat Adjuster			
Calais Coupe, Calais Sedan	125	96	97
Fleetwood Seventy-Five Sedan	93	72	73
Padded Vinyl Roof, Fleetwood Eldorado Coupe	162	125	127
Calais Coupe, Calais Sedan, Coupe de Ville, Sedan de Ville	156	120	122
Fleetwood Seventy-Five Sedan & Seventy-Five Limousine	745	574	580
Front Shoulder Belts, Pair, Fleetwood Eldorado Convertible	35	27	28
Tilt & Telescope Steering Wheel	98	75	76
Painted Sunroof	738	568	574
W/full Vinyl Roof	668	514	520
Theft Deterrent System	108	83	84
Thermometer, Left Outside Mirror	17	13	14
Track Master	250	192	194
Trailering Package	68	52	53
Trumpet Horn	18	14	15
Remote Trunk Lock	65	50	51
Trunk Mat	10	6	7
Twilight Sentinel	45	35	36
Expanded Vinyl Upholstery	45	35	36
Special Wheel Discs	43	33	34

Dual Comfort Seat 50/50	125	96	97
Eldorado Cabriolet	413	318	322
Eldorado Cabriolet Astroroof	1326	1021	1032
Eldorado Cabriolet Sunroof	1151	886	895
Electronic Fuel Injection	600	462	467
Firemist Color	139	107	109
Fleetwood Talisman	1788	1377	1391
Carpeted Rubber Floor Mats			
Twin, Front & Rear	36	28	29
One Piece, Front & Rear	42	32	33
Twin, Front	24	18	19
Fuel Monitor	25	19	20
Two Piece Hard Boot	50	38	39
Guide-Matic Headlamp Control	52	40	41
Heavy Duty Cooling System	23	18	19
Illuminated Entry System	50	38	39
Leather Upholstery			
Coupe de Ville, Sedan de Ville	200	154	156
Fleetwood Sixty Special Brougham			
Fleetwood Eldorado Coupe	212	163	165
One License Frame	7	5	6
Two License Frames	14	9	10
Illuminated Vanity Mirror, Passenger Side	50	38	39
Fleetwood Eldorado Convertible	43	33	34
Right Side Remote Mirror	29	22	23
Opera Lamps	56	43	44
Power Antenna Radios			
AM/FM Stereo w/Integral Tape Player	89	69	70
Fleetwood Eldorado Coupe, Eldorado			
Convertible, Sixty Special Brougham	229	176	178

AUTOMOBILES

CHEVROLET

BEL AIR

4 Dr. Sedan 6 passenger	$4358	$3391	$3591

IMPALA

Custom Coupe, 6 Passenger	4639	3607	3807
Sport Coupe, 6 Passenger	4588	3567	3767
Sport Sedan, 6 Passenger	4644	3611	3811
4 Dr Sedan, 6 Passenger	4561	3546	3746

CAPRICE CLASSIC

Coupe, 6 Passenger	4850	3772	3972
Sport Sedan, 6 Passenger	4904	3814	4014
4 Dr. Sedan, 6 Passenger	4832	3758	3958
Convertible, 6 Passenger	5126	3985	4185

CHEVROLET ACCESSORIES

Air Conditioning			
Four-Season	$458	$357	$361
Comfortron	535	417	422
Positraction Rear Axle	51	40	41
Axle Ratios	12	9	10
Heavy Duty Battery	15	12	13
Custom Deluxe Seat & Shoulder Belts			
Coupes & Sedans	16	12	13
Convertible	12	9	10
Heavy Duty Brakes	36	28	29
Bumper Equipment			
Deluxe Bumper	27	21	22

AUTOMOBILES

CHEVROLET BEL AIR, IMPALA & CAPRICE ESTATE WAGONS ACCESSORIES

	Retail Price	Dealer Cost	Low Price
BEL AIR			
4 Dr Station Wagon, 2 Seat	$4891	$3801	$4101
4 Dr. Station Wagon, 3 Seat	5011	3895	4195
IMPALA			
4 Dr Station Wagon, 2-Seat	$5014	$3897	$4197
4 Dr Station Wagon, 3-Seat	5134	3990	4290
CAPRICE ESTATE			
4 Dr Estate Wagon, 2-Seat	$5244	$4077	$4377
4 Dr Estate Wagon, 3 Seat	5364	4170	4470
Air conditioning			
Four Season	$458	$357	$361
Comfortron	535	417	422
Positraction Rear Axle	51	40	41
Axle Ratios	12	9	10
Heavy Duty Battery	15	12	13
Custom Deluxe Seat & Shoulder Belts			
2-Seat Wagons	16	12	13
3-Seat Wagons	19	15	16
Heavy Duty Brakes	18	14	15
Deluxe Bumpers	27	21	22
Bumper Guards	40	31	32
California Emission Certification	45	35	36
Roof Carrier	77	60	61
Electric Clock	18	14	15
Litter Container	5	4	5
Rear Window Defogger	45	35	36

	Retail Price	Dealer Cost	Low Price
Bumper Guards	40	31	32
California Emission Certification	45	35	36
Electric Clock	18	14	15
Litter Container	5	4	5
Rear Window Defogger			
Coupes & Sedans	41	32	33
Convertible	45	35	36
Power Door Lock System			
Coupes	56	44	45
Sedans	82	64	65
Econominder Gauge Package	32	25	26
Engines			
350-4 BBL V8	54	42	43
400-4 BBL V8	113	88	89
454-4 BBL V8 Caprice Classic	291	227	230
454-4 BBL V8 Bel Air & Impala	315	246	249
61-Amp Delcotron Generator	26	20	21
Soft-Ray Tinted Glass	60	47	48
Dual Horns	4	3	4
Deluxe Luggage Compartment	33	26	27
Color-Keyed Floor Mats	14	11	12
Mirrors			
Left & Right Outside Remote Control	41	32	33
Left Outside Remote Control	14	11	12
Sport, Twin Remote, Body-colored	46	36	37
Body Side Molding	38	30	31
Deluxe Body Side Molding	25	20	21
Door Edge Guard			
Coupe & Convertible	7	5	6

40   CONSUMER GUIDE

AUTOMOBILES

Sedan	11	9	10	32	35	36
Roof Drip	15	12	13			
Wheel Opening	18	14	15			
Two-Tone Paint	31	24	25			
Quiet Sound Group						
Power Door Lock System						
Econominder Gauge Package				172	134	136
Engines						
454 4BBL V8				56	44	45
Deluxe Load Floor Carpeting	44	34	35	40	31	32
Removable Load Floor Carpeting	28	22	23	14	11	12
Color-Keyed Floor	32	25	26	26	20	21
61-Amp Delcotron Generator				60	47	48
Soft-Ray Tinted Glass				4	3	4
Pushbutton Radios				13	10	11
Dual Horns						
AM	69	54	55			
AM/FM	139	108	110			
AM/FM Stereo	233	182	184			
Dome Reading Light						
Auxiliary Lighting						
Bel Air & Impala				19	15	16
Stereo Tape System w/AM	215	168	170			
Stereo Tape System w/AM/FM Stereo	363	283	286			
Caprice Estate				23	18	19
Rear Seat Speaker	19	15	16			
Rearview Left and Right Outside Remote Control Mirrors				36	28	29
Vinyl Roof Cover	109	85	86			
Power Seat	113	88	89			
Rearview Left Remote Control Mirror				14	11	12
Rear Fender Skirts	31	24	25			
Twin Remote Sport Mirror				41	32	33
Cruise-Master Speed Control	69	54	55			
Visor Vanity				3	2	3
Comfortilt Steering Wheel	49	38	39			
Body Side Moldings				38	30	31
Superlift Rear Shock Absorbers	41	32	33			
Deluxe Body Side Moldings				35	27	28
Radial Tuned Suspension	17	13	14			
Door Edge Guard Moldings				11	9	10
Roof Drip Moldings				22	17	18
Sport Suspension						
Caprice Classic	6	5	6			
Wheel Opening Moldings				18	14	15
Bel Air & Impala	30	23	24			
Two-Tone Exterior Paint				31	24	25
Vinyl Interior Trim						
Quiet Sound Group						
Coupes & Sedans	19	15	16			
Bel Air				44	34	35
50/50 Reclining Passenger Seat	133	104	106			
Impala				23	18	19
Power Trunk Opener	16	12	13			
Heavy Duty Radiator				32	25	26
Power Windows	149	116	118			
Pushbutton Radios						
Caprice Classic Cpe. & Impala Cust. Cpe.	99	77	78	AM	69	54	55
Windshield Wiper System	26	20	21	AM/FM	139	108	110

CONSUMER GUIDE

AUTOMOBILES

	Retail Price	Dealer Cost	Low Price
Stereo Tape System w/AM	215	168	170
Stereo Tape System w/AM/FM Stereo	363	283	286
Rear Seat Speaker	19	15	16
Vinyl Roof Cover	138	108	110
Power Seat	113	88	89
Speed Control	69	54	55
Tilt Steering Wheel	49	38	39
Shock Absorbers	41	32	33
Heavy Duty Suspension	17	13	14
Power Tailgate	49	38	39
Interior Trim			
50/50 Reclining Passenger Seat	133	104	106
Power Windows	149	116	118
Intermittent Windshield Wiper System	26	20	21

CAMARO

	Retail Price	Dealer Cost	Low Price
Sport Coupe, 4-Passenger, 6 Cylinder	$3553	$3028	$3228
Sport Coupe, 4 Passenger, 8 Cylinder	3698	3156	3456
Type LT Coupe, 4 Passenger, 8 Cylinder	4070	3479	3779

CAMARO ACCESSORIES

	Retail Price	Dealer Cost	Low Price
Four Season Air Conditioning	$435	$339	$343
Positraction, Rear Axle	49	38	39
Axle Ratios	12	9	10
Trailering or High Altitude	43	34	35
Heavy-Duty Battery	15	12	13
Color-Keyed Seat & Shoulder Belts	16	12	13
Sports Decor Package			
Sports Coupe	42	33	34
Sports Coupe w/Style Trim	40	31	32
Type LT	15	12	13
Type LT w/Style Trim	13	10	11
Comfortilt Steering Wheel	49	38	39
Striping	77	60	61
Style Trim	55	43	44
Transmissions			
Turbo Hydra-matic	235	193	195
4 Speed	219	180	182
Leather Interior Trim	216	162	170
Wheel Trim			
Full Wheelcovers	30	23	24
Rally Wheels	46	36	37
Turbine I Wheels, Sport Coupe	111	86	87
Turbine I Wheels, Type LT Coupe	75	59	60
Power Windows	91	71	72
Hide-A-Way Windshield Wipers	21	16	17

CHEVELLE MALIBU AND MALIBU CLASSIC COUPES AND SEDANS

MALIBU 6-CYLINDER

	Retail Price	Dealer Cost	Low Price
Colonnade Hardtop, 6 Passenger	$3420	$2794	$2994
Colonnade Hardtop Dedan, 6 Passenger	3415	2796	2996

MALIBU CLASSIC 6-CYLINDER

	Retail Price	Dealer Cost	Low Price
Colonnade Hardtop Coupe 6 Passenger	3711	3031	3231
Colonnade Hardtop Landau Coupe Psngr	3943	3218	3418
Colonnade Hardtop Sedan, 6 Passenger	3708	3034	3234

AUTOMOBILES

MALIBU 8-CYLINDER

Colonnade Hardtop Coupe, 6 Passenger	3670	2994	3194
Colonnade Hardtop Sedan, 6 Passenger	3665	2996	3196

MALIBU CLASSIC 8-CYLINDER

Colonnade Hardtop Coupe, 6 Passenger	3961	3231	3431
Colonnade Hardtop Landau Coupe, 6 Psngr	4193	3417	3617
Colonnade Hardtop Sedan, 6 Passenger	3958	3234	3434

CHEVELLE MALIBU AND MALIBU CLASSIC ACCESSORIES

Four Season Air Conditioning	$505	$394	$398
W/o 250-1 BBL V8 or 454-4 BBL V8 Engine	450	351	355
W/454-4 BBL V8 Engine	579	452	457
W/250-1 BBL V6	49	38	39
Positraction Rear Axle	12	9	10
High Altitude Axle Ratio	12	9	10
Highway Axle Ratio	15	12	13
Heavy-Duty Battery			
Custom Deluxe Seat & Shoulder Belts	16	12	13
Bench Seat	15	12	13
Bucket Seats	55	43	44
Power Brakes	27	21	22
Deluxe Bumpers	34	27	28
Bumper Guards	45	35	36
California Emission Certification	18	14	15
Electric Clock	68	53	54
Console	5	4	5
Litter Container	41	32	33
Rear Window Defogger			
Power Door Lock System			
2 Door	56	44	45
Power Brakes	55	43	44
Bumper Equipment	34	27	28
California Emission Certification	45	35	36
Electric Clock	17	13	14
Console	68	53	54
Rear Window Defogger	41	32	33
Power Door Lock System	56	44	45
350-4BBL V8 Engine	54	42	43
Floor Covering			
Deluxe Carpet	30	23	24
Color-Keyed Floor Mats	14	11	12
Soft-Ray Tinted Glass, All Windows	45	35	36
Special Instrumentation	88	69	70
Interior Decor/Quiet Sound Group	35	27	28
Auxiliary Lighting, Sport Coupe w/o Interior Decor/Quiet Sound Group	23	18	19
Auxiliary Lighting Sport Coupe w/Interior Decor/Quiet Sound Group	20	16	17
Sport Mirrors	27	21	22
Body Side Moldings	38	30	31
Heavy Duty Radiator	15	12	13
Pushbutton Radio			
AM	69	54	55
AM/FM	135	105	107
AM/FM Stereo	233	182	184
Stereo Tape System w/AM	199	155	157
Stereo Tape System w/AM/FM Stereo	363	283	286
Rear Seat Speaker	19	15	16
Vinyl Roof Cover	87	68	69
Adjustable Seat Back	18	14	15
Space Saver Spare Tire	14	12	13
Spoilers	77	60	61

CONSUMER GUIDE

AUTOMOBILES

	Retail Price	Dealer Cost	Low Price
4 Door	82	64	65
Engines			
350-4 BBL V8	54	42	43
400-4 BBL V8	113	88	89
454-4 BBL V8	340	265	268
Exterior Decor			
W/o Vinyl roof	49	38	39
W/Vinyl roof	34	27	28
61-Amp Delcotron Generator	26	20	21
Soft-Ray Tinted Glass	48	37	38
Dual Horns	4	3	4
Instrumentation			
Econominder	43	33	34
Special	88	69	70
Color-Keyed Floor Mats	14	11	12
Mirrors			
Outside R-View, Left Remote-Control	14	11	12
Outside R-View, Left & Right Remote-Control	41	32	33
Sport	27	21	22
Twin Remote Sport Mirror			
Malibu Classic Landau	19	15	16
Malibu & Malibu Classic	46	36	37
Body Side Moldings	38	30	31
Door Edge Guard Moldings			
2 Door	7	5	6
4 Door	11	9	10
Heavy-Duty Radiator			
6 Cylinder	15	12	13

	Retail Price	Dealer Cost	Low Price
4-Dr. Station Wagon, 3-Seat	4476	3654	3954
MALIBU CLASSIC STATION WAGONS			
4-Dr. Station Wagon, 2-Seat	4569	3729	4029
4-Dr. Station Wagon, 3-Seat	4714	3847	4147
MALIBU CLASSIC ESTATE STATION WAGONS			
4-Dr. Wagon, 2-Seat	4761	3883	4183
4-Dr. Wagon, 3-Seat	4906	4001	4301
MALIBU, MALIBU CLASSIC, MALIBU CLASSIC ESTATE WAGONS ACCESSORIES			
Four-Season Air Conditioning	450	351	355
Rear Window Air Deflector	22	17	18
Positraction, Rear Axle	49	38	39
Axle Ratios	12	9	10
Heavy-Duty Battery	15	12	13
Custom Deluxe Seat & Shoulder Belts, 2-Seat Wagons			
W/Bench Seat	16	12	13
W/Bucket Seats	14	11	12
Custom Deluxe Seat & Shoulder Belts, 3-Seat Wagons			
W/Bench Seat	19	15	16
W/Bucket Seats	17	14	15
Deluxe Bumpers	27	21	22
Bumper Guards	17	13	14
California Emission Certification	45	35	36
Roof Carrier	65	51	52
Electric Clock	18	14	15

AUTOMOBILES

8 Cylinder	22	17	18	
Pushbutton Radios				
AM	69	54	55	
AM/FM	135	105	107	
AM/FM Stereo	233	182	184	
Stereo Tape System with AM	199	155	157	
Stereo Tape System with AM/FM Stereo	363	283	286	
Rear Seat Speaker	19	15	16	
Vinyl Roof Cover	96	75	76	
Power Seat	113	88	89	
Sky Roof	350	273	276	
Speed Control	69	54	55	
Power Steering	129	101	103	
Steering Wheels				
Comfortilt	49	38	39	
Sport	15	12	13	
Special Suspension Equipment	17	13	14	
Turbo Hydra-matic Transmission	235	193	195	
Interior Trim				
Vinyl Bench Seat	19	15	16	
Strato-bucket Front Seat Interior Trim				
Malibu	133	104	106	
Malibu Classic	97	76	77	
Power Windows				
2 Door	91	71	72	
4 Door	132	103	105	

Litter Container	5	4	5	
Rear Window Defogger	45	35	36	
Power Door Lock System	82	64	65	
Engines				
350-4 BBL V8	54	42	43	
400-4 BBL V8	113	88	89	
454-4 BBL V8	285	222	225	
Exterior Decor	50	39	40	
Floor Covering				
Removable Load Floor Carpeting	40	31	32	
Color-Keyed Floor Mats	14	11	12	
61 Amp Delcotron Gnerator	26	20	21	
Soft-Ray Tinted Glass	48	37	38	
Dual Horns	4	3	4	
Instrumentation, Econominder Gauge Package	42	33	34	
Auxiliary Lighting, Malibu				
2-Seat Wagons	36	28	29	
3-Seat Wagons	26	20	21	
Aux. Lighting, Malibu Classic & Classic Estate				
2-Seat Wagons	32	25	26	
3-Seat Wagons	22	18	19	
Mirrors				
R-View, Left & Right Outside Remote-Control	41	32	33	
R-View, Left Outside Remote-Control	14	11	12	
Sport	27	21	22	
Twin Remote Sport	46	36	37	
Moldings				
Body Side	38	30	31	
Door Edge Guard	11	9	10	

MALIBU STATION WAGONS

4-Dr. Station Wagon, 2-Seat	$4331	$3535	$3835

AUTOMOBILES

	Retail Price	Dealer Cost	Low Price
Pushbutton Radios			
AM	69	54	55
AM/FM	135	105	107
AM/FM Stereo	233	182	184
Stereo Tape System w/AM	199	155	157
Stereo Tape System w/AM/FM Stereo	363	283	286
Rear Seat Speaker	19	15	16
Power Seat	113	88	89
Speed Control	69	54	55
Steering Wheels			
Comfortilt	49	38	39
Sport	15	12	13
Power Tailgate Release	16	12	13
Strato-bucket Front Seat Interior Trim			
Malibu	133	104	106
Malibu Classic & Malibu Classic Estate	97	76	77
Power Windows	132	103	105
Swing-Out Windows	44	34	35
Intermittent Windshield Wiper System	26	20	21

CORVETTE

	Retail Price	Dealer Cost	Low Price
Coupe, 2-Passenger	$6810	$5314	$6014
Convertible, 2-Passenger	6550	5112	5812

CORVETTE ACCESSORIES

	Retail Price	Dealer Cost	Low Price
Four-Season Air Conditioning	$490	$382	$386
Axle Ratios	12	9	10
w/Bucket seats, 5 seat & 2 front shoulder	15	11	12
Front & Rear Bumper Equipment			
Deluxe	27	21	22
Guards	34	27	28
California Emission Certification	45	35	36
Console	68	53	54
Rear Window Defogger	41	32	33
Power Door Lock System	56	44	45
Engines			
350-4 BBL. V8	54	42	43
400-4 BBL. V8	113	88	89
454-4 BBL. V8	285	222	225
61-Amp Delcotron Generator	26	20	21
Soft-Ray Tinted Glass, All Windows	51	40	41
Instrumentation	43	33	34
Color-Keyed Floor Mats	14	11	12
Mirrors			
Outside Rearview, Left Remote Control	14	11	12
Outside R-View, Left & Right Remote Control	41	32	33
Sport, Body-colored Left Remote Control & Right Manual	27	21	22
Sport, Twin Remote	46	36	37
Sport, Twin Remote w/Landau Top	19	15	16
Deluxe Body Side Moldings	49	38	39
Heavy Duty Radiator	22	17	18
Pushbutton Radio			
AM	69	54	55

AUTOMOBILES

Heavy-Duty Battery	15	12	13
Custom Deluxe Belts	41	32	33
Power Brakes	55	43	44
California Emission Certification	45	35	36
Rear Window Defogger	46	36	37
Special 350-4 BBL V8 Engine	336	262	265
Off-Road Handling Package	403	314	318
Radio			
AM/FM	178	139	141
AM/FM Stereo	284	222	225
Vinyl Roof Cover	350	273	276
Power Steering	129	101	103
Tilt-Telescopic Steering Wheel	82	64	65
Auxiliary Top	267	208	211
Turbo Hydra-matic Transmission w/Special 350-4 BBL V8 engine	120	98	99
Custom Interior Trim	154	120	122
Power Windows	93	73	74

MONTE CARLO

Coupe, 6 Passenger	$4262	$3492	$3692
Landau Coupe, 6 Passenger	4532	3712	3912

MONTE CARLO ACCESSORIES

Four Season Air Conditioning	$450	$351	$355
Positraction Rear Axle	49	38	39
Axle Ratios	12	9	10
Heavy-Duty Battery	15	12	13
Custom Deluxe & Shoulder Belts w/Bench seat, 6 seat & 2 front shoulder	16	12	13
AM/FM	139	108	110
AM/FM Stereo	233	182	184
Stereo Tape System w/AM	215	168	170
Stereo Tape System w/AM/FM Stereo	363	283	286
Rear Seat Speaker	19	15	16
Vinyl Roof Cover	123	96	97
Power Seat	113	88	89
Sky Roof	350	273	276
Cruise-Master Speed Control	69	54	55
Steering Wheel	49	38	39
Suspension Equipment	17	13	14
Turbo Hydra-matic Transmission	235	193	195
Interior Trim			
Vinyl Bench Seat	19	15	16
Luxury Cloth 50/50 Bench Seat	260	203	206
Strato-bucket Front Seats	133	104	106
Luxury Cloth Strato-bucket Front Seats	252	197	199
Power Trunk Opener	16	12	13
Deluxe Wheel Covers	19	15	16
Rally Wheels	32	25	26
Wire Wheel Covers	75	59	60
Power Windows	91	71	72
Windshield Wiper System	26	20	21

NOVA 6-CYLINDER

Hatchback Coupe, 6 Passenger	$3360	$2886	$3086
2 Dr. Coupe, 6 Passenger	3218	2762	2962
4 Dr. Sedan, 6 Passenger	3222	2766	2966

NOVA CUSTOM 6-CYLINDER

Hatchback Coupe, 6 Passenger	3554	3054	3254
2 Dr. Coupe, 6 Passenger	3415	2933	3133

AUTOMOBILES

	Retail Price	Dealer Cost	Low Price
4 Dr. Sedan, 6 Passenger	3428	2944	3144
NOVA LN 6-CYLINDER			
Coupe, 6 Passenger	3795	3256	3456
4 Dr. Sedan, 6 Passenger	3808	3267	3467
NOVA 8-CYLINDER			
Hatchback Coupe, 6 Passenger	3435	2951	3151
2 Dr. Coupe, 6 Passenger	3293	2827	3027
4 Dr. Sedan, 6 Passenger	3297	2831	3031
NOVA CUSTOM 8-CYLINDER			
Hatchback Coupe, 6 Passenger	3629	3118	3318
2 Dr. Coupe, 6 Passenger	3490	2997	3197
4 Dr. Sedan, 6 Passenger	3503	3009	3209
NOVA LN 8-CYLINDER			
Coupe, 6 Passenger	3870	3320	3520
4 Dr. Sedan, 6 Passenger	3883	3332	3532

NOVA ACCESSORIES

	Retail Price	Dealer Cost	Low Price
Four-Season Air Conditioning	$435	$339	$343
Positraction Rear Axle	49	38	39
Axle Ratios	12	9	10
Heavy-Duty Battery	15	12	13
Custom Deluxe Belts			
Coupes & Sedans w/Bench Seat	16	13	14
Coupes w/Bucket Seats	14	11	12
Power Brakes	55	43	44
Bumper Equipment	59	46	47
California Emission Certification	45	35	36
Nova	178	139	141
Heavy-Duty Radiator	17	13	14
Pushbutton Radios			
AM	69	54	55
AM/FM	135	105	107
AM/FM Stereo	233	182	184
Stereo Tape System w/AM	199	155	157
Stereo Tape System w/AM/FM Stereo	363	283	286
Rear Seat Speaker	19	15	16
Vinyl Roof Cover	87	68	69
Floor-Mounted Shift Lever	27	22	23
Space Saver Spare Tire	14	12	13
Power Steering	129	101	103
Steering Wheel			
Comfortilt	49	38	39
Sport	15	12	13
Nova Suspension Equipment	30	23	24
W/SS Equipment	24	19	20
Transmissions			
Turbo Hydra-matic	235	193	195
4-Speed Wide-Range	219	180	182
Nova & Nova Custom Interior Trim	19	15	16
Strato-bucket Front Seats	75	59	60
Power Windows			
2 Door	91	71	72
4 Door	132	103	105
Swing-Out Windows	44	34	35
Windshield Wiper System	26	20	21

AUTOMOBILES

Roof Carrier	60	47	48	
Electric Clock	17	13	14	
Console	68	53	54	
Rear Window Defogger	41	32	33	
Power Door Lock System				
Engines				
2 Door	56	44	45	
4 Door	82	64	65	
350 2 BBL. V8	50	39	40	
350 4 BBL. V8	104	81	82	
Exterior Decor Package	73	57	58	
Soft-Ray Tinted Glass, All Windows	45	35	36	
Special Instrumentation				
w/o Nova LN	152	119	121	
w/Nova LN	135	105	107	
Interior Decor/Quiet Sound Group	39	30	31	
Econominder Light	15	12	13	
Color-Keyed Floor Mats	14	11	12	
Inside Rearview Day-Night Mirror	6	5	6	
Outside Rearview Mirror, Left Remote Control	14	11	12	
Sport Mirrors				
Left Remote, Right Manual	27	21	22	
Turn Remote, Body Colored	46	36	37	
Turn Remote, Body Colored w/SS Equip.	19	15	16	
Body Side Moldings	38	30	31	
Door Edge Guard				
2 Door	7	5	6	
4 Door	11	9	10	
Wheel Opening	18	14	15	
Nova SS Equipment				
Nova Custom	162	126	128	

MONZA
Monza 2 + 2—4-Passenger $3966 $3378 $3578

MONZA ACCESSORIES

Four-Season Air Conditioning	$398	$338	$342
Positraction, Rear Axle	45	38	39
Axle Ratio	11	9	10
Heavy-Duty Battery	14	12	13
Custom Deluxe Belts	15	12	13
Power Brakes	51	43	44
California Emission Certification	45	38	39
Rear Window Defogger	60	51	52
4.3 Litre 2-BBL. V8 Engine	198	168	170
Soft-Ray Tinted Glass, All Windows	42	36	37
Auxiliary Lighting	12	10	11
Color-Keyed Floor Mats	13	11	12
Sport Mirrors, Left Remote-Control & Right Manual	25	21	22
Body Side Moldings	36	30	31
Heavy-Duty Radiator	16	14	15
Pushbutton Radio			
AM	63	54	55
AM/FM	129	110	112
AM/FM Stereo	213	181	183
Rear Seat Speaker	18	15	16
Adjustable Seat Back, Driver's Seat	16	14	15
Power Steering	111	94	95
Comfortilt Steering Wheel	45	38	39
Turbo Hydra-matic Transmission	235	200	202
Leather Interior Trim	198	168	170

CONSUMER GUIDE

AUTOMOBILES

	Retail Price	Dealer Cost	Low Price
Aluminum Wheels	153	130	132

VEGA

	Retail Price	Dealer Cost	Low Price
Notchback Coupe, 4 Passenger	$2799	$2418	$2618
Notchback Coupe, 4 Passenger	3132	2701	2901
Hatchback Coupe, 4 Passenger	2912	2515	2715
Wagon, 2 Seat	3029	2615	2815
Estate Wagon, 2 Seat	3257	2809	3009

VEGA ACCESSORIES

	Retail Price	Dealer Cost	Low Price
Four-Season Air Conditioning	$398	$338	$342
Rear Window Air Deflector	21	18	19
Positraction Rear Axle	45	38	39
High Altitude Axle Ratio	11	9	10
Heavy-Duty Battery	14	12	13
Custom Deluxe Belts	15	12	13
Power Brakes	51	43	44
Bumper Equipment			
Deluxe Bumpers	41	34	35
Deluxe Guards	16	13	14
California Emission Certification	45	38	39
Roof Carrier	50	42	43
Electric Clock	15	13	14
Custom Exterior			
Hatchback	82	70	71
Notchback	82	70	71
Wagon	55	47	48
Custom Interior, Hatchback	134	114	116
W/o GT			
AM/FM	129	110	112
AM/FM Stereo	213	181	183
Rear Seat Speaker	18	15	16
Vinyl Roof Cover	79	67	68
Adjustable Seat Back	16	14	15
Power Steering	111	94	95
Steering Wheel			
Sport	14	11	12
Comfortilt	45	38	39
Sport Stripes	70	60	61
Sport Suspension	131	110	112
Transmission			
4-Speed	56	48	49
Turbo Hydra-matic	235	200	202

BLAZER

	Retail Price	Dealer Cost	Low Price
C10 Series 2-Wheel Drive, 6-Cylinder			
Utility w/o Top	$3358	$2764	$2964
Utility w/Top	3787	3111	3311
K10 Series 4-Wheel Drive, 6-Cylinder			
Utility w/o Top	4188	3440	3640
Utility w/Top	4617	3787	3987
C10 Series 2-Wheel Drive, 8-Cylinder			
Utility w/o Top	3498	2877	3077
Utility w/Top	3926	3225	3425
K10 Series 4-Wheel Drive, 8-Cylinder			
Utility w/o Top	4569	3717	3917
Utility w/Top	4998	4065	4265

CONSUMER GUIDE

AUTOMOBILES

W/GT	124	105	107			
Custom Interior, Notchback						
W/o LX	134	114	116			
Custom Interior, Wagon						
W/o GT	113	96	97			
W/GT	103	88	89			
Decor Group						
W/o Custom Interior or Custom Exterior	32	27	28			
W/Custom Interior	27	23	24			
W/Custom Exterior	5	4	5			
Rear Window Defogger	60	51	52			
140-2 BBL L4 Engine	50	43	44			
Soft-Ray Tinted Glass, All Windows	42	36	37			
GT Hatchback	425	361	365			
GT Wagon						
W/o Estate	399	339	343			
W/Estate	316	268	271			
Special Instrumentation						
Notchback, Hatchback, Wagon & Estate Wagon	67	57	58			
Notchback LX	52	44	45			
Color-Keyed Floor Mats	13	11	12			
Inside Rearview, Day-Night Mirror	6	5	6			
Sport Mirror, Left Hand Remote, Right Hand Manual	25	21	22			
Body Side Moldings	36	30	31			
Door Edge Guard Moldings	7	6	7			
Wheel Opening Moldings	18	15	16			
Heavy-Duty Radiator	16	14	15			
Pushbutton Radios						
AM	63	54	55			

BLAZER ACCESSORIES

	$12	$9	$10
Poly-Wrap Air Cleaner	$12	$9	$10
All-Weather Air Conditioning	458	357	361
Rear Axles			
Optional Ratio	14	11	12
Locking Differential	145	113	115
Padded Roll Bar	89	69	70
Batteries			
Auxiliary	61	44	45
Heavy-Duty	18	14	15
Heavy-Duty Power Brakes	48	37	38
Chromed Bumper Equipment			
Front & Rear	36	28	29
Front Bumper Guards	20	16	17
California Emission Certification			
K10 Series	75	59	60
C10 Series or K10 Series w/250 1 BBL. Engine	45	35	36
Wheelhouse Carpeting	17	13	14
Cheyenne			
C10 Series w/o Top	429	335	339
K10	432	337	341
C10 Series w/Top	530	413	418
K10	533	416	421
Electric Clock	38	30	31
W/Cheyenne	21	16	17
Cold-Climate Package	88	69	70
W/Trailering Special	71	55	56
Engine Oil Cooler	74	58	59
Radiator Cooling	30	23	24
350 4 BBL. V8 Engine, C10 Series	25	20	21

CONSUMER GUIDE

AUTOMOBILES

	Retail Price	Dealer Cost	Low Price
Temperature & Oil Pressure Ammeter	17	13	14
Tachometer	67	52	53
W/Cheyenne	50	39	40
42-Amp Delcotron	27	21	22
61-Amp Delcotron	35	27	28
Sliding Side Window Glass	142	111	113
Soft Ray Tinted Glass, All Windows			
W/o Top	25	20	21
W/Top	39	30	31
Chromed Grille	22	17	18
Trailer Wiring Harness	23	18	19
Front Free-Wheeling Hubs	85	66	67
Wood-Grained Instrument Panel	30	23	24
Below-Eye-Line Mirror			
Painted	23	18	19
Stainless Steel	41	32	33
Camper Type Mirror	58	45	46
Moldings			
Body Side Spear	50	39	40
Body Side Upper	52	41	42
Body Side Upper & Lower	126	98	99
Exterior Paints			
Special Two-Tone	199	155	157
Special Two-Tone w/Cheyenne	73	57	58
Fuel Tank Shield Plate			
C10 Series	31	24	25
K10 Series	58	45	46

CHRYSLER

	Retail Price	Dealer Cost	Low Price
NEWPORT			
2 Door Hardtop	$4937	$3833	$4083
4 Door Sedan	4854	3768	4018
4 Door Hardtop	5008	3888	4138
NEWPORT CUSTOM			
2 Door Hardtop	5329	4132	4382
4 Door Sedan	5254	4076	4326
4 Door Hardtop	5423	4207	4457
NEW YORKER BROUGHAM			
2 Door Hardtop	6334	4907	5157
4 Door Sedan	6277	4863	5113
4 Door Hardtop	6424	4977	5227
TOWN AND COUNTRY			
4 Door Wagon, 2 Seat	6099	4715	5015
4 Door Wagon, 3 Seat	6244	4838	5138

AUTOMOBILES

NEWPORT, NEW YORKER, TOWN AND COUNTRY ACCESSORIES

Pushbutton Radios			
AM	69	54	55
AM/FM	151	118	120
Front Auxiliary, 1-Passenger Seat	87	68	69
Front Custom Vinyl, Driver & Passenger Seat			
W/o Top, w/o Rear 3 Passenger Seat	168	131	133
W/o Top, w/Rear 3 Passenger Seat	202	158	160
W/Top, w/o Rear 3 Passenger Seat	198	154	156
W/Top, w/Rear 3 Passenger Seat	232	181	183
Front Custom Cloth, Driver & Passenger			
W/Top, w/Rear 3 Passenger Seat	34	27	28
Rear 3 Passenger Seat	153	119	121
Heavy-Duty Shock Absorbers			
Front & Rear	18	14	15
Rear	10	8	9
Speed & Cruise Control	69	54	55
Heavy-Duty Springs			
Front Capacity 1625-lb. Each C10 Series	7	5	6
Front Capacity 1900-lb. Each K10 Series	36	28	29
Rear Capacity 1700-lb. Each C10 Series	21	16	17
Stabilizers			
Front 1" Diameter	20	16	17
Front, Heavy-Duty 1.25" Diameter	6	5	6
Power Steering			
C10 Series	153	119	121
K10 Series	170	133	135
Steering Wheels			
Comfortilt	61	48	49
Custom	11	9	10
Fuel Tank, Approximately 30-gallon capacity	21	16	17
Manual Throttle Control	16	12	13
Vinyl Roof	$137	$103	$105
Vinyl Side Moulding	41	31	32
St. Regis Package, 2 Dr. Hardtop	569	427	432
W/Easy Order Package	432	324	328
Bench Seats			
Vinyl	29	22	23
Cloth & Vinyl	80	60	61
50/50 Vinyl w/Shag Carpets	27	20	21
400 CID 4 BBL w/Calif. Emission Control & Testing	40	32	33
440 CID 4 BBL	165	132	134
Light Package			
Newport & Newport Custom	71	53	54
Town and Country	35	26	27
Deluxe Wiper/Washer Package	15	11	12
Basic Group			
Newport, Newport Custom	820	639	646
New Yorker Brougham	661	519	525
Town and Country	875	680	687
Easy Order Package			
Newport & Newport Custom	1140	828	837
New Yorker Brougham	1267	924	934
Town and Country	1275	930	940
Town and Country Package	111	83	84
Light Trailer Towing Package	72	54	55
Heavy Trailer Towing Package	288	216	219
Manual Control Air Conditioning	475	380	384
Automatic Temp Control Air Conditioning	552	441	446

AUTOMOBILES

	Retail Price	Dealer Cost	Low Price
Automatic Temp Control w/Basic Group, or Easy Order Package	77	61	62
Optional Axle Ratio	15	11	12
Sure Grip Differential	55	41	42
Battery	28	21	22
Electric Clock	21	16	17
Electronic Digital Clock	23	17	18
Newport & Newport Custom	44	33	34
Tinted Glass, All Windows	63	48	49
Tinted Glass, Windshield Only	49	37	38
Manual Vent Windows	39	29	30
Engine Block Heater	17	13	14
Lights, Cornering	41	31	32
Lights, Safeguard Sentinel	39	29	30
Accessory Floor Mats	18	14	15
Vanity Mirror	43	32	33
Left Remote Control Mirror	15	11	12
Right Remote Control Mirror	29	22	23
Left & Right Remote Control Mirror	45	33	34
Door Edge Protector Mouldings			
2 Door	7	5	6
4 Door	13	10	11
Upper Door Frame, 4 Door Sedan	28	21	22
Wheel House Opening Skirts	41	31	32
6 Way Bench Seat	121	91	92
6 Way Left 50/50 Seat	121	91	92
6 Way Left & Right 50/50 Seat	243	182	184
W/Easy Order Package	121	91	92
Power Windows	157	118	120
Steering Wheels			
W/Partial Horn Ring	16	12	13
Tilt & Telescope	97	73	74
Tilt & Telescope w/Easy Order Package	82	61	62
Power Sunroof			
W/Vinyl Roof	781	586	592
W/Easy Order Pkg.	644	484	489
Heavy Duty Suspension			
Town & Country	20	15	16
Other	27	20	21
Automatic Height Control	100	75	76
Trunk Dress Up			
Brougham	20	15	16
Others	43	32	33
Undercoating w/Hood Insulator Pad	33	25	26

CORDOBA

	Retail Price	Dealer Cost	Low Price
2 Door Specialty Hardtop V8	$5072	$4169	$4469

CORDOBA ACCESSORIES

	Retail Price	Dealer Cost	Low Price
Full Vinyl Roof	$109	$83	$84
W/Easy Order Package	15	11	12
Full Landau Roof	95	72	73
Vinyl Side Moulding	38	29	30
Cloth & Vinyl Bench Seat w/Center Folding Arm Rest	17	13	14

AUTOMOBILES

Door Locks					
2 Door	61	46	47	Leather Bucket Seats w/Center Seat Cushion	
4 Door	88	66	67	w/Folding Center Arm Rest	187 142 144
Deck Lid Release	19	14	15	360 CID 8 4 BBL Single Exhaust	40 32 33
Radio				360 CID 8 4 BBL	153 123 125
AM	99	74	75	400 CID 8 2 BBL Single Exhaust	44 35 36
AM/FM Stereo Search Tune	159	119	121	400 CID 8 4 BBL Single Exhaust	73 58 59
AM/FM Stereo w/Stereo Tape 8 Track	318	239	242	Easy Order Package	760 560 566
AM/FM Stereo w/Stereo Tape 8 Track	409	307	311	Light Trailer Towing Package	71 54 55
Radios w/Basic Group				Heavy Trailer Towing Package	284 216 219
AM/FM	60	45	46	Air Conditioning	437 350 354
AM/FM Stereo Search Tune	219	164	166	Optional Axle Ratio	15 11 12
AM/FM Stereo w/Stereo Tape 8 Track	310	232	235	Sure Grip Differential Axle	50 38 39
Radios w/Easy Order Package, All Except				500 AMP Long Life Battery	28 21 22
Brougham & Town & Country				Console	17 13 14
AM/FM	60	45	46	Rear Window Defroster	73 55 56
AM/FM Stereo Search Tune	198	149	151	Emission Control System & Testing	58 44 45
AM/FM Stereo w/Stereo Tape 8 Track	289	217	220	Fender Mounted Turn Signal Indicators	12 9 10
Radios w/Easy Order Package, Town				Fuel Pacer System	32 24 25
& Country Only				Tinted Glass, All Windows	51 39 40
AM/FM	60	45	46	Tinted Glass, Windshield Only	36 28 29
AM/FM Stereo Search Tune	190	145	147	Accessory Floor Mats	17 13 14
AM/FM Stereo w/Stereo Tape 8 Track	280	210	213	Left Remote Control Chrome Mirror	15 11 12
Radios w/Easy Order Package, Brougham Only				Left & Right Remote Control Chrome Mirror	44 34 35
AM/FM Stereo w/Stero Tape 8 Track	91	68	69	W/Easy Order Package	29 22 23
Rear Seat Speaker				Dual Remote Control Chrome Sport	
Sedans & Hardtops	21	16	17	Mirrors	52 39 40
Wagons	30	22	23	W/Easy Order Package	37 28 29
Power Antenna	37	28	29	Dual Remote Control Painted Sport Mirrors	52 39 40
Security Alarm System	114	85	86	W/Easy Order Package	37 28 29
Automatic Speed Control	77	58	59	Power Bench Seat	117 89 90
Station Wagon Rear Bumper Step Pads	13	10	11	Left Power Bucket Seat	117 89 90
				Power Windows	97 74 75

CONSUMER GUIDE 55

AUTOMOBILES

DODGE

	Retail Price	Dealer Cost	Low Price
MONACO — V8			
2 Door Hardtop	$4631	$3607	$3857
4 Door Sedan	4605	3587	3837
2 Seat Wagon	5109	3981	4231
ROYAL MONACO — V8			
2 Door Hardtop	4868	3781	4031
4 Door Sedan	4848	3766	4016
4 Door Hardtop	4951	3846	4096
2 Seat Wagon	5292	4110	4360
3 Seat Wagon	5415	4209	4459
ROYAL MONACO BROUGHAM — V8			
2 Door Hardtop	5460	4246	4496
4 Door Sedan	5262	4092	4342
4 Door Hardtop	5382	4185	4435
2 Seat Wagon	5779	4488	4788
3 Seat Wagon	5905	4585	4885

MONACO ACCESSORIES

	Retail Price	Dealer Cost	Low Price
Vinyl Roof	$117	$89	$90
Vinyl Body Side Moldings	20	17	16
Vinyl Bench Seat	20	15	16
Vinyl Bench Seat w/Center Arm Rest	40	32	31
50/50 Cloth & Vinyl Bench Seat	151	117	115
360 CID 2 BBL Engine	40	32	33

	Retail Price	Dealer Cost	Low Price
Power Door Locks	60	46	47
Power Deck Release	18	14	15
AM Radio	72	55	56
AM/FM Radio	149	113	115
W/Easy Order Package	77	58	59
AM Radio w/8 Track Stereo Tape	214	163	165
W/Easy Order Package	121	92	93
AM/FM Stereo Radio	254	193	195
W/Easy Order Package	161	123	125
AM/FM Stereo Radio w/8 Track Stereo Tape	304	231	234
W/Easy Order Package	397	302	306
AM/FM Stereo Radio w/Search Tune	314	239	242
W/Easy Order Package	221	168	170
Single Rear Speaker	20	16	17
Automatic Speed Control	72	55	56
"Tuff" Steering Wheel	13	10	11
Manual Sun Roof	296	225	228
Heavy Duty Suspension	24	18	19
Tachometer	59	45	46
Undercoating	29	22	23
Strato Ventilation	19	15	16

LE BARON

	Retail Price	Dealer Cost	Low Price
2 Dr. Hardtop	$8698	$6757	$7057
4 Dr. Hardtop	8844	6871	7171

IMPERIAL LE BARON ACCESSORIES

	Retail Price	Dealer Cost	Low Price
Vinyl Side Moulding	$41	$31	$32

CONSUMER GUIDE

AUTOMOBILES

Crown Coupe Package	569	427	432	44	35	36
Interior Trim	200	150	152			
Imperial Accessory Group						
2 Door	55	41	42	84	67	68
4 Door	60	45	46	40	32	33
Heavy Trailer Towing Package	288	216	219			
Sure Grip Differential Axle	62	47	48	194	156	158
Rear Window Electric Defroster	76	57	58	151	121	123
Emission Control System & Testing	59	44	45			
Fuel Pacer System	34	25	26	63	48	49
Manual Vent Windows	39	29	30	66	50	51
Engine Block Heater	17	13	14	60	45	46
Auto Headlight Dimmer	55	42	43	55	41	42
Safeguard Sentinel	45	34	35	57	43	44
Left 6 Way Power 50/50 Bench Seat	127	95	96	48	36	37
Left & Right 6 Way Power 50/50 Bench Seat	253	190	192	15	11	12
Door Locks						
2 Door	61	46	47	435	295	298
4 Door	88	66	67	437	297	300
Deck Lid Release	39	29	30			
Radios				439	298	301
AM/FM	202	152	154			
AM/FM Stereo w/Search Tuner	347	260	263	441	300	303
AM/FM Stereo w/Stereo Tape 8 Track	451	338	342	410	276	279
Security Alarm System	114	85	86	317	206	209
Automatic Speed Control	105	79	80	434	295	298
Tilt & Telescope Steering Wheel	104	78	79	403	271	274
Power Sun Roof	668	501	507			
Heavy Duty Suspension	21	16	17	1583	1120	1132
				1612	1143	1155

400 CID 2 BBL Engine
400 CID 4 BBL Monaco & Royal Monaco
 Sedans/Hardtops
 Wagons & Brougham
440 CID 4 BBL Monaco & Royal Monaco
 Sedans/Hardtops
 Wagons & Brougham
Light Package
 Monaco 2 Door Hardtop
 Monaco Sedan
 Monaco 2 Seat Wagon
 Royal Monaco 2 Door Hardtop
 Royal Monaco Sedan, 4 Dr. Hdtp & Wagons
 All Brougham Models
Deluxe Wiper/Washer Pkg.
Easy Order Package
 Royal Monaco 2 Dr. Hardtop
 Royal Monaco Sedan & 4 Dr. Hardtop
 Royal Monaco 2 Dr. Hardtop w/400 or 440
  CID Engine
 Royal Monaco Sedan & 4 Dr. Hardtop
  w/400 or 440 CID Engine
 Royal Monaco Wagons
 Brougham 2 Dr. Hardtop
 Brougham Sedan & 4 Dr. Hardtop
 Brougham Wagons
Luxury Equipment Package
 Royal Monaco 2 Dr. Hardtop
 Royal Monaco Sedan & 4 Dr. Hardtop

AUTOMOBILES

	Retail Price	Dealer Cost	Low Price
Royal Monaco 2 Dr. Hardtop /400 or 440 CID Engine	1586	1123	1135
Royal Monaco Sedan & 4 Dr. Hardtop W/400 or 440 CID Engine	1616	1146	1158
Royal Monaco Wagons	1638	1162	1174
Brougham 2 Dr. Hardtop	1361	952	962
Brougham Sedan & 4 Dr. Hardtop	1550	1096	1107
Brougham Wagons	1513	1067	1078
Wagon Package	59	45	46
Light Trailer Towing Package	71	54	55
Heavy Trailer Towing Package	284	216	219
Manual Control Air Conditioner	445	356	360
Automatic Temperature Control	522	417	422
W/Luxury Equipment Pkg.	77	61	62
3.21 Axle Ratio	15	11	12
Sure Grip Differential Axle	52	40	41
Battery	28	21	22
Electric Clock	19	14	15
Electric Digital Clock	43	33	34
Rear Window Defroster	73	55	56
Emissions Control System & Testing	58	44	45
Engine Temperature & Oil Pressure Gauges W/o Easy Order or Luxury Eqpt. Pkg.	19	14	15
Fuel Pacer System	32	24	25
W/Light, Easy Order & Luxury Eqpt. Pkg.	20	15	16
Tinted Glass, All Windows	63	48	49
Tinted Glass, Windshield Only	48	37	38
Manual Tinted Vent Windows	38	29	30
Engine Block Heater	17	13	14
W/Luxury Eqpt. Pkg.	247	188	190
Single Rear Speaker	20	16	17
Security Alarm System	112	85	86
Automatic Speed Control	72	55	56
Station Wagon Items			
Assist Handles	21	16	17
Tailgate Auto Lock	33	25	26
Luggage Rack	79	60	61
Rear Bumper Step Pads	13	10	11
Tilt & Telescope Steering Wheels	96	73	74
W/Luxury Eqpt. Pkg.	81	61	62
Deluxe Steering Wheel w/Partial Horn Rim	16	12	13
Sun Roof w/Vinyl Roof, Power Operated	634	482	487
W/Easy Order or Luxury Eqpt. Pkg.	517	393	397
Heavy Duty Suspension			
Sedans/Hardtops	24	18	19
Wagons	17	13	14
Automatic Height Control	99	75	76
Trunk Dress-Up	42	32	33
Undercoating	29	22	23
CORONET — SIX			
2 Door Hardtop	$3591	$2947	$3147
4 Door Sedan	3641	2988	3188
CORONET — V8			
2 Door Hardtop	3719	3056	3256
4 Door Sedan	3769	3097	3297
2 Seat Wagon	4358	3572	3772
CORONET CUSTOM — SIX			
2 Door Hardtop	3777	3094	3294

AUTOMOBILES

Cornering Lights	41	31	32	
Accessory Floor Mats	17	13	14	
Left Remote Control Mirror	15	11	12	
Left & Right Remote Control Mirrors	44	34	35	
W/Easy Order Pkg.	29	22	23	
Door Edge Protector Mouldings				
2 Dr. Models	7	5	6	
4 Dr. Models	13	10	11	
Upper Door Frame Mldgs. Sedans & Wagons	29	22	23	
Power Bench Seat	117	89	90	
Left Power Seat	117	89	90	
Power Windows	150	114	116	
Brougham 2 Dr. Hardtop	105	80	81	
4 Door Sedan		3754	3076	3276
CORONET CUSTOM — V8				
2 Door Hardtop		3904	3202	3402
4 Door Sedan		3883	3185	3385
2 Seat Wagon		4560	3727	3977
3 Seat Wagon		4674	3831	4081
CORONET BROUGHAM — V8				
2 Door Hardtop		4154	3406	3656
CRESTWOOD — V8				
2 Seat Wagon		4826	3939	4189
3 Seat Wagon		4918	4026	4276

CORONET ACCESSORIES

Power Door Locks				
2 Dr. Models	60	46	47	
4 Dr. Models	87	66	67	
Power Deck Lid Release	18	14	15	
AM Radio	72	55	56	
AM/FM Radio	149	113	115	
W/Easy Order Pkg.	77	58	59	
AM Radio w/8 Track Stereo Tape				
W/o Easy Order or Luxury Eqpt. Pkg.	214	163	165	
W/Easy Order Pkg.	142	108	110	
W/Luxury Eqpt. Pkg.	65	49	50	
AM/FM Stereo Radio				
W/o Easy Order or Luxury Eqpt. Pkg.	254	193	195	
W/Easy Order Pkg.	182	138	140	
W/Luxury Eqpt. Pkg.	105	80	81	
AM/FM Stereo Radio w/8 Track Stereo Tape				
W/o Easy Order or Luxury Eqpt. Pkg.	397	302	306	
W/Easy Order Pkg.	324	247	250	
Vinyl Roofs				
Full, 4 Dr. Coronet & Coronet Custom		$103	$78	$79
Full, 2 Dr. Models		109	83	84
Full w/Easy Order or Luxury Eqpt. Pkg.				
Coronet Custom, Brougham or Crestwood		31	23	24
Canopy		79	60	61
Vinyl Side Moulding				
Coronet		38	29	30
Coronet Custom		19	15	16
Stripes				
Lower Body Side Tape Stripe		38	29	30
Door, Qtr. & Hood Tape Stripe		19	15	16
Cloth & Vinyl Bench Seat w/Padded Door				
Trim Panels		50	38	39
Cloth & Vinyl Bucket Seat w/Padded Door				
Trim Panels				
Coronet Custom Models		226	171	173

CONSUMER GUIDE

AUTOMOBILES

	Retail Price	Dealer Cost	Low Price
Coronet Brougham Models.	29	22	23
Vinyl Bucket Seat w/Shag Carpets	197	149	151
Vinyl Center Arm Rest Bench Seat	40	31	32
360 CID 8 Cylinder 2 BBL Single Exhaust	49	39	40
360 CID 8 Cylinder 4 BBL Single Exhaust			
All Models	89	71	72
W/Rallye Pkg. Only 2 Dr. Coronet & 2 Dr. Custom	202	162	164
360 CID 8 Cylinder 4 BBL Dual Exhaust	202	162	164
400 CID 8 Cylinder 2 BBL Single Exhaust	93	74	75
400 CID 8 Cylinder 4 BBL Single Exhaust	122	98	99
Torqueflite Transmissions			
W/225, 318, 360 & 400 Single Exhaust Engine	241	193	195
W/360 CID Dual Exhaust Engine	264	211	214
Light Package			
2 Door Models	40	30	31
3 Seat Wagons	40	27	28
4 Door Models	43	32	33
Easy Order Package w/Single Exhaust Engine			
Coronet Custom Hardtop	803	585	591
Coronet Custom Sedan	815	594	600
Coronet Custom 2 Seat Wagon	484	333	337
Coronet Custom 3 Seat Wagon	478	328	332
Coronet Brougham Hardtop	765	556	562
Crestwood 2 Seat Wagon	447	304	308
Crestwood 3 Seat Wagon	440	299	302
Easy Order Package w/360 Dual Exhaust Eng.			
Coronet Custom Hardtop	826	603	610

	Retail Price	Dealer Cost	Low Price
Brougham Package w/Patterned or Valour Body Cloth	230	175	177
Vinyl Bucket Seat w/o Easy Order or Luxury Eqpt. Pkg.	164	124	126
W/Easy Order Pkg.	134	102	104
W/Luxury Eqpt. Pkg.	53	40	41
Deluxe Sound Insulation Package	437	350	354
Air Conditioning	15	11	12
Optional Axle Ratio	50	38	39
Sure Grip Differential Axle	28	21	22
500 AMP Long Life Battery	15	11	12
Front Protective Rub Strips	29	22	23
Front & Rear Protective Rub Strips	20	15	16
Electric Clock	17	13	14
Console	73	55	56
Rear Window Defroster	58	44	45
Emission Control System & Testing	32	24	25
Fuel Pacer System	20	15	16
W/Light Pkg.	51	39	40
Tinted Glass, All Windows	36	28	29
Tinted Glass, Windshield Only	11	9	10
Inside Hood Release	17	13	14
Accessory Floor Mats	15	11	12
Left Remote Control Chrome Mirror	44	34	35
Left & Right Remote Control Chrome Mirrors	29	22	23
W/Easy Order or Luxury Eqpt. Pkgs.	52	39	40
Dual Remote Control Sport Styled Mirrors	37	28	29
W/Easy Order or Luxury Eqpt. Pkgs.			
Door Edge Protectors 2 Dr. Models	7	5	6

CONSUMER GUIDE

AUTOMOBILES

	788	574	580	13	10	11
Coronet Brougham Hardtop				29	22	23
Luxury Equipment Package w/Single Exhaust Engine						
Coronet Custom Hardtop	1656	1185	1197	36	27	28
Coronet Custom Sedan	1669	1195	1207	24	18	19
Coronet Custom 2 Seat Wagon	1461	1027	1038	15	12	13
Coronet Custom 3 Seat Wagon	1428	1002	1013	26	20	21
Coronet Brougham Hardtop	1599	1142	1154	136	103	105
Crestwood 2 Seat Wagon	1353	945	955	58	44	45
Crestwood 3 Seat Wagon	1346	940	950	117	89	90
Luxury Equipment Package w/360 Dual Exhaust Engine				117	89	90
Coronet Custom Hardtop	1679	1203	1216	139	105	107
Coronet Brougham Hardtop	1622	1160	1172	60	45	47
				72	55	56
AM Radio				149	113	115
AM/FM Radio				77	58	59
Deluxe Package						
Coronet Hardtop	56	43	44	214	163	165
Coronet Sedan & Wagon	100	76	77	142	108	110
Light Trailer Towing Package	71	54	55	44	34	35
Heavy Trailer Towing Package	284	216	219	254	193	195
				182	138	140
Rallye Package				84	64	65
Coronet Hardtop w/400 CID Engine	207	157	159	397	302	306
Coronet Hardtop w/o 400 CID Engine	225	171	173	324	247	250
Coronet Custom Hardtop w/o 400 CID Engine or Easy Order Pkg	206	156	158	227	173	175
Coronet Custom Hardtop w/400 CID Engine w/o Easy Order Pkg	188	143	145	20	16	17
Coronet Custom Hardtop w/Easy Order Pkg. w/o 400 CID Engine	138	105	107	72	55	56
Coronet Custom Hardtop w/400 CID Engine & Easy Order Pkg	121	92	93	24	19	20
				33	25	26
				26	20	21

4 Dr. Models
Upper Door Frame Mouldings
 Sedan
 Wagons
Sill Moulding
Belt Moulding
Performance Hood Treatment
Power Steering
Front Power Disc Brakes
Power Bench Seat
Left Power Bucket Seat
Power Windows
Power Door Locks
AM Radio
AM/FM Radio
 W/Easy Order Pkg.
AM Radio w/8 Track Stereo Tape
 W/Easy Order Pkg.
 W/Luxury Eqpt. Pkg.
AM/FM Stereo Radio
 W/Easy Order Pkg.
 W/Luxury Eqpt. Pkg.
AM/FM Stereo Radio w/8 Track Stereo Tape
 W/Easy Order Pkg.
 W/Luxury Eqpt. Pkg.
Single Rear Speaker
Automatic Speed Control
Station Wagon Items
 Air Deflectors
 Auto-Lock Tailgate
 Cargo Compartment Carpets

CONSUMER GUIDE

AUTOMOBILES

	Retail Price	Dealer Cost	Low Price		Retail Price	Dealer Cost	Low Price
Luggage Rack	67	51	52	Left & Right Remote Control, Chrome	44	34	35
Power Tailgate Window	39	30	31	Left & Right Remote Control, Chrome			
Deluxe Steering Wheel w/Partial Horn Ring				w/Easy Order Package			
Coronet Models	21	16	17	Dual Sport Style Remote Control, Chrome	29	22	23
Other Models	10	8	9	Dual Sport Style Remote Control, Chrome	52	39	40
"Tuff" Steering Wheel				w/Easy Order Package			
Coronet Models	34	26	27	Dual Sport Style Remote Control, Painted	37	28	29
Models w/Luxury Eqpt. or Brougham Pkg.	13	10	11	Dual Sport Style Remote Control, Painted	52	39	40
Models w/o Luxury Eqpt. or Brougham Pkg	23	18	19	w/Easy Order Package			
Manual Sun Roof	296	225	228	Power Bench Seat	37	28	29
Heavy Duty Suspension	24	18	19	Power Bucket Seat, Left	117	89	90
Tachometer	59	45	46	Power Windows	117	89	90
W/Luxury Eqpt. Pkg.	40	30	31	Power Door Locks	97	74	75
Trunk Dress-Up	42	32	33	Power Deck Release	60	46	47
Undercoating	29	22	23	AM Radio	18	14	15
Forced Upper Air Ventilation	19	15	16	AM/FM Radio	72	55	56
3 Speed Windshield Wipers	9	7	8	W/Easy Order Package	149	113	115
				AM Radio W/8 Track Stereo Tape	77	58	59
CHARGER SPECIAL EDITION				AM Radio W/8 Track Stereo Tape	214	163	165
2 Dr. Specialty Hardtop	$4903	$4131	$4281	W/Easy Order Package	121	92	93
				AM/FM Stereo Radio	254	193	195
CHARGER SPECIAL EDITION ACCESSORIES				W/Easy Order Package	161	123	125
				AM/FM Stereo Radio w/8 Track Stereo Tape	397	302	306
				W/Easy Order Package	304	231	234
				AM/FM Stereo Radio w/Search Tune	314	239	242
				W/Easy Order Package	221	168	170
Vinyl Roofs				Single Rear Speaker	20	16	17
Full	$109	$83	$84	Automatic Speed Control	72	55	56
Full w/Easy Order Pkg.	15	11	12	Tuff Steering Wheel	13	10	11

62   CONSUMER GUIDE

Landau	95	72	73	Manually Operated Sun Roof	296 225 228
Stripes	38	29	30	Heavy Duty Shock Absorbers	7 5 6
Interior Trims				Heavy Duty Suspension	24 18 19
Cloth & Vinyl Bench Seat w/Center				Tachometer	59 45 46
Folding Arm Rest	17	13	14	Trunk Dress-Up	43 32 33
Engines				Undercoating	29 22 23
360 CID 8 Cylinder 4 BBL, Single Exhaust	40	32	33	Forced Upper Air Ventilation	19 15 16
360 CID 8 Cylinder 4 BBL	153	123	125	"15" Wire Wheel Covers, Set of 4	58 44 45
400 CID 8 Cylinder 2 BBL, Single Exhaust	44	35	36	"15" Styled Road Wheels, Set of 5	109 83 84
400 CID 8 Cylinder 4 BBL, Single Exhaust	73	58	59	3 Speed Windshield Wipers	9 7 8
Light Package	36	27	28	**DART SERIES SIX**	
Easy Order Package	812	599	605	4 Dr. Sedan	$3269 $2842 $3042
Light Trailer Towing Package	71	54	55	**DART SERIES EIGHT**	
Heavy Trailer Towing Package	284	216	219	4 Dr. Sedan	3390 2947 3147
Brougham Pkg. w/B3 Trim	81	61	62	**SPORT SERIES SIX**	
Brougham Pkg. w/E3 Trim	98	74	75	2 Dr. Coupe	3297 2867 3067
Air Conditioning	437	350	354	**SPORT SERIES EIGHT**	
Optional Axle Ratio	15	11	12	2 Dr. Coupe	3420 2973 3173
Sure Grip Differential Axle	50	38	39	**SWINGER SPECIAL SERIES SIX**	
500 AMP Long Life Battery	28	21	22	2 Dr. Hardtop	3341 2905 3105
Front & Rear Protective Rub Strips	29	22	23	**SWINGER SPECIAL SERIES EIGHT**	
Console	17	13	14	2 Dr. Hardtop	3463 3010 3210
Rear Window Electric Heated Defroster	73	55	56	**"360" SPORT EIGHT**	
Emission Control System & Testing	58	44	45	2 Dr. Coupe	4014 3482 3732
Fuel Pacer System	32	24	25	**SWINGER SERIES SIX**	
W/Light Package	20	15	16	2 Dr. Hardtop	3518 3056 3256
Locking Gas Cap	6	4	5	**SWINGER SERIES EIGHT**	
Tinted Glass, All Windows	51	39	40	2 Dr. Hardtop	3640 3161 3361
Tinted Glass, Windshield Only	36	28	29	**CUSTOM SERIES SIX**	
Accessory Floor Mats	17	13	14	4 Dr. Sedan	3444 2992 3192
Mirrors				**CUSTOM SERIES EIGHT**	
Left Remote Control, Chrome	15	11	12	4 Dr. Sedan	3566 3097 3297

AUTOMOBILES

	Retail Price	Dealer Cost	Low Price
SPECIAL EDITION SIX			
2 Dr. Hardtop	4232	3667	3917
4 Dr. Sedan	4159	3604	3854
SPECIAL EDITION EIGHT			
2 Dr. Hardtop	4328	3750	4000
4 Dr. Sedan	4256	3688	3938

DODGE ACCESSORIES

	Retail Price	Dealer Cost	Low Price
Vinyl Roofs			
Canopy	$72	$60	$61
Full	88	73	74
Vinyl Side Moulding			
Sport, Swinger Special & Dart Series	35	29	30
Swinger, Custom, "360" Sport, Special Edition Series	18	15	16
Vinyl Bench Seat			
"360" Sport	30	25	26
Vinyl Bench Seat W/Center Fold Arm Rest			
W/Interior Decor Group	93	77	78
Sport Series & "360" Sport	30	25	26
W/Sport Topper Pkg., "360" Sport	63	52	53
W/Rallye Pkg., "360" Sport	37	31	32
Custom & Swinger Series			
Cloth & Vinyl Bench Seat W/Center Fold Arm Rest W/Interior Decor Group	68	57	58
Custom & Swinger Series	37	31	32
Sport Series	82	68	69
Interior Decor Group	33	27	28
Sport Series W/Rallye Pkg.	23	19	20
Deluxe Insulation Package			
Sport, Swinger & Custom Series	48	40	41
"360" Sport	41	34	35
Fold Down Seat Package	99	82	83
Air Conditioning	407	337	341
Axle Ratio			
2.76 Ratio, w/318 Eng. & Torqueflite Trans.	13	11	12
Axle Suregrip Differential	46	38	39
50 AMP Long Life Battery	26	21	22
Manual Front Disc Brakes	24	20	21
Carpets	19	16	17
Console	62	52	53
Rear Window Defogger			
Forced Air	39	32	33
Electric Heated	67	55	56
Emissions Control System & Testing	53	44	45
Fuel Pacer System	30	24	25
W/Light Pkg.	18	15	16
Tinted Glass, All Windows	44	36	37
Tinted Glass, Windshield Only	33	28	29
Inside Hood Release	10	9	10
Accessory Floor Mats	15	13	14
Inside Day/Night Mirror	7	6	7
Left Remote Control Mirror	14	11	12
Dual Sport Style Remote Cont. Chrome Mirrors	29	24	25
W/Basic Group	15	12	13

AUTOMOBILES

Caravan Trim Vinyl Bench Seat	30	26		
Vinyl Bucket Seats W/Interior Decor Group				
"360" Sport	133	112	29	25
W/Sports Topper Pkg. Sport Series	63	53	15	13
W/Rallye Pkg. Sport Series	103	86		
Vinyl Bucket Seats W/Center Folding Arm Rest				
Custom & Swinger Series	122	103		
Torqueflite Transmission	233	195	6	6
Floor Mounted 3 Speed Manual Trans.	27	23	11	10
Light Package	31	27	27	23
W/Sport Topper Pkg.	20	17	14	12
Basic Group	273	229	15	14
Merchandising Package Swinger Series			16	15
6 Cylinder	554	464	124	105
8 Cylinder	530	445		
Merchandising Package Custom Series			77	65
6 Cylinder	580	486	53	45
8 Cylinder	556	467	66	56
Protection Group			137	115
W/Merchandising Pkg.	20	17		
Models	10	9	70	59
Trailer Towing Package	65	55	19	17
Radial Tire Roadability Package	17	15	66	56
Sport Topper Package	251	211	10	10
Rallye Pkg.	161	135	178	149
Custom Package	595	498		
"360" Sport	108	91	22	19
Sport Series	115	97	8	8
Custom Package W/Special Trim			13	12
"360" Sport	75	63	27	23
			29	25
			53	45

Dual Sport Style Remote Cont., Painted Mirrors		
W/Basic Group		
Door Edge Protector Mouldings		
2 Dr. Models		
4 Dr. Models		
Upper Door Frame Moulding		
Drip Rail		
Sill		
Wheel Lip		
Power Steering		
Front Disc Brakes		
6 Cylinder Models		
8 or 6 Cylinder Models W/Merchand. Pkg.		
AM Radio		
AM/FM Radio		
W/Basic & Merchandising Pkg. & Premium Models		
Rear Speaker		
Automatic Speed Control		
Deluxe Steering Wheel		
Manual Sun Roof		
Heavy Duty Suspension		
W/Rallye & Trailer Towing Pkg.		
W/Radial Tire Pkg. & Special Edition Mdls.		
Front Sway Bar		
Undercoating		
Deluxe Wheel Covers — Set of 4		
Wire Wheel Covers		

CONSUMER GUIDE

AUTOMOBILES

FORD

	Retail Price	Dealer Cost	Low Price
FORD LTD			
2 Dr. Pillared Hardtop	$4753	$3683	$3883
4 Dr. Pillared Hardtop	4712	3651	3851
FORD LTD BROUGHAM			
2 Dr. Pillared Hardtop	5133	3977	4227
4 Dr. Pillared Hardtop	5099	3953	4303
FORD LTD LANDAU			
2 Dr. Pillared Hardtop	5484	4229	4479
4 Dr. Pillared Hardtop	5453	4205	4455
FORD LTD STATION WAGONS			
LTD Wagon (Non-Woodgrain) 6 Passenger	5158	3998	4248
LTD Country Squire, 6 Passenger	5440	4216	4466

FORD ACCESSORIES

	Retail Price	Dealer Cost	Low Price
400 CID 2V 8 Cylinder	$87	$68	$69
460 CID 4V 8 Cylinder			
Country Squire & LTD Wagon models	236	184	186
All other models	322	251	254
Selectaire Air Conditioner	478	373	377
Selectaire Air Conditioner w/Auto Temp Con.	555	433	438
Anti-Theft Alarm System	93	73	74
All other models	77	60	61
Fuel Monitor Warning Light	19	15	16
Automatic Load Adjuster	89	69	70
Security Lock Group	17	13	14
Electric Power Door Locks			
2 Dr. Models	59	46	47
4 Dr. & Station Wagon w/Convenience Group or Landau Luxury Group	85	66	67
Station Wagon Models w/o Convenience Group or Landau Luxury Group	100	78	79
Lockable Side Stowage Compartment	39	30	31
Luggage Compartment Trim	34	26	27
Deluxe Luggage Rack	89	69	70
Outside Left Remote Control Mirror	14	11	12
Vinyl Insert Bodyside Moldings	38	30	31
Metallic Glow Paint	54	42	43
Tu-Tone Paint	31	24	25
Dual Accent Paint Stripes	27	21	22
Protection Group			
2 Dr. Models	45	35	36
All Other Models	54	42	43
Radio			
AM	72	56	57
AM/FM Stereo w/Two Front Door Mounted & Dual Rear Seat Speakers	246	192	194
AM/FM Stereo w/Tape Player w/2 F Door Mounted & Dual Rear Seat Speakers	379	296	299
Recreation Table w/Magnetized Checkers	49	38	39

66 CONSUMER GUIDE

AUTOMOBILES

Heavy-Duty Battery	16	13	13	14	14
Color-Keyed Deluxe Belts	17				
Deluxe Bumper Group					
Models w/Rear Bumper Guards Standard	31	24	25		
Models w/o Rear Bumper Guards Standard	50	39	40		
Rear Bumper Guards	19	15	16		
Deluxe Cargo Area					
W/Extended Range Fuel Tank, w/o Lockable Side Stowage Compartment	66	52	53		
W/o Extended Range Fuel Tank, w/Lockable Side Stowage Compartment	86	67	68		
Digital Clock					
LTD Brougham, LTD Landau, Country Squire, & LTD Wagons w/Brougham option	22	17	18		
LTD & LTD Wagon models	24	19	20		
Convenience Group	95	74	75		
Front Cornering Lamps	44	34	35		
Rear Window Defogger	44	34	35		
Electric Rear Window Defroster	68	53	54		
California Emission Equipment	71	55	56		
Fender Skirts	38	30	31		
Fuel Sentry Vacuum Gauge	32	25	26		
Extended Range Fuel Tank	94	73	74		
Complete Tinted Glass	60	47	48		
Landau Luxury Group					
LTD Landau models	472	368	372		
Country Squire model	683	533	539		
Light Group					
LTD Brougham, LTD Landau, Country Squire, LTD Wagon w/Brougham Option	72	56	57		

All Other Models	113	88	89
6-Way Driver Only Power Seat	120	94	95
6-Way Driver & Passenger Power Seat	234	182	184
6-Way Full Width Power Seat	120	94	95
Automatic Seat Back Release	28	22	23
Dual Facing Rear Seats	125	98	99
Split Bench w/Manual Pass. Recliner Seats	122	95	96
Dual Rear Seat Speakers	36	28	29
Fingertip Speed Control			
Models w/Landau Luxury Group	66	52	53
All Other Models	108	84	85
Squire Brougham Option	266	208	210
Luxury Steering Wheel	42	33	34
Tilt Steering Wheel	56	44	45
Power Operated Sunroof	564	440	445
Heavy Duty Suspension	24	19	20
Class I Trailer Towing Package	39	30	31
Class II Trailer Towing Package			
W/o Load Equalizer Hitch Platform	42	33	34
W/Load Equalizer Hitch Platform	139	108	110
Class III Trailer Towing Package			
W/o Load Equalizer Hitch Platform	127	99	100
W/Load Equalizer Hitch Platform	224	175	177
Leather Seat Trim	193	151	153
Vinyl Seat Trim	26	20	21
Duraweave Vinyl Trim	50	39	40
LTD Wagon Brougham Option	378	295	298
Full Wheel Covers	36	28	29
Deluxe Wheel Covers			
Models w/Full Wheel Covers Standard	61	48	49
All Other Models	94	73	74

CONSUMER GUIDE

AUTOMOBILES

	Retail Price	Dealer Cost	Low Price
Color-Keyed Wheel Covers			
Models w/Full Wheel Covers Standard	61	48	49
All Other Models	94	73	74
Power Side Windows			
2 Dr. Models	104	81	82
All Other Models	154	120	122
Power Mini-Vent & Side Windows	216	169	171

MAVERICK 6-CYLINDER

	Retail Price	Dealer Cost	Low Price
2 Dr. Sedan	$3025	$2636	$2786
4 Dr. Sedan	3061	2664	2814
2 Dr. Grabber Sport Sedan	3282	2855	3005

MAVERICK 8-CYLINDER

	Retail Price	Dealer Cost	Low Price
2 Dr. Sedan	3147	2741	2891
4 Dr. Sedan	3183	2768	2918
2 Dr. Grabber Sport Sedan	3404	2959	3109

MAVERICK ACCESSORIES

	Retail Price	Dealer Cost	Low Price
Extra Charge Over 200 CID IV 6-Cylinder	$42	$36	$37
250 CID IV 6-Cylinder	239	203	206
Selectshift Cruise-O-Matic	417	354	358
Selectaire Air Conditioner	14	12	13
Heavy-Duty Battery	17	14	15
Deluxe Color-Keyed Belts	37	31	32
Manual Front Disc Brakes			

	Retail Price	Dealer Cost	Low Price
Dual Color-Keyed Outside Mirrors			
Models w/Conven. Group or Luxury Decor	13	11	12
All Other Models	25	21	22
Metallic Glow Paint	49	42	43
Protection Group			
Models w/Luxury Decor Option	20	17	18
2 Dr. Models	29	25	26
4 Dr. Models	37	31	32
Radio			
AM	65	55	56
AM/FM Monaural	136	116	118
AM/FM Stereo	225	191	193
Vinyl Roof	83	71	72
Grabber Bucket Reclining Seats	129	110	112
Power Steering	124	105	107
Bodyside Accent Paint Stripe	24	20	21
Heavy-Duty Suspension	15	13	14
Vinyl Seat Trim	25	21	22

MUSTANG II 4-CYLINDER

	Retail Price	Dealer Cost	Low Price
2 Dr. Hardtop	$3529	$3018	$3218
3 Dr. 2+2	3818	3264	3464
2 Dr. Ghia	3938	3366	3566

MUSTANG II 6-CYLINDER

	Retail Price	Dealer Cost	Low Price
3 Dr. Mach I	4188	3579	3779

MUSTANG II ACCESSORIES

	Retail Price	Dealer Cost	Low Price
Extra Charge Over 2.3 Liter 1-4 2.8 Liter V-6 6 Cylinder	$272	$231	$234

CONSUMER GUIDE

AUTOMOBILES

Power Front Disc Brakes	76	65	66	203	173	175
Deluxe Bumper Group						
Models w/Luxury Decor Option	26	22	23	217	184	186
All Other Models	58	49	50	239	203	206
Front Bumper Guards	16	14	15	162	138	140
Rear Bumper Guards	16	14	15	417	354	358
Convenience Group						
Grabber Sport Sedan w/Interior Decor Grp.	12	10	11	76	65	66
All Other Models w/Interior Decor Group	25	21	22	46	39	40
Grabber Sport Sedan w/o Interior				14	12	13
Decor Grp	27	23	24	17	14	15
All Other Models w/o Interior Decor Group	42	36	37	55	47	48
Exterior Decor Group	90	76	77	35	30	31
Interior Decor Group				40	34	35
Grabber Sport Sedan	57	48	49	63	54	55
All Other Models	96	82	83			
Luxury Decor Option	462	393	397	46	39	40
Rear Window Defogger	38	32	33			
California Emission Equipment	41	35	36	14	12	13
Floor Shift	26	22	23	70	59	60
Complete Tinted Glass				63	54	55
Grabber Sport Sedan & Models w/Exterior				41	35	36
Decor or Luxury Decor	41	35	36	19	16	17
All Other Models	57	48	49	41	35	36
Light Group				35	30	31
Models w/Luxury Decor Option	19	16	17	19	16	17
All Other Models	30	25	26	15	13	14
Fuel Monitor Warning Light	19	16	17	46	39	40
Security Lock Group	12	10	11	106	90	91
Deck Lid Luggage Rack	46	39	40	162	138	140
				48	41	42

302 CID 2V 8 Cylinder
  Mach I Model
  All Other Models
Selectshift Cruise-O-Matic
Exterior Accent Group
Selectaire Air Conditioner
Anti-Theft Alarm System
Traction-Lok Differential Axle
Heavy-Duty Battery
Deluxe Color-Keyed Belts
Power Front Brakes
Front & Rear Bumper Guards
Digital Quartz Crystal Clock
Console
Convenience Group
  Models w/Luxury Interior Group
  Mach I, Models w/Rallye Package or
    Exterior Accent Group
  All Other Models
Electric Rear Window Defroster
California Emission Equipment
Extended Range Fuel Tank
Tinted Complete Glass
Light Group
Fuel Monitor Warning Light
Security Lock Group
Decklid Luggage Rack
Luxury Interior Group
Ghia Silver Luxury Group
Maintenance Group

AUTOMOBILES

	Retail Price	Dealer Cost	Low Price
Outside Dual Color-Keyed Mirrors	39	33	34
Rocker Panel Molding	19	16	17
Color-Keyed Vinyl Insert Bodyside Molding	51	43	44
Silver Glass Moonroof	454	386	390
Radio			
AM	65	55	56
AM/FM Monaural	136	116	118
AM/FM Stereo	225	191	193
AM/FM Stereo w/Tape Player	347	295	298
Rallye Package			
Mach I Model	141	120	122
3 Dr. 2+2 Model	195	166	168
All Other Models	282	240	243
Glamour Paint	49	42	43
Protection Group			
Mach I Model	20	17	18
All Other Models	29	25	26
Vinyl Roof	83	71	72
Fold Down Rear Seat	66	56	57
Power Rack & Pinion Steering	117	99	100
Leather Wrapped Steering Wheel	32	27	28
Pin Stripes	24	20	21
Manual Operated Sunroof	210	178	180
Competition Suspension			
Ghia or Models w/Exterior Accent Group	43	37	38
Mach I Model	25	21	22
All Other Models	55	47	48
Velour Cloth Trim	88	75	76
All Other Models	233	198	200
Rear Window Defogger	40	34	35
Rear Window Electric Defroster	68	58	59
California Emissions Equipment	41	35	36
Floor Shift	29	25	26
Tinted Complete Glass	43	37	38
Light Group	35	30	31
Fuel Monitor Warning Light	19	16	17
Security Lock Group	15	13	14
Luggage Compartment Dress-Up	32	27	28
Decklid Mounted Luggage Rack	46	39	40
Illuminated Visor Vanity Mirror	37	31	32
Bodyside/Decklid Accent Moldings	26	22	23
Vinyl Insert Bodyside Moldings	35	30	31
Metallic Glow Paint	49	42	43
Protection Group			
2 Dr. Sedan Model	29	25	26
4 Dr. Sedan Model	37	31	32
Ghia Models	20	17	18
Radio			
AM	65	55	56
AM/FM Monaural	151	128	130
AM/FM Stereo	225	191	193
AM/FM Stereo W/Tape Player	347	295	298
Vinyl Roof	92	78	79
Leather Trim Seats	160	136	138
Leather Wrapped Steering Wheel	32	27	28
Power Steering	124	105	107

AUTOMOBILES

GRANADA

2 Dr. Sedan	$3698	$3145	$3345		
4 Dr. Sedan	3756	3194	3394		
2 Dr. Ghia Sedan	4225	3594	3794		
4 Dr. Ghia Sedan	4283	3643	3843		

GRANADA ACCESSORIES

Extra Charge Over Base 6 Cylinder	$42	$36	$37
250 CID IV 8 Cylinder			
302 CID 2V 8 Cylinder			
Ghia Models	86	73	74
All Other Models	128	109	111
351 CID 2V 8 Cylinder			
Ghia Models	134	114	116
All Other Models	176	150	152
Selectshift Cruise-O-Matic	239	203	206
Selectaire Air Conditioner	430	365	369
Anti-Theft Alarm System	76	65	66
Heavy-Duty Battery	15	13	14
Deluxe Color-Keyed Belts	16	14	15
Power Front Disc Brakes	55	47	48
Deluxe Bumper Group	59	50	51
Digital Clock	40	34	35
Convenience Group			
Ghia Models	29	25	26
All Other Models	66	56	57
Exterior Decor Group	128	109	111
Interior Decor Group			
Models w/Convenience Group	210	178	180
Space Saver Spare Tire	14	12	13
Class I Trailer Towing Hitch	36	31	32
Seat/Door Deluxe Cloth Trim	75	64	65
Simulated Spoke Aluminum Wheels			
Ghia Models	140	119	121
All Other Models	166	141	143
Power Side Windows			
2 Dr. Models	91	77	78
4 Dr. Models	129	110	112

PINTO 4-CYLINDER

2 Dr. Sedan	$2769	$2409	$2559
3 Dr. Runabout	3068	2665	2815
2 Dr. Station Wagon	3237	2812	2962

PINTO 6-CYLINDER

3 Dr. Runabout	3340	2897	3047
2 Dr. Station Wagon	3509	3043	3193

PINTO ACCESSORIES

Selectshift Cruise-O-Matic	$202	$172	$174
Accent Group	51	43	44
Selectaire Air Conditioner	416	354	358
Traction-Lok Differential Axle	46	39	40
Heavy-Duty Battery	14	12	13
Color-Keyed Deluxe Belts	17	14	15
Power Front Disc Brakes	55	47	48
Deluxe Bumper Group	58	49	50
Front Bumper Guards	17	14	15
Rear Bumper Guards	17	14	15
Passenger Compart. Color-Keyed Carpeting	20	17	18

CONSUMER GUIDE

AUTOMOBILES

	Retail Price	Dealer Cost	Low Price
Convenience Group			
Models w/Luxury Decor, Sports Accent			
& Squire Option	48	41	42
All Other Models	70	59	60
Exterior Decor Group			
Station Wagon Model	105	89	90
All Other Models	127	108	110
Luxury Decor Group			
Station Wagon Model	152	129	131
Runabout Model	194	165	167
2 Dr. Sedan Model	228	194	196
Rear Window Defogger	35	30	31
Electric Rear Window Defroster	60	51	52
California Emission Equipment	45	38	39
Complete Tinted Glass	42	36	37
Light Group	33	28	29
Fuel Monitor Warning Light	19	16	17
Security Lock Group	15	13	14
Roof Luggage Rack			
Station Wagon Model	71	60	61
All Other Models	50	43	44
Wide Color-Keyed Vinyl Insert Bodyside			
Mldgs.	55	47	48
Vinyl Insert Bodyside Moldings	36	31	32
Metallic Glow Paint	49	42	43
Protection Group	32	27	28
Pivoting Quarter Window			
Models w/Accent, Luxury Decor, Exterior			
Decor, or Sports Accent Group	32	27	28

	Retail Price	Dealer Cost	Low Price
Optional Ratio Axle	13	10	11
Traction-Lok Differential Axle	50	39	40
Four Wheel Disc Brakes	184	143	145
Sure-Track Brake Control System	378	295	298
Convenience Group	55	43	44
Electric Rear Window Defroster	91	71	72
Electric Windshield/Rear Window Defrost.	337	263	266
California Emission Equipment	45	35	36
Dual Exhaust	53	41	42
Light Group	111	87	88
Fuel Monitor Warning Light	19	15	16
Power Lock Group	74	58	59
Security Lock Group	12	9	10
Luggage Compartment Dress Up	57	44	45
Copper Luxury Group			
Models w/Velour Trim	651	508	514
Models w/Leather Trim	724	565	571
Silver Luxury Group			
Models w/Velour Trim	542	423	428
Models w/Leather Trim	615	480	485
Wide Vinyl Insert Bodyside Molding	112	87	88
Power Moonroof	859	670	677
Starfire Paint	185	144	146
Protection Group			
Models w/Wide Vinyl Insert			
Bodyside Mldg.	72	56	57
All Other Models	81	63	64
AM/FM Stereo Radio w/Tape Player	175	136	138
Manual Reclining Passenger Seat	63	49	50

72 CONSUMER GUIDE

AUTOMOBILES

All Other Models	54	46	47	
Radio				
AM	65	55	56	
AM/FM Monaural	141	120	122	
AM/FM Stereo	225	191	193	
Vinyl Roof	83	71	72	
Super Sound Package	46	39	40	
Sports Accent Group				
Station Wagon Model w/Squire Option	164	139	141	
Station Wagon Model w/o Squire Option	299	254	257	
All Other Models	417	354	358	
Squire Option	241	205	208	
Power Steering	117	99	100	
Dual Accent Paint Stripe	24	20	21	
Durawave Vinyl Trim				
Runabout & Station Wagon Models	46	39	40	
Runabout Model Equipped w/Luxury Decor Group	19	16	17	
Station Wagon Model Equipped w/Squire Option or Luxury Decor Group	19	16	17	
Wheel Covers	30	25	26	
Steel-Belted Radial Tires	84	72	73	

THUNDERBIRD

2 Dr. Hardtop	$7701	$5962	$6262		

THUNDERBIRD ACCESSORIES

Selectaire Air Conditioner w/Automatic Temperature Control	$99	$77	$78		
Power Antenna	34	26	27		
Anti-Theft Alarm System	77	60	61		

ELITE

2 Dr. Hardtop	$4767	$3872	$4122	

ELITE ACCESSORIES

6-Way Driver Only Power Seat	124	97	98
6-Way Driver & Passenger Power Seat	234	182	184
Fingertip Speed Control	113	88	89
Tilt Steering Wheel	66	52	53
Dual Bodyside & Hood Paint Stripes	31	24	25
Power Sunroof	611	477	482
Heavy-Duty Suspension	28	22	23
Space Saver Spare Tire	78	61	62
Class III Trailer Towing Package	86	67	68
Leather Trim	221	172	174
Turnpike Group	156	122	124
Power Mini Vent Windows	75	58	59
Deluxe Wheel Covers	67	52	53
Simulated Wire Wheel Covers			
Models w/Silver Luxury Group	24	19	20
Models w/Copper Luxury Group	(132)	(103)	(105)
All Other Models	88	69	70

400 CID 2V 8 Cylinder	$87	$68	$69
460 CID 4V 8 Cylinder	292	228	231
Selectaire Air Conditioner	470	367	371
Selectaire W/Automatic Temperature Control Air Conditioner	547	427	432
Anti-Theft Alarm System	88	69	70
Optional Ratio Axle	13	10	11
Traction-Lok Differential Axle	50	39	40

AUTOMOBILES

	Retail Price	Dealer Cost	Low Price
GRAN TORINO SPORT			
2 Dr. Hardtop	$4790	$3903	$4153

TORINO & GRAN TORINO ACCESSORIES

	Retail Price	Dealer Cost	Low Price
400 CID 2V 8 Cylinder	$87	$68	$69
460 CID 4V 8 Cylinder	292	228	231
Accent Group	33	26	27
Selectaire Air Conditioner	470	367	371
Selectaire W/Automatic Temperature Control			
Air Conditioner	547	427	432
Anti-Theft Alarm System	88	69	70
Optional Ratio Axle	13	10	11
Traction-Lok Differential Axle	50	39	40
Deluxe Color-Keyed Belts	17	13	14
Deluxe Bumper Group			
Station Wagon Models	48	37	38
All Other Models	65	51	52
Front Bumper Guards	17	13	14
Rear Bumper Guards	17	13	14
Electric Clock	18	14	15
Console	68	53	54
Convenience Group			
Gran Torino Sport or Models Ordered w/Outside Color-Keyed Remote			
Control Mirrors	30	23	24
Station Wagon Models	79	62	63
All Other Models	72	56	57
Rear Window Electric Defroster	73	57	58

	Retail Price	Dealer Cost	Low Price
Deluxe Bumper Group	48	37	38
Rear Bumper Guards	17	13	14
Convenience Group	45	35	36
Interior Decor Group	384	299	302
Rear Window Electric Defroster	73	57	58
Heavy Duty Electrical System			
351 CID 2V Engine w/o Rear Window Electric Defroster	56	44	45
351 CID 2V Engine & Rear Window Electric Defroster, & 400 CID 2V or 460 CID 4V Engines w/o Rear Window Electric Defroster & Trailer Towing Package, Class III	28	22	23
California Emission Equipment	71	55	56
Fuel Sentry Vacuum Gauge	13	10	11
Complete Tinted Glass	48	37	38
Fuel Monitor Warning Light	19	15	16
Light Group	44	34	35
Electric Power Door Locks	59	46	47
Luggage Compartment Trim	36	28	29
Outside Color-Keyed Remote Control Mirrors	42	33	34
Outside Left Chrome Remote Control Mirror	14	11	12
Illuminated Visor Vanity Mirror	40	31	32
Power Operated Glass Moonroof	859	670	677
Metallic Glow Paint	54	42	43
Dual Accent Bodyside Paint Stripes	27	21	22
Protection Group	32	25	26
Radio			
AM	72	56	57
AM/FM Stereo	230	179	181

AUTOMOBILES

AM/FM Stereo W/Tape Player	376	293	296	
Automatic Seat Back Release	28	22	23	
6-Way Driver Only Power Seat	120	94	95	
6-Way Full Width Power Seat	120	94	95	
Manual Reclining Passenger Seat	63	49	50	
Security Lock Group	17	13	14	
Dual Rear Seat Speakers	36	28	29	
Fingertip Speed Control	108	84	85	
Leather Wrapped Steering Wheel	29	23	24	
Luxury Steering Wheel	35	27	28	
Tilt Steering Wheel	56	44	45	
Power Operated Sunroof	525	410	415	
Handling Suspension	83	65	66	
Pleated Vinyl Bench Seat Trim	26	20	21	
Four Deepdish Forged Aluminum Wheels	220	172	174	
Wire Wheel Covers	93	73	74	
Luxury Wheel Covers	55	43	44	
Power Side Windows	99	77	78	
Heavy-Duty Electrical System				
351 CID 2V Engine w/o Rear Window Electric Defroster	56	44	45	
351 CID 2V Engine w/Rear Window Electric Defroster, & 400 CID 2V or 460 CID 4V Engines w/o R Window Electric Defroster & Trailer Towing Package-Class III	28	22	23	
Fuel Sentry Vacuum Gauge				
Gran Torino Brougham, Gran Torino Sport & Models w/Squire Brougham Option	13	10	11	
All Other Models	32	25	26	
Complete Tinted Glass	48	37	38	
Fuel Monitor Warning Light	19	15	16	
Light Group	44	34	35	
Power Door Electric Locks				
2 Dr. Models	59	46	47	
4 Dr. Models	85	66	67	
Station Wagon models	101	79	80	
Luggage Compartment Trim	36	28	29	
Deluxe Luggage Rack	87	68	69	
Outside Color-Keyed Remote Control Mirrors	42	33	34	
Outside Left Chrome Remote Control Mirror	14	11	12	
Vinyl Insert Bodyside Moldings	38	30	31	
Opera Windows	50	39	40	
Metallic Glow Paint	54	42	43	
Protection Group				
Gran Torino Squire model	24	19	20	
2 Dr. Models	32	25	26	
All Other Models	40	31	32	
Radio				
AM	72	56	57	

TORINO

2 Dr. Hardtop	$3954	$3227	$3427
4 Dr. Pillared Hardtop	3957	3229	3429
4 Dr. Station Wagon	4336	3544	3744

GRAN TORINO

2 Dr. Hardtop	$4314	$3515	$3715
4 Dr. Pillared Hardtop	4338	3532	3732
4 Dr. Station Wagon	4673	3818	4018

GRAN TORINO BROUGHAM

2 Dr. Hardtop	$4805	$3910	$4160
4 Dr. Pillared Hardtop	4837	3935	4185

GRAN TORINO SQUIRE

4 Dr. Squire Station Wagon	$4952	$4037	$4287

AUTOMOBILES

	Retail Price	Dealer Cost	Low Price
AM/FM Stereo	230	179	181
AM/FM Stereo W/Tape Player	376	293	296
Vinyl Roof	100	78	79
Automatic Seat Back Release	28	22	23
6-Way Driver Only Power Seat	120	94	95
6-Way Full Width Power Seat	120	94	95
Rear Facing Third Seat	88	69	70
Manual Reclining Passenger Seat	63	49	50
Security Lock Group	17	13	14
Dual Rear Seat Speakers	36	28	29
Fingertip Speed Control	108	84	85
Squire Brougham Option	184	143	145
Leather Wrapped Steering Wheel			
Gran Torino Brougham, Gran Torino			
Squire, or Gran Torino Sport Models	29	23	24
All Other Models	36	28	29
Luxury Steering Wheel			
Gran Torino Brougham, Gran Torino			
Squire, or Gran Torino Sport Models	35	27	28
All Other Models	42	33	34
Tilt Steering Wheel	56	44	45
Dual Accent Bodyside Paint Stripes	27	21	22
Power Operated Sunroof	525	410	415
Heavy-Duty Handling Suspension			
Station Wagon Models	18	14	15
All Other Models	31	24	25
Trailer Towing Package, Class II			
Station Wagon Models	43	34	35
All Other Models	57	44	45

	Retail Price	Dealer Cost	Low Price
Continental Mark IV	11082	8443	9443

LINCOLN ACCESSORIES

	Retail Price	Dealer Cost	Low Price
Diamond Fire Paint	$193	$149	$151
Moondust Paint	141	109	111
Leather Interior	200	154	156
Town Car/Town Coupe Option	532	410	415
Town Car/Coupe Velour Interior	200	154	156
Twin Comfort Lounge Seats	237	183	185
Twin Comfort Seats w/Passenger Recliner	319	245	248
Bench Seat w/Passenger Recliner	69	53	54
Wide Band White Sidewall Tires	38	30	31
Higher Ratio Rear Axle	31	24	25
Traction Lok Differential	60	46	47
4-Wheel Disc Power Brakes	172	132	134
Sure Track Brakes	249	192	194
Glass Panel Power Moonroof	843	649	656
Steel Panel Power Sunroof	668	514	520
Power Vent Windows	76	59	60
Anti-Theft Alarm System			
W/Security Lock Group	104	80	81
W/o Security Lock Group	108	83	84
Security Lock Group	13	10	11
Coach Lamps	60	46	47
Electric Rear Window Defroster	87	67	68
Fuel Economy Reminder Light	25	20	21
Extended Range Fuel Tank	95	73	74
Headlamp Convenience Group	95	73	74

AUTOMOBILES

Trailer Towing Package, Class III			
Station Wagon Models	87	68	69
All Other Models	111	87	88
Duraweave Vinyl Seat Trim	50	39	40
Pleated Vinyl Bench Seat Trim	26	20	21
Five Magnum 500 Wheels Trim Rings			
Gran Torino Sport & Gran Torino Brougham Models	130	101	103
All Other Models	169	132	134
Wheel Covers	33	26	27
Deluxe Wheel Covers			
Gran Torino Squire Model	12	9	10
All Other Models	39	30	31
Luxury Wheel Covers			
Gran Torino Sport & Gran Torino Brougham Models, & Models w/Squire Brougham Option or Exterior Decor Group	55	43	44
Gran Torino Squire Model	67	52	53
All Other Models	94	73	74
Power Side Windows			
2 Dr. Models	99	77	78
All Other Models	140	109	111
Power Tailgate Window	39	30	31
Luggage Compartment Trim Option	61	47	48
Right Hand Remote Control Mirror	29	23	24
Illuminated Visor Vanity Mirrors	100	77	78
AM/FM/MPX Radio w/Stereo Tape	139	107	109
Speed Control	100	77	78
Luxury Wheel Covers	83	64	65
Interval Select Windshield Wipers	27	21	22
California Emissions System	45	35	36

MARK IV ACCESSORIES

Moondust Paint	$141	$109	$111
Diamond Fire Paint	193	149	151
Landau 3/4 Vinyl Roof	500	385	389
Leather Interior	212	163	165
Blue Diamond Luxury Group	516	397	401
Saddle/White Luxury Group	465	358	362
Silver Luxury Group	516	397	401
Gold Luxury Group	516	397	401
Lipstick/White Luxury Group	465	358	362
Higher Ratio Rear Axle	31	24	25
Traction Lok Differential	60	46	47
Space Saver Spare Tire	88	68	69
Power Lumbar Seat	87	67	68
Power Vent Windows	76	59	60
Steel Panel Power Sun Roof	668	514	520
Glass Panel Power Moon Roof	843	649	656
Anti-Theft Alarm System			
W/Security Lock Group	104	80	81
W/o Security Lock Group	108	83	84
Security Lock Group	13	10	11
Electric Rear Window Defroster	87	67	68

LINCOLN

LINCOLN CONTINENTAL

2 Door Coupe	$9214	$7007	$8007
4 Door Sedan	9656	7344	8344

CONSUMER GUIDE

AUTOMOBILES

	Retail Price	Dealer Cost	Low Price
Quick Defrost Defroster	344	265	268
Dual Exhausts	59	45	46
Fuel Economy Light	25	20	21
Headlamp Convenience Group	95	73	74
Right Hand Remote Control Mirror	29	23	24
Illuminated Visor Vanity Mirrors	100	77	78
Protective Bodyside Moldings	39	30	31
Premium Bodyside Moldings	129	100	101
AM/FM/MPX Radio Stereo Tape	139	107	109
Passenger Side Reclining Seat	69	53	54
Trailer Towing Package, Class III	73	56	57
5 Forged Aluminum Wheels	287	221	224
Interval Windshield Wipers	27	21	22
California Emission System	45	35	36

MERCURY

	Retail Price	Dealer Cost	Low Price
MARQUIS			
2 Door Hardtop	$5049	$3905	$4155
4 Door Pillared Hardtop	5115	3955	4205
MARQUIS BROUGHAM			
2 Door Hardtop	5972	4621	4921
4 Door Pillared Hardtop	6037	4671	4971
GRAND MARQUIS			
2 Door Hardtop	6403	4952	5252
4 Door Pillared Hardtop	6469	5002	5302

	Retail Price	Dealer Cost	Low Price
Anti-Theft Alarm System			
2 Door & 4 Door Models	90	70	71
Station Wagons	95	74	75
Security Lock Group			
W/o Anti-Theft Alarm System	17	13	14
W/Anti-Theft Alarm System	7	5	6
Appearance Protection Group			
2 Door Models	46	36	37
4 Dr. Models & Station Wagons	50	39	40
Heavy-Duty Battery	13	10	11
Bumper Protection Group			
2 & 4 Door Models	47	37	38
Station Wagons	32	25	26
California Emissions System	71	55	56
Clock, Digital			
Marquis & Marquis Wagon	22	17	18
Brougham & Colony Park	22	17	18
Electric Clock	19	14	15
Cross-Country Ride Package	24	18	19
Electric Rear Window Defroster	70	54	55
Fender Skirts	41	32	33
Front & Rear Floor Mats	30	24	25
Extended Range Fuel Tank	94	73	74
Cornering Lamps	40	31	32
Automatic Load Levelers	84	66	67
Fuel Economy Light	19	14	15
Luggage Compartment Trim Option	46	36	37
Protective Bodyside Molding	36	28	29
Paint Stripes	26	21	22

STATION WAGONS

Marquis	5411	4186	4436	74	57	58
Colony Park	5598	4330	4580	249	194	196

MERCURY ACCESSORIES

460-4V V8 Engine w/Dual Exhausts	$196	$153	$155	383	299	302
Glamour Metallic Paint	51	40	41	34	27	28
Grand Marquis Trim Option	278	217	220	37	29	30
Twin Comfort Lounge Seats	82	64	65	19	14	15
Vinyl Bench Seats	29	23	24	103	80	81
Vinyl Roofs,				55	43	44
2 & 4 Door Hardtops	124	96	97	99	77	78
Station Wagons	147	115	117			
Higher Ratio Rear Axle w/Class III Tow Pkg.	14	11	12	40	31	32
Traction-Lok Differential	55	43	44	105	82	83
Sure-Track Brakes	197	154	156			
4-Wheel Disc Brakes	170	132	134	91	71	72
Lock Convenience Group				99	77	78
2 Door Models	66	51	52	75	59	60
4 Door Models	91	71	72			
Power Side Windows	154	120	122	61	47	48
Power Bench Seat, 6-Way	124	96	97			
Power Seat, 6-Way Driver Only	124	96	97	21	16	17
Power Seats, 6-Way/6-Way	247	193	195	69	53	54
Reclining Passenger Seat	45	35	36	47	37	38
Power Sunroof	637	497	502	26	21	22
Power Vent Windows	72	56	57			
Automatic Temperature Control Air Cond	541	422	427	86	67	68
Manual Control Air Conditioning	504	393	397	66	51	52
Complete Tinted Glass	(61)	(47)	(48)	37	29	30

AUTOMOBILES

Radios			
AM	74	57	58
AM/FM/Multiplex	249	194	196
AM/FM/Multiplex w/Stereo Tape	383	299	302
Power Antenna	34	27	28
Dual Rear Seat Speakers	37	29	30
Deluxe Seat Belts	19	14	15
Speed Control	103	80	81
Tilt Steering Wheel	55	43	44
Trailer Hitch, Equalizer Platform	99	77	78
Trailer Towing Package			
Class I & II	40	31	32
Class III	105	82	83
Visibility Light Group			
Marquis	91	71	72
Marquis Wagon	99	77	78
Brougham & Colony Park	75	59	60
Grand Marquis & Colony Park w/Grand			
Marquis Trim	61	47	48
Wheel Covers			
Brougham	21	16	17
Luxury, over Deluxe Wheel Covers	69	53	54
Over Brougham Wheel Covers	47	37	38
Interval Windshield Wipers	26	21	22
Station Wagon Options			
Deluxe Cargo Area Trim w/o Extended			
Range Fuel Tank	86	67	68
W/Extended Range Fuel Tank	66	51	52
Lockable Stowage Compartment	37	29	30
Luggage Carrier w/Air Deflector	96	75	76
Rear Seats, Dual Facing	127	98	99

CONSUMER GUIDE

AUTOMOBILES

	Retail Price	Dealer Cost	Low Price
Rear Seat Recreation Table	57	44	45

COMET, 6-CYLINDER

	Retail Price	Dealer Cost	Low Price
2 Door	$3113	$2711	$2861
4 Door	3147	2737	2887

COMET, 8-CYLINDER

	Retail Price	Dealer Cost	Low Price
2 Door	3236	2816	2966
4 Door	3270	2842	2992

COMET ACCESSORIES

	Retail Price	Dealer Cost	Low Price
250-IV Engine	$42	$36	$37
Glamour Paint	47	40	41
Tutone Paint	33	28	29
Vinyl Roof	88	75	76
Vinyl Interior	21	17	18
Custom Option	456	387	391
GT Package	354	301	305
Transmissions			
Select-Shift Automatic	241	205	208
Floor-Mounted Selector	25	22	23
Power Front Disc Brakes	74	62	63
Power Steering	124	105	107
Air Conditioning	416	353	357
Complete Tinted Glass	41	35	36
Appearance Protection Group			
2 Door	31	27	28
4 Door	35	30	31
Security Lock Group	12	10	11

	Retail Price	Dealer Cost	Low Price
Over Custom	74	62	63
California Emissions System	41	35	36

MONARCH

	Retail Price	Dealer Cost	Low Price
2 Door	$3764	$3202	$3402
4 Door	3822	3251	3451

MONARCH GHIA

	Retail Price	Dealer Cost	Low Price
2 Door	4291	3650	3900
4 Door	4349	3699	3949

MONARCH ACCESSORIES

	Retail Price	Dealer Cost	Low Price
Engines			
250-IV	$42	$36	$37
302-2V, Monarch	128	109	111
302-2V, Ghia	86	73	74
351-2V, Monarch	176	150	152
351-2V, Ghia	134	114	116
Glamour Paint	49	42	43
Luxury Cloth Trim	75	63	64
Interior Decor Option			
W/Visibility Light Group	211	179	181
W/o Visibility Light Group	234	199	201
Leather Trim Bucket Seats	160	136	138
Full Vinyl Roof	92	78	79
Select-Shift Automatic Transmission	239	203	206

AUTOMOBILES

Option					
Deluxe Color-Keyed Belts	16	13	14	Floor Mounted Transmission Selector	29	25	26
Heavy-Duty Battery	15	12	13	Power Front Disc Brakes	54	46	47
Front Manual Disc Brakes	34	29	30	Power Windows			
Bumper Protection Group				2 Door Models	90	77	78
W/Custom Option	29	25	26	4 Door Models	129	110	112
W/o Custom Option	59	50	51	Power Steering	124	105	107
Front Bumper Guards	16	13	14	Power Seats, 4 Way, Driver Only	104	88	89
Convenience Group w/Dual Racing Mirrors				Power Steel Sunroof	517	439	444
or GT Package	43	37	38	Power Glass Moonroof	762	647	654
Other	51	43	44	Air Conditioning, Manual Control	430	366	370
Rear Window Defogger	37	32	33	Tinted Glass, Complete	43	37	38
Fuel Economy Warning Light	17	14	15	Anti-Theft Alarm System			
Deck Lid Luggage Carrier	51	43	44	W/Security Lock Group	68	58	59
Dual Racing Mirrors				W/o Security Lock Group	76	65	66
W/Custom Option	13	11	12	Appearance Protection Group	16	13	14
W/o Custom Option	25	22	23	Security Lock Group			
Protective Bodyside Molding	33	28	29	2 Door	29	25	26
Radios				4 Door	36	31	32
AM	65	55	56	Ghia, All Models	23	19	20
AM/FM Multiplex	218	185	187	Heavy Duty Battery	15	12	13
AM/FM Monaural	129	110	112	Bumper Protection Group	59	50	51
Leather Wrapped Steering Wheel	33	28	29	Rear Window Defogger	40	34	35
Heavy Duty Suspension	15	12	13	Rear Window Electric Defroster	68	57	58
Deluxe Wheel Covers				Digital Clock	40	34	35
Over Hubs	30	26	27	Fuel Economy Reminder Light	19	16	17
W/GT Package	74	62	63	Illuminated Visor Vanity Mirror	36	31	32
Forged Aluminum Wheels				Deck Lid Luggage Rack	46	39	40
Over Hubs	186	158	160	Luggage Compartment Trim	33	28	29
W/GT Package	82	70	71	Dual Bright Mirrors			
Over Custom	156	132	134	Monarch	36	31	32
Styled Steel Wheels				Ghia	24	20	21
Over Hubs	104	88	89	Protective Bodyside Molding	35	30	31

AUTOMOBILES

	Retail Price	Dealer Cost	Low Price
Radios			
AM	65	55	56
AM/FM Monaural	151	128	130
AM/FM Multiplex	225	192	194
AM/FM MPX w/Stereo Tape	347	295	298
Deluxe Color-Keyed Seat Belts	16	13	14
Leather Wrapped Steering Wheel	33	28	29
Trailer Towing Package, Class I	36	31	32
Visibility/Convenience Group			
Monarch w/Illum. Visor Vanity Mirror	98	83	84
Monarch w/o Illum. Visor Mirror	101	86	87
Ghia w/Illum. Visor Vanity Mirror	62	52	53
Ghia w/o Illum. Visor Vanity Mirror	65	55	56
Cast Aluminum Spoked Wheels			
Monarch	165	140	142
Ghia	146	124	126
California Emissions System	41	35	36

COUGAR XR-7

	Retail Price	Dealer Cost	Low Price
2 Door Hardtop	$5218	$4233	$4483

COUGAR XR-7 ACCESSORIES

	Retail Price	Dealer Cost	Low Price
Engines			
400-2V	$86	$67	$68
460-4V	247	193	195
Glamour Paint	51	40	41
Full Vinyl Roof	41	32	33
Leather Trim	203	158	160
AM/FM/Multiplex	238	186	188
AM/FM/Multiplex w/Stereo Tape Player	383	299	302
Deluxe Color-Keyed Seat Belts	16	12	13
Dual Rear Speakers	37	29	30
Speed Control	103	80	81
Tilt Steering Column	55	43	44
Leather Wrapped Steering Wheel	36	28	29
Cross-Country Suspension	17	13	14
Trailer Towing Package Class II	37	29	30
Trailer Towing Package Class III	132	103	105
Visibility Light Group	70	54	55
Interval Windshield Wipers	26	21	22
California Emissions System	71	55	56

MONTEGO

	Retail Price	Dealer Cost	Low Price
2 Door Hardtop	$4092	$3338	$3538
4 Door Pillared Hardtop	4128	3366	3566

MONTEGO MX

	Retail Price	Dealer Cost	Low Price
2 Door Hardtop	4304	3508	3758
4 Door Pillared Hardtop	4328	3524	3774

MONTEGO MX BROUGHAM

	Retail Price	Dealer Cost	Low Price
2 Door Hardtop	4453	3628	3878
4 Door Pillared Hardtop	4498	3663	3913

STATION WAGONS

	Retail Price	Dealer Cost	Low Price
MX	4674	3810	4060

AUTOMOBILES

			MX Villager
Velour Cloth Trim	88	69	70
Higher Ratio Rear Axle	15	11	12
Traction-Lok Differential	50	39	40
Power Windows	100	78	79
Power Door Locks	59	46	47
Twin Comfort Power Seat	124	96	97
Steel Panel Power Sun Roof	525	410	415
Glass Panel Power Moonroof	832	649	656
Automatic Temperature Air Conditioning	507	395	399
Manual Air Conditioning	467	364	368
Complete Tinted Glass	51	40	41
Anti-Theft Alarm System			
W/Security Lock Group	90	70	71
W/o Security Lock Group	81	62	63
Security Lock Group	17	13	14
Appearance Protection Group	34	27	28
Bumper Protection Group	47	37	38
Convenience Group			
W/Visibility Light Group	45	35	36
W/o Visibility Light Group	49	38	39
Electric Rear Window Defroster	70	54	55
Heavy Duty Electrical System	29	23	24
Fuel Economy Reminder Light	19	14	15
Luggage Compartment Trim	36	28	29
Left Hand Remote Control Mirror	13	10	11
Dual Racing Mirrors			
W/Convenience Group	37	29	30
W/o Convenience Group	49	38	39
Protective Bodyside Molding	36	28	29
Radios			
AM	74	57	58

MONTEGO ACCESSORIES

	4909	4002	4302
Engines			
400-2V	$86	$67	$68
460-4V	247	193	195
Glamour Paint	51	40	41
Brougham Custom Trim Option	384	300	303
Villager Custom Trim Option	138	108	110
Full Vinyl Roof	103	80	81
Vinyl Roof, Embassy, on 2 Dr. Models Only	132	103	105
3/4 Vinyl Roof	103	80	81
Plush Loom Polyknit Trim	45	35	36
Higher Ratio Axle	15	11	12
Traction-Lok Axle	53	41	42
Power Side Windows			
2 Door	100	78	79
4 Door & Station Wagons	138	108	110
Power Door Locks			
2 Door	59	46	47
4 Door	84	66	67
Station Wagons	94	73	74
6-Way Bench Power Seat	124	96	97
6-Way Split Bench Power Seats	124	96	97
Automatic Temperature Air Conditioning	507	395	399
Manual Air Conditioning	467	364	368
Complete Tinted Glass	47	37	38
Anti-Theft Alarm System			
W/Security Lock Group	74	57	58
W/o Security Lock Group	83	65	66

AUTOMOBILES

	Retail Price	Dealer Cost	Low Price
Security Lock Group	17	13	14
Appearance Protection Group			
2 Door	34	27	28
4 Door & Station Wagons	38	30	31
Bumper Protection Group			
2 & 4 Door	47	37	38
Station Wagons	32	25	26
Electric Clock	19	14	15
Convenience Group			
2 Door	61	47	48
4 Door	33	26	27
Station Wagons	33	26	27
Electric Rear Window Defroster	70	54	55
Heavy Duty Electrical System	29	23	24
Fuel Economy Reminder Light	19	14	15
Fuel Sentry Vacuum Gauge	32	25	26
Left Hand Remote Control Mirror	13	10	11
Dual Racing Mirrors	49	38	39
W/Convenience Group	36	28	29
Protective Bodyside Molding	36	28	29
Opera Window	50	39	40
Radios			
AM	74	57	58
AM/FM/MPX	238	186	188
AM/FM/MPX w/Stereo Tape Player	383	299	302
Deluxe Color-Keyed Seat Belts	16	12	13
Dual Rear Speakers	37	29	30
Speed Control	103	80	81

	Retail Price	Dealer Cost	Low Price
Coupe	4194	3593	3793
Sedan	4205	3602	3802
CUTLASS			
Colonnade Hardtop Coupe	3756	3069	3269
Colonnade Hardtop Sedan	3831	3130	3330
"S" Colonnade Hardtop Coupe	3853	3148	3348
CUTLASS SUPREME			
2 Seat Cruiser	4678	3818	4018
3 Seat Cruiser	4791	3910	4110
Colonnade Hardtop Sedan	4105	3361	3561
Colonnade Hardtop Coupe	4048	3314	3514
VISTA CRUISER			
2 Seat	4888	3988	4188
3 Seat	5001	4080	4280
CUTLASS SALON			
Colonnade Hardtop Sedan	4726	3863	4063
Colonnade Hardtop Coupe	4654	3804	4004

STARFIRE, OMEGA, OMEGA SALON, CUTLASS, CUTLASS SUPREME, VISTA CRUISER AND CUTLASS SALON ACCESSORIES

	Retail Price	Dealer Cost	Low Price
6-Way Power Seat	$117	$91	$92
Vista Vent Roof Ventilator	99	77	78
Vista Vent (Deduct)	(99)	(77)	(78)
Deluxe Front And Rear Seat Belts	12	10	11
Bucket Seats	14	11	12
Bench Seat			

CONSUMER GUIDE

AUTOMOBILES

Sports Appearance Group	247	193	195	Bench Seat, Starfire	12	10	11
W/Convenience Group	261	203	206	Bench Seat, Cutlass Supreme 3 Seat			
W/o Convenience Group	55	43	44	Cruiser, 3 Seat Vista Cruiser	17	13	14
Tilt Column Steering Wheel	36	28	29	Seats			
Leather Wrapped Steering Wheel	25	20	21	Bucket, Omega Hardtop Coupes	75	58	59
Cross Country Suspension	37	29	30	Divided 60/40 Front w/Dual Controls	81	63	64
Trailer Towing Package, Class II				Shell Type Swivel Bucket, Cutlass "S"	75	58	59
Trailer Towing Package, Class III				Colonnade Hardtop Coupe	133	104	106
2 & 4 Door Models	132	103	105	Seat Back Adjuster, Left Side, Starfire	16	14	15
Station Wagons	92	72	73	Power Door Locks			
Visibility Light Group	70	54	55	2 Door	56	44	45
Interval Windshield Wipers	26	21	22	4 Door	82	64	65
Station Wagon Options				Soft Ray Tinted Windows			
Luggage Carrier	94	73	74	Omega	45	35	36
Power Rear Window	38	30	31	Starfire	42	36	37
Third Seat	86	70	71	Cutlass, Cutlass Supreme, Vista Cruiser,			
Rear Window Defogger	32	25	26	Cutlass Salon	48	37	38
California Emissions System	71	55	56	Swing-out Rear Quarter Vent Window	44	34	35
				Power Side Windows			
				2 Doors	91	71	72
				4 Doors	132	103	105
				Power Trunk Lid Release	16	12	13
				Cut Pile Floor Carpeting	22	17	18
				Front Auxiliary Floor Mats			

OLDSMOBILE

				Omega, Omega Salon	6	5	6
				Custlass, Cutlass Supreme, Vista Cruiser,			
STARFIRE				Cutlass Salon	7	6	7
Sport Coupe	$4157	$3542	$3742	Luggage Compartment Floor Mat	9	7	8
OMEGA				Rear Auxiliary Floor Mats			
Hatchback Coupe	3559	3056	3256	Omega, Omega Salon	6	5	6
Coupe	3435	2948	3148	Cutlass, Cutlass Supreme, Vista Cruiser,			
Sedan	3463	2972	3172	Cutlass Salon	7	6	7
OMEGA SALON							
Hatchback Coupe	4311	3695	3895				

AUTOMOBILES

	Retail Price	Dealer Cost	Low Price
Front And Rear Floor Mats	13	11	12
Cargo Area Carpeting	21	16	17
Bright Roof Drip Moldings	14	11	12
Rocker Panel Moldings	14	11	12
Protective Side Moldings			
Starfire	36	31	32
Omega	35	27	28
Cutlass, Cutlass Supreme Colonnades, Cutlass Salon	42	33	34
Bright Door-Edge Guard Moldings			
Starfire	7	6	7
Hardtop Coupes	7	5	6
Sedans and Vista Cruisers	11	9	10
Vinyl Landau Roof	110	86	87
Pulse Wiper System	26	20	21
Vinyl Rooftop Covering (includes Bright Roof Drip Moldings)			
Omega, Omega Salon	87	68	69
Other Models	103	80	81
Electric Rear Window Defogger			
Starfire	60	51	52
Other Models	73	57	58
Forced Air Rear Window Defogger	41	32	33
Rear Window Air Deflector	23	18	19
Four Season Air Conditioner			
Starfire	398	338	342
Omega, Omega Salon	435	339	343
Other Models	453	353	357
Tempmatic Air Conditioner	490	382	386
Locking Gas Cap	6	5	6
Tilt Away Steering Wheel	49	38	39
Starfire	45	38	39
Custom Sport Steering Wheel	33	26	27
Vari-Ratio Power Steering			
Starfire	111	94	95
Omega, Omega Salon	129	101	103
Heavy-Duty Battery	14	12	13
AM Radio w/Stereo Tape Player	203	158	160
Omega Omega Salon	199	155	157
AM/FM Stereo Radio w/Stereo Tape Player	363	283	286
AM/FM Stereo Radio	233	182	184
Starfire	214	182	184
AM Radio	73	57	58
Starfire	63	54	55
Omega, Omega Salon	69	54	55
AM/FM Radio	135	105	107
Starfire	129	110	112
Rear Radio Speaker	19	15	16
Starfire	18	15	16
Fuel Economy Meter	24	19	20
Instrument Panel Gauges	33	26	27
Electric Clock	19	15	16
Omega, Omega Salon	17	13	14
5 Wire Trailer Electrical Wiring Harness	15	12	13
7 Wire Trailer Electrical Wiring Harness	25	19	20
Bumper Rub Strips	27	21	22
Special Rear Bumper	16	12	13
California Emission Test	45	35	36

CONSUMER GUIDE

AUTOMOBILES

			Description			
13	10	11	Remote Control Outside Mirror	16	14	15
25	21	22	Sports Styled Outside Rearview Mirrors	17	13	14
68	53	54	Sports Console			
37	29	30	Illuminated Visor Vanity Mirror			
5	4	5	Firm Ride Front & Rear Shock Absorbers	50	42	43
22	17	18	Heavy-Duty Use Suspension System	68	53	54
43	34	35	Superlift Rear Shock Absorbers	60	47	48
49	38	39	Anti-spin Rear Axle	13	10	11
45	38	39	Starfire	198	168	170
55	43	44	Power Front Disc Brakes			
11	9	10	Engine Block Heater	168	131	133
69	54	55	Automatic Cruise Control	178	139	141
79	61	62	260 V8 2 BBL Engine			
130	101	103	350 V8 2 BBL Engine	128	100	102
			350 V8 BBL Engine	61	48	49
180	140	142	Cutlass, Cutlass Supreme Colonnades			
102	80	81	Cutlass Salon			
298	232	235	455 V8 4 BBL Engine			
119	93	94	Cutlass, Cutlass Supreme Colonnades			
220	172	174	Cutlass Supreme Cruisers, Vista Cruisers			
			Cutlass Salon			
180	140	142	350 V8 4 BBL Engine			
27	21	22	Omega, Omega Salon			
			3-Speed Floor Shift Control			
			Turbo-Hydramatic 350 Transmission			
235	200	203	Starfire			
237	194	196	Other Models			
			Turbo-Hydramatic Transmission Cutlass,			
259	212	215	Cutlass Supreme Colonnade Hdtps.,			
			Cutlass Supreme Cruisers, Vista Cruiser,			
22	18	19	Cutlass Salon			

Description			
Heavy Duty Radiator			
Starfire	11	14	15
Omega, Omega Salon	22	13	14
Rooftop Luggage Carrier	54		
Starfire	30		
Cutlass Supreme Cruisers, Vista Cruisers	5	42	43
Other Models	18	53	54
Rear Storage Compartment Lock And Trim	35	47	48
Custom Leather Trim	39	10	11
Omega "S" Sports Package	39	168	170
Omega Coupe, Omega Hatchback Coupe	44		
W/o Space Saver Spare Tire, Omega Cpe.	10	131	133
4-4-2 Appearance And Handling Package	55	139	141
Cutlass Colonnade Hardtop Coupe	62		
Cutlass "S" Colonnade Hardtop Coupe	103	100	102
		48	49

DELTA 88

Model			
Hardtop Sedan	$4904	$3811	$4011
Hardtop Coupe	4843	3764	3964
Town Sedan	4787	3720	3920

DELTA 88 ROYALE

Model			
Hardtop Sedan	5064	3936	4136
Hardtop Coupe	4998	3882	4082
Convertible	5213	4051	4251
Town Sedan	4927	3831	4031

CUSTOM CRUISER

Model			
2 Seat	5426	4218	4418
3 Seat	5565	4326	4526
2 Seat	5581	4337	4537
3 Seat	5720	4445	4645

AUTOMOBILES

	Retail Price	Dealer Cost	Low Price
NINETY-EIGHT			
Luxury Coupe	5963	4639	4939
Luxury Sedan	6104	4748	5048
Regency Coupe	6225	4841	5141
Regency Sedan	6366	4951	5251
TORONADO			
Custom Hardtop Coupe	6536	5101	5451
Brougham Hardtop Coupe	6766	5278	5628

DELTA 88, DELTA 88 ROYALE, CUSTOM CRUISER, NINETY-EIGHT AND TORONADO ACCESSORIES

	Retail Price	Dealer Cost	Low Price
6-Way Power Seat Adjuster, Left Side	$117	$91	$92
Divided Seat, Other Models	90	70	71
Divided Seat, Ninety-Eight	117	91	92
6-Way Power Seat Adjuster, Right Side	117	91	92
6-Way Power Seat Adjuster			
Bench, Other Models	117	91	92
Bench, Ninety-Eight Luxury Sedan & Coupe	90	70	71
Deluxe Front And Rear Seat Belts	14	11	12
3 Seat Custom Cruisers	17	13	14
Divided Front Seat w/Dual Controls	81	63	64
Delta 88 Royale Town Sedan, Cus. Cruiser	119	93	94
Air Cushion Restraint System	300	234	237
Power Door Locks			
2 Doors	56	44	45
4 Doors	82	64	65
Custom Cruiser	22	17	18
Remote Control Outside Mirror	13	10	11
Sports Styled Outside Rearview Mirrors			
Delta 88, Delta 88 Royale	25	19	20
Custom Cruiser	20	16	17
Illuminated Visor Vanity Mirror, Right Side	37	29	30
Remote Control Outside Rearview Mirror w/Illumin. Outside Temperature Indicator Left Side	31	24	25
Ninety-Eight, Toronado	18	14	15
Illuminated Visor Vanity, Left Side	37	29	30
Special Solid Color Oldsmobile Paint	119	93	94
Two Tone Magic Mirror			
Custom Cruiser	33	26	27
Delta 88 and Delta 88 Royale Sedans	45	35	36
Heavy Duty Use Suspension System	22	17	18
Superlift Rear Shock Absorbers	43	34	35
Anti-Spin Rear Axle	51	40	41
True-Track Braking	220	172	174
Heavy Duty Power w/Front Disc Brakes	30	23	24
Engine Block Heater	11	9	10
Automatic Cruise Control	74	58	59
Engines			
400 V8 4BBL Carburetor	62	48	49
455 V8 4BBL Carburetor	135	105	107
Locking Gas Cap	6	5	6
Tilt-Away Steering Wheel	49	38	39
Tilt-And-Telescope Steering Wheel	89	69	70

CONSUMER GUIDE

AUTOMOBILES

Soft-Ray Tinted Windows	60	47	48		
Power Side Windows	149	116	118		
Deluxe Lap Belts	11	9	10		
Rear Storage Compartment Lock			11		
Auxiliary Front Floor Mats	13	10	11		
Toronado	8	7	8		
Auxiliary Rear Floor Mats	10	8	9		
Luggage Compartment Floor Mat	7	6	7		
Cargo Area Carpeting, Custom Cruiser	9	7	8		
Protective Side Moldings	56	44	45		
Delta 88	42	33	34		
Custom Cruiser, Ninety-Eight	36	28	29		
Toronado	27	21	22		
Bright Side-Window Frame Moldings	25	19	20		
Bright Door-Edge Guard Moldings					
Coupes	7	5	6		
Sedans and Convertible	11	9	10		
Vinyl Opera Roof	142	111	113		
Padded Vinyl Rooftop Covering, Halo	154	120	122		
Pulse Wiper System	26	20	21		
Padded Vinyl Rooftop Covering					
Delta 88, Delta 88 Royale Coupe & Sedans	127	99	100		
Ninety-Eight Sedans	142	111	113		
Power Operated Glide-Away Tailgate	49	38	39		
Electric Rear Window Defogger	73	57	58		
Four Season Air Conditioning	487	380	384		
Tempmatic Air Conditioner	524	409	414		
Front Door Courtesy/Warning Lamps	17	13	14		
Combination Dome & Reading Lamps	14	11	12		
Illumination Package, Front Door Locks	45	35	36		
Remote Control Outside Rearview Mirror, Right Side	27	21	22		
Heavy Duty 15" Wheels					10
Deluxe 15" Wheel Discs					28
Maintenance-Free Battery					22
Cornering Lamps					31
Theft Deterrent System					85
Trip Odometer & Safety Sentinel					15
Electric Digital Clock					32
Ninety-Eight Luxury Sedan & Coupe					17
Electronic Lamp Monitor					32
Radios					
AM w/Stereo Tape Player	215	168	170		
AM/FM Stereo w/Stereo Tape Player	363	283	286		
AM/FM Stereo	233	182	184		
AM	85	66	67		
AM/FM Monaural	144	112	114		
Rear Radio Speaker	19	15	16		
Fuel Economy Meter	24	19	20		
Electric Clock	19	15	16		
Rooftop Luggage Carrier	89	69	70		
5-Wire Trailer Electrical Wiring Harness	15	12	13		
7-Wire Trailer Electrical Wiring Harness	25	20	21		
Special Rear Bumper	12	9	10		
California Emission Test	45	35	36		

PLYMOUTH

FURY SIX
2 Dr. Hardtop	$3542	$2907	$3107
4 Dr. Sedan	3591	2947	3147

CONSUMER GUIDE

89

AUTOMOBILES

	Retail Price	Dealer Cost	Low Price
FURY V8			
2 Dr. Hardtop	3672	3018	3218
4 Dr. Sedan	3720	3057	3257
ROAD RUNNER V8			
2 Dr. Hardtop	3973	3262	3462
FURY CUSTOM SIX			
2 Dr. Hardtop	3711	3041	3241
4 Dr. Sedan	3704	3035	3235
FURY CUSTOM V8			
2 Dr. Hardtop	3840	3150	3350
4 Dr. Sedan	3834	3145	3345
FURY SPORT V8			
2 Dr. Hardtop	4105	3366	3616
FURY SUBURBAN V8			
2 Seat Wagon	4309	3532	3782
FURY CUSTOM SUBURBAN V8			
2 Seat Wagon	4512	3688	3938
3 Seat Wagon	4632	3797	4047
FURY SPORT SUBURBAN V8			
2 Seat Wagon	4770	3894	4144
3 Seat Wagon	4867	3984	4234

FURY ACCESSORIES

	Retail Price	Dealer Cost	Low Price
Vinyl Roofs			
Full, 2 Dr. Fury & Sport	$103	$78	$79
Full, 4 Dr.	109	83	84
Full w/Easy Order or Luxury Equip. Pkg.	31	23	24
Easy Order Package w/360 4 BBL Engine			
Fury Custom Hardtop	826	603	610
Fury Sport Hardtop	788	574	580
Luxury Equipment Package			
Fury Custom Hardtop	1676	1272	1285
Fury Custom Sedans	1688	1209	1222
Fury Sport Hardtop	1599	1142	1154
Fury Custom Suburban, 2 Seat Wagon	1480	1041	1052
Fury Custom Suburban, 3 Seat Wagon	1447	1017	1028
Fury Sport Suburban, 2 Seat Wagon	1377	964	974
Fury Sport Suburban, 3 Seat Wagon	1371	959	969
Luxury Equipment Package			
Fury Custom Hardtop	1698	1290	1303
Fury Sport Hardtop	1622	1160	1172
Deluxe Package			
Fury Hardtop	56	43	44
Fury Sedan & Wagon	100	76	77
Light Trailer Towing Package	71	54	55
Heavy Trailer Towing Package	284	216	219
Salon Package			
W/o Easy Order or Luxury Equipment Pkg.	230	175	177
W/Easy Order Package	164	124	126
W/Luxury Equipment Package	153	117	119
Salon Package w/Velour Body Cloth			
Easy Order or Luxury Equipment Package	230	175	177
W/Easy Order Package	164	124	126
W/Luxury Eqpt. Package	153	117	119
Exterior Decor Package	116	89	90
Deluxe Sound Insulation Package	53	40	41

AUTOMOBILES

Canopy	79	60	61	354
Vinyl Side Moulding	38	29	30	12
Stripes	17	13	14	39
Cloth & Vinyl Bucket Seats				22
Road Runner	139	106	108	
Fury Sport	29	22	23	12
Cloth & Vinyl Bench Seat				23
Fury Custom	50	38	39	16
Vinyl Bench Seat				16
Fury Custom	40	31	32	
360 CID 8 Cylinder 4 BBL, Single Exhaust	89	71	72	82
Road Runner	202	162	164	14
360 CID 8 Cylinder 2 BBL, Single Exhaust	49	39	40	14
360 CID 8 Cylinder 4 BBL, Dual Exhaust	202	162	164	69
400 CID 8 Cylinder 2 BBL, Single Exhaust	93	74	75	56
400 CID 8 Cylinder 4 BBL, Single Exhaust	122	98	99	45
Torqueflite Transmissions				
W/225, 318, 160, & 400 Single Exh.				16
Engines	241	193	195	25
W/360 CID	264	211	214	40
Light Package				29
2 Dr. Models	40	30	31	10
3 Seat Wagons	36	27	28	5
Other 4 Dr. Models	43	32	33	14
Easy Order Package				12
Fury Custom Hardtop	803	585	591	35
Fury Custom Sedans	815	594	600	23
Fury Sport Hardtop	765	556	562	40
Fury Custom Suburban, 2 Seat Wagon	484	333	337	29
W/Easy Order or Luxury Equipment Pkg.	478	328	332	
Fury Custom Suburban, 3 Seat Wagon	447	304	308	6
Fury Sport Suburban, 2 Seat Wagon	440	299	302	11
Fury Sport Suburban, 3 Seat Wagon				

Air Conditioning	437	350		
Optional Axle Ratio	15	11		
Sure Grip Differential Axle	50	38		
500 AMP Long Life Battery	28	21		
Bumper Protection				
Front Protective Rub Strips	15	11		
Front & Rear Proctective Rub Strips	29	22		
Carpets	21	15		
Electric Clock	20	15		
Console				
Roadrunner W/o Trim	107	81		
Roadrunner w/trim	17	13		
Fury Sport Model Only	17	13		
Cushion Center w/Folding Arm Rest	89	68		
Rear Window Electric Defroster	73	55		
Emission Control System & Testing	58	44		
Fuel Pacer System				
W/Light Package	20	15		
W/o Light Package	32	24		
Tinted Glass, All Windows	51	39		
Tinted Glass, Windshield Only	36	28		
Inside Hood Release	11	9		
Dual Horns	6	4		
Accessory Floor Mats	17	13		
Left Remote Control Chrome Mirror	15	11		
Left & Right Remote Control Chrome Mirror	44	34		
W/Easy Order or Luxury Equipment Pkg.	29	22		
Dual Remote Control Sport Styled Mirrors	52	39		
W/Easy Order or Luxury Equipment Pkg.	37	28		
Door Edge Protector Mouldings				
2 Dr. Models	7	5		
4 Dr. Models	13	10		

CONSUMER GUIDE

AUTOMOBILES

	Retail Price	Dealer Cost	Low Price
4 Door Hardtop	4837	3766	3966
GRAN FURY BROUGHAM			
2 Door Hardtop	5146	4011	4261
4 Door Hardtop	5067	3950	4200
GRAN FURY SUBURBAN			
4 Door Wagon, 2 Seat	5067	3948	4198
GRAN FURY CUSTOM SUBURBAN			
4 Door Wagon, 2 Seat	5176	4033	4283
4 Door Wagon, 3 Seat	5294	4132	4382
GRAN FURY SPORT SUBURBAN			
4 Door Wagon, 2 Seat	5455	4245	4495
4 Door Wagon, 3 Seat	5573	4343	4593

GRAN FURY ACCESSORIES

	Retail Price	Dealer Cost	Low Price
Air Conditioner			
Manual Control	$445	$356	$360
Automatic Temp. Control w/o Luxury Equipment Package	522	417	422
W/Luxury Equipment Package	77	61	62
Axle Ratio	15	11	12
Sure Grip Differential Axle	52	40	41
500 AMP Extended Life Battery	28	21	22
Carpets	21	16	17
Electric Clocks	19	14	15
Electronic Digital Clocks			
Models w/o Easy Order or Luxury Equip.	43	33	34
Packages	25	19	20
Models w/Easy Order Package			

	Retail Price	Dealer Cost	Low Price
Upper Dr. Frame Mouldings			
Sedans	29	22	23
Wagons	36	27	28
Sill Mouldings	24	18	19
Belt Mouldings	15	12	13
Performance Hood Treatment	26	20	21
Power Steering	136	103	105
Front Power Disc Brakes	58	44	45
Power Bench Seat	117	89	90
Left Power Bucket Seat	117	89	90
Power Windows	139	105	107
Power Door Locks	60	46	47
AM Radio	73	55	56
AM/FM Radio			
W/o Easy Order Package	149	113	115
W/Easy Order Package	77	58	59
AM Radio w/8 Track Stereo Tape			
Models W/o Easy Order or Luxury Equipment Package	214	163	165
Models W/Easy Order Package	142	108	110
Models W/Luxury Eqpt. Package	44	34	35
AM/FM Stereo Radio			
W/o Easy Order or Luxury Eqpt. Pkg.	254	193	195
W/Easy Order Pkg.	182	138	140
W/Luxury Eqpt. Pkg.	84	64	65
AM/FM Stereo w/8 Track Stereo Tape			
W/o Easy Order or Luxury Equipment Pkg.	397	302	306
W/Easy Order Package	324	247	250
W/Luxury Eqpt. Package	227	173	175

AUTOMOBILES

Single Rear Speaker	20	16	17	
Automatic Speed Control	72	55	56	
Electric Rear Window Defroster	73	55	56	
Emissions Control Systems & Testing	58	44	45	
Station Wagon Items				
Air Deflector	24	19	20	
Auto. Lock Tailgate	33	25	26	
Cargo Compartment Carpets	26	20	21	
Luggage Rack	67	51	52	
Power Tailgate Window	39	30	31	
Engines				
360 CID 4-BBL	40	32	33	
400 CID 2-BBL	44	35	36	
400 CID 4-BBL	84	67	68	
400 CID 4-BBL w/Emission Control Systems & Testing	40	32	33	
440 CID 4-BBL	194	156	158	
440 CID 4-BBL	151	121	123	
Deluxe Steering Wheels				
Fury Models	21	16	17	
Other Models	10	8	9	
Engine Temperature & Oil Pressure Gauges				
W/o Easy Order or Lux. Equip. Pkgs.	19	14	15	
Custom w/Luxury Equipment Package	25	19	20	
Tuff Steering Wheel				
Fury Models	34	26	27	
Models W/o Luxury Equipment Package or Salon Package	13	10	11	
Brougham & Sport Suburban w/Easy Order or Lux. Equip. Pkgs.	25	19	20	
Fuel Pacer System				
Models W/Luxury Equipment Package or Salon Package				
W/o Light, Easy Order or Luxury Equip. Packages	23	18	19	
Manual Sun Roof	296	225	228	
W/Equipment Packages Above	24	18	19	
Heavy Duty Suspension	59	45	46	
Locking Gas Cap	6	4	5	
Tachometer	40	30	31	
Glass				
W/Luxury Equipment Package				
Trunk Dress-Up	42	32	33	
Tinted, All Windows	32	24	25	
Undercoating	29	22	23	
Tinted Windshield	20	15	16	
Strato Ventilation	19	15	16	
Vent Windows, Manual	6	4	5	
3 Speed Windshield Wipers	9	7	8	
Light Package				
GRAN FURY				
Gran Fury Sedan	63	48	49	
4 Door Sedan	$4565	$3556	$3756	
Suburban 2 Seat Wagon	57	43	44	
Custom 2 Door Hardtop	52	40	41	
GRAN FURY CUSTOM				
Custom Sedan 4 Dr. H.T. & Custom Sub.	55	41	42	
2 Door Hardtop	4781	3721	3921	
2 & 3 St. Wgns.	50	38	39	
4 Door Sedan	4761	3707	3907	
All Brougham & Spt. Sub. Models	15	11	12	
Deluxe Wiper/Washer Package				

CONSUMER GUIDE

AUTOMOBILES

Item	Retail Price	Dealer Cost	Low Price
Easy Order Package			
Custom 2 Door Hardtop	432	293	296
Custom 4 Dr. Sedan/Hardtop	435	295	298
Custom Subrbn. 2 & 3 St. Wgns.	407	274	277
Brougham 2 Door Hardtop	319	207	210
Brougham 4 Door Hardtop	436	296	299
Sport Subrbn. 2 & 3 St. Wgns.	405	272	275
Luxury Equipment Package			
Custom 2 Door Hardtop	1580	1118	1130
Custom Sedan/4 Dr. Hardtop	1610	1141	1153
Custom Subrbn. 2 & 3 St. Wgns.	1635	1160	1172
Brougham 2 Door Hardtop	1363	953	963
Brougham 4 Door Hardtop	1552	1097	1108
Sport Suburban 2 & 3 St. Wgns.	1574	1114	1126
Wagon Package	59	45	46
Light Trailer Towing Package	71	54	55
Heavy Trailer Towing Package	284	216	219
Engine Block Heater	17	13	14
Dual Horns	6	4	5
Interior Trim			
Vinyl Bench Seat	27	21	22
Vinyl Bench Seat w/Center Arm Rest	40	31	32
50/50 Cloth & Vinyl Bench Seat w/Passenger Recliner	174	132	134
50/50 Vinyl Bench Seat w/ Passenger Recliner	174	132	134
Voyager Trim Package, Cloth & Vinyl			
Bench Seat w/Center Arm Rest	53	40	41
Accessory Floor Mats	17	13	14
Models w/Easy Order Package	182	138	140
Models w/Luxury Equip. Package	105	80	81
AM/FM Stereo w/8-Trk. Stereo Tape inc. 2 Spkrs. Front & 2 Rear			
Models w/o Easy Order or Luxury Equipment Packages	397	302	306
Models w/Easy Order Package	324	247	250
Models w/Luxury Equip. Package	247	188	190
Rear Seat Speaker	20	16	17
Power Operated Vinyl Sun Roof			
Models w/o Easy Order or Luxury Equipment Packages	634	482	487
Models w/o Easy Order or Luxury Equipment Packages	517	393	397
Vinyl Roof	117	89	90
Security Alarm System	112	85	86
Automatic Speed Control	72	55	56
Station Wagon Items			
Assist Handles	21	16	17
Auto Lock, Tailgate	33	25	26
Luggage Rack	79	60	61
Rear Bumper Step Pads	13	10	11
Tilt/Telescope Steering Wheel			
Models w/o Luxury Equip. Pkg.	96	73	74
Models w/Luxury Equip. Pkg.	81	61	62
Deluxe Steering Wheel w/ Partial Horn Rim	16	12	13
Heavy Duty Shock Absorbers, Front & Rear	7	5	6
Heavy Duty Suspension			
Sedans & Hardtops	24	18	19

AUTOMOBILES

Mirrors						
Left Remote Control	15	11	12	Wagons	17	13	14
Left & Right Remote Control	44	34	35	Automatic Height Control Suspension	99	75	76
Models w/Easy Order Package	29	22	23	Trunk Dress-Up	42	32	33
Door Edge Protectors				Undercoating w/Hood Silencer Pad	29	22	23
2 Door Models	7	5	6				
4 Door Models	13	10	11	**DUSTER SIX**			
Upper Door Frame Mouldings	29	22	23	2 Door Sport Coupe	$3243	$2821	$3021
Vinyl Side Mouldings				**DUSTER V8**			
Gran Fury & Gran Fury Custom	20	16	17	2 Door Sport Coupe	3364	2926	3126
Brougham Only	29	22	23	**VALIANT SIX**			
Power Seat	117	89	90	4 Door Sedan	3247	2824	3024
Power Windows				**VALIANT V8**			
All Exc. Brougham 2 Dr. H.T.	150	114	116	4 Door Sedan	3369	2929	3129
Brougham 2 Door Hardtop	105	80	81	**SCAMP SIX**			
Power Door Locks				2 Door Hardtop	3518	3056	3256
2 Door Models	60	46	47				
4 Door Models	87	66	67	**SCAMP V8**			
Power Deck Lid Release	18	14	15	2 Door Hardtop	3640	3161	3361
AM Radio	72	55	56	**DUSTER CUSTOM SIX**			
AM/FM Radio				2 Door Sport Coupe	3418	2971	3171
W/o Easy Order Package	149	113	115				
W/ Easy Order Package	77	58	59	**DUSTER CUSTOM V8**			
AM Radio w/8-Track Stereo Tape, includes				2 Door Sport Coupe	3539	3076	3276
2 Speakers Front & 2 Rear							
Models w/o Easy Order or Luxury Equip.				**VALIANT CUSTOM SIX**			
Packages	214	163	165	4 Door Sedan	3422	2974	3174
Models w/Easy Order Package	142	108	110				
Models w/Luxury Equip. Package	65	49	50				
AM/FM Stereo Radio, inc. 2 Spkrs. F. & 2 R.							
Models w/o Easy Order or Lux. Equip.							
Pkgs.	254	193	195				

CONSUMER GUIDE

AUTOMOBILES

	Retail Price	Dealer Cost	Low Price
VALIANT CUSTOM V8			
4 Door Sedan	3544	3079	3279
DUSTER 360 V8			
2 Door Sport Coupe	3979	3451	3701
BROUGHAM SERIES SIX			
2 Door Hardtop	4232	3667	3917
4 Door Sedan	4139	3586	3836
BROUGHAM SERIES V8			
2 Door Hardtop	4328	3750	4000
4 Door Sedan	4235	3669	3919

VALIANT, DUSTER, SCAMP ACCESSORIES

	Retail Price	Dealer Cost	Low Price
Canopy Vinyl Roof	$72	$60	$61
Full Vinyl Roof	88	73	74
Body Side Performance Tape Stripe	30	25	26
Vinyl Side Moulding	18	15	16
Body Side Tape Stripe	30	25	26
Lower Deck Panel Tape Stripe	15	13	14
Interior Trim			
Vinyl Bench Seat	30	25	26
Vinyl Caravan Trim, Bench Seat w/Carpeting	49	41	42
Vinyl Bench Seat, Split Back w/Center Arm	37	31	32
Vinyl Bench Seat, Slit Back Bench w/Ctr.			
Arm Rest, Wdgrn. Dr. Trim & Cptg.	88	73	74
Deluxe Sound Insulation Package	48	40	41
W/Duster 360 V8 Model	41	34	35
Space Duster Pak, Folding Rear Seat	99	82	83
Air Conditioning	407	337	341
Axle — Optional Ratio	13	11	12
Suregrip Differential Axle	46	38	39
500 Amp. Long Life Battery	26	21	22
Manual Front Disc Brakes	24	20	21
Carpets	19	16	17
Cigarette Lighter	5	4	5
Console	62	52	53
Rear Window Defogger			
Forced Air	39	32	33
Electric Heated	67	55	56
Emission Control System & Testing	53	44	45
Fuel Pacer System	30	24	25
W/Light Pkg. & Brougham Models	18	15	16
Tinted Glass, all Windows	44	36	37
Tinted Glass, Windshield Only	33	28	29
Inside Hood Release	10	8	9
Lock-Glove Box	4	3	3
Accessory Floor Mats	15	13	14
Mirrors			
Inside Day-Night	7	6	7
Left Remote Control	14	11	12
Remote Control Chrome, Dual Sport Style	29	24	25
W/Basic Group Package	15	12	13

96   CONSUMER GUIDE

Vinyl Bucket Seats	83	69	70
Vinyl Bucket Seats w/Wdgrn. Dr. Trim Panels & Carpeting	127	106	108
Vinyl Bucket Seats, Center Cushion w/Folding Arm Rest	122	101	103
Transmissions			
Torqueflite	233	193	195
3 Speed Manual Floor Mounted Shift	27	22	23
4 Speed Manual Floor Mounted Shift w/318 Engine & 2 Dr. Models Only	217	180	182
Light Package	31	26	27
Basic Group	125	103	105
Basic Group w/Decorator Special Pkg.	95	79	80
Merchandising Package Scamp			
6 Cylinder	538	446	451
8 Cylinder	514	426	431
Merchandising Package, Valiant			
6 Cylinder	580	481	486
8 Cylinder	556	462	467
Protection Group	20	16	17
W/Merchandising Package	10	8	9
Custom Sport Package	54	45	46
W/Vinyl Bench Seat w/Ctr. Arm Rest or w/Bucket Seats	48	40	41
Trailer Towing Package	65	54	55
Radial Tire Roadability Package	17	14	15
W/Brougham Series Models	4	3	4
Decorator Special Package	272	226	229
W/Duster 360 V8 Model	293	243	246
Gold Duster Package	181	150	152
Remote Control Painted, Dual Spt. Style	29	24	25
W/Basic Group Package	15	12	13
Door Edge Protectors			
2 Door Models	6	5	6
4 Door Models	11	9	10
Sill Mouldings	15	13	14
Wheel Lip Moulding	16	14	15
Power Steering	124	103	105
Front Disc Power Brakes			
6 Cylinder Models	77	64	65
8 Cylinder Models	53	44	45
Radios			
AM	66	55	56
AM/FM	137	113	115
Rear Seat Speaker	19	16	17
Speed Control	66	55	56
Sterring Wheels			
"Tuff"	31	26	27
W/Scamp, Duster & Valiant Models	21	17	18
W/Brougham Series Models	10	9	10
Deluxe	10	9	10
Manual Sun Roof	178	147	149
Heavy Duty Suspension	22	18	19
W/Radiel Tire roadability Pkg. & Brougham Series Models	8	7	8
Front Sway Bar	13	11	12
Undercoating	27	22	23
Deluxe Wheel Covers	29	24	25
Wire Wheel Covers	53	44	45
Windshield Wipers, 3 Speed	8	6	7

PONTIAC

	Retail Price	Dealer Cost	Low Price
SAFARI			
2 Seat	$5162	$4016	$4266
3 Seat	5308	4130	4380
CATALINA			
Hardtop Coupe	4713	3667	3917
4 Door Sedan	4625	3599	3849
GRAND SAFARI			
2 Seat	5446	4240	4490
3 Seat	5593	4355	4605
BONNEVILLE			
Hardtop Coupe	5098	3963	4213
4 Door Hardtop	5166	4016	4266
GRAND VILLE BROUGHAM			
Hardtop Coupe	5742	4459	4709
4 Door Hardtop	5909	4588	4838
Convertible	5871	4569	4819

CATALINA, BONNEVILLE GRAND VILLE BROUGHAM ACCESSORIES

	Retail Price	Dealer Cost	Low Price
Cordova Top			
Bonneville & Grand Ville	$141	$110	$112
Catalina Coupe & Sedan, Bonneville 4 Door	119	93	94
Wagons	44	34	35
Left Remote Control Chrome Mirror	13	10	11
Custom Seat Belts w/Soft-Tone Warning	17	13	14
Safari & Grand Safari 3 Seat Grand Ville			
Brougham Coupe & Sedan	20	16	17
Custom Cushion Steering Wheel	16	12	13
Deluxe Wheel Covers	30	23	24
Side Window Reveal Moldings			
Safari	32	25	26
Catalina 4 Door Sedan	27	21	22
Window Sill Moldings	21	16	17
Wheel Opening Moldings	16	12	13
Door Edge Guards			
4 Doors	11	9	10
2 Doors	7	5	6
Body Side Moldings	35	27	28
Electric Clock	18	14	15
Tilt Steering Wheel	49	38	39
Woodgrain Safari Siding	154	120	122
Power Tailgate	49	38	39
Spare Tire Cover & Luggage Compart. Trim	13	10	11
Luggage Carrier	89	69	70
California Emission Equipment & Testing	45	35	36
Power Windows	149	116	118
Bonneville Coupe	91	71	72
2 Door Power Door Locks w/Seat Back Locks	82	64	65
Saf-T-Lok Power Door Locks			
4 Doors	82	64	65
2 Doors	56	44	45

AUTOMOBILES

Wagons	141	110	112	6 Way Power Seat	117	91	92
Two Tone Regular Paint	42	33	34	Cruise Control	74	58	59
Vinyl Trim	27	21	22	Soft Ray Glass, All Windows	60	47	48
Custom Interior Trim Group	95	74	75	Delco X Maintenance Free Battery	27	21	22
60/40 Notchback Seat	81	63	64	Auto Temp Control Air Conditioning	524	409	414
2 BBL 400 V8 Engine (Deduct)	(66)	(51)	(52)	Custom Air Conditioning	487	380	384
4 BBL 400 V8 Engine	66	51	52	Additional Acoustical Insulation	25	20	21
4 BBL 455 V8 Engine				Heavy Duty Battery	11	9	10
Wagons	62	48	49	Electric Rear Window Defroster	41	32	33
Catalina & Bonneville	128	100	101	Rear Window Defogger	41	32	33
Grand Ville Brougham	62	48	49	Wagons	45	35	36
Safe-T Track Differential	51	40	41	Engine Block Heater	11	9	10
				Heavy Duty Air Cleaner	11	9	10
Radios				Load Floor Carpet Covering	56	44	45
AM	85	66	67	Carpeted Front Floor Mats	13	10	11
AM/FM	144	112	114	Accent Stripes	38	30	31
AM/FM Stereo	233	182	184	Automatic Level Control	84	66	67
AMw/Stereo 8 Tape Player	215	168	170	W/Trailer Group	41	32	33
AM/FM w/Stereo 8 Tape Player	363	283	286	Super Lift Shock Absorbers, Rear Only	43	34	35
Controlled Cycle Windshield Wipers	26	20	21	Remote Control Deck Lid Release	16	12	13
Left & Right Remote Control Chrome Mirrors				Firm Ride Package, Springs & Shocks	9	7	8
Catalina & Bonneville	40	31	32	Front Bumper Guards	17	13	14
Grand Ville Brougham	27	21	22	Rear Bumper Guards	17	13	14
Wagons	35	27	28	Kilo Speedometer & Clock			
Left Remote Cont. Sport Mirrors, Right Fixed				Safari, Catalina, Grand Ville Brougham	23	18	19
Catalina & Bonneville	27	21	22	Medium Trailer Group	117	91	92
Grand Ville Brougham	14	11	12	Heavy Trailer Group	157	122	124
Wagons	22	17	18	Heavy Duty Alternator	40	31	32
Left & Right Remote Control Sport Mirrors				Roof Wiring Harness	9	7	8
Catalina & Bonneville	49	38	39	Trailer Hitch	25	20	21
Grand Ville Brougham	36	28	29				

AUTOMOBILES

	Retail Price	Dealer Cost	Low Price
5 Wire Light Cable	15	12	13
7 Wire Trailer Light Cable	10	8	9

FIREBIRD
	Retail Price	Dealer Cost	Low Price
Hardtop Coupe	$3726	$3188	$3438

ESPRIT
Hardtop Coupe	3971	3396	3646

FORMULA
Hardtop Coupe	4362	3736	3986

TRANS AM
Hardtop Coupe	4753	4075	4325

FIREBIRD, ESPIRIT, FORMULA, TRANS AM ACCESSORIES

	Retail Price	Dealer Cost	Low Price
Cordova Top	$99	$77	$78
Custom Trim Group	81	63	64
4 BBL 350 V8 Engine	180	140	142
2 BBL 350 V8 Engine	130	101	103
4 BBL 400 V8 Engine	50	44	45
4 Speed Manual Transmission	219	180	182
Turbo Hydramatic Transmission	237	194	196
Safe-T-Track Differential	49	38	39
Radios			
AM	69	54	55
AM/FM	135	105	107
AM/FM Stereo	233	182	184
Rear Seat Speaker	19	15	16
Stereo 8 Tape Player	130	101	103
Saf-T-Lok Power Door Locks	56	44	45
Soft Ray Glass, All Windows	43	34	35
Soft Ray Glass, Windshield Only	34	27	28
Custom Air Conditioning	435	339	343
Additional Acoustical Insulation	20	16	17
Heavy Duty Battery	11	9	10
Electric Rear Window Defroster	70	55	56
Rear Window Defogger	41	32	33
Engine Block Heater	11	9	10
Heavy Duty Air Cleaner	11	9	10
Front Floor Mats	8	6	7
Rear Floor Mats	7	5	6
Accent Stripes	43	34	35
Lamp Group	12	9	10
Rear Air Spoiler	45	35	36
Fuel Economy Vacuum Gauge	23	18	19
Electric Clock	16	12	13
Rally Gauge Cluster, Clock	50	39	40
Rayy Gauge Cluster, Clock & Tach.	99	77	78
Kilo Speedometer & Clock	21	16	17
Heavy Duty Alternator	40	31	32

PONTIAC GRAND PRIX
	Retail Price	Dealer Cost	Low Price
Hardtop Coupe	$5309	$4145	$4395

PONTIAC GRAND PRIX ACCESSORIES
	Retail Price	Dealer Cost	Low Price
Left Front Power Bucket Seat	$117	$91	$92
6 Way Power Seat Adjuster, Driver Seat	117	91	92

CONSUMER GUIDE

AUTOMOBILES

Option					
Recessed Windshield Wipers	18	14	5		
Sport Mirror, Left Hand Remote Control, Right Hand Fixed	27	21	22		
Rear Seat Console	41	32	33		
Front Seat Console	68	53	54		
Right Hand Visor Vanity Mirror	3	2	3		
Custom Seat Belts w/Soft-Tone Warning	19	15	16		
Headlamp Warning Buzzer	6	5	6		
Custom Cushion Steering Wheel	16	12	13		
Formula Steering Wheel					
Firebird Coupe	57	44	45		
Esprit & Formula Coupe	41	32	33		
Wheel Trim Rings	30	23	24		
Custom Finned Wheel Covers					
Firebird & Formula	54	42	43		
Esprit	24	19	20		
Rally II Wheels & Trim Rings					
Firebird & Formula	91	71	72		
Firebird & Formula w/Space Saver Tire	79	61	62		
Esprit	61	48	49		
Esprit w/Space Saver Spare Tire	49	38	39		
Deluxe Wheel Covers	30	23	24		
Roof Drip Moldings	15	12	13		
Window Sill w/Hood Rear Edge Moldings	21	16	17		
Wheel Opening Moldings	16	12	13		
Door Edge Guards	7	5	6		
Body Side Moldings	35	27	28		
Power Front Disc Brakes	55	43	44		
Tilt Steering Wheel	49	38	39		
Hood Decal	55	43	44		
California Emission Equipment & Testing	45	35	36		
Power Windows	91	71	72		
60/40 Notchback Seat	13	10	11		
Reclining Bucket Seat, Right Hand	49	38	39		
Saf-T-Lok Power Door Locks	56	44	45		
Soft Ray Glass, All Windows	60	47	48		
Power Windows	91	71	72		
Remote Control Deck Lid Release	16	12	13		
Carpeted Front Floor Mats	13	10	11		
Front Floor Mats	8	6	7		
Rear Floor Mats	7	5	6		
Body Side Moldings	35	27	28		
Door Edge Guards	7	5	6		
Electric Sunroof	350	273	276		
Landau Cordova Top	119	93	94		
Windshield Wipers, Controlled Cycle	26	20	21		
Manual Sunroof	300	234	237		
Cordova Top	119	93	94		
Electric Rear Window Defroster	70	55	56		
Custom Air Conditioning	487	380	384		
Auto Temp Control Air Conditioning	524	409	414		
Door Courtesy Lamp	26	20	21		
Dome Reading Lamp	15	12	13		
Left Hand & Right Hand Remote Control Chrome Mirrors	40	31	32		
Left Hand & Right Hand Remote Control Sport Mirrors					
W/o LJ or SJ Options	40	31	32		
W/ LJ or SJ Options	49	38	39		
Left Hand Remote Control Chrome Mirror	22	17	18		
Left Hand Remote Control Sport Mirror, Right Hand Fixed	13	10	11		
Accent Stripes	27	21	22		
Rear Super Lift Shock Absorbers	38	30	31		
	43	34	35		

CONSUMER GUIDE

AUTOMOBILES

	Retail Price	Dealer Cost	Low Price
Saf-T-Track Differential	51	40	41
Engine Block Heater	11	9	10
Cruise Control	74	58	59
Heavy Duty Air Cleaner	11	9	10
2 BBL 400 V8 Engine	50	48	49
4 BBL 455 V8 Engine	62	48	49
Custom Sport Steering Wheel	41	32	33
Tilt Steering Wheel	49	38	39
Rally II Wheels & Trim Rings	61	48	49
W/Space Saver Spare Tire, without SJ or SJ Option	49	38	39
W/LJ Option, w/o Space Saver Spare Tire	37	29	30
W/LJ Option T/W Space Saver	25	19	20
Custom Finned Wheel Covers	24	18	19
Delco X Maintenance Free Battery	27	21	22
Headlamp Warning Buzzer	6	5	6
Cornering Lamps	39	30	31
Heavy Duty Battery	11	9	10
Radios			
AM w/Stereo 8 Tape Player	215	168	170
AM/FM w/Stereo 8 Tape Player	363	283	286
AM/FM Stereo	233	182	184
AM	85	66	67
AM/FM	144	112	114
Rear Seat Speaker	19	15	16
Fuel Economy Vacuum Gauge	23	18	19
Kilo Speedometer	5	4	5
California Emission Equipment & Testing	45	35	36
Front Bumper Guards	17	13	14

GRAND LEMANS

	Retail Price	Dealer Cost	Low Price
4 Door Colonnade Hardtop	$4170	$3394	$3594
Safari 2 Seat	4762	3884	4084
2 Door Colonnade Hardtop	4114	3359	3559
Safari 3 Seat	4895	3993	4193

GRAND AM

	Retail Price	Dealer Cost	Low Price
4 Door Colonnade Hardtop	$4989	$4087	$4287
2 Door Colonnade Hardtop	4900	4015	4215

LEMANS, LEMANS SPORT COUPE, GRAND LEMANS, GRAND AM ACCESSORIES

	Retail Price	Dealer Cost	Low Price
Cordova Top	$99	$77	$78
Regular Two Tone Paint	42	33	34
Special Solid Paint	116	90	91
W/Cordova Top	100	78	79
Special Two Tone Paint	155	121	122
Vinyl Trim	27	21	22
60/40 Notchback Seat	81	63	64
Grand AM (Deduct)	(44)	(34)	(35)
Custom Trim Group	83	65	66
Safe-T-Track Differential	49	38	39
GT Option Lemans 2 Dr. Colonnade or Sport Cpe.	257	200	202

102   CONSUMER GUIDE

AUTOMOBILES

Rear Bumper Guards	17	13	14	227	176	160
LJ Option				237	185	187
Special Two Tone Paint	699	545	551	211	155	157
Special Two Tone Paint w/Notchback Seat	677	528	534	180	140	142
Special Solid Paint	649	506	512	130	101	103
Special Solid Paint w/Notchback Seat	627	489	494			
Standard Paint	599	467	477	236	184	186
Standard Paint w/Notchback Seat	577	450	455	50	39	40
Lamp Group	41	32	33	112	87	88
Firm Ride Package, Springs & Shocks	9	7	8	237	194	196
SJ Option	277	216	219	259	212	215
W/Space Saver SpareTire, w/o Notchback Seat				22	18	19
W/Notchback Seat, w/o Space Saver Spare	261	203	206			
W/Notchback Seat, T/W Space Saver Spare	269	210	213	69	54	55
5-Wire Trailer Light Cable	253	197	199	135	105	107
7-Wire Trailer Light Cable	15	12	13	233	182	184
Trailer Hitch	10	8	9	199	155	157
Medium Trailer Group	25	20	21	363	283	286
W/o Air Conditioning	111	87	88	19	15	16
W/Air Conditioning	90	70	71	22	17	18
				26	20	21
W/Space Saver Spare Tire & w/o Air Cond.						
W/Air Cond. & w/o Space Saver Spare Tire				40	31	32
W/Air Cond. & w/Space Saver Spare Tire				13	10	11
4 BBL 350 V8 Engine						
2 BBL 350 V8 Engine				49	38	39
4 BBL 400 V8 Engine				27	21	22
Lemans Hardtops				68	53	54
Safari & Grand AM				99	77	78
4 BBL 455 V8 Engine				350	273	276
Turbo Hydramatic Transmission				300	234	237
Lemans Colonnade Hardtops				16	12	13
Grand Lemans Colonnade Hardtops						
Radios						
AM						
AM/FM						
AM/FM Stereo						
AM w/Stereo 8 Tape Player						
AM/FM Stereo w/Stereo 8 Tape Player						
Rear Seat Speaker						
All Wagons						
Controlled Cycle Windshield Wipers						
Chrome Mirrors						
Left & Right Remote Control						
Left Remote Control						
Sport Mirrors						
Left & Right Remote Control						
Left Remote, Right Fixed						
Front Seat Console						
Landau Cordova Top						
Electric Sunroof						
Manual Sunroof						
Custom Cushion Steering Wheel						

LEMANS

4 Door Colonnade Hardtop	$3625	$2972	$3072
Safari 2 Seat	4569	3724	3924
2 Door Colonnade Hardtop	3603	2945	3145
Safari 3 Seat	4701	3833	4033

LEMANS SPORT COUPE

2 Door Colonnade Hardtop	$3721	$3040	$3240

CONSUMER GUIDE

AUTOMOBILES

	Retail Price	Dealer Cost	Low Price
Custom Sport Steering Wheel			
Lemans Colonnade, Safari & Sport Coupe	57	44	45
Grand Lemans	41	32	33
Wheel Trim Rings	30	23	24
Deluxe Wheel Covers	30	23	24
Hood RR Edge & Fender Extension Moldings	10	8	9
Wheel Opening Moldings	16	12	13
Door Edge Guards			
2 Drs.	7	5	6
4 Drs.	11	9	10
Body Side Moldings	35	27	28
Variable Ratio Power Steering	129	101	103
Power Front Disc Brakes	55	43	44
Tilt Steering Wheel	49	38	39
Woodgrain Safari Siding	154	120	122
Rear Window Wind Deflector	26	20	21
Swing-Out Rear Vent Window	44	34	35
Remote Electric Tailgate Release	16	12	13
Spare Tire Cover & Luggage Compt. Trim	13	10	11
Luggage Carrier	68	53	54
Bumper Impact Protection			
Wagons	17	13	14
Grand AM	5	4	5
Calif. Emission Equipment & Testing	45	35	36
Power Windows			
2 Drs.	91	71	72
4 Drs.	132	103	105
W/Front Seat Console	42	33	34
Medium Trailer Group	112	87	88
W/Air Cond.	91	71	72
Heavy Duty Alternator	40	31	32
Trailer Hitch	25	20	21
5 Wire Trailer Light Cable	15	12	13
7 Wire Trailer Light Cable	10	8	9
Firm Ride Package, Springs & Shocks	9	7	8
Front Bumper Guards	17	13	14
Rear Bumper Guards	17	13	14
Protective Rubber Bumper Strips	27	21	22
Kilo Speedometer & Clock	24	19	20

ASTRE

	Retail Price	Dealer Cost	Low Price
Safari	$3188	$2751	$2951
Hatchback Coupe	3092	2668	2868

ASTRE SJ

	Retail Price	Dealer Cost	Low Price
Safari	$3699	$3184	$3384
Hatchback Coupe	3623	3118	3318

PONTIAC ASTRE, ASTRE SJ ACCESSORIES

	Retail Price	Dealer Cost	Low Price
Cordova Top	$79	$67	$68
Special Solid Paint	92	78	79
GT Option			
Astre Safari	408	347	351
Astre Hatchback Coupe	434	369	373

AUTOMOBILES

Saf-T-Lok Power Door Locks					
2 Drs.	56	44	45	55	47	48
4 Drs.	82	64	65	82	70	71
Left Front Power Seat Bucket Seat	117	91	92	50	42	43
6-Way Power Seat Adjuster Driver Seat	117	91	92	56	48	49
6-Way Power Bench Seat	117	91	92			
Cruise Control	69	54	55			
Soft Ray Glass, All Windows	48	37	38	235	200	202
Soft Ray Glass, Windshield Only	34	27	28	179	152	154
Delco X Maint. Free Battery	27	21	22	45	38	39
Auto Temp. Control Air Conditioning	487	380	384	11	9	10
Custom Air Conditioning	450	351	355			
Additional Acoustical Insulation	20	16	17	63	54	55
Heavy Duty Battery	11	9	10	129	110	112
Electric Rear Window Defroster	70	55	56	213	181	183
Rear Window Defogger	41	32	33	18	15	16
Engine Block Heater	11	9	10			
Heavy Duty Air Cleaner	11	9	10	25	21	22
Rear Wheel Opening Cover	35	27	28	14	12	13
Load Floor Carpet Covering	21	16	17	15	13	14
Carpeted Front Floor Mats	13	10	11	21	18	19
Front Floor Mats	8	6	7	36	31	32
Rear Floor Mats	7	5	6	30	26	27
Accent Stripes	35	27	28	75	64	65
Super Lift Shock Absorbers, Rear Only	43	34	35	75	64	65
Cornering Lamps	39	30	31	27	23	24
Hood Air Scoop	35	27	28	35	30	31
Remote Control Deck Lid Release	16	12	13	111	94	95
Fuel Economy Vacuum Gauge	23	18	19	51	43	44
Electric Clock	19	15	16	45	38	39
Rally Gauge Cluster & Clock	53	41	42	136	116	118
W/o Front Seat Console	34	27	28	21	18	19
				32	27	28

Custom Exterior Group			
Astre Safari			
Astre Hatchback			
2 BBL 140 4 Cylinder Engine			
4 Speed Manual Transmission			
Turbo Hydramatic Transmission			
Astre			
Astre SJ			
Safe-T-Track Differential			
Performance Axle			
Radio			
AM			
AM/FM			
AM/FM Stereo			
Rear Seat Speaker			
Sport Mirror, Right Hand Fixed, Left Hand			
Remote Control			
Custom Seat Belts w/Front Shoulder			
Custom Cushion Steering Wheel			
Formula Steering Wheel			
Astre Safari & Hatchback w/o GT Option			
Wheel Trim Rings			
Rally III Wheels			
Rally Wheels & Trim Rings			
Deluxe Wheel Covers			
Body Side Moldings			
Variable Ratio Power Steering			
Power Disc Brakes			
Tilt Steering Wheel			
Exterior Woodgrain Paneling			
Rear Window Wind Deflector			
Swing-out Rear Vent Window			

CONSUMER GUIDE

AUTOMOBILES

	Retail Price	Dealer Cost	Low Price
Luggage Carrier	49	42	43
California Emission Equipment & Testing	45	38	39
Adjustable Seat Back	16	14	15
Soft Ray Glass, All Windows	42	36	37
Soft Ray Glass, Windshield Only	28	24	25
Custom Air Conditioning	398	338	342
Additional Acoustical Insulation	20	17	18
Heavy Duty Battery	14	12	13
Electric Rear Window Defroster	60	51	52
Engine Block Heater	9	8	9
Front And Rear Floor Mats	13	11	12
GT Stripes	40	34	35
Accent Stripes	40	34	35
Electric Clock	15	13	14
Rally Gauge Cluster, Clock & Tachometer	67	57	58
Ride & Handling	12	10	11
Front Bumper Guards	15	13	14
Protective Rubber Bumper Strips	25	21	22
Heavy Duty Radiator	16	14	15

VENTURA

	Retail Price	Dealer Cost	Low Price
2 Door Hatchback Coupe	$3445	$2959	$3159
2 Door Coupe	3306	2837	3037
4 Door Sedan	3317	2847	3047

VENTURA CUSTOM

	Retail Price	Dealer Cost	Low Price
2 Door Hatchback Coupe	$3606	$3096	$3296

	Retail Price	Dealer Cost	Low Price
Spare Tire	130	101	103
Ventura Coupe w/Space Saver Spare Tire	186	145	147
Ventura Custom Cpe. w/Space Saver Spare Tire	118	92	93
Radios			
AM	69	54	55
AM/FM	135	105	107
AM/FM Stereo	233	182	184
AM Radio & Stereo 8 Tape Player	199	155	157
AM/FM Stereo Radio & Stereo 8 Tape Player	363	283	286
Rear Seat Speaker	19	15	16
Controlled Cycle Windshield Wipers	26	20	21
Sport Mirror			
Left Remote, Right Fixed	27	21	22
Left & Right Remote Control	49	38	39
Left & Right Remote Control w/Sprint Option	22	17	18
Left Remote Control Chrome Mirror	13	10	11
Front Seat Console	68	53	54
Front & Rear Custom Seat Belts & Front Shoulder W/Bucket Seats	16	12	13
Custom Cushion Steering Wheel	14	11	12
Custom Sport Steering Wheel	16	12	13
Ventura w/o Sprint Option	41	32	33
Wheel Trim Rings	57	44	45
Deluxe Wheel Covers	30	23	24
Side Window Reveal Moldings	30	23	24
Ventura 2 Door	22	17	18
Ventura 4 Door	27	21	22
Rocker Panel Molding	14	11	12

AUTOMOBILES

2 Door Coupe	3462	2970	3170	
4 door Sedan	3477	2983	3183	

VENTURA SJ

2 Door Hatchback Coupe	$3974	$3408	$3608
2 Door Coupe	3842	3293	3493
4 Door Sedan	3859	3308	3508

VENTURA, VENTURA CUSTOM, VENTURA SJ ACCESSORIES

4 BBL 350 V8 Engine	$180	$140	$142
2 BBL 260 V8 Engine	78	61	62
2 BBL 350 V8 Engine	130	101	103
3 Speed Manual Transmission, Floor Shift	27	21	22
Turbo Hydramatic Transmission	237	194	196
Safe-T-Track Differential	49	38	39
Two Tone Regular Paint	34	27	28
Special Solid Paint	100	78	79
Special Two-Tone Paint	141	110	112
Cordova Top	87	68	69
Bucket Seats			
Ventura	140	110	112
Ventura Custom	75	59	60
Right Reclining Bucket Seat	49	38	39
Sprint Option			
Ventura Hatchback	207	161	163
Ventura Coupe w/o Space Saver Spare Tire	198	154	156
Ventura Custom Hatchback	118	92	93
Ventura Custom Coupe w/o Space Saver			
Wheel Opening Moldings	16	12	13
Door Edge Guards			
2 Door	7	5	6
4 Door	11	9	10
Body Side Moldings	35	27	28
Variable Ratio Power Steering	129	101	103
Power Front Disc Brakes	55	43	44
Tilt Steering Wheel	49	38	39
Swing-Out Rear Vent Window	44	34	35
Luggage Carrier	60	47	48
California Emission Equipment & Testing	45	35	36
Power Windows			
2 Doors	91	71	72
4 Doors	132	103	105
Saf-T-Lok Power Door Locks			
2 Doors	56	44	45
4 Doors	82	64	65
Soft Ray Glass, All Windows	45	35	36
Soft Ray Glass, Windshield Only	34	26	27
Custom Air Conditioning	435	339	343
Additional Acoustical Insulation	20	16	17
Heavy Duty Battery	16	12	13
Rear Window Defogger	41	32	33
Engine Block Heater	11	9	10
Heavy Duty Air Cleaner	11	9	10
Load Floor Carpet Covering	21	16	17
Accent Stripes	43	34	35
Electric Clock	17	13	14
Firm Ride Package, Springs & Shocks	9	7	8
Rear Bumper Guards	17	13	14
Bumper Protection Strips & Front Guards	44	34	35
Heavy Duty Radiator	17	13	14

HI-FI COMPONENTS

HI-FI COMPONENTS

HARD TIMES will force the hi-fi component industry to go to the history books for its next great idea. For the high-fidelity component industry, 1974 was "the year of 4-channel sound." However it seems—at first glance—that 1975 will be the year of an idea whose time has come, gone—and returned. That idea is 2-channel stereo. This regression must be understood in the light of the continuing problems of a world-wide inflation, electronics parts and plastic shortages, and, perhaps most important, the apparent failure of the phonograph record makers to agree on an acceptable standard format for quadraphonic discs. The initial enthusiasm on the parts of both component manufacturers and record companies for 4-channel sound has waned, primarily because retail sales have failed to meet expectations. Quadraphonic components account for only 15 to 20 percent of new system audio sales.

Despite the poor sales record of quadraphonic equipment, the high-fidelity industry is not cutting back. In fact, it continues to expand more rapidly than any other leisure-oriented product category in the United States. It is estimated that sales of audio component equipment for 1975 will approach the one billion dollar mark. Many dealers in major market areas, in responding to a CONSUMER GUIDE Magazine poll,

HI-FI COMPONENTS

reported increasing sales of stereo components, coupled with static and even decreasing sales of 4-channel systems. This would indicate continued interest on the part of the consumer—at least for 2-channel stereo systems. New models—such as stereo receivers, high-performance record players (both in the record changer and manual turntable categories), tape decks, and speaker systems—have largely been concentrated in the higher-price categories.

Rising Prices

A YEAR AGO, a consumer could have easily assembled a satisfactory stereo component system for just over $300. Today, the starting point for anyone seriously considering the purchase of an audio component system would probably be more than $400. At that, such a system would likely contain only record playing facilities, its central electronic component being an integrated amplifier rather than a complete receiver with FM stereo and AM radio included. Suggested retail prices of nearly all stereo components (whether produced in the United States, Europe, or the Orient) have risen between 10 and 20 percent during 1974—a figure not inconsistent with the inflation rate for all consumer items.

Manufacturers of components have attempted, often with great success, to justify price increases by adding features that offer additional control and flexibility, but which cost the manufacturer very little. This can work to the benefit of the consumer. For example, the addition of a second tape-monitoring set of jacks costs just pennies—but it allows you to record from one tape deck to another, and provides you with a place to connect one or more of the many accessory products which help to upgrade a system. Thus, while just about all audio products have increased in price, the so-called "cost/performance" ratio has remained about the same and has even been improved in many instances. CONSUMER GUIDE Magazine is always concerned with performance as it relates to price, and—for the moment at least—we feel that a consumer with a limited budget is better off purchasing a good quality stereo component system rather than a minimal quality 4-channel system.

Even if you have the money to spend upwards of 75 percent more for 4-channel components, but cannot decide whether to invest in a stereo system or 4-channel, you can actually have both. Some of the manufacturers, such as Harman-Kardon or MX, who produce 4-channel receivers have devised circuitry which permits enjoyment of the product in a stereo mode (using just two speakers) initially. All available audio power is directed to the two speakers, and the system operates much like any other stereo component setup. If, at some future date, you wish to add another pair of speakers and convert fully to quadraphonic sound, all you have to do is throw a switch on the front or back panel of the receiver. Power is then divided among four amplification channels, with each channel driving one of the loudspeaker systems.

When you do decide to convert to 4-channel sound (either by buying

HI-FI COMPONENTS

one of the 2/4 channel receivers or by adding a second stereo amplifier plus decoders), you should know that your present stereo cartridge will not be able to track the new CD-4 records. No matter how expensive or high-performing your stereo cartridge is, you will need a cartridge specifically designed for quadraphonic sound. The Stanton 681 EEE, for example, is a fairly expensive ($82.00) and highly rated pickup, but it cannot play Quadradiscs (another name for the new CD-4 records). Such cartridges as Audio-Technica's AT-15S or Pickering's UV-2000Q, on the other hand, are designed specifically for CD-4 use, and they work perfectly with conventional stereo discs as well.

To keep readers knowledgeable of the latest trends in each component category, CONSUMER GUIDE Magazine surveyed the audio market and discussed buying trends with leading experts at the manufacturing and retail levels. Here are capsule summaries of what we see as the major trends in each component category.

Turntable Trends

IT MAY COME as a surprise to audiophiles to learn that not a single Japanese manufacturer makes what Americans call a "record changer." Ever since the invention of the long-playing 33-1/3 rpm record, Japanese audio buffs have preferred to play their records on single-play turntables, regarding machines that handle many records sequentially as basically inferior. Up until a short time ago, the so-called record changer was the undisputed favorite with both serious and casual music listeners in the United States and in Great Britain. Indeed, recent technological improvements resulted in record changers that played records as carefully and as precisely as the more rugged manual turntables.

Nevertheless, there is suddenly a growing interest in two basic types of single-play turntable systems. These are the completely manual types, in which all operations—such as tone-arm set-down, start of motor, etc.—are performed by hand; and semiautomatic systems which, while lacking record changing facilities, offer some of the automatic features of the record changer. There are, for example, some manual turntables which—at the press of a button—begin rotation, index the tone-arm to the starting groove of the record, bring the arm back to its rest position at the conclusion of play, and even shut off the entire mechanism. Manufacturers of these single-play devices have begun calling them "automatic turntables," but that designation is confusing. Years ago, when the term "record changer" became unfashionable and suggestive of lower quality performance, the name was changed to "automatic turntables." When shopping you should make certain that the automatic turntable you choose is the machine that provides the features and performance you are seeking.

CONSUMER GUIDE Magazine does not prefer either record changers or single play turntables. We have tested excellent units in the manual, semiautomatic, and fully automatic categories; our recom-

HI-FI COMPONENTS

mendations are based primarily upon such operating criteria as speed accuracy, rumble, wow and flutter, tone-arm action, antiskate features, tracking force adjustment, and the range and effectiveness of cueing controls (if any).

In turntable nomenclature, vibrations from the motor or other sources is known as rumble. The lower the rumble, the better. If you are seeking the lowest rumble characteristics in a turntable, you may be interested in checking one of the many new direct-drive units (the most advanced in design) now available. In such units as the Dual 701 or the Technics SL-1200—both single-play—special new slow-speed motors rotate at the required 33-1/3 or 45 rpm speeds to eliminate the need for any belts or speed-reduction pulleys and idler wheels. Direct-drive motors (whose shafts are connected directly to the center hole of the turntable) are invariably driven by electronic circuitry rather than being connected directly across the 120-volt power line. Some of them offer speed or pitch control, with stroboscope indicators to permit precise speed adjustment—and, therefore, perfect musical pitch.

While the direct-drive approach has not been applied to fully automatic record changers, one company (British Industries of Westbury, New York—the former distributors of the Garrard line of changers from England) has begun production of a new line of automatic multiple-record handling turntables which utilizes belt-drive and moderately slow-speed motors (300 rpm instead of the more usual 1800 rpm) for reduced rumble and wow and flutter. CONSUMER GUIDE Magazine has not had an opportunity to test these new machines, but from preliminary data supplied by the company, the belt-drive automatics seem to offer performance rivaling that of the best belt-driven manual units.

The sudden popularity of manual turntables has prompted such well-known foreign manufacturers as Sansui, Pioneer, Technics by Panasonic, and Philips (of Holland) to introduce high-priced models in the United States—models which had originally been developed for their home market where single-play turntables have always been the rule rather than the exception. Old firms such as Thorens (of Switzerland) and Acoustic Research (in New England) have also profited from the sudden popularity of a single-play turntable. Acoustic Research has upgraded its successful model XA turntable to a model XB which now includes a cueing control. The XB turntable represents one of the best values in a single-play no-nonsense turntable, offering excellent specifications and the XA's good reputation for long life and reliability.

Cartridge Trends

STEREO EQUIPMENT manufacturers love to re-engineer their products. While this occurs in every field, cartridges do not undergo the annual redesign to the same degree. The tried-and-true models from such companies as Pickering, Shure, Empire, and other domestic manufacturers are usually just modified slightly for better performance. A good example is Shure's new V-15 III, successor to the V-15 II "Improved" and the V-15 II.

HI-FI COMPONENTS

What is significant in the cartridge field is that after a late start, domestic and European manufacturers are now offering CD-4 type cartridges which are equal or superior to the early "discrete 4-channel" pickups available from such Japanese sources as Audio-Technica, JVC, and Panasonic. Models as Pickering's V-15 2000Q and its more costly V-15 2400Q employ a new stylus tip shape which the company calls Quadrahedral. This new tip shape—like the popular Shibata stylus developed for Japanese cartridges—properly tracks the high frequencies contained in CD-4 discs. The new cartridges, therefore, are able to reproduce frequencies up to and including 45,000 Hz—a requirement for properly unscrambling CD-4 records into four separate signals. Bang and Olufsen of Denmark recently introduced a CD-4 cartridge, Model MMC6000. Empire, in the United States, introduced a series of three new cartridges to add to its extensive line which includes the 999 TE/X unit and the 2000 series. The new cartridges, dubbed the 4000 series, include units priced from about $70 on up; all three models are expressly designed for playing CD-4 as well as conventional stereo records.

CONSUMER GUIDE Magazine suggests that you not be guided by tracking force specifications alone. It is true that low tracking force (below 1½ grams or so) contributes to the long life of your records. However, purchasing a cartridge with super-compliance and low tracking force and then trying to use it in a low-cost changer or turntable for which it was not designed can cause you more grief than joy. Generally, lower cost record changers have higher tone-arm bearing friction, and there are cartridges that are specifically designed to be used at the higher tracking forces (around 2 grams or so) for such machines. The light-tracking (1 gram and under) cartridges should be used only with top-of-the-line automatic turntables or manual machines.

Receiver Trends

POWER OUTPUT levels formerly associated only with separate, basic amplifiers are now commonplace in the all-in-one stereo receiver, which continues to be the most popular single component. It is the basis around which most people assemble a complete sound system. In 1975 many electronic component manufacturers are offering higher powered, more feature-laden 2-channel receivers to make up the sales volume that they could not achieve with earlier quadraphonic entries.

In addition to more power, the new receivers are laden with control features and flexibility that were previously found only on the more sophisticated separate integrated amplifiers, preamplifiers, and tuners. Consider, for example, the Kenwood KR-6400 and the Tandberg TR-1055. CONSUMER GUIDE Magazine measured 53-watts per channel for the former and 56-watts per channel for the latter. At $450 and $600 such receivers are not intended for budget systems, but they and others like them can be relied upon to drive even the low-efficiency speaker systems that remain favorites as space-savers in small apartments or wherever floor space is at a premium.

HI-FI COMPONENTS

Fisher Radio is one of the few firms that continues to make a total commitment to 4-channel sound. The Fisher Studio Standard series, introduced some years ago, has been continuously updated. You can now purchase Model 4060 which produces about 17-watts per channel in quad and more than 35-watts per channel when operated in the so-called "strapped" mode (stereo, but with quadraphonic potential when you add more speakers later). Newer Fisher models, such as the 314B, now include built-in CD-4 demodulator circuitry for playing 4-channel discs.

Speaker Trends

SPEAKERS MAY be the most important part of a stereo sytem but their performance levels are difficult to define. This is because there are no standards that are universally recognized by the industry for measuring and reporting the performance of loudspeakers. CONSUMER GUIDE Magazine has always rated speakers on the basis of extensive listening tests, price (in relation to quality), and, lastly, on the basis of published specifications.

Some speaker manufacturers have recently begun stressing one important operating parameter—efficiency. They have been specifying the minimum power required to produce adequate sound from their products, as well as the maximum power which a given speaker can safely handle without emitting high orders of distortion or even being "burned out" or destroyed. A few manufacturers, in an effort to be even more definitive, are specifying the sound pressure level in dB (decibels) that a given amount of audio power will produce at a prescribed distance from the loudspeaker. Most quote the test distance as one meter (a bit over three feet) from the speaker. Since you generally sit a bit further from the speaker than that, you should subtract about five dB from the number given.

As a frame of reference, 80 dB is a comfortable but not very loud listening level. The level at which most people listen seriously to reproduced music is 90 dB. 100-dB levels represent quite a loud listening level in a home environment, while ear-shattering discotheque levels have been measured at 110 dB and even higher. At the 120-dB level or thereabouts, sound actually becomes painful; your hearing can be impaired permanently if you are subjected to such listening levels for even a relatively short period of time.

Although speakers contribute the greatest amount of coloration to what you hear in a sound system, they remain the most difficult items to judge objectively. CONSUMER GUIDE Magazine suggests that you examine our "Best Buy" recommendations in terms of price and basic design type, but above all spend some time listening to speakers in an audio equipment store before you make your final selection.

The Vanishing Compact System

WHEN CONSUMER GUIDE Magazine first began publishing data on

HI-FI COMPONENTS

stereo hi-fi systems some years ago, at least one quarter of our test reporting covered compact music systems—that halfway category between the all-in-one console radio phonograph (which audio buffs regard disparagingly) and true hi-fi components. In the late 1960's and early 1970's, it was possible to purchase a compact system (usually consisting of a preassembled receiver-record player combination with speakers supplied separately) which reproduced acceptable quality music and took the guesswork out of choosing the right components. Recently, however, CONSUMER GUIDE Magazine has devoted less and less space to reviewing compact systems in its Stereo Equipment Quarterlies. There are, of course, hundreds of compact models still available, but most of them are marketed by little-known importers who have them specially built overseas.

The few well-known component makers who formerly offered compacts—such as Harman-Kardon—have abandoned them altogether, while such companies as Fisher Radio, Panasonic, and Sony continue to sell them (but usually through distribution facilities other than the special audio shops). Walk through any radio and phonograph department of a mass-merchandise department store and you will see and hear plenty of compact models. With few exceptions, these systems include record changers of low price and quality, small speakers mounted in open-backed or perforated-back speaker enclosures, etc.

We wish to point out, however, that if you are fearful about choosing the right set of components that will work well with each other, there is another alternative open to you. Many audio dealers, recognizing the plight of the neophyte audiophile, go to great lengths to assemble what they believe to be compatible systems. They feature these systems in working displays which you can hear, and—more often than not—they offer these complete packages at prices which are particularly attractive compared to the sum of the prices for the individual components included. Even some fair-traded components (in states which recognize and enforce fair-trade pricing practices) can be purchased through this hidden discount arrangement. A dealer may discount a system that includes fair-trade items so long as the final price to you is no lower than the full retail price of the fair-traded item plus the wholesale cost for the other components in the package. Thus, dealers who are particularly anxious to make a sale may offer preselected packages of components at very substantial discounts. Providing the dealer's knowledge and reputation are good, CONSUMER GUIDE Magazine recommends the package deals—especially if you feel that you cannot judge each component on its own merits.

Headphone Trends

HEADPHONES continue to grow in popularity, and it is no wonder. They offer the advantages of isolating the listener from the acoustics of the listening room (which often can upset reproduction faithfulness to an amazing degree) and from disturbing other people. At the same time, however, they offer the disadvantage of significant discomfort if you

HI-FI COMPONENTS

wear them for long periods of time. Consequently, CONSUMER GUIDE Magazine judges headphones not only for their ability to reproduce sound faithfully, but also for their comfort during long listening sessions.

Koss Corporation (of Milwaukee) is credited with introducing the audio enthusiast to the joys of headphone stereo listening; the Koss ESP-9—though more expensive (at $175 retail) than many speaker systems—is still the best set of phones around. The ESP-9 is an electrostatic set of headphones, completely different from conventional dynamic phones which operate more like miniature loudspeaker systems. Less affluent headphone buffs may find that the Koss PRO-5Q phones, which retail at about $75, answer their needs for both stereo and 4-channel sound. You can hear 4-channel sound through headphones, provided that the phones have two transducers properly oriented in each earpiece; the Koss PRO-5Q phones are properly oriented for 4-channel sound.

A somewhat new approach to headphone design has appeared in recent years. The so-called open-air design does not require that you have a perfect air seal between your ear and the phone's earpiece. Many listeners report that the open-air design tends to make them feel less confined when wearing headphones. Many of the open-air headphones, such as Pickering's Model OA-1, are much lighter in weight than the conventional sealed types. On the other hand, CONSUMER GUIDE Magazine has yet to test an open-air design that provides the same kind of rich, true bass that is possible with the sealed-to-your-ear models.

SPECIAL INFORMATION SERVICE
A Bonus for Readers of this CONSUMER GUIDE

CONSUMER GUIDE offers a special bonus to its readers who are interested in obtaining information as to where they can find low prices on specific products listed in this guide. Simply fill out the form and mail. Please include 25 cents for postage and handling.

Please send me information on:

Product _____ Model Number _____

Manufacturer _____

Your Name _____

Address _____

City _____ State _____ Zip Code _____

CONSUMER GUIDE Magazine
3323 West Main, Skokie, Illinois 60076

HI-FI COMPONENTS

HI-FI COMPONENTS BEST BUYS

IN RATING hi-fi equipment, CONSUMER GUIDE Magazine selected a number of leading brands for review. Our "Best Buys" ratings are based on: (1) a technical analysis of design, construction, and performance; (2) a trial period of actual use; and (3) a comparison of control features and functions within each price range.

STEREO RECEIVERS

Sony STR-7055 *can be classified as a medium-high-power stereo receiver. Like the many other Sony products tested by CONSUMER GUIDE Magazine over the past few years, it lives up to expectations for good-looking front panels, orderly control arrangement, and well-designed circuitry.*
Suggested Retail Price: $449.50   **Low Price: $350.60**

Tandberg TR-1055 *is the company's best receiver effort to date and is highly recommended by CONSUMER GUIDE Magazine. FM performance, and particularly stereo FM, is excellent. As for the amplifier section, the availability of full power at low frequencies makes a positive difference in driving standard low-efficiency speaker systems to loud listening levels.*
Suggested Retail Price: $599.90   **Low Price: Not Available**

QUADRAPHONIC RECEIVERS

Harman-Kardon 800+ Quad Receiver *has a clean, functional layout and retains control flexibility. Every cubic inch of chassis space is efficiently utilized. Both measurements and listening tests showed performance to be quite good. The 800+ is loaded with features and power capability, yet it is no larger than the best integrated stereo receivers, and it is smaller than some.*
Fair Trade Price: $499.95   **Low Price: $374.95**

JVC 4VR-5446 Quad Receiver *may offer only moderate power output when compared to stereo receivers costing considerably less, but it packs lots of four-channel circuitry into a single chassis. If four-channel sound (CD-4) is what you are after, this receiver will certainly provide good reproduction of that kind of program source. But if you want the*

HI-FI COMPONENTS

best possible matrix disc reproduction and great amounts of power output, you may want to build your system of separate components.
Fair Trade Price: $679.95   **Low Price: $469.20**

Pioneer QX-949 is an excellent, "do-everything," two-channel/four channel receiver. Its long, low panel has controls aplenty, and yet it presents an uncluttered and uncomplicated look. Modular circuitry is used throughout the QX-949, and extensive shielding is used around radio-frequency (RF) and intermediate frequency (IF) tuner sections.
Fair Trade Price: $749.95   **Low Price: $599.95**

Sansui QRX-3500 Quad Receiver delivers just about the best kind of matrix logic we have heard, but it does not include CD-4 demodulation circuitry. Going by the number of discs available, matrix facilities are more important than CD-4 facilities at this time. For really superb reproduction of matrix discs, you need a receiver or amplifier that has a well-thought-out logic scheme for increasing instantaneous apparent separation between the four channels.
Fair Trade price: $549.95   **Low Price: $467.45**

TUNERS

Dynaco AF-6 AM/FM Tuner is a tremendous value for those willing to invest a bit of time in building it from a kit. In wired form, we find its price a bit too high in light of other state-of-the-art tuner products currently available (unless you include the reputation and reliability factor of this particular manufacturer).
Suggested Retail Price (Kit): $245.00   **Low Price: $183.75**

Kenwood KT-6005 AM/FM Tuner is one notch below Kenwood's top-of-the-line KT-8005, which retails for about $100 more. CONSUMER GUIDE Magazine believes that, all in all, the Kenwood KT-6005 represents excellent value in its price range for those interested in a separate tuner.
Fair Trade Price: $289.95   **Low Price: $246**

Pioneer TX-9100 Tuner gives us pause. Not every audiophile is prepared to pay its price for a separate AM/FM tuner. For those who like their AM and FM in a separate unit, however, the TX-9100 equals or exceeds the performance of tuners costing twice as much, or even more. This unit has won plaudits from audio equipment reviewers throughout the country, and justly so.
Fair Trade Price: $349.95   **Low Price: $279**

TURNTABLES

PE 3060, manufactured by the West German Company, Perpetuum-Ebner, has extremely accurate turntable speed. There is no audible

HI-FI COMPONENTS

wow or flutter, even on long, sustained musical passages. It runs at three speeds and may be used as a single-play or as a stack-and-change unit. You can start it either automatically or manually. It comes with two spindles–a short one for single-play, and a longer one for holding up to six records at a time.
Suggested Retail Price: $199.95 **Low Price: Not Available**

Acoustic Research AR-XB *is a two-speed, manual, single-play model, with no automatic options whatsoever. The AR-XB does not have an antiskating adjustment; it seems that Acoustic Research does not believe it is needed. Further, there is no variable speed or "vernier" pitch adjustment. Although it has no fine-speed adjustment, the AR-XB hardly needs it because it has inherent high-speed accuracy. CONSUMER GUIDE Magazine concludes that the AR-XB performs as claimed and is an excellent manual record player, despite its lack of certain features that have become familiar on many other brands.*
(without cartridge)
Suggested Retail Price: $119.95 **Low Price: $89.95**

Philips GA-212, *in common with many of the newer turntables, uses an electronic system for speed control. But, unlike most other models, it features "touch-to-operate" buttons that make for effortless handling, unprecendented in consumer audio gear. It is a superior manual (single-play) record player that, at its price, leaves most of its competition at the starting line.*
Fair Trade Price: $179.50 **Low Price: $149**

Yamaha YP-701 *is a two-speed, belt-driven, single-play turntable, integrated with an S-shaped arm of advanced design. The turntable lacks a fine-speed adjustment, but a check of speed accuracy showed that the unit ran true at both 33 and 45 rpm. CONSUMER GUIDE Magazine testers found performance to be quite good.*
Suggested Retail Price: $220 **Low Price: $178**

CARTRIDGES

Pickering UV-15/2000Q *is a cartridge designed to play discrete quadraphonic discs. CONSUMER GUIDE Magazine finds that its quadraphonic capacity ranks with considerably more expensive foreign quad entries.*
Suggested Retail Price: $69.90 **Low Price: $32**

Shure V-15 Type III *gave both excellent laboratory measurements and listening tests. Highs were noteworthy for their lack of "fuzziness." We could detect no "peaks" in response; and distortion, if heard at all, was largely a function of the recordings themselves. CONSUMER GUIDE Magazine recommends this Shure entry to anyone seeking the finest in stereo record-reproduction facilities and willing to utilize a record player or turntable/tone-arm combination worthy of its installation.*
Sug. Retail Price: $72.50 **Low Price: $50**

HI-FI COMPONENTS

Stanton 681 EEE *has smooth frequency response beyond the limits of audibility, low harmonic and IM distortion, and excellent tracking capability, which make this cartridge a top performer in its price category.*
Fair Trade Price: $72 **Low Price: $40**

SPEAKERS

Acoustic Research AR-7 *is a low-priced bookshelf model. This unit's modest cost and dimensions, can put you off, but for its size and price, it is an astonishingly good speaker.*
Suggested Retail : $69 (per speaker) **Low Price: $51.75**

Avid 103 *is a high-quality speaker system that seems to be broad enough in aural scope to appeal to a variety of listeners, regardless of preferred musical tastes. It is an "all-purpose" speaker with plenty of clean, honest, uncolored response to reproduce accurately all manner of program material, and it performs well with both modest and super-powerhouse amplifiers. Quality of Avid 103 is evident in sound and in construction.*
Suggested Retail : $145 (per speaker) **Low Price: Not Available**

Bose 501 Series II *is an improved version of the earlier 501, which was a novel design. You can place it on the floor or on a low bench or similar mounting—just remember to leave some space on either side for the tweeters.*
Fair Trade Price: $139 (per speaker) **Low Price: Not Available**

Heath AS-104 *is a speaker kit. The enclosure itself comes fully assembled and finished in walnut veneer. The buyer, however, does the soldering and installing. About two hours should be enough to do the job. When you have finished, you will have a good speaker system that would normally cost considerably more than you will pay for the AS-104.*
Suggested Retail : $99.95 (per speaker) Low Price: Not Available

Dynaco A-35 *is not a rock speaker in the sense that higher efficiency units are. It will not long survive extremely high levels in larger rooms. But in a small apartment living room, the A-35 will give you as much good volume as you (or your neighbors) can stand. With the room size restriction as the only negative factor, CONSUMER GUIDE Magazine heartily recommends the A-35.*
Suggested Retail Price: $120 **Low Price: $85**

EPI Microtower II *is the realization of a particular design concept in search of a low-cost good performing unit of modest but attractive proportions. In CONSUMER GUIDE Magazine's opinion, that quest has been successfully achieved.*
Suggested Retail: $129.95 (per speaker) Low Price: Not Available

TAPE RECORDERS

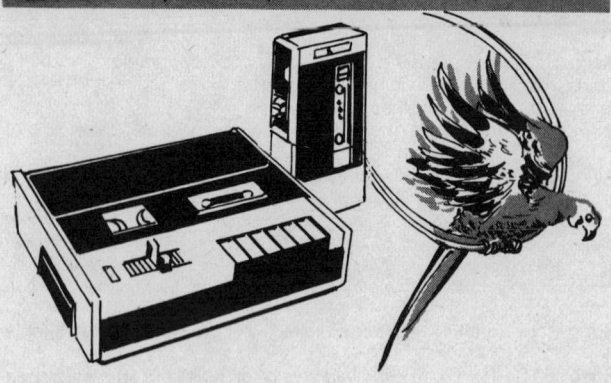

1975 TAPE RECORDERS

IN THE WORLD of sound, the tape medium enjoys a unique position: It has many applications. The portable cassette machine, for example, is used in the business world to record dictation, in journalism to record interviews, and in schools to record lecturers. Tape machines, unlike record players which are strictly playback media, serve both as a playback and a recording medium. Consequently, when you buy a tape recorder for your stereo system, you are purchasing not only another program source, but also the means to make your own programs—from disc recordings, radio broadcasts, or live performances via microphones.

The choice of a tape recorder is, therefore, far more involved than for other sound equipment. You must consider such features as ips, Dolby, four-channel play, microphone mix, peak level, and two- and three-head recorders. To further complicate the picture, there are three distinct forms of tape equipment.

The first, which appeared as a professional tool in recording and broadcasting shortly after World War II, is the open-reel tape recorder. It continues today as the first choice of the professional, the serious amateur, and the advanced hobbyist. At its best, open-reel provides the best sound quality and the most versatility. The second format is the cassette, which at its best can sound virtually as good as open-reel, but it still cannot match open-reel in terms of versatility. The third format is the cartridge which remains, in the opinion of CONSUMER GUIDE Magazine, in third place in terms of both audio quality and versatility.

TAPE RECORDERS

Open-Reel Tape

IN AN OPEN-REEL format, the tape is spooled off one reel, the supply reel, onto another reel, the take-up reel, while it runs past magnetic heads. The normal head arrangement is designed to perform three basic functions—erase, record, and play, in that order. In the case of open-reel tape machines, three-heads are better than two, for in the process of making a recording, the erase head demagnetizes any previously recorded material on the tape; the record head impresses the new signal onto the tape; and the play head then reproduces what has been put onto the tape. If the play head is a separate entity, the operator can monitor what is being recorded as it is being recorded. If the play head is combined with the record head, monitoring is impossible. The operator must wait until the actual recording is finished, rewind the tape to its starting position, and switch the machine to the playback mode in order to hear what has been recorded.

Separate heads for the two functions of record and play also permit added versatility for multiple-track recording, echo effects, and so on. It enables the designer of the tape machine to maximize each head for its one intended function instead of compromising in order to have one head perform two distinctly different functions. For these reasons, CONSUMER GUIDE Magazine feels that if a buyer is interested enough in tape to consider buying an open-reel machine, he should choose one that has separate heads for record and play.

In addition to moving the tape at normal speeds, the tape machine typically has provisions for fast-wind operations, both forward and back (rewind). Fast wind is a great convenience because it permits the operator to get to a specific part of a tape very quickly; but it must be used with some caution. Some tapes on some machines lap unevenly during fast wind. Moreover, the tightness of the successive layers of tape during fast wind can cause mischief with the recorded signal, such as "print-through" whereby a faint signal is transferred from one section of the tape to another, causing distortion and a confused sound. CONSUMER GUIDE Magazine recommends that you test the fast-wind operation before you make a purchase.

Professional-quality open-reel machines run at relatively high speeds (30 to 15 inches-per-second). To get an appreciable amount of recording time onto a reel, large-size reels must be used: the so-called NAB reels, which are 10½ inches in diameter. Consumer-quality open-reel machines typically run at 7½ or 3-3/4 inches-per-second. At 7½ ips, a seven-inch reel will hold as much program material as a 10½-inch reel running at 15 ips. At 3-3/4 the same seven-inch reel will hold twice as much material. A faster recording speed means better sound reproduction with less audible interference.

Finally, most open-reel decks have an automatic shutoff that stops the mechanism at the end of the tape. And few machines offer automatic reversing and head switching to reverse the direction of the tracks.

TAPE RECORDERS

Cassettes

IN THE CASSETTE format, the tape is enclosed in a small packet that actually includes the equivalent of miniature supply and takeup reels. The standard speed in cassettes is only 1⅞ inches-per-second, a "voice-only" speed on most open-reel machines. But ingenious design advances have enabled cassettes and cassette recorders to provide audio response surprisingly close to what one would expect from an open-reel machine operating at faster speeds.

Without a doubt, the most telling single advance in cassette quality has been the Dolby noise-reduction system which is now incorporated in all top-quality cassette recorders. The net result is that noise from cassette tape is quite low. A related development, which works in conjunction with the Dolby system, is the general improvement in cassette tapes themselves. Thus, a cassette recorder can sound nearly as good as an open-reel machine.

Not to be overlooked either are the improvements in the mechanical portions of the latest cassette models. Although the cassette machine's transport mechanism is much smaller than that used in an open-reel model, it can provide smooth and steady tape motion with no wavering—either rapidly ("flutter") or slowly ("wow").

Difficulties or troubles with the tape as it moves in the cassette are generally not caused by a defect in the recorder, but rather are the result of imperfectly fabricated cassette housings. The plastic cover of a cassette is a two-piece affair, with several small windows that permit the capstans and the heads of the machine to engage the tape. Several kinds of imperfections in the cassette can cause trouble. If, for example, the two sections of the cassette housing are not precisely matched, or if the windows are imperfectly formed, or if there are small burrs or tiny projections anywhere along the edge of the cassette that face the capstans and heads of the recorder, trouble can develop in the form of snagged tape, backlash, failure to wind properly, and so on. These troubles often are blamed—incorrectly—on the cassette recorder when they are actually the result of an imperfectly made cassette. For this reason, CONSUMER GUIDE Magazine strongly advises that a cassette-machine owner avoid the temptation to use bargain cassettes. Stick to such widely accepted brand names as Advent, Ampex, Audio Magnetics, BASF, Capitol, Certron, Maxell, Memorex, Scotch, Sony, and TDK.

Most cassette recorders use a combined record/play head, although a few late models have separate heads for these functions. All cassette models offer fast wind, but you need not be as careful with cassette fast wind as you do with the open-reel machines. Still, to prevent "print-through", it is wise not to store a cassette in the fast-wind mode.

Cartridge Format

IN THE CARTRIDGE tape format (popularly known as "stereo-8" or "eight-track"), the tape is one long continuous loop that moves by

TAPE RECORDERS

literally sliding over itself. It is always being taken up on the same hub from which it plays out. While the system is ingenious and easy to operate, it is also inherently tricky and subject to mechanical difficulties. The tape itself is coated with a special lubricant to facilitate its movement, and when this lubricant dries up, trouble can develop.

The cartridge tape format was originally developed as an aid to broadcasters. Unfortunately, its adaptation as a consumer product seems to have been more of a rush to cash in on an idea than to research and perfect it fully in consumer-product terms. Aside from mechanical difficulties, the tape cartridge system does not sound as good as the cassette system—despite the fact that the cartridge runs at the faster speed of 3¾ ips. In addition, the cartridge format is not as inherently versatile as the other tape formats. Relatively few cartridge tape machines can record, and even fewer offer fast-forward wind. Rewind is ruled out by the nature of the cartridge.

Within the cartridge tape field, one company—Wollensak—appears to be making a serious effort to upgrade the format. Wollensak offers units that—in CONSUMER GUIDE Magazine's opinion—are a notch above most others in terms of mechanical and audio performance. Wollensak reportedly has been designing its new cartridge recorders to deliver top performance when used with 3M's new "Classic" line of cartridge recording tapes. On the basis of the evidence to date, it would appear that a buyer who is determined to have the cartridge tape format should investigate one of the new Wollensak models and to use the 3M brand Classic tape with it. Such a buyer, however, should still not expect the high performance he or she would get from a good cassette machine equipped with Dolby.

Four-Channel Sound and Tape

FOUR-CHANNEL, or quadraphonic, sound originated as an open-reel tape medium. Tape is, of course, the natural and preferred medium for multi-channel sound since it permits the recording of independent (discrete) sound tracks next to one another. No encoding (converting four channels of signals to two) is required, and each sound track can be fully captured without compromise. A disc groove has but two sidewalls, and the only way more than two sound channels can be impressed onto those walls is by some form of encoding.

Four-channel tape equipment falls into one of two distinctly different marketing approaches, both of which any prospective tape-equipment buyer should be aware. At one quality extreme are many new open-reel tape decks of near-professional caliber and unprecendented versatility. Priced, as a rule, well above the $500 mark, these machines not only permit full, discrete four-channel recording and playback, but —because they have four complete tape paths (in terms of inputs and outputs, head assemblies, and related electronics)—they also are readily usable for stereo (two-channel) or mono (one-channel) recording. The open-reel quadraphonic decks provide almost unlimited facilities for special effects such as sound-with-sound, elaborate mix-

TAPE RECORDERS

ing, controlled echo, and the like. Their high audio performance, versatility, and cost have put these units in a new class of home tape equipment that has come to be known as the "semi-pro" category.

Exact sales figures are impossible to come by, but it is CONSUMER GUIDE Magazine's understanding that the industry is very optimistic about consumer reaction to these products. They are being vigorously promoted, and the models tested by CONSUMER GUIDE Magazine have been found to deliver the goods. These machines are being bought primarily as recorders by the advanced active hobbyist, however, rather than as players by the serious music listener because there are very few prerecorded four-channel open-reel tapes to play on such machines.

At the other quality extreme (distinctly lower) are cartridge quadraphonic tape models. Most of these machines, if they provide the recording function at all, do so only for stereo. From a four-channel standpoint, therefore, quadraphonic cartridge machines are purchased as playback devices only. As you might expect, there are far more prerecorded four-channel cartridge tapes than four-channel open-reel tapes. The sonic quality of the cartridge tapes is variable, however, and the repertoire is devoted primarily to popular music with little emphasis on classical.

Selecting a Tape Format

IN CONSUMER GUIDE Magazine's opinion, the buyer who is seeking the best in both sonic performance and tape-recording versatility should, if his budget permits, choose one of the late-model open-reel tape decks. Such a machine provides the means for a variety of self-recording activities, and it does a great playback job on the prerecorded tapes that are available.

The latest top-of-the-line cassette models come surprisingly close in sonic quality, although their recording and editing abilities are limited when compared to open-reel decks. Even so, the cassettes do provide adequate facilities for making very good tape copies of other program sources (live or recorded), and should suffice for most home users, except the semi-pros or advanced hobbyists.

There is good news if you like listening more than recording on a cassette model—a wide variety of material is available on prerecorded cassettes, with a high proportion devoted to classical music. The widely acclaimed Deutsche Gramophon library is now on cassettes processed with Dolby noise reduction. The new prerecorded cassettes released by Advent (Dolbyized and on chromium-dioxide tape) lend added emphasis to the cassette format as a high-quality program format of interest to the serious music listener.

The cartridge tape format remains in third place from every standpoint (except that of its four-channel availability). However, 1975 may witness an upgrading of the cartridge format as a result of the Wollensak/3M thrust.

TAPE RECORDERS

Battery Portable And Mobile Compact Tape Machines

RELIABLE PORTABLE tape-recorders that are powered by batteries are available for under $100. In most cases, these are monophonic cassette models with built-in microphones that are surprisingly sensitive and well-suited for noncritical recording such as interviewing and other "spoken-voice" work. For recording music, for accuracy, and in stereo, however, the cost of a truly portable battery-operated tape machine becomes astronomical—ranging from such units as the $2600 stereo Nagra IV-SD and the $5730 quadraphonic Stellavox SQ-7. These imported machines are in limited supply and are clearly intended for professional use. A somewhat broader selection of portable stereo recorders priced below $250 is also available, but in general, these models should only be considered for convenience rather than for sound quality.

If a battery-powered portable interests you, here is something to remember: Flashlight batteries should never be used in portable tape recorders. The preferred battery is an alkaline cell, and the best manufacturers are Eveready and Mallory. Alkaline batteries in a recorder last five to ten times longer than flashlight batteries. Alkaline batteries also have a much longer life than do conventional batteries. If a recorder is used only occasionally, it is essential that you remove even so-called leak-proof alkaline batteries from the recorder during periods of storage. Another point to remember about batteries is that the heaviest drain on battery-driven machines comes when the motor works hardest—during fast forward or rewind; thus, obtaining maximum life from the batteries is realized by laying-off the fast wind button.

Most portable machines are equipped with inexpensive dynamic microphones. In most cases, however, you can achieve better musical recordings by substituting higher quality microphones. Many of the microphones supplied with the machines also contain start and stop switches to operate the recorder, a nice feature.

Anyone who likes listening to music in the car will appreciate the freedom offered by a mobile tape player. Most cars have space for a portable player somewhere in the front seat area. Players are available with mounting plates that attach to the dashboard of many cars; others have brackets that attach under the dashboard, in the glove compartment, and even under the roof. Because mobile players are vulnerable to theft, the safest mounting system uses fasteners that enable you to take the player with you when you leave your car. Because of the simplicity of the mobile compact formats and the minimal number of controls needed, DC-powered units for cars and boats tend to be similar in features and appearance. Mobile tape players nearly always contain their own power amplifiers, and the amount of power they deliver is a factor in the large price differences between two apparently identical models. None of them can deliver more than minimal power, but most mobile tape players have enough to make loud and reasonably clear sound in a car. Generally, though, the higher the power the better the player will sound at all volume levels.

CONSUMER GUIDE

TAPE RECORDERS

CONSUMER GUIDE Magazine feels that the factory built-in unit is the most practical way to have tape sound—or even radio—in a car. Such installations are professional and fit the car as if they belong (they do). Built-ins are a marked contrast to the so-called permanent installations, many of which look as if they were pasted in place and ready to come loose at any second. CONSUMER GUIDE Magazine strongly recommends that if you have a permanent unit installed, it should be done professionally and put in as inconspicuous a location as possible. Never leave tapes lying about in sight—they are a nearly irresistible temptation to a thief.

Cartridge tape may have been the first format to be adapted for mobile use, but its preeminence in this area has been challenged by recent cassette models, with some rather high quality units from reputable manufacturers. For instance, Teac has offered the first automotive Dolby playback unit—the AC-10. With the Teac AC-10, sound may actually be getting too good for cars. Remember that the car does not provide the quiet ambiance that the home does (or should).

Two series of decks, both for cassette players, which meet the quality standards that CONSUMER GUIDE Magazine demands are from Sony and Teac. The Sony TC-10 has high quality stereo sound and low flutter, even by home-deck standards. Cassettes are fed into a slot in the unit, and operation is automatic. A deluxe version, the TC-30, incorporates automatic reverse. Teac also manufactures several fine stereo cassette car units. They range from the AC-5 with automatic reverse, through the deluxe AC-9 with tape-direction indicating lamps, to the top-of-the-line AC-10, already mentioned, which features Dolby and FM stereo.

SPECIAL INFORMATION SERVICE
A Bonus for Readers of this CONSUMER GUIDE

CONSUMER GUIDE offers a special bonus to its readers who are interested in obtaining information as to where they can find low prices on specific products listed in this guide. Simply fill out the form and mail. Please include 25 cents for postage and handling.

Please send me information on:

Product _____ Model Number _____

Manufacturer _____

Your Name _____

Address _____

City _____ State _____ Zip Code _____

CONSUMER GUIDE Magazine
3323 West Main, Skokie, Illinois 60076

TAPE RECORDERS

TAPE RECORDERS BEST BUYS

IN JUDGING the following tape equipment as Best Buys, CONSUMER GUIDE Magazine has paid special consideration to price in relation to the following features and performance characteristics: wow and flutter; frequency response in record and playback; signal-to-noise ratio of record and playback electronics; harmonic distortion, relative to signal level applied to the tape; and overall construction and design.

REEL-TO-REEL TAPE RECORDERS

Sony TC-377 is a three-head, four-track, single-motor tape deck. Its electrical properties are outstanding, and in most home-recording applications its sound could not be distinguished from that of the finest three-motor machines selling for up to three times its price. Similarly, the low distortion and noise level of this recorder are excellent. Yet, as with most single-motor machines, the TC-377's transport-control knob requires an appreciable physical effort, and its fast-forward and rewind times are exasperatingly long. The tape transport has a flutter level about as low as we have ever seen on a single motor recorder, and its speed accuracy is certainly good enough for any nonprofessional purpose.

Fair Trade Price: $399.95 **Low Price: $331.95**

Pioneer RT-1020L, at its fastest speed meets the most stringent high fidelity performance standards with respect to frequency response, noise, and distortion. CONSUMER GUIDE Magazine found the playback performance to be excellent with either two-channel or four-channel commercially recorded tapes. This recorder requires a little more familiarization than most because of its unusual switching flexibility, but it is actually quite easy to use. The tape-transport logic system worked well, with the tape stopping from a fast speed in a fraction of a second when the "play" button was pressed. There was a pause of about 5 seconds before it resumed play at normal speed. This seemed interminably long, but compensating for it is the assurance that the recorder will not damage or spill a tape, no matter how carelessly it is

TAPE RECORDERS

handled. One rarely finds either a four-channel playback ability or the capacity to hold 10-1/2 inch reels; it is, therefore, a pleasant surprise to find both features in a moderately priced recorder, whose construction and general quality resemble those of much more expensive units.
Fair Trade Price: $649.95   **Low Price: $519.95**

Sony TC-388-4 *is available for four-channel recording or dubbing. This one has many of the professional features at a relatively low price. It has two-speeds, four-digit tape counter, tape-speed selector, and a locking pause control. Its 34-pound weight makes it quite suitable for field as well as home use. If you have never owned a tape deck before, and if you are interested in four-channel recording, the Sony TC-388-4 might be just the machine you are looking for. Only open-reel units and 8-track decks have that capability, and only open-reel machines offer high fidelity quadraphonic sound.*
Fair Trade Price: $679.95   **Low Price: $564.35**

CASSETTE TAPE RECORDERS

Heath AD-1530, *when considered on its own merits, is one of the better cassette recorders on the market, comparable in performance to units in the $280 to $350 price range. It is not significantly cheaper, however, than many equally good machines that can be bought at a discount (and it must be assembled from a kit, although this is not particularly difficult). In spite of this, there are some unique advantages to the AD-1530. It can be adjusted for optimum performance with any tape the builder chooses to use and also have the assurance that the Dolby circuits are operating as they were meant to. Should any service ever be required, the AD-1530 was designed to be serviced by its builder.*
Factory Mail Order: $259.95   **Low Price: Not Available**

Teac 450 *has operating controls on the front panel, facing the user, while the cassette loads on top of the deck in the usual manner. The tape transport control levers can be operated from above or from the front with dual markings that can be read from either position. We found that the Teac 450 was much less "fussy" to set up than most cassette machines, probably because of its extra recording "headroom." So long as the meters were kept on scale, there was no tendency to overload or distort. The flutter and noise level were both inaudible when recording from records or FM broadcasts. In fact, we were never able to hear any difference between the program source and the recorder's playback in a direct comparison. The bonus feature of being able to decode Dolby FM broadcasts (even when not making a recording) is an important plus for the Teac 450. Its motor runs continuously when the power is applied, however. If it had been possible to shut off the motor (to reduce unnecessary wear) when decoding Dolby FM signals, we would have found ourselves with no criticisms whatever of this machine.*
Fair Trade Price: $449.50   **Low Price: $385.00**

TAPE RECORDERS

Fisher SR-110 *is a straight-forward, no frills model which gives the home music system owner enough of a machine to make and play acceptable recordings at a reasonable price. When used with chromium dioxide tape and with the Dolby switched in, the Fisher SR-110 made recordings that were virtually indistinguishable from the original source, whether stereo FM or stereo records. We encountered no mechanical difficulties during our tests of the Fisher SR-110, and all controls worked smoothly and responsively.*
Fair Trade Price: $249.95 **Low Price: $179.00**

Kenwood KX-710 *is a moderately priced unit with certain internal design techniques that make for a generally commendable performance. For instance, its use of a DC-servo motor and an unusually massive fly-wheel can be credited, in CONSUMER GUIDE Magazine's judgment, with achieving excellent speed accuracy, combined with very low wow and flutter. Mechanical virtues are well balanced with electrical performance in terms of extended, low-distortion response. The ancillary features (automatic level control, memory rewind, etc.) may or may not interest you; but they are present, and they do work as intended.*
Fair Trade Price: $249.95 **Low Price: $212.45**

Tandberg TCD-310 *has no playback control or "rewind memory" feature because Tandberg obviously decided to trade off certain frills in favor of going after high audio performance, while still keeping the price from hitting astronomical levels. The result is that you must adjust playback levels by using the volume control(s) on whatever external amplifier or receiver the TCD-310 is connected to. In CONSUMER GUIDE Magazine's view, these omissions are more than offset by the genuinely superior performance of the TCD-310, which results from a canny combination of excellent transport action and unusually smooth, extended frequency response, with extremely low distortion and noise. In short, the TCD-310 is a superb cassette recorder.*
Fair Trade Price: $499.00 **Low Price: Not Available**

CARTRIDGE TAPE RECORDERS

Lafayette RK-82 *has a response that is reasonably wide and linear, and low enough in distortion and noise, so that when it is played through a high fidelity component system, the sound is pleasant and listenable. CONSUMER GUIDE Magazine estimates that this unit covers an appreciable part of the total audible band with no audible distortion. Mechanically, the RK-82 did exactly what it is supposed to do: It played the tapes at required speed, with no dragging and no wow or flutter. The program-change button worked satisfactorily, even when subjected to several rapid-fire pushes of a kind more intense than you would expect in normal use. In general the RK-82, playing through a powerful and wide-range system, sounded as good as most FM stations do.*
Suggested Retail Price: $49.94 **Low Price: Not Available**

1975 Hi Fi Components and Tape Recorder Prices

ACOUSTIC RESEARCH

SPEAKERS

Model	Description	Retail	Discount
AR-3a	3-Way System Oil. Wal.	$285.00	$213.75
AR-5	3-Way System Oil. Wal.	199.00	149.25
AR-2ax	3-Way System Wal. Gr.	149.00	111.75
AR-8	2-Way System Wal. Gr.	119.00	87.00
AR-6	2-Way System Wal. Gr.	95.00	71.25
AR-4xa	2-Way System Wal. Gr.	79.00	59.25
AR-7	2-Way System Wal. Gr.	69.00	51.75
AR-LST		600.00	—
AR-LST2		400.00	—

TURNTABLES

Model	Description	Retail	Discount
XA	Two Speed	$110.00	$80.00
XAU/Universal	110/220v, 50/60 Cycles	106.95	83.00
XA.91	AR—XA w/Shure M91ED Cart.	165.00	97.00
AR-XB		119.95	89.95

ADC

LOUDSPEAKERS

Model	Description	Retail	Discount
ADC-XT10	2-Way, 3-Driver Bookshelf	$115.00	$88.00
ADC-303AX	2-Way Bookshelf System	100.00	77.00
ADC-XT6	Mini 2-Way Bookshelf	58.00	45.00

HI-FI COMPONENTS & TAPE RECORDERS

Model	Description	Retail	Discount
CS-33D	Stereo Cassette w/Dolby	209.95	157.45
GXC-38D	Deluxe w/Dolby System	269.95	205.00
GXC-46D	Advance Stereo Deck	319.95	243.00
GXC-65D	Auto-Reverse Deck	349.95	266.00
GXC-75D	With Dolby	429.95	322.45
CR-81D	Deluxe 8-Track Stereo	209.95	157.45
GXR-82D	Deluxe 8-Track Record	249.95	187.45

4-CHANNEL CARTRIDGE/REEL-to-REEL DECKS

Model	Description	Retail	Discount
CR-80DSS	8-Track 4/2 Channel	$329.95	$250.00
GX-280DSS	Deluxe 4 Channel Stereo	850.00	646.00
GX-400DSS	4 Channel, Reel-to-Reel	1495.00	1121.25
1730-DSS	4/2 Channel Stereo	419.95	314.95

RECEIVERS

Model	Description	Retail	Discount
AA-910	AM/FM, 36 Watts, RMS	$249.95	$187.45
AA-910DB	AM/FM w/Dolby, 36 Watts	349.95	262.45
AA-930	AM/FM, 75 Watts RMS	399.95	285.00
AS-960	4-Channel AM/FM	499.95	345.00
AS-970	4-Channel AM/FM	599.95	414.00
AS-980	4-Channel AM/FM	850.00	637.50

SPEAKER SYSTEMS

Model	Description	Retail	Discount
SW-175	5-Way 15" System	$295.00	$212.00
SW-161	3-Way 10" System	200.00	144.00
SW-155	4-Way 12" System	175.00	126.00
SW-135	3-Way 10" System	130.00	94.00

HI-FI COMPONENTS & TAPE RECORDERS

ADVENT*

SPEAKERS
Loudspeaker	$125.00
Loudspeaker, Utility Cabinet	110.00
Smaller Loudspeaker	76.00
Advent/2 Loudspeaker	59.50

TAPE DECKS
201	$299.95
202	132.00
202hp	152.00

AKAI*

STEREO REEL-to-REEL DECKS
GX-210D	2 Head Auto-Reverse Deck	$459.95 $344.95
GX-600D		625.00 468.75
GX-600DB	With Dolby	725.00 543.75
4000DB	With Dolby	369.95 277.00
4000DS	3 Head	299.95 224.95
4400		369.95 277.45
4000-DS	3 Head Stereo Tape Deck	299.95 224.95

STEREO REEL-to-REEL TAPE SYSTEMS
1721-W	Economy w/Walnut Cab.	$314.95 $236.20

STEREO CASSETTE/CARTRIDGE DECKS
CS-30D	Stereo Cassette Deck	$169.95 $127.45

	3-Way 10 System	145.00 104.00
SW-125		90.00 65.00
SW-35	Horn-Loaded System	55.00 40.00
SW-30	Horn-Loaded System	125.00 90.00
NDS-70	Omni Directional 6 Spkr.	

COMBINATION REEL-to-REEL/CASSETTE/ CARTRIDGE SYSTEMS/DECKS
GX-1900D	Reel-to-Reel/Cassette	$519.95 $395.00

ALTEC*

STEREO COMPONENTS
724A	AM/FM Tuner-Preamp.	$499.00 $401.00
725A	AM/FM Receiver	599.00 482.50
770A	Electronic Crossover Biamp.	284.00 229.00
42161	Cabinet for 725A, 724A	29.95 24.00
42162	Cabinet for 714A, 710A	29.95 24.00

EQUALIZERS
EQE	Concept EQ Speaker	$150.00 $120.00
729A	Acqusta Voicette Stereo	875.00 704.00

FINISHED SPEAKER SYSTEMS
EQ5	Concept Equalized Sys.	$499.00 $399.20
EQS	Concept EQ Spkr. Sys.	195.00 156.00
2873A	Barcelona Biamp/Spkr. Sys.	850.00 652.00
2878B	Santiago Biamp/Spkr. Sys.	699.00 536.00
819A	Stonehenge I.	329.00 263.20
846B	Valencia System (Walnut)	425.00 340.00
873A	Barcelona Spkr. System	699.00 559.20

*With fair-traded stereo components, low prices are available only when a complete music system is purchased.

HI-FI COMPONENTS & TAPE RECORDERS

		Retail	Discount
874A	Segovia Speaker System	275.00	220.00
878B	Santiago Speaker System	499.00	444.10
879A	Santana Speaker System	249.00	199.20
887A	Capri Speaker System	89.00	71.20
891A	Bookshelf Sys. (Walnut)	149.00	119.20
891V	Bookshelf Sys. (Wood Grain Vinyl)	119.00	95.20

BANG & OLUFSEN*

CARTRIDGES
	Retail	Discount
SP-10	$75.00	—
SP-12	85.00	—
SP-14	45.00	—
MMC6000	85.00	—

REPLACEMENT STYLI
SS-10	$30.00	—
SS-12	40.00	—
SS-14	22.00	—

TURNTABLES
3000	Beogram w/SP-12 Cartridge	$300.00
4002	Beogram w/MMC 6000 Cartridge	650.00

RECEIVERS
3000-2	Beomaster	$475.00
4000	Beomaster	575.00

SPEAKERS
| 1203 | Beovox Pair | $170.00 |

BOZAK*

SPEAKER SYSTEMS WITH CABINETS
		Retail	Discount
B-201	Sonora	$99.50	$147.35
B301A	Tempo No. 2 Vinyl	165.50	124.15
B401/B402	Rhapsody	283.00	57.00
B-407	Monitor C	514.00	51.25
B-4000A	Symphony No. 1—Modern	664.00	45.55
B-4000A	Symphony No. 1—Classic	758.50	43.40
B-4000A	Symphony No. 1—Moorish	780.00	38.30
B-4005	Symphony No. 2—Century	680.00	31.30
B-4005	Symphony No. 2—Moorish	795.00	30.45
B-310B	Concert Grand—Contemporary	1166.00	
B-410	Concert Grand—Classic	1195.50	
B-410	Concert Grand—Moorish	1253.00	
B-1000	The Bard	99.50	

BSR

TURNTABLES
		Retail	Discount
810/X	Total Magnetic Turntable	$219.95	
710/X	Total Magnetic Turntable	179.95	
620A/X	Total Magnetic Turntable	99.95	
610A/X	Total Magnetic Turntable	89.95	
520A/X	Total Magnetic Turntable	79.95	
510A/X	Total Magnetic Turntable	74.85	
310A/XE	Total Magnetic Turntable	64.95	
260A/X	Total Magnetic Turntable	54.95	
6500A/X	Total Ceramic Turntable	44.95	

HI-FI COMPONENTS & TAPE RECORDERS

3702	Beovox, Pair	200.00
4703	Beovox, Pair	250.00
5700	Beovox, Pair	440.00
	Beovox, Pair	600.00
5500A/X	Total Ceramic Turntable	44.95 / 26.95
4800A/X	Total Ceramic Turntable	39.95 / 22.75
2000A/X	Total Ceramic Turntable	29.95 / 19.45

BENJAMIN ELAC/MIRACORD*

AUTOMATIC MANUAL TURNTABLES

625	Automatic Turntables	$129.95 / $92.00
660H	Deluxe w/Hysteresis Motor	179.95 / 126.00
50H	Mark II w/Hysteresis Motor	259.95 / 172.00
760	Deluxe Automatic	199.95 / 139.00
50H	Mark II	259.95 / 181.95
770H	Hysteresis Motor, Variable	279.95 / 196.00

BOSE*

SPEAKERS

501	Standard Speaker	$149.00
901	Standard Speakers, Pair, Direct Reflecting	550.00
901	Series II, Pair	566.00
901	Bose 901* Continental	635.00

AMPLIFIER

1801	W/LED	986.00

DOKORDER*

TAPE DECKS

7100	Tape Deck, 2-Channel	$429.95 / $325.00
7200	Auto. Continuous Rev. Repeat	499.95 / 375.00
7500	4-Track Stereo Deck	599.95 / 450.00
9200	Pushbutton Controls, Bi-Directional Recording	899.95 / 600.00
7140	Tape Deck, 2/4-Channel Stereo	629.95 / 425.00
1140 (H)	4-Channel (10-1/2")	1,199.95 / 899.95
1120V	Reel-to-Reel (10-1/2")	649.95 / 485.00
MK-60	Cassette	329.95 / 250.00

DYNACO

APERIODIC LOUDSPEAKER SYSTEMS

A-10	2-Way, Oiled Walnut, matched pair	$124.00 / $93.00
A10VW	2-Way, Vinyl Walnut, matched pair	115.00 / 86.25
A-25	2-Way, Oiled Walnut	94.00 / 70.50
A-25R	2-Way, Rosewood Finish	104.00 / 78.00
A-25T	2-Way, Teak Finish	104.00 / 78.00
A-25VW	2-Way, Vinyl Walnut	83.95 / 62.95
A-25XL	2-Way, Oiled Walnut	104.00 / 78.00

*With fair-traded stereo components, low prices are available only when a complete music system is purchased.

HI-FI COMPONENTS & TAPE RECORDERS

		Retail	Discount
A-35	2-Way, Oiled Walnut	125.00	93.75
A-50	3-Spkr. System, Oiled Walnut	194.00	145.50

DYNAKITS

		Retail	Discount
AF-6	AM/Stereo FM Multiplex Tuner	$245.00	$183.75
FM-5	Stereo FM Multiplex Tuner	180.00	135.00
SCA-80 Q	4-Dimen. Stereo Dual-40W Control Amp.	190.00	142.50
PAT-4	Stereo Preamplifier	124.00	93.00
PAT-5	Stereo Preamplifier	184.00	138.00
Stereo 80	Stereo Dual-40W. Amplifier	144.00	108.00
Stereo 120	Stereo Dual-60W. Amplifier	184.00	138.00
Stereo 150	Stereo Dual-75W. Amplifier	230.00	172.50
Stereo 400	Stereo Dual-200W. Amplifier	459.00	344.25
QSA 300	Quad/Stereo 4x75 W. Amplifier	409.00	306.75
SCA-35	Stereo Dual-17.5W. Amplifier	134.00	100.50
PAS-3X	Stereo Preamplifier	124.00	93.00
Stereo 70	Stereo Dual-35W. Amplifier	134.00	100.50
Mark III	Mono 60W. Amplifier	129.00	96.75
Mark III-70	Mono 60W. Amplifier	139.00	104.25
Mark III-500	Mono 60W. Amplifier	149.00	111.75

ASSEMBLED DYNACO COMPONENTS

		Retail	Discount
AF-6/A	AM/Stereo FM Multiplex Tuner	$355.00	$266.25
FM-5/A	Stereo FM Multiplex Tuner	284.00	213.00
SCA-80	4-Dimen. Stereo Dual-40W. Amp.	304.00	228.00
Q/A	Stereo Preamplifier	204.00	153.00

		Retail	Discount
999 TE/X	.2 x .7 Elliptical	64.95	24.00

4 CHANNEL CARTRIDGES

		Retail	Discount
4000 D/III	Professional	$149.95	$85.00
4000 D/II	Deluxe	124.95	73.00
400 D/I	Standard	84.95	52.00

SUPER QUALITY SERIES CARTRIDGES

		Retail	Discount
2000 E/III		$69.95	$17.00
2000 E/II		54.95	16.50
2000 E/I		39.95	14.00
2000 E		34.95	11.00
2000		24.95	10.00

ROYAL GRENADIER SPEAKER SYSTEMS

		Retail	Discount
9500MII	3-Way, 6 Driver System w/Walnut Finish, Marble Tops	$349.95	$235.00
9500II	3-Way, 6 Driver System w/Walnut Fin., Walnut Top	319.95	225.00

GRENADIER SPEAKER SYSTEMS

		Retail	Discount
7500M II	3-Way Divergent Lens, Marble Top	$199.95	$140.00
7500 II	3-Way Divergent Lens, Walnut Top	184.95	134.00
6000M II	3-Way Wide Angle Lens, Marble Top	129.95	95.00
6000 II	3-Way Wide Angle Lens, Walnut Top	119.95	89.00

HI-FI COMPONENTS & TAPE RECORDERS

PAT-5/A Stereo	Stereo Preamplifier	294.00	220.50
80/A Stereo	Dual-40W. Amplifier	204.00	153.00
120/A Stereo	Dual-60W. Amplifier	254.00	190.50
150/A Stereo	Dual-75W. Amplifier	330.00	247.50
400/A Stereo	Dual-200W. Amplifier	609.00	456.75
400M/A	Stereo 400 w/mounted illuminated Output Meters	679.00	509.25
QSA-300 M/A	Quad/Stereo 4x75W. Amplifier w/4-Meters	609.00	456.75
Mark III/A	60W. Power Amplifier	174.00	130.50
Mark III-70/A	60W. Power Amplifier	184.00	138.00
Mark III-500/A	60W. Power Amplifier	194.00	145.50

4-DIMENSIONAL DECODERS

QD-1	Kit Quadaptor	$23.65	$17.75
QD-1/A	Assembled Quadaptor	31.45	23.60

EMPIRE*

STEREO CARTRIDGES

1DGO 2E/X	.2 x .7 Elliptical	$99.95	$55.00
999 VE/X	.2 x .7 Elliptical	79.95	45.00

JUPITER SPEAKER SYSTEMS

6500 II	3-Way Wide Angle Lens 12" Woofer (White)	$149.95	$110.00
6500 II	Same as above (Blue, Yellow, Bittersweet)	164.95	121.25

TURNTABLES

598 III	Complete System w/4000 D3 Cartridge, 4-Channel	$399.95	$294.00

FISHER*

STEREO & 4-CHANNEL RECEIVERS

170	AM/FM Stereo	$199.95	$150.00
180	AM/FM Stereo	249.95	187.00
4020	4/2 Channel AM/FM	299.95	225.00
4060	4/2 Channel AM/FM	369.95	277.50
304	2/4 Channel, AM/FM	369.95	278.00
304B	2/4 Channel, AM/FM	399.95	299.95
404	2/4 Channel, AM/FM	499.95	374.95
504	2/4 Channel, AM/FM	599.95	449.95
304X	2/4 Channel, AM/FM, CD-4 Adaptable	449.95	322.30
404X	2/4 Channel, AM/FM, CD-4 Adaptable	549.95	393.80
504X	2/4 Channel, AM/FM, CD-4 Adaptable	649.95	465.30
314	2/Channel, AM/FM w/CD-4 & SQ	549.95	393.80
414	2/4 Channel, AM/FM w/CD-4 & SQ	649.95	465.30
514	2/4 Channel, AM/FM w/CD-4 & SQ	749.95	536.80
122	AM/FM Stereo	199.95	159.95
222	AM/FM Stereo	249.95	199.95

*With fair-traded stereo components, low prices are available only when a complete music system is purchased.

HI-FI COMPONENTS & TAPE RECORDERS

		Retail	Discount
234	2/4 Channel, AM/FM w/SQ	349.95	279.95
334	2/4 Channel, AM/FM w/SQ & CD-4	499.95	399.95
434	2/4 Channel, AM/FM	599.95	479.95
534	w/SQ/Logic & CD-4	699.95	559.95
	2/4 Channel AM/FM		
634	w/SQ/Logic & CD-4	799.95	639.95
	2/4 Channel, AM/FM		
	w/SQ/Logic & CD-4		

SPEAKER SYSTEMS

		Retail	Discount
XP-44-S	2-Way Speaker	$49.95	$41.00
XP-55-S	2-Way Speaker	69.95	52.45
XP-56-S	2-Way Speaker	89.95	63.00
XP-65-S	3-Way Speaker	109.95	77.00
XP-7-S	3-Way Speaker	169.95	119.00
XP-9-C	4-Way 5 Speaker	219.95	165.00
ST-425	2-Way, 2-Speaker System	89.95	67.45
ST-445	3-Way, 3-Speaker System	109.95	82.45
ST-465	3-Way, 3-Speaker System	199.95	149.95
ST-500	3-Way, 4-Speaker System	199.95	139.00
ST-530	3-Way, 6-Speaker System	249.95	175.00
ST-550	3-Way, 7-Speaker System	349.95	245.00

GARRARD

TURNTABLES

		Retail	Discount
Zero 100C	Auto. Transcription Turntable	$209.95	$134.00
Zero 92	Auto. Transcription Turntable	169.95	108.00

		Retail	Discount
100+		399.95	291.95
150+		489.95	357.65
800+		499.95	374.95
900+		749.95	563.00

TAPE DECK

		Retail	Discount
HK 1000	Prof. Cassette Deck w/Dolby	$349.95	$255.00

SPEAKERS

		Retail	Discount
HK 20	2-Way Air Suspension Speaker	$60.00	$44.00
HK 40		99.95	72.95

CARTRIDGE PLAYER DECK

		Retail	Discount
8+	8-Track Stereo/Quad Player	$89.95	$66.00

INFINITY SYSTEMS*

SPEAKERS

		Retail	Discount
POS 2	Each	$98.00	—
1001A	Each	139.00	—
2000AXT	Each	299.00	—
	Column, Each	239.00	—

JANSZEN*

ELECTROSTATIC BOOKSHELF SYSTEMS

	Retail	Discount
Z-210a	$119.95	$88.00

136   CONSUMER GUIDE

HI-FI COMPONENTS & TAPE RECORDERS

Model 82	Auto. Transcription Turntable	119.95	149.95
Model 70	Auto. Transcription Turntable	89.95	179.95
Model 62	Auto. Transcription Turntable	69.95	249.95
40B	Automatic Turntable	49.95	299.95
Model 30	Automatic Turntable	44.95	645.00
SP20B	Manual Turntable	42.95	

Z-210ah	76.00	110.00
Z-410	57.00	135.00
Z-412a	45.00	185.00
Z-412hp	32.00	225.00
Z-824	29.00	486.50
	28.00	

PRE-PACKS

70M	$139.95	$66.00
42M	94.85	44.00
42C	77.90	37.75

HARMAN-KARDON*

CITATION SERIES

11	Solid State Preamp. Center	$395.00	$289.00
12 Wired	120 Watt S.S. Power Amp.	295.00	216.00
12 Deluxe	120 Watt S.S. Power Amp.	340.00	249.00
14	Solid State FM/Stereo Tuner	525.00	385.00
15	Solid State FM/Stereo Tuner	395.00	289.00

RECEIVERS

330B	AM/Stereo FM	$199.95	$146.00
630	AM/Stereo FM	359.95	257.00
930	AM/Stereo FM	479.95	343.00

MULTICHANNEL RECEIVERS

50+		$199.95	$146.00
75+		329.95	240.85

ELECTROSTATIC ARRAYS

130	$199.95	$154.00
132	99.95	74.95
134	149.95	110.00
134a	179.95	135.00
134hp	199.95	149.95
138	299.99	225.00

JBL*

SPEAKERS & ACCESSORIES

Paragon		$3000.00	$2400.00
Olympus	Encl. w/S7R Loudspeaker Sys.	837.00	669.60
Olympus	Encl. w/S8R Loudspeaker Sys.	1080.00	864.00
Delphi	Equipment Cabinet	525.00	420.00
Sov. I	Encl. w/S7R Loudspeaker Sys.	837.00	669.60
Sov. III	Encl. w/S8R Loudspeaker Sys.	1080.00	864.00
L45	Equip. Cabinet	525.00	420.00
55	Flair	471.00	376.80
L65	Lancer	276.00	221.00
L200	Jubal	396.00	316.00
	Studio Master	657.00	525.60
L100	Century	297.00	237.60

*With fair-traded stereo components, low prices are available only when a complete music system is purchased.

HI-FI COMPONENTS & TAPE RECORDERS

		Retail	Discount
Aqu. 4	Oiled Walnut or Satin White	210.00	168.00

JENSEN*

SPEAKERS IN FURNITURE CABINETS

		Retail	Discount
1	2-Element 8" Full Range	$42.00	$35.70
2	2-Way 2-Speaker 8"	69.00	58.65
3	2-Way 2-Speaker 10"	99.00	84.15
4	3-Way 3-Speaker 10"	129.00	109.65
5	3-Way 4-Speaker 12"	189.00	160.65
6	4-Way 4-Speaker 15"	249.00	211.65
15	4-Way 5-Speaker 15"	426.00	362.10

UNITARY LOUDSPEAKERS

		Retail	Discount
7	8" Dual Cone	$24.00	$23.40
8	8" 2-Way Coaxial	42.00	39.05
9	12" Dual Cone	36.00	34.20
10	12" 2-Way 3-Element Coaxial	51.00	43.35
11	12" 2-Way Multicell Horn Coaxial	81.00	65.60
12	12" 3-Way Triaxial	117.00	93.60
13	G-600 15" 3-Way Triaxial	231.00	170.95
14	G-610B 15" 3-Way Triaxial	438.00	321.95

JVC*

LABORATORY SERIES RECEIVERS

		Retail	Discount
VR-5660	Digital Readout FM Stereo	$599.95	$431.95

AUDIO SERIES RECEIVERS

		Retail	Discount
4VR-5456	FM/AM 4-Channel Stereo	$799.95	$552.00
4VR-5446	FM/AM 4-Channel Stereo	679.95	469.20
4VR-5436	FM/AM 4-Channel Stereo	569.95	393.30
VR-5426	FM/AM 4-Channel Stereo	399.95	288.00
4VR-5406	FM/AM 4-Channel Stereo	299.95	185.95
4VR-5404	FM/AM 4-Channel Stereo	229.95	158.75
VR-5535	FM/AM Stereo w/SEA	429.95	296.70
VR-5525	FM/AM Stereo w/SEA	369.95	255.30
VR-5515	FM/AM Stereo Receiver	299.95	207.00
VR-5505	40 Watt FM/AM Stereo	199.95	149.50

AUDIO SERIES REEL-TO-REEL DECKS

		Retail	Discount
4RD-1406	4-Channel Tape Deck	$429.95	$322.00
RD-1696	Stereo Tape Deck	249.95	186.85
RD-1695	Stereo Tape Deck	229.95	158.70

AUDIO SERIES CASSETTE DECKS

		Retail	Discount
CD-1667-2	Stereo Cassette w/ANRS	$299.95	$207.00
CD-1667	Stereo Cassette w/ANRS	249.95	186.85
CD-1656	Stereo Cassette w/ANRS	229.95	171.90
CD-1655	Stereo Cassette Deck	149.95	112.10

AUDIO SERIES 8-TRACK DECKS

		Retail	Discount
4ED-1205	4-Channel, 8-Track Deck	$229.95	$166.00
ED-1245	8-Track Cart. Player w/ANRS	249.95	172.50
ED-1240	8-Track Cart. Player w/Mode Selector	169.95	135.00

HI-FI COMPONENTS & TAPE RECORDERS

KENWOOD*

STEREO RECEIVERS

KR-7400	63 Watts, AM/FM	$519.95	$441.95
KR-6400	45 Watts, AM/FM	449.95	382.45
KR-5400	35 Watts, AM/FM	379.95	322.95
KR-4400	25 Watts, AM/FM	299.95	254.95
KR-3400	22 Watts, AM/FM	259.95	220.95
KR-2400	16 Watts, AM/FM	219.95	186.95
KR-1400	10 Watts, AM/FM	179.95	152.95

4-CHANNEL RECEIVERS

KR-9340	40 Watts, 4-Channel/44 Watts, 2-Channel	$749.95	$637.45
KR-8340	25 Watts, 4-Channel/60 Watts, 2-Channel	569.95	484.45
KR-6340	20 Watts, 4-Channel/50 Watts, 2-Channel	389.95	331.45
KR-5340	12 Watts, 4-Channel/30 Watts, 2-Channel	299.95	254.95
KR-9940	4-Channel/50 Watts per Channel	974.95	828.70
KR-8840	4-Channel/40 Watts per Channel	849.95	722.45

STEREO AMPLIFIERS

KA-8004	60 Watts	$389.95	$332.00
KA-6004	40 Watts	299.95	255.00
KA-4004	18 Watts	189.95	162.00
KA-2002A	13 Watts	119.95	102.00

LABORATORY SERIES, PREAMPLIFIERS/AMPLIFIERS

4VN-990	4-Channel Integrated Amp.	$599.95	$414.00
4VM-770	4-Channel Integrated Amp.	279.95	202.00
VN-900	220W. Stereo Integrated Amp.	399.95	275.95
VN-700	140W.S.S. Integrated Amp.	299.95	248.95

LABORATORY SERIES, STEREO TUNERS

VT-900	FM Digital Stereo Tuner	$399.95	$288.00
VT-700	FM/AM Stereo Tuner	249.95	180.00

LABORATORY SERIES TAPE DECKS, REEL-to-REEL

RD-1555	Auto. Reverse Tape Deck	$499.95	$345.00
RD-1553	3-Motor, 3-Head Stereo Deck	$499.95	360.00
RD-1552	3-Motor, 3-Head Stereo Deck	399.95	288.00

LABORATORY SERIES CASSETTE DECKS

CD-1669	Deluxe Stereo Deck w/ANRS	$499.95	$345.00
CD-1668	Deluxe Stereo Deck w/ANRS	329.95	227.65

LABORATORY SERIES MANUAL PLAYER

VL-8	2-Sp. Servo Motor Turntable	$269.95	$201.80
JLB-44	2-Sp. Direct Drive Turntable	349.95	241.50

LABORATORY SERIES SPEAKER SYSTEMS

VS-5313	8-Spkr. Omni-Directional, Dlx.	$229.95	$158.70
SX-3	Open Baffle, Wide Dir. Dlx.	159.95	115.00

AUDIO SERIES AMPLIFIERS

VN-5101	4-Channel Stereo Add-On	$239.95	$191.95

*With fair-traded stereo components, low prices are available only when a complete music system is purchased.

CONSUMER GUIDE

HI-FI COMPONENTS & TAPE RECORDERS

	Retail	Discount
KA-8006 70 watts	439.95	373.95
KA-6006 48 Watts	359.95	305.95
KA-4006 32 Watts	259.95	220.95
KA-1400G 14 Watts	159.95	135.95

STEREO TUNERS

	Retail	Discount
KT-8005 FM/AM	$389.95	$332.00
KT-6005 FM/AM	289.95	246.00
KT-4005 FM/AM	189.95	162.00
KT-2001A FM/AM	119.95	102.00
KT-8007 FM/AM	419.95	356.95
KT-6007 FM/AM	319.95	271.95
KT-4007 FM/AM	229.95	195.45
KT-1300G FM/AM	139.95	118.95
KT-700T Frequency Synthesizing	749.95	637.45

STEREO CASSETTE DECK

	Retail	Discount
KX-910 W/Dolby Noise Reduction	$299.95	$254.95
KX-710 W/Dolby Noise Reduction	249.95	212.45

4-CHANNEL COMPONENTS

	Retail	Discount
KCD-2 CD-4 Demodulator	$79.95	$68.00

SPEAKER SYSTEMS

	Retail	Discount
KE-3 2-Way/2-Speakers, Pair	$79.95	$68.00
KL-77 3-Way System, Each	129.95	110.45
KL-55 2-Way System, Each	89.95	76.45
KL-44 2-Way System, Each	69.95	59.45

	Retail	Discount
557 W/2 M-17 Speakers	399.85	270.90

For Model 55A Receiver Systems add $20.00 to above prices.

Model 55 4-Piece Systems RC-4 changer, base, cover & cartridge.

	Retail	Discount
5514	$404.90	$273.75
5524	429.95	285.50
5584	454.90	299.35
5574	484.85	320.80

For Model 52A Receiver Systems, add $20.00 to above prices.

Model 52 3-Piece Systems

	Retail	Discount
521 W/1 pair M-31 Speakers	$419.90	$286.90
528 W/1 pair M-38 Speakers	469.90	297.95
527 W/2 M-17 Speakers	499.85	316.45
526 W/2 M-6 Speakers	619.85	387.45

Model 52A Receiver Systems add $18.00 to above prices.

Model 52 4-Piece Systems w/RC-4 changer, base, cover & cartridge.

	Retail	Discount
5214	$504.90	$336.80
5284	554.90	347.85
5274	584.85	366.35
5264	704.85	437.35

For Model 52 Receiver Systems add $18.00 to above prices.

	Retail	Discount
RC-4 Record Changer Module (Complete)	$85.00	$55.35

HEADPHONE

	Retail	Discount
Eighty	$43.95	$33.00

HI-FI COMPONENTS & TAPE RECORDERS

TURNTABLES
KP-5022	Direct Drive Automatic	$299.95	$254.95
KP-3022	Dual Motor Automatic	199.95	169.95

KLH

RECEIVERS
Fifty-Two A	$349.95	$231.00
Fifty-Two	319.95	211.00
Fifty-Five A	259.95	172.00
Fifty-Five	219.95	152.00

SPEAKERS
Five	$225.00	$155.25
Six	149.95	93.75
Six-V	129.95	97.45
Nine	1495.00	1061.45
Seventeen	89.95	53.95
Seventeen X	89.95	67.45
Twenty-Three	119.95	80.00
Thirty-Two Pair	125.00	83.75
Thirty-Three	110.00	78.00
Thirty-Eight Pair	149.95	92.95

RECEIVER/SPEAKER SYSTEMS
Model 55 3-Piece Systems
551	W/1 pair M-31 Speakers	$319.90	$223.95
552	W/1 pair M-32 Speakers	344.95	235.55
558	W/1 pair M-38 Speakers	369.95	249.95

With fair-traded stereo components, low prices are available only when a complete music system is purchased.

KOSS

ELECTROSTATIC STEREOPHONES
ESP 6A	Electrostatic Stereophones	$130.00	$87.00
ESP-9	Electrostatic Stereophones	175.00	117.00

HIGH VELOCITY STEREOPHONE
HV-1	High Velocity Microweight	$44.95	$30.55
HU-1LC		54.95	38.45
HV-1A	High Velocity Decilite	49.95	34.95

DYNAMIC STEREOPHONES
SP-3XC	Stereophones	$15.95	$10.00
K-6	Stereophones	19.95	13.00
K-6LC	Stereophones/Volume Control	29.95	20.00
KO-727B	Wide Range Stereophones	34.95	24.00
PRO-4AA	Professional Wide Range	65.00	43.55
PRO-600AA	600 OHM Professional	70.00	47.60
Phase/2	Panoramic Source Controls	75.00	51.00

QUADRAFONES
K-6LC/Q	Quadrafones	$49.95	$33.45
PRO-5/Q	Quadrafones	75.00	50.00
K2+2	Quadrafones	92.00	60.30

PROFESSIONAL VOLUME CONTROL STEREOPHONE
Pro/5LC	$70.00	$47.00

CONSUMER GUIDE

HI-FI COMPONENTS & TAPE RECORDERS

MARANTZ*

RECEIVERS

Model	Description	Retail	Discount
2325	AM/FM Stereo, 125 Watts per Channel, Dolby	$799.95	$639.95
2275	AM/FM Stereo 75 Watts per Channel	649.95	519.95
2240	AM/FM Stereo 40 Watts per Channel	499.95	399.95
220B	AM/FM Stereo, 20 Watts per Channel	349.95	279.95
2015	AM/FM Stereo, 15 Watts per Channel	249.95	199.95

AM/FM QUADRADIAL RECEIVERS

Model	Description	Retail	Discount
4430	AM/FM Quad. 120 Watts	$599.95	$480.00
4415	AM/FM Quad. 60 Watts	399.95	320.00

AM/FM STEREO 2+ QUADRADIAL 4 RECEIVERS

Model	Description	Retail	Discount
4300	AM/FM Stereo 2+, 200 Watts	$899.95	$720.00
4270	AM/FM Stereo 2+, 140 Watts	699.95	560.00
4240	AM/FM Stereo 2+, 80 Watts	579.95	464.00
4230	AM/FM Stereo 2+, 60 Watts	479.95	384.00
4220	AM/FM Stereo 2+, 40 Watts	299.95	240.00
4400	AM/FM Stereo 2+, 250 Watts	1250.00	1000.00

PREAMPLIFIERS

Model	Description	Retail	Discount
3300	Stereo Control Console	$449.95	$359.95
3800	Pre-Amp w/Dolby	$649.95	$519.95
3600	Pre-Amp w/Dolby	499.95	399.95

BASIC AMPLIFIERS

Model	Description	Retail	Discount
500	Stereo Power, 500 Watts	$1200.00	$960.00

Model	Description	Retail	Discount
Imperial 5	2-Way System	79.99	64.00
Imperial 5G	2-Way System	99.00	79.00
Imperial 6	2-Way System	119.00	95.00
Imperial 6G	2-Way System	139.00	111.00
Imperial 7	3-Way System	199.95	159.95
Imperial 8	3-Way Floor System	319.95	255.95
Imperial 9	3-Way, Floor System	499.95	399.95

PANASONIC*

PORTABLE TAPE RECORDERS

Model	Description	Retail	Discount
RQ-711S	Cassette Tape Recorder	$32.88	$26.95
RQ-309	Cassette Tape Recorder	39.95	32.75
RP-9309	Case for RQ-309	5.95	4.00
RQ-410S	Cassette Recorder	54.95	45.05
RQ-413S	Cassette Tape Recorder	69.95	54.95
RP-092	Rechargeable Battery for RQ-413S	16.95	13.00
RQ-212DS	Cassette Tape Recorder	79.95	65.55
RP-9212	Rechargeable Battery for RQ-212S	11.95	9.00
RQ-228S	Cassette Tape Recorder	129.95	106.55
RQ-320S	Cassette Tape Recorder	129.95	106.55
RQ-430S	Cassette w/Radio	59.95	45.00
RQ-432S	Cassette w/Radio	69.95	57.35
RQ-444S	Cassette w/Radio	119.95	98.35
RQ446S	Cassette w/Radio	99.95	81.95
RQ-438S	Cassette w/Radio	139.95	114.75

HI-FI COMPONENTS & TAPE RECORDERS

250	Stereo Power, 250 Watts	499.95	399.95
240	Stereo Power, 250 Watts	429.95	343.95
400M	Stereo Power, 400 Watts	699.95	559.95
400	Stereo Power, 400 Watts	599.95	479.95

CONSOLE AMPLIFIERS

1200B	Stereo Console, 200 Watts	$699.95	$559.95
4140	Stereo 2+ Quad. 140 Watts	549.95	440.00
4100	Quad. 4 Console, 100 Watts	399.95	320.00
1120	Stereo Console, 120 Watts	449.95	359.95
4070	Stereo 2+ Quad. 4, 70 Watts	299.95	240.00
4060	Quad. 4 Console, 60 Watts	229.95	184.00
1060	Stereo Console, 60 Watts	229.95	184.00
1030	Stereo Console, 30 Watts	169.95	136.00
1070	Stereo Console, 70 Watts	269.95	215.95
1040	Stereo Console, 40 Watts	199.95	159.95

TUNERS

120B	AM/FM Stereo Tuner	$549.95	$440.00
115B	AM/FM Stereo Tuner	299.95	239.95
105B	AM/FM Stereo Tuner	169.95	135.95
150	AM/FM Stereo Tuner	599.95	480.00
125	AM/FM Stereo Tuner	329.95	263.95

PRE-AMPLIFIER/AMPLIFIER ADAPTORS

4000	Quad. Pre-Amplifier	$249.95	$200.00

SPEAKER SYSTEMS

Imperial			
4G	2-Way System	$59.95	$47.00

RQ-448S	Cassette w/AM-FM Radio	149.95	122.95
RP-091	Rechargeable Battery for RQ-448S	29.95	24.95
RS-451S	Cassette w/FM/AM/FM Stereo	199.95	163.95
RF-7100	8-Track w/Radio	129.95	106.55

TAPE DECKS

RS-26IUS	Stereo Cassette Deck	$88.88	$72.88
RS-260US	Stereo Cassette Deck	99.95	81.95
RS-296US	Stereo Cassette Deck	499.95	409.95
RS-801US	Stereo 8-Track Deck	49.95	40.95
RS-844US	Stereo 8-Track Deck	99.95	81.95
RS-8Q5US	Stereo 8-Track Deck	99.95	81.95
RS-855US	Stereo 8-Track Deck	179.95	147.55

STEREO HOME ENTERTAINMENT SYSTEMS

RE-8134	FM/AM/FM Stereo w/8-Track	$159.95	$131.15
RS-828S	FM/AM/FM Stereo w/8-Track	299.95	245.95
SE-817S	FM/AM/FM Stereo w/8-Track	179.95	147.55
SE-1040D	FM/AM/FM w/Phono & Cass	229.95	188.55
SE-2150D	FM/AM/FM w/Phono & Cass	329.95	270.55

4-CHANNEL HOME ENTERTAINMENT SYSTEMS

RE-7880	FM/AM/FM Stereo Radio	$259.95	$213.15
RS-862	FM/AM/FM Stereo w/8-Trk	399.95	327.95
SE-5050	FM/AM/FM Radio w/Phono	329.95	270.55
SE-5070	FM/AM/FM Radio w/Phono	439.95	360.75
SE-5070D	FM/AM/FM Radio w/Phono	459.95	377.15
RE-8585	FM/AM/FM w/Phono & 8-Trk	429.95	352.55
SE-4440	FM/AM/FM w/Phono & 8-Trk.	349.95	286.95

*With fair-traded stereo components, low prices are available only when a complete music system is purchased.

HI-FI COMPONENTS & TAPE RECORDERS

PANASONIC/TECHNICS*

STEREO COMPONENT RECEIVERS

Model	Description	Retail	Discount
SA-5200A	26 Watt FM/AM	$219.95	$186.95
SA-5400X	68 Watt FM/AM	319.95	271.95
SA-6000X	140 Watt FM/AM	399.95	339.95
SA-8000X	160 Watt FM/AM	549.95	467.45
SA-6700X	240 Watt FM/AM	669.95	569.45
SA-7300X	40 Watt FM/AM	529.95	450.45
SA-8500X	136 Watt FM/AM	739.95	628.95

4-CHANNEL ACOUSTIC FIELD DIMENSION SCOPE

Model	Description	Retail	Discount
SH-3433	4-Channel Audio Scope	$259.95	$220.95

ULTRA HI-FIDELITY TURNTABLES

Model	Description	Retail	Discount
SL110A		$299.95	$254.95
SL-1100A	Direct Drive Turntable	359.95	309.00
SP-10	2-Speed Turntable	419.95	356.95

STEREO TAPE DECK

Model	Description	Retail	Discount
RS-1030US	10" Reel, Prof. Stereo	$999.95	$849.95

STEREO CASSETTE DECKS

Model	Description	Retail	Discount
RS-263US	Dolby Noise Reduction Unit	$199.95	$169.95
RS-610US	Dolby Noise Reduction Unit	249.95	212.45
RS-676US	Dolby Noise Reduction Unit	459.95	390.95
RP-9275	Opt. Remote control for RS-276US & RS-279US	34.95	29.70

PICKERING

Model	Description	Retail	Discount
GA-212	Record Player w/Electronic Brain	$199.50	$165.60
GA-407	Record Player	119.00	99.00

CARTRIDGES

Model	Retail	Discount
XV-15/1200E	$79.95	$39.00
XV-15/750E	65.00	33.00
XV-15/400E	54.95	23.00
XV-15/200E	49.95	21.00

MICRO IV MICRO-MAGNETIC SERIES

Model	Retail	Discount
V-15 Micro IV AME	$49.95	$20.00
V-15 Micro IV ATE	39.95	17.00
V-15 Micro IV ACE	29.95	15.00
V-15 Micro IV AM	34.95	15.00
V-15 Micro IV AT	29.95	14.00
V-15 Micro IV AC	24.95	13.00

PIONEER*

STEREO RECEIVERS

Model	Description	Retail	Discount
SX-1010	100W x 2	$699.95	$559.95

HI-FI COMPONENTS & TAPE RECORDERS

RS-279US	3-Head Sys. w/Dolby Noise Reduction Unit	499.95	424.95

STEREO 8-TRACK DECK

RS-858US	8-Track Quadrasonic	$299.95	$259.00

HIGH FIDELITY HEADPHONE

EAH-80A	"Electret" Electrostatic	$79.95	$67.95

HIGH-FIDELITY SPEAKERS

T-200	2-Way System	$99.95	$84.95
T-300	3-Way System	179.95	152.95
T-400	4-Way System	279.95	237.95
T-500	4-Way System	429.95	365.45

PHASE LINEAR*

MODEL			
700B		$799.00	$570.00
400		499.00	370.00
Cabinet		37.00	30.00
Preamp.	Model 4000	599.00	475.00

SX-939	70W x 2	599.95	479.95
SX-838	50W x 2	499.95	399.95
SX-737	35W x 2	399.95	320.00
SX-636	25W x 2	349.95	279.95
SX-535	20W x 2	299.95	240.00
SX-434	15W x 2	239.95	191.95
Sound Project	300 7W x 2	189.95	151.95

STEREO AMPLIFIERS

SA-9100	60W x 2	$449.95	$359.95
SA-8100	40W x 2	349.95	279.95
SA-7100	20W x 2	249.95	200.00
SA-5200	10W x 2	139.95	112.00
SR-202W	Stereo Reverb. Amp.	139.95	112.00
SD-1100	Quad/Stereo Display	599.95	480.00

STEREO TUNERS

TX-9100	AM/FM	$349.95	$279.00
TX-8100	AM/FM	249.95	200.00
TX-7100	AM/FM	199.95	159.95
TX-6200	AM/FM	139.95	112.00

4-CHANNEL COMPONENTS

QX-949	40W x 4 Receiver	$749.95	$599.95
QX-747	20W x 4 Receiver	649.95	519.95
QX-646	10W x 4 Receiver	499.95	399.95
QA-800A	20W x 4 Amplifier	399.95	320.00
QM-800A	30W x 4 Power Amplifier	349.95	279.95
QC-800A	4-Channel Pre-Amp	279.95	223.95
PC-Q1	CD-4 Cartridge	69.95	55.95

PHILIPS*

TURNTABLES & ARM

GA-209S		$349.50	$290.10

*With fair-traded stereo components, lcw prices are available only when a complete music system is purchased.

HI-FI COMPONENTS & TAPE RECORDERS

SPEAKER SYSTEMS

Model	Description	Retail	Discount
R-700	12" 3-Way	$249.95	$199.95
R-500B	10" 3-Way	169.95	135.95
R-300	10" 2-Way	119.95	96.00
CS-63DX	15" 4-Way	279.95	223.95
CS-99A	15" 5-Way	239.95	191.95
CS-A700	12" 3-Way	199.95	159.95
CS-A600	10" 3-Way	149.95	120.00
CS-66G	10" 3-Way	119.95	96.00
CS-44G	8" 2-Way	79.95	63.95
Project 100	10" 2-Way	129.95	103.95
Project 80	10" 2-Way	99.95	80.00
Project 60	8" 2-Way	79.95	63.95

TURNTABLES

Model	Description	Retail	Discount
PL-71	2-Speed, Direct Drive	$299.95	$240.00
PL-51	2-Speed, Direct-Drive	249.95	200.00
PL-A45D	2-Speed Automatic	169.95	135.95
PL-12D	2-Speed Hysteresis Synch	119.95	95.95
PL-10	2-Speed Hysteresis Synch	99.95	80.00

TAPE DECKS

Model	Description	Retail	Discount
RT-1050	3-Motor, 3-Head	$699.95	$559.95
RT-1020/H	3-Motor, 3-Head	649.95	519.95
RT-1020/L	3-Motor, 3-Head	649.95	519.95
RT-1011/L	3-Motor, 3-Head	599.95	479.95
1322	2-Track, Metal Case w/Amps	1066.00	938.10
1324	4-Track, Metal Case w/Amps	1066.00	938.10
1222	2-Track, w/Speakers & Amps	1140.00	1003.20
1224	4-Track, w/Speakers & Amps	1140.00	1003.20

A77/DOLBY B

Model	Description	Retail	Discount
1132DB	2-Track, Walnut Deck	$1172.00	$1031.35
1134GB	4-Track, Walnut Deck	1172.00	1031.35
1332DB	2-Track, Metal Case, Deck Only	1172.00	1031.35
1334DB	4-Track, Metal Case, Deck Only	1172.00	1031.35

A77 HIGH SPEED

Model	Description	Retail	Discount
1102HS	2-Track, Walnut Deck	$1069.00	$940.70
1104HS	4-Track, Walnut Deck	1069.00	940.70
1122HS	2-Track, Walnut w/Amp.s	1069.00	940.70
1124HS	4-Track, Walnut w/Amp.s	1069.00	940.70
1222HS	2-Track, w/Amps. & Speakers	1144.00	1006.70
1224HS	4-Track, w/Amps & Speakers	1144.00	1006.70
1202HS	2-Track, Speakers w/o Amps.	1176.00	1034.90
1204HS	4-Track, Speakers w/o Amps.	1176.00	1034.90
1302HS	2-Track, Metal Case, Deck Only	1176.00	1034.90
1304HS	4-Track, Metal Case, Deck Only	1176.00	1034.90
1322HS	2-Track, Metal w/Amps.	1250.00	1100.00
1324HS	4-Track, Metal w/Amps.	1250.00	1100.00

AMPLIFIER & TUNER

Model	Description	Retail	Discount
A76	Tuner	$690.00	$607.20
A78	Amplifier	530.00	466.40

(Stainless Steel Plate available on Standard Speed and Dolby B at a slightly higher price.)

CONSUMER GUIDE

HI-FI COMPONENTS & TAPE RECORDERS

CT-F7171	Dolby Cassette Deck	369.95	295.95
CT-5151	Dolby Cassette Deck	269.95	215.95
CT-4141A	Dolby Cassette Deck	239.95	191.95
CT-3131A	Dual Bias Cassette Deck	179.95	143.95

RECTILINEAR

SPEAKERS

XIa	$99.00	$79.20
Mini-III	109.00	81.75
IIIA	279.00	223.20
XII	159.00	127.20
5	299.00	239.20
7	399.00	319.20

REVOX*

TAPE DECKS

A77 STANDARD SPEED

1102	2-Track, Walnut Deck	$959.00	$843.90
1104	4-Track, Walnut Deck	959.00	843.90
1302	2-Track, Metal Case, Deck Only	959.00	843.90
1304	4-Track, Metal Case, Deck Only	959.00	843.90
1202	2-Track, Speakers w/o Amps	1034.00	909.90
1204	4-Track, Speakers w/o Amps	1034.00	909.90
1122	2-Track, Walnut w/Amps	1066.00	938.10
1124	4-Track, Walnut w/Amps	1066.00	938.10

*With fair-traded stereo components, low prices are available only when a complete music system is purchased.

SANSUI*

SPEAKER SYSTEM

SP-3500	4-Way 6-Spkr. Multi-Direct.	$269.95	$229.50
SP-2500	3-Way, 5-Spkr. Multi-Direct.	229.95	195.45
SP-1700	3-Way 5-Spkr. Multi-Direct.	199.95	169.50
SP-1200	3-Way 5-Spkr. Multi-Direct.	179.95	152.95

OMNI-DIMENSIONAL SPEAKERS

SF-2	2-Way Omni-Radial	$199.95	$166.00
SF-1	2-Way Omni-Radial	159.95	134.95

STEREO RECEIVERS

771	40W x 2 (RMS 8 Ohms)	379.95	319.95
661	30W x 2 (RMS 8 Ohms)	329.95	279.95
210	10W x 2 (RMS 8 Ohms)	179.95	140.35
441	11W x 2 (RMS 8 Ohms)	219.95	171.55
551	16W x 2 (RMS 8 Ohms)	259.75	202.75
881	60W x 2 (RMS 8 Ohms)	499.95	424.95

STEREO AMPLIFIERS & TUNERS

AU-9500	80W x 2 (RMS 8 Ohms)	$549.95	$465.00
AU-7500	40W x 2 (RMS 8 Ohms)	399.95	319.95
AU-505	25W x 2 (RMS 8 Ohms)	189.95	159.95
AU-101	15W x 2 (RMS 8 Ohms)	129.95	109.95
TU-9500	AM/FM Stereo Tuner	349.95	295.00
TU-505	AM/FM Stereo Tuner	179.95	152.95
AU-6600	42W x 2 (RMS 8 Ohms)	349.95	297.45
AU-5500	32W x 2 (RMS 8 Ohms)	299.95	254.95

HI-FI COMPONENTS & TAPE RECORDERS

		Retail	Discount
TU-7700	AM/FM Tuner	329.95	280.45
TU-5500	AM/FM Tuner	279.95	237.95

CASSETTE DECKS

		Retail	Discount
SC-737	Stereo Cassette Deck, Dolbyized	$299.95	$249.00
SC-700	Stereo Cassette Deck, Dolbyized	199.95	169.95

STEREO HEADPHONE

		Retail	Discount
SS-2		$16.95	$14.00

4-CHANNEL RECEIVER, AMPLIFIER, TAPE DECK

		Retail	Discount
QRX-3500	180W (IHF)	549.95	467.45
QRX-3000	100W (IHF)	429.95	365.45
QR-1500	100W (IHF)	249.95	212.45
QA-7000	108W (IHF)	499.95	424.95
QD-5500	4-Ch/2-Ch Tape Deck	799.95	679.95
QRX-7001		$879.95	$637.95
QRX-6001		759.95	550.95

4-CHANNEL MUSIC SYSTEM

		Retail	Discount
MQ-2000	74W 4-Ch. Receiver, Auto. Changer	$270.00	—
QC04	CD-4 Demodulator	129.95	94.20

TURNTABLES

		Retail	Discount
SR-212	2-Sp. Automatic	$159.95	$135.95
SR-717	Direct Drive 2-Sp.	319.95	271.95
SR-313	Belt Driven 2-Sp.	199.95	119.95

ACCESSORIES

		Retail	Discount
MQC-2	Dust Cover for MQ-2000	$10.00	$8.00

SPEAKERS

		Retail	Discount
S-42	Deluxe Two-Way, 8" Woofer	$79.95	$45.20
S-10B	Deluxe Two-Way, 10" Woofer	99.95	55.95
S-15	Three-Way, 10" Woofer	134.95	62.05
S-52	Deluxe Two-Way, 10" Woofer	114.95	64.35
S-11D	Deluxe Three-Way, 10" Woofer	149.95	68.95
S-61	Deluxe Three-Way, 10" Woofer	169.95	95.15
S-71	Deluxe Four-Way, 12" Woofer	199.95	111.95

SHERWOOD

RECEIVERS

		Retail	Discount
S-7900A	Stereo Dynaquad FM/AM	479.95	333.00
S-8900A	Stereo Dynaquad FM	449.95	310.00
S-7200	Stereo FM/AM	359.95	265.00
S-7100A	Stereo FM/AM	235.95	180.00
S-7050	Stereo FM/AM	179.95	140.00
S-7244	2/4 Channel, Sterequad FM/AM	495.95	345.00
S-7310	Stereo FM/AM	369.95	260.45
S-7210	Stereo FM/AM	229.95	211.15
S-7110	Stereo FM/AM	229.95	169.00
S-7010	Stereo FM/AM	179.95	140.00

TUNERS

		Retail	Discount
SEL-300	Deluxe FM Digital Readout	$499.00	$344.00
S-2400	AM/FM Stereo	229.95	169.00

AMPLIFIERS

		Retail	Discount
S-9400	Stereo Dynaquad	$259.95	$191.00

HI-FI COMPONENTS & TAPE RECORDERS

SDC-5	Dust Cover for QD-5500	23.00	19.00	
QBL-100	4-Ch. Bal/Vol. Control for QRX-3500 & QRX-5500	35.00	29.00	
SEL-400	Stereo/Dynaquad	399.95	276.00	

SCOTT

STEREO RECEIVERS
R-33S	AM/FM, 18W/Ch., RMS	$249.95	$168.00
R-36S	AM/FM, 30W/Ch., RMS	299.95	201.60
R-74S	AM/FM, 40W/Ch., RMS	399.95	268.80
R-75S	AM/FM, 50W/Ch., RMS	499.95	336.00
R-77S	AM/FM, 70W/Ch., RMS	599.95	403.20

TUNERS
431	AM/FM Stereo	$219.95	$147.85
433	FM Digital Frequency Synthesizer	549.95	369.60

AMPLIFIERS
235S	Integrated Stereo Amp., 15W/Ch., RMS	$159.95	$107.50
255S	Integrated Stereo Amp., 30W/Ch., RMS	229.95	154.55
490	Integrated Stereo Amp., 70W/Ch., RMS	299.95	201.60

COMPACT UNITS
2506-42	Deluxe AM/FM Phono w/Speakers	$466.95	$315.20
2506-10	Deluxe AM/FM Phono w/Speakers	499.95	337.45
2506-15	Deluxe AM/FM Phono w/Speakers	524.95	388.45

SHURE

CARTRIDGES WITH ELLIPTICAL STYLI
M93E		$39.95	$16.00
M93E-EP		39.95	16.00
M91E		49.95	19.00
M91E-EP		49.95	19.00
M91ED		54.95	21.00
M91ED-EP		54.95	21.00
M75ECS		34.95	14.00
M75ECS-EP		34.95	14.00
M75ECS-M8		34.95	13.00
M75ED			
Type 2		54.95	21.00
M75ED			
T2-EP		54.95	21.00
M75EJ			
Type 2		44.95	18.00
M75EJ			
T2-EP		44.95	18.00
M55E		29.95	14.00
M55E-EP		29.95	14.00
M55E-MB		29.95	14.00
M44E		24.95	13.00
M44E-EP		24.95	13.00
M44E-MB		24.95	13.00

*With fair-traded stereo components, low prices are available only when a complete music system is purchased.

HI-FI COMPONENTS & TAPE RECORDERS

	Retail	Discount
CARTRIDGES WITH SPHERICAL STYLI		
M91GD	$44.95	$18.00
M91GD-EP	44.95	18.00
M75B-T2	33.45	16.00
M75B-T2-EP	33.45	15.00
M75B-T2-		
MB	33.45	15.00
M75G		
Type 2	38.45	17.00
M75G T2-EP	38.45	17.00
M75CS	24.50	12.00
M75CS-EP	24.50	12.00
M75-6S	27.50	13.00
M75-6S-EP	27.50	13.00
M44-7	19.95	12.00
M44-7EP	19.95	12.00
M44-7MB	19.95	12.00
M44C	17.95	11.00
M44C-EP	17.95	11.00
M44G	19.95	12.00
M44G-EP	19.95	12.00
M7/N21D	17.95	11.00
M7/N21D		
EP	17.95	11.00
M3D	15.75	11.00
M3D-M	15.75	10.00
M3D-BP	15.75	10.00
M3D-MB	15.75	10.00

	Retail	Discount
V15 III TYPE CARTRIDGES & REPLACEMENT STYLI		
V15 Type III	$72.50	$50.00
V15 III-G	67.50	47.00
VN35E	29.00	24.00
VN78E	28.00	23.00
VN3G	27.00	22.00
V15 III-DL	73.00	51.00
V15 III-GZ	73.00	51.00
V15 III-GSL	73.00	51.00
TONE ARMS		
M232	$32.75	$28.00
M236	35.00	26.00
3009		
Improved	135.00	86.00
3009 S2		
Improved	147.00	94.00
3012	128.00	82.00

SONY*

	Retail	Discount
HIGH FIDELITY COMPONENTS		
ST-5555 FM Stereo/FM Tuner	$1699.50	$1212.10
ST-5130 FM Stereo/FM-AM Tuner	369.50	267.95
ST-5150 FM Stereo/FM-AM Tuner	269.50	198.95
ST-5055 FM Stereo/FM-AM Tuner	199.50	155.60
ST-5066 FM Stereo/FM-AM Tuner	159.50	124.40

HI-FI COMPONENTS & TAPE RECORDERS

PRE-MOUNTED CARTRIDGES

M93E-	$39.95
D12-MB	$16.00
M93E-	16.00
GSL-MB	39.95
M91E-D12	51.25
M91E-	20.00
D12-MB	49.95
M91ED-DL	56.25
M91ED-	21.00
DL-MB	54.95
M91E-GSL	51.25
M91E-	20.00
GSL-MB	49.95
M91ED-GS	56.25
M91ED-	21.00
GS-MB	54.95
M91ED-GZ	56.25
M91ED-	20.00
GZ-MB	54.95
M91E-50H	51.25
M91E-	20.00
50H-MB	49.95
M91ED-BJ	56.25
M91ED-	21.00
BJ-MB	54.95
M44E-GSL	26.25
M44E-	13.00
GSL-MB	24.95
	12.00

Model	Description	Price 1	Price 2
STR-7065	FM Stereo/FM-AM Receiver	549.50	428.60
STR-7055	FM Stereo/FM-AM Receiver	449.50	350.60
STR-7045	FM Stereo/FM-AM Receiver	369.50	288.20
STR-6046A	FM Stereo/FM-AM Receiver	279.50	205.85
HQR-600	AM/FM Receiver	229.50	169.05
SQR-6650	4-Channel Receiver	219.50	164.45
SQA-2030	96W, 4-Channel FM/FM/AM Rec.	329.50	243.00
TA-1130	4-Channel Receiver	249.50	194.60
TA-1150	230 Watt S.S. Integrated Amp.	429.50	307.05
TA-1055	150 Watt S.S. Integrated Amp.	269.50	198.95
TA-1066	90 Watt S.S. Integrated Amp.	199.50	155.60
STC-7000	15W per Channel, Integrated Amp.	159.50	124.40
	FM Stereo FM/AM Tuner Control		
TA-2000F	Preamplifier	589.50	420.00
TA-3200F	S.S. Stereo Control Preamp.	579.50	413.00
TA-3140F	500 Watt S.S. Power Amp.	369.50	263.00
SQD-2020	35W per Channel Power Amp.	199.50	147.20
	Full Logic Stereo/Quad.		
SQD-2070	Decoder/Preamp.	229.50	163.00
PS-5520	Front/Back SQ Logic Decoder	99.50	77.60
PS-2251/LA	Stereo Turntable, Playback	169.50	132.20
2251	Direct Drive Turntable.	349.50	272.60
	Turntable w/Arm.	429.50	335.00

SPEAKER SYSTEMS

Model	Description	Price 1	Price 2
SSU-1000	2-Way, Acoustic Suspension Sys., Pair	$99.50	$69.00
SSU-1200	2-Way, Acoustic Suspension Sys.	79.50	55.20
SSU-1400	3-Way, Acoustic Suspension Sys.	109.50	75.90
SSU-1600	3-Way, Acoustic Suspension Sys.	149.50	103.50

*With fair-traded stereo components, low prices are available only when a complete music system is purchased.

CONSUMER GUIDE 151

HI-FI COMPONENTS & TAPE RECORDERS

		Retail	Discount
SSU-1800	3-Way, 4-Driver, Acoustic Suspension System	199.50	138.00

SONY/SUPERSCOPE*

MONAURAL CASSETTE-CORDERS

		Retail	Discount
TC-42	Mini, Battery-Operated	$129.95	$107.85
TC-45	Mini, Battery-Operated	139.95	116.15
TC-55	Sub-Min. Battery-Operated	169.95	141.00
TC-66	Economy Portable	74.95	62.20
TC-90A	Portable Cassette-Corder	109.95	91.25
TC-92	Portable Cassette-Corder	149.95	124.45
TC-95A	Executive Cassette-Corder	129.95	107.85
TC-110A	Portable Cassette-Corder	139.95	116.15
TC-140	Deluxe Portable Recorder	149.95	124.00
TC-142	3 Head Port. Cassette-Corder	199.95	165.95
TC-180AV	Monophonic Cassette-Corder	179.95	149.00
TC-182AV	Monophonic Cassette-Corder	299.95	248.95

STEREO CASSETTE/CARTRIDGE RECORDERS

		Retail	Discount
TC-121A	Economy Stereo Deck	$129.95	$107.85
TC-126	Portable Stereo Corder	209.95	174.25
TC-126CS	Port. Stereo Corder System	239.95	199.15
TC-129	Stereo Cassette Deck	149.95	124.00
TC-131SD	Economy Stereo Cass. Deck	239.95	199.15
TC-162SD	Port. Stereo Cass. Deck	349.95	290.45
TC-161SD	Adv. Stereo Cassette Deck	299.95	249.00
TC-177SD	Adv. 3 Head Deck	699.95	580.95

		Retail	Discount
TC-756	Prof. 3-Motor Deck	899.95	746.95
TC-756-2	Prof. 3-Motor 2 Track 2 Channel	889.95	736.95
TC-758	Deluxe 3-Motor Auto. Reverse	999.95	833.95

CASSETTE-CORDER/RADIO COMBINATIONS

		Retail	Discount
CF-310	Cassette AM/FM Radio Comb.	$139.95	$116.15
CF-320	Cassette AM/FM Radio Comb.	149.95	124.45
CF-350	Cassette AM/FM Radio Comb.	149.95	124.45
CF-420	Deluxe Cassette/AM/FM/PSB Radio Combination	189.95	157.65
CF-450	Deluxe Cassette/AM/FM Radio Comb. w/TMS	179.95	149.35

CASSETTE-CORDER/AM-FM STEREO SYSTEMS

		Retail	Discount
CF-550A	Port. 1-Point Stereo AM/FM Radio Combination	$269.95	$224.00

QUADRADIAL REEL-TO-REEL CARTRIDGE

		Retail	Discount
TC-258	Economy Quad/8-Track Playback Deck	$119.95	$100.00
TC-277-4	Quadradial Tape Deck	465.95	390.00
TC-388-4	Deluxe Quad. 3-Head Tape	679.95	564.35
TC-788-4	Prof. 3-Motor Quad Tape Deck	1,399.95	1,161.95

SOUNDCRAFTSMEN*

MODEL		Retail	Discount
20-12	Stereo Audio Frequency Equalizer	$299.50	$240.00

152   CONSUMER GUIDE

HI-FI COMPONENTS & TAPE RECORDERS

TC-208 Economy 8-Track Cartridge Playback Deck		89.95
TC-224 Port. Stereo System w/TMS		199.95
TC-228 8-Track Stereo Cartridge Recorder/Playback Deck		199.95

CAR STEREO CASSETTE/CARTRIDGE PLAYERS

TC-10 Car Cassette Stereo Player		$119.95
TC-25F Car Stereo Cassette Player		169.95
TC-30 Deluxe Car Stereo Cassette		169.95

MONAURAL REEL-TO-REEL RECORDERS

TC-105A Deluxe 1/4 Track Recorder		$229.95
TC-106AV 1/2 Track Recorder		199.95
TC-800B Servo Control Portable		299.95

STEREO REEL-TO-REEL TAPE SYSTEMS

TC-270 Economy Stereo System		$379.95
TC-353 Economy 3-Head System		399.95
TC-630 Deluxe Stereo Sys/Control.		499.95

STEREO REEL-TO-REEL TAPE DECKS

TC-280 Economy Stereo Deck		$249.95
TC-353D Economy 3-Head Tape Deck		319.95
TC-377 Deluxe 3-Head Tape Deck		399.95
TC-458 Auto. Reverse Stereo Deck.		499.95
TC-558 3-Motor Auto. Reverse Deck.		769.95
TC-580 Deluxe Auto. Reverse		599.95
TC-640B 3-Motor 3-Head Deck		449.95
TC-755 Deluxe 3-Motor Tape Deck		699.95

	Single Channel Record Playback, Prof.	
	Audio Frequency Equalizer	349.50
	Stereo Audio Frequency Equalizer	349.50
20-12/600 Reflectrostatic 3-Way Speaker System (Pair)		799.00
SC-12ES Acoustic Suspension 3-Way Speakers		229.30
SC7 22-17 Preamplifier		499.50

STANTON*

CALIBRATION STANDARD CARTRIDGES

681A		$66.00
681EE		72.00
681SE		66.00
681 EEE		82.00

BROADCAST STANDARD CARTRIDGES

600A		$45.00
600E		50.00
600EE		55.00

500 SERIES CARTRIDGES

500 EE		$40.00
500 E		35.00
500 AA		35.00
500 A		30.00
500 AL		30.00

DYNAPHASE HEADPHONES

5760 Dynaphase 60		59.95

Prices column (right): 275.00, 275.00, 640.00, 183.60, 362.15, $39.00, 40.00, 39.00, 59.45, $19.00, 21.00, 22.00, $29.00, 25.35, 25.35, 21.75, 21.75, 48.00

*With fair-traded stereo components, low prices are available only when a complete music system is purchased.

HI-FI COMPONENTS & TAPE RECORDERS

		Retail	Discount
5751	Dynaphase 50	49.95	39.95
5740	Dynaphase 40	39.95	31.95
5741	Dynaphase Control Box	19.95	15.95
5765	Dynaphase 65-4C	64.95	51.95

DISCRETE CARTRIDGES AND STYLI

		Retail	Discount
780/4DQ	Cartridge	$125.00	$100.00
4DQ	Stylus	45.00	36.00
780/Q	Cartridge	75.00	60.00
Q	Stylus	33.00	26.40

SUPERSCOPE*

COMPACT MUSIC SYSTEMS

		Retail	Discount
SMS-1016	Stereo System w/Quadraphase	$249.95	$212.00
SMS-1816	Stereo System w/8-Track Player & Quadraphase	299.95	255.00
SMS-3026	Stereo System w/Quadraphase	299.95	255.00
SMS-3826	Stereo System w/8-Track Player & Quadraphase	349.95	290.45
SMS-6026	Deluxe Stereo System w/Quadraphase	349.95	290.45

RECEIVERS & COMPONENTS

		Retail	Discount
A-235	Integrated Stereo Amp	89.95	74.65
A-245	Integrated Stereo Amp	119.95	99.55
A-260	Integrated Stereo Amp. w/Quad.	189.95	157.65
T-210	FM/AM Stereo Tuner	119.95	99.55

SERIES 9200XD, WALNUT

		Retail	Discount
9241XD	4 Track	$949.00	—

SERIES 3300X, WALNUT

		Retail	Discount
3341X	4 Track	$469.90	—

Series 3600XD, WALNUT

		Retail	Discount
3641XD	4 Track	$599.50	—

STEREO CASSETTE DECK

		Retail	Discount
TCD-310		$499.00	—
Series	9200XD, Walnut 9241XD 4 Track	$949.00	—

REEL-TO-REEL

		Retail	Discount
3641XD	Reel-to-Reel w/Dolby	$599.50	—

RECEIVERS

		Retail	Discount
TR-1020A	AM/FM, Walnut	$529.90	—
TR-1055A	AM/FM, Walnut	599.90	—

TEAC*

CASSETTES

		Retail	Discount
AC-5		$159.50	$136.00
AC-9		199.50	175.00
140	Stereo-Cassette Deck	199.50	173.00
160	Dolby Stereo Cassette	249.50	215.00
250		279.50	239.00

CONSUMER GUIDE

HI-FI COMPONENTS & TAPE RECORDERS

T-220	FM/AM Deluxe Stereo Tuner	179.95	355		249.50	212.05
R-330	FM/AM/FM MPX Stereo Receiver	219.95	360S		379.50	325.00
R-340	FM/AM/FM MPX Receiver w/Quad.	259.95	450	Dolby Stereo Cassette	449.50	385.00
R-350	FM/AM/FM MPX Receiver w/Quad.	299.95				
QA-450	Stereo 2/Quadrascope 4 Amp.	299.95	**COMPONENTS**			
QRT-440	Stereo 2/Quadrascope 4 Rec. w/2/4 Channel 8-Track Player	329.95	AN-60		$99.50	$85.00
			AN-80		169.50	144.00
STEREO CASSETTE & 8-TRACK TAPE DECKS/PLAYERS			AN-180		329.50	280.00
CD-301	Stereo Cassette Deck	$139.95	AN-300		429.50	370.00
CD-302	Stereo Cassette Deck w/Noise Reduction System	189.95	AX-300		399.50	340.00
			AT-100		229.50	196.00
TD-28	2 Channel 8-Track Player	74.95	**SPEAKERS**			
TD-48	2/4 Channel 8-Track Player	99.95	LS-1	(Pair)	$29.50	$26.00
			LS-30		99.50	85.00
SPEAKER SYSTEMS			LS-80		159.50	136.00
S-18	Extended Range System (Pair)	99.95				
S-28	2-Way Hi-Compliance System	79.95	**REEL-TO-REEL TAPE DECKS**			
S-212	2-Way Hi-Compliance System	119.95	4010 GSL		$599.50	$509.00
S-310	3-Way Hi-Definition System	169.95	6010 GSL		949.50	807.00
S-16	Extended Range System (Pair)	59.95	7030 GSL		1099.50	934.00
S-26	2-Way Hi-Efficiency System (Pair)	69.95	7010 GSL		1149.50	977.00
			4070G		729.50	620.00
ACCESSORY			2340		899.50	765.00
CC-1580	FM Car Radio Converter	29.95	2300S	Stereo Tape Deck	469.50	400.00
			3300S	Stereo Tape Deck	699.50	595.00
TANDBERG*			3300-SZT	Stereo Tape Deck	739.50	629.00
			4300	Stereo w/Auto. Reverse Play	679.50	577.00
SERIES 9100X, WALNUT			5300	Stereo w/Auto. Reverse Play	769.50	655.00
9141X	4 Track	$799.00	5500	Dolby Stereo w/Auto. Reverse	899.50	765.00
			3340S	4-Channel Simul-Sync Deck.	1099.50	935.00

*With fair-traded stereo components, low prices are available only when a complete music system is purchased.

CONSUMER GUIDE

HI-FI COMPONENTS & TAPE RECORDERS

Model	Description	Retail	Discount
2340R	4-Channel Tape Deck w/2 Channel Auto-Reverse Play	899.50	765.00

THORENS*

TRANSCRIPTION TURNTABLES

Model	Description	Retail	Discount
TD-125MkII	3-Speed	$290.00	$246.50
TD-125BMkII	3-Speed w/Base	305.00	259.25
TD-125ABMkII	3-Speed w/Arm, Base	410.00	348.50
TD-160C	2-Speed w/Tonearm, Base	230.00	195.50
TD-165C	Dust Cover	199.95	169.95

ACCESSORIES

Model	Description	Retail	Discount
WB-125	Walnut Base for TD-125	$17.50	$15.00
WB-160	Walnut Base for TD-160	17.50	15.00
TX-25	Dust Cover, Tinted	35.00	29.75
TX-44	Dust Cover, Clear	17.50	15.00
CE-509	Mounting Bracket	20.00	17.00

UNITED AUDIO*

DUAL AUTOMATIC TURNTABLES

Model	Description	Retail	Discount
1229-Q	Professional Auto. Turntable	$259.95	$173.00
1228	Auto/Prof. Turntable	189.95	127.00

EIGHT TRACK/STEREO-PLAY/RECORD-PREAMP DECK

Model	Description	Retail	Discount
8060	4-Channel Play, 2-Channel Record/Play, Matrix/Discrete Switch, Digital Time Counter	$289.95	$240.65
8055		249.95	206.20
8075		339.95	280.45
8080		399.95	329.95
8054		119.95	98.95

YAMAHA**

RECEIVERS

Model	Description	Retail	Discount
CR-1000	70W x 2 RMS	$850.00	$680.00
CR-800	45W x 2 RMS	580.00	464.00
CR-600	30W x 2 RMS	460.00	368.00
CR-400	16W x 2 RMS	330.00	264.00
CS-70R	2/4 Channel Receiver w/Digital Clock/Timer	370.00	296.00

AMPLIFIERS

Model	Description	Retail	Discount
CA-1000	70W x 2 RMS	$600.00	$480.00
CA-800	45W x 2 RMS	470.00	380.00
CA-600	30W x 2 RMS	330.00	264.00
CA-400		270.00	216.00
UD-500	4-Channel Adapter/Amplifier 15/15 W RMS	200.00	160.00

HI-FI COMPONENTS & TAPE RECORDERS

1226	Auto/Standard Turntable	159.95	107.15
1225	Automatic Turntable	129.95	87.00

PE TURNTABLES
3044		$109.95	$73.65
3046		149.95	100.45
3048		169.95	113.85
3060		199.95	133.95

WOLLENSAK*

CASSETTE RECORDERS/STEREO-PREAMP DECK-DOLBY
4765	Dolby FM Switch, Line Mike-Mix Switch, Ferrite Heads, Bias Switch	$409.95	$338.20
4775	IC Dolby Chip, Line-Mic-Mix Switch, Bias Switch	314.95	267.70
402K		154.95	127.85

TUNER
CT-7000	FM Stereo Tuner	$1200.00	$960.00
CT-800	Stereo Tuner	370.00	296.00
CT-600	Stereo Tuner	270.00	216.00

TURNTABLE
YP701	W/Cartridge, Base, Dust Cover	$220.00	$176.00
YP800	Direct Drive, No Cartridge	500.00	400.00

CASSETTE TAPE DECK
TB-700	Dolby Stereo Cassette Tape Deck	$340.00	$272.00

SPEAKERS
NS-570	Speaker System, Floor Model	$500.00	$400.00
NS-550	Speaker System, Floor Model	400.00	320.00

*With fair-traded stereo components, low prices are available only when a complete music system is purchased.

TELEVISIONS

1975 TELEVISIONS

NOWADAYS, one would be more likely to find a television in every home than a chicken in every pot. Television sales each year continue to break the record of the previous years, most of those sales are for color television sets. Sales of black-and-white sets have been diminishing every year.

The person buying a television in 1975 has certainly picked the right time. CONSUMER GUIDE Magazine has found that the 1975 models deliver surprising new highs in performance—brighter, sharper pictures than ever before. That is not all. New technology used in '75 models means you can buy a lot more TV reliability, and there are more models and more features to choose from. All this, of course, makes it increasingly difficult for the consumer to decide which set to buy. Adding to the dilemma is the fact that the television shopper in 1975 will be faced with higher prices.

Although the cost of manufacturing a television set has risen sharply in the past few years, there have been only a few minor price increases. Unfortunately, this situation has changed and the manufacturers have been forced to raise their prices substantially on their 1975 lines. In the past, when large manufacturers have raised prices, small companies have held to their lower prices in order to lure the bargain seeker. But even the small manufacturers are raising their prices along with the big

TELEVISIONS

corporations. Everyone is now more interested in profit-per-sale than in building a volume business.

Portable or Console?

THE FIRST decision you will probably make when shopping for a television is whether to get a portable version or a console model. Portable televisions are less expensive than either consoles or table models; however, in the case of color portables, do not be surprised to find that they are anything but portable, even though they may have a handle on the top. Portable color televisions are bulky and heavy, sometimes weighing as much as 60 to 80 pounds. Consequently, you will not be able to move these sets easily from room to room except with the aid of a cart—and that costs extra. Most color portable televisions, because of their bulk, probably will not be able to fit on an average bookshelf. If portability does not concern you and it is simply a matter of price, you can save a lot of money buying a portable color set. An example of an attractive portable is Admiral's Model 19C1307. It is designed to fit so beautifully into its stand that it almost looks like a console.

However, if it is real portability that you want, and color is only a secondary consideration, look for a black-and-white set. Black-and-white sets are extremely inexpensive, particularly when compared to the color sets, and they are quite light and trim. They can normally be carried in one arm and can fit almost anywhere.

The major trend in black-and-white portables for 1975 is toward the personal television. The advertising thrust is that these sets are so inexpensive and can be so small, that everyone can have his or her own personal set. One company, Panasonic, has become so carried away by the concept of the personal television that they are marketing a set that is no bigger than a portable radio. With a 1 1/2-inch screen, it is the smallest television in the world, and also the most expensive black-and-white portable. It carries a price that is at least $100 more than most 22-inch consoles.

If it is not a portable TV that you want, you have a choice between a table model or a console. As the name implies, a table model TV must be set on a table; a console is an entire cabinet that sits on the floor—a separate piece of furniture. Often there is little difference between a manufacturer's table models and consoles; they are basically the same televisions. The only difference is in the cabinet, and that difference can add $100 or more to the price of the set. A few manufacturers—such as Magnavox and Sylvania—still offer consoles which contain a TV and Stereo combination. As might be expected, these are quite expensive going up as high as $2000.

Solid State or Tubes

ONCE YOU have decided whether you will get a portable, a table model, or a console, you will have to make a choice between a solid

CONSUMER GUIDE 159

TELEVISIONS

state or tube set. A solid state chassis is made up of transistors instead of vacuum tubes. The only tube in a solid-state TV is the picture tube. Slightly less expensive than the totally solid state set is the so-called hybrid set, which is partially solid state and partially tubes.

There are two basic advantages of solid state televisions: They are less expensive to operate than hybrid models, and they are much more reliable. Over the course of ten years, a solid state set will save the user from $75 to $100 in electricity consumption alone. The exact amount saved depends on utility rates, screen size, the amount of use the set gets, and the particular design of the chassis.

While tubes burn out and have to be replaced in the same way that lightbulbs do, transistors fail only if they are overstressed, abused, or improperly made. CONSUMER GUIDE Magazine estimates that hybrid sets require an average of one service call every one or two years, but a solid state set requires service only once in three to five years. The savings in electrical consumption and in service calls more than make up for the extra $50 to $100 that solid state costs. Almost all manufacturers offer fairly complete lines of solid state sets. Hitachi and RCA, leaders in the solid-state movement, offer only solid state sets.

Another money-saving feature of solid state sets is that they normally have modular construction. Each module, a small circuit board that plugs in and out, contains all of the components related to a given function of the set. The service technician can easily tell which module is faulty by looking at the performance of the TV. So the repair is a simple job of removing the faulty module and replacing it with a new one. Labor and time charges are held to a minimum. Some sets contain fewer modules which encompass more functions than do others. A set with fewer modules will be easier to repair, so time and labor charges will be lower, but the individual modules will be more expensive to replace. CONSUMER GUIDE Magazine recommends that you not be overly concerned with the number of modules, but simply be sure that the set has some form of modular construction.

Which Color Picture Tube?

WHEN YOU SHOP for a color television set, you will hear terms like slot-mask, in-line, and negative matrix. If you are as unfamiliar with electronics as most people are, it will be pretty confusing to you. Familiarizing yourself with these features can make your buying choice easier.

The original color picture tubes were made up of hundreds of thousands of dots of phosphor. Three electronic guns, set in a triangular formation, convert the signals coming from the TV station into electrons. When these electrons hit the phosphor dots, they glow red, green, blue, and all the blendings in between.

An improvement on the phosphor dot system is the slot-mask system. Instead of dots, the screen is made up of extremely thin vertical color stripes. The use of stripes instead of dots reduces the chance of the electron beam hitting the wrong phosphor color. Most of the leading

TELEVISIONS

models of 1975 televisions have slot-mask picture tubes. Sets with slot-mask tubes are lighter, slimmer, and have a more uniform brightness; but, up until 1974 some slot-mask tubes have tended to develop color errors in "hot spots," extemely bright areas of the screen.

A color picture tube improvement by General Electric in 1965 is the in-line tube. Most slot-mask picture tubes are also in-line. The improvement is in the configuration the three electronic guns, which are now arranged in a straight line instead of in a triangular pattern. Television sets with slot-mask picture tubes cost less, and the in-line systems reduces or eliminates the need for convergence controls, the delicate adjustment made by the factory or by a service technician. The elimination of the need for this step in the manufacturing process or warranty requirement means a reduction in manufacturing costs.

Negative matrix refers to the system wherein the dots or stripes are fully illuminated and are surrounded by a light-absorbing black material. This contributes to the brightness of the picture. The negative matrix system originated with Zenith's Chromacolor sets, and it is quickly becoming standard on most large screen units. Less expensive sets may have a system called positive guardband black matrix, and a few have no matrix at all. Beware: Some nonmatrix sets are often advertised as having a "super bright picture tube." This does not necessarily mean that they have a negative matrix tube.

The one exception to the rule that negative matrix is better than nonmatrix is the Sony Trinitron tube. Until recently, Japanese manufacturers were prevented by patent restrictions to market negative matrix sets in the United States. But they managed to circumvent this restriction. While the Trinitron tube is not as bright as negative matrix tubes, it is certainly bright enough.

The only new development in picture tubes for 1975 is Sylvania's Dark-Light picture tube. This is actually a combination of two older developments: negative matrix and darkly tinted glass. The tinted glass reduces the brightness slightly, but it improves contrast.

How Automatic?

ALMOST ALL major television manufacturers have adopted a single-button tuning system on some of their sets. In most cases when you activate the automatic tuning you disconnect the brightness, contrast, color, and tint controls on the front of the set and turn over control of these functions to a duplicate set of controls at the back of the set.

In spite of manufacturers' claims, there is no such thing as a "single button that locks in perfect color every time" nor is there a "completely self-adjusting TV." Some of the automatic systems are more effective than others, but there is still no substitute for good manual controls. The basic problem with one-button tuning is that no one setting of picture controls is correct for all conditions. If there were no need to change color, brightness, and contrast settings, picture controls would not have been put on TV sets in the first place. The facts are, however, that stations change cameras and viewers with different tastes use the same

TELEVISIONS

set. These facts require that you be able to adjust the picture.

A real problem with automatic tuning on a color set is that it is most often coupled with the flesh tone circuit. The result is that the skin tones are correct, but everything else is the wrong color. The theory behind the flesh tone circuit is that viewers will not mind some distortion because they know what color flesh tones are supposed to be, and can accept furniture, houses, cars, clothing, etc. of any color. The theory breaks down when you notice that golf courses appear blue instead of green, and apples are orange instead of red.

The important thing to look for in an automatic system is one that does not interfere with the set's normal operation. Some automatic tuning systems can get in your way. The most annoying types are those that combine the single-button control with automatic fine tuning. With these sets, you cannot enjoy the benefits of automatic fine tuning unless you are willing to give up the use of the other controls. Nearly all manufacturers provide a way to turn off automatic fine tuning when the single tuning button is engaged, but there are a few who make it possible to enjoy automatic fine tuning with the button disengaged. Ideally, automatic fine tuning should be on a completely independent switch.

When the automatic tuning button is not activated, you have to use the manual controls. Unfortunately, many manufacturers have used the advent of one-button tuning as an excuse to degrade the quality of manual controls. Good manual controls should be conveniently located, logically grouped, clearly labeled, and not crowded together. Most importantly, they should effect a smooth and continuous change in the functions they regulate. A control that produces no change throughout much of its rotation and then suddenly produces a dramatic change at one point is a bad control. Moreover, the middle position on each control should be roughly the correct one for most viewing conditions, if the set is properly aligned. Controls should be protected behind a door or tilt-out bin, so that they cannot accidentally be moved.

In addition to a choice of tuning controls, there is the matter of channel selection controls. Basically, the choice is between a channel selection dial and push buttons. The push buttons, like the buttons on elevators, are part of a varactor tuner system. The advantage of varactor tuners over the more conventional selector dials is that they are all electronic; therefore, less subject to wear.

A new approach to channel selecting appears on some of Zenith's 1975 sets. Zenith is doing away with the push buttons on some of its 19-inch varactor sets and replacing them with a sliding selector. The channel numbers lie along the length of the selector's path, and a channel is chosen by sliding the selector to the desired number.

Another channel-selecting feature to look for in 1975 is ease of tuning in UHF channels. In the past, one tuned in a UHF channel by turning the channel indicator to a stop called UHF, and then dialing in the desired UHF station with another control. However, the FCC has ruled that on all sets manufactured since July 1974, UHF channels must be as easy to tune in as VHF channels.

TELEVISIONS

Other Features

INSTANT-ON eliminates warm-up delay; therefore, the picture appears the instant the set is turned on. The way it works is that a small amount of electricity is constantly being used to keep the picture tube filament warm. Some TV manufacturers, because of the energy crisis, are wisely eliminating this feature from their sets. In hybrid sets, the instant-on feature requires an inexcusable amount of energy in view of the world's limited energy resources. However, the amount of energy the instant-on feature uses in a solid state set is negligible.

An advantage of the instant-on feature is its picture-tube-saving property. A picture tube suffers the greatest stress when it heats up or cools down. By keeping the filaments warm all the time, the thermal shock to which it would be subjected is reduced. Therefore, in a solid state set, the benefits of the instant-on feature outweigh the extra energy cost.

Remote Control is purchased by fewer than five percent of all television buyers, yet those who have it swear by it. Studies show that the same consumers buy remote control with each new set they purchase. It can add as little as $50, or as much as $150, to the price of the set. The less sophisticated remotes offer only channel-changing capability and volume control. Those in the $100 range control picture adjustments, and the most expensive units provide prominent on-screen display of the channel number.

Independent On/Off is useful because most people use the same volume control setting day after day. If their television set allows them to turn the set on and off without affecting the volume setting, the volume control never needs to be touched. On many sets this is accomplished by making On/Off a completely separate switch from the volume control. Pull the knob to turn the set on; push it to turn the set off. Rotating the same knob adjusts volume.

Earphones are provided with many small-screen sets. It is a good idea, but often impractical. Most people like to put the TV set across the room, or at least at the foot of the bed, and the earphone cord is rarely long enough. A longer cord or less distance between the set and the viewer are the only available solutions and not very good ones at that.

Audiojacks are designed for music lovers who are forever disappointed in the audio quality of their television sets. The manufacturers explain that putting better amplifiers and speakers into television receivers would only show how bad the transmissions are in the audio department. The broadcasters say they see no reason to upgrade the quality of audio transmissions as long as TV sets have such inferior audio quality. And so it goes.

Nevertheless, one manufacturer—Quasar—does provide jacks on its console sets for playing the sound through your hi-fi amplifier and speakers or just through the speakers, using the TV amplifier. In tests of the Quasar, CONSUMER GUIDE Magazine found that some music programming sounded much better through an external hi-fi speaker, while most other shows sounded almost as bad as ever.

TELEVISIONS

Extended warranty may not seem like a "frill" to most purchasers, but that is exactly what it is—it is far and away the most expensive extra you can buy with your TV. A manufacturer can offer any length warranty he wants without improving the set one bit. All he has to do is raise the price enough to cover the expected cost of service during the warranty period. The length and strength of the warranty should be closely examined by the shopper and weighed against the price in comparison to other, similar sets with differing warranties.

Every TV set has at least 90 days full coverage of parts and labor; most also cover parts for the first year and the picture tube for two years. Evaluate additional labor coverage beyond the first 90 days at the rate of about $25 per year. The salesperson may argue that a service contract for a year costs $75 and so the extended warranty should be valued at that rate, but such reasoning is only valid if you intend to buy a service contract in the first place. Otherwise, the potential cost of service in the course of a year is about $25, according to a recent major university study of TV ownership costs.

How to Shop

PICKING THE right set is only half the battle when shopping for a television; the other half is getting a good price. To do that, you have to pick the right time and the right place to do your TV shopping.

The right time for TV shopping is after Christmas. The peak buying season for television sets has just ended, and retailers and manufacturers traditionally begin lowering prices. Immediately after Christmas, there should still be a good selection of models in the showrooms. Later, in spring and summer, prices may go still lower, but many models may be out of stock. In the fall, the new models are introduced and the prices are at their highest again.

No one type of retailer consistently has the best prices. Some of the lowest prices are found in the mail-order catalogs of Sears, J. C. Penney, and Montgomery Ward. But shipping costs can add substantially to these prices, and all of the major catalog houses offer only their own brands. Discounters and promotional department stores often have the lowest prices in town, but aggressive independent appliance-TV stores can frequently match or better them and provide you with better service to boot.

Purchasing a television is almost like buying a car; do not be reluctant to bargain. Many television salesmen are authorized to lower prices to close a sale, so do not assume that the price tag is the final word. Even so-called fair-trade items are often discounted.

Before bargaining it is helpful to arrive at an estimate in your own mind of what the set cost the store. This will give you an idea of how low the salesperson can reduce the price. The retailer's cost on most television sets is 70 to 80 percent of the list price. Therefore, a discount of 10 to 15 percent off list price is not an unrealistic expectation. If you really want to drive a hard bargain, wait until late in the model year, and shop at a time of day when the store is not busy.

TELEVISIONS

BEST BUYS

CONSUMER GUIDE Magazine has examined televisions of all manufacturers. The following "Best Buys" have been chosen on the basis of price in relation to performance, particularly in regards to sharpness, color accuracy (contrast on black-and-white sets), operation of controls, and weak-signal performance.

COLOR PORTABLES

General Electric YA6308WD is a solid-state portable with a 17-inch screen. It has a handle on top for carrying, and, at 50 pounds, is not too heavy for most adults to move from place to place. In addition to being solid state, this set has an in-line picture tube, and instant-on – all of which make this a reliable set. For people who want to save electricity, the instant-on feature can be turned off. The picture is bright and sharp, and colors are true to life.
Suggested Retail Price: $409.95   Low Price: $351.15

General Electric YA5508WD is a 13-inch portable designed to take up a minimum amount of space. It weighs only 40 pounds, but because the handles are on the side instead of on the top, it is not as easy to carry as other models. This set is designed for long life: it is solid state, has instant-on (which can be switched off), and has an in-line picture tube. The controls, particularly the Custom Picture Control, are extremely easy to use.
Suggested Retail Price: $369.95   Low Price: $309.65

Magnavox CD4230 has an extraordinarily bright and sharp picture. This 17-inch set is solid state, has a slotted-mask negative matrix picture tube, separate on/off control, automatic fine tuning, lighted channel numbers, and an electric eye that monitors the amount of light in the room and automatically adjusts the picture accordingly. The only drawbacks are that the set is not easy to move although it weighs the same as others, and that the controls are inconveniently located at the back of the set.
Fair Trade Price: $399.95   Low Price: $360.00

Panasonic CT-301 has a small screen (13 inches) but it has everything else you could want: solid state, automatic fine tuning, pre-set color

TELEVISIONS

button, clickstop channel selector, lighted channel numbers, convenient carrying handle, sharpness and tone controls which are normally found only on consoles, remarkable color reproduction, and a sharp picture. Although the set has a non-matrix picture tube, the brightness is more than adequate.

Suggested Retail Price: $349.95 **Low Price: $306.20**

RCA ET355 *is comfortable enough for easy carrying and the 15-inch screen is large enough for comfortable viewing. There are no "gadget features" but most of the usual deluxe features are included: lighted channel numbers, pre-set color button, automatic fine tuning, independent on/off switch, solid state chassis, and a slot-mask negative matrix picture tube. RCA has eliminated the instant-on feature from their 1975 sets in the interest of energy conservation.*

Suggested Retail Price: $404.95 **Low Price: $347.60**

Sony KV1722 *is expensive, but it is one of the finest quality portables on the market. Few sets can match its color accuracy, smoothness and convenience of controls, or weak signal performance. In addition, it has the widest-angle picture tube of any set in the world, which not only improves the picture sharpness, but makes it slimmer by four to five inches. It has all the other deluxe features also, such as automatic fine tuning, lighted channel numbers, and independent on/off control.*

Fair Trade Price: $499.95 **Low Price: $434.05**

Toshiba C335, *with a 13-inch screen and weighing only 30 pounds, is one of the easiest sets to carry around. With the exception of lighted channel numbers, there is not a deluxe feature missing from this set. A serious design flaw, however, is that the automatic fine tuning can only be activated when the pre-set color button is engaged. Unfortunately, when the pre-set color button is engaged, color accuracy suffers because of its flesh tone emphasizing circuits.*

Suggested Retail Price: $379.95 **Low Price: $322.95**

COLOR CONSOLES

General Electric MC9222MP *is an Early American-styled 25-inch console with solid state chassis, independent on/off control, instant-on (and and switch for disengaging it to save energy), and lighted channel numbers. The controls are hidden behind a pop-out drawer which was the best arrangement for concealed controls on any set CONSUMER GUIDE Magazine tested. The set's only flaw is its "Custom Picture Control" which did not maintain proper balance between brightness, color, and contrast, as it was supposed to.*

Suggested Retail Price: $729.95 **Low Price: $624.25**

Magnavox CE4756PE *has all the deluxe features you could want, and even a few that you may not want, like a light sensor which adjusts the brightness, contrast, and color intensity according to the light in the*

TELEVISIONS

room. The cabinet is Mediterranean-styled, and, like the other Magnavox top-of-the-line models for 1975, this one is available with the new "Star" remote control system. This model lacks only an instant-on feature.

Fair Trade Price: $649.95   **Low Price: $585.00**

Philco C2451FMA *is lower in price than most 25-inch consoles, but it still gives a bright, sharp picture with outstanding color accuracy. This unit has all the features found on deluxe sets; the reason for the low price is the cabinet. Instead of wood, the Early American-styled cabinet is made of plastic to look like wood. (But you cannot tell that it is plastic unless you examine the cabinet closely.) The only flaw in this set is in the controls. For one thing, the pre-set color button has been combined with the automatic fine tuning. Also, the controls do not work smoothly – at some points in the knob's rotation there is enormous change while at other points there is none.*

Suggested Retail Price: $569.95   **Low Price: $484.45**

Sylvania CE4193K *is a 21-inch console with an Early American-styled cabinet. This is the perfect set for the person who cannot tune a color TV; the GT-Matic II system adjusts the color and can be pre-set for a low or high degree of flesh tone. The viewer who wants to adjust the color to his or her own taste will have trouble though. The controls, bare plastic shafts, are difficult to use and are hidden behind a spring-loaded cover which keeps trying to snap shut. All of the other deluxe features are available on this set, including instant-on.*

Suggested Retail Price: $579.95   **Low Price: $485**

Zenith F4084, *with its 19-inch screen, is one of the most compact consoles on the market today. The modern styling features chrome legs with casters and a cane backing. The set is solid state and has all the deluxe features except instant-on. The picture is bright, with accurate color reproduction and good contrast, and it is easy to tune. A particularly nice feature is that the pre-set buttons do not get in the way of the automatic fine tuning.*

Suggested Retail Price: $569.95   **Low Price: $501.00**

BLACK AND WHITE

RCA AT193W *is a 19-inch portable with a picture that is sharply detailed, bright, with good contrast and little snow. Controls are easy to find and operate smoothly. Unlike many black-and-white receivers, this model has a dipole antenna (two rabbit ears instead of one), which provides extra signal strength and a little directionality to reject ghosts. Reliability of the chassis should be outstanding because it is solid state.*

Suggested Retail Price: $169.95   **Low Price: $146.30**

TELEVISIONS

1975 Television Prices

ADMIRAL

COLOR MODELS

Model	Size	Retail	Discount
2427P	12"	—	$249.00
3117P	13"	—	265.00
6447P	16"	—	299.00
56457P	16"	—	329.00
7059P	17" Solid State	399.95	369.00
7057PC	17"	419.95	379.00
8T1150	18"	—	309.00
19T981	19"	369.90	349.00
19T991C	19"	—	369.00
19T937	19" Solid State	429.95	389.00
19T947C	19" Solid State	459.95	409.00
19T957C	19" Solid State	489.95	439.00
19T959B	19" Solid State	—	459.00
19T5967C	19" Solid State	—	539.00
19C1301	19" Solid State	—	519.00
19C1307	19" Solid State	—	519.00
25L01	25"	—	499.00
25L05	25"	—	529.00
25L11M	25" Solid State	—	549.00
25L25	25" Solid State	—	579.00
25L28	25" Solid State	—	579.00
S25L38	25" Solid State	—	659.00
25L41	25" Solid State	599.00	569.00
25L53	25" Solid State	699.95	629.00

Model	Size	Retail	Discount
YA6308WD	17"	409.95	351.15
CD7302BG	19"	—	287.10
CD7304WD	19"	339.95	288.20
CD7314RW	19"	349.95	305.25
CD7316WD	19"	359.95	310.75
QB7420WD	19"	439.95	381.15
QB7422WD	19"	459.95	392.15
QB7478WD	19"	469.95	399.55

PORTABLE COLOR CONSOLE MODELS

Model	Size	Retail	Discount
MB9202WD	25"	$ —	$545.60
MB9203MP	25"	—	545.60
MB9204PN	25"	—	545.60
MB9205WD	25"	659.95	569.80
MB9206MP	25"	659.95	569.80
MB9207PN	25"	659.95	569.80
MB9207DS	25"	659.95	569.80
MB9212AP	25"	689.95	590.40
MC9220WD	25"	729.95	624.25
MC9222MP	25"	729.95	624.25
MC9224PN	25"	729.95	624.25
MC9224DS	25"	729.95	624.25
MC9226AP	25"	759.95	646.25
MC9232MP	25"	809.95	685.00
MC9234PN	25"	809.95	685.00

MONOCHROME TELEVISION MODELS

Model	Size	Retail	Discount
BA1202VY	5" Solid State	$139.95	$111.65

TELEVISIONS

25L55	25" Solid State	TRL20RY	629.00	119.05
25L77	25" Solid State	SF1600BG	669.00	70.10
25L91	25" Solid State	SF1602VY	699.00	72.30
25L98	25" Solid State	SF1608VY	699.00	75.60
		SF1702YL		77.80

BLACK & WHITE MODELS

		SF2100GY		75.60
12P647	12" Solid State w/Earphone and Pedestal Base	SF2101SL	$95.00	76.45
12P620	12" Solid State w/Earphone and Pedestal Base	SF2105EB	109.00	79.45
12P637	12" Solid State w/Earphone and Pedestal Base	SF2106VY	109.00	79.45
		SF2220BG		83.05
		SF2402VY		84.40
16P640	16"	Series	109.00	
16P657C	16"	SF2326WD	135.00	85.80
19P857C	19"	SF2330RW	145.00	88.00
19P889C	19"	SF3102VY	147.00	89.65
19P897C	19"	SF3202BW	159.95	94.05
22T331C	22"	SF3124BK	167.00	93.50
22C341	22"	SF3126VY	209.00	95.70
22C345	22"	SF3304BW	219.00	97.35
22C343	22"	SF3306WD	239.00	99.00
		SF3308RD	249.95	102.30

GENERAL ELECTRIC

		UA4201BG		112.45
		UA4126WD	144.95	120.45
		UA4153WD	144.95	120.45

PORTABLE COLOR MODELS

HE5202GR	10"	XA4201BG	$190.55	117.95
HE5206WD	10"	XA4216WD	190.85	124.85
HE5216WD	10"	XA4317WD	203.20	124.85
HE5218RW	10"	UA4802WD	207.05	166.10
YA5504WD	13"	UA4812WD	295.05	185.35
YA5508WD	13"	UA4822MP	309.65	189.75
YA6304WD	17"	XA4804WD	336.60	168.30

CONSUMER GUIDE 169

TELEVISIONS

		Retail	Discount
XA4824MP	22"................................	239.95	191.95
XA4834PN	22"................................	239.90	191.95

JVC

COLOR

		Retail	Discount
7830	19" Diag., 100% Solid State......	$569.95	$450.00
7130	13" Diag., 100% Solid State......	399.95	324.00
7140	13" Diag., 100% Solid State......	429.95	351.00

BLACK & WHITE

		Retail	Discount
3020	5" Diag., Mini Vis., Elec. Tun.....	$119.95	$86.40
3030	5" Diag., Mini Vis., Elec. Tun.....	129.95	94.32
3100R	7" Diag., Built-In FM/AM Radio...	269.95	86.00
3100D	7" Diag., Port. w/Built-In Dig. Clock	259.95	176.40
3231	9" Diag., w/Up/Down & Swivel Base	139.95	108.00
3240	9" Diag., Video Sphere...........	179.95	129.60
3241	9" Diag., w/Dig. Clock............	199.95	138.00
3250	9" Diag.........................	199.95	138.00
3251	9" Diag. w/FM/AM Radio.........	259.95	177.60
3430	12" Diag........................	149.95	109.20
3410	12" Diag........................	129.95	96.00
3510	13" Diag., Solid State............	159.95	112.32

MAGNAVOX*

BLACK & WHITE MODELS

		Retail	Discount
5050	12" Portable.....................	$84.95	$76.50

COLOR

		Retail	Discount
4730	25" Solid State..................	649.95	585.00
4731	25" Solid State..................	699.95	630.00
4734	25" Solid State..................	599.95	540.00
4735	25" Solid State..................	699.95	630.00
4736	25" Solid State..................	599.95	540.00
4737	25" Solid State..................	699.95	630.00
4752	25" Solid State..................	649.95	585.00
4754	25" Solid State..................	649.95	585.00
4755	25" Solid State..................	749.95	675.00
4756	25" Solid State..................	649.95	585.00
4757	25" Solid State..................	749.95	675.00
4758	25" Solid State..................	649.95	585.00
4758	25" Solid State..................	669.95	603.00
4760	25" Solid State, Pecan...........	649.95	585.00
4760	25" Solid State, Milano...........	669.95	603.00
4784	25" Solid State..................	749.95	675.00
4786	25" Solid State..................	749.95	675.00
4787	25" Solid State..................	849.95	765.00
4790	25" Solid State..................	799.95	720.80
4798	25" Solid State, Pecan...........	799.95	720.00
4798	25" Solid State, Genoa...........	825.00	743.00
4799	25" Solid State, Pecan...........	899.95	810.00
4799	25" Solid State, Genoa...........	925.00	833.00

COLOR STAR SYSTEM MODELS

		Retail	Discount
4875	25" Solid State..................	$995.00	$895.00
4877	25" Solid State..................	995.00	895.00
4891	25" Solid State..................	1195.00	1080.00
4895	25" Solid State..................	1295.00	1165.00

TELEVISIONS

5056	12" Portable	99.95
5110	16" Portable	124.95
5111	16" Portable	139.95
5140	19" Portable	129.95
5141	19" Portable w/Mobile Cart	139.95

COLOR PORTABLE MODELS

4080	13" Solid State	$299.95
4090	13" Solid State	359.95
4160	15" Solid State	379.95
4220	17" Solid State	329.95
4230	17" Solid State	399.95
4237	17" Solid State	499.95
4300	19" Solid State	329.95
4350	19" Solid State	399.95
4352	19" Solid state w/Base	449.95
4360	19" Solid State	449.95

COLOR TABLE MODELS

4367	19" Solid State	$549.95
4452	19" Solid State	499.95
4454	19" Solid State	499.95
4456	19" Solid State, Pecan	499.95
4456	19" Solid State, Ivy	519.95
4463	19" Solid State	599.95
4465	19" Solid State	599.95
4467	19" Solid State, Pecan	599.95
4467	19" Solid State, Ivy	619.95

COLOR CONSOLE MODELS

4722	25" Solid State	$549.95

MOTOROLA QUASAR

BLACK & WHITE PORTABLE MODELS

WP5546LW	19" Solid St. Walnut, AM-FM Radio w/Cart	$449.94

		89.95
		112.50
		126.00
		117.00
		126.00

	$270.00
	324.00
	342.00
	297.00
	360.00
	450.00
	297.00
	360.00
	405.00
	405.00

	$495.00
	450.00
	450.00
	450.00
	468.00
	540.00
	540.00
	540.00
	558.00

	$495.00

$418.00

COLOR PORTABLE MODELS

WP4502KW	16" Walnut	$319.95
TP5505LW	18", Walnut, Remote Cont. w/Cart	388.88
WP589KW	19" Solid St., Walnut w/Cart	399.95
WP5500KW	19" Walnut	—
WP5506KP	19" Boca Pecan w/Cart	419.95
WP5508KP	19" Solid St., Boca Pecan w/Pedestal Base	469.95

	$294.80
	354.90
	384.95
	316.80
	378.40
	413.60

COLOR TABLE MODELS

TT6101KW	21" Walnut, Remote Cont.	$529.95
WT6102KW	21" Royal Walnut, w/Base	599.95
WT6110KW	21" Walnut	479.95

	$489.50
	533.50
	443.30

COLOR CONSOLE MODELS

WU8008KP	23", Classic Pecan	$499.95
WL8010KP	23", Classic Pecan w/Dual Speakers	579.95
WU918JP	25" Mission Pecan, Instamatic	629.95
TU9105KW	25" Solid St., Walnut, Remote Cont.	579.95
WU8016LS	23" Solid St., Amer. Trad. Maple	589.95
WU8018LP	23" Solid St., Classic Pecan	589.95
WL8024LP	23" Solid St., Classic Pecan	629.95

	$471.90
	520.30
	525.80
	528.00
	544.50
	544.50
	566.50

TELEVISIONS

PANASONIC

		Retail	Discount
WU9126KW	25", Royal Walnut w/Base	539.95	489.50
TU9127KW	25", Royal Walnut, Remote Cont.	619.95	540.05
WU9134KP	25", Classic Pecan	589.95	532.40
WU9140KW	25" Solid St., Royal Walnut w/Base	579.95	527.45
TU9141KW	25" Solid St., Royal Walnut, Remote Cont. w/Base	629.95	571.45
WU9144KS	25" Solid St., Heritage Maple	649.95	567.60
TU9145KS	25" Solid St., Heritage Maple, Remote Cont.	699.95	614.90
TL9151KP	25" Solid St., Rico Pecan, Remote Cont., Dual Speakers	799.95	684.20
TL9153KS	25" Solid St., Heritage Maple, Remote Cont., Dual Speakers	799.95	684.20
TL9155KP	25" Solid St., Classic Pecan, Remote Cont., Dual Speakers	799.95	684.20

SOLID-STATE COLOR

	Retail	Discount
CT-551	$469.95	$411.20
CT-772	299.95	262.45
CT-994	339.95	297.45
CT-301	349.95	306.20
CT-314	349.95	306.20
CT-324	369.95	323.70
CT-714	409.95	358.70
CT-914	429.95	376.20
CT-974	569.95	498.70

PHILCO-FORD

		Retail	Discount
25-INCH-DIAGONAL BOSS 300 COLOR CONSOLES			
C2507FPC	Modern w/Pedestal Base	$639.95	$541.00
C2507FWH	Same as Above, White	639.95	541.00
C2510FWA	Contemporary, Walnut	669.95	562.75
C2511FMA	Early Amer., Antiqued	669.95	562.75
C2512FPC	Mediterranean, Pecan	669.95	562.75
C2513FAW	Mediterranean, Antiqued White	669.95	562.75
C2520FWA	Contemporary, Walnut	719.95	601.15
C2521FPN	Early Amer., Knotty Pine Top	719.95	601.15
C2522FPC	Mediterranean, Antiqued Pecan	719.95	601.15
C2532FPC	Mediterranean, Antiqued Pecan	759.95	628.85
C2550FPC	Ultra Modern, Pecan	799.95	660.00

25-INCH-DIAGONAL BOSS 300 HOME THEATER COMBINATIONS

		Retail	Discount
C8232FLK	Quadraphonic, 8-Track Stereo Tape, FM Stereo, FM/AM Radio, Auto. Changer, 6 Speakers	$1195.00	$932.10
C8242FLK	Same as Above, Amoire	1195.00	932.10

25-INCH-DIAGONAL BOSS 300 COLOR TABLE MODELS

		Retail	Discount
C2500FWA	Contemporary, Walnut	$619.95	$526.95

25-INCH-DIAGONAL BOSS COLOR CONSOLES

		Retail	Discount
C2450FWA	Contemporary, Walnut	$569.95	$484.45
C2451FMA	Early Amer., Maple	569.95	484.45

TELEVISIONS

MODULAR-SOLID STATE COLOR

CT-910		$399.95
CT-924		479.95
CT-934		499.95
CT-944	W/Cart.	499.95
CT-954		569.95
CT-912R		599.95
CT-254		599.95
CT-2514		629.95
CT-2524		649.95
CT-2534		679.95

SOLID-STATE BLACK AND WHITE PORTABLE

TR-001	$359.95
TR-475	179.95
TR-729	99.95
TR-499	169.95
TR-622	99.88
TR-622U	99.88
TR-562	109.95
TR-562U	109.95
TR-632	114.95
TR-632U	119.95
TR-642	114.95
TR-642U	129.95
TR-542	129.95
TR-542U	129.95

BLACK AND WHITE PORTABLE

TR-276	$144.95
TR-559	154.95
TR-569	169.95

		$349.95
		419.95
		437.45
		437.45
		498.70
		524.95
		524.95
		551.20
		568.70
		594.95

	$314.95
	157.45
	87.45
	148.70
	87.40
	87.40
	96.20
	96.20
	100.60
	104.95
	100.60
	113.70
	113.70
	113.70

	$126.85
	135.60
	148.70

19-INCH-DIAGONAL BOSS COLOR PORTABLES

C1900FBE	Trim, Compact, Beige, A.C.T.	—
C1907FWA	Contemporary, Walnut, A.C.T.	399.95
C1908FWA	Contemporary, Furniture-Styled Walnut	429.95
C1913FWA	Contoured Walnut, A.T.S.	439.95
C1922FRW	Contoured, Rosewood, Hands Off Tuning	469.95

		339.95
		365.45
		373.95
		399.45

13-INCH-DIAGONAL COLOR PORTABLE

C1301FRW	Solid St, Rosewood, A.C.T.	$329.95	$280.45

RCA

BLACK & WHITE PORTABLES

AT059Y	Lunar I 5″ w/AM-FM Radio/Digital Clock	$179.95
AT091	Series Jaunty	89.88
AT097B	Carryette 9″	139.95
AT121	Series Headliner 12″	104.88
AT127E	12″	114.95
AT128E	Sportsman 12″	149.95
AT166W	Rogue 16″	129.95
AT192W	Modernist 19″	149.95
AT193W	Innovator 19″	169.95

$155.38
81.95
118.80
90.75
99.00
127.05
115.50
130.90
146.30

BLACK & WHITE TABLE MODEL

BT221W-EN	Royale 22″	$229.95	$194.70

BLACK & WHITE CONSOLE MODELS

CT222W	Woodruff 22″	$244.95	$207.90

CONSUMER GUIDE

TELEVISIONS

Model	Description	Retail	Discount
CT223L	Taunton 22"	249.95	212.30

COLOR PORTABLE MODELS
Model	Description	Retail	Discount
ET353B	Projecta 15, Walnut/Beige	$379.88	$327.80
ET355E	Projecta 15, Charcoal Bronze	$404.95	347.60
ET355Y	Projecta 15, Fog White	404.95	347.60
ET395W	Projecta 17, Walnut Grain	409.88	349.80
ET396W	Projecta 17, Walnut Grain/Plat. Mist	434.95	374.55
E396Y	Projecta 17, Fog White/Plat. Mist	434.95	374.55
ET396WR	Projecta 17, Walnut Grain/Plat. Mist	514.95	443.85

COLOR TABLE MODELS
Model	Description	Retail	Discount
FT480W	Abbott 19"	$509.95	$442.20
FT480WR	Abbott 19"	589.95	508.20
FT484L	Brandywine 19"	529.95	454.85
FT788D	Martinez 19", Oak	529.95	454.85
FT488S	Martinez 19", Pecan	529.95	454.85

COLOR TABLE MODEL
Model	Description	Retail	Discount
FT505W	Cosmos 21"	$539.95	$466.95

CONSOLETTE COLOR TABLE MODEL
Model	Description	Retail	Discount
FT518W-EN	Gladwin 25"	$619.95	$536.80

COLOR CONSOLE
Model	Description	Retail	Discount
GT540W	Lambert 21"	$589.95	$506.00

Model	Retail	Discount
31C36	329.50	280.10
51C51R	359.50	305.55
91C53/63	389.50	331.10
91C56	409.50	348.10
91C57N	419.50	356.55
91C54	439.50	373.55
91C59S	479.50	407.55
91C73	499.50	424.55
91C75	549.50	467.10

BLACK AND WHITE MODELS
Model	Retail	Discount
61V53	129.95	110.45
91V87	149.95	127.45
91T49	169.95	144.45

SONY*

BLACK & WHITE PORTABLE MODELS
Model	Description	Retail	Discount
TV-760	7" Indoor/Outdoor View	$129.95	$113.55
TV-750	7" Portable w/Recharg. Bat.	139.95	119.90
TV-950	8" Indoor/Outdoor View	139.95	119.05
TV-960	8"	139.95	119.05
TV-115	11" Solid State	149.95	129.30
TV-520	5" Smoke Filter Screen	126.95	109.75

SOLID STATE COLOR MODELS
Model	Description	Retail	Discount
KV-1520R	15" Auto. Color, Hue Fine Tng.	489.95	425.40
KV-1710	17" Auto. Color/Fine Tuning	469.95	410.70

CONSUMER GUIDE

TELEVISIONS

GT544L	Princeton 21"	599.95	KY-1711	17" Auto. Color/Fine Tuning	489.95	428.20
GT548S	Lamancha	599.95	KY-1722	17" Auto. Color, Hue, Fine Tng.	499.95	434.05
GT660WR	Donley 25"	739.95	KY-1730R	17" Auto. Color, Hue, Fine Tng.	569.95	485.00
GT702W	Glendale 25"	649.95	KY-1910	19" Auto. Color, Hue, Fine Tng.	549.95	474.30
GT704L	Lexington 25"	649.95	KY-5000	5" Auto-Color, Hue, Fine Tng.	419.95	352.55
GT708S	Carrera 25"	669.95	KY-9200	9" Instant-On Defeat Switch	389.95	331.85
GT720W	Selkirk 25"	719.95	KY-1201	12" Auto. Color Control	359.95	314.60
GT720WR	Selkirk 25"	799.95	KY-1203	12"	359.95	314.60
GT723W	Atherton 25"	669.95	KY-1212	12" Auto. Color, Fine Tuning	379.95	327.70
GT724L	Leesburg 25"	729.95	KY-1214	12" Auto. Color, Fine Tuning	379.95	327.70
GT724LR	Leesburg 25"	809.95	KV-1500	15" Auto. Color Control	409.95	363.00
GT728D	Gerona 25", Oak	729.95	KV-1510	15" Auto. Color, Hue Fine Tng.	429.95	375.75
GT728S	Gerona 25", Pecan	729.95				
GT728SR	Gerona 25", Pecan	809.95	*Fair Trade			
GT794L	Fitchburg 25"	789.95				
GT795H	Cumberland 25"	789.95		**SYLVANIA***		
GT798S	Marafino 25"	789.95				
GT802W	Stockholm 25"	849.95				
GT803Y	Ramsgate 25"	849.95	**COLOR MODELS**			
GT830M	Allison 25"	899.95	CA411BG	13" Diag. Portable GT-101	$299.95	$259.00
GT834L	Pawtucket 25"	899.95	CA411BW	13" Diag. Portable GT-Matic	329.95	275.00
GT835H	Bordentown 25"	899.95	C84137W	15" Diag. Portable GT-Matic	359.95	310.00
GT838D	Vincennes 25"	899.95	CC1157WR	15" Diag. Portable Gibraltar 95	399.95	330.00
GT838D	Marengo 25", Oak	899.95	CC4152W	17" Diag. Portable GT-101	369.95	313.00
			CC4154W	17" Diag. Portable GT-Matic	399.95	334.00
			CC4160W	19" Diag. Portable Gibraltar 95	338.88	290.00
	SANYO		CX217WR		449.95	365.00
			CX4161W	19" Diag. Portable GT-101	399.95	336.00
SOLID STATE COLOR MODELS			CX4164W	19" Diag. Portable GT-Matic	429.95	357.00
31C35		$329.50 $280.10	CX4166TK	19" Diag. Table GT-Matic II	469.95	390.00
			CE4181W	21" Diag. Table GT-Matic II	519.95	434.00
			CE4193K	21" Diag. Console GT-Matic II	579.95	485.00

CONSUMER GUIDE

TELEVISIONS

		Retail	Discount
CL202W	25" Diag. Table Gibraltar 90	499.95	428.00
CL4302WR	25" Diag. Table Gibraltar 90	559.05	479.00
CL4204W	25" Diag. Consolette GT-Matic II	569.95	482.00
CL4241	Series: 25" Diag. Console GT-Matic Varactor	599.95	507.00
CL4251	Series: 25" Diag. Console GT-Matic II	669.95	555.00
CL4411W	25" Diag. Console GT-Matic II	669.95	555.00
CL4511WR	25" Diag. Console GT-Matic II Varactor	769.95	640.00
CL4432	Series: 25" Diag. Console GT-Matic II Varactor	749.95	620.00
CL4532	Series: 25" Diag. Console GT-Matic II Varactor	849.95	700.00
CL4453K	Series: 25" Diag. Console GT-Matic Varactor	$850.00	$700.00
CL4553	Series: 25" Diag. Console GT-Matic II Varactor	950.00	770.00
CL4456	Series: 25" Diag. Console GT-Matic II Varactor	850.00	700.00
CL4568	Series: 25" Diag. Console GT-Matic II Varactor	1095.00	895.00
CL4471W	25" Diag. H.E.C. GT-Matic II	995.00	800.00
CL4473	25" Diag. H.E.C. GT-Matic II	1095.00	895.00
CL4585PR	25" Diag. H.E.C. GT-Matic II	1495.00	1200.00

*Fair Trade

		Retail	Discount
F2475M	22" Cambridge	249.95	220.64
F2427P	22" Casablanca	259.95	230.72
F2477P	22" Morocco	269.95	238.56

COLOR PORTABLE MODELS

		Retail	Discount
S2905W	14" Blake	$298.88	$266.00
F3721L	16" Hals	318.88	287.00
F3852L	17" Raeburn	398.88	362.00
F3855W	17" Bertram	419.95	372.00
F3858W	17" Allston	419.95	372.00
F3860W	17" Matisse	449.95	399.00
F3860R	17" Matisse	449.95	399.00
T2834W	17" Marin	429.95	383.00
F4002W	19" Steen	398.88	348.00
F4015L	19" Degas	459.95	407.00
F4025W	19" Stuart	489.95	434.00
F4028W	19" Kirchner	509.95	439.00
F4030X	19" Braque	529.95	457.00
F4033X	19" Braque	529.95	457.00
F4035P	19" Mondrian	529.95	457.00
F4037M	19" Goya	529.95	457.00
T2838W	19" Sargent	459.95	388.00
T2840W	19" Jamaica	509.95	439.00
	19" Courbet		

COLOR TABLE MODELS

		Retail	Discount
F4541W	23" Bingham	$559.95	$508.00

TELEVISIONS

ZENITH

BLACK & WHITE PORTABLE MODELS

Model	Name	Price 1	Price 2
F1335C	12" Palette	$98.88	$89.60
F1335D	12" Palette	98.88	89.60
F1335F	12" Palette	98.88	89.60
F1335L	12" Palette	98.88	89.60
F1335P	12" Palette	98.88	89.60
F1335V	12" Palette	98.88	89.60
F1340W	12" Resort	109.95	99.12
F1343B	12" Sidekick	109.95	99.12
F1345X	12" Olympus	119.95	108.65
F1345Y	12" Olympus	119.95	108.65
F1850C	16" Brent, Solid State	138.88	126.50
F1850L	16" Brent, Solid State	138.88	126.50
F1860N	16" Blaine, Solid State	148.88	135.50
F2040W	19" Ashington	138.88	131.00
F2050J	19" Camelot, Solid State	148.88	140.00
F2055W	19" Falmouth, Solid State	148.88	140.00
F2060N	19" Southampton, Solid State	159.95	149.00
F2070X	19" Carlisle, Solid State	169.95	157.00

BLACK & WHITE TABLE MODELS

Model	Name	Price 1	Price 2
F2411W	22" Lynn	$198.88	$182.50
F2461W	22" Lancaster	209.95	187.00

BLACK & WHITE CONSOLES

Model	Name	Price 1	Price 2
F2471W	22" Norfolk	$238.88	$210.56
	25" Van Gogh	639.95	570.00
F4740W			

COLOR CONSOLE MODELS

Model	Name	Price 1	Price 2
F4086M	19" Audubon, Solid State	$539.95	$473.00
F4088DE	19" Titian, Solid State	539.95	473.00
F4088P	19" Titian, Solid State	539.95	473.00
F4082X	19" Avante X, Solid State	569.95	501.00
F4084P	19" Lyman, Solid State	569.95	501.00
F4543W	23" Manet	588.88	521.00
F4545W	23" Watteau	599.95	530.00
F4547M	23" Lawrence	639.95	565.00
F4549DE	23" Bassano	639.95	565.00
R4549P	23" Bassano	639.95	565.00
F4550DE	23" Ribera	659.95	585.00
F4550P	23" Ribera	659.95	585.00
F4560P	23" Veronese	659.95	585.00
T2858W	23" Van Dyck	629.95	551.00
T2860DE	23" Giorgione	639.95	558.00
T2860P	23" Giorgione	639.95	558.00
F4714W	25" Millet	548.88	499.00
F4718M	25" Sisley	579.95	515.00
F4720DE	25" Utrillo	589.95	524.00
F4720P	25" Utrillo	589.95	524.00
F4742W	25" Holbein, Solid State	659.95	583.00
F4744P	25" Vermeer, Solid State	699.95	611.00
F4746M	25" Copley, Solid State	709.95	620.00
F4748DE	25" Rubens, Solid State	709.95	620.00
F4748P	25" Rubens, Solid State	709.95	620.00
F4752P	25" Reynolds, Solid State	749.95	647.00
F4754E	25" Gainsborough, Solid State	749.95	647.00

CONSUMER GUIDE

TELEVISIONS

Model	Description	Retail	Discount
F4756M	25" Cassatt, Solid State	749.95	647.00
F4757PN	25" Peale, Solid State	749.95	647.00
F4758DE	25" Florentino, Solid State	749.95	647.00
F4758P	25" Florentino, Solid State	749.95	647.00
F4759X	25" Renoir, Solid State	770.00	655.00
F4760X	25" Avante XII, Solid State	785.00	668.00
F4761P	25" Raphael, Solid State	785.00	668.00
T2873P	25" Lebrun, Solid State	759.95	647.00
T2875M	25" Putnam, Solid State	759.95	647.00
T2877DE	25" Bronzino, Solid State	759.95	647.00
T2877P	25" Bronzino, Solid State	759.95	647.00
T2881DE	25" Giotto, Solid State	809.95	680.00
T2881P	25" Giotto, Solid State	809.95	680.00
F8748P	25" Correggio	1095.00	918.00

COLOR PORTABLES W/REMOTE CONTROL

Model	Description	Retail	Discount
SF1750R	17" Daumier	$499.95	$448.00
SF1960R	19" Hilliard	609.95	530.00
SF1962X	19" Bonnard	609.95	530.00

COLOR TABLE MODELS W/SPACE COMMAND REMOTE CONTROL 25" PICTURE

Model	Description	Retail	Discount
SF2560W	25" Velasquez	$739.95	$653.00
SF2560X	25" Velasquez	739.95	653.00

COLOR CONSOLES W/SPACE COMMAND REMOTE CONTROL 19" PICTURE

Model	Description	Retail	Discount
SF1964X	19" Avante XI	$649.95	$565.00
SF1966P	19" Gauguin	649.95	565.00
SF2561P	25" Millais, Solid State	799.95	683.00
SF2562M	25" Inness, Solid State	809.95	692.00
SF2563DE	25" Botticelli, Solid State	809.95	692.00
SF2563P	25" Botticelli, Solid State	809.95	692.00
SF2564X	25" Avante XIV, Solid State	870.00	741.00
SF2568W	25" Zorn, Solid State	920.00	774.00
SF2569P	25" Cezanne, Solid State	920.00	774.00
SF2570DE	25" Tintoretto, Solid State	920.00	774.00
SF2570P	25" Tintoretto, Solid State	920.00	774.00
SF2590X	25" Avante XV Color	1500.00	1254.00

COLOR CONSOLE COMBINATION

Model	Description	Retail	Discount
SF2595P	25" Michelangelo	$1600.00	$1338.00

TELEVISIONS

TELEVISION PERFORMANCE RATINGS

manufacturer/model	sharpness	brightness	color accuracy/contrast (b&w)	operation of controls	weak signal performance
COLOR PORTABLES					
Admiral 19T959B	G	VG	E	F	G
General Electric HE5206	F	G	G	VG	G
General Electric YA6308WD	E	VG	E	G	E
General Electric YA5508WD	E	VG	E	E	E
Magnavox CD4230	E	E	VG	G	E
Panasonic CT-910	G	VG	E	E	G
Panasonic CT-301	VG	VG	E	E	VG
RCA ET355	E	VG	E	VG	E
Sears 57H41991N	VG	VG	E	E	G
Sharp C-1541	E	E	E	VG	E
Sony KV1722	E	VG	S	S	S
Toshiba C335	E	VG	G	E	E
COLOR CONSOLES					
General Electric MC9222MP	E	E	E	VG	VG
Magnavox CE4756PE	E	E	E	VG	VG
Magnavox CD4736	VG	E	VG	G	E
Philco C2451FMA	VG	E	E	F	VG
Quasar WU9232	E	E	E	G	VG
Sylvania CE4193K	E	G	S	F	E
Zenith F4084	VG	E	E	VG	E
BLACK AND WHITE					
General Electric SF2101GD	E	E	F	G	VG
RCA AT193W	E	E	E	E	E
Sylvania MU4060S	VG	E	E	VG	VG

Television Performance Rating Codes: *S - Superior; E - Excellent; VG - Very Good; G - Good; F - Fair.*

RADIOS

1975

THE RADIO market has always been a high-volume one which has always seen a load of annual new offerings. But for 1975, the radio manufacturers are facing the same problems everyone else is: parts shortages, rising production costs, and tight money. For 1975, radio manufacturers have increased their wholesale prices by five percent. And in an attempt to save manufacturing costs, some manufacturers will no longer be including batteries in the price of their models. Others will supply batteries in their portable-only units, but in none others. RCA, Philco, Motorola, and Westinghouse have stopped production of this low-ticket commodity all together, and are concentrating their expenditures where they will reap more profit. So, for 1975, you will find only a sprinkling of new models amid the many conventional sets that have sold well in the past.

Features for 1975

THE NEW look in radios for 1975 is the military one: a tall, narrow cabinet, shoulder strap, speaker grille designed to look like rugged metal slits, and the other stark outlines of a battlefield radio. The new design is meant to satisfy the recent rage for British desert uniforms, tank commander caps, and cartridge belts. Of all the military-look portables on the market, probably the most gimmicky is JVC's model 8240, with a fairly useless woofer, tweeter, and joystick tone control.

RADIOS

From the electronic point of view, the greatest expansion of new models is in the areas of multiband and digital clock radios. Until recently, "multiband" referred to the shortwave portion of the dial that picked up the overseas broadcasts of the BBC, Radio Japan, Radio Moscow, or a thousand other international stations transmitted to North America. But now "multiband" has come to refer to a radio that intercepts local public-safety stations that operate on two-way radio: police, fire, ambulance, taxis, trucks, civil defense, aircraft, Coast Guard, and dozens of others.

If you intend to do much listening to the multiband portion of your set, you should consider paying the extra cost for the squelch control. Mobile radios transmit only brief messages with long intervals of static in between. The squelch control will silence those long intervals. Panasonic offers a portable with a weatherband (Model RF-822) that incorporates another interesting feature—it floats. That should make this multiband unit of special interest to boat owners. It also has a microphone mixing feature: you plug in a mike, sing with the radio, and your voice comes out of the speaker.

Of all clock radios sold in 1974, 70 percent were digital. So for 1975, all manufacturers are adding new digital clock radios to their line-up. Zenith, for example, has doubled the number of digital clock radios in its '75 line. Most of the digitals are actually mechanical movements with flip-card numerals, an illuminated tape, or rotating number drums. If you choose a model with flip cards, test the unit to make sure the numbers flip quietly. That click of the cards which occurs every minute could be disturbing to a light sleeper.

The greatest number of complaints about digital clock radios have been about the illumination of the numbers. Because they are usually placed by the bedside, the complaints have been that the numbers are either too bright for comfort, or too dim for clarity. You will have to test the unit of your choice at home before you will know if it falls into either of those catagories. For 1975, General Electric is offering a "blacklight" feature on its clock radios. This spooky display causes the digits to glow in the dark for good visibility at night. Hitachi is offering a somewhat expensive dimmer switch which controls the display's brightness. A most unusual and versatile clock radio is being manufactured by MGA (Model RWD-90). This one features a piggyback arrangement between the clock and the radio. You can listen to the radio while away from home by lifting out the top section, which is a small portable radio.

The great popularity of digital clocks has not meant the demise of the dial-and-hands versions that consumers have become so used to. Most manufacturers still have these units in their line-up, at least for the moment. But the digital-clock-radio boom has meant a lowering of the prices on these "old-fashioned" models, so they now offer the best bargains.

The low-priced novelty portables also remain popular for 1975. These are normally under $10 and are AM only. Admiral offers a "bike" AM that fastens to a bicycle, and General Electric sells a portable that looks like a can of Coke, Pepsi, Budweiser, and other brews.

RADIOS
Choosing a Radio

THE MATTERS that should concern you the most when shopping for a radio are the particular unit's intelligibility, sensitivity, ease of tuning, antenna effectiveness, and its power source. Most of these features cannot be tested in a showroom, but must be taken home and tried out in your own environment. Therefore, buy a radio only from a reputable dealer who will allow you to return an unsatisfactory model for refund or exchange.

Radios typically have speakers that run in size from about two to six inches in diameter. You can normally generalize that wider speakers deliver more pleasing musical sounds. But it is not so easy to determine the quality of sound a speaker will deliver during spoken transmission—its intelligibility. The way to test the intelligibility of a unit is to take the radio home and tune it to a program carrying a speaking voice. Listen to the words. Turn up the volume in a series of small increases, and critically appraise whether you can still understand each syllable. Some radios simply cannot sustain higher volume levels without the audio breaking into a mushy distortion that is annoying or incomprehensible to the ear. Of course, good intelligibility also improves the quality of musical programs. This may be an important factor if you plan to use the radio outdoors, in a workshop, or anywhere else it must compete with other sounds.

Sensitivity refers to the number of stations a radio can pick up, and from what distance. On the lowest-price sets, expect to hear only nearby stations on the AM band. If you do not get good reception there is little you can do to improve matters—short of returning the radio for a more sensitive model. On FM, however, you may be able to improve a set that picks up too few stations. You can adjust the telescoping whip antenna, or place the radio in another part of the room, or, if it has a line-cord antenna, reroute the wire to find stronger signals, or, as a last resort, install an outdoor antenna. If none of these tactics work, the radio does not have sufficient sensitivity to satisfy your needs, and you should exchange it.

Some radios operate with too much sensitivity, and this can be just as annoying. An over-sensitive set cannot handle a too-strong FM signal. If you live near an FM station, the receiver may be unable to control the signal strength effectively, and the result will be highly distorted audio in the loudspeaker. Cross-modulation is a closely related problem. The symptom is easy to hear: the same station appears at many points along the dial. A problem experienced by people who live near airports or near the antenna of a fire or police station is a false response, called "image." While listening to a favorite program, you may suddenly hear something like "out of 10 for 4." What you hare hearing are the voices of pilots speaking on an adjacent aircraft band that gets trapped within the circuits of your FM set. Image normally occurs with inexpensive FM sets only. If you experience any of these problems, your FM set is too sensitive; if it is annoying to you, you will have to exchange the set for another, less sensitive, one.

RADIOS

The most important physical feature of a radio is its dial and knob layout. Try each knob on the radio; grasp each control to see if it has a sufficient depth for comfortable feel. Be wary of multiband sets with band-changing knobs that hurt the fingers because of stiff resistance and poor leverage. Try the sliding levers that have now replaced the familiar rotating controls on many radios; some people find these levers difficult to adjust.

Since the tuning dial is the most frequently used control of all, give it special scrutiny. As a general rule, as the price goes up, the rate at which the tuning dial moves goes down. Frequently, when you turn the dial of a low-cost radio, so many stations whiz by that tuning becomes a tricky chore. Better sets have mechanical gearing that slows the tuning rate to help separate the stations on the dial. More expensive receivers have a slide-rule arrangement, in which a pointer moves in a straight line across a numbered dial face. A good test for AM radios is to check how easily you can tune and separate stations which lie in the upper half of the standard broadcast band (between 100 and 160 on the dial). Accuracy of the dial numbers may improve with price, but after a few days' listening you will learn the location of your favorite stations on any AM or FM bands.

Another technical problem that involves tuning, but which is also in the realm of sensitivity is poor selectivity. Selectivity is a measure of a radio's ability to separate stations that are closely spaced on the dial. Poor selectivity causes you to hear two signals at once.

Whether or not you should be concerned about an antenna is dependent upon your geographic location. If you live in an urban area with many satisfying local stations an antenna is often unimportant. However, if your tastes spill beyond your town (especially for FM), a radio's antenna provisions become important.

The most common FM antenna for table radios is the line-cord, which taps into the radio's power cord plugged into the wall outlet. This may work well when your home is within the FM station's primary service area—about 25 to 50 miles. To squeeze the most from a line-cord antenna in a fringe area, however, you may have to place the cord in different positions until you discover a good compromise between the least static and the most stations received.

If you live a great distance from FM transmissions or want to receive the most stations with greatest clarity, an external or outdoor antenna can bring vast improvement. Turn the radio around and look at the back panel to see if there is a place for an external FM antenna. With most radios there are simple instructions which explain how to remove the line-cord connection and replace it with an external antenna, which can be anything from TV rabbit ears to a true FM antenna mounted outdoors.

FM portables are fitted with telescoping whip antennas, clearly visible at the tops of the cases, which are a distinct advantage for receivers that are carried outdoors or shifted among rooms in a home. The whip is mounted on a swivel, permitting you to angle the antenna for best reception. The same antenna is frequently used for reception on the various high-frequency bands that capture weather.

CONSUMER GUIDE

RADIOS

The type of power source is another basic item to check before buying. The radio's back cover is usually detachable to allow you to inspect the markings and determine the battery type. The smallest sets are cells—which give longer life or help drive a larger speaker—are also common. D cells (flashlight size) are occasionally found in very large sets. Since big portables can also double as table radios at home, many include a built-in AC connection to operate from house current. In deluxe models, a built-in charger can rejuvenate worn batteries from house current. One accessory of interest to boat and car owners who want to use their sets in motion is a DC adaptor, or special cord, which plugs into the 12-volt source (through the cigarette lighter) and provides the correct operating voltage.

Finally, even the best manufacturers suffer occasional lapses in quality control; therefore, inspect the radio you are buying for a crack in the cabinet, loose trim, broken knobs, faulty dial dirve, and other obvious mechanical and structural defects. Before you leave the store listen to the radio at several volume settings, and run the dial back and forth fully. Have the salesperson, if possible, install the batteries or plug in the line cord. Auditioning a radio out of the carton not only exposes gross electronic defects but also uncovers another notorious problem: a radio that has been returned as defective by an earlier customer. More than one bad radio has been mistakenly returned to "good" stock.

SPECIAL INFORMATION SERVICE
A Bonus for Readers of this CONSUMER GUIDE

CONSUMER GUIDE offers a special bonus to its readers who are interested in obtaining information as to where they can find the low prices on specific products listed in this guide. Simply fill out the form and mail. Please include 25 cents for postage and handling.

Please send me information on:

Product _____ Model Number _____

Manufacturer _____

Product _____ Model Number _____

Manufacturer _____

Your Name _____

Address _____

City _____ State _____ Zip Code _____

CONSUMER GUIDE Magazine
3323 West Main, Skokie, Illinois 60076

RADIOS

BEST BUYS — RADIOS

CONSUMER GUIDE Magazine has examined the lines of all the major manufacturers of radios, and has judged them in terms of their styling and performance. The following Best Buys are those that excelled in such features as sensitivity, intelligibility, and ease of control.

PORTABLE RADIO

Zenith E74J is a noteworthy AM-FM portable fitted with a large speaker (3x5-inch), which delivers an excellent tone quality from a moderate-size cabinet. Unlike some personal-size sets, there is no hiss and screech, and a built-in AC cord enables this model to do double-duty as a portable and as a table radio. Although there is no provision for an outside antenna–which may be a problem if you are some distance from the station–there is a built-in telescoping whip that should pull in all but the most remote stations. The controls are well-marked and up front, making the E74J a pleasure to adjust, but it may take a while to grow accustomed to the cramped slide-type levels.

Suggested Retail Price: $39.95   Low Price: $34.75

TABLE RADIOS

JVC 8806 produced consistently good audio. The fine sound is achieved through a spacious cabinet with enough vertical area to accommodate front-facing 4- and 2-inch speakers. The sides of the cabinet are tapered to form a broad base that eliminates the danger of tipping which is inherent in tall radios. Controls are a pleasure to grasp and turn; the dial drum has clear, softly illuminated numbers; and a molded-in handle makes the radio easy to tote. "Front-end" sensitivity of the circuit snared plenty of fringe-area FM stations on the line cord alone, but there is provision for an external antenna as well. The JVC 8806 comes with an earphone.

Fair Trade Price: $59.95   Low Price: $42.00

Sony TFM-9450 is a radio for people who are not satisfied with the routine sound of a table model, but who do not want to pay for an expensive hi-fi receiver. The TFM-9450 can be thought of as a gap-filler, with price and performance falling somewhere between major catagories. As an AM-FM table radio, it is among the most costly in its

CONSUMER GUIDE

RADIOS

class, but it delivers a musical performance that is clearly superior to most others. The hefty 6-1/2-inch speaker and a solid, spacious wood cabinet are responsible for the TFM-9450's superior performance. Its circuits offer loudness compensation to boost highs and lows at soft listening levels, and it has an effective tone control. Illuminated dial and switchable AFC are also included.

Fair Trade Price: $59.95   **Low Price: $51.78**

CLOCK RADIOS

General Electric C2425 *illustrates how a budget buyer can find a surprising value at the bottom of a clock radio line. Model C2425 is AM-only, and the clock uses the old-fashioned dial-and-hands movement, yet it includes the important wake-to-music function. The cabinet, which measures 8x5x4, houses a 4-inch speaker, and the dial operates on a convenient slide-rule drive. Although GE offers one of the most elaborate and complete clock radio lines in the industry, the C2425 is worth considering if you want the most function for the least number of dollars.*

Suggested Retail Price: $15.95   **Low Price: $13.43**

Hitachi KC-783 *AM-FM clock radio is a small contemporary cube which can sit on a bedside table without taking much room. Despite its small cabinet area, tone quality is acceptable and free of the stridency heard in many small radios. Only the clock numerals are illuminated, not the radio dial. The dial face follows a recent (but not new) trend to place station frequencies on a rotating drum and to keep the dial pointer stationary; a system that makes tuning easy. Most controls, however, are mounted on the cabinet side, and their labels are hidden from view (unless you rotate the radio). Since it takes a while to memorize what each control does, their location must be considered a minor inconvenience. The FM section has an AFC circuit to pin down stations electronically, but the AFC can be defeated if it interferes with weak-signal reception. In addition, the KC-783 features a 24-hour alarm timer and a 60-minute sleep switch.*

Suggested Retail Price: $59.95   **Low Price: $48.00**

MULTIBAND RADIOS

Lafayette Guardian 6600 *features a good mix of bands and functions that should prove especially attractive to the boater. In addition to AM and FM bands, the Lafayette Guardian 6600 pulls in marine beacon stations, the high public-service band which also harbors a new marine band for boat communications. Because of the rotating antenna atop its case, the Guardian 6600 can also be used as a simple radio-direction finder for the small-boat navigators who must find their way by radio beacons in fog or darkness. In fact, there is a tuning meter whose needle dips to signal compass bearings. Other features are a squelch*

RADIOS

control, telescoping whip antenna, large slide-rule dial, and VHF weather channel.
Suggested Retail Price: $99.95 **Low Price: Not Available**

Zenith RE94Y *concentrates on the public-service bands as part of its multi-band feature, and also turns in a creditable performance on FM and AM. The RE94Y eliminates the numerical confusion of some receivers and presents clearly marked bands in the three important VHF categories (Lo, Hi, and Aircraft)–plus the latest UHF coverage. The crucial bandswitch is a mechanical pleasure to operate, as a red indicator instantly signals the band in operation; this can be ambiguous on other models. A fine-tuning dial aids in seeking out elusive high-band stations, and other features include squelch and tone control, headphone, and built-in AC cord. Because of its outstanding music reproduction and its intelligent panel layout, the RE94Y definitely deserves a "Best Buy" rating.*
Suggested Retail Price: $99.95 **Low Price: $81.70**

SPECIAL INFORMATION SERVICE
A Bonus for Readers of this CONSUMER GUIDE

CONSUMER GUIDE offers a special bonus to its readers who are interested in obtaining information as to where they can find the low prices on specific products listed in this guide. Simply fill out the form and mail. Please include 25 cents for postage and handling.

Please send me information on:

Product _____ Model Number _____

Manufacturer _____

Product _____ Model Number _____

Manufacturer _____

Product _____ Model Number _____

Manufacturer _____
(PLEASE PRINT)

Your Name _____

Address _____

City _____ State _____ Zip Code _____

CONSUMER GUIDE Magazine
3323 West Main, Skokie, Illinois 60076

RADIOS

1975 Radio Prices

ADMIRAL

DIGITAL CLOCK RADIOS
CRF281	AM/FM	$29.95
CRF1123	AM/FM	39.95

MULTIBAND DIGITAL CLOCK RADIOS
CRM1131	4-Band	$49.95
CRM1143	4-Band	59.95
CRM1151	4-Band	69.95

PORTABLE RADIOS
PR293	AM, Pocket	$6.95
PRF1103	AM/FM, Pocket	14.95
PRF971	AM/FM, Pocket	15.95

MULTIBAND RADIOS
PRM941	4-Band, Portable	$23.95
PRM1127	5-Band, AC-DC	39.95
PRM1137	6-Band, AC-DC	49.95
PRM1141	9-Band, AC-DC	79.95

	$27.70
	36.00

	$43.00
	52.00
	59.95

	$6.50
	12.95
	13.95

	$20.95
	35.95
	42.95
	69.95

GENERAL ELECTRIC

AM MINIATURE PORTABLE RADIO
P2710	Long-Range, Direct Tuning	$11.95	$9.56

P1783	Pabst, AM Portable	12.95	8.96
P2780	Coke, AM Portable	12.95	8.96
P2786	Pepsi, AM Portable	12.95	8.96
P4792	Budweiser	12.95	8.96

AM TABLE RADIO
T2105	Solid State	$13.95	$11.36

FM/AM TABLE RADIOS
T2310	Compact	$19.95	$16.16
T2320	4" Magnet Speaker	23.95	19.16
T2330	3-dimensional grille design	34.95	27.56

AM CLOCK RADIOS
C2425	Compact	$15.95	$13.43
C2430	Wake-to-Music or Music Alarm	23.95	19.16

FM/AM CLOCK RADIOS
C4501	Wake-to-Music	$24.95	$20.36
C4506	Wake-to-Music or Music Alarm	37.95	29.36
C4530	Wake-to-Music or Music Alarm	37.95	29.36

AM DIGITAL CLOCK RADIO
C4205	Large Lighted Numerals	$32.95	$26.36

FM/AM DIGITAL CLOCK
C4315	Lighted Numerals	$35.95	$29.96

RADIOS

FM/AM MINIATURE PORTABLE RADIOS
P4715	W/Outboard Antenna	$14.95	$11.96
P4716	W/Outboard Antenna	14.95	11.96
P4717	W/Outboard Antenna	14.95	11.96

FM/AM PERSONAL PORTABLE RADIOS
P4810	2-Way Power w/Build-in-Cord	$25.95	$21.56
P977	Vertical Style, 2-Way Power	32.95	26.36

FM/AM/INSTANT WEATHER
P4845	Slide Rule Dial	29.95	23.96

FM/AM/TV-AUDIO RADIOS
P4930	Receives FM/AM,TV Audio VHF Channels 2-13	29.95	23.96
P4931	Receives FM/AM,TV Audio VHF Channels 2-13	29.95	23.96

MULTI-BAND PORTABLE RADIOS
P4910	3-Band w/Weather, 2-Way Power	$32.95	$26.36
P4920	3-Band 2/Weather, 2-Way Power	32.95	26.36
P4950	5 Band w/Squelch Control on FM	48.95	38.96
P4960	8 Band w/Instant Weather, Shortwave	74.95	58.76
P4970	10 Band w/Squelch control for UHF	104.95	80.36

DESIGN SERIES
P2755	Soundscene, Change Pictures	$7.95	$5.96
P2775	UFO Sound Saucer, AM	15.95	11.96
P2765	Orbiter, Spins Freely on Base	15.95	11.96

CAN RADIOS
P1780	Schlitz, AM Portable	$12.95	$8.96

C4310	Large Lighted Numerals	41.95	33.56
C4321	Large Lighted Numerals	48.95	38.36

JVC

PORTABLE
8240	VHF/FM/AM, AC/DC	$109.95	$75.60
8220	FM/AM, AC/DC	64.95	46.20
8205b	FM/AM, AC/DC	59.95	42.00
8210	FM/AM, AC/DC	54.95	37.80
8202	FM/AM, AC/DC	44.95	31.08
8000	AM, DC	15.95	10.44

TABLE RADIOS
8008	AM, DC	$19.95	$13.44
8806	FM/AM, Solid State	59.95	42.00
8805	Square Sound FM/AM	49.95	34.56

DIGITAL CLOCK
9031	Solid State FM/AM	$64.95	$46.20

PORTABLE FM/AM RADIO W/CASSETTE RECORDERS
9407	Deluxe w/Review System	$159.95	$113.40
9425	Deluxe w/Built-In Condensor Mic.	149.95	109.20
9403	W/Anti-Rolling Device, Sleep Timer	129.95	92.40
9310	W/Review System, ALC	119.95	84.00
9402	W/Built-In Condensor Microphone	109.95	75.60
9406	W/Automatic Head Cleaning	99.95	71.40
9401	W/Built-In Condensor Microphone	89.95	67.20

RADIOS

PANASONIC

	Retail	Discount
TECH SERIES - INFORMATION BAND RADIOS		
PSB-VHF High-VHF Low-UHF		
RF-1004/	$59.95	$49.95
Tech-200		
RF-1060/	69.95	59.95
Tech-400		
RF-940/	109.95	89.95
Tech-700		
RF-888/	125.00	99.95
Tech-800		
RD-9844	59.95	49.95
FM/AM MULTIBAND PORTABLE		
RF-1700	$169.95	$149.95
FM/AM PORTABLE		
RF-508	$21.95	$19.88
RF-519	32.95	27.88
RF-564	42.95	32.95
RF-594	52.95	42.95
RF-933	59.95	49.95
RF-900	69.96	59.95
RF-973	99.95	79.95
SPECIAL FM RADIO HEADSET		
RF-40	$104.95	$85.00

RCA

		Retail	Discount
AM PORTABLE			
R-1013		$11.95	$ 9.88
R-1052		13.95	11.88
R-5252		13.95	11.88
R-1492		18.95	16.88
R-1493		24.95	22.88
AM TRANSISTOR PORTABLE MODELS			
RZG101J	Gray	$ 6.99	$ 6.05
RZG102N	Sun Gold	6.99	6.05
RZG117E	Black	19.95	16.45
RZG338J	Gray (Earphone Only)	6.99	6.05
AM/FM TRANSISTOR PORTABLE MODELS			
RZM142JB	Gray/Black	$17.95	$15.25
RZM158E	Black/Brown	25.95	21.95
RWM168E	Black	34.95	28.50
RWM172A	Blue Denim	47.95	39.00
RWM173E	Black	42.95	35.15
RWM179E	Black	54.95	44.00
RWM68EV	Black	42.95	35.15
MULTI-BAND PORTABLE MODEL			
RWM690EV	Black	$47.95	$39.00
TABLE AM RADIO			
RZA203T	Brown	$16.95	$14.25

RADIOS

DIGITAL CLOCK RADIOS
RC-1103	$39.95
RC-8003	49.95
RC-6004	56.95
RC-6253	59.95
RC-6234	64.95
RC-6354	74.95
RC-7053	79.95
RC-6304	79.95
RC-6493	99.95
RC-7462	99.95
RC-7254	99.95

SPECIAL CLOCK RADIOS
RC-7243	$69.95
RC-6500	84.95
RC-6900	169.95

MONAURAL TABLE RADIOS
R-70	$14.95
R-7007	14.95
R-72	—
R-7272	—
R-63	17.95
RF-93	27.95
RE-6192	27.95
RE-6283	49.95
RE-6513	59.95
RE-7273	69.95

	$29.95
	39.95
	46.95
	49.95
	54.95
	59.95
	69.95
	69.95
	79.95
	79.95
	79.95

	$59.95
	75.00
	149.95

	$11.88
	11.88
	—
	—
	14.88
	24.88
	24.88
	39.95
	49.95
	59.95

TABLE AM/FM RADIO
RZC221Y	White	$27.95
RWC229Y	White	34.95
RZC723WV	Walnut Grain	29.95

AM CLOCK MODELS
RZD405B	Tan	$21.95
RWD423Y	White	31.95
RWD427W	Walnut Grain	34.95

AM/FM CLOCK MODELS
RWS441W	Walnut Grain	$34.88
RWS449W	Walnut Grain	39.95
RWS450A	Blue Denim	49.95
RWS450B	Tan/Brown	49.95
RWS453R	Rosewood Grain	54.95
RWS470W	Walnut	59.95

$23.05
28.55
24.75

$18.15
26.35
28.55

$28.55
32.95
40.65
40.65
43.95
49.00

SANYO

RADIO/PHONO PORTABLE STEREOCAST RADIOS
Model	Price	Price
RP5210		$17.95
RP5310		22.45
RP5000	$23.95	26.95
RP9210	31.95	26.95
RP5350	34.95	26.95
RP6000	34.95	35.95
RP7410	34.95	35.95
RP8120	44.95	35.95
	44.95	
	44.95	

CONSUMER GUIDE

RADIOS

	Retail	Discount
RP7220	54.95	44.95

CLOCK RADIOS
RM5320	$44.95	$35.95
RM7320	54.95	44.95

RADIO/PHONOGRAPHS
SPT1100	$44.95	$35.95
RPT1200	44.95	35.95

SONY

CLOCK MODELS
		Retail	Discount
TR-C340	Mini AM Digimatic	$24.95	$21.84
TFM-C430W	Compact FM/AM Digimatic	44.95	39.36
TFM-C444W	FM/AM Digimatic	44.95	39.36
TFM-C450W	3 Band Digimatic	49.95	43.74
8 FC-100W	Compact FM/AM Digimatic	49.95	43.74
TFM-C550W	Compact FM/AM/VHF Weather Digimatic	54.95	47.46
TFM-C650W	FM/AM Digimatic	59.95	53.22
TFM-C660W	FM/AM Day-Date Digimatic	69.95	62.10
TFT-C770W	FM/AM Day-Date Digimatic	79.95	69.06
TFM-C390W	Space-Saving FM/AM	29.95	26.22
TFM-C490W	Compact FM/AM	39.95	34.98

ZENITH

		Retail	Discount
AM SOLID STATE RADIOS			
E210P	Gold	$16.95	$14.84
E210W	White	16.95	14.84
F214W	Walnut	16.95	14.84
E214W	Walnut	18.95	16.52
FM/AM SOLID STATE TABLE RADIOS			
F410P	Gold	$29.95	$25.76
F420W	Walnut	36.95	31.85
F425W	Walnut	59.95	50.40
E430W	Walnut	79.95	63.84
AM SOLID STATE CLOCK RADIOS			
E258P	Gold	$19.95	$17.92
E258W	White	19.95	17.92
F252W	Walnut	24.95	22.40
E266W	Walnut	24.95	22.40
DIGITAL AM SOLID STATE CLOCK RADIOS			
F260P	Gold	$32.95	$28.00
F260W	White	32.95	28.00
F262R	Rosewood	36.95	31.36
FM/AM CLOCK RADIOS			
F450P	Gold	$34.95	$30.25
F452W	Walnut	39.95	33.88

RADIOS

DESK & TABLE MODELS
TFM-1859W	FM/AM Desk Top	$29.95
TFM-9430W	FM/AM Table on Pedestal	39.95
TFM-9440W	FM/AM Table	49.95
TFM-9450W	FM/AM Table Radio	59.95

PORTABLE MODELS
TR-4100	Deluxe AM Pocketable	$ 9.95
TFM-3750W	FM/AM Pocketable Radio	24.95
TFM-3950W	VHF Weather, FM/AM Band	29.95
TR-6500	High Power AM	29.95
TFM-7150W	Compact, Lightweight FM/AM	34.95
TFM-7250W	FM/AM	44.95
TFM-7350W	FM/AM/VHR Lightweight Weather	54.95

MATRIX MODELS
MR-9100W	Compact, Lightweight FM Stereo, AM/FM	$79.95
MR-9400W	Compact, Lightweight FM Stereo, FM/AM	99.95

MULTI-BAND MODELS
ICF-5500W	Ultra-Compact 3-Band Port.	$99.95
ICF-8100WA	FM/AM & Continuous Weather	84.95
TFM-8000W	Powerful 6-Band Portable	149.95
CRF-5100	Deluxe Portable w/10 Band Receptions	279.95

TRANSCEIVERS
ICB-300W	All Weather Transistor	$79.95
ICB-1000W	All Weather Transistor	99.95

DIGITAL FM/AM SOLID STATE CLOCK RADIOS
F460P	Gold	$44.95
F460W	White	44.95
E465W	Walnut	44.95
F462W	Walnut	49.95
F462Y	Ebony	49.95
F472W	Walnut	59.95
F474W	Walnut	74.95

DIGITAL FM/AM SOLID STATE CLOCK RADIOS W/WEATHER BAND
F476W	Walnut	$79.95
F476Y	Ebony	79.95

DIGITAL FM/AM STEREO FM CLOCK RADIO
F480W	Walnut	$89.95

MINIATURE AM PORTABLES
RE10L	Beige	$ 9.95
RE10P	Gold	9.95
RE10W	White	9.95
RE16L-1	Beige	12.95
RE16Y-1	Ebony	12.95

PERSONAL FM/AM PORTABLES
RE20V	Orange	$16.95
RE20W	White	16.95
RE26W	Rosewood	29.95
RE26Y	Ebony	29.95

$25.50	$38.00
34.98	38.00
43.74	38.00
51.78	42.50
	42.50
$ 8.82	48.75
22.14	62.00
26.22	
26.22	$65.00
30.60	65.00
39.36	
47.46	$74.00
$69.06	$ 8.50
	8.50
85.14	8.50
	10.97
$80.34	10.97
72.36	
124.14	$15.00
	15.00
225.06	24.75
	24.75
$63.30	
79.14	

CONSUMER GUIDE

RADIOS

	Retail	Discount
FULL SIZE AM PORTABLE		
RE71J Brown	$32.95	$28.00
FULL SIZE FM/AM PORTABLES		
RF42J Brown	$32.95	$28.50
RF42P Yellow	32.95	28.50
RF42V Orange	32.95	28.50
RE47W Walnut	39.95	34.75
RE74J Brown	39.95	34.75
FULL SIZE FM/AM PORTABLE W/WEATHER BAND		
RF51Y Ebony	$44.95	$38.00
FM/AM PORTABLE — RECHARGEABLE		
RE27Y Ebony	$39.95	$33.75
MULTI-BAND PUBLIC SERVICE		
RF86Y Ebony	$69.95	$57.00
RF88Y Ebony	79.95	65.35
RE94Y Ebony	99.95	81.75
MULTI-BAND TRANSOCEANIC		
RD7000Y-1 Ebony	$329.95	$246.00

Prices are accurate at time of printing; subject to manufacturer's change.

SPECIAL INFORMATION SERVICE
A Bonus for Readers of this CONSUMER GUIDE

CONSUMER GUIDE offers a special bonus to its readers who are interested in obtaining information as to where they can find the low prices on sspecific products listed in this guide. Simply fill out the form and mail. Please include 25 cents for postage and handling.

Please send me information on:

Product _____ Model Number _____

Manufacturer _____
(PLEASE PRINT)
Your Name _____

Address _____

City _____ State _____ Zip Code _____

CONSUMER GUIDE Magazine 3323 West Main, Skokie, Illinois 60076

PERSONAL CARE

1975 PERSONAL CARE APPLIANCES

THE MOST obvious trend in consumer personal care products is toward professional-type equipment. The newest appliances—from high powered pistol-grip dryers to hot shaving lather dispensers—are designed to allow the user to handle his or her personal grooming at home with professional equipment that provides better results. From head to toe, there is now an electrical appliance to take care of every aspect of personal grooming and beauty—saunas for our complexions, massagers for our muscles, styling combs for our hair, and even wrinkle-chasers for our clothes. These portable, relatively inexpensive electric products help us look better, feel better and feel that we look better.

In this inflationary era, personal care products have become increasingly important—Americans are becoming more and more a do-it-yourself people. We need professional equipment for styling our hair at home instead of relying on the beauty or barber shop; irons and steam "guns" eliminate the need for having our clothes pressed by the dry cleaners, and dental aids help us keep our teeth in good condition and lessen our trips to the dentist.

Because of the proliferation of new products, new models, and new innovations on old models, shopping for a personal care appliance is

PERSONAL CARE

more difficult today than it has ever been. Consequently, it is important for the consumer to know just what is in the marketplace before making that all-important buying decision.

Following is a rundown of the wide, wide spectrum of 1975 personal care appliances. And although this report centers much attention on hair care—where there are more new products than ever before—it covers all the major categories including makeup mirrors, facial saunas, men's and women's shavers, hot lather dispensers, massagers, automatic toothbrushes, and irons.

HAIR CARE PRODUCTS

Pistol-Grip Hair Dryers

THE PISTOL-GRIP hair dryer, a direct descendant of the hand-held dryer/styler, is the one used professionally in beauty salons. It requires the user to hold the dryer in one hand while he or she styles the hair with a comb or brush (not included with the dryer) held in the other. Although the pistol-grip dryers are more awkward to use than the hand-held dryer/stylers, they have the advantage of greater drying speed. Most of the pistol-grip dryers are 1000 watts.

Until 1974 CONSUMER GUIDE Magazine would not recommend any hand-held dryer with a wattage rating of over 800. But as the wattage continued to rise, Underwriters Laboratories ordered stiffer requirements before dryer manufacturers could receive their approval. UL requires that the units be of heavy enough plastic to withstand the high temperatures produced by the powerful units, and that they have a thermostat and safety cutoff to prevent overheating. In addition, many manufacturers have eliminated from their units the exposed metal nozzles in order to prevent an accidentally burned hand.

But even with these safety precautions, CONSUMER GUIDE Magazine offers this advice to anyone considering purchase of one of these high-powered units:
- 1000 watts produce a lot of heat; therefore, such units can be dangerous for people with sensitive scalps or children.
- Two heat and air-flow settings are a must. The high heat and strong air-flow are used for drying; the low heat and slow air-flow are needed for styling.
- The pistol-grip dryers work best with a simple hair style. And they are not desirable for frizzy or thin and sparse hair.
- Higher wattage also means higher price. The wattage rating refers only to the highest speed and heat setting; considerably less wattage is used at the lower setting. If you do not really have much need for 1000 watts (if your hair is very short and dries quickly), save money by buying a lower-powered unit.
- Most of the 1000-watt units are alike. Therefore, when making your selection, buy the one with the lowest price—providing, of course, that it has the approval of Underwriters Laboratories.

Because most of the pistol-grip dryers work equally well, the man-

PERSONAL CARE

ufacturers have concentrated on other features besides the wattage to help sell their products.

General Electric, for example, has tried to solve the problem of having to hold the entire drying unit in one hand while drying and styling your hair. Their "Power Pro" comes with a stand which can cradle the dryer, directing the air flow at your head, thus leaving both hands free for styling.

GE's "Superblow Hair Care Center" combines a separate table-top power unit with four attachments that fit on the end of a hose coming from the power unit. The advantage is that you only have to hold the weight of the attachment instead of the weight of the entire dryer, motor and all. The disadvantage is that the hose coming from the power base is more confining than most cords. Another disadvantage is the price—the Superblow is the most expensive pistol-grip dryer on the market.

The special feature on Clairol's "Pro-Gun 1000" is its simple system of heat and air-flow control; it has push buttons, much like those found on blenders. The buttons are much easier to use than the rocker controls that are found on so many of the units. The rocker controls are two separate switches set side-by-side that can be used separately or together to create varying levels of heat and air-flow. Both the rocker controls and the push buttons offer more versatility than a single high-low switch.

If it is real professionalism you want, then look for the products of Continental Hair Products, a beauty salon supplier. They offer a variety of models under a number of brand names. The Conair Pro Styler (Model 060) with 1050 watts and two speeds is widely used in hair salons. The only difficulty you may encounter is finding the Continental products in a retail store.

Hand-Held Dryers

A HAND-HELD dryer/styler is a drying unit that comes with styling tools that attach right to the unit. The advantage of the styler/dryer over the pistol-grip dryer is that it is easier to use. The entire styling and drying process can be done with one hand.

Up until now, the major disadvantage of the hand-held dryers over the pistol-grips was the drying time. In general, the hand-held dryer/stylers have a much lower wattage than the pistol-grips. But that is changing. Several manufacturers have introduced styler/dryers for 1975 that approach the 1000-watt mark. Both Remington's new "Power Control" and Sunbeam's "Power Plus 900" have 900 watts of power. Both units are recommended to people who feel they need the drying power the high-wattage units offer. Both units are far more versatile and easy to use than the pistol-grip dryers. However, as with the pistol-grip dryers, CONSUMER GUIDE Magazine must warn against their use by children or by people with sensitive scalps.

The most common attachments found with the styler/dryers are a comb and a brush. But additional attachments are also offered by some

PERSONAL CARE

manufacturers. For example, Sunbeam's new "Triplet" has a detangler attachment; Gillette's "Super Curl 3 in 1" comes with two sizes of rollers; and Remington's "Power Control," mentioned earlier, has an optional mist attachment. Incidentally, if you do not need a high level of heat, but want the mist feature, look for Sunbeam's "Power Mist" for a real bargain.

When shopping for a styler/dryer, make sure that you do not buy more attachments than you will have need for; that would be a waste of money. Be certain that the attachments are substantial in design and fit the unit securely. And make sure that the unit is comfortable to hold.

Hard-Top and Bonnet Dryers

FOR THE WOMAN who sets her hair with rollers and who wants the same professionalism of the pistol-grip dryers, there are the hard-top dryers. Just as with the other dryers on the market, an important consideration of the hard-top dryers is their wattage. The newer hard-top dryers offer even higher wattage than do the pistol-grip dryers. But remember, a dryer with a high wattage rating MUST offer a variety of heat choices; few people could bear sitting under such uncomfortably hot heat for an entire drying process.

Another feature available on some of the newer models is mist. Schick's "Time Machine" can be bought with such a feature—it is also available without. CONSUMER GUIDE Magazine does not see any great advantage to a mist feature on any of the hair-care appliances. The same purpose can be accomplished by spraying the hair lightly with water. However, the "Time Machine" without mist is a versatile dryer. At 1400 watts, it has four heat settings and two wig settings. Another versatile unit is the General Electric "Touch 'N Tilt." With 1200 watts, it is a quick-drying unit, and the "Touch 'N Tilt" feature allows the hood to be adjusted to a variety of positions.

Worthy of special consideration is the Sunbeam Model HD25, once considered the fastest drying unit on the market. However, it was long ago surpassed by the newer high-powered machines. Still, this unit is highly recommended for people who are more interested in value than in extra-fast drying speed and extra-fancy features.

Before the portable hard-top dryers came on the market, there were the soft-bonnet dryers. Although these dryers generally do not dry as quickly as do the hard-top models, they offer the conveniences of mobility. With most of the bonnet dryers, a woman can move around the room while she is drying her hair. Another advantage of the soft-bonnet dryers is their price—they are generally less expensive than the hard-top variety.

Schick is the only company to introduce a new soft-bonnet dryer for 1975. With 750 watts, it is considerably more powerful than the other units on the market. In addition, its extra-long cord gives greater mobility. One of the most comfortable soft-bonnet dryers is Gillette's "Max Hatter." The motor is built into the top of the bonnet, which floats slightly from the head. Another nice feature of this machine is its price.

PERSONAL CARE

Sunbeam's "Jet Set Flair" is an interesting unit. It was recently updated to accept styling attachments, including a mist comb. Thus, it has become a combination bonnet dryer and styler/dryer.

Roller Hair Setters

ELECTRIC ROLLERS come in either dry or mist versions, and with either 20 or 27 rollers. As stated earlier, CONSUMER GUIDE Magazine does not think the mist feature is a very important one. The same job can be done easily with a spray bottle. Therefore, a person looking for economy should look at the dry units. Also, we have found that 20 rollers are usually sufficient, and that the larger units are more expensive without being very much more convenient to use.

An important thought to keep in mind when thinking of purchasing a set of rollers is that a hair style set with electric rollers, whether with mist or without, probably will not last longer than four hours. Only those women whose hair holds a set exceptionally well will have greater success with these units. The electric rollers are terrific to use for a quick set before going out for the evening or afternoon. But if you use them to set your hair in the morning, do not expect the set to last all day.

Clairol still offers the original electric rollers, the "Clairol 20", but for 1975 they have improved the rollers. The chief objection to the Clairol unit was that the hair inevitably got caught on the pointed prongs of the rollers, causing hair damage. Clairol has replaced the pointed prongs with spade-shaped ribs that hold the hair on the roller without causing tangling. They also have added a rim to the edge of the roller to keep the hair from slipping off. This is still one of the best units on the market because of its economical price and quick heat-up time.

If you are set on having a mist curler, look at Schick's "Lasting Curl." This is a mist-only unit that makes excellent use of space. And if you want a choice between mist and dry sets, there is Sunbeam's economical "Duet Set."

Curler/Stylers

THIS UPDATED VERSION of the old curling iron shares the number-one spot on the popularity polls with the pistol-grip dryers. Almost every manufacturer is introducing its version of this new appliance for 1975. In general, the features to look for are a heat-proof tip to prevent burned fingers, a swivel cord, and a coated rod to prevent the hair from sticking. Another important feature to look for is a heat-proof stand, either attached to the curler/styler or as a separate piece. You will find all of these features available on a multitude of units.

In 1974, Clairol introduced the first curler/styler with a no-stick finish. For 1975, they have come out with an economy version of that model. Priced 40 percent lower than the original, it lacks only the mist feature. Other units, such as the General Electric "Touch 'N Curl" and the Gillette "Super Curl" offer a variety of heat settings to control the tightness of the curl. Grandinetti offers a deluxe unit, the "Mark III"

PERSONAL CARE

which comes with three sizes of curlers, thus, combining the features of a curler/styler and electric rollers. Remember, each feature that you add to a unit adds to the price, so don't buy more features than you really need.

Features you can definitely avoid are an on/off switch and a cordless feature. No curler/styler should be left plugged in when it is not in use; therefore, the on/off switch is unnecessary. And the cordless feature adds a great deal of expense without adding much convenience. The only convenience is that the curler itself, which is heated by being inserted into a separate heating unit, does not have a cord to get in the way. But the swivel cord available on most units keeps the cord pretty much out of the way anyway. A real disadvantage of the cordless feature is that it takes much longer to curl your hair with such a unit because the curling wand must be occasionally reheated during the process.

Detangling Combs

A DETANGLING COMB, shaped like a giant toothbrush, has two rows of teeth that move back-and-forth to take tangles out of the hair. It is specifically designed for people with long hair. The most prominent unit on the market is Gillette's "Purrr." When the unit retailed for close to $20, even at discount, CONSUMER GUIDE Magazine felt that it was too expensive. But now that Gillette has cut the price more than in half, you might find it a useful item, especially for combing the long, tangled hair of children.

FACIAL AND BODY CARE

Lighted Makeup Mirrors

THE MINIMUM FEATURE a lighted makeup mirror must have is a choice of light settings. It should adjust to simulate office light, home light, day, and evening. Without this feature, there is no advantage of a separate lighted makeup mirror over the wall mirror that comes equipped in your bathroom. Another convenient feature to look for is a rotating mirror that can be switched from a regular mirror to a magnifying one.

Other features are available, but they all add to the price. You will find units that have adjustable side mirrors, a storage drawer, a travel case, or an electric outlet. Do not buy a unit with any of these features unless you feel you absolutely need them.

Two basic lighted makeup mirrors are Clairol's "True-to-Light V" and General Electric's Model IM-1. Both feature the four recommended light settings and a magnifying mirror. The G.E. unit also can be wall-mounted, which is a possible advantage. Clairol has added a new mirror to its line for 1975. The "Mirror Mirror" is simply a round mirror surrounded by a circle of light. It does not have adjustable light settings, making it undesirable for applying makeup. However, it has an attractively low price and might be considered by a man who wants the extra light and magnification for shaving.

PERSONAL CARE

Facial Saunas

THE PRIMARY PURPOSE of the facial sauna is to open the pores to allow complete removal of dirt and oils from the skin. The facial sauna is an exceedingly expensive way to do this; a hot, wet washcloth held on the face will accomplish the same thing. Therefore, CONSUMER GUIDE Magazine does not recommend the purchase of a facial sauna except for the most luxury-minded people. If you are one of those people, you might want to look at the Schick and Panasonic models. Both have cushioned-rimmed masks and a choice of heat settings.

Clairol's "Skin Machine" is a motorized brush designed to scrub the skin clean. It is particularly advertised to be used by adolescents. However, many dermatologists strictly forbid their adolescent patients from using a brush, or even a washcloth, on their faces, believing that such bacteria-laden articles can do more harm than good.

Men's Shavers

ALL OF THE recent improvements in men's shavers have been in the same direction: to try to match the closeness of a blade shave. No one has as yet succeeded. Norelco came close with their floating-head system. The Norelco Tripleheader (Model 35-T) is still one of the best shavers available, although the more expensive models in the Tripleheader line offer not as good a value. They offer a choice of closeness settings, but few people use any but the closest setting.

The flexible screen, or foil head, shavers also offer a close, comfortable shave. You must be cautious when using such shavers, though, to insure against damaging the soft flexible (replaceable) screens. Both Schick, with their "Fleximatic" line, and Ronson, with their 1000XL, offer excellent foil-head shavers.

Remington is introducing a new line of shavers for 1975, the "Radial Shaver." The big improvement over their previous shavers is that the head of the new model is angled and thus follows the contours of the face and neck better. As with the other Remington shavers, the blades are replaceable, this year with chromium.

Women's Shavers

THERE IS LITTLE new that has been developed for women in shavers. A few years ago, manufacturers started offering built-in lights in their units, but nothing to improve the shaving action. Norelco is the first manufacturer to develop a woman's shaver to match their men's shaver. Their new model 30LT is a Tripleheader for women. Remington also offers a woman's shaver to match their men's. The Lady Remington (Models MS-160 and MS-140) have the same angled head as the new Radial Shaver. But in this case the design of the men's shaver was probably taken from the design of the women's.

PERSONAL CARE

Hot Lather Dispensers

FOR THE MEN AND WOMEN who use blade shavers, there is the hot lather dispenser. These units are designed to hold an aerosol can of shaving cream, which it heats. All do an adequate job of heating the lather, so the primary features to look for is a unit that will accommodate your favorite shaving cream (take a can with you when you shop), and one that fits conveniently in the space you have available for it. One of the least expensive units on the market is Sunbeam's new "Lather Man," which is not much larger than the can it is designed to hold.

Massagers

MASSAGERS are available in two types: the Swedish-type which is a compact unit that fits over the back of the hand, so that the hand does the actual manipulating; and the handled version, which is a massager at the end of a long handle. The Swedish-type massager does a better job, but the handled-type allows you to reach out-of-the-way places, like your back. Some units offer a heat feature. The additional comfort the heat offers is minimal, so you can save money by forgoing that extra luxury. The most complete line of massagers, both Swedish-type and handled, is offered by Oster.

DENTAL CARE

Automatic Toothbrushes

AUTOMATIC TOOTHBRUSHES are available in several models: cord or cordless, and single action or dual action. The corded models are more efficient than their battery-operated counterparts because they do not run down and have to be recharged. Although the corded models are quite safe, many people still feel uncomfortable putting such a unit in their mouths. For them we recommend the cordless versions. There is no distinct advantage of a dual-action toothbrush over a single-action version as long as that single action is up-and-down, not side-to-side.

The original automatic toothbrush, the Broxodent, was introduced by Squibb more than 12 years ago, and it is still one of the best units on the market.

Water Pulsating Devices

DESIGNED TO SUPPLEMENT the toothbrush, not replace it, the water pulsating devices are often recommended by dentists. The device directs a narrow jet of water between the teeth, which helps to dislodge food particles and massages the gums. Both the Water Pik (Model 37) and Sunbeam's "Oral Jet Rinse" are recommended because of their compactness and ease to use.

PERSONAL CARE

CLOTHING CARE

Irons

THERE ARE PROBABLY more irons on the market than all the other personal care appliances put together. Irons are manufactured by at least a dozen companies and are available from the most simple —steam and dry—to the most complex—with steam, dry, spray, burst of steam, and self-cleaning features. How sophisticated a model you choose depends on how much ironing you do. If you do a lot of ironing, you can probably make use of all the features; if you iron only occasionally, a simple steam and dry iron will probably be adequate. If you live in an area with hard water, you may be particularly interested in the self-cleaning feature.

Other features that are available are Hamilton Beach's "No-Scorch" system, which indicates when the iron has reached the proper heat; and a non-stick coated soleplate, as that on the Panasonic irons. Proctor-Silex' Mary Proctor line of irons are made of a modular design so they can be easily repaired by simply replacing a module. In addition, all of the Proctor-Silex irons come with a unique guarantee which promises over-the-counter replacement for a defective iron instead of having to send it to a sometimes-inconveniently-located service center.

SPECIAL INFORMATION SERVICE
A Bonus for Readers of this CONSUMER GUIDE

CONSUMER GUIDE offers a special bonus to its readers who are interested in obtaining information as to where they can find the low prices on specific products listed in this guide. Simply fill out the form and mail. Please include 25 cents for postage and handling.

Please send me information on:

Product _____ Model Number _____

Manufacturer _____

Product _____ Model Number _____

Manufacturer _____

Your Name _____

Address _____

City _____ State _____ Zip Code _____

CONSUMER GUIDE Magazine
3323 West Main, Skokie, Illinois 60076

PERSONAL CARE

PERSONAL CARE BEST BUYS

The number of personal-care appliances on the market today is enormous. Here CONSUMER GUIDE Magazine lists just a few of what we consider to be the best of each kind of appliance. In judging what is best, we have taken into consideration construction, efficiency, price, and warranty.

PISTOL-GRIP DRYERS

General Electric Power Pro-1 *has four heat settings, an extra-wide nozzle for broad coverage, and a separate concentrator attachment for spot drying. A separate stand can cradle the dryer, leaving both hands free for styling.*
Suggested Retail Price: $28.98   **Low Price: $20.35**

Gillette Pro-Max *offers greater styling control than the G. E. model because of its three heat settings and two air speeds. In addition, a shorter nozzle than that found on most units makes this model particularly easy to handle. It, too, has an extra-wide nozzle and separate concentrator attachment.*
Suggested Retail Price: $31.99   **Low Price: $24.50**

HAND-HELD DRYERS

Clairol Air Brush Model AB-1, AB-2 *is rated at only 500 watts, but thanks to its superior air flow it performs better and faster than many higher-powered units. The unit is compact, easy to hold, and is ideal for traveling. There are two heat and air-flow settings.*
Suggested Retail Price: $23.99   **Low Price $17.98**

Sunbeam Power Mist 52-34, *with only 350 watts, is the slowest drying hand-held dryer tested. But with two heat settings and a mist feature, this is one of the best bargains available and is highly recommended for people whose hair dries quickly.*
Suggested Retail Price: $21.98   **Low Price: $15.42**

HARD-TOP DRYERS

General Electric Touch 'N Tilt HD-61SS *is the fastest hair dryer available. It has 1200 watts and four temperature settings. In addition, the*

PERSONAL CARE

versatile Touch 'N Tilt hood can be adjusted to a number of positions.
Suggested Retail Price: $33.98   **Low Price: $23.65**

Sunbeam 51-24 *is a bargain for people with finer hair that dries easily or for people with sensitive scalps which cannot tolerate the temperatures of the more powerful units. This unit has 725 watts, four heat settings, and a large hood to accommodate large rollers.*
Suggested Retail Price: $28.98   **Low Price: $19.83**

SOFT-BONNET DRYERS

Gillette Max Hatter *is one of the most comfortable bonnet dryers available. Its 15-foot cord also makes it one of the most mobile. With two heat settings, drying time is about average for bonnet dryers.*
Suggested Retail Price: $23.99   **Low Price: $17.99**

Ronson Escort Deluxe 35321 *is consistently highly rated for its high level of performance, comfort, and quietness. It comes in a luggage-type case, is extremely light, and has the added convenience of coming with styling attachments.*
Suggested Retail Price: $32.50   **Low Price: $21.14**

ROLLER HAIR SETTERS

Clairol 20 C-20-S, *with its new, improved rollers that are gentle with the hair, is one of the easiest and fastest to use. This is a dry-only unit. Although mist setters are the best sellers, it is not a certainty that they produce a better set or are better for the hair.*
Suggested Retail Price: $16.99   **Low Price: $12.93**

Sunbeam Duet Set 62-14 *is for the person who wants a choice between dry and mist setting at a low price.*
Suggested Retail Price: $27.98   **Low Price: $18.14**

CURLER/STYLERS

General Electric Touch 'N Curl CS-1 *offers the most features for the lowest price. In addition to the non-stick coating on the curling wand, there is a non-stick coating on the clamp that holds the curl on the wand. An indicator light shows when the unit is plugged in, the mist feature can be filled directly from the tap, and the heat-proof stand is built right into the handle. There are two heat settings.*
Suggested Retail Price: $20.98   **Low Price: $14.30**

Lady Schick Quick Curls C1-3 *is one of the few no-mist curlers on the market, and therefore, one of the least expensive. Although missing a light to indicate that the unit is plugged in, it has the other standard features.*
Suggested Retail Price: $14.98   **Low Price: $10.49**

PERSONAL CARE

DETANGLING COMBS

Gillette Purrr Power, we found, helps straighten curly hair, aids in styling Afro-type hair styles, and is ideal for combing children's long hair. Now that the price has been cut more than in half, CONSUMER GUIDE Magazine feels more comfortable about recommending it for these specialized uses.
Suggested Retail Price: $7.95   Low Price: $4.95

LIGHTED MAKEUP MIRRORS

Clairol True-to-Light V (LM-2) adjusts to four light settings. The mirror swivels from regular to magnifying and can be tilted so both mirror and light are always directed at the face.
Suggested Retail Price: $19.99   Low Price: $13.93

General Electric IM-1 is slightly bulkier and more expensive than Clairol's mirror, but offers an advantage that the Clairol mirror does not: a bracket for wall mounting, an advantageous feature for the person who has no counter space in the washroom. Two vertical rows of light adjust to the four standard light settings, and the mirror swivels from regular to magnifying.
Suggested Retail Price: $23.98   Low Price: $17.05

MEN'S AND WOMEN'S SHAVERS

Norelco Tripleheader 35T gives a close, comfortable shave using three floating shaving heads. In addition, there is a pop-up trimmer, dual voltage for traveling, and flip-top cleaning.
Suggested Retail Price: $35.00   Low Price: $28.68

Schick Flexamatic 400 has a super-thin flexible head that allows the blades to provide an exceptionally close shave. However, you must take special care not to damage the flexible screen (which can be replaced for $1.95). It also features an extra-wide trimmer.
Suggested Retail Price: $39.95   Low Price: $28.81

Lady Remington MS-160 and MS-140 is easy to maneuver, with their tapered handles and angled heads. There are two heads: one for legs and one for underarms, and replaceable chromium blades are available.
Suggested Retail Price: Not Available   Low Price: $15.55

HOT LATHER DISPENSERS

Sunbeam Lather Man 74-23 is one of the lowest priced units on the market. Although not much larger than the aerosal can it holds, it has all the standard features: on/off switch, ready light, and controlled heat.
Suggested Retail Price: $16.50   Low Price: $11.42

PERSONAL CARE

General Electric SCD-1 *is bulkier than the Sunbeam unit, but for not much more money offers a few extra features that are worthwhile. The G.E. unit can be wall-mounted, has a cord storage area, and, best of all, has a heating system which shuts off automatically, eliminating the possibility of leaving the unit on all day.*
Suggested Retail Price: $18.98   Low Price: $13.20

AUTOMATIC TOOTHBRUSHES

Squibb Broxodent, *the original automatic toothbrush, is available in a number of styles with several different types of brushes. It is a remarkably reliable unit with good brushing effectiveness.*
Suggested Retail Price: $22.95   Low Price: $15.99

IRONS

Sunbeam Today *is one of the most versatile of the steam and spray irons. It is compact and lightweight and can be used horizontally as a steamer. It is an ideal traveling iron as well as a handy iron for people who do only occassional ironing.*
Suggested Retail Price: $19.75   Low Price: $13.83

General Electric F110WHT *is for the person who irons regularly. It has all the conveniences one could need, but no unnecessary gimmicks. It is a steam, spray, or dry iron with a self-cleaning feature, built-in water-level indicator, fabric guide, and cord lift to allow ironing from both left and right. The G.E. model F92 is almost the same unit, lacking only the self-cleaning feature, but is less expensive.*
Suggested Retail Price: $33.98   Low Price: $22.75

1975 Personal Care Appliances Prices

DAZEY

		Retail	Discount
CURLING WAND			
1025	Beauty Curl	$9.95	$6.10
MASSAGERS			
1170	Back Massager	$34.95	$20.14
102	Hand Massager	14.95	8.91
4711	Heat Massager	14.95	8.91

DOMINION

		Retail	Discount
HAIR DRYERS			
3801	Dominion I, portable	$15.95	$10.24
3802	Dominion II, portable	19.95	12.81
3803	Mistie, portable w/Mist Comb &Dry	28.95	17.94
1837	Styling attachment	21.95	14.09
1845	Portable	26.95	17.29
1847	Salon, 750 watts	30.95	19.86
1850	Salon Mist, 750 watts	30.95	19.86
1855	Salon, 1000 watts		
	Salon w/Remote Control console, 1000 watts	34.95	22.42
1856	Salon Mist, 1000 watts	39.95	25.63

		Retail	Discount
IM2		28.98	20.65
SHAVE CREAM DISPENSER			
SCD1		$18.98	$13.20
STYLING COMBS			
STC1		8.98	6.60
STC1A		11.98	8.80
STC2		10.98	7.70
STYLING DRYERS			
SD1		$14.98	$10.90
SD2		14.98	10.90
SD4		18.98	13.45
SD3		21.98	15.65
PD1		23.98	17.05
DD1		27.98	19.80
PRO-1		28.98	20.35
SUPERBLOW THE HAIR CARE CENTER			
SB1		$36.98	$26.40
TOOTHBRUSHES			
TB5PK12		$14.98	$10.45
TB10		17.98	12.65

PERSONAL CARE

CURLERS & COMBS
1891	Gold Crown Carousel Mist Hair Setter	$26.95
3856	Comb Free Untangler	19.95
3850	Comb'n Dry Styling Brush Dryer	16.95

GENERAL ELECTRIC

CURLER/STYLER
CS-1	$20.98	$14.30

DETANGLER
DT1	$12.98	$9.65

HAIR DRYERS
HD19	$22.98	$15.95
HD2A	24.98	17.60
HD18	28.98	20.35
HD51	23.98	17.05
HD56	29.98	20.90
HD60	29.98	20.90
HD61SS	33.98	23.65
HD63SS	42.98	30.25
HD63	39.98	28.50

HAIRSETTER
HCD4	27.98	19.80
HCD5	22.98	15.95

LIGHTED MAKE-UP MIRRORS
IM1	$23.98	$17.05

TB9	22.98	15.95
TBC20	18.98	13.20
TBC21	22.98	15.95

WRINKLE REMOVER
WR1	$—	$3.55

IRONS
F110WHT	$33.98	$22.75
F110WH	30.98	21.75
F101WHT	27.98	19.85
F101	22.98	16.45
F95AV	23.98	17.00
F95AVT	25.50	18.05
F92WHT	20.98	15.65
F92	17.50	12.85
F118HRT	27.98	19.70
F78WHT	17.98	13.05
F78WH	16.98	12.35
F77	15.50	11.45
F79WH	17.50	13.20
F63T	13.98	10.35
F120HR	30.98	21.75
F116BL	23.98	17.05
F64	13.50	9.65

GRANDINETTI

DRYER/STYLERS
82	Professional Bio-Styler	$31.95	$23.95
72	Original Bio-Styler	30.00	22.50

CONSUMER GUIDE

PERSONAL CARE

		Retail	Discount
HB 7600	Mist 'N Dry 750 for men	29.95	21.22
HB 7601	Mist 'N Dry 750 for women	29.95	21.22
HB 6600	Shape 'N Dry 750	25.95	18.73
HB 5600	Quick Dry 750	19.95	14.35
HC 1107	Mod Comb	14.95	9.98
HP 4416	Untangler	18.95	12.48
HP 4606	Lady Norelco Hair Dryer	29.95	21.22

NORTHERN ELECTRIC COMPANY

LATHER DISPENSER
8301	Lather-Up	$16.95	$10.60

STYLING COMBS
1400	The Untangler	$17.95	$11.25
2302	Mist Styling Curling Wand	18.95	11.85
1596	Groommate	14.95	9.35
1595	Mister-Mist Grooming	21.95	13.75
1592	Mist 'n Curl Beauty	21.95	13.75

HAIR DRYERS & STYLERS
1836	The Northern "700", 700 watts	$23.95	$14.95
1851	The Northern "850", 850 watts	25.95	16.25
1852	The Northern "850", 850 Watts w/Mist	27.95	17.45
1821	Pro. Blower/Dryer, 700 watts	24.95	15.60
1826	Pro. Blower/Dryer, 1000 watts	29.95	18.70
1575	Carefree Floating Soft Bonnet Hair Dryers	19.95	12.45

		Retail	Discount
265	Traveler	25.00	18.75

CURLING IRONS
974	Mark III Multi-Size Kit	$30.00	$22.50
874	Dry Curl Professional	15.00	11.25
674	Dry Curl Hi-Style	10.00	7.50

HAMILTON BEACH

IRONS
876	No Scorch, Self-Clean, Burst-of-Steam/Spray, 65 Steam Vents	33.90	20.94
878	No Scorch, Self-Clean, Spray/Steam, Burst-of-Steam, 65 Steam Vents	33.99	20.99
869	No Scorch, Self-Clean, Burst-of-Steam, 65 Steam Vents	29.98	18.52
863	No Scorch, Spray/Steam, 44 Steam Vents	30.98	19.13
856	Steam/Dry, 21 Vent	19.98	12.34

HOOVER

IRONS
3900	Dry Iron	$11.95	$8.95
3961	Travel Iron, Spray/Steam/Dry	16.95	12.70
4001-01	Dry Iron, Channel-Steam	14.95	11.20
4018	Steam-Dry Iron, 25 Vents	15.95	11.95
4431	Spray/Steam/Dry, 46 Vents	19.95	14.95

PERSONAL CARE

4521	Spray/Steam/Dry, Wager Gauge		25.95 19.45
4526	Jetstream Spray Dry Iron		28.95 21.70
P3043	Steam/Dry Iron, Self Clean		21.95 16.45
P4051	Spray/Steam/Dry, Self Clean		24.95 18.70

HAIR DRYERS
G3501	Professional Type	$24.95	$18.70
G3503	Professional Type w/Manicure	29.95	22.45

NORELCO

SHAVERS
HP1304G	Rechargeable Tripleheader 50 V.I.P. Cord/Cordless	—	$39.95
HP1309G	Rechargeable Tripleheader III Deluxe		
	45RT Cord/Cordless	—	34.45
HP1118G	Tripleheader 40 V.I.P.	—	32.95
HP1119G	Tripleheader III 35T	—	28.68
HP1124G	Speedshaver II 20	—	17.45
HP1214G	Speed Shaver II Cordless 20B	—	14.95
HP2121	Lady Norelco Home Beauty Salon	—	23.95
HP2117	Lady Norelco Tripleheader 30LT	—	21.75
HP2114	Ladybug 20LB	—	15.55
HP2126	Ladybug 17LB	—	12.45
HP2108	Lady Shave 10L	—	7.95

HAIR CARE PRODUCTS
HB 1600	Curly Q	$19.95	$14.98
HP 1700	Quick Dry 1000	29.95	22.48

HAIRSETTERS
1528	Deluxe "Mist 20"	$22.95	$14.35
1536	The Switch Set, Mist or Dry	23.95	14.95
1533	The Switchable, Mist or Dry	29.95	18.70

LIGHTED MAKE-UP MIRRORS
1688	Standard Model	$11.95	$7.45
1600	Light 'n Look Lovely	16.95	10.60
1604	The Perfect Touch	29.95	18.70

FACIAL SAUNA
6204	Deluxe Beauty Mist	$15.95	$9.95

ORAL WATER JETS
6250	Standard Unit	$23.95	$14.95
6265	Standard Unit w/On/Off "Flo-Control"	27.95	17.45
6270	Deluxe w/On/Off "Flo-Control"	29.95	18.70

OSTER

WRINKLE REMOVERS/SEWING AIDS
690-01	Steam Wand	$19.95	$13.75
690-03	Steam Wand w/Case	24.95	17.70

ELECTRIC CLIPPER HAIRTRIMMING SETS
617-14	Oster 14-pc. Adj. Pivot Mtr. Set w/Light	$34.95	23.70

PERSONAL CARE

		Retail	Discount
606-14	Oster 14-pc. Adj. Pivot Mtr. Set	31.95	22.40
606-10	Oster 10-pc. Adj. Pivot Motor Set	25.95	17.90
284-16	Raycine 16-pc. Adj. Magnetic Motor Set	15.95	9.60
254-16	Raycine 16-pc. Magnetic Motor Set	13.95	8.50

ELECTRIC SHAVERS
325-02	Pro. Shaver for Men	$30.95	$21.50

ELECTRIC ANIMAL CLIPPER KITS
182-11	Raycine Adjustable Dog Trim, 11 pc.	$16.95	$12.00
96-10	Oster Pivot-Motor, Detach. Blade, 10 pc. Dog Trim	32.95	23.80
96-20	Oster Pivot-Motor, Detach. Blade, 10 pc. Dog Trim w/3 Grooming Aids	36.95	25.00

HAIR CARE PRODUCTS
381-05	Mist Set Curler Wand	$22.95	$15.90
376-01	Beauty Salon Dryer, Remote Control	29.95	20.60
366-01	Encore Hand Held Styler Dryer	28.95	20.20
366-11	Encore Hand Held Styler Dryer W/Attachments	32.95	23.10

STYLING SET
160-06	Deluxe Styler/Shaper Set	$24.95	$17.30

MASSAGE INSTRUMENTS
218-01	Infra-Red Heat	$14.95	$10.50
268-01	Infra-Red Massagett	28.95	20.20

		Retail	Discount
I-705H	Super-Steam, Spray, Steam, Dry w/Self Clean	28.95	18.80
I-706H	Super-Steam Iron, Steam, Dry w/Self Clean	25.95	16.85
I-629H	Modular Spray, Steam, Dry Iron w/Temp-o-Guide Chart	21.95	14.15
I-503H	Modular Steam & Dry Iron	18.95	12.05
I-101H	Steam & Dry Iron	15.95	10.40
I-812H	Auto. Dry Iron	12.95	8.30

REMINGTON

SHAVERS
RR-1	Radial Rechargeable World-Wide	—	$37.75
RC-5	Radial Cord Shaver	—	29.95
MK-4	Mark IV World-Wide Rechargeable	—	34.75
MK-C	Mark-C Compact Rechargeable	—	31.15
MK-3	Mark III Cord Shaver	—	27.55
MK-1	Mark I Cord Shaver	—	23.95
SF-2	Soft Foil World-Wide	—	26.35
MS-180	Lady Remington Cordless	—	20.35
MS-160	Lady Remington Cord Shaver	—	15.55
MS-140	Lady Remington Cord Shaver	—	15.55
MS-120	Lady Remington Cord Shaver	—	9.55

HAIR DRYERS, WANDS AND COMBS
PD-900	Power Control Dryer	$32.98	$22.25
PD-850R	Hand-Held Hair Dryer	26.98	17.60

PERSONAL CARE

754-01	Back	44.95	31.50
751-04	Hydro-Lax Foot	21.95	15.88
759-04	Hydro-Whirl Foot	34.95	24.50
146-01	Ultra Scientific Variable Intensity	54.95	38.00
136-01	Scientific II Two-Intensity	44.95	32.40
126-01	Scientific I Swedish Style	41.95	29.50
395-01	Infra-Red Heat, Long Handle	19.95	14.10
393-01	Massager, Long Handle	15.95	11.50

PANASONIC

ELECTRIC SPRAY, STEAM AND DRY IRONS

NI-01D	Dry Iron, Non-Stick Soleplate, Dial Selector	$19.95	$12.88
NI-02SH	Steam/Dry, Auto. Clean, Non-Stick Soleplate	24.95	17.88
NI-03SH	Power Spray, Auto. Clean, Non-Stick Soleplate	28.95	20.95
NI-05SH	Booster Steam, Dual Settings, Auto. Clean, Push-Button	33.95	23.95
NI-07SS	Power Spray, Auto. Clean, Booster Steam, Dual Settings	35.95	26.95

PROCTOR-SILEX

STARFLITE IRONS

I-704H	Super Steam Iron, Spray, Steam, Dry/Self Clean Action, Teflon Soleplate	$31.95	$20.75

PD-850M	Mist Hand-Held Dryer	28.98	18.98
PD-600	Super Hand-Held Dryer	23.98	15.88
CW-1	Lady Remington Curling Wand	22.98	15.25
HP-1000	Hot Pistol Blower/Dryer	31.98	21.20
HW-4	Mist Air Hot Comb	12.98	8.20
HW-1B	Lady Remington Mist Air Hot Comb	12.98	8.20
HW-3	Hot Comb	10.98	7.00
HC-8	Lady Remington Mist Hair Curler	17.48	11.50
UC-1	Lady Remington Untangle Comb	17.98	11.98

RONSON

SHAVERS

22601	1000 Electric	$27.50	$19.30
22602	1000XL Electric	32.50	22.81
22202	Cobra Cordless Elec.	39.50	28.68
22218	Cobra Cordless Elec.	49.50	35.63

PORTABLE HAIR DRYERS

35321	Escort Deluxe	$32.50	$21.14
35901	Jetstar Hair Dryer	19.95	13.14
35601	Coiffeur Deluxe	34.95	21.23

RIGID HOOD HAIR DRYERS

35504	Salon Mode/Standard	$79.95	$56.08
35502	Salon Mode/Deluxe	99.50	67.06

ELECTRIC SHOE POLISHERS

77210	Roto-Shine Magnetic	$29.50	$19.42
77217	2-Speed Deluxe Roto-Shine	37.50	24.83

PERSONAL CARE

ELECTRIC TOOTHBRUSHES

		Retail	Discount
71011	Cordless Rechargeable, Std.	$27.50	$18.12
71010	Cordless Rechargeable, Deluxe	32.50	21.80

SCHICK

HAIR DRYERS

		Retail	Discount
2001	Lady Schick Time Machine	$39.98	27.98
2002	Lady Schick Time Machine w/Mist	49.98	31.57
322	Lady Schick Beauty Salon	37.98	25.68
316	Lady Schick Deluxe Capri Consolette	35.98	23.60
317	Lady Schick Consolette	28.98	18.52
327	Lady Schick Style Dryer	24.98	16.34
325	Lady Schick Tote N Dry	19.98	12.66
1776	Freedom Machine	24.98	17.49
337	Lady Schick Free Style Dryer	19.98	12.91

MEN'S STYLING DRYERS

		Retail	Discount
361	Samson Mist Styling	$28.98	$19.68
351	Samson Styling	25.98	17.48
339	Schick Styling	19.98	13.76
336	Schick Styling	15.98	10.49

LADIES' STYLING DRYERS

		Retail	Discount
362	Lady Schick Mist Speed	$28.98	$19.68
352	Lady Schick Speed	25.98	17.48
340	Lady Schick Air	19.98	13.76
338	Lady Schick Styling	15.98	10.49

		Retail	Discount
50-18	Flair Hair Dryer, Slim Silhouette Style Case	18.50	12.62
50-24	Jet Set Flair Dryer/Mist Styler, Silhouette Style Case	28.50	19.51
51-24	Portable Pro. Type Hair Dryer	28.98	19.83
51-84	Mist & Sauna Pro. Type Hair Dryer w/Sauna	45.98	31.35
51-64	Deluxe Pro. Type Hair Dryer/Wig Dryer	32.98	22.44
51-94	Mist Pro. Type Hair Dryer	35.50	24.32

HAND-HELD HAIR DRYERS/STYLERS

		Retail	Discount
52-13	Beauty Breeze	$17.98	$12.97
52-49	Power Beeeze	17.98	12.97
52-34	Power Mist	21.98	15.42
52-61	Power Breeze "700" Deluxe 700 Watt	23.98	16.50
	Power Plus, 900 Watt	25.50	17.39
52-87	Mist Super Styler, 700 Watt	29.98	20.32
52-73	Professionaire Blower/Styler 1000 Watt	29.98	19.65
52-91			
52-101	Triplet Detangler	29.98	22.04

CURLER/STYLERS

		Retail	Discount
54-44	Curl Stick, 30 Watt	$12.98	$ 8.81
54-13	Mist stick	18.98	13.44
54-28	Deluxe Mist Stick	21.98	14.85
54-33	Cordless Mist Stick	27.98	19.44

PERSONAL CARE

HAIRSETTERS AND WANDS
75-LC	Lady Schick Lasting Curls	$31.98
71-LC	Lady Schick Lasting Curls	24.98
CI-2	Lady Schick Cordless Quick Curls	24.98
CI-3	Schick Quick Curl	14.98

FACIAL SAUNA
60B	The Facial w/Beaut. Mist	$27.98

COSMETIC MIRROR
LL-4	Schick Love Light	$24.98

SHAVERS
900	Flexamatic Cord-Cordless	$49.95
400	Flexamatic Deluxe Cord	39.95
300	Flexamatic Standard Cord	32.95
X10	Lady Schick Shaving Wand	23.95
109	Lady Schick Jewel	13.95

SUNBEAM

DENTAL PRODUCTS
165-18	Travel Elect. Toothbrush	$16.99
65-24	Cordless Elect. Toothbrush	20.50
65-34	Cordless Elect. Toothbrush	21.50
66-24	Oral Jet Rinse, Deluxe	27.98

HAIR DRYERS
50-44	Floating Free Hair Dryer	$19.98

MANICURE SET
59-18	Manicurist	$22.19
		17.51
		17.49
		10.49

ELECTRIC MIRROR
58-18	Lighted Makeup Mirror	$19.07

HAIR CURLER
62-14	Duet Set Mist & Dry Hair Curler	$16.44

LATHER DISPENSER
74-23	Lather Man Lather Dispenser	

HAIR GROOMING COMBS
55-19	Hair Groomer for Men	$35.00
55-21	Comb & Dry Hair Styler for Women	28.81
55-38	Jet Mist Comb for Men	22.93
55-43	Jet Mist Comb for Women	16.58
		9.39

TANGLE FREE COMB
56-13	Tangle Free Comb	

ELECTRIC STEAM BRUSH
61-12	Electric Steam Brush	$12.01

MASSAGERS
MA1	Massagers	13.95
MA3H	Deluxe Heat Massager	14.60
		18.36

HAIR CLIPPERS
63-18	10-Pc. Clipmaster Kit	$14.55
63-28	17-Pc. Clipmaster Kit	

	$26.50
	17.50
	27.98
	16.50
	15.98
	15.98
	23.98
	23.98
	24.98
	15.98
	$10.48
	15.48
	$10.98
	14.98

	$18.15
	12.01
	18.14
	11.42
	$11.63
	11.63
	16.55
	16.55
	$15.88
	$11.63
	$ 7.70
	11.37
	$7.37
	9.99

PERSONAL CARE

MEN'S SHAVERS

		Retail	Discount
75-19	Shavemaster w/Groomer	$43.95	$30.53
SM7	Shavemaster	36.95	25.82
SM7M	Shavemaster Multi-Volt	38.95	27.00
SM8	Shavemaster Cord/Cordless	46.95	32.65
75-29	Shavemaster w/Groomer, Multi Volt	45.95	31.71
75-39	Shavemaster w/Groomer, Cord/Cordless	53.95	37.59
75-179	Shavemaster w/Trimmer	36.95	25.82
75-72	Shavemaster in Gift Case	26.95	18.47
75-102	Shavemaster Cord/Cordless	41.95	29.34
75-118	Shavemaster	21.95	15.43

LADIES' SHAVERS

		Retail	Discount
76-14	Lady Sunbeam Twin Head, Presentation Case	$22.95	$14.67
76-27	Lady Sunbeam Twin Head, Boudoir Case	22.95	14.67
76-31	Lady Sunbeam Shaver	15.95	11.06
76-61	Lady Sunbeam Shaver, A.C. Only, Boudoir Case	11.95	8.02
76-67	Lady Sunbeam Shaver	11.95	8.02

VISTA PERSONAL CARE PRODUCTS

		Retail	Discount
750-34	Lady Sunbeam Vista Soft Bonnet Hair Dryer w/Carrying Case	$14.94	$10.91
751-70	Lady Sunbeam Vista Hard Hat Hair Dryer	24.94	18.21
765-61	Sunbeam Vista Cordless Toothbrush	16.94	11.64

IRONS

		Retail	Discount
10-14	Today Shot of Steam Iron w/Hand Steamer	$19.75	$13.83
13-10	Ironmaster Dry	14.50	10.15
11-31	Steam or Dry, 31 Holes	18.75	13.13
11-51	Steam or Dry, 61 Holes	21.50	15.05
11-61	Steam or Dry, Non-Stick, 61 Holes	22.50	15.75
12-21	Spray Mist	25.25	17.68
12-31	Spray Mist, Teflon II Coated, 61 Holes	26.25	18.38
11-104	Self-Cleaning Shot of Steam	28.25	19.76
12-41	Self-Cleaning Spray Mist/Shot of Steam Super	31.75	22.23

TOASTMASTER

IRONS

		Retail	Discount
409	Steam & Dry Travel Iron	$18.50	$12.50
407	Compact Dry Iron w/foldaway handle, 120 Volt	14.50	9.62
408	Compact Dry Iron w/foldaway handle, 230 Volt	14.50	9.62
461	Prestige Spray-Steam-Dry Iron w/Stainless Steel soleplate	29.50	19.68
460W	Prestige Spray-Steam-Dry Iron w/Stainless Steel Soleplate	27.50	18.53
424	Steam and Dry Iron w/Aluminum Soleplate	—	9.87
404	Lightweight Dry Iron	—	8.01
499	Portable Steamer	17.50	11.86

Trash Compactors

ONE OF the newest appliances on the market is the trash compactor. And some of the best-known and most respected manufacturers have added compactors to their appliance lines.

You can find compactors bearing the names Amana, Caloric, Frigidaire, General Electric, Hotpoint, Roper, Whirlpool, and others. Most of these manufacturers are promoting this new appliance as the answer for people who hate to take out the garbage. And appliance dealers try to sell compactors with garbage disposers to make a complete waste disposal center.

If you have been enticed by the compactor advertising, CONSUMER GUIDE Magazine suggests you think carefully about whether you really need one. We are completely opposed to garbage compactors, both for economical and ecological reasons. Therefore, we do not rate any compactors as "Best Buys."

Compactors simply are not the great, useful items that the manufacturers claim they are. What the manufacturers do not tell you in their ads and what you do not find out until you read the appliance's instruction booklet is that compactors are not designed to handle wet, smelly food waste. In addition you cannot discard combustible items in them; and the way some of them unload makes it unsafe to discard glass in them. No wonder the manufacturers are able to advertise the amazing effectiveness of the deodorizers that are utilized by the compactors. There are not many smells that they have to combat. Considering the rather high purchase price of compactors (about $250), the cost of the refill bags (about 35 cents each), and the cost of the deodorizer (about $2 a can), a compactor is a very expensive wastebasket for cans and paper refuse.

The ecological considerations for ignoring compactor advertisements are just as important. A compactor is comprised of a ram assembly which exerts from 2000 to over 3000 pounds of force upon the garbage. This force compacts the garbage so tightly that the compactor can hold a week's worth of garbage produced by a family of four. The problem is that compacted garbage, in which there is no air space, is difficult to incinerate. An additional problem is caused by the deodorant that is sprayed on the garbage every time the compactor is opened and closed. The deodorant not only retards the development of odors, but it also retards the decomposition of the garbage after it is discarded. Therefore, garbage which is discarded into a compactor and which is compressed into a solid brick of waste is a real problem for community refuse departments—they cannot burn it, and it will not rot.

Perhaps the garbage compactor manufacturers will find a solution for this ecological problem. Or perhaps they will discover a new clever use for these compacted blocks of garbage. Until they do, CONSUMER GUIDE Magazine suggests you spend that $250 differently.

FOOD PREPARATION

FOOD PREPARATION APPLIANCES

THE TREND in 1975 in entertainment is staying home. As restaurant prices soar, more people are rediscovering the joy of cooking for friends. Another trend is related to inflation, but also to the wave of nostalgia infecting us all. We are not only saving money by eating at home, but are saving money by cooking from scratch (as in the good old days) instead of paying the high prices for convenience foods.

Most people today lead active lives which include a variety of commitments that take them out of the home—from car-pool duty to hospital volunteer work, to league bowling, to career. Although more people are interested in cooking exciting meals for friends and family, few are willing or able to spend the long hours in the kitchen that some of this cooking calls for. Thanks to more and more sophisticated food preparation appliances, it is no longer necessary to choose between delicious home-cooked meals and fulfilling away-from-home activities. Many appliances today do much of the cooking on their own—either slowly or quickly—but always conveniently.

There is an appliance for every cooking need—one to sharpen knives, one to open cans, one to mix, one to blend, one to broil, one to

FOOD PREPARATION

roast, one to fry, one to brew, etc. With so many useful appliances, it would not take long for the cook to be completely crowded out of the kitchen, leaving no one to push the buttons. Manufacturers have listened to the cries of homemakers who are quickly running out of counter space, and now they are combining several functions in one appliance. For example, Ronson has a Can Do that combines a can opener, hand mixer, whipper, potato masher, and knife sharpener in one unit with various attachments. And the Oster Kitchen Center combines a stand mixer, blender, and grinder.

The only unattractive aspect of food preparation appliances is their price. Like all other segments of the economy, the food appliance manufacturers are feeling the pinch of inflation. They are now just catching up to the soaring costs of new materials and labor by hiking their prices. The full impact at the retail level will hit during 1975 and send the prices for food preparation appliances skyrocketing. Therefore, you should think carefully before deciding to buy that appliance you have had in mind.

For example, if you are thinking about buying a new toaster because your old one does not work well, CONSUMER GUIDE Magazine suggests that you try to get it fixed before rushing out for a new model. In addition, we urge you to consider carefully just how much use you will derive from the appliance. Buying an Oster Kitchen Center would be a waste of money if you already own a mixer and a blender. And if you have a good frypan, do you really need a device that is limited to cooking bacon? On the other hand, there is no substitute for a waffle baker.

But if you are certain that you want to buy a food appliance, that you have a real need for it, we urge you not to wait. The lower price that you may be waiting for is not likely to appear.

What to Look For

ONCE YOU have made the decision to buy an appliance, you will want to shop and compare models and prices. When examining different models, the first thing to look for is the Underwriters Laboratory seal of approval. Underwriters Laboratories tests appliances to make certain that they meet certain safety standards established by UL. The UL seal on an appliance is your assurance that the appliance has met those standards. If the seal is not on the unit, do not buy it, no matter how much of a bargain it seems. Do not accept any excuses that may be offered by the salesperson. If the UL seal is not on a unit it is because the manufacturer did not submit the model for testing or because the model did not pass the UL tests. No manufacturer would "forget" to put the UL seal on a product if it had been earned.

Another matter to check is the model's easiness to clean. A convenience appliance is not very convenient if it takes great effort to keep it clean. The easiest-to-clean appliances are those that are completely immersible. Another aid to cleanability is a nonstick coating. Toasters, can openers, broiler ovens, and mixers should have removable parts

FOOD PREPARATION

that are easy to assemble and disassemble.

The construction of the model you are looking at should be good. Make sure that covers fit well, knobs and handles are not loose, controls are easy to reach, and temperature settings are easy to read. Also determine whether the appliance is sturdy enough to handle its work load. There is nothing quite as maddening as a stand mixer that continually wants to jump off the counter when you raise the beaters from the bowl.

You will also want to be aware of the size of the models you are examining. Measure how much space you have available before you go shopping, and then buy an appliance that fits within those measurements. Usually you have a choice of different sizes, so pick the appliance that—all other things being equal—best suits the amount of cabinet or counter space you can spare.

Another important consideration when comparing models is the guarantee. Most guarantees on food preparation appliances cover the product for one year. What you really need to find out is what you must do to get the product repaired. Some manufacturers provide for over-the-counter replacement from your local retailer within a year of the purchase date if the product proves to be defective. But if no replacement is allowed, there are normally two different repair policies that you will find. One requires you to take the appliance to an authorized repair center (normally listed in the instruction booklet). But the other requires you to box and ship the defective merchandise back to the factory at your expense. CONSUMER GUIDE Magazine definitely feels that this latter policy is an inferior guarantee. First of all, if you have to pay to ship the appliance, have to pay money out of your pocket, then the repair is not really free for you. In addition, most consumers do not have proper materials for packing and wrapping an appliance for shipment. If you ever do have to return an appliance, however, make sure you surround it with crumpled newspaper—both inside and out. Crushed quilted plastic wrap and foam plastic are even better, if you have them.

Blenders

IF YOU think a blender is just for mixing and blending, then your blender will sit idle most of the time and will not be worth the money you pay for it. But if you get a multi-speed blender and read the instruction booklet to discover all the jobs it can do, you will find that a blender can be one of the most versatile and useful appliances in your kitchen. It chops, grinds, stirs, whips, grates, purees, liquefies, and blends. It works on vegetables, potatoes, meats, breads, cheeses, and nuts along with many other foods.

The biggest names in blenders are Oster—which made "Osterizer" a household word—Waring, and Hamilton Beach. Other manufacturers are Proctor Silex, Ronson, Van Wyck, Sunbeam, Hoover, Rival, and Toastmaster. With so many manufacturers competing, it is the consumer who benefits. One obvious area of competition is price. Some deluxe blenders cost over $100, but you can also find models that

FOOD PREPARATION

perform well for under $20. For example, Waring's 7-speed Nova I blender, model 51, is a good buy at $16.84.

Some manufacturers try to outsell the competition by adding extra features, some of which are useful but many of which are gimmicks designed only to boost sales. An example of a helpful extra feature is the mini container (usually a half pint) that Oster and Waring (among others) are offering. These small containers are ideal for blending small portions of baby foods, sandwich spreads, salad dressings, etc. The containers, which are often made of heat- and cold-resistant glass or Lexan, can be stored for future use.

Oster has gone further along the attachment route by offering a citrus juicer, food grinder, mixer, and icer; each attachment fits on top of any Oster blender. Not to be outdone, Ronson has introduced the power center blender with 24 speed ranges that can combine five appliances into one. Available attachments can turn the Ronson blender into a coffee mill, juicer, knife and scissors sharpener, and ice crusher—as well as a blender, of course. CONSUMER GUIDE Magazine, however, cannot recommend the Ronson power center blender because of its high price. The power centers with the glass carafes range (in suggested retail price) from $69.50 for model 44401 to $95.00 for model 44405. Add to these figures the price of the attachments, which run from $14.95 for the knife and scissors sharpener to $29.95 for the coffee mill. Although the Ronson power centers are heavyweight, high quality machines, they represent exactly what we mean about spending too much money for more appliance than you really need.

Similarly, CONSUMER GUIDE Magazine does not recommend Ronson's 10-speed Cook 'N Stir blender, model 42102. While this appliance can perform many tasks — as a regular blender, an ice crusher, a popcorn popper, and even heat foods up to 375 degrees — it carries a $100 price tag. It is doubtful whether many consumers can derive enough use out of the Ronson Cook 'N Stir blender to justify that sort of expenditure.

Another gimmick is "The Stripper" from Waring. Retailing from between $10 to $15, this blender attachment is designed to peel fruit and vegetables automatically. Unfortunately, the idea works better in theory than in practice. You still have to get the eyes out of the potatoes after you put them through the Waring Stripper.

Some manufacturers have tried to make their blenders more attractive by offering extra speeds, but CONSUMER GUIDE Magazine recommends that you stay away from the 14- to 24-speed models. Usually the gradations are so minimal that what you are doing is spending money to have a great many buttons on your blender. For normal use, all you need are five- to ten-speeds, especially if the blender includes a pulse control. Blender effectiveness depends more on its power, the way its blades circulate, and the shape of its jar, than it does on the number of its speeds. On the other hand, blenders with just high and low buttons are not versatile enough for most homemakers' needs. They are adequate for mixing drinks, but you need a five to ten-speed model for anything more complicated.

FOOD PREPARATION

CONSUMER GUIDE Magazine suggests that you buy a blender with a timer; a timer is very useful in preventing overblending. Moreover, look for a removable blade assembly in any blender that you consider buying; a removable blade assembly makes cleaning much easier.

Broilers

BROILERS (or oven-broilers) are ideal for the informal entertaining of small numbers of people that has become so popular. Since these units are lightweight, they can be moved easily from the kitchen to the family room or even to the patio — in short, anywhere there is an electrical outlet. Oven-broilers also require much less electricity to operate than do standard ovens, as they heat up much faster than regular ovens do.

Like many modern standard ovens, most oven-broilers offer a continuous clean feature that eliminates the need for strenuous cleaning with chemicals and abrasives. These oven-broilers clean themselves continually when operating at normal cooking temperatures. A catalytic porcelain enamel finish makes spills and spatters disappear as you cook. In most units, however, you still have to wipe clean the oven door, racks, and drip trays.

Since broilers range from large to small, CONSUMER GUIDE Magazine suggests that you evaluate your needs carefully before you select any broiler model. If you are searching for a large oven to use in a recreational room, then look at the Black Angus model 008820. It is a deluxe combination unit that serves as a broiler, rotisserie, oven, and grill, and has a four-hour built-in timer and a pilot light. You can use the grill above the cabinet as a warming tray for foods, while the king-size broiler can accommodate big turkeys and roasts.

If you are looking for a small, portable broiler to use in the dining room or to take with you to a vacation home, check the Broil King model 135. It broils both sides of foods simultaneously, and — with a change in setting — it can bake bread, cookies, or muffins. The Broil-King 135 is a self-cleaning Broiler.

If you notice any similiarity between Nesco oven-broilers and Hoover models, you are right; both lines are made by Hoover. Two attractive Nesco units are the BA505 — which has a rotisserie — and the BA005 — which does not have a rotisserie. Designed in shiny chrome with black end panels and walnut wood handles, neither of these Nesco broilers are large. Nevertheless, they can accommodate a steak or a rolled roast on a spit. Their smaller size, moreover, makes them easy to store.

Toastmaster also makes a handsome unit in chrome, model 5233. Featuring tubular-type elements that are similar to those on full-size electric ranges, this oven-broiler maintains temperatures selected from 200 degrees to 475 degrees. What makes the Toastmaster 5233 unusual is that it converts from a broiler to an oven simply by flipping over. The full-view glass door, chrome tray, and baking rack are removable for easy cleaning.

If you like the idea of broiling away from the range, but have no use for the oven portion of an oven-broiler, CONSUMER GUIDE Magazine

FOOD PREPARATION

recommends the smokeless open-type broilers — often referred to as rotisserie broilers. Although you can purchase an open-type broiler without a rotisserie and save money, the rotisserie greatly expands the variety of cooking you can do.

The big name in open-type broilers is Farberware. Coining the term "Open Hearth," Farberware captured the market with its rotisserie model 455A. The Open Hearth weighs 15 pounds, has a large (10 x 15-inch) broiling surface, and provides an aluminum drip tray to absorb the heat from the fat. Farberware also offers a shish-kebab accessory, consisting of five skewers in a rack.

The Farberware Open Hearth is the most deluxe unit available, but there are many other open broilers that work as well and cost considerably less. Mirro, Dominion, and Toastmaster all offer economical rotisserie-broilers. The Mirro-Matic (model W7303-MO346-37) is a fine unit made of Mirro Aluminum. The Dominion model 2565 has a low silhouette that eases storage problems. The Toastmaster model 5256 has a stainless steel drip pan and removable legs. Although it offers only three adjustable positions, it can handle just about any cooking task.

Can Openers

THE ELECTRIC can opener is certainly a great labor-saving appliance. Anyone who has ever had to go around the circumference of a coffee can lid with a manual can opener will vouch for that statement. It must be admitted, however, that an electrical appliance designed only to cut the lids off of cans takes up a disproportionate amount of space on the countertop. As a result, electric can openers are now equipped to perform many other functions: knife and scissor sharpening, ice crushing, and juice squeezing.

Ronson has taken a fresh approach with its Can Do. The Can Do is shaped more like a hand mixer than a can opener. Available in two versions, the Can Do model 36012 is CONSUMER GUIDE Magazine's choice. This unit has a whipper-mixer attachment, a knife sharpener, a potato masher, and a plastic drink mixer — in addition, of course, to the basic can opener. The Can Do makes storage easy with its wooden rack for wall mounting.

It seems that for the moment can opener manufacturers are stressing cleanability rather than new feature combinations. CONSUMER GUIDE Magazine welcomes this change of emphasis. The easiest to clean can opener presently on the market is "Click 'N' Clean" by Rival. When you push a button, the cutting mechanism blades click off for easy rinsing.

CONSUMER GUIDE Magazine recommends Rival's model 707 as a good combination unit. A Click 'N' Clean unit, the Rival 707 can opener has a citrus juicer with two reamers, a pulp barrier, a fairly large bowl, and a dust cover. It performs far better than Oster's can opener/juicer combinations (models 576 and 577). Although the Oster units offer adequate performance, the cutting mechanisms are not removable like the Rival Click 'N' Clean.

FOOD PREPARATION

The less expensive Rival can openers are not fully automatic. By fully automatic we mean that all you have to do is position the can and pierce the lid; the opener completes the work, including shutting off the motor. A can opener performs just as well if it is semiautomatic which requires you to hold the lever down for cutting and to remove the can in order to stop the motor.

Coffeemakers

NOW THERE is big news for any coffee lover. It is the single-pass coffeemaker. The single-pass coffeemaker passes heated tap water from a tank at the top to a basket, where either a paper or permanent filter device traps the sediment from the coffee. Then, the filtered brew drips into the waiting carafe below. Coffee tastes better when sediment is trapped instead of being perked round and round and round.

North American Systems was the first on the market a few years back with its Mr. Coffee. Since then several manufacturers have introduced single-pass coffeemakers, including Norelco, West Bend, Sunbeam, Melitta, and Cory under the Nicro name.

Mr. Coffee (model MC 1) is one of the best selling single pass coffeemakers on the market. It has a 1 to 10 cup capacity (50 ounce maximum) and weighs 6½ pounds. Individual warmer and brewer switches control the operations. Included in the package is a calibrated water measuring pitcher, a coffee measuring spoon, and a hot water funnel attachment that is used when you just want hot water for tea, soup, gelatins. The water tank is self-cleaning.

There are two unattractive features about Mr. Coffee. One is disposable paper filters, and the other is the price. Most retail stores across the country sell Mr. Coffee at $49.99, which is the highest price of all the single-pass coffeemakers. CONSUMER GUIDE Magazine does not see any features on this appliance that warrant the high price tag. North American Systems tried to solve the price problem by introducing Mr. Coffee II, model CB 500 priced as low as $23.88. The unit works much the same as Mr. Coffee I. They differ primarily in styling. Mr. Coffee II has only one switch for brewing and warming whereas Mr. Coffee I has two separate switches. Mr. Coffee II is an inch shorter (12½ inches high) and about an inch wider (nearly 10 inches) than Mr. Coffee I. Both of these coffeemakers are made of white plastic, and both require disposable paper filters (about two cents apiece).

If you do not like the look of plastic, Norelco offers an aluminum single-pass coffeemaker. As far as the taste of the coffee is concerned, it makes no difference whether the tank is plastic or metal. Norelco's 10-cup model HD 5135 makes 10 cups of coffee in eight minutes.

It is almost impossible to tell coffee from one unit to the other. They all produce coffee that tastes far superior to that which you brew in any pot or percolator. The glass carafes or pots that each manufacturer includes, however, do not match the quality of the coffeemaker. When rinsing a Mr. Coffee glass carafe under running water, for example, we accidentally tapped it against the water faucet and it broke. While these

FOOD PREPARATION

glass containers may look nice, they are a hazard for cleaning.

Similarly, glass percolators — like the Proctor-Silex "See-Thru" line — also can cause problems. After breaking a glass bowl on Proctor's model P-102N, we shopped unsuccessfully for a replacement. We finally gave up, and ordered a new one from the factory. A glass pot is tops for coffee taste, but the price you must pay in breakage cannot be overlooked.

That a glass coffeemaker does not have to cause breakage problems is proved by the Corning line of electric coffeemakers. Made of much heavier glass, the Corning units make the finest coffee next to the single-pass coffeemakers.

If you prefer a metal coffeemaker, CONSUMER GUIDE Magazine suggests that you buy an all-stainless steel pot. Since it is less porous than other metals, stainless steel is less likely to retain the foul odor of trapped coffee oils from which many metal pots suffer. To keep a stainless steel pot clean, use a solution of baking soda and warm water rather than detergent. Of course, make sure that any stainless steel coffeemaker you consider purchasing is immersible and that all parts — including the coffee basket, pump, and well — are stainless. Stainless steel is more expensive than metal or plastic; be certain that you get your money's worth in value.

If you are on a severe budget but want an immersible coffeemaker, look at General Electric's model P-15. It is a good value, featuring a Peek-A-Brew gauge — which shows the amount of coffee remaining in the pot — a hot water setting, and a flavor selector. The P-15 is equipped to handle up to 9 cups, but the minibrew basket (standard) allows you to make as few as two or three cups at a time.

Corn Poppers

TODAY, there are dozens of self-buttering corn poppers on the market, including units from Regal Ware, Presto, Empire, West Bend, Hamilton Beach, Mirro, Cornwall, Sunbeam, Robeson, and Dominion. Most of these poppers have the butter cup on the top of the cover. As the corn pops, the butter, theoretically, melts and drips down on the corn. However, not enough heat makes it to the top of the popper to effectively melt the butter. All too often, at the end of the popping process, a lump of butter is still left in the butter melter, unmelted. You can more effectively melt butter on top of the stove or even right in the popper after you remove the corn. Therefore, CONSUMER GUIDE Magazine sees little reason to pay extra for a feature that does so little.

CONSUMER GUIDE Magazine does, however, recommend the combination serving dish/cover found on many of the newer corn poppers. It eliminates extra dirty dishes. The clear glass covers, moreover, allow children to watch the corn as it pops.

Other labor saving aspects of the new electric corn poppers are the linings with a nonstick coating, and electric cords that remove so that the popper is immersible. Since popcorn is a fun snack food, there is no reason that clean-up should be difficult.

FOOD PREPARATION
Electric Knives

ALTHOUGH it is something that most homemakers do not buy for themselves, most cooks really appreciate the ease and convenience that an electric knife provides. An electric knife can do more than merely carve a roast or turkey. It can also dice vegetables, carve freshly baked bread, cut fruits, and slice cheese — even the crumbly kind. You should use the knife for all of these purposes; otherwise, you will not use the electric knife to its fullest advantage.

When buying an electric knife be sure that it fits comfortably in your hand. Hamilton Beach's "Hole-in-the-handle" makes holding and using the appliance easy. Similarly, the General Electric electric knives feature lightweight handles. We would not recommend the Sunbeam line however, because the oversized bodies make them difficult to hold.

CONSUMER GUIDE Magazine advises that activator buttons should be easy to operate, and that blades should be simple to insert and remove. While we approved of the overall performance of the Ronson electric knife, model 34123, we did find that it was difficult to hold the button in for extensive slicing. This is a definite disadvantage when you are tackling a 10-pound turkey.

CONSUMER GUIDE Magazine believes that two sets of blades are an unnecessary expense. On many higher priced units — such as General Electric's model EK 7 — the manufacturer offers long blades for carving and short blades for paring, but one set of blades will get the work done. We also see no purpose in having two speeds. Sunbeam's model 6-21 has two speeds, raising the price of the unit unnecessarily. One speed is adequate for all types of slicing and cutting.

Frypans

AN ELECTRIC frypan is one of the most useful appliances for use in the kitchen or right on the table. CONSUMER GUIDE Magazine believes that immersible frypans are a necessity, You should be able to scrub all parts of the pan — including the undersurface, which will certainly become quite greasy. We also recommend frypans that are coated with a nonstick material, like DuPont's Teflon II, to facilitate easy clean-up. Although the nonstick coating boosts the price of the frypan, it is worth the investment.

Although the primary purpose of a frypan is to fry, you will also want to use your frypan with the lid on to roast or braise. Because they allow a greater variety of cooking, high-dome frypans are superior; they are, however, more difficult to store.

An important feature of a frypan is its temperature control. Make sure that the temperature control allows you to do anything from a steady simmer to a fast fry. Do not compromise on the control, even to save on the purchase price, or you will defeat the function of the frypan. Also make sure that the temperature control detaches along with the legs and handles. Once these parts have been removed, the frypan can be placed in the dishwasher or in hot sudsy water.

FOOD PREPARATION

Another feature available on some units is removable legs and handles. This is another aid to easy cleanability. The General Electric SK27, for example, has an ejector button that releases the legs and handles so the rest of the frypan can be put in the dishwasher if desired.

A popular combination product on the market is the frypan/broiler. The broiler element is inside the hinged lid that can be set at the desired angle for broiling. Hamilton Beach's Panastic Plus, model 476, met most of our testing requirements for frypan/broilers. It has a Duralon III nonstick interior, removable handles, and a plug-in temperature control.

Corning's "Electromatic" skillet line is actually just a Corning dish set on a hot plate. Attractive enough to sit on any table, the Corning skillets are elegantly designed in a white glass-ceramic material called "Pyroceram." The heating element is completely sealed, making for easy cleanability by eliminating food particles and spills from being trapped inside. We particularly recommend model E-1310. This table range can braise, pan-grill, brown, stew, boil, simmer, warm, roast, or thaw. The glass cover allows you to see exactly what's going on inside. Since the heating base and dish are separate on the Corning Electromatic skillet, you can use the base as a warming tray for foods while the dish is in the oven, on top of the range, or under the broiler.

Griddles

AN ELECTRIC griddle is less versatile than an electric frypan, and cannot accommodate any foods that require a cover for cooking. CONSUMER GUIDE Magazine does not recommend buying a griddle unless you need a large cooking surface frequently. On the other hand, the griddle does have a place in the kitchen if you prepare large quantities of pancakes, bacon, fried eggs, hamburgers, chops, etc.

When shopping for a griddle, look for a nonstick surface, stay-cool handles on either end, a removable temperature control, and a tray or some receptacle for catching grease. While many cooking surfaces on griddles are about 20 inches (which is difficult to store), you can find smaller units. Manning-Bowman offers an 11-inch square griddle, model 415002. It has a grease trench around the periphery, a run-off spout for drainage, and is Teflon coated. The 20-inch griddle from Manning-Bowman, model 415004, has a grease trench that drains into a removable plastic tray. CONSUMER GUIDE Magazine wonders how long the plastic will endure with hot grease rolling into it, and, therefore, we do not recommend the Manning-Bowman 415004 griddle.

A large, economy griddle is available from West Bend. Model 3545 offers a cooking surface of 12⅜ inches by 19⅝ inches. The handles are easy to use and the heat control is detachable for immersibility.

Oster's "Super Grill" has one important defect. Its cooking surface is a circle with a 16-inch diameter. Anyone who has ever owned a large, round appliance will agree that storage is just too difficult. Although the Super Grill (model 730) has many excellent features — a removable temperature control, nonstick coating, and grease pouring lip — it is

FOOD PREPARATION

overpriced at around $40. The round-shaped griddle from Black Angus also cannot be recommended, even though it costs less (around $25 when discounted). Like the Oster Super Grill, the Black Angus's shape leads to storage problems that make this griddle impractical.

Mixers

THERE ARE two types of mixers: stand mixers and portable mixers. The type you select should correspond to the type of cook you are. If you enjoy making foods from scratch — like cookies, breads, and muffins — then we suggest that you buy a durable stand mixer that will last for years. If you need to use a mixer only occasionally, then we feel that a portable mixer is your best choice. Stand mixers take up considerable storage space and usually cost much more.

A stand mixer should be, above all, sturdily constructed. It should remain firmly planted when you lift the beaters from the bowl. The beaters should just clear the bottom of the bowl when mixing, even if the unit operates with only one beater. You also should make sure the stand mixer you want has an ejector button for the beaters. Another feature that CONSUMER GUIDE Magazine recommends is a removable beater unit that can be taken away from the stand mixer's bowl.

It also would be to your advantage to see if attachments come with the mixer unit, or whether they must be purchased separately. Some of the attachments available are grinders, juicers, bread kneaders, blenders, ice crushers, sausage stuffers, and salad makers.

For attachments to work well on a stand mixer, the appliance must have a powerful motor. The most efficient way to determine the power of the motor is to check the wattage of the unit. In most cases, the higher the wattage, the more powerful the motor. The number of speeds on a mixer has little to do with the effectiveness of the motor.

The best heavy-duty stand mixers are made by Hobart, of KitchenAid appliances. KitchenAid prices are very high however. A 10-speed stand mixer with a stainless steel bowl, model K5-A, retails around $200, although you can find it in some stores for about $150. Obviously, no one but the homemaker who does plenty of mixing should consider paying that kind of price. If you feel that your needs justify the expense, however, the KitchenAid K5-A will provide a lifetime of fine performance for you.

However, CONSUMER GUIDE Magazine cautions the serious cook to stay away from the KitchenAid model 4-C. Although this stand mixer is less expensive, it cannot be recommended for kneading heavy doughs. Therefore, we do not think that it is worth its still considerable purchase price.

If you want a stand mixer but do not want to pay the high KitchenAid prices, CONSUMER GUIDE Magazine recommends the Sunbeam line of Mixmasters. The 2-12 Mixmaster, a good buy between $20 and $30, is equipped with a glass bowl, a 150-watt motor, a pushbutton beater ejector, and a built-in mixing guide. The mixer removes from the stand for use as a portable.

FOOD PREPARATION

The Sunbeam model 2-12 also has a 12-position infinite control setting. Even though the control is marked for 12 specific settings, there is a wide choice of settings in between. An advantage to the infinite type of control is that you can slow down the action to a gentle stirring motion, which comes in handy for folding egg whites or for stirring a sauce.

Slow Cookers

WITH FOOD prices skyrocketing, the slow cooker helps extend even the most limited budget. Less expensive cuts of meat prepared in a slow cooker come out tender and juicy and with a minimum loss due to shrinkage. Even where money is not a problem, slow cookers are beneficial because cooking at slow temperatures imparts a better flavor to food.

In addition, they free the cook from the kitchen. You can start dinner before leaving the house in the morning, and it will be ready when you return in the evening. Neither pot watching nor stirring is ever needed. Food will not burn since there are no hot spots in a slow cooker. You can make a wide variety of foods — including roasts, chicken, stews, vegetables, fruit, breads, and cakes — all in your slow cooker.

There are two types of slow cookers on the market. One kind has a crockery or stoneware lining, and the other has some type of nonstick material for the inside lining. Another major difference in slow cookers is that the coils are either wrapped around the sides or they are located at the base of the appliance. Nearly all have a simple high, medium, and low control knob.

The big name in slow cookers is the Rival "Crock-Pot". Lined with stoneware and having the coils wrapped around the sides, the Rival units are glazed on the inside to prevent porous leakage which could short circuit the heating element. The clear cover on the Rival Crock-Pots allows you to peek inside without opening the unit. Rival's slow cooker line ranges from small to large, consisting of 2-quart, 3½-quart, and 5-quart stoneware cookers.

The newer Crock-Pots are definitely superior to Rival's older units. Although the performance of the Crock-Pots has always been excellent, the newer models 3300 (3-quart) and 3300 (5-quart) have detachable heating controls. The stoneware bowl on the Model 3500 lifts out and is dishwasher safe. In addition, the Lexan outer container and covers remain cool to the touch.

A new innovation in slow cookers comes from Hamilton Beach. Called "The Crock Watcher," model 449 has an auto shift that can cook food at roughly 190 degrees for about 1¾ hours before shifting to an intermediate heat setting. The Crock Watcher also has high and low settings.

Although CONSUMER GUIDE Magazine prefers slow cookers to have the coils wrapped around the side for better performance, there are some advantages to having the coils at the base. In making chili, for instance, our testers found that some recipes called for browning the

FOOD PREPARATION

hamburger and some of the other ingredients before simmering. Browning can be done quickly and efficiently in slow cookers that have the coils at the base.

If you want this type of flexibility, CONSUMER GUIDE Magazine recommends Regal's "Pot-O-Plenty," which has eight temperature settings. The Pot-O-Plenty can double as a deep-fat fryer and comes with the required metal basket. We must point out, however, that the Regal Pot-O-Plenty is made of aluminum and lined with Teflon II. We feel that for the best slow cooking, you are better off with a stoneware interior.

Specialty Appliance

THE LIST OF specialty appliances grows longer each month. Some of these appliances seem absurd and a waste of electricity, storage space, and money. Others, however, may deserve a place in your kitchen. Be sure you have a need for these appliances before purchasing them.

The "Whiz-Grid" (model M-0363) by Mirro-Matic offers a new idea in cooking, which the company has termed "froiling" — a combination of frying and broiling. Twin grids slanted at 10 degrees allow cooking fat to drain away from the food into a removable Lexan grease tray. Thus, you get the taste of frying combined with the benefits of grease-free broiling. Since heat is concentrated over the grid area (each grid is roughly 11x6 inches), foods are "froiled" fast. Four hot dogs, three hamburgers, and two sandwiches can be "froiled" in three minutes each.

While CONSUMER GUIDE Magazine likes the idea, we found in testing the "Whiz-Grid" that food often slides off the slanted frying areas along with the grease. We also found that the appliance is much too small for serious cooking. It can only froil three slices of bacon, for instance, at one time.

Although the fondue fad has died down, these appliances continue to be useful for social gatherings. An electric fondue that CONSUMER GUIDE Magazine would advise you to avoid is the Nesco unit. In our testing we found that the handles became hot and that oil spattered. Moreover, the prongs on the six forks were too short.

Farberware's Turbo-Oven is the only unit of its kind on the market. Designed to seal in juices and flavor with less meat shrinkage, turbo cooking circulates hot air around food surfaces while maintaining an even temperature. It roasts one-third faster than conventional ovens, and a rotisserie is not needed. In terms of cleanability, the Turbo Oven's interior is lined with a stay-clean coating that vaporizes most food spatters during cooking. There is also a drip-tray, and the oven door is removable.

There are, however, some general drawbacks to the Turbo-Oven. In CONSUMER GUIDE Magazine testing, we found that the outside of the oven gets very hot to the touch. And although the Turbo-Oven can accommodate a 20-pound turkey, it is too small for two 9-inch cake pans. These facts, coupled with a high price tag—around

FOOD PREPARATION

$160—should cause anyone to reconsider before buying this item.

Toaster Oven

TOASTER OVENS are increasingly popular because they serve not only as a toaster, but also as an extra oven. They are especially appealing to small families since they eliminate the need to heat up an entire oven for small quantities of food. In addition to toasting regular bread, toaster ovens also toast large slices of bread that would not fit into a standard toaster. They also are ideal for top-browning open-face sandwiches and hors d'oeuvres, but they do not broil.

General Electric was responsible for marketing the first toaster oven, and GE's old standby — the T93B Toast-R-Oven — is still a good buy. We prefer the T93B over GE's king-size Toast 'N' Serve model T95. Offering basically the same features as the T93B, the T95 is not really a king-size unit. In our testing, a standard 9-inch pie was crowded between the back wall and the glass door. CONSUMER GUIDE Magazine feels that you would be better off spending less money for GE's T93B, unless you need to toast four slices of bread at the same time. The T93B can only toast two slices simultaneously.

The Toastmaster toaster oven has better controls, although its appearance is not as nice as the GE T93B, Toastmaster's model 311 combines push-button controls with a temperature dial. The temperature range is fairly standard, from 200 to 500 degrees. The Toastmaster 311 includes a baking pan and an oven tray.

Nesco's portable speed-oven, model N146, is worth your consideration. It has a 60-minute timer and a Teflon-coated baking pan. Like the Toastmaster unit, however, the Nesco toaster oven is not as attractive as the GE T93B. The Proctor-Silex toaster oven definitely cannot be recommended. The unit is split; the toaster slot is on the top half and the oven is on the lower half. Our objection to the Proctor-Silex toaster oven is that the split design results in an oven portion that is too small.

Toasters

TOASTERS ARE becoming more useful. While its primary purpose continues to be toasting bread, the toaster is taking on a whole new character in frozen food preparation. Toasters now accommodate sandwiches, pizzas, breakfast foods, and desserts. While it is true that you can prepare some of these foods in your old toaster, many require a pastry setting for warming without burning or drying them out.

These pastry settings hike the cost of the all-purpose toasters. If you do not eat these frozen foods, then you would be better off buying a traditional toaster. If you need a toaster that can handle the frozen foods, however, CONSUMER GUIDE Magazine recommends the economical Proctor-Silex 2-slice bread/pastry toaster, featuring the "Select-ronic" color control. Proctor-Silex also offers basically the same toaster in a 4-slice model with individual controls.

Proctor-Silex offers a no-frills toaster at an economical price. Model

FOOD PREPARATION

T-614H is a 2-slice toaster that does what it is supposed to do—toast bread.

All Proctor-Silex toasters have a snap-out tray in the bottom to facilitate crumb cleaning. Another fine feature is the Proctor-Silex guarantee. The company offers an over-the-counter replacement if any defect in workmanship occurs during the first year.

The big name in the toaster field is Toastmaster, maker of a wide variety of 2-slice and 4-slice models. You can count on the Toastmaster name, in most cases, for smooth operation and for reliable heat control at modest cost.

Two new Toastmaster toasters (2-slot model B146HG and 4-slot model D166HG) come in harvest gold and feature an abstract garden design on a heat-resistent front panel. Controls are up-front, and on the 4-slice unit each pair of slots can be operated separately to toast light and dark at the same time. Both units can accommodate frozen foods, both provide a hinged crumb tray for easy cleaning.

Manning-Bowman has a line of toasters that closely resembles the Toastmaster line, though usually sold at lower price. The resemblance of the lines is to be expected, since both companies are owned by McGraw-Edison. Investigate the Manning-Bowman toasters carefully before you decide to buy any of the Toastmaster models.

Panasonic's "Shutter Seal," model NT115, might seem like a gimmick at first glance, but it proved to be a valuable feature in our tests. The toaster's sliding top slips into place over the slots as you push the lever to lower the bread, the purpose of this seal is to hold in heat and moisture. As the toast pops up, the sliding top moves aside. The result is toast that is evenly browned on the outside and not dried out on the inside.

Waffle Bakers

A WAFFLE BAKER is an appliance for which there is just no substitute. You cannot fry a waffle on top of the stove or bake it in an oven. Frozen waffles from the grocery store, of course, cannot match the taste of those made at home from scratch or from a mix. CONSUMER GUIDE Magazine urges you to buy a waffle baker with a nonstick coating, which will cost you more money initially but save you plenty of time and effort when clean-up time comes.

If you plan to use a waffle baker for parties, buy a square model for its large cooking surface. Toastmaster offers an excellent Teflon-coated square unit, model 265, which doubles as a grill. All you do is reverse the grid for foods like grilled sandwiches. The temperature control has a range from high, to medium, to low.

Two other similar units that combine waffle baking and grilling are the Black Angus 950843 and the General Electric G-46T. The Black Angus unit is coated with Teflon II and can handle four waffles at a time. Our testers grilled steaks 1½-inches thick with the lid closed, and fried bacon with less shrinkage than usually occurs. Superbly versatile, the Black Angus 950843 constitutes an excellent value.

FOOD PREPARATION

BEST BUYS: FOOD PREPARATION APPLIANCES

CONSUMER GUIDE Magazine's food appliance experts tested many products under actual kitchen conditions and judged each on its performance, cleanability, and construction. In addition, the experts tested the claims manufacturers made for their units, to see if they lived up to their advertising. In light of all these attributes, and in relation to their prices, the following products are considered "Best Buys."

BLENDERS

OSTER 878 "Cyclomatic" features automatic cycling to prevent overblending. This means that you set the dial to the number of cycles your recipe calls for, and then select the indicated push-button speed from any of the seven low-range speeds or any of the seven high-range speeds. From then on the control automatically cycles on and off. Although we think that 14 speeds are more than necessary, we found the Oster 878's blending action to be superb. While the design is more compact than on many other blenders, the Oster's base is solid. Clean-up is made simple by the removable cutting blade.
Fair Trade Price: $68.95   **Low Price: $64.87**

Sunbeam 4-13, an 8-speed blender, performed well in our tests. It has a 5-cup glass container and a removable cutting assembly. The lid on our test model was too large and did not fit snugly into the container. We encourage you, therefore, to check the lid before buying a Sunbeam 4-13 blender. We found no other imperfections; the overall construction is good. The unit is operated well, providing excellent speed control. Sunbeam provides an interesting recipe book.
Suggested Retail Price: $37.50   **Low Price: $26.25**

BROILERS

Farberware 455A "Open Hearth" is probably the most deluxe opentype broiler available. It has a large broiling surface and an aluminum

FOOD PREPARATION

drip pan which absorbs the heat from the fat. The rotisserie has 14 adjustable positions, which is more than you need, and an optional shish-kebab accessory is available. A smaller version, Model 445, has only an 8-1/2 x 12-inch broiling surface, too small if you have a family.
Fair Trade Price: $54.99 **Low Price: $49.49**

Toastmaster 5231 *is an oven-broiler with a continuous cleaning feature. A thermostat maintains temperatures selected from 200 to 475 degrees. It can be converted from a broiler to an oven by flipping it over. The full-view glass door, chrome tray, and baking rack are removable for easy cleaning.*
Suggested Retail Price: $27.75 **Low Price: $18.91**

CAN OPENERS

Hamilton Beach 831 *has an easy-to-remove cutting assembly which makes cleaning a snap, and the unit itself is sturdy for both opening cans and sharpening knives. All operations with the Hamilton Beach 831 were efficient and fast.*
Suggested Retail Price: $14.98 **Low Price: $9.25**

Oster 566 *requires little pressure to open cans of various sizes. Never once did the magnetic lid drop a can. Although the unit is lightweight, it is sturdy enough in use. A nice extra feature is the ice crusher, which we found to work as well as the cutting action.*
Fair Trade Price: $26.95 **Low Price: $24.87**

Rival 707 *is a combination can opener and juicer with two reamers, a pulp barrier, and a fairly large bowl. It performs well, and the Click "N" Clean features mean easy cutting mechanism removal for easy cleaning. This is the easiest-to-clean can opener on the market.*
Suggested Retail Price: $29.95 **Low Price: $19.83**

Ronson Can-Do 36012 *is a combination hand-held electric can opener, knife sharpener, whipper/mixer, potato masher, and plastic beater-drink mixer. It also features a wooden rack for wall mounting. The appliance is offered in white and chrome only. Our testers found that most of the attachments as well as the basic can opener work quickly and efficiently. We had no problem opening any type of cans; the unit never stalled. The Can-Do made it simple to whip and mix sauces, and it sharpened knives well. The only difficulty we had was with the masher attachment; it produced only fair results in mashing small quantities.*
Suggested Retail Price: $37.50 **Low Price: $24.83**

Waring CO-1 *in addition to its operating quietly and taking up a minimum amount of counter space, is easy to assemble and disassemble for cleaning. It is heavy enough to stand without moving when opening cans; you must, however, hold down the starting lever the full*

FOOD PREPARATION

time that the can is being opened. The Waring CO-1 is, consequently, a basic can opener that pierces lids easily, but–with the exception of a cord storage compartment–has few extra features.

Suggested Retail Price: $12.95　　　　　　　　**Low Price: $7.50**

COFFEEMAKERS

Corning E-1210 *is a glass coffeemaker that makes some of the finest coffee we have tested. Only the single-pass coffeemakers can exceed it. The Corning E-1210 percolates fast, has a lock-in basket and lid, a plug receptacle underneath the handle, and is easily dissembled for washing. The design is excellent, with lines that are sleek and simple, featuring a light touch of color on a pure white background.*

Suggested Retail Price: $32.95　　　　**Low Price: Not Available**

General Electric SSP12 *is a stainless steel 12-cup coffeemaker, and stainless steel is preferable to other metals for making excellent tasting coffee. The mini-brew basket is handy in that it allows you to perk two or three cups of coffee. The spout filter helps to trap sediment, a worthwhile feature. We also approve of the "Peek-A-Brew" gauge that lets you see the amount of coffee remaining in the pot.*

Suggested Retail Price: $40.98　　　　　　**Low Price: $29.55**

North American Systems Mr. Coffee MC 1 *is a single-pass coffeemaker that drips tap water from the top on the unit through the filter basket and into a waiting glass carafe. Mr. Coffee stands about 13 inches high and is difficult to store. You probably should plan on giving a permanent part of your countertop to Mr. Coffee. It can brew from 1 to 10 cups of coffee faster than you can get your eyes open in the morning (brewing time for 5 or 6 cups is about five minutes). Included with the unit is a Pyrex measuring cup for the tap water, a measuring spoon for the coffee, and a hot water funnel for making instant foods or hot beverages.*

You must operate two controls to turn on the unit: a brewer switch and a warming switch. Once brewing is completed, you turn off the brewer switch – leaving only the warming plate on – and dump the used coffee grounds. If you do not dump the grounds, dripping from the filter basket will occur every time you lift the carafe off the warming tray.

Mr. Coffee is only available in a white plastic housing with a partial wood-like front panel. It can be easily disassembled for cleaning, but the cord cannot be detached. Although it requires you to operate two switches, dump the coffee grounds, and purchase paper filters, we still rate Mr. Coffee as a "Best Buy" because it makes superb coffee.

Suggested Retail Price: $49.95　　　　　　**Low Price: $39.95**

CORN POPPERS

CORNWALL 5614 *corn popper does not have a butter cup, a feature that we find unnecessary. The unit is fast, but we noted that the corn*

FOOD PREPARATION

burned badly when oil was not evenly distributed on the bottom before popping began. The Cornwall 5614 was easy to clean. Both the automatic shut-off and the see-through cover are nice convenience features.
Suggested Retail Price: $17.95   **Low Price: $13.37**

Sunbeam 18-19 *is for the person who insists on a self-buttering popper. It is lined with a Teflon II coating for easy cleaning and makes up to four quarts of popcorn. The lightly tinted cover doubles as a serving bowl.*
Suggested Retail Price: $17.50   **Low Price: $12.25**

ELECTRIC KNIVES

Hamilton Beach 360 *is light in weight and convenient to hold, featuring the "hole-in-the-handle" design. And it comes in a storage tray that can be mounted on a wall, sit upright, or store flat in a drawer. The tray features a scabbard blade holder and cord storage. Although only minimal pressure operates the power button, you need to apply a good deal of pressure to the knife itself to cut through many meats, especially roast beef. The Hamilton Beach 360 has rotating blades for carving sideways as well as downward – a feature we recommend. It does not, however, cut as well as does the Ronson 34123. We suggest therefore, that you try both models to determine which is more important to you: cutting ease or rotating blades.*
Suggested Retail Price: $29.95   **Low Price: $19.13**

Ronson 34123 *is easy to hold and maneuver, but suffers from a power button that requires considerable pressure to keep the knife in operation. The cutting action was so excellent, however, that it overcame any objection. The Ronson 34123 electric knife is relatively quiet; the cord is long; and the overall weight is good.*
Suggested Retail Price: $27.50   **Low Price: $18.79**

FRY PANS

Corning Table Range E-1310 *is an appliance that stands alone; its modern and simple design can be compared to none, and it will enhance any buffet. The heat range goes from 250 to 500 degrees, which makes it possible to warm and to cook meals right at the table. Corning provides a 2-1/2 quart dish with glass lid that may be used in the oven first and then placed atop the E-1310 Table Range for serving.*
Suggested Retail Price: $42.95   **Low Price: Not Available**

General Electric SK27, *designed for convenience, has a leg/handles section that snaps off for easy cleaning and storage, and an ejector button makes it simple to remove the plug control when it gets hot. Our testers found that the SK27 provided even heat to all corners of the attractive Teflon-coated pan. A tilt-leg feature for basting and draining makes for added convenience.*
Suggested Retail Price: $29.98   **Low Price: $21.60**

FOOD PREPARATION

Sunbeam Crocker Frypan 9-13 is a crockery vessel and a frypan combination that fries, simmers, and bakes. With a temperature range from 180 to 420 degrees, the Sunbeam Crocker Frypan 9-13 has a signal light that goes out when it reaches the desired cooking temperature – a feature we like. The frypan itself is coated in Teflon II. Our testers found that the 9-13 heats evenly and that both the frypan and the crockery vessel work well. The frypan unscrews from the cradle handle, making for convenient cleaning, and the crockery vessel can be placed in the cradle for serving purposes.

Suggested Retail Price: $45.95   **Low Price: $32.17**

MIXERS

KitchenAid K45 is sturdy and heavy enough to last a lifetime. It features KitchenAid's "round the bowl mixing": the single beater moves completely around the bowl as it mixes, from the center to the edges. This adds up to an efficient mixing job, whether you are whipping a cup of cream or a full bowl of ingredients. The KitchenAid beats, whips, stirs, blends, folds, and mixes – and does it all with only one beater to wash.

The dough hook that comes with the K45 can mix dough batter until the batter clings to the hook. The hook then carries the batter around and around, kneading it against the sides of the bowl. The dough hook cuts the average kneading time from 20 minutes to 10. KitchenAid offers a wide range of attachments – a can opener, food grater, knife sharpener, colander, meat grinder, sausage maker, grain mill, and shredder – that you can purchase separately.

Model K45 is very expensive, but not as costly as the KitchenAid K5-A, the top of the line. While we found that the higher priced unit performed extraordinarily well, so did the K45. Model K45 is a "Best Buy" because it is the most mixer the average homemaker should ever need to use.

Suggested Retail Price: $139.95   **Low Price: $97.10**

Sunbeam 2-12 is a stand mixer and a portable mixer in one. It comes with one large heat-resistant pour-spout glass bowl. We found it simple to insert and eject the beaters. Although this Sunbeam Mixmaster is easy to use, the cook must check the mixing guide for a key to proper speed selection, and then go back to the dial to set the proper number. This involves two steps rather than one. On the positive side, the cord is removable and the stand is so light that moving it for cleaning is no problem. Not as large as a standard heavy-duty Mixmaster, the 2-12 must be considered a full-size portable.

Suggested Retail Price: $29.75   **Low Price: $20.83**

Sunbeam Mixmaster 1-20 is expensive, but it is so well constructed that we think it is worth the money. It is heavier than many models on the market, but not so heavy that you will have difficulty lifting it on and off the countertop. A convertible unit, the mixer top detaches for use as a portable. It has an infinite speed dial that does what it is supposed to

FOOD PREPARATION

do. The Sunbeam Mixmaster 1-20 gave immediate response when mixing various weights of batter, and it mixed batter evenly in all of our tests. Well designed, the unit comes with two stainless steel mixing bowls.

Suggested Retail Price: $88.95   **Low Price: $62.27**

Waring HS15 *is a convertible hand/stand mixer which comes with two dishwasher-safe glass bowls in 1-1/2 and 2-1/2 quart sizes. Our testers found that the 2-1/2 quart bowl was too small. When mixing a cake mix, the batter nearly ran over the sides, coming 1/2 inch from the top of the bowl. The cord is not detachable, which is a detriment in cleanup. If you can put up with these inconveniences, however, the turntable of the Waring HS15 revolves better than the Sunbeam M12 Mixmaster. We also liked the fact that the Waring mixer has an off position between each of its 12 speeds—handy when you are mixing at higher speeds. Another plus for the Waring HS15 is that the mixing guide, which matches the proper speed to the unit's numbers, is on the top of the handle, placing it on the same level with the fingertip speed-control dial.*

Suggested Retail Price: $26.95   **Low Price: $15.59**

TOASTER OVENS

General Electric Toaster Oven T94 *is a good appliance if you need to replace your toaster. The T94 not only toasts regular and irregular size breads but also bakes, warms, and top-browns foods. It gives off little heat and is generally well constructed. Controls are easy to set and read. Its low profile makes storage easy.*

Suggested Retail Price: $46.98   **Low Price: $33.45**

Toastmaster 311 *can toast four slices of bread at a time. An easy-to-reach crumb tray and a removable door window make it an easy job to keep this unit clean. Like the G. E. model, the Toastmaster 311 has a thermostat which automatically maintains preselected temperatures from 200-500 degrees.*

Suggested Retail Price: $46.50   **Low Price: $31.73**

TOASTER

Panasonic NT 115 *features a sliding shutter, called the "Shutter Seal," that does an excellent job of retaining heat and moisture inside the browned toast. We found it easy to clean the Panasonic NT 115, and we appreciated the simple lines of this toaster.*

Suggested Retail Price: $27.95   **Low Price: $19.95**

WAFFLE BAKERS

Black Angus 950843 *features reversible grids for waffle baking or*

FOOD PREPARATION

grilling. It can cook four excellent waffle squares at one time, grill 1-1/2 inch thick steaks, and fry bacon with less shrinkage than occurs in ordinary frying. It is made of stainless steel. Clean-up is easy since the removable grids are coated with duPont's Teflon II, and there is a groove around the unit to catch excess batter.
Suggested Retail Price: $37.95   **Low Price: $23.70**

Dominion 1251 *is a well-balanced and sturdy unit and one of the best waffle bakers we tested. It delivered consistently well-browned and evenly cooked waffles. We regret, however, that the instruction booklet has only one recipe.*
Suggested Retail Price: $44.95   **Low Price: $28.83**

SLOW COOKERS

Oster Super Pan 697 *is a versatile cooking appliance. It includes a base heating unit, a water pan for warming, a cooking pan and cover, a tempura ring and skewers, and fondue forks. It also acts as a slow cooker. We highly recommend the Oster Super Pan 697 because it provides superb temperature control for simmer-to-boil cooking. We also like the unit's elegant design.*
Suggested Retail Price: $45.95   **Low Price: $42.87**

Rival Crock Pot 3500 *has a 10-inch stoneware interior bowl that is removable, dishwasher safe, and oven-proof. The control cord is detachable for easy serving. It's low profile means it is easy to store. The Rival 3500's coils are wrapped around the sides, resulting in true slow cooking. It can be left unattended for the entire day, needing no stirring. Meat cooked for 10 hours did not burn; in fact, it was delicious. An economical appliance, the Rival Crock Pot can operate all day for roughly three cents worth of electricity.*
Suggested Retail Price: $39.95   **Low Price: $25.94**

YOGURT MAKER

Electric Char-B-Que NYM-1, *the "natural yogurt maker" is a six-jar unit that has a very good instruction booklet. We made smooth and thick yogurt with no previous experience on our first attempt. Although the company's deluxe unit, NYM-2T, has an automatic timer that can be set from 5 hours (for delicate yogurt) to 10 hours (for piquant yogurt), the NYM-1's "take out" dial reminds you when to shut it off. A good gift item, the Electric Char-B-Que unit makes yogurt at home for less than one-fourth of the supermarket price.*
Suggested Retail Price: $9.95   **Low Price: Not Available**

1975 Food Preparation Appliances Prices

BLACK ANGUS

		Retail	Discount
BROILER/TOASTER/OVENS			
044821	Petite Broiler Warmer w/Continous Clean	$37.95	$23.75
044820	Petite Broiler/Warmer	31.95	19.50
330821	Petite Broiler/Oven/Warmer w/Cont. Clean	47.95	29.50
330820	Petite Broiler/Oven/Warmer	38.95	23.88
332821	Petite Plus w/Cont. Clean	49.95	31.25
333821	Petite Chef w/Cont. Clean & Push Button Controls	58.95	36.56
100825	Open Pit Broiler/Rotisserie	81.95	51.25
005821	Lido Rotisserie/Broiler/Grill w/Cont. Clean	121.95	76.25
005820	Lido Rotisserie/Broiler/Grill	107.95	67.50
711821	Silver Chef Rotisserie/Broiler/Oven w/Cont. Clean & Push Button Controls	117.95	73.75
711820	Silver Chef Rotisserie/Broiler/Oven & Push Button Controls	103.95	65.00
008821	Malibu Rotisserie/Broiler/Oven/Grill w/Cont. Clean	133.95	83.75
008820	Malibu Rotisserie Broiler/Oven/Grill	117.95	73.75

WAFFLER/GRILLS			
950829	Square w/Teflon II Coated Rev. Grids	36.95	23.00

		Retail	Discount
7000	Seal-A-Meal II	16.75	11.95
4200	Food Slicer	49.95	31.17
671	Can Opener	12.95	7.77
672	Can Opener/Knife Sharpener	15.95	8.88

DOMINION

SANDWICH TOASTER/WAFFLE IRONS			
1316	Auto. Waffle Iron, 7-1/2" Grids	$23.95	$15.37
1251	Gourmet Comb. Sandwich Toaster/Waffle Iron	44.95	28.83

ELECTRIC GRIDDLE			
3306	Non-Stick Coated	$33.95	$21.14

BUFFET RANGES, TABLE RANGES			
1460	Series Single Range-Type Heating Element, Table	$12.95	$7.94
3410	Series Single Burner, Table	14.95	9.60
1451	W/Single Range-type Heating Element, Buffet	18.95	11.53
3420	Deluxe Single Element, Buffet	23.95	14.86
1457	Double Element Range-Type, Buffet	26.95	16.65
3430	Deluxe Double Element, Buffet	33.95	21.26

BUFFET SKILLETS			
2261	11" Immersible	$25.95	$16.65

240   CONSUMER GUIDE

FOOD PREPARATION

950820	Square, Reversible Grids	30.95	19.44
932829	Twin-Size w/Teflon II Coated Rev. Grids	27.95	17.50
950843	Steak Griller & Waffile Iron w/Teflon Coated Rev. Grids	37.95	23.70
920820	Pizzelle Wafer Maker & Grill	27.95	17.63
920829	Pizzelle w/Teflon Coating	33.95	21.06

GRIDDLE & WARMER
550829	Hard Coat Teflon II	$42.95	$26.88
560829	18" Round w/Hard Coat Teflon II	39.50	24.69

COOKER/FRYER
866832	6 Qt., Hard Coat Teflon	$39.95	$25.00

TOASTERS
674820	4-Slice, Front-Control, Auto.	$26.95	$16.88
672820	2-Slice, Front-Control, Auto.	17.95	11.25

DAZEY

COUNTRY MANOR APPLIANCES
DC01	Can Opener	$14.95	$9.06
DCS2	Can Opener/Knife Sharpener	16.95	10.99
DIC3	Ice Crusher	24.95	17.46
DMG4	Food Grinder	32.95	23.06
DCP5	Chef's Pot	26.95	18.86
DSM6	Seal-A-Meal	14.95	9.99

DAZEY KITCHEN APPLIANCES
5000	Seal-A-Meal	$14.95	$9.72
2262	Series: 11" Immersible	26.95	17.95
3242	11" Pol. Alum., Immersible	29.95	19.06
2282	Series: 12" Non-Stick/Non-Scour Coating	34.95	21.63
3270	12" Immersible Broiler Fry Pan	41.95	26.91

TOASTERS
3160	Chrome	$17.95	$11.53
1170	Series: 4-Slice Pop-Up	23.95	15.37

CORN POPPERS
1703	4-Quart	$13.95	$8.49
1720	Automatic Self-Buttering	19.95	12.80

THE L'OVEN OVENS
3502	Cont. Clean Compact Oven Broiler	$30.95	$19.44
3503	Cont. Clean Deluxe Oven Broiler	38.95	24.63
3504	Cont. Clean Family Size Portable Oven	59.95	38.90
2521	Chrome Finish "Flip-Flop" Oven Broiler	26.95	16.82
2523	Series: "Flip-Flop" Oven /Broiler	25.95	16.19
2530	Auto. Combo. Oven & Broiler	34.95	22.00
2532	Series: Auto. Combo. Oven & Broiler	33.95	21.38
2506	Series: Auto. Portable Oven, Broiler	54.95	34.37

ROTISSERIE/BROILER
2559	Smokeless Broiler w/Magic Mirror	$29.95	$19.22
2560	Smokeless Rotisserie-Broiler	45.95	29.47
2565	Smokeless Rotisserie-Broiler with Hard Wood Cutting Board	54.95	35.24

FOOD PREPARATION

		Retail	Discount
BACONER			
3310	Chrome Sides, Wood Handles	29.99	26.99

		Retail	Discount
ELECTRIC HAND MIXER			
277	3-Speed	$11.99	$10.79
	• Fair Trade		

GENERAL ELECTRIC

		Retail	Discount
CAN OPENERS			
EC32	Series	$11.98	$9.10
EC33	Series	16.98	12.25
EC41	Series	24.98	18.05
COFFEEMAKERS			
CM9		$14.98	$10.75
CM11		17.98	12.70
CM15AV		23.98	16.70
P15	Series	25.98	18.10
DCM1		36.98	27.05
SSP10		35.98	26.00
SSP12		40.98	29.55
COFFEE URNS			
CU3		$25.98	$18.85
CU1		45.98	32.75
GRIDDLES			
EG1		$34.98	$24.75
EG1T		38.98	28.00

		Retail	Discount
ELECTRIC KETTLES			
1635	Stainless Steel 2-1/2 Qt. Auto.	$15.95	$9.68
1636,	2-1/2-Qt. Automatic	16.95	10.49
COFFEEMAKERS			
3640	2-10 Cup Aluminum	$18.95	$11.53
3650	Aluminum, 2-10 Cup, Pressure-Flo.	24.95	15.37
3660	Gleaming Chrome 2-10 Cup, Pressure-Flo, Teflon	28.95	17.94
3670	Stainless Steel, Imm. 2:10 Cup	31.95	19.87

FARBERWARE

		Retail	Discount
ELECTRIC FRY PANS			
300A	10-1/2" Round, Stainless Steel	$29.99	$26.99
310A	12" Round, Stainless Steel	36.99	33.29
312SP	12" Round w/High Dome Cover, Stainless Steel	39.99	35.99
320A	5-Qt. "Pot-Pourri"	39.99	35.99
330A	3-Qt. "Pot-Pourri"	28.99	26.09
335SP	12" Buffet w/High Dome Cover, Stainless Steel	44.99	40.49
BROILERS, BROILER ROTISSERIES & TURBO-OVEN			
441	"Open Hearth" Electric Broiler	$27.99	$25.19
444	Rotisserie Assembly Only	22.99	20.69

242   CONSUMER GUIDE

FOOD PREPARATION

450A	Comb.	39.99	G44	35.99	$29.98	$21.60
	"Open Hearth" Elec. Broiler	37.99	G44T	34.19	34.98	24.80
454A	Rotisserie Assembly Only	24.99	F54AV	22.49	12.98	9.60
455A	"Open Hearth" Broiler & Rotisserie		F54		12.98	9.60
456	Comb.	54.99	F49	49.49	20.98	14.85
	"Open Hearth" Shish Kebab	14.99	F47	13.49	17.98	12.70
460	Turbo-Oven	159.99	F87	143.99	17.98	12.70

AUTOMATIC COFFEEMAKERS

			KETTLE			
122B	12-Cup, Stainless Steel	$39.99	K52	$35.99	$20.98	$15.45
134	4-Cup, Stainless Steel	22.99		20.69		
138	8-Cup, Stainless Steel	27.99		25.19		
142	12-Cup, Stainless Steel	29.99		26.99		

AUTOMATIC URNS

			KNIVES			
130A	30-Cup, Stainless Steel	$54.99	EK9	$49.49	$18.98	$13.40
155A	55-Cup, Stainless Steel	64.99	EK8	58.49	26.98	19.35
			EK7		33.98	24.10

ELECTRIC CAN OPENERS

			MIXERS			
1234	Automatic	$14.99	M24 Series	$13.49	$11.98	$9.05
244	W/Knife Sharpener	19.99	M47 Series	17.99	16.98	12.00
			M22 Series		18.98	13.65
			M68 Series		22.98	16.45
			M44 Series		27.98	21.60
			M45WH Series		33.98	25.10
			M46 Series		43.98	31.55

GRIDDLE/WAFFLER

			SKILLETS			
260SP	Elec. Griddle & Control, Alum.	$34.99	SK26	$31.49		
290	Waffler & Grill	32.99	SK26AVT	29.69		

TOASTERS

271	2-Slice Automatic	$16.99	SK26HRT	$15.29	23.98	17.50
275	2-Slice Automatic, Chrome	19.99	SK27AV	17.99	27.98	20.25
276	4-Slice Automatic, Chrome	29.99		26.99	27.98	20.25
					27.98	20.30

FOOD PREPARATION

	Retail	Discount
SK27AVT	29.98	21.60
SK27HRT	29.98	21.60
SK29T	31.98	23.60
SK29AVT	35.98	25.90
SK29FT	34.08	25.90

THE CREATIVE ENTERTAINER COLLECTION
SFC3TY	$32.00	$29.09

TOAST-R-OVEN TOASTER
T93B	$39.98	$28.00
T94	46.98	33.45
T95	52.98	38.20

TOASTERS
T17	$16.98	$12.85
T16	21.98	15.45
T86 Series	21.98	15.85
T127	25.98	19.10
T146	24.98	18.00
T124HR	27.98	21.00
T125	29.98	22.30
T128	36.98	26.40

GRANDINETTI

CROCKERY CASSEROLE & SERVER

	Retail	Discount
ROTISSERIE/BROILERS		
325A W/Motor and Spit	$45.98	$28.40
331P W/Motor and Adj. Spit	39.98	24.69
330P Broiler with Chrome Grid	23.98	14.81
SKILLETS		
476 Pantastic Plus 11"x16" Broiler	$49.90	$30.82
548 Hi Dome 12" Broiler	41.99	25.90
540 Hi Dome 12"	37.95	23.44
BACONER		
474G Automatic Control	$29.98	$18.52
CORN POPPER		
505D Gourmet "Butter-Up" Self-Buttering	$20.99	$12.97

HOOVER/NESCO

	Retail	Discount
BROILER-OVENS/ROTISSERIES		
B1007 Broiler-Oven, Self Clean	$44.95	$33.70
B1507 Broiler-Oven w/Rotisserie, Self Clean	$69.95	$52.45
TOASTERS		
8509 2-Slice, Recessed Handles	$16.95	$12.70
8528 4-Slice, Recessed Handles	23.95	17.95
8530 2-4 Slice, Twin-Long Slow, Recessed Handles	25.95	19.45

FOOD PREPARATION

CROCKERY COOK-POTS
632	The All American 5-Qt.	$25.00
532	The All American 3-1/2-Qt.	30.00

HAMILTON BEACH

ELECTRIC KNIVES
164	Mix-N-Carve Knife/Mixer Comb.	$36.95
360	Deluxe Switchable	29.95
359	Switchable	26.98
296	Custom Utility	20.95

BLENDERS
631	System 1, Auto. or Timed	$42.95
688	Blender Plus, 14 Speeds	31.95
613	8 Push-Button Switch	28.98

STAND MIXER
36	10 Position	$48.95
40CT	Deluxe All Chrome, Auto.	66.98

HAND MIXERS
091-2T	12-Speed Power Dial	$26.98
108	Deluxe 5-Speed	15.95
107	Deluxe 3-Speed	14.98

CAN OPENERS
831	Insta-Clean Opener/Knife Sharpener	$14.98
829	Insta-Clean	13.98

FONDUE & FRY PANS
B3001-7	Mini Fry Pan	$16.95
8610-40	Mini Fry Pan/Fondue Set w/Forks	25.95
B3003	Fry Pan, Alum. w/Rem. Handles	22.95
B3005	Fry Pan, Alum. Warm. Try w/Rem. Handles	26.95
B3007	Fry Pan, Stainless Steel, Warm Tray w/Rem. Handles	35.95
B3009	Fry Pan, Stainless Steel, Broiler Lid, Warm Tray w/Removable Handles	43.95

BLENDERS
K6009	2-Speed	$19.95
K6007	6-Speed, Pushbutton, Spatula	24.95
K6005	6-Speed Custom	32.95
K6003	6-Speed Deluxe	39.95

KITCHENAID

MIXERS
4C	Heat Resis. Glass Bowl w/All-Purpose Beater	$84.95
K45	Stainless Steel Bowl, Beater, Whip & Dough Hook	139.95
K5A	Stainless Steel Bowl, Beater, Whip & Dough Hook	194.95

COFFEE MILL
KCM	Coffee Mill	$28.95

Second price column:

CROCKERY COOK-POTS
$16.50
19.50

HAMILTON BEACH
ELECTRIC KNIVES
$22.86
19.13
16.66
13.58

BLENDERS
$27.16
19.75
17.90

STAND MIXER
$32.10
41.99

HAND MIXERS
$16.66
9.85
9.25

CAN OPENERS
$9.25
8.63

FONDUE & FRY PANS
$12.70
19.45
17.20
20.20
26.95
32.95

BLENDERS
$14.95
18.70
24.70
29.95

KITCHENAID
MIXERS
$54.70
97.10
135.80

COFFEE MILL
$21.60

CONSUMER GUIDE

FOOD PREPARATION

NATIONAL PRESTO

FOUR QUART PRESSURE COOKERS

		Retail	Discount
PCA4	Pressed Aluminum	$20.30	$13.53
PCC4	Cast Aluminum	20.20	13.47
PCC4A,H	Color-Bright	21.20	14.13
PCS4	Stainless Steel	30.90	20.60
PCE4	Control Master	37.98	23.50
PCE4A,H	Control Master	40.98	25.36

SIX QUART PRESSURE COOKERS

		Retail	Discount
PCA6	Pressed Aluminum	$23.98	$15.99
PCC6	Cast Aluminum	24.90	16.60
PCC6A,H	Color-Bright	25.90	17.27
PCS6	Stainless Steel	34.90	23.27
PCE6	Control Master	41.60	27.74
PCE6A,H	Control Master	44.60	27.60

PRESSURE CANNERS

		Retail	Discount
CA16	16-Qt. Cooker-Canner	$59.90	$39.93
CA21	21-Qt. Cooker-Canner	65.90	43.93

COFFEEMAKERS

		Retail	Discount
CM9	9-Cup Super Speed	$31.90	$19.74
CM12	12-Cup Super Speed	35.90	22.22
CM10	10-Cup	32.40	20.05

		Retail	Discount
730	Super Grill Griddle	39.95	28.20
694	Super Pan Galaxie		
	Buffet/Cooker/Server	49.95	34.70
670	8-Qt. Super Pot All Purpose Cooker	49.95	34.70
681	Fondue	30.95	21.50
682	Heating & Serving Kettle Only	12.95	8.30
535	Touch-A-Matic Can Opener	16.95	11.30
557	Touch-A-Matic Can Opener/Knife/& Scissor Sharpener	19.95	14.10
577	Touch-A-Matic Can Opener/Citrus Juicer	26.95	18.85
567	Touch-A-Matic Can Opener/Ice Crusher	26.95	18.85
367	Automatic Citrus Juicer	19.95	13.75
362	Stainless Steel Juice Extractor	89.95	61.00

PANASONIC

TOASTERS

		Retail	Discount
NT-101	2-Slice Auto., Pastry Set, Radiant Cont.	$19.95	$13.88
NT-105	2-Slice Deluxe Auto., Pastry Set, Radiant Cont.	21.95	14.95
NT-114	2-Slice Auto., Keep Warm Feature, Pastry Set., Radiant Cont.	23.95	16.95
NT-115	2-Slice Auto., Shutter Seal, Pastry Set, Radiant Cont.	27.95	19.95

FOOD PREPARATION

NORELCO

COFFEEMAKERS
HD 5135	12-Cup Auto. Drip Filter	$39.95 $29.98
HB 5130	8-Cup Auto. Drip Filter	34.95 24.95
HB 5145	Plus 12 Warming Plate & 12-Cup Service	18.95 12.48
NT-3000	4-Slice Auto., Pastry Set, Radiant Cont.	27.95 19.88
NT-3005	4-Slice Auto., Pastry Set, Radiant Cont.	29.95 21.95

ICE CRUSHER
MK-285	Heavy-Duty, 5 Settings, Stainless Steel Blades	$33.95 $24.95

HAND MIXER
MK-125	Solid State, 8 Speeds, Push Button Btr. Eject, 150 Watts.	$29.95 $21.95

CAN OPENERS
MK-103	Lever w/Cutter & Remov. Floating Magnet	$17.95 $10.88
MK-111	Auto., Push-Button, Floating Magnet w/Remov. Cutter.	18.95 12.95
MK-107	W/Knife Sharpener, Lever w/Cutter & Remov. Fltg. Magnet.	19.95 13.88
MK-112	Auto., Deluxe w/Knife Sharpener, Floating Magnet w/Remov. Cutter	$23.95 $16.95

BLENDERS
MX-350	7-Speed, Solid State, Stainless Steel Blades.	$41.95 $31.95
MX-360	Auto. Recipe Blending, Solid State, Stainless Steel Blades	54.95 44.95
MX-370	Auto. Recipe Blending, Pana Blend Cycle, Solid State, Stainless Steel Blades.	59.95 49.95

OSTER

OSTERIZER BLENDERS
877	10-Speed Cyclomatic	$74.95 $52.25
857	16-Speed Dual-Range Pulse-Matic	54.95 38.70
847	10-Speed Cycle-Blend	42.95 29.50
833	10-Speed Dual Range	34.95 24.30
828	10-Speed Osterizer	29.95 20.50

MISCELLANEOUS ELECTRIC HOUSEWARES
551	"Snoflake" Ice Crusher	$26.95 $18.60
985	Kitchen Center	144.95 101.00
355	Deluxe 5-Sp. Hand Mixer	16.95 11.30
995	Food Grinder	46.95 32.30
473	Salad Maker Attachment	19.95 13.75
581	Automatic Egg Cooker.	26.95 18.60
631	Transparent 10-Cup Coffeemaker	30.95 21.50
529	Cutlery Center w/Knives	25.95 17.90
529	Cutlery Center w/o Knives	14.95 10.50
587	Salad Maker	34.95 24.50

FOOD PREPARATION

STEAMER MATICS

Model	Description	Retail	Discount
SR-10ZH	2-1/2-Qt. Multi-Purpose w/Therm	59.95	39.63
SR-16ZH	4-Qt. Multi-Purpose W/Therm	35.95	23.21
	Budget Grinder/Salad Maker	49.95	34.15

RICE COOKERS

Model	Description	Retail	Discount
SR-6E	1-1/2-Qt. Push Button w/Therm	$39.95	$29.88
SR-10EG	2-1/2-Qt. Push Button w/Therm	42.95	32.95
SR-15EG	4-Qt. Push Button w/Therm	49.95	39.95
SR-18EG	4-1/2-Qt. Push Button w/Therm	54.95	44.95

ELECTRIC BLENDERS

Model	Description	Retail	Discount
933	Touch Blend 7-Speed	$34.95	$21.89
944	Push-Button 4-Speed	29.95	18.30
939	Push-Button 2-Speed	24.95	15.51

AUTOMATIC WAFFLER/GRILLS & PIZZELLE/WAFFLER

Model	Description	Retail	Discount
90	Waffler/Grill w/Teflon Coated Rev. Grids	$37.95	$24.43
92	Mini Waffler/Grill w/Teflon Rev. Grids	28.95	18.84
95	Pizzelle Maker/Waffler Baker	30.95	20.14

PORTABLE ELECTRIC BUFFET RANGES

Model	Description	Retail	Discount
604	Single Burner	$21.80	$14.17
605	Double Burners	35.70	23.20

ELECTRIC JUICER

Model	Description	Retail	Discount
960	Juice-O-Matic w/2 Cones	$21.95	$14.29

ELECTRIC KNIVES

Model	Description	Retail	Discount
1220	Slimline, Stainless Steel Blades	$19.95	$12.98
1223	Deluxe, Stainless Steel Blades	22.95	14.29

ELECTRIC FOOD SLICERS

Model	Description	Retail	Discount
1030VC	Protect-O-Matic Deluxe Family Size	$69.95	$45.48
1037A	Slice-Crafter	59.95	38.98

PROCTOR-SILEX

STARFLITE TOASTER OVEN & TOASTERS

Model	Description	Retail	Discount
0-350H	Deluxe Toaster Oven	$38.95	$25.85
T-901H	Auto. 4-Slice Bread/Pastry	35.95	23.35
T001H	Auto. 4-Slice	32.95	21.40
T-506H	Auto. 4-Slice	25.95	16.85
T-703H	Auto. 2-Slice Bread/Pastry	21.95	14.00
T-303H	Auto. 2-Slice Bread/Pastry	19.95	12.70
T-609H	Auto. 2-Slice Bread/Pastry	16.95	11.00
T-614H	2-Slice Auto.	14.95	9.80

STARFLITE COFFEEMAKERS

Model	Description	Retail	Discount
P-102N	Auto. 12-Cup Perc., Glass Bowl	$27.95	$18.05
P-202H	Auto. 12-Cup Perc., Glass Bowl	21.95	14.20
P-003H	Auto. 10-Cup Perc., Glass Bowl	19.95	12.85
P-004B	Auto. 10-Cup Perc., Glass Bowl	18.95	12.30

STARFLITE BLENDERS & JUICER

Model	Description	Retail	Discount
B-505	8-Button, 12-Speed Solid State	$27.95	$18.20

FOOD PREPARATION

B-506	8-Button, 7-Speed Solid State	26.95	17.55
B-409	8-Button, 7-Speed Solid State	23.95	15.85
B-410W	6-Button, 5-Speed Solid State	22.95	15.20
J-118C	Auto. "Jucit" Juicer	19.95	13.00
J-108H	Same features as J-118C	17.95	11.30

RIVAL

ELECTRIC CLICK 'N CLEAN CAN OPENERS

711	Auto. Can-O-Matic Comb./Knife Sharpener	$26.50	$17.10
730	Can-O-Matic	15.95	9.90
731	Can-O-Matic/Knife Sharpener	18.95	12.30
790	Can-O-Matic Auto.	19.95	12.99
791	Can-O-Matic Auto./Knife Sharpener	24.95	16.39
752R	Knife Sharpener	15.95	10.02
753R		13.95	8.60
782	Knife Sharpener	16.95	10.92
794	Auto.	17.95	11.62
795	Auto/Knife Sharpener	20.95	13.66
703	Comb. Salad Maker/Can Opener	28.95	19.10
702R	Comb. Ice Crusher/Can Opener	28.50	18.46
707	Comb. Juicer/Can Opener	29.95	19.83

ELECTRIC ICE CRUSHERS

800	Ice-O-Matic	$37.95	$24.61
824	Ice-O-Matic w/Lift-O-Matic	25.50	16.39

ELECTRIC MEAT GRINDER-FOOD CHOPPERS

2100	Grind-O-Matic w/Removable Hopper	$48.50	$31.46

1038A	Slimline Budget	45.95	31.42
1101IEC	All Chrome	51.95	33.78

CROCK-POT ELECTRIC S-L-O-W COOKERS

3100	3-1/2-Qt. Cooker/Server, Detach.	$26.50	$17.10
3101	3-1/2-Qt. Cooker/Server, Detach. Cord	29.95	19.45
3102	2-Qt.	20.95	13.56
3300	Deluxe 5-Qt. Cooker/Server	39.95	25.94
3500	Casserole, 3-Qt. Cooker/Server, Removable Stoneware	39.95	25.94

RONSON

48408	Quintisserie Rotisserie, Griddle, Grille, Broiler, Fryer	$119.50	$79.80
48402	Quintisserie w/Shish Kebab	135.00	90.16
48103	19" Broiler Oven w/Cont. Self Clean.	84.50	54.29
42102	Cook 'N' Stir Blender	109.50	79.18
34123	Carve "N" Slice Electric Knife	27.50	18.79
67401	Deluxe Motorized Juicer	34.50	24.28
67301	Motorized Ice Crusher	32.50	21.14

APPLIANCE POWER CENTERS

44401	Multi-Speed Whisper Drive	$69.50	$47.45
44402	7-Speed Whisper Drive	75.00	50.97
44404	24-Speed Whisper Drive	87.50	59.38
44405	24-Speed Whisper Drive	95.00	64.39

FOOD PREPARATION

SALTON

PORTABLE MULTI-PURPOSE APPLIANCE

Model	Description	Retail	Discount
36013	Can-Do Can Opener	$32.50	$21.80
36012	Can-Do Deluxe Can Opener	37.50	24.83

HOTRAY FOOD WARMERS

Model	Size	Retail	Discount
H-907	10"x7-3/4"	$9.50	$6.35
H-910	14-3/4"x7-3/4"	13.95	9.35
H-920	17-1/4"x9-1/4"	19.95	13.35
H-926	24-3/4"x9-1/4"	27.50	18.40
H-930	20-1/4"x11"	33.95	22.75
H-940	24-1/4"x13-1/2"	39.95	26.75
H-950	29-1/2"x15-1/2"	54.50	36.50
H-960	32-1/2"x16-1/2"	63.00	42.20
H-934	20-1/4"x11"x4-1/2"H	38.95	26.10
H-944	24-1/4"x13-1/2"x4-1/2"H	47.50	31.80

HOTABLE SERVING CARTS

Model	Size	Retail	Discount
H-958	29"x16-1/2"x29-1/2"H	$89.00	$59.63
H-966	32"x17-1/4"x30"H	135.00	90.45
H-969	46"x17-1/4"x29"H	290.00	194.30

DOMES

Model	Fits	Retail	Discount
D-530	Fits, H-930, H-934	$19.95	$13.35
D-540	Fits, H-940, H-944	24.95	16.70
D-550	Fits, H-950, H-958	29.95	20.05

BUN WARMERS AND PARTY SERVER

Model	Size	Retail	Discount
WB-5	14-1/2"x9"x5"	$10.95	$7.35

BLENDERS

Model	Description	Retail	Discount
3-61	Deluxe 5-Speed	18.75	13.13
3-71	Deluxe 5-Speed Burst of Power	20.95	14.67
3-121	Deluxe 12 Pos. Inf. Speed	22.75	15.93
4-11	Deluxe 8-Speed Push Button Solid State	$37.50	$26.25
4-21	Deluxe 16-Sp. Solid State	40.50	28.35
4-30	Bar Blender, 2-Speed	43.95	30.77

CAN OPENERS

Model	Description	Retail	Discount
5-12	Auto. w/Knife Sharpener	$13.95	$9.77
5-32	Deluxe Auto. w/Knife Sharpener	17.95	12.57
5-91	Deluxe Auto. Total Clean, w/Knife Shrpn.	20.95	14.67
5-52	Deluxe Auto w/Ice Crusher	25.50	17.85

ELECTRIC SLICING KNIVES

Model	Description	Retail	Discount
6-11	Electric Slicing Knife	$19.75	$13.83
6-21	Deluxe Solid State, 2-Sp.	27.95	19.57

CORN POPPER

Model	Description	Retail	Discount
18-19	Self-Buttering, 4-Quart	$17.50	$12.25

FRYPANS

Model	Description	Retail	Discount
7-22	Cook & Clean Multi-Cooker	$36.95	$25.87
7-52	Decorator Teflon II Gourmet	37.95	26.57
7-30	Stainless Steel Multi-Cooker	38.95	27.27
7-40	Aluminum Multi-Cooker	24.95	17.47
7-100	Broiler Cover	38.95	27.27

CONSUMER GUIDE

FOOD PREPARATION

WB-4	14-1/2″ x9″ x5″		8.00
WS-3	22-1/2″ x19-1/2″ x4-1/2″		10.00

EGG COOKER
ER-IT	Auto. Time/Temp. Control	$16.70

YOGURT MAKER
GM-5	1-Qt., Thermostatically Cont.	$6.65

ICE CREAM MACHINE
IC-4	1-Qt. Automatic	$14.70

COFFEE-MAKERS & GRINDERS
CE-12	4-10 Cups, Glass Carafe	$6.65
CE-14	Coffee Extractor w/Warmer	12.70
GC-1	Auto. Measures & Grinds	23.40
GC-2	Quick-Mill	12.70

SUNBEAM

MIXMASTER MIXERS AND ATTACHMENTS
1-11	Deluxe w/o Juicer	$48.97
1-20	Deluxe w/o Juicer, Chrome Plated, Stainless Steel Bowls	62.27
2-12	12-Position, Inf. Speed	20.83
94-20	Meat Grinder	10.85
94-30	Power Unit	10.85

MIXMASTER HAND MIXERS
3-52	5-Speed	$11.03

CROCKER FRYPAN
7-152	Cook & Clean Multi Cooker w/Removable Crockery	$32.55

COOKER-FRYERS
9-42	Black Teflon II Auto. Porcelain	$29.75
9-30	Black Teflon II Auto. 5-Qt. Alum.	29.05
9-20	5-Qt. Automatic, Aluminum	27.65
9-12	Black Teflon II w/Removable 5-Qt. Crockery	32.17

BEVERAGE MAKER
17-13	Hot Shot	$13.83

COFFEEMAKERS
15-203	Clear Brew Auto. Drip-Type	$23.77
15-213	Coffeemaster Auto. Drip	23.77
15-109	11-Cup Auto., Glass	14.53
15-122	11-Cup Auto., Glass	15.93
15-52	11-Cup Auto. Percolator	10.85
15-62	11-Cup Auto. Percolator	15.05
15-10	11-Cup Auto. Perc., Pol. Alum.	13.83
15-20	7-Cup Auto. Percolator, Stainless Steel	18.17
15-30	12-Cup Auto. Perc., Stainless Steel	23.98
16-10	30-Cup Party Perc., Alum.	17.15
16-20	30 Cup Party Perc., Stainless Steel	33.95

GRIDDLE
21-10	Black Teflon II	$27.27

FOOD PREPARATION

		Retail	Discount
EGG COOKER			
23-10	Auto. w/Poacher Attach.	$27.75	$19.43
WAFFLE BAKERS			
22-20	Waffle Baker & Grill	$33.50	$23.45
22-30	Non-Stick	41.50	29.05
TOASTERS			
20-30	Radiant Cont. Self Lower	$37.95	$26.57
20-20	Deluxe 2-Slice	18.75	13.13
20-510	Deluxe 4-Slice	24.95	17.47

TOASTMASTER

		Retail	Discount
4-SLOT FOOD TOASTERS			
D109D110	Decor. Porcelain	$33.00	$24.70
D114	Deluxe Auto., Dual Cont., Chrome.	40.50	27.88
D103D104	Deluxe Auto., Dual Cont.	40.50	27.88
D127	Single Control "Up Front"	31.50	21.47
D132	"Astra" Dual Controls	—	23.65
2-SLOT FOOD TOASTERS			
B185	Deluxe Auto. "Up Front" Control, Chrome	$25.75	$17.88
B113B115	Deluxe Auto. "Up Front"	25.75	17.88
B120B121	Decor Porcelain	21.00	15.75
B150	Deluxe "Up Front"	16.00	12.08
B141	Automatic, End Controls	—	14.29

		Retail	Discount
5209	Steak 'N' Chop Broiler w/Auto. Thermostat	21.50	14.42
5206	"Mini Broiler" w/Auto. Thermostat.	—	10.58
5241	Deluxe Oven-Broiler w/Auto. Therm. & Timer.	38.00	28.39
5232	Reversible Tabletop Oven-Broiler, Auto. Therm., 1400 Watts	—	17.14
5225	Reversible Tabletop Oven-Broiler, Auto. Therm., 1000 Watts	19.95	14.94
ELECTRIC ICE CRUSHER			
6550	Deluxe.	—	$14.04
TEFLON WAFFLE BAKERS & GRILLS			
259	Deluxe w/Rev. Grids.	$36.95	$25.45
263/267268	Deluxe w/Rev. Grids.	29.95	20.83
266	Deluxe Waffle Baker.	24.95	16.99
W252	Deluxe Waffle Baker w/Auto. Thermostat	20.50	14.04
265	Deluxe w/Rev. Grids.	25.00	18.75
W258	Round Waffle Baker	16.00	12.08
POPCORN POPPERS			
6208	Deluxe Self-Butter. Auto.	$16.95	$11.47
6201	Deluxe Automatic.	—	8.33
6205	3-Qt. Non-Automatic.		5.10
GRIDDLES & FRY PANS WITH TEFLON			
871	Deluxe Griddle.	$33.95	$23.01

FOOD PREPARATION

311 Deluxe, Sep. Dual Elements ... $46.50

DELUXE STAINLESS STEEL COFFEE MAKERS
522A	4 to 12 Cup	$31.50
519	4 to 10 Cup	28.75
506	4 to 10 Cup	—
M552	8 to 30 Cup Buffet Urn	36.95

STAINLESS STEEL ELECTRIC TEA KETTLE
599 2-1/2 Quart ... $18.75

CAN OPENER/KNIFE SHARPENERS
2213/2212	Deluxe Combination	$20.95
2204/2203	Deluxe Can Opener	—

ELECTRIC CARVING KNIVES
6105/6106 Stainless Steel Blades ... —

TABLETOP OVENS & BROILERS
5256	Deluxe Broiler-Rotisserie	$46.50
5245	Deluxe Oven/Rotisserie	75.95
5242	Deluxe Pushbutton, Cont. Clean	
	Oven/Broiler	52.50
5247	Deluxe Oven/Broiler w/Auto. Therm., Pushbutton	42.95
5233	Deluxe "Flip Over" Cont. Clean	32.50
5231	Deluxe "Flip Over" Broiler-Oven w/Auto Thermostat	27.75
5212	Steak 'N' Chop Broiler w/Auto. Thermostat	23.50

	Deluxe Fry Pan	32.95
	Deluxe Fry Pan	32.95

BLENDERS
1024	Deluxe Solid State w/Variable Speed	$44.95
1021	Deluxe Solid State, 7 Speeds	—
1020	Deluxe Solid State, 7-Speeds, Tyril Plastic Food Container	

PORTABLE HAND MIXERS
1712	Deluxe 5-Speed	$15.50
1706	Deluxe 3-Speed	—

AUTOMATIC EGG COOKER
6501 Deluxe w/Auto. Signal Light ... $18.75

BUFFET RANGES
6400	Deluxe Double Burner Unit	$29.95
6401	Deluxe Single Unit Burner	18.75
6404	Double Burner w/Toggle Switches	21.95
6405	Single Burn w/Toggle Switch	13.95

WARING

BLENDERS
97-56	Chroma, 14-Speed Chrome Timer-Blender	$49.95
9356	Chroma, Blend Control, 8 Button, Chrome	41.95

FOOD PREPARATION

		Retail	Discount
57	14-Speed w/Timekeeper	42.95	24.31
55	Nova 1, 8 Pushbutton w/Dyna Blend.	36.95	20.40
51	Nova 1, 8 Pushbutton, 7 Speeds	28.95	16.84
94	14-Speed Timer Blender w/Flash Blend	41.95	24.59
91	8 Pushbutton Automatic Timer	34.95	19.79
79	14-Speed Color Coordinated	33.95	18.59
81	8 Pushbuttons w/Power Pitcher	27.95	17.38
C-80	8 Pushbutton Color Coordinated	26.95	16.20
NN-41	3 Pushbutton Power Pitcher	23.95	13.80

STAND MIXERS

		Retail	Discount
WS-155	Custom 250 Chrome, 10 Position, Infinite Speed	$59.95	$34.00
WS-151	10 Position, Infinite Speed	49.95	26.70

HAND MIXERS

		Retail	Discount
HM-121	12-Speed Solid State	$16.95	$9.71
HM-161	12-Speed Custom	19.95	11.62
HM-41	3-Speed Economy	12.95	7.80
HM-61	6-Speed	13.95	8.40
HM-81	6-Speed Deluxe	14.95	8.70

2 WAY HAND/STAND MIXERS

		Retail	Discount
HS-91	6-Speed	$19.95	$13.19
HS-151	12-Speed	26.95	15.59

CAN OPENERS

		Retail	Discount
CO-52	Maxi Clean, Knife Sharpener	$23.95	$13.63
CO-21	Auto., Knife Sharpener w/Push Button Clean Opener	18.95	10.30
CO-41	Deluxe Auto. w/Push Button Clean Opener	15.95	9.70
CO-11	Pushbutton Clean Opener	12.95	7.50
CO-31	Clean Opener w/Knife Sharpener	15.95	8.99

WEST BEND

AUTOMATIC COFFEEMAKERS

		Retail	Discount
9466A	9-Cup Economy Perk	$12.95	$7.75
5938A	9-Cup Poly Percolator	12.95	7.75
9470A	9-Cup High Speed Perk	16.95	10.15
3253A	Instant Hot Pot	14.95	8.95
3410A	25-Cup Party Perk	15.95	9.95
5960A	8-Cup Quik Drip, Decorated	43.95	27.55
5850A	Automatic Drip	43.95	27.55
5940	8-Cup Flavo-Drip	63.95	40.01
27210A	Double Quik-Drip II	54.95	40.10
33525A	30-Cup Automatic	23.95	14.35
11838A	30-Cup Insulated Party Perk	17.95	10.75
43536A	30-Cup Aluminum Percolator	27.95	16.75
13500A	36-Cup Auto. Institutional Perk	52.95	31.70
33600A	55-Cup Auto. Institutional Perk	59.95	35.90
39408A	100-Cup Auto. Institutional Perk	19.95	11.95
5920A	36-Cup Party Percolator	16.95	10.15
	20-Cup Poly Perk		

Prices are accurate at time of printing; subject to manufacturer's change.

FLOOR CARE

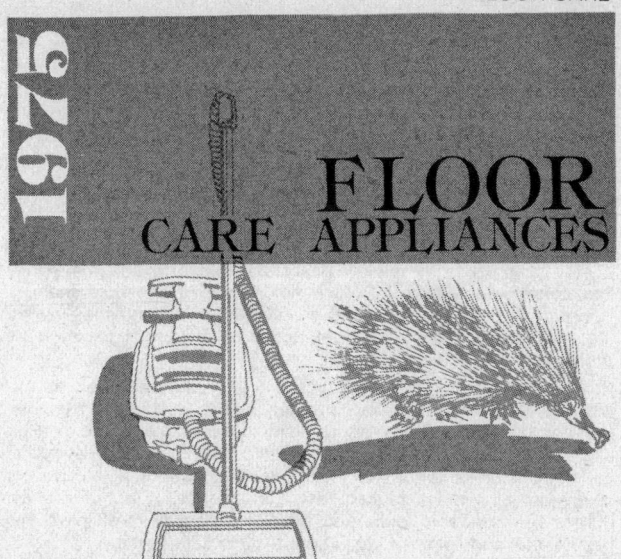

1975 FLOOR CARE APPLIANCES

THERE ARE hundreds of models of vacuum cleaners on the market today. These include canister vacuums, uprights, lightweights, hand potables, and shop-type. There is a variety of models within each of these catagories, many of which appear to be alike. Within its own line, Eureka, for example, offers many models that are very similar to one another. Some are different only in that they have extra chrome or optional attachment tools. CONSUMER GUIDE Magazine is opposed to such a marketing procedure because it makes price comparison for the average shopper nearly impossible.

During 1975, the consumer will have more models to choose from than ever before, but at the same time, there are fewer manufacturers building those models. General Electric, Westinghouse, and Shetland/Lewyt have discontinued their lines of vacuum cleaners. Consequently, Sunbeam is the only full-line portable appliance manufacturer still in the vacuum cleaner business. The G.E. and Shetland models have not left the market, however; they are now being manufactured by Premier Electric, an old name in vacuum cleaners. They are marketed under the brand name Premier (in department stores) and Whirlwind (in discount stores). Vacuum cleaners sold by J. C. Penney and Montgomery Ward are not of their own manufacture. J. C. Penney's models are supplied primarily by Hoover; Eureka Williams makes the vacuum cleaners sold under the Montgomery Ward label. In addition, both manufacturers offer the most complete lines in the business under their own names.

FLOOR CARE
Types and Prices

VACUUM CLEANERS cover a wide price range, from about $20 to more than $200. This price spread is not just between lightweight stick-types and deluxe canisters; it also represents the difference from low-end canisters to high-end canisters. Before deciding how much you want to spend, however, you should decide what type of vacuum cleaner you need to buy.

Dollar for dollar an upright vacuum cleaner outperforms the equivalent canister vacuum cleaner when it comes to cleaning carpets. Hoover manufactures the most complete line of uprights. Uprights have beater-bar-brushes that rotate to beat and brush up dirt and grime while canisters must rely largely on suction power alone for carpet cleaning. However, if you have extremely high, thick velvet, or long shag carpeting, you may find that the beater brush of an upright makes more problems than it solves.

The canister and tank-type vacs are generally regarded as all-purpose vacuum cleaners that can clean bare floors, carpeting, upholstery, and draperies with its various attachments. Some deluxe canister units, in fact, feature a motorized revolving brush built into the nozzle, giving them the same superior carpet cleaning power that the uprights have—but at a much higher cost. For example, Electrolux units, Eureka's Power-Team units, and the Sears Best units all have this feature and range in price from about $150 to $200 or more.

It is possible, of course, to buy attachments for some upright models, adding the flexibility of the canisters to their already superior carpet-cleaning powers. But it is usually more complicated to attach accessory parts to an upright than it is to put them on a canister or tank-type vacuum cleaner.

Canisters and uprights differ in their maneuverability also. Canisters and tank-type cleaners are generally easier to maneuver over door sills, under low furniture, and near baseboards. They are also better for cleaning stairs because you can usually reach at least halfway up or down the stairs with the hose and wands. Uprights are, for the most part, quite heavy, and you may experience some difficulty in carrying one with you to another floor of the house; but on the other hand, they are easy to wheel from room to room. Canisters are also easy to wheel from room to room, but you can just as easily pick one up and carry it wherever you are going.

Lightweight or stick-type vacuum cleaners are designed mainly as second vacs for quick daily sweepings. The best-known vacs of this sort are made by Regina—the Electrikbroom—but Bissell, long famous for its manual carpet sweeper, now has a line of lightweight vacs that are sturdily built and which perform as well as any on the market. The portable, or hand vacs, are also useful primarily as second vacs. Sears markets one that is as powerful as many canisters and which has optional floor attachments.

Both the lightweight vacs and hand vacs are suction-only machines, and, therefore, cannot do an adequate cleaning job on carpeting. But

FLOOR CARE

you can use them to pick up surface litter during intervals between regular cleanings with a more efficient vacuum cleaner. The lightweight vacs are particularly useful as an alternative to a broom for bare wood, tile, and linoleum floors.

The shop-type vacuum cleaner is a heavy-duty model designed for use in the home workshop, basement, and patio. It also is terrific for simplifying the chore of cleaning out the fireplace. The best-known name in shop-type vacs is Shop-Vac. They offer inexpensive drum-type models that provide sufficient capacity for most home uses. They also market wet-and-dry pickup machines, called Aqua-Vac, which feature an automatic float shutoff to prevent overflowing.

Horsepower Ratings

MOST VACUUM CLEANER manufacturers still rate their canister models—the largest-selling, all-purpose types—on the basis of peak horsepower, a practice which CONSUMER GUIDE Magazine has condemned for years as misleading. Peak horsepower performance is not based on the constant power level you can expect; instead, it represents the best the motor could do in laboratory tests.

The Vacuum Cleaner Manufacturers Association (VCMA), following years of prodding, finally came up with a better horsepower rating system. While CONSUMER GUIDE Magazine has a number of reservations about the VCMA rating system, we do recognize it as an attempt to rate the actual horsepower of the motor used in the vacuum cleaner.

If you can find the VCMA horsepower rating when you go shopping for a vacuum cleaner, it is almost surely to be in very small print. Manufacturers—and retailers too—are still promoting the peak-horsepower figures. The reason is simple: the VCMA horsepower rating is about half the peak horsepower rating. For example, a canister vacuum cleaner with a 1.7 peak horsepower rating qualifies for a .75 horsepower rating under the VCMA system.

The new VCMA rating system, however, is less than satisfactory for two major reasons: (1) The industry has failed to support it; manufacturers persist in listing their peak horsepower claims. (2) The rating system is still based on the horsepower performance of the motor rather than on the true cleaning power of the vacuum cleaner. There can be a big difference between the vacuum cleaner's motor power and its suction power.

Test the suction power of a vacuum cleaner by cupping your hand over the end of the hose and then pulling your hand away. Picking up cigarette butts may not be the most scientific means of testing, but it can serve as a guide. In fact, the way a vacuum cleaner picks up cigarette butts will give you a better idea of the machine's in-home performance than any sort of horsepower ratings.

How Many Vacuum Cleaners Do You Need?

ALTHOUGH CONSUMER GUIDE Magazine would not normally suggest buying two of any appliance, with vacuum cleaners two may be

FLOOR CARE

cheaper than one. Most people need a vacuum to perform two separate functions: to clean carpets and to do above-floor cleaning, like upholstery and drapes. To perform both functions well, you need either an upright with inconvenient-to-use attachments for the other cleaning chores, or a canister or tank-type model that performs well on carpets. The former will cost $100 or more; the latter ranges from $150 to over $200. A third alternative is to purchase an upright that performs well on carpeting ($60) and a canister that performs well everywhere else ($40). Or buy one now and add the other one later.

There are several advantages to the two-vac approach: one unit can be stored upstairs and the other downstairs in multi-level houses; if one ever has to go to the repair shop, the other one is there to carry you through; and you always have the right machine for the job. There are some disadvantages, however. By spending the same amount for two vacs instead of one deluxe unit, you may not get all the convenience features that you might get with a single deluxe unit; you may have trouble finding the space to store two machines; and you probably will have to keep two types of disposable bags on hand.

Floor Polishers and Rug Shampooers

FLOOR POLISHERS and rug shampooers generally can be rented through supermarkets or local hardware-housewares stores for a few dollars. The low rental rate is designed to induce you to buy the more profitable shampoo and liquid floor polish. If you have wall-to-wall carpeting that soils easily, you may want to invest in a home machine; but for most people, renting makes more sense. Improvements in liquid floor polishes have eliminated the need for regular polishing and buffing of hard-surface floors, while the advent of rug shampoos in aerosol cans has in large measure reduced the need for a home machine or for professional-quality carpet cleaning more than once or twice a year.

Nevertheless, if you decide that you should own your own machine, Bissell markets a Spinfoam electric rug shampooer that is shaped like—and is as easy to use as—a carpet sweeper. Designated model 3080, it features a powered roller-style brush that applies the shampoo as foam and massages it into the carpet fibers. There is a slightly more deluxe and more powerful Spinfoam model, 3054B, which is better for cleaning shag carpeting.

The traditional, dual-brush rug shampooers/floor polishers are five appliances in one—they scrub, wax, polish, buff, and shampoo. Regina offers a well-constructed line, including the popular model P1025. Two more expensive units have the same motor but offer a choice of speeds.

For the ultimate in floor and carpet care, Hoover markets its Floor-A-Matic (model 3614) which power scrubs floors, picks up the water, polishes, and buffs—as well as shampoos carpets—all for under $100. Hoover also makes separate rug shampooers and shampooer/polishers. Although they feature dual brushes, these Hoover machines are both easy to handle and effective. Model 5308 is a shampooer; model 5488 is a shampooer/polisher.

FLOOR CARE

BEST BUYS: FLOOR CARE APPLIANCES

CONSUMER GUIDE Magazine experts tested more than 30 vacuum cleaners on bare and hard-surface flooring, and on all types of carpeting–from low-pile indoor/outdoor to standard broadloom to high-pile shag. In addition, the cleaners were tested for their ability to clean draperies, upholstered furniture, and other above-floor furnishings. We looked for sufficient suction power to perform the cleaning function expected according to the price of the vac. Budget-priced canisters, for example, were judged on their ability to pick up surface dirt and lint on carpeting, while deluxe canisters were expected to do a more thorough, deep-down cleaning job. Upright vacs were expected to excel in carpet cleaning, with above-floor cleaning ability of secondary importance. Naturally, we also judged the units on the basis of durability of overall construction and attachments, convenience in use, and special features–particularly in relation to the price.

BUDGET-PRICED CANISTER VACUUMS

Sunbeam VC635, a well-constructed machine with an all-steel body, is without frills but offers good suction power at this price range. Attachments include an all-purpose rug-floor nozzle, adequate for picking up most surface dirt. Large wheels make maneuvering easy; a flick of the toe turns the machine on and off. Tools can be stored inside, and the large dust bags are convenient to use and replace. A basic vac with no extra features and priced accordingly, the VC635 is no longer in production, but you may still be able to find it in stock. The VC1 is Sunbeam's new budget-priced canister vac.
Suggested Retail Price: $59.95   Low Price: $43.79

Premier Electric P6-C-14 or Whirlwind WI-C350 are basically identical models designed for all-purpose cleaning rather than for deep-down carpet care. The Premier Electric and Whirlwind machines are the Swivel-Top vacs formerly marketed by General Electric. Suction power is adequate for surface cleaning and the rotating hose swivels 360 degrees for convenience in use. A foot control turns the vac on and off, while a fingertip control on the hose regulates suction. A nice money-saving feature–you can use these Premier Electric and Whirl-

FLOOR CARE

wind machines with or without disposable bags. You will probably find the Whirlwind model at a greater discount.

Premier Electric P6-C-14
Suggested Retail Price: Open   Low Price: $29.72
Whirlwind WI-C350
Suggested Retail Price: $29.99   Low Price: $22.97

Hoover Constellation 843 or Celebrity S3005 *both glide along the floor on a cushion of exhaust air with no wheels or runners. The Constellation 843 is more expensive than the Celebrity S3005, but the latter provides particularly good suction power and a 10-quart capacity bag. The Constellation comes with a better floor/rug nozzle and carries its own tools. Both offer excellent value for their prices.*

Constellation 843
Suggested Retail Price: $49.95   Low Price: $37.45
Celebrity S3005
Suggested Retail Price: $44.95   Low Price: $33.70

MID-PRICED CANISTER VACUUMS

Hoover Portable 2204 *lacks the suction and cleaning power of the Celebrity Deluxe, but it rates high for convenience features and for its all-purpose cleaning ability; it is adequate for surface cleaning carpets. The 2204 is, of course, considerably less expensive than the S3003. Styled like a suitcase and able to store everything inside – including hose and wands – the 2204 is the perfect canister vac to use in an apartment. Well constructed of high-impact plastic over a steel base, this slim machine is easy to use for cleaning stairs. An automatic cord reel is standard.*
Suggested Retail Price: $69.95   Low Price: $52.45

Regina V379 *offers a good combination of suction power and features for its price. The unit is not as powerful as the Hoover Celebrity, but it can do a good job on most carpeting. Push-button controls provide easy adjustment of suction power when switching from floors to dusting or cleaning draperies. A dial control converts the nozzle easily for varying carpet piles and for edge cleaning. The well-constructed all-steel case stores accessories inside.*
Suggested Retail Price: $99.95   Low Price: $63.33

Premier Electric P2-C-18A, *with plenty of power for all-round cleaning, has push buttons to make it easy to regulate suction for cleaning floors and draperies, and for dusting above-floor furnishings. The swivel-top design greatly enhances convenience, as do the piggy-back tool carrier, cord reel, and bag indicator light. A floor-rug nozzle and seven-piece attachment set are included. The cloth filter bag can be used with or without disposable paper bags. Although the disposable bags increase your operational costs, they do save you the mess of emptying the cloth bag.*
Suggested Retail Price: $89.99   Low Price: $61.99

FLOOR CARE

HIGHER-PRICED CANISTERS

Eureka Power-Team 1255, *a two-motor canister, is not as powerful as the more expensive models in the Power-Team line. Nevertheless, the 1255's suction power – when combined with the motorized beater-bar-brush roll in the nozzle – is highly effective in cleaning carpeting. It is not, however, as effective as the more powerful Hoover Celebrity for above-floor cleaning. On the other hand, the power nozzle has the Edge Kleener feature, and it adjusts automatically to varying carpet piles.*
Suggested Retail Price: $119.95   Low Price: $93.24

Sunbeam 40-118 *not only delivers more than adequate suction power, but it also comes complete with a number of deluxe features. The eight-piece attachment set includes a shag brush, and all accessories – in addition to wands and hose – are stored and carried piggy back. A 25-foot cord, full-bag indicator, and five suction controls are standard. Exclusive features in this Sunbeam canister vac include a stair-lock wheel base and "wheelbarrow" transportation with the wand serving as a handle. The unit stores compactly, and total weight is less than 20 pounds.*
Suggested Retail Price: $102.99   Low Price: $77.24

UPRIGHT VACUUM CLEANERS

Hoover U4003 Custom's *"beats-as-it-sweeps-as-it-cleans" action for carpeting does a highly effective job in getting carpeting deep cleaned. The U4003 Custom features a two-speed motor that automatically shifts into high when above-floor tools are attached to provide 50 percent more suction power offered by comparably priced canisters. It is sufficient, nonetheless, for dusting and most other light chores; single-speed Hoover uprights, on the other hand, are not recommended for use with attachments. The Hoover U4003 Custom has a lever for carpet pile adjustment, a somewhat less convenient control than Eureka's dial. Although attachments cost extra, the U4003 has die-cast aluminum housing and a headlight. The outer vinyl bag zips open and shut.*
Suggested Retail Price: $89.95   Low Price: $67.45

Eureka 1416 *is for anyone wanting an upright merely for cleaning carpets; it is not recommended, however, for use with attachments. The 12-inch beater bar/brush roll effectively beats and sweeps up imbedded dirt. A four-way dial adjusts from low to normal to high to shag according to the height of the carpet pile. A basic upright vac without many frills, the Eureka 1416 does include the Edge Kleener feature and a foot-controlled on/off switch. It lacks a headlight, however.*
Suggested Retail Price: $59.95   Low Price: $53.28

Premier Electric P3-U4, *like any good upright vac, has a beater-bar that effectively loosens imbedded dirt. Unlike many uprights, however,*

FLOOR CARE

this Premier Electric model also possesses sufficient suction power for above-floor cleaning. A foot-control switch operates the two-speed motor for high suction with attachments. For carpet cleaning, the Premier Electric P3-U4 has a four-position carpet pile adjustment and an edger attachment. The vinyl outer bag is opened and closed via a full-length zipper. Like the other vacs from Premier Electric, this model carries a one-year over-the-counter replacement warranty.
Suggested Retail Price: $79.99   Low Price: $55.97

Sears 3456, *a one-speed budget-priced upright, has beater-bar-brush action to loosen deep dirt and sufficient suction power to get it up. Although there are only two height adjustments, those may be sufficient for most users. The 3456 possesses a large dust bag, larger even than some more expensive Sears uprights. Recommended for people seeking an inexpensive vac for carpet cleaning only, the Sears 3456 has a plastic body and vinyl outer zippered bag.*
Catalog Price: $52.95

LIGHTWEIGHT VACUUM CLEANERS

Hoover Handivac *broom-type vac can be pulled apart and used as a portable (hand) vacuum cleaner. It is powerful enough for quick cleanups and for kitchen spills. Available in several models that are comparable in performance but differ in features – model S2003 features a more deluxe floor nozzle than models S2005 and S2007 – the Hoover Handivac can be used with optional attachments for above-floor dusting.*
S2003
Suggested Retail Price: $29.95   Low Price: $22.45
S2005
Suggested Retail Price: $27.95   Low Price: $20.95
S2007
Suggested Retail Price: $24.95   Low Price: $80.70

Regina Electrikbroom B4518, *like the other models in the Electrikbroom line uses a plastic dust cup instead of disposable bags. The dust cup saves money, but it is messier to empty and needs to be emptied more frequently than do the disposable paper bags. The Electrikbroom line features a cloth outer bag (rather than plastic housing as on most lightweights), which may have to be shaken from time to time to get the dust to drop into the cup. Able to hang like a broom from a hook in the closet, the Regina Electrikbroom generates sufficient suction power for quick run-throughs. The two-speed models are not worth their substantially higher prices.*
Suggested Retail Price: $52.95   Low Price: $29.06

Sears Kwik-Sweep Vac 6316 *is more powerful than the Regina Electrikbroom, but is very similar in most other respects. It has a dust cup*

FLOOR CARE

and cloth bag. The deluxe floor nozzle has a dial with three settings for adjusting to carpet height or to bare floors.
Catalog Price: $31.95

Hoover 409 Swingette *is a portable vac that can be used as a canister. It is actually as powerful as many under-$50 canisters–and is priced like one, but attachments are included. Its compact pocketbook styling–it can be carried easily by its handle–gives no clue to the 409's substantial suction power. Convenient for reaching into corners and high places that need dusting, the unit can also slide along the floor like a canister. Due to its cleaning power in relation to its size, the Hoover 409 Swingette is particularly recommended for people living in small apartments; it later can become a second vac in a home.*
Suggested Retail Price: $49.95   Low Price: $37.45

COMBINATION VACUUM CLEANERS

Hoover Dial-A-Matic 1149, *an upright-styled combination vac, has a molded plastic outer housing rather than the vinyl outer bag found on most uprights. The Dial-A-Matic takes its name from a dial in the middle of the back of the outer plastic housing; the above-floor cleaning hose attaches here, and the dial controls the degree of suction. The hose which attaches to the back of the machine provides extended reach through attachments (optional at extra charge) and telescoping wands. Unsurpassed for carpet cleaning – and the most convenient and most powerful upright for use with above-floor attachments – the Hoover Dial-A-Matic offers a full-bag indicator and lever adjustment for carpet pile height, and it uses extra-large disposable bags.*
Suggested Retail Price: $124.95   Low Price: $93.70

Eureka Power-Team 1261 *is the more powerful version of the Power-Team 1255. Model 1261 offers considerably more power for increased suction, making it particularly useful for both floor and above-floor cleaning. The power-driven nozzle looks different than the one on model 1255, although it works in basically the same way. The Eureka Power-Team 1261 also has the Edge Kleener feature in addition to an even larger dust bag than found on model 1255.*
Suggested Retail Price: $139.95   Low Price: $113.30

Sears Powermate 2491L *provides almost as much suction power as Sears' "Best" Powermate which lists in the catalog for $214.95. But the 2491L retails for $70 less. This machine also features a floor nozzle with a motor-driven bar that beats and sweeps up dirt from carpeting, similar to an upright vac; strong suction power enables it to perform equally as well for above-floor and all-round cleaning as for carpet. Model 2491L comes complete with attachments and features an automatic cord reel. The all-plastic body has twin attachment ports –one for suction and one for blowing – and open tool storage on top.*
Catalog Price: $144.95

1975 Home Care Appliances Prices

FLOOR CARE

BISSELL

		Retail	Discount
FLOOR CARE ELECTRICS			
3044-1	Sweep Master, Deluxe	$—	$22.80
3045-1	Sweep Master, 2 speed	—	29.40
3054B	Electrofoam Shampooer	—	35.88
3080	Spinfoam Shampooer	—	24.60
SWEEPERS			
2155	Regency, All Floor Sweeper	$—	$14.25
2601A	Series: Gemini, All Floor Sweeper	—	13.12
2220A	The Shagger	—	12.18
2208	Series: Grand Rapids	—	10.93
2501	Series: Vanity	—	8.75
2424	Daisy	—	8.25
2425	Flowergarden	—	8.25

EUREKA

		Retail	Discount
UPRIGHTS & ATTACHMENTS			
1404-A		$49.95	$44.80
1406-A		54.95	48.84
1416-A		59.95	53.28
1421-A		69.95	61.05
2013-A		69.95	58.83
2023-A		79.95	67.71

HOOVER

		Retail	Discount
150-A		29.95	23.52
150-AT		39.95	30.24
UPRIGHT			
U4003	Convertible, w/Headlight	$89.95	$67.45
U4005	Convertible		
1348	Lightweight, Rug Adj.		
COMBINATION			
1149	Dial-A-Matic	$124.95	$93.70
U6007	Dial-A-Matic, Power Dr. w/Headlight	209.95	157.45
COMMERCIAL			
344/348	Lightweight	$99.95	$74.95
918	Heavy Duty, Rug Adj., 3-Prong	199.95	149.95
CANISTER COMPLETE			
409	Swingette	$49.95	$37.45
843	Constellation, Tools/Rack	49.95	37.45
858	Constellation	44.95	33.70
S3001	Celebrity Custom	129.95	97.45
S3003	Celebrity Deluxe	99.95	74.95
S3005	Celebrity Air-Ride	44.95	33.70
S3013	Portable, Tools, Cord Reel	69.95	52.45

FLOOR CARE

Model	Price 1	Price 2	Description	Price 3	Price 4
2033-A	89.95	77.70	S3015 Portable, Tools, Cord Reel, Wheels	79.95	59.95
2042-B	99.95	78.81	S3023 Slimline Deluxe, Cord Reel, Tools/Rack		
2053-A	109.95	84.36	2017 Slimline	54.95	41.20
2073-A	119.95	91.02	2120 Portable, Tools	39.95	29.95
2083-A	149.95	106.56	2204 Portable, Tools, Cord Reel	59.95	44.95
2625-B	19.95	11.20	2266 Portable, Tools, Cord Reel, Wheels	69.95	52.45
2675-B	24.95	17.92		74.95	56.20
405-E	169.95	103.04	**HAND/STICK**		
C1625-A	129.95	76.16	2800 Pixie, w/Tools	$34.95	$26.20
C2035	129.95	86.58	S2007 Handivac	24.95	18.70
C2045	149.95	99.90	S2005 Handivac Deluxe	27.95	20.95
C2055	159.95	109.89	S2003 Handivac Custom, Single Speed	29.95	22.45
C2065	169.95	113.22			

CANISTERS & LIGHTWEIGHTS

Model	Price 1	Price 2	Description	Price 3	Price 4
500-BT	$39.95	$35.52	**POLISHERS & SHAMPOOERS**		
755-A	44.95	41.07	5158 Polisher, 2 Brushes, 2 Pads	$29.95	$22.45
736-A	49.95	43.85	5168 Shampoo-Polisher, 1½-qt. Tank	34.95	26.20
738-B	54.95	46.62	5308 Deluxe Rug Shampooer, 3-qt. Tank	39.95	29.95
780-A	54.95	46.62	5488 Shampoo-Polisher, 3-qt. Tank	49.95	37.45
1630-A	69.95	55.50	5498 Shampoo-Polisher, 3-qt. Tank w/Headlight	54.95	41.20
1660B	89.95	73.26			
1680-B	104.95	82.14	**RUG & FLOOR CONDITIONERS**		
1255-A	119.95	93.24	3614 Floor-A-Matic w/Water Pickup	$74.95	$56.20
1260-A	139.95	104.34	3616 Floor-A-Matic, w/Headlight	89.95	67.45
1265-A	169.95	127.65			
1285-A	219.95	163.17	**PREMIER**		
95-S	25.95	20.72			
100-B	33.95	25.20	**CANISTERS**		
107-A	36.95	26.88	P2C-17 Two Stage, Swivel Top	$69.99	$51.25
102-A	39.95	29.68			

CONSUMER GUIDE

FLOOR CARE

		Retail	Discount
P2C-17A	Two Stage, Swivel Top, w/Shag Rug Cleaning Tool	79.99	55.99
P2C-18A	Two Stage, Swivel Top	89.99	61.99

SWEEPERS
		Retail	Discount
SB-3	2-Speed Sweeper Broom	$29.99	$21.25
SB-3A	2-Speed Sweeper Broom	34.99	23.97

UPRIGHT VACUUM CLEANERS
		Retail	Discount
P1-U10	1-Speed Upright	$59.99	$43.99
P4-U5	2-Speed Upright	64.99	46.47
P3-U4	2-Speed Upright Vacuum w/Floor Level Headlight	79.99	55.97
P9-U7	2-Speed Deluxe Upright w/Floor Level Headlight & Auto. Cord Rewind	99.99	68.97

PORTABLE
		Retail	Discount
P4-MV-2	Mighty Vac Deluxe	$26.99	$19.97

CANISTERS
		Retail	Discount
P7C-16	Single Stage, Swivel Top	$44.99	$33.47
P1C-21	Single Stage, Swivel Top	49.99	37.99
P3C-15	Two Stage, Swivel Top	59.99	42.99
P3C-15A	Two Stage, Swivel Top, w/Shag Rug Cleaning Tool	69.99	47.99

REGINA

ELECTRIKBROOM VACUUM CLEANERS
		Retail	Discount
B-7524	Power Cont. Nozzle, 2 Speed, 350 Watt	$39.95	$27.88

SHOP-VAC

		Retail	Discount

SHOP VACUUM CLEANERS
		Retail	Discount
22201	5 Gallon	$37.95	$30.35
22301	Deluxe 5 Gallon	44.95	35.95
77701	10 Gallon	42.95	34.35
77801	Deluxe 10 Gallon	49.95	39.95
44001	Bulldog	49.95	39.95
99900	Hippo	39.95	31.95
99901	"His" Hippo	44.95	35.95
99902	"Hers" Hippo	44.95	35.95
99903	Hippo w/"His" & "Hers" Acc.	51.95	41.55
46001	Aqua-Vac w/Cart.	99.50	79.60
46101	Aqua-Vac w/Cart.	124.50	99.60
40001	10 Gal. Stainless Steel Wet & Dry	189.50	151.60
93001	20 Gallon Wet & Dry	169.50	135.60
33301	18 Gallon Dust Collector	49.50	39.60
41101	28 Gallon Dust Collector	49.60	39.60
91101	30 Gallon Steel	99.50	79.60
94001	Dustman	139.50	111.60
22101	55 Gallon Dual	125.00	100.00
99601	Hippo Blower	49.95	39.95

SUNBEAM

CHALLENGER VACUUM CLEANERS
		Retail	Discount
40-118	2.3 H.P. motor w/Stair-Lock	$102.99	$77.24

CONSUMER GUIDE

FLOOR CARE

B-4518	Rug Pile Dial Edge Tool Nozzle, 1 Speed, 425 Watt	52.95	40.98	1-1/4 H.P. w/Stair-Lock 73.99 55.49
RB-5628	Rug Pile Dial Nozzle w/Power Edge Suction w/900210 Shag Rake	59.95	34.96	

CANISTER VACUUM CLEANERS

40-18	1 H.P. Special Value	$42.99	$32.24
40-38	1-1/2 H.P. Round Canister	54.99	41.24
40-58	1-1/2 H.P. Round Canister	64.99	48.74
WC4000C	Vista Canister w/4-Way Suction	49.94	36.46
740-84	Vista Canister w/Auto Cord Reel	56.94	41.57

B-4629	Air Pulse Nozzle w/Rug Pile Dial & Edge Suction, 2 Speed	64.95	36.88
B-4639	Air Pulse Nozzle w/Rug Pile Dial & Edge Suction	72.95	41.97

UPRIGHT VACUUM CLEANERS

41-12	4/5 H.P. Special Value	$64.99	$48.74
41-28	2 Sp. Custom Deluxe, 4-Pos.	93.99	70.49
41-38	2 Sp. Custom Deluxe Cord Reel	105.99	79.49
743-64	Vista Lightweight	35.94	26.24
741-64	Vista Upright	59.94	43.76
741-54	2 Sp. Vista Upright	79.94	58.36

POWER LINE CANISTER VACUUM

RV-455	2 Peak H.P., 8 Piece Acc.	$84.95	$56.43
V-379	2-1/3 Peak H.P., 7 Piece Acc.	99.95	63.33
V.477	2-3/4 Peak H.P., 7 Piece Acc.	119.95	77.37
V.496	2-3/4 Peak H.P., 2 Speed 8 Piece Acc.	134.95	91.42

OUTDOOR/INDOOR HEAVY DUTY VACS

42-18	1 H.P. 5 Gal. Tank, Dry	$41.99	$31.49
42-28	1-1/2 H.P. Deluxe, Dry	48.99	36.74
42-31	5 Gal. Deluxe Wet/Dry	63.99	47.99
742-44	Vista Heavy Duty 5 Gal.	34.94	25.51

2-IN-1 POWER COMBINATION DUO-VAC

V.550	2 Peak H.P., 8 Piece Acc.	$169.95	$126.93
V.570	2-1/3 Peak H.P., 8 Piece Acc.	189.95	141.22
V0590	2-3/4 Peak H.P., 9 Piece Acc.	204.95	169.86

HEAVY DUTY VACS

43-53	"Power 4" Vacuum Broom	$27.99	$20.99
43-11	Special Value Vacuum Broom	33.99	24.47
43-31	Deluxe Vacuum Broom	37.99	28.49
43-41	Super Deluxe Vacuum Broom	45.99	33.11
740-124	Vista Heavy Duty Vacuum	81.94	59.82

ALL-PURPOSE WET/DRY VACS

APV-21	Heavy-duty, Over 7-U.S.gal. tank, 8 Piece Acc.	$64.95	$41.96
APV-23	Heavy-duty, 14 piece Acc.	74.95	47.71

12-INCH 2-SPEED RUG SHAMPOOER/FLOOR POLISHER

P1033	90-Oz. "Touch-O-Matic"	$52.95	$33.35
P862	120-Oz. "Automatic Internal"	59.95	41.20

BUDGET UPRIGHT VACUUM

U940	3.5 Amp Rated Motor	$59.95	$33.92

Prices are accurate at time of printing; subject to manufacturer's change.

WASHERS / DRYERS

WASHERS/DRYERS

TODAY'S LAUNDRY equipment does more automatically than ever before. And more demands are made on today's laundry equipment. Newer fabrics and special finishes require specific care—varying water and drying temperatures; selective wash, spin, and dry speeds; special settings for permanent press, no-iron fabrics, wools, and knits. New washers and dryers are designed to launder and dry, in the best way possible, each of the various wash loads found in the laundry basket, whether it be for one or two people, or for a large family; whether you live in an apartment, a single-family house, or a mobile home—even in a dormitory room. Features are many, capacities vary, and prices are influenced by both factors. Your choice of home laundry products is wide, and with such a variety, it is easy to become confused in the marketplace.

CONSUMER GUIDE Magazine does not feel that it is necessary to purchase the top-of-the-line, full-featured programmed model to achieve good washability. The best values and those that offer overall practical convenience for most people fall within the middle-of-the-line models. There are some economy-priced models that offer flexibility for your varying loads, but for the most part they offer very little convenience past getting the job done. And getting the job done today is not enough. With new fabrics and finishes, changing family needs and individual lifestyles, concern about energy consumption and the need for increased efficiency, you may be happier with a model which offers more choice in selective convenience.

WASHERS / DRYERS

As far as size is concerned, you will find both full size and compact laundry equipment—and portable units in both sizes. Whatever your lifestyle or particular needs may be, there will be just the washer or dryer for you somewhere on the market. But you must shop around and compare features versus convenience in relation to price. Defining both in terms of your needs, you will be better able to make the right decision.

Before buying laundry appliances, overall needs must be projected over the life of the equipment. After all, both a washer and a dryer represent a sizeable investment, and the average life span for an automatic washer is around 11 years and for a dryer about 14 years. So, try to anticipate any future needs, such as how much your family is likely to grow or shrink in the next few years.

It would be wise for you to analyze the contents of your laundry basket to determine what types of fabrics and loads you will normally launder. It was not so many years ago that the natural fibers of cottons and linens were all housewives had to contend with. Then along came manufactured fibers, each with separate laundering needs resulting from the kind of fiber and the fabric finish. For a time, appliance manufacturers felt that a separate cycle had to be designed for each one of these special requirements. The result caused more confusion than help. The truth is that while there may be hundreds if not thousands of different brand names of fabrics, there really are only a few categories and types; thus, relatively few different laundering procedures are required. The manufacturers have recognized the trend, so now there are more machines with simple controls, cycles, and the entire laundering procedure has been simplified.

Another key consideration when buying a washer is the need for a good supply of hot water; therefore, you should give some thought to the adequacy of your water heater. Ask about the two types available—the standard storage type and the quick recovery design—and the advantages and disadvantages of both in relation to a continuous supply of hot water. And how about softened water? Inquire about how hard the water is in your area and the ways it can be softened if necessary.

PURCHASING TIPS: WASHERS

Top Load or Front Load

WASHERS ARE available primarily in top-loading designs with the washing action accomplished by means of an agitator. One manufacturer—Westinghouse—offers a front-loading type which performs by means of a tub or drum which tumbles the loads. While they offer several standard-size models in a front-loading design, the compact Westinghouse Space Mates offer you the option of installing a washer and dryer side-by-side under a counter or as stackables, one on top of the other.

Top-loading washers are convenient to load and unload. They also allow you to add clothes and check the load to assure free movement during the wash cycles. Top-loaders are available with lids that open to

WASHERS/DRYERS

the side or to the back. Those that open to the side offer several advantages: On many of these machines the lid can be used as a landing spot for loading and unloading, and controls are easier to get at if the lid opens to the side. On the other hand, a side-opening lid may be an obstacle if the washer is in a tight-fitting space, such as along a wall.

Front-loading washers use less water than the top loaders, and they hold more clothes because no space is taken up with an agitator. In addition, a front-loading machine offers greater convenience in installation for tight space requirements, such as in under-counter kitchen arrangements or in narrow spaces that necessitate stacking the washer and dryer. A special feature available on Westinghouse's Space Mate is a built-in scale in the door for weighing laundry loads.

As for any differences in washability performance and cleaning powers of varying designs in agitators and tub formations, generally they all do a satisfactory job. The important factor in cleaning performance lies in using the proper amount and kind of detergent, in meticulous sorting, in adjusting the amount of clothes to the size of the tub, and in the ability of the items to move about the tub freely. Again, the temperature of the water (140° - 160°) and its condition in terms of how hard or soft it is are primary factors.

Decide What Capacity You Will Need

CAPACITY is usually expressed in pounds of dry clothes. Up until a few years ago, standard capacity for a washer was 8 pounds. Today, standard-size machines are available in capacities anywhere from 14 to 20 pounds. The 18-pound capacity has become fairly standard throughout the industry, and allows you to vary the size of your load from 1 to 18 pounds. Norge has a washer that will wash as little as 2 pounds and as much as 20.

The trend toward larger capacity machines stems from the desire for flexibility in doing either small or large loads, depending upon family size and the variety of loads in fabric types, finishes, and colors. Many feel that a larger machine is a great advantage in that it provides better performance in handling bulky or larger loads. Also, with the growing popularity of no-iron fabrics, larger capacity machines offer less wrinkling. On the other hand, large capacity washers use a lot more water, an important consideration if your water is metered and also has to be heated. The size of your load will depend upon the kind of sorting you do, according to types of fabric and how they should be laundered. If you have a large family and your properly sorted loads are large, then you should consider a large capacity machine. On the other hand, if your loads are small, a smaller capacity will do just as good a job.

How Much Automation?

THE OLD-fashioned wringer and spinner washers are still popular in many areas. Both are portable, being mounted on casters. They cost less than the automatic washers, use less water, and cost less to

WASHERS/DRYERS

operate. On most units, the washer and wringer are power- or motor-driven; no longer do you need to turn the wringer by hand. Maytag has a wringer washer whose wringer can be operated by a foot control.

Automatic washers have a variety of controls and push buttons to regulate speeds, temperatures, washing time, etc. There are generally two types of automatics: manually-controlled and programmed. The manually-controlled automatic washers are for people who want the flexibility and responsibility of making thse decisions themselves. They range from inexpensive machines with just the basic components for good performance, to top-of-the-line designs with every convenience feature for specialized washing. The basic models offer one or two speeds, a choice of wash and rinse temperatures for varying loads, and possibly a bleach dispenser. Middle-of-the-line machines, in addition to the basic components, offer a wider choice of wash and rinse temperatures, specialized fabric cycles, and dispensing systems. Prices will range as features and convenience increase anywhere from about $25 to over $60 or $65.

If you want to leave the decision-making to the machine itself consider the programmed type. These models allow you to set a single control or push a button for any one of a number of specialized loads —regular or normal, delicate, permanent-press, knits, woolens, bright colors, heavy-duty, etc. These washer controls are pre-set to make all the strategic decisions about water temperature, water level, agitation and spin speeds, etc., automatically. You do not have to do the thinking.

Although these units offer the greatest convenience, CONSUMER GUIDE Magazine questions their overall value. They are expensive (they are the top-of-the-line models); and they cannot be reprogrammed to meet new washing demands. If you know what kinds of fabrics are in your laundry basket, we suggest you save money by looking at units with specific cycle controls for the loads you will be laundering. Instruction manuals will guide you until the proper settings become second nature to you.

How Much Flexibility?

MOST AUTOMATIC WASHERS offer a choice of wash and spin speeds: regular for normal loads and gentle/slow for delicate items. There are single-speed washers available, but CONSUMER GUIDE Magazine considers the two-speed worth the extra $25 to $30 you will pay, as they offer greater flexibility in the choice of garments and items you can wash. We also find that machines with several wash/rinse water temperatures offer choice of greater flexibility for laundering a wider variety of fabrics. The recommended choice of temperature combinations are cold/cold, warm/cold, hot/cold, warm/warm and hot/warm. Such flexibility in choice is important, particularly in view of the fact that in July of 1972 the Federal Trade Commission ruled that all wearing apparel manufactured after that date must have a permanent label that carries care instructions. With this law and with such a choice of water temperatures, you can be prepared for any washing situation.

WASHERS/DRYERS

How Much Space?

BECAUSE MANY homes have space limitations, the compact and portable washers and dryers are excellent choices. Virtually all leading manufacturers now have a compact machine in their lines. Compact washers and dryers, often referred to as "stackables," are pint-sized versions of major designs. They measure from 21 to 27 inches wide. The dryer can be mounted or stacked on top of the washer by means of a rack designed for the purpose, or it may be wall-mounted. Or both units can be conveniently installed side-by-side under a counter. These units are a good solution to space problems. They do a satisfactory job if you have no other alternative or if you are not critical to a fault, but they do not offer the full-convenience performance that their standard counterparts do. Some washers, like the Maytag Porta-Washer require hand transfer of clothes to a separate spin drum, while others wash and spin them in a single tub. Load capacity ranges from 5 to 8 pounds.

Portable washers are available in both standard and compact sizes. They are caster-mounted for portability and hideaway storage, can be plugged into a 115-volt outlet, and must be rolled to a sink or tub for filling and draining.

In addition to the "stackables," several even smaller units are on the market. Hoover has a table-top washer with an optional wringer attachment which does a 1½-pound load in about 12 minutes, then shuts off automatically. It sells for approximately $45, and is an excellent choice for students who live in dormitories, or for campers. Another tabletop washer, the "Wash-O-Matic" made by Rival, a small appliance manufacturer, retails for about $43. While both of these units are solutions to real space problems, neither can offer the good washability that even the compacts do.

There is an increasing growth in compact portable laundry appliances manufactured and sold in the United States. More of them are automatic... offering many of the convenience features that their larger counterparts do. If the growth of metropolitan areas increases and the amount of space available for each family unit decreases, the importance of this growing market in compacts may become even more significant.

CONSUMER GUIDE Magazine recommends that a large family with unlimited space should consider a permanently installed, full-size washer and/or dryer, with a variety of selective controls. If space is limited, but the capacity of a full-size machine is needed, consider a washer and/or dryer which stacks one on top of the other or a standard-size portable unit on casters. An apartment dweller, mobile home, or vacation home owner should consider a smaller washer and/or dryer or one which does not require permanent installation. A compact machine is a good choice. However, with vacation homes, there may be the need to do large quantities of laundry. In this case, standard-size machines are best. If you live in a studio-apartment, a dormitory, or have need for a washer in an office set-up you may want to consider one of the table-top designs.

WASHERS/DRYERS

Available Features

Pre-soak. There is a renewed belief in the idea that presoaking of certain types of laundry loads will reduce the time and effort of pre-treating. Hence, the growing number of pre-soak features on washing machines. If your wash load is normally heavily soiled, a pre-soak feature will be useful for you.

Water level and temperature controls give you the option of varying the amount of water and temperature for the wash and rinse cycles —cold, warm, hot, and variations of each. These are essential in giving you the flexibility for washing any fabric or combination of fabrics in any given load, and are a basic and important feature found on most machines.

Automatic dispensers eliminate the need for waiting for the final rinse in order to pour in fabric conditioner. This feature allows the homemaker to fill the dispenser when loading and starting the machine. The dispenser will then automatically release the conditioner into the machine at the proper time. This is a great time-saving feature. If you want to save money on the feature, you can just use one of the several rinses on the market that can be poured into the machine at the beginning of the wash cycle.

Adjustable wash times to control the number of minutes you want to wash the loads are available on some machines. Unless your wash loads normally vary a great deal in terms of dirtiness, this is not a necessity.

Unbalanced load corrector—an automatic stop and reset device or specially designed tub to offset unbalanced loads is a basic component on most machines. Do not buy a machine that lacks this feature.

Variable wash and spin cycles set up the proper washing time and water temperatures for specific loads, such as regular, permanent press, and delicate. Basic machines have regular and permanent press cycles. In addition to these there are cycles for knits, woolens, pre-wash and soak. For $20 to $30 more you will buy more flexibility in cycle selection.

Extra rinses for heavily soiled clothes. If you have many loads of extra-soiled fabrics this feature may be worth the extra $25 to $30 you will pay. Virtually all manufacturers offer this feature on their more expensive models.

Multiple agitation and spin speeds. Slower agitation speeds are important for delicate fabrics, slower spin speeds for permanent-press items. Most washers offer a selection of two to four speeds. Some with solid-state controls have an infinite range of speeds. However, CONSUMER GUIDE Magazine has found that the delicate cycles are too rough on delicate items. If you wash a fair amount of delicate clothes regularly, CONSUMER GUIDE Magazine suggests that you look at special features that cater to this need. General Electric's "mini-basket" handles up to 2½ pounds of delicate items. And Westinghouse's hand agitator, smaller than the standard agitator, moves very slowly and gently.

WASHERS/DRYERS

Safety lid switch shuts off the spin cycles when the lid is raised; or there is a device that prevents the lid from opening during the spin cycles. One or the other of these safety features is a must, but CONSUMER GUIDE Magazine feels that the type that cannot be opened during the spin cycles is best if you have small children.

Weighing lid or door is a feature on some Westinghouse washers. CONSUMER GUIDE Magazine feels that this is not really necessary as you will get to know what your own average loads are in time and will not need to weigh them.

Variety of colors are important only if you are trying to color-coordinate or decorate areas such as utility rooms, family rooms, or kitchens.

Illuminated controls and basket interiors can add to the cost of the machine. Illumination is essential to any task, but if your laundry area is adequately lighted, you should forgo this luxury.

Operating instructions on the lid are generally found on middle-of-the-line to top models. These are handy reminder instructions, though you will get used to your machine as you use it and will not really need to refer to the instructions often. The same instructions are in the instruction book.

Easy access to parts for servicing, such as snap removal of control panels, etc., eliminate the moving of the machine away from the wall.

Porcelain tub and enamel cabinet are durable, easy to care for, and resistant to rust, corrosion and laundry aids. Speed Queen offers a stainless steel tub, an unnecessary luxury. A porcelain tub will last as long as you need it to, providing you do not drop a brick in it. A stainless steel tub will last forever; unfortunately, the rest of the machine will not.

PURCHASING TIPS: DRYERS

Suit Your Convenience and Pocketbook

THE MOST EXPENSIVE dryers are sensor-controlled; next are the thermostat-controlled; and finally, there are the time-controlled models. An automatic sensor-control or dryness control such as in Maytag's "Halo of Heat" dryers, has electronic sensings which "feel" the moisture in your clothes and turn off the dryer when they are dry. It depends upon the degree of moisture in the fabrics as to how long it takes the load to dry. While this sounds like a foolproof way of preventing overdrying, it is not. If there is any moisture left in any of the load, even the exposed elastic of some underwear, it is possible that the dryer will keep running, and that the other items in the load may overdry. Of course, it is important that like items be dried together. These dryers cost anywhere from $40 to $60 more than the least expensive time-controlled dryers. This is a dryer for people who do not want to make any decisions and who do not have any special drying problems.

A thermostat or temperature-controlled type offers a selection of different heat levels, from high to medium to low. They are generally indicated by the type of fabric or load—regular, permanent press, knit,

WASHERS/DRYERS

and delicate are the most common. These sell from $15 to $25 more than the least expensive time-controlled type.

A time-controlled design turns the dryer off at the end of a specific length of time which you set manually. The times for various types of loads are indicated in the instruction manual. This design is good for limited budgets. If you do not mind determining the time it takes to dry your average load, it could be your best buy. However, if you do not take the time to study how long it takes to dry the specific loads in your laundry basket, you could overdry your laundry creating dryness wrinkles that are hard to remove. Many time-controlled machines are also temperature-controlled.

Installation Requirements

DRYERS COME in both gas and electric models. Both types do a good job, but installation may be your deciding factor. Gas dryers cost about $25 to $30 more, but are normally less expensive to operate. If you already have gas appliances, you can have a gas feed line run to an expected dryer location for around $30 to $50. All gas dryers have a pilot light. Most are located at the base of the unit, covered by a small door, though Speed Queen places its pilot light at the top, beneath a hinged lid.

Most electric dryers require a separate 30-ampere, 3-wire, 240-volt circuit. (Some metropolitan areas, such as New York City, require 208 volts.) If you already have this capacity in your home (you do if you have an electric range or water heater), running a 220/240 volt circuit to the expected dryer location should cost between $40 to $75, depending on its distance from the service entrance. If you do not have 220/240 volt service, it will be a fairly expensive proposition to rewire. Some compact electric dryers can be plugged into a standard 115-volt outlet, if properly grounded.

Another concern is venting. All gas and electric dryers must be vented to remove hot air and moisture. For the greatest efficiency and, particularly, for safety, CONSUMER GUIDE Magazine recommends that all dryers be vented to the outside. Installation charges will be less expensive if you locate the dryer on an outside wall.

Available Features

Lint filters on dryers are basic to every dryer and are extremely important. A clogged filter can cause poor or no air circulation and a build-up of heat concentration, eventually leading to serious service problems. Lint filters should be accessible and easily removed. Blackstone offers a wide screen which encircles the entire port opening assuring adequate airflow and encourages regular and easy removal of lint.

Automatic electric ignition for gas dryers should have an automatic shut off in case gas or electrical service is interrupted.

Larger opening or porthole means easier loading and unloading,

WASHERS/DRYERS

such as the type found on Frigidaire, General Electric, and Whirlpool. Doors that open downward can provide a convenient landing shelf, but avoid overloading them. New dryers bearing the UL seal will turn off when the door is opened and will not start again until the door is closed and a button is pushed.

Interior drum finishes of porcelain enamel, acrylic or zinc-coated steel, and similar finishes offer smooth, no-snag surfaces, resistant to rust and corrosion.

Variety of temperature settings for specific fabrics or loads usually offer air only, no-heat cycles and permanent press cycles with a cool-down period to reduce wrinkling. CONSUMER GUIDE Magazine finds this a real advantage in meeting the needs of today's mixed laundry basket.

Indicator light or bell signal for end-of-cycle such as the chime offered by Maytag, could be a decided advantage if you are drying permanent-press and other items which should be removed immediately to reduce wrinkling. However, this can also be an annoying feature (except on the Westinghouse dryers, on which the loudness of the signal can be controlled). On a time-controlled machine, a signal is not really needed since you will have set the drying time yourself and so will know when the dryer will turn off.

Retractable hanger rod on which to hang clothes just removed from the dryer can be handy, but is also not really necessary. It is just as easy to hang them on a doorknob, a clothes line, or a hook put in the wall.

Stationary drying rack for drying items without tumbling, such as stuffed animals, sneakers, sweaters, and knit items, is a useful feature only if you do a lot of that kind of washing. Otherwise, it is just as easy and less expensive to lay these items to dry on a rack or towel.

WASHERS/DRYERS BEST BUYS

WASHERS AND dryers have been rated according to durability of construction, operating performance, and special features–in relation to price. The following "Best Buys" represent the finest quality and best values available. And because the following models are made by well-known manufacturers, you are assured of serviceability.

WASHERS

General Electric WWA 8330P is a two-speed large capacity washer. This model handles up to 18 pounds of laundry, but the water can be adjusted to four different levels for those times when smaller loads are washed. There is no re-set button for unbalanced loads, so the machine will continue the wash cycle although the load is unbalanced. However, in this case, the machine shakes quite a bit, so it would be wise to locate the machine somewhere where it has room to shake without harming anything.
SPECIFICATIONS: Height, 43 1/2"; Width, 27"; Depth, 25"; Speeds, 2; Cycles, 4; Dry Load (pounds), 1-18; Volts, 115; Amps, 15. FEATURES: Water Level Selector; Water Temperature Selector.
Suggested Retail Price: $299.95   **Low Price: $231**

Maytag A606 is a large capacity unit that is able to do small loads by an adjustment of the water level. This two-speed model has a separate soak cycle, and a fabric softener dispenser. This is a basic, dependable washer with no frills. It is available in decorator colors, but colors cost extra.
SPECIFICATIONS: Height, 43 1/8"; Width, 25 1/2"; Depth, 27"; Speeds, 2; Cycles, 3; Volts, 115; Amps, 15; Motor H. P. 1/3. FEATURES: Water Level Selector; Water Temperature Selector; Load Selector.

Suggested Retail Price: Not Available   **Low Price: $288.75**

Speed Queen DA3500 is a dependable basic washer with all the features you need to do a good job with your laundry. There are two wash cycles–one for normal loads and one for permanent press–plus there is a pre-soak cycle for heavily soiled items. There are three water temperature selections and three water level selections, making this as versatile a unit as you will need. The top and front panel can be removed for easy servicing, so the machine does not have to be moved

WASHERS/DRYERS

away from the wall for a service check. This model is available in white only.

SPECIFICATIONS: Height, *42"*; Width, *25 5/8"*; Depth, *28"*; Speeds, *1*; Cycles, *2*; Volts, *120*; Motor H. P., *1/2*. FEATURES: Water Level Selector; Water Temperature Selector.

Suggested Retail Price: Not Available   Low Price: $224.90

Gas Dryers

General Electric DDG 7180P *is a most deluxe gas dryer. There are three temperature settings, and there are three drying cycles: an automatic cycle for normal loads, an automatic cycle for permanent press loads, and a timed cycle (up to 60 minutes). An automatic sensor control ends the cycle when the clothes are dry. When the cycle ends, a signal sounds.*

SPECIFICATIONS: Height, *43 1/2"*; Width, *27"*; Depth, *25"*; Cycles, *3*; Cabinet Vented, *2-way*; Volts, *115*; Amps, *6*. FEATURES: Type, *gas*; Temperature Settings; Lint Trap Location, *front*.

Suggested Retail Price: $259.95   Low Price: $196.90

Maytag DG406 *features drying cycles for permanent press (with a cool-down period) and for regular loads. There is also an air fluff cycle for tumbling without heat. The pilot light is behind a door in the front of the unit for easy access. To order this unit in colors costs $7 extra.*

SPECIFICATIONS: Height, *43 1/8"*; Width, *28 1/2"*; Depth, *27"*; Cycles, *3*; Cabinet Vented, *3-way*; Volts, *115*. FEATURES: Type, *gas*; Temperature Settings.

Suggested Retail Price: Not Available   Low Price: $199.90

Speed Queen DG 6181 *has four heat selections plus an air fluff setting that has no heat. The dryer can be set either on one of several automatic settings (for normal loads or delicate loads) or can be set on a timer which can be set for from 10 to 75 minutes. A buzzer sounds when the drying cycle has ended. A handy feature is that the loudness of the buzzer can be controlled and it can even be turned off.*

SPECIFICATIONS: Height, *43 1/2"*; Width, *30"*; Depth, *28 1/8"*; Cycles, *3*; Cabinet Vented, *4-way*; Volts, *120*; Amps, *5.3*. FEATURES: Type, *gas*; Temperature Settings; Lint Trap Location, *in door*.

Suggested Retail Price: Not Available   Low Price: $222.40

ELECTRIC DRYERS

General Electric DDE 7100P *is the electric version of the Model DDG 7180P described earlier. This unit has all of the same features as the gas model except that it can be vented from four different locations. The gas model can be vented from three. As with the gas model, this one features thermostatically controlled heat.*

SPECIFICATIONS: Height, *43 1/2"*; Width, *27"*; Depth, *25"*; Cycles, *3*; Cabinet

WASHERS/DRYERS

Vented, *2-way;* Volts, *120;* Amps, *24.* FEATURES: Type, *electric;* Temperature Settings; Lint Trap Location, *front.*
Suggested Retail Price: $219.95   Low Price: $165

Maytag DE406 *is exactly the same as the Model DG406, except this is an electric dryer. Both units can be vented from three different locations. Because these models have simple lines and only one dial, they are exceptionally easy to keep clean.*
SPECIFICATIONS: Height, *43 1/8";* Width, *28 1/2";* Depth, *27";* Cycles, *3;* Cabinet Vented, *3-way;* Volts, *115.* FEATURES: Type, *electric;* Temperature Settings.
Suggested Retail Price: Not Available   Low Price: $122.40

Whirlpool LAE 7800, *like the gas Model LAI 7801 has the lint trap set behind a hinged door on the top of the dryer, which makes it particularly easy to reach to clean. The end-of-cycle buzzer cannot be controlled in terms of loudness–a consideration if the laundry area is near the nursery.*
SPECIFICATIONS: Height, *43";* Width, *29";* Depth, *25 1/2";* Cycles, *3;* Volts, *120/240.* FEATURES: Type, *electric;* Temperature Settings; Lint Trap Location, *top.*
Suggested Retail Price: Not Available   Low Price: $171.60

COMPACT WASHERS AND DRYERS

Whirlpool LAC 4900 *is only 24 inches wide. It features two wash speeds and four wash cycles. A soak setting allows for prebuilt in or used as a portable, needing only one hose connection to the faucet of a sink. The unit can be adjusted for six different water levels. Although small in size, this unit clearly has all the features necessary for effective and economical operation.*
SPECIFICATIONS: Height, *32 1/2";* Width, *23 7/8";* Speeds, *2;* Cycles, *5;* Volts, *120;* Motor H. P., *1/2.* FEATURES: Water Level Selector; Water Temperature Selector; Load Selector.
Suggested Retail Price: Not Available   Low Price: $236.50

Whirlpool LAE 4900 *is the electric dryer which pairs with the Model LAC 4900 washer. No special wiring is needed, so this portable can be plugged into any 120-volt outlet. The dryer features three cycles: one for normal loads, one for permanent press, and one that is air only for tumbling items without heat. These units can be used side-by-side, or the dryer can be hung on a wall (an optional hanging kit is available), or the dryer can be mounted on a tubular metal rack above the washer. The rack is also available as an optional feature.*
SPECIFICATIONS: Height, *32";* Width, *23 7/8";* Depth, *20 1/2";* Cycles, *3;* Cabinet Vented, *rear;* Volts, *120.* FEATURES: Type, *electric;* Lint Trap Location, *back.*
Suggested Retail Price: $169.00   Low Price: $140.80

WASHERS / DRYERS

1975 Washer and Dryer Prices

FRIGIDAIRE

		Retail	Discount
WASHERS			
WCDA	2 Speed, 16 lbs.	$299.95	$231.00
WCD	2 Speed, 18 lbs.	319.95	243.10
WIA	2 Speed, 18 lbs.	334.95	253.00
WCI	3 Speed, 18 lbs.	109.95	308.00
W3-24	24 Inch	—	183.70
W3-224	24 Inch	—	192.50
ELECTRIC DRYERS			
DA	Timed Dry, 18 lbs.	$199.95	$157.30
DCD	Timed Dry, 18 lbs.	224.95	166.10
DIA	Auto Dry, 18 lbs.	249.95	183.70
DCI	Auto Dry, 18 lbs.	299.95	226.60
D-24	24 Inch		129.80
GAS DRYERS			
DAG	Timed Dry, 18 lbs.	$239.95	$190.30
DCDG	Timed Dry, 18 lbs.	264.95	199.10
DIAG	Auto Dry, 18 lbs.	289.95	216.70
DCIG	Auto Dry, 18 lbs.	339.95	259.60
LAUNDRY CENTERS			
LC-2	2 Speed, 240V	$439.95	$354.20
LCT-120	2 Speed, 120V	439.95	354.20

		Retail	Discount
DDG 7180P		259.95	196.90
DDG 8280P		279.95	220.00
DDG 9280P		319.95	245.30

HOOVER

SPIN DRY WASHERS
9519	Series: Deluxe Poly Tub, Auto. Rinse	$209.95	$157.45
T1001-1	Poly Tub	179.95	134.95
T1003	Series: Poly Tub	199.95	149.95

PORTABLE DRYERS
0920	Series: Portable Electric	$149.95	$112.45

TABLE TOP WASHER
W1003-2	Washer	$44.95	$33.70
168691	Wringer	15.95	11.95

HOTPOINT

FAMILY SIZE WASHERS
	Retail	Discount
WLW2020	$188.00	$170.75
WLW1500P	219.95	187.55
WLW2500P	239.95	198.25

18 LB. MULTI-SPEED WASHERS
	Retail	Discount
WLW3600	$269.95	$212.85

280 CONSUMER GUIDE

WASHERS/DRYERS

LCA-120	Merch. Model 120V	389.95	WLW5880P	299.95 245.85
LC-2WG	Woodgrain, 240V	449.95 326.70	WLW5900	329.95 247.20
LCT-120WG	Woodgrain, 120V	449.95 359.70		
			359.70	

GENERAL ELECTRIC

COMPACT WASHER

WLP1010 .... $239.95 $191.95

AUTOMATIC WASHERS

WWP1000N	$259.95	$204.60
WWA5400P	249.95	190.30
WWA7000P	239.95	185.90
WWA7030P	269.95	206.80
WWA7300P	269.95	207.90
WWA8310P	299.95	227.70
WWA8330P	299.95	231.00
WWA8350P	319.95	246.40
WWA8400P	339.95	261.80
WWA8500P	369.95	262.90

ELECTRIC DRYERS

DLB1020	$144.95	$122.10
DLB1550P	169.95	144.10
DLB2550P	189.95	157.55
DLB2750	209.95	166.35
DLB2980	229.95	179.55

GAS DRYERS

DLL1020	$184.95	$154.25
DLL1550P	209.95	176.25
DLL2550P	229.95	189.75
DLL2750	249.95	198.25
DLL2980	269.95	211.75

GAS AND ELECTRIC DRYERS

DDP 1200P	$159.95	$123.20
DDE 3000P	169.95	129.80
DDE 5200P	189.95	148.50
DDE 6200P	204.95	156.20
DDE 7100P	219.95	165.00
DDE 8200P	239.95	188.10
DDE 9200P	279.95	213.40

COMPACT DRYER

DLP1050 .... $144.95 $115.50

GAS DRYERS

DDG 5283P	$229.95	$180.40
DDG 6280P	244.95	188.10

MAYTAG

PORTABLE LAUNDRY APPLIANCE

A50	Porta-Washer	$— $167.45
DE 50	Porta-Dryer	— 113.70

AUTOMATIC WASHERS

A806	Large Tub, 2 Speed, Deluxe	$— $326.15

CONSUMER GUIDE

WASHERS/DRYERS

		Retail	Discount
A806S	W/Suds Return System		377.15
A606	Large Tub, 2 Speed, Chrome		288.75
A606S	W/Suds Return System		299.75
A407	Large Tub, Single Speed, Chrome		270.60
A407S	W/Suds Return System		281.60
A207	Standard Tub, 2 Speed, Chrome		256.30
A207S	W/Suds Return System		267.30
A107	Standard Tub, Single Speed		235.95
A107S	W/Suds Return System		246.95
A106	Standard Tub, Single Speed		229.90
A106S	W/Suds Return System		240.90

ELECTRIC DRYERS
		Retail	Discount
DE806	Elect. Cont., Deluxe, Drum Light	$—	$237.85
DE606	Elect. Cont., Chrome, Signal Light	—	217.50
DE407	Auto. Dry Cont., Chrome, Signal Light		
		—	194.95
DE406	Time Dry Cont., Chrome	—	122.40
DE306	Time Dry Cont., Neutral	—	169.10

GAS DRYERS
		Retail	Discount
DG806	Elect. Cont., Deluxe, Drum Light	$—	$265.35
DG606	Elect. Cont., Chrome, Signal Light	—	245.00
DG407	Auto. Dry Cont., Chrome, Signal Light		
		—	222.45
DG406	Time Dry Cont., Chrome	—	199.90
DG306	Time Dry Cont., Neutral	—	196.60

ELECTRIC DRYERS
	Retail	Discount
DE9021	$—	$206.45
DE6171	—	197.35
DE6231	—	189.85
DE3670	—	167.95
DE1020	—	161.10

GAS DRYERS
	Retail	Discount
DG9031	$—	$231.45
DG6181	—	222.40
DG6241	—	215.65
DG3680	—	194.40

WRINGER WASHERS
	Retail	Discount
DW9053	$—	$186.35
DW6132	—	186.35
DW6132	—	171.60
DW3092	—	167.10
DW3090	—	157.30

PORTABLES
	Retail	Discount
DH1150	$—	$179.80
DE1160	—	88.00

Additional charge for colors

WASHERS / DRYERS

WRINGER WASHERS

E2L	Square Aluminum Tub	$191.40
E2LP	W/Pump	200.20
E2M	W/Gas Engine	229.90
N2L	Round Porcelain Tub	166.65
N2LP	W/Pump	175.45
N2M	W/Gas Engine	205.15

PANASONIC

WASHER NA-7050P	Portable, 4-Wheels, Single Tub, Auto., Safety Switch	$229.95 $219.95
DRYER NH-550B	Portable, Compact, Timer Temp. Cont.	$149.95 $139.95

SPEED QUEEN

AUTOMATIC WASHERS

DA9103	$320.75
DA9101	299.40
DA6191	272.80
DA6123	283.90
DA6121	258.85
DA3690	238.40
DA3500	224.90
DA1040	224.90

WESTINGHOUSE

AGITATOR MODELS

LA270P	$197.00
LA370P	197.00
LA470P	211.00
LA495P	229.00
LA501P	239.00
LA570P	255.00
LA870P	310.00

TUMBLER MODELS

LT470P	$267.00
LT570P	300.00
LT870P	322.00

ELECTRIC DRYERS

DE270P	$135.00
DE370P	154.00
DE470P	159.00
DE495P	162.00
DE500P	175.00
DE570P	203.00
DE870P	232.00

GAS DRYERS

DG370P	$189.00
DG470P	191.00
DG475P	197.00

WASHERS/DRYERS

Model	Description	Retail	Discount
DG500P		—	228.80
DG570P		—	232.10
DG870P		—	246.40
		—	242.00
		—	257.40

SPACE MATE MODELS

Model	Description	Retail	Discount
LT100P	Washer	—	249.70
DE100P	Electric Dryer	—	264.00
LT170P	Washer		
DE170P	Electric Dryer	—	267.30
DG170P	Gas Dryer	—	281.60

MINI-MATE MODELS

Model	Description	Retail	Discount
LS200P	Washer	—	301.40
DE200P	Electric Dryer	249.00	207.90

WHIRLPOOL

SUPER SIZE LAUNDRY SPECIALS

Model	Description	Retail	Discount
LXA 7800	Supreme 80, 2 Speed, 4 Cycle, 5 Water Temp.	$169.00	$140.80
LXA 7805	Same as Above w/Suds Miser	—	154.00
LXI 7801	Gas, 5 Drying Temps.	—	145.20
LXE 7800	Electric, Same as Above	—	171.60
LAA 7800	2 Speed, 5 Cycle, 18 lb Cap.	—	147.40
LAA 7885	Same as above w/Suds Miser	—	173.80
LAI 7881	Gas, 5 Drying Temps.	—	161.70
LAE 7880	Electric, Same as Above	—	171.60

Model	Description	Retail	Discount
LAA 5705	Same as Above w/Suds Miser	$—	207.00
LAA 5800	4 Cycle, 2 Speed, 3 Temps.	—	238.00
LAA 5805	Same as Above w/Suds Miser	—	269.00
LAA 7700	5 Cycle, 2 Speed, 5 Temps.		
LAA 7705	Same as Above w/Suds Miser		
LAA 7800	5 Cycle, 2 Speed, 5 Temps., X-Large Cap.	$—	$263.00
LAA 7805	Same as Above w/Suds Miser	—	187.00
LAA 8800	6 Cycle, 2 Speed, 5 Temps., X-Large Cap.	—	300.00
		—	235.00
		—	272.00
LAA 8805	Same as Above w/Suds Miser		
LAA 9800	6 Cycle, 3 Speed, 5 Temps., X-Large Cap.		
LAA 5500	3 Cycle, 2 Speed, 3 Temps.	$—	145.15
		—	107.70

DRYERS

Model	Description	Retail	Discount
LAE 4900	Elec., 1 Speed, 2 Temps., Por.		$226.50
LAE 4920	Elec., 1 Spd., 2 Temps., Por.	—	240.90
LAE 5500	Elec., 1 Speed, 3 Temps.	—	189.20
LAE 5501	Gas, 1 Speed, 3 Temps.	—	162.80
LAE 5700	Elec., 1 Speed, 3 Temps.	—	250.80
LAI 5701	Gas, 1 Speed, 3 Temps., Custom Dry Cont.	—	265.10
LAE 5800	Elec., 1 Speed, 3 Temps., Custom Dry Cont.		
LAI 5801	Gas, 1 Speed, 3 Temps., Custom Dry Cont.	—	201.30
LAE 7800	Elec., 1 Speed, 5 Temps., Custom Dry Cont.	—	174.90

AUTOMATIC WASHERS

LAC 4100	Compact Portable, "Wash 'n Spin"	$229.00
LAC 4500	3 Cycle, 1 Speed, 3 Temps.	—
LAC 4700	3 Cycle, 2 Speed, Compact Portable	—
LAC 4900	4 Cycle, 2 Speed, 5 Temps., Conv. Portable	—
LAB 5300	3 Cycle, 1 Speed, 3 Temps., 24" Auto.	229.00
LAB 7750	5 Cycle, 2 Speed, 5 Temps., 24" Auto.	—
LAA 5300	3 Cycle, 1 Speed, 3 Temps.	—
LAA 5380	3 Cycle, 1 Speed, 3 Temps., X-Large Cap.	—
LAA 5700	4 Cycle, 2 Speed, 4 Temps.	—

WASHERS/DRYERS

LAI 7801	Gas, 1 Speed, 5 Temps., Custom Dry Cont.	$189.20
LAE 8810	Elec., 3 Speed, 5 Temps., Custom Dry Cont.	209.00
LAI 8811	Gas, 3 Speed, 5 Temps., Custom Dry Cont.	225.50
LAE 9810	Elec., 3 Speed, 5 Temps.	236.50
LAI 9811	Gas, 3 Speed, 5 Temps.	191.40
FALL LARGE CAPACITY DRYER SPECIAL		
LAE 5910	Elec., 1 Speed, 3 Temps., Custom Dry Cont.	228.80
LAI 5911	Gas, 1 Speed, 3 Temps., Custom Dry Cont.	198.00
		214.50
		214.50

	Price
	198.00
	190.30
	216.70
	239.80
	266.20
	$166.10
	192.50

SPECIAL INFORMATION SERVICE

A Bonus for Readers of this CONSUMER GUIDE

CONSUMER GUIDE offers a special bonus to its readers who are interested in obtaining information as to where they can find the low prices on sspecific products listed in this guide. Simply fill out the form and mail. Please include 25 cents for postage and handling.

Please send me information on:

Product _____ Model Number _____

Manufacturer _____
(PLEASE PRINT)
Your Name _____

Address _____

City _____ State _____ Zip Code _____

CONSUMER GUIDE Magazine 3323 West Main, Skokie, Illinois 60076

DISHWASHERS

JUST A FEW short years ago, the number of wired homes with dishwashers was only a little over 10 percent. But dishwashers are slowly coming into their own, due to the advantages they offer, not only in convenience, but in sanitization. The average homemaker washes and dries over a million-and-a-half pieces of kitchenware in a lifetime. Almost 24 million of these homemakers have decided to make this chore easier.

How a Dishwasher Sanitizes

"WE HAVEN'T had a cold this year since we bought our dishwasher. And we have five small children." "We got our first dishwasher a year ago and haven't passed around colds anywhere nearly as much as we used to." "We're cold-free. We just don't seem to catch them since we've had a dishwasher." Three women with the same story and each in separate parts of the country. Each had a different brand of dishwasher. Yet when asked if they thought their dishwasher had made any difference in their family's health, each answered, "yes."

There is research to suggest they are right. And therein lies good news for every family—especially every young family who is afflicted with an unbroken cycle of coughs, sore throats, and fever. Since household dishwashers first started to become really popular, there have been several scientific studies to determine how effective they are in sanitizing dishes, glasses, silverware, and cooking utensils. All have

DISHWASHERS

come to the same general conclusions: Although a dishwasher does not sterilize utensils, it destroys so many of the bacteria left on them that, with very rare exceptions, they easily meet the accepted standard for sanitary eating utensils, set by public health officials to reduce the transmission of disease by utensils in public eating places and hospitals. Few dishes washed by hand meet this standard.

The high degree of sanitization is accomplished by two things: hot water and alkaline detergent. Heat kills bacteria better than almost anything else, and in a dishwasher the heat is high throughout the entire dishwashing cycle. The normal temperature of the water in dishwashers is 140°F to 160°F, much too hot for human hands. The normal temperature of the water used in hand washing is around 110°F.

The dishwashing detergent used in hand dishwashing must be neutral in order to be kind to hands. In fact, most detergent manufacturers advertise the gentleness of their products. Unfortunately, bacteria is not destroyed in such a neutral atmosphere. Dishwasher detergents on the other hand do not have to be so gentle. Thus, they include chlorine in their formulations and are more alkaline, both of which add to the dishwasher's bacteria-killing properties.

Top-Loading or Front-Loading—Portable or Built-In

EVEN THOUGH there is a wide choice of dishwasher models to choose from, there is very little difference between them. The primary choice you will have to make is between top-loading and front-loading dishwashers, and between a portable unit that has to be rolled up to the sink to be used, or a built-in model.

Built-in dishwashers should be considered only by people who own their own homes. Renters who install built-in dishwashers pay a lot of money to improve their landlord's property. The renter will not be able to take the dishwasher along when he or she moves without doing considerable damage to the rented property. If you own your own home and are planning to install your first built-in dishwasher, you will find that it is an expensive undertaking. You will need the services of a carpenter and a plumber. If you are replacing a worn-out built-in dishwasher, your installation cost will be between $50 and $75. Some dealers' prices include installation. If that is the case, call a plumber to determine what the installation cost would be. Then subtract that from the dealer's price to determine if the price of the machine itself is fair.

For the renter or for the homeowner who does not want expensive installation costs, there is the portable dishwasher. Portable dishwashers are available in either top-loading versions or front-loading designs. Top-loading models are normally less expensive than front-loaders because they do not need the extra weight to balance the opening of the door and they do not need tracks and rollers for sliding racks. The racks on a top-loading washer are stationary. Top-loading washers are also more compact—a plus if you are tight on space. The basic disadvantage of a top-loading dishwasher is its comparative inconvenience to load. In order to get a plate into the lower rack, you

DISHWASHERS

have to maneuver it through an opening in the middle of the top rack. The only other alternative is to remove the top rack entirely.

The major advantage of a front-loading portable is its easy loading. Both the top and bottom racks roll out, so there is easy access to both. Some front-loading portables are called convertibles. This means that it can be used as a portable, but can also be installed as a built-in at some future date if desired. Convertible dishwashers are more expensive than portables. If you do not have definite plans for future installation of the unit, save some money and buy a portable.

If space limitation is the only thing that is keeping you from building in a dishwasher, several manufacturers have come up with a solution. Speed Queen manufactures a unit that is a combination range/dishwasher. It has an eye-level oven, and the dishwasher is located where the lower oven would normally be. General Electric's GSS 200 is a special under-sink model which utilizes either a single or double sink. Kitchen Aid also has a sink/dishwasher combination. It is a stainless steel sink and drainboard, with a dishwasher located beneath the drainboard. All of these units are expensive because they contain more than one appliance, but either could be just the answer for a small kitchen.

Washing and Drying Systems

EARLY DESIGNS of dishwashers used an impeller that rotated in a pool of water, spraying the dishes loaded in racks above it. They sprayed water in specific directional patterns, which called for regimental loading habits. To overcome this disadvantage, manufacturers have changed to rotating spray-arm systems. These systems consist of a pump, which draws water from a sump in the bottom of the tub and pumps it through a rotating arm which sprays the water onto items in racks above. Water falls back into the sump and is recirculated. Generally these newer dishwashers include a rotating arm under the lower rack to allow water to reach the dishes above. And still others, like Maytag and Waste King, have added spraying devices in the top of the dishwasher. Considering the small area that comprises the interior of a dishwasher, one rotating arm (with two spokes), like that found on the Westinghouse units is adequate.

There are two types of drying systems: forced air and convection or natural draft. Forced air systems operate by a fan which blows air over a heating element and onto the items loaded on the rack. This system provides the fastest and most complete drying as a result of increased and better circulation. However, the forced air systems are more expensive and normally available only on top-of-the-line models. Natural draft systems use convection currents created by a heating element in the bottom of the tub to circulate air through a venting system and over the racks. They work well on flat items and silverware but tend to leave some water on the bottoms of glassware and other surfaces on which water can collect. General Electric's new deluxe Potscrubber II provides both systems and allows you to choose one depending on how

DISHWASHERS

quickly you need a particular load of dishes. We must mention here that some concave designs on dishes and glassware collect water to such a degree that neither drying system will take care of it adequately. In the selection of dinnerware and glassware, it is wise to think about design in relation to its use in a dishwasher.

Available Features

Varied dishwashing cycles. Dishwashers offer a wide choice of cycles these days—normal or regular, rinse-and-hold, heavy-duty, pots and pans, short wash, china and crystal, plate warming, and sani-cycle. Generally, the more cycles a machine offers, the more expensive it is, and only the most deluxe offer all of them.

The most important cycle to concern yourself with is the regular cycle. All dishwashers have at least this cycle. The next most popular cycle is the rinse-and-hold. If you are loading dishes into the dishwasher but do not intend to run the dishwasher until later, when it is full, the rinse-and-hold cycle will just pour water over the dishes to clean off the food. Many economy models, like Caloric's Model 2202, provide this cycle in addition to the regular cycle. However, the rinse-and-hold cycle is not really necessary. Most dishes have to be scraped clean anyway, and it does not take much more effort to rinse them under the faucet. Most dishwasher owners that CONSUMER GUIDE Magazine spoke to did not use the rinse-and-hold cycle even though it was on their machine.

The other cycles do little more than add to the cost of the dishwasher. A dishwasher really can do little to control the temperature of the water in the machine. So the basic difference between the different cycles is their length. Manufacturers who offer a sani-cycle claim that the water temperature is increased in the last rinse for better sanitization. The way this is done is that a coil heats up; as the water hits the coil, it too is heated. But if you have ever seen a demonstration of a working dishwasher, you know that the water is splashing around with such ferocity that it cannot be touching the coil for longer than a split second. That the water can be heated up considerably in this time is highly doubtful. In addition, to properly use the various cycles as they are intended would seem to imply a need for sorting your dishes and utensils in the same manner that you sort your laundry, and running several different loads. That would be quite a time-consuming task when considering the time for each full wash cycle and the added time needed for the dishes to cool off enough for you to empty the machine and reload it. And it is certainly wasteful of water, electrical energy, and money.

The plate warming cycle seems to be the dishwasher manufacturer's attempt to add versatility to their product. On this cycle, no water is poured into the machine; the drying coil, the most energy-consuming part of the machine, heats up to warm the dishes. You already have an appliance that will do a beautiful job of heating your dishes; it is your oven. If you are warming your dishes, it is because you are about to put hot food on them. Your oven is probably already turned on, cooking the

DISHWASHERS

food, so popping the dishes in the already hot oven is the most practical and economical way to achieve what you want.

Rack features which offer flexibility in loading. All convertible and built-in dishwashers are exactly the same size. This is so contractors can plan kitchens without concerning themselves about appliance brands. Portable dishwashers may be smaller than convertibles or built-ins, but they are never larger. So when manufacturers talk about the capacity of their dishwasners, they are really talking about the designs of the racks. You want racks that can hold large items, like platters, and which offer versatility. If you have small children, you know that by the end of the day you have more dirty glasses than anything else. Most dishwashers are designed to hold glasses in the upper rack, but that usually is not enough space. So make certain that you will have the flexibility to also load glasses on the lower rack. Some models are quite deluxe in their loading versatility; for example, General Electric has a dial-a-level rack that can be raised, lowered, or tilted.

Automatic rinse agent dispensers. In an area with hard water, some kind of rinsing agent will probably be needed to keep dishes and, particularly, glassware from spotting. Most middle range and top-of-the-line machines have an automatic dispenser which squirts a measured amount of rinsing agent into the last rinse. People who want to save money and buy a good, basic machine, can still have the benefit of the rinsing agent. A solid form is sold in the supermarket under the name Jet Dry. It comes in a little plastic basket that can be hung from the upper rack. The solid agent has to be replaced more often than the automatic dispenser has to be refilled because the plastic basket is subjected to the water that goes through the machine during all of the wash and rinse cycles, not just the final rinse. But the difference in price between using the solid or liquid agent is not enough to justify buying a more expensive unit just for a dispenser feature.

Convenient cord for portables. A portable unit, whether portable or convertible, will have to be rolled over to the sink when it is to be used, and it will have to be plugged in near the sink. Locate the electrical outlet closest to your sink. When you shop for a portable, make sure that the power cord is long enough to comfortably reach your outlet. Also, the cord should be provided with a 3-prong grounding plug for your safety. The machine should provide some sort of convenient storage for the cord when the machine is not in use. The most convenient storage is an automatic reel which stores the cord in the cabinet and is available on a variety of portables including Hotpoint's.

Connection hose on portables. One of the most important features on a portable is the hose that connects the machine to the faucet for use. It goes without saying that the hose must have a strong connection that will attach to the faucet securely. It should also have a bypass valve, which allows you to use the sink even though the dishwasher is con-

DISHWASHERS

nected to it. After all, the total dishwashing process is a fairly long one, and you do not want to be deprived of the use of that water source for that full time. A bypass valve is standard on most portable units at all price levels.

Filter screens and grinding mechanisms. At one time all dishwashers had filter screens. Any food that is washed off the dishes is caught in the screen so it cannot pump through the spray arms again. The screens should be cleaned regularly to prevent plugging and impaired pumping ability. As people demanded that dishwashers do more of the work for them, some manufacturers removed the screens so more food soil could be removed from dishes without blocking the pump. Maytag introduced its micro-mesh system, a self-cleaning filter system. Some manufacturers, like Caloric, have replaced the screens with some kind of grinding mechanism which purports to grind up food wastes and flush them away. Although it sounds like they are offering a combination dishwasher and garbage disposal, they are not. All of the manufacturers are careful to specify that their machines can handle only soft waste, and CONSUMER GUIDE Magazine adds this warning: You still must first scrape dishes clean before putting them in the dishwasher; if you overload the food waste disposal system, you will have problems.

Water-overflow protection devices. Most dishwashers have float- or pressure-operated switches that close the inlet valve if the water level in the tub gets too high. This is an extremely important feature if you want to avoid the possibility of a flooded kitchen.

Warranty. Warranties on dishwashers generally cover service-parts and labor for one year, although there are some exceptions. Maytag covers parts for two years, labor for one; Waste King warrants its stainless-steel tub for twenty years, its electronic timer for five, but labor for only one year; Speed Queen, on the other hand, offers a full two-year parts and labor warranty.

DISHWASHERS

DISHWASHERS BEST BUYS

WHEN SHOPPING for automatic dishwashers, it is not always easy to discern quality by looking at price. The most expensive units are the ones with the most cycles – and not all of those cycles are ones which you will use. The following Best Buys represent examples of good, basic models as well as the most luxurious many-cycled models.

PORTABLE

General Electric GSM560 is a top-loading compact portable. This is a deluxe portable featuring General Electric's Power Scrub cycle, which they call the Potscrubber. When the lid of the dishwasher is raised, the top rack rises with it, which facilitates the loading of the bottom rack. Other useful features are a rinse-aid dispenser and a bypass control on the faucet connection, so the sink can be used while the dishwasher is in operation. Although this unit supplies more cycles and wash levels than are really necessary, this is a fine machine for the person looking for luxury in a portable.

SPECIFICATIONS: Height, *34 1/2"*; Width, *22"*; Depth, *29 3/8"*; Heating Element Wattage, *700*; Volts, *115*; Level Wash Action, *3*; Cycles, *4*; Spray Arm, *1*; Regular Wash (gallons), *16.2*. FEATURES: Type Loading, *top*; Selector Type, *push button & dial*; Soft Food Particle Elimination; Water Spray System, *revolving arm*.

Suggested Retail Price: $279.95   Low Price: $220

Kitchenaid KDC-7EC is a good basic top-loading portable. There is only one wash arm, which is adequate, and only two wash cycles, which will do almost all the wash jobs you will want. A slight plus for this model is that it uses less water than most other dishwashers. On the average, a dishwasher uses 15 gallons for a normal wash cycle. This Kitchenaid uses 12. Over a period of time, and with regular dishwasher use, that can amount to a healthy savings if you pay for your own water and own water heating. What this unit lacks in luxury features, it makes up for in quality.

SPECIFICATIONS: Height, *36 1/4"*; Width, *22 1/2"*; Depth, *26 3/4"*; Heating Element Wattage, *1300*; Volts, *120*; Level Wash Action, *1*; Cycles, *2*; Spray Arm, *1*; Regular Wash (gallons), *12*. FEATURES: Type Loading, *top*; Selector Type, *dial*; Soft Food Particle Elimination; Water Spray System, *revolving arm*.

Suggested Retail Price: $239   Low Price: $222.90

DISHWASHERS

CONVERTIBLE

Frigidaire DW-IM *is a deluxe convertible. This is the Imperial model which features four wash levels and five wash cycles. The top of the dishwasher is an attractive and very useful cherrywood chopping block. A bypass control on the faucet connection makes the faucet usable even when the dishwasher is in operation. And an automatic cord reel makes putting the dishwasher away an easy job.*

SPECIFICATIONS: Height, *37 5/8";* Width, *24 1/4";* Depth, *49 3/4";* Heating Element Wattage, *950;* Volts, *115;* Level Wash Action, *4;* Cycles, *6;* Spray Arm, *1;* Regular Wash (gallons), *14.6*. **FEATURES:** Type Loading, *front;* Selector Type, *dial;* Soft Food Particle Elimination; Water Spray System, *spray impeller.*

Suggested Retail Price: $339.95   Low Price: $273.90

Hotpoint HDB672 *is an economical convertible that has all the features necessary for convenience. There are three wash cycles, a soft food disposer, and rinse dispenser. This is a basic unit that will bring years of satisfaction.*

SPECIFICATIONS: Height, *36 3/4";* Width, *24 3/8";* Depth, *25";* Volts, *115;* Level Wash Action, *3;* Cycles, *3;* Spray Arm, *1*. **FEATURES:** Type Loading, *front;* Selector Type, *push button & dial;* Soft Food Particle Elimination; Water Spray System, *spray & revolving arm.*

Suggested Retail Price: $244.95   Low Price: $191.95

BUILT-IN

Admiral DU-2449 *is a top-of-the-line deluxe built-in. There are six cycles including a double wash for large and heavily soiled loads. There are eight indicator lights to tell you at what point in the entire wash cycle the load is. There are two spray arms and a soft food disposer. This is for the person who wants everything.*

SPECIFICATIONS: Height, *34-34 1/2";* Width, *24";* Depth, *23 1/2";* Heating Element Wattage, *1000;* Volts, *115;* Cycles, *6;* Spray Arm, *2*. **FEATURES:** Type Loading, *front;* Selector Type, *push button;* Soft Food Particle Elimination; Water Spray System; *revolving arms.*

Suggested Retail Price: $265.95   Low Price: $239.95

Frigidaire DW-DU *is a basic, economical built-in. Although this unit does not have all the extra cycles and other fancy gimmickry found on the more expensive models, the DW-DU can be depended on to do a good, reliable job. There are two wash cycles – a double and a single – and two wash levels.*

SPECIFICATIONS: Height, *34 1/8";* Width, *24 1/8";* Depth, *23 3/8";* Heating Element Wattage, *950;* Volts, *115;* Level Wash Action, *2;* Cycles, *2;* Spray Arm, *1;* Regular Wash (gallons), *14.6*. **FEATURES:** Type Loading, *front;* Selector Type, *dial;* Soft Food Particle Elimination; Water Spray System, *spray impeller.*

Suggested Retail Price: $244.95   Low Price: $185.90

DISHWASHERS

1975 Dishwasher Prices

FRIGIDAIRE

FRONT LOADING MOBILE

Model	Description	Retail	Discount
DW-CDM	Formica Top, Dial	$279.95	$231.00
DW-1M	Wood Top, Dial	339.95	273.90
DW-C1M	Wood Top, Pushbutton	419.95	335.50

UNDERCOUNTER

Model	Description	Retail	Discount
DW-DU	Dial, 2 Cycles	$244.95	$185.90
DW-CDU	Dial, 5 Cycles	289.95	214.50
DW-1U	Dial, 5 Cycles	349.95	251.90
DW-C1U	Pushbutton, 7 Cycles	439.95	317.90

GENERAL ELECTRIC

Model	Retail	Discount
GSM 560	$279.95	$220.00

FRONT LOADING CONVERTIBLES

Model	Retail	Discount
GSC 250	$249.95	$187.00
GSC 411	249.95	189.20
GSC 445	299.95	227.70
GSC 461	319.95	240.90
GSC 861	359.95	281.60

UNDERCOUNTER

Model	Retail	Discount
GSS 200 NP	$229.95	$182.60

SINK COMBINATION

Model	Description	Retail	Discount
KDC-37A	Custom, Stainless Steel Top & Faucet	$539.00	$476.00
KDS-37A	Superba, Stainless Steel Top & Faucet	629.00	560.00

MAYTAG

FRONT LOADING PORTABLE CONVERTIBLE

Model	Description	Retail	Discount
WC400		$—	$337.70
WC200		—	316.40

BUILT-IN

Model	Description	Retail	Discount
WU600	All Push Button Control	$—	$306.90
WU400	Timer Dial & 3 Pushbutton Control	—	281.70
WU200	Easy to Operate Timer Dial	—	257.60

WASTE KING

UNDERCOUNTER

Model	Description	Retail	Discount
OSS575-001	Pop-Up Hydro Tower, 1/2 HP Motor, 3 Pushbuttons, 2 Cycles, Full & Rinse & Hold	$234.95	$191.55
OSS777-200	1/2 HP Motor	289.95	230.05
OSS811-001	Same as OSS777-200 w/5 year Warranty	299.95	240.75

CONSUMER GUIDE

DISHWASHERS

Model		Price
GSD 251		189.20
GSD 281		194.70
GSD 441		203.50
GSD 461		240.90
GSD 661		280.50
GSD 950		290.40
GSD 1050		312.40

KITCHENAID

UNDERCOUNTER UNITS

KDC-17A	Custom, Porcelain Tank	$319.00
KDI-17A	Imperial, Porcelain Tank	349.00
KDS-17A	Superba, Porcelain Tank	389.00
KDSS-17A	Superba, Stainless Steel Tank	469.00

TOP LOADING PORTABLES

KDC-7	Electra, Formica Top	$239.00
KDA-7	Vari-Cycle, Formica Top	279.00
KDW-7	Vari-Cycle, Maple Top	299.00

FRONT LOADING PORTABLES

KDD-67	Deluxe, Porcelain Top	$309.00
KDR-67	Regency, Maple Top	339.00

CONVERTIBLE PORTABLES

Model	Description	Price
KDC-57A	Custom, Maple Top	$359.00
KDI-57A	Imperial, Maple Top	389.00
KDS-57A	Superba, Maple Top	419.00

Model	Description	Price
OSS878-200	Same as OSS811-001 w/ 4 Pushbuttons, 3 cycles	339.95
OSS911-250	Same as OSS878-200 w/ 5 Pushbuttons, 4 Cycles	399.95
OSS979-250	Same as OSS911-250 w/ 8 Pushbuttons, 7 Cycles	449.95

CONVERTIBLE/PORTABLE

CP575-001	Same features as OSS575-001 above.	$289.95
CP777-200	Same features as OSS777-200 above.	354.95
CP811-200	Same features as OSS811-270 above.	364.95
CP878-200	Same features as OSS878-200 above.	399.95
CP911-250	Same features as OSS911-250 above.	459.95
CP979-250	Same features as OSS979-250 above.	519.95

WHIRLPOOL

PORTABLE

Model	Description	Price
SAF 300	Custom, 1 Cycle	$219.00
SAF 325	Deluxe, 2 Cycle	—
SAF 440	Supreme, 4 Cycles	—
SAF 500	Imperial, 5 Cycles, 2 Speeds	—
SAF 600	Mark Six, 6 Cycles, 2 Speeds	—

UNDERCOUNTER

Model	Description	Price
SAU 300	Custom, 1 Cycle	$—
SAU 325	Deluxe, 2 Cycle	—
SAU 440	Supreme, 4 Cycles, 2 Speeds	—
SAU 500	Imperial, 5 Cycles, 2 Speeds	—
SAU 600	Mark Six, 6 Cycles, 2 Speeds	—

	266.45
	316.70
	358.45

	$267.70
	301.30
	334.90
	414.40

	$222.90
	249.75
	278.90

	$280.00
	302.40

	$324.80
	352.80
	386.40

	$219.00
	262.00
	270.00
	296.00
	337.00
	378.00

	$184.80
	201.30
	244.20
	273.90
	290.40

	$173.80
	190.30
	233.20
	262.90
	279.40

REFRIGERATORS

1975

ONE OF the hardiest appliances you will ever own is your refrigerator. The life expectancy is approximately 15 years. What this means, first of all, is that you will want to choose one that will fulfill your needs well into the future. What it also means is that if you are buying a refrigerator this year, you are probably replacing one that is quite old. A lot has changed in refrigerators since the last time you bought one. They are larger, use new materials, have different shapes, and offer a variety of new features.

Basic Models

THE BASIC choice you will have to make is between a single-door model and a combination model. The single-door refrigerator is the oldest style around and is also the least convenient. One door gives you access to both the refrigerator and freezer compartment, which means that the freezer is exposed to the warm room air every time you open the refrigerator. The freezer holds a temperature ranging from 10 to 15 degrees, so should be used only for short-time storage of frozen foods and for making ice cubes. Adding to the inconvenience is the fact that all single-door models require manual defrosting of the freezer. On the other hand, the single-door refrigerators are the least expensive full-

REFRIGERATORS

size refrigerators on the market, ranging in price from $150 to $275 depending on size. CONSUMER GUIDE Magazine recommends the single-door refrigerator as an economical second refrigerator or for use in a vacation home where you do not need long-term freezer storage capabilities.

The combination models combine a refrigerator that maintains storage temperatures ranging from 37 to 40 degrees and a separate freezer which maintains temperatures ranging from -5 to $+5$ degrees. The combinations are available in three styles: top-freezer, bottom-freezer, and side-by-side.

The first combination refrigerator/freezers to appear on the market were the top-freezer models, and they are still the most popular. Top-freezer models are available in a variety of sizes, ranging from 11 cubic feet to 20 cubic feet and are priced from $300 to $750 dollars. Although the freezer capacity on these models is usually less than on either the bottom-freezer or side-by-side models, manufacturers are working to increase the freezer capacity to meet today's needs for greater frozen food storage. Considering price and available convenience features, CONSUMER GUIDE Magazine has found that the top-mounted freezer models offer the best overall value.

Bottom-freezer models were popular a number of years ago for people who wanted enlarged freezer capacity. These are more expensive than the top-freezer units, but salespeople justified that expense by pointing out that with the freezer on the bottom, the refrigerator was moved off the ground and no one would have to stoop down to get things from the bottom of the refrigerator anymore. In addition, the freezer of the bottom-mount normally has a basket to hold the more frequently used items so no one has to dig through the whole freezer to find something. As the capacity of the top-mounted freezers has grown, and with the advent of the side-by-side refrigerator/freezer, the bottom-freezer models have all but disappeared from the scene. Only Amana still manufactures one.

About 20 years ago Kelvinator introduced the "Fooderama," the first combination refrigerator/freezer for home use with separate full-length vertical refrigerator and freezer sections. Unfortunately, the unit was 41 inches wide, which limited its sales to only those who had the tremendous kitchen space to accommodate it. In 1964 Admiral improved on the concept by presenting the convenience of the two separate vertical units in a narrower body—36 inches. It was an instant success, and now every major refrigerator manufacturer has introduced one or several side-by-side models into their lines. Realizing that the key to the side-by-side's sudden popularity was making them narrow enough to fit into conventional refrigerator spaces, some manufacturers have made their units even narrower—as narrow as 28 inches. CONSUMER GUIDE Magazine does not recommend the very narrow side-by-side units. Remember, only half of that width is refrigerator; the other half is freezer. With such narrow compartments, you will have a hard time fitting a large platter of food in the refrigerator (like the cold-cut-platter you want to fix ahead for your buffet supper), or a large item in the freezer (like the

REFRIGERATORS

Thanksgiving turkey). Admiral, Frigidaire, Tappan and Westinghouse have taken the two-door convenience feature one step further and are now offering units with three doors. The freezer side is divided into two sections: the bottom for frozen foods storage and the top for ice cubes. The theory is that you open your freezer most often to get ice cubes; by putting the ice cubes behind a separate door, you will not disturb the temperature level of the rest of the freezer section whenever it is just an ice cube that you need. Side-by-side refrigerator/freezers are the most expensive models on the market. They range in price from $500 to $800. The third door adds approximately $25.

Another model of refrigerator that is available is the compact. The market for these small units has grown considerably in the last few years; however, they offer very little in convenience features other than an ice cube compartment and door shelves. They are best used as a second refrigerator.

Manual or Automatic

IF YOU are one of those people who think that defrosting the refrigerator is the most awful chore in the world, you will want to choose a self-defrosting refrigerator. This is quickly becoming the most popular refrigerator feature, so much so that manual defrost refrigerators are slowly disappearing from the appliance scene. The self-defrosting feature goes under a number of different names: frostless, no-frost, frost-free, etc. Be certain you know what you are buying. Amana and Hotpoint, for example, have frost-free and cycle defrost models. Only the frost-free one is self-defrosting.

The cooling coils in a manual-defrost freezer section are in direct contact with the liner of the freezer. Moisture condenses on the cold surface of the liner and frost collects. Eventually, the frost has to be removed (two or three times a year). In a self-defrosting freezer section, frost never forms in the freezer. The coils are behind the rear wall of the freezer section and a fan circulates the cold air through the compartment. The moisture and frost collect on the coils, not in the freezer. About twice a day a heater coil turns on to melt the accumulated frost; then the cooling cycle begins again.

The self-defrosting feature adds about $35 to the price of a refrigerator, but it adds a great deal more than that in operating costs. Because of the alternating cooling and heating system of the self-defrosting feature, the compressor must run almost continually. This adds to the noise the refrigerator produces, and it also adds considerably to the amount of electricity that is consumed annually. However, manufacturers are concentrating on improving the efficiency of their units, and because of the popularity of the self-defrosting refrigerators, most of their improvements will be on these models.

Efficiency

UNTIL NOW there has been no way for a consumer to compare the

REFRIGERATORS

energy consumption of one refrigerator to another. Although all models are required on their nameplates to list the rate of current used by that unit, the rating never took into account how long the compressor has to run on a given model to maintain proper temperature. So a model with a low current rating that has to run most of the time could cost more to operate than one with a higher rating if it has to run only sporadically. Soon all that will be changing. The Association of Home Appliance Manufacturers (AHAM) has proposed to the National Bureau of Standards a new rating system that does take into account running time. The AHAM rating will begin appearing on new refrigerator models this year. The new energy ratings will be expressed in average kilowatt-hours. To figure out how much the unit will cost to run, you simply multiply the kwhr rating by the cost per kwhr you are charged on your electric bill. The real boon, as CONSUMER GUIDE Magazine sees it, will be your ability to compare the efficiency of two units that are alike in most other respects.

However, efficiency can be estimated by doing more than checking a nameplate. The most important contributor to high efficiency is adequate insulation—to keep the cold in and the warm out. Refrigerators were originally insulated with a glass fiber material. Most manufacturers used a three-inch thickness of this insulation. It did an adequate job, but thicker insulation would have been more efficient. As you will recall, these old refrigerators had heavy thick doors. The refrigerators looked like enormous units, but when you opened them up, you found that the bulk was made up mostly of wall and door thickness and there was a lot less storage space than you wanted. It is no wonder the manufacturers did not try adding even more insulation.

Then foam insulation was discovered. The foam, it was found, was twice as effective as the glass fiber. Where three inches was used before, half of that thickness could be used now. Refrigerator manufacturers were able to maintain the size of their units, but, with thin-wall construction, they could increase the capacity of storage area. However, by cutting the thickness of insulation in half, they were maintaining the same efficiency that the glass-fiber-insulated units had. Manufacturers have now learned that by increasing the thickness of the foam, they can improve the insulation and efficiency of their units tremendously—without taking away much storage space. Amana, for example, has introduced for 1975 several high-efficiency top-freezer models that have three-inch foam insulation. This is double what thin-wall construction models have—equivalent to six inches of glass fiber. Any unit with thicker insulation can cause a dramatic change on your electric bill. It has been proven in independent tests that a well-insulated model can save over $50 per year in operating costs over a thin-wall model. Appliance manufacturers are quick to point out that the model has foam insulation. But make sure that the purpose of the foam is added insulation, not thin-wall construction. Ask how thick the insulation is. If the salesperson does not know, ask to see the dealer's catalog sheet for that model. The catalog sheets are not confidential information, so no dealer should object to showing it to you. If the insulation is

REFRIGERATORS

thick enough to be meaningful for efficiency, the manufacturer will be sure to mention it on that sheet.

There are other characteristics to look for in an efficient refrigerator. Most larger refrigerators have an automatic heater system which is designed to prevent sweating in humid environments. The operation of this heater raises energy use by as much as 25 percent. However, CONSUMER GUIDE Magazine has found that this system is unnecessary in many areas—in air-conditioned homes, for example, or during the winter in cold climates. At least five manufacturers—Admiral, Amana, General Electric, Hotpoint, and Philco now provide power-saver switches on some of their models. This allows you to turn the heater system off during those times of the year when it is not needed.

Another energy-saving tool is separate temperature controls for the freezer and refrigerator. With separate controls, you can turn up the temperature in the freezer section when there is very little food being stored there. That way the compressor will not have to operate as often to maintain the super-cold temperature needed when the freezer is full. Or you can save energy by raising the temperature of refrigerator section when you go away for vacation and there are no perishables left there—and still keep the freezer cold enough to preserve the food you have stored there.

Size

WHEN YOU are talking about the size of a refrigerator you are talking about two things: the amount of room the unit will take up in your kitchen and the food storage capacity.

Before shopping for a refrigerator, you should take some measurements in your kitchen. Measure the height and width of the space in which you want to put the refrigerator. Remember that you will want to buy a refrigerator that is smaller than that space so there will be adequate space above, behind, and on both sides for free air circulation. If you buy a unit that has forced air ventilation around the condenser (a fan that circulates air around the condenser and blows it out through the bottom of the refrigerator), you do not have to worry about this air space and can buy a model to fit flush in the space you have. Also check how much space you have to accommodate the opening of the door. If your space is particularly narrow, as in a pantry, you might be happier with a side-by-side refrigerator with its narrow doors which do not open too far into the room. Also check whether you need a refrigerator whose door opens to the left or to the right. If the refrigerator will be alongside a wall, you will probably want it to be hinged on the opposite side. Some refrigerators are available only with right- or left-hinged doors; some can be ordered either way; some are convertible and can be switched at any time. If you are planning to move soon and will want to take your refrigerator with you, the convertible models will be worth your consideration to insure that the refrigerator you buy now will work well in your new home. The world seems biased towards the right-handed person, so you will find many more right-hinged models

REFRIGERATORS

than left. Amana even charges an extra $15 for hinging a door on the left.

Capacity is a much more difficult thing to measure. All refrigerator capacities are measured in cubic feet. The total cubic-foot figure includes both the refrigerator and freezer. Normally, the manufacturer then breaks that figure down and indicates the cubic-foot capacity of the freezer. Most people have no idea what the cubic-foot measurement means except that a 20-cubic-foot refrigerator is larger than a 17-cubic-foot model. No manufacturer tells you how much food each of those sizes will hold. Manufacturers suggest that food storage compartments should provide at least 8 cubic feet for a family of two and that you should add one cubic foot for each additional person. If you do a great deal of entertaining, they suggest adding two extra cubic feet. The freezer should supply about two cubic feet per person. It all sounds very scientific, but it is not. CONSUMER GUIDE Magazine found that several refrigerators with the same cubic footage actually had different storage capacities.

The difference, of course, is shelf space. The important figure to look for is shelf capacity. After all, a lot of the cubic footage is air space. Air space in the refrigerator is necessary for storing bulky items, like a large casserole, but shelf space is the all-important item. If the shelves are full, you are not going to get that casserole into the refrigerator, no matter how much air space is available. Some manufacturers are now indicating the square-foot size of the shelves in their refrigerators.

Probably the best way to choose a refrigerator is to choose the capacity you need according to the manufacturers' suggestion. Then compare the shelf space of several models that have that capacity and also have the other features you want. Buy the model that has the greatest shelf space. You will probably have to take a tape measure along to determine shelf capacity.

Other Considerations

ANOTHER important consideration when choosing a refrigerator is the unit's construction. We have already discussed the importance of adequate insulation, but you should also be aware of such things as the materials used and how the shelves are attached.

At one time the entire interior of refrigerators was made of enamel-clad steel. The metal was sturdy, helped maintain the cold, and was easy to clean. Its only major drawbacks were that if you dropped something sharp and heavy on it, the enamel could chip, and it was impossible to mold into complicated shapes. Crosley was the first to introduce an interior door panel molded of plastic. After Crosley's patent ran out, every manufacturer in the industry replaced the metal door interiors with plastic. The plastic could be molded into a variety of shapes allowing for the inclusion of butter and cheese storers, egg trays, and more convenient shelf attachment—the shelves can be molded out of the same sheet, eliminating the need for any attachment at all. Today, all interior door panels are of a molded plastic.

REFRIGERATORS

Some manufacturers have taken the idea of using plastic a step further—perhaps a step too far. Some manufacturers have replaced the metal refrigerator lining with plastic.

CONSUMER GUIDE Magazine does not recommend any refrigerator with this kind of lining. Plastic can scratch in the cleaning of it, which makes it difficult to clean ever after and retains odors. In addition, after being subjected to the cold temperatures of a refrigerator for some time, the plastic can become brittle and crack. Admiral is one of those manufacturers who have been using plastic linings in their refrigerators, and the complaints have been many and loud. The liner is warrantied for only one year. What good is a machine that will last 15 years, if the interior will not last also? Until Admiral and other manufacturers improve the interior lining of their plastic-lined units—to the point that they have enough confidence in them to fully warranty them — CONSUMER GUIDE Magazine recommends staying away from these units.

Also check the shelf construction of a model you are interested in. Make sure that the studs that will support the shelf are imbedded securely in the side of the refrigerator. And make sure that the shelf supports stick out far enough to hold the shelf securely. Apply pressure to the center of the shelf; it should not sag. If it does, it is not adequately supported. A few manufacturers, such as Hotpoint, have gone back to the old glass shelves. The new version is breakproof and much easier to keep clean than the standard wire shelves although they have to be cleaned more often.

Convenience Features

A VARIETY of "convenience" features are available on today's refrigerators, all adding to the cost of the unit. Some really are conveniences; others are just luxuries. Whether a particular feature is a convenience or a luxury may depend on your lifestyle and particular needs. But CONSUMER GUIDE Magazine's steadfast rule holds true here: Do not buy more features than you really need. Be certain that you will get enough use out of a feature to justify its extra cost.

REFRIGERATORS

BEST BUYS

THE following list of refrigerators represents what CONSUMER GUIDE Magazine's experts rate the best in terms of construction, convenience features, performance, and warranty. In addition, there is the important consideration of price.

SINGLE/DOOR

Whirlpool EAL12CT is a small economy unit perfect as a second refrigerator or for a vacation home. Although only 12.4 cubic feet, this compact model has many of the features found on more deluxe models: adjustable shelves, adjustable temperature control, door storage space. The freezer is small, making it useful only for ice cubes and small food storage, but the 15.3 square feet of shelf space in the fresh-food section is more than adequate for limited use. Like all other single-door units, this one requires manual defrosting. The only drawback is that there are no wheels for facilitating cleaning.

SPECIFICATIONS: Total Capacity (cubic feet), *12.4;* Freezer Capacity (cubic feet), *1.27;* Shelf Capacity (square feet),*15.3;* Height, *57 1/4";* Width, *24";* Depth, *30 5/8";* Defrost, *manual.* FEATURES: Type, *1 dr. w/freezer;* Adjustable Shelves, *slide-out;* Adjustable Temperature Control.

Suggested Retail Price: $239.95   Low Price: $216.15

TOP-FREEZER

Amana ESRF-16 is Amana's latest offering for 1975. This is a super-efficient unit that can cut your electrical costs by $50. The secret is increased insulation and a power-saver switch that allows you to turn off the humidity control heater when it is not needed. This is a 15.6 cubic-foot, self-defrosting model. Although it is not any taller than other comparable-size units, it is about 2 inches wider – about as wide as a 20-cubic-foot model. This is because of the added insulation. For the person even more economy minded, there is the ESR-16. This is a manual defrost model (Amana calls it cycle defrost), and can save you even $20 more on your electric bill.

SPECIFICATIONS: Total Capacity (cubic feet), *15.6;* Freezer Capacity (cubic feet), *3.3;* Shelf Capacity (square feet), *19.4;* Height, *63";* Width, *32";* Depth, *29 1/4";* Defrost, *Free-O-Frost.* FEATURES: Type, *top freezer;* Adjustable Shelves; Adjustable Left or Right Hand Door; Roll Wheels; Adjustable Temperature Control Fresh Meat Storage; Cold Control, *2;* Power Saver Switch.

Fair Trade Price: $499.00   Low Price: $439.95

CONSUMER GUIDE

REFRIGERATORS

Frigidaire FPCI170T *is a 17 cubic-foot model. The fresh food section measures 12.25 cubic feet, and the freezer section is 7.45 cubic feet. This is a middle-of-the-line refrigerator with some top-of-the-line features: attractive interior trim, cantilever shelves, frost-free, roller wheels, freezer shelf, and reversible doors. This model comes with two flexible ice trays, but an optional automatic ice maker can be added on.*
SPECIFICATIONS: Total Capacity (cubic feet), *17;* **Freezer Capacity (cubic feet),** *7.45;* **Shelf Capacity (square feet),** *12.26;* **Height,** *65 7/8";* **Width,** *30";* **Depth,** *29 1/2";* **Defrost,** *frost proof.* **FEATURES: Type,** *top freezer;* **Adjustable Shelves,** *3;* **Adjustable Left or Right Hand Door; Roll Wheels; Adjustable Temperature Control Fresh Meat Storage; Power Saver Switch.**
Suggested Retail Price: $469.95   Low Price: $387.50

General Electric TBF-18SR *is an excellent middle-of-the-line unit. It is a 17.6 cubic-foot model that comes equipped with self-defrosting, a power-saver switch, removable egg storage container, and cantilever shelves. An automatic ice maker can be added on at extra cost. The door shelves on this unit are wide enough to hold a half-gallon carton of milk, which does a lot to free up space in the refrigerator. A handy efficiency feature is a separate control for refrigerator and freezer temperatures.*
SPECIFICATIONS: Total Capacity (cubic feet), *17.6;* **Freezer Capacity (cubic feet),** *4.65;* **Shelf Capacity (square feet),** *20.8;* **Height,** *66";* **Width,** *30 1/2";* **Depth,** *30 1/4";* **Defrost,** *no frost.* **FEATURES: Type,** *top freezer;* **Adjustable Shelves; Roll Wheels; Cold Control; Power Saver Switch.**
Suggested Retail Price: $419.99   Low Price: $337.15

Hotpoint CTF16CR *is a 15.7 cubic-foot no-frost refrigerator which is a basic, low-cost model. There are some nice touches, like ice cube storage bin, ability to add on optional automatic ice maker, roller wheels, power-saver switch, cantilever shelves. A freezer shelf is considered a useful feature, but the removable shelf on this unit was judged less handy than others.*
SPECIFICATIONS: Total Capacity (cubic feet), *15.7;* **Freezer Capacity (cubic feet),** *4.37;* **Shelf Capacity (square feet),** *22.7;* **Height,** *64";* **Width,** *30 1/2";* **Depth,** *na;* **Defrost,** *no frost.* **FEATURES: Type,** *top freezer;* **Adjustable Shelves,** *3;* **Cold Control,** *2;* **Power Saver Switch.**
Suggested Retail Price: Not Available   Low Price: $304.65

SIDE-BY-SIDE

General Electric TFF-24RR *is one of the largest— and one of the most expensive refrigerators on the market. This is a refrigerator for the person who wants everything and is willing to pay for it. This 23.6 cubic-foot model takes plenty of space–almost 36 inches, but the same features are available on a slightly smaller model, the TFF-22rr which is 21.6 cubic-feet and is 33 inches wide. Both are self-defrosting models which are equipped with glass shelves instead of wire. Set in the freezer door is an ice dispenser (set it for cubes or crushed ice) and a cold water dispenser. There are separate temperature controls for the re-*

REFRIGERATORS

frigerator and freezer, and there is a power-saver switch. The meat keeper in the refrigerator section has its own temperature.

SPECIFICATIONS: Total Capacity (cubic feet), *23.6;* Freezer Capacity (cubic feet), *8.58;* Shelf Coapcity (square feet), *15.01;* Height, *66 1/4";* Width, *35 33/4";* Depth, *31";* Defrost, *no frost.* **FEATURES: Type,** *side-by-side;* **Adjustable Shelves,** *4;* **Roll Wheels; Adjustable Temperature Control Fresh Meat Storage; Cold Control,** *2;* **Power Saver Switch.**

Suggested Retail Price: $1099.00   **Low Price: $859.65**

Tappan 95-2284 *is a three-door side-by-side. The freezer is divided into two separate sections: one for ice, and one for regular food storage. This 22 cubic-foot unit is 33 inches wide–the same as G.E.'s TFF-22RR but has more than a square foot less shelf area. However the Tappan is like the G.E. in most other respects. It is self-defrosting, has tempered glass shelves, and an adjustable meat storage area. There is no ice and water dispenser, which makes this a more economical unit.*

SPECIFICATIONS: Total Capacity (cubic feet), *22;* **Freezer Capacity (cubic feet),** *6.78;* **Shelf Capacity (square feet),** *27.6;* **Height,** *66 1/4";* **Width,** *33";* **Depth,** *29";* **Defrost,** *no frost.* **FEATURES: Type,** *side-by-side;* **Adjustable Shelves; Roll Wheels; Adjustable Temperature Control Fresh Meat Storage; Cold Control,** *2;* **Power Saver Switch.**

Suggested Retail Price: Not Available   **Low Price: $601.70**

Westinghouse RS194R *is a smaller side-by-side–19.1 cubic feet and 31 inches wide. This is not a super-fancy unit, but there are enough features to let you feel that you have a deluxe model. It is completely frost-free, there are separate refrigerator and freezer temperature controls, deep door shelves, and glide-out rollers. An automatic ice maker is an available option. There is a meat keeper in the refrigerator, but there is no means of controlling its temperature.*

SPECIFICATIONS: Total Capacity (cubic feet), *19.1;* **Freezer Capacity (cubic feet),** *8.3;* **Shelf Capacity (square feet),** *26.4;* **Height,** *64 1/2";* **Width,** *31";* **Depth,** *27 3/4";* **Defrost,** *frost free.* **FEATURES: Type,** *side-by-side;* **Adjustable Shelves; Roll Wheels; Adjustable Temperature Control Fresh Meat Storage.**

Suggested Retail Price: Not Available   **Low Price: $511.00**

Whirlpool EAD19PT *is a 19 cubic-foot model that has all the features standard on other side-by-side units: self-defrost, deep door shelves, roller wheels, separate temperature controls for refrigerator and freezer. The meat keeper in this Whirlpool has no special meat-keeping qualities, so do not plan to store meat for more than a few days in it. It would be better used as a second vegetable bin. What this model has that others do not is that the automatic ice maker is standard and included in the price.*

SPECIFICATIONS: Total Capacity (cubic feet), *19.0;* **Freezer Capacity (cubic feet),** *6.34;* **Shelf Capacity (square feet),** *25.5;* **Height,** *66 1/4";* **Width,** *32 3/4";* **Depth,** *29 1/2";* **Defrost,** *no frost.* **FEATURES: Type,** *side-by-side;* **Adjustable Shelves; Roll Wheels; Adjustable Temperature Control Fresh Meat Storage; Cold Control,** *2;* **Power Saver Switch.**

Suggested Retail Price: $589.95   **Low Price: $493.90**

REFRIGERATORS

1975 Refrigerator Prices

ADMIRAL

Model	Description	Retail	Discount
C1255	12.2 Cu. Ft. Single Door	$—	$239.00
T1354	12.2 Cu. Ft. Double Door	—	289.00
NT1554	15.0 Cu. Ft. Two Door	—	354.00
NT1656	15.5 Cu. Ft. Two Door	—	374.00
NT1858	18.0 Cu. Ft. Two Door	—	399.00
NT2159	21.4 Cu. Ft. Two Door	—	474.00
INT2159	21.3 Cu. Ft. 2 Dr. w/Ice Maker	—	534.00

DUPLEX MODELS

Model	Description	Retail	Discount
ND1954	19.3 Cu. Ft.	$—	$514.00
ND1958	19.4 Cu. Ft.	—	579.00
IND2059	20.1 Cu. Ft. w/Ice Maker	—	664.00
IND2259	21.7 Cu. Ft. w/Ice Maker	—	759.00
IND2459	23.7 Cu. Ft. w/Ice Maker	—	804.00
IND2859	27.8 Cu. Ft. w/Ice Maker	—	929.00

Model	Description	Retail	Discount
FPCI-152T	15.2 Cu. Ft., Frost Proof	429.95	359.50
FPI-170T	17.0 Cu. Ft., Frost Proof	434.95	365.10
FPCI-170T	17.0 Cu. Ft., Frost Proof	469.95	387.50
FPCI-206T	20.6 Cu. Ft., Frost Proof	519.95	428.95
FPF-200TI	20.0 Cu. Ft., Frost Proof	759.95	629.45
FPI-152T	15.2 Cu. Ft., Frost Proof	399.95	341.60

SIDE-BY-SIDE MODELS

Model	Description	Retail	Discount
FPCI-165V	16.5 Cu. Ft., Frost Proof	$539.95	$455.85
FPCI-203V	20.3 Cu. Ft., Frost Proof	659.95	553.30
FPCI-203V3	20.3 Cu. Ft., Frost Proof	689.95	576.80
FPCI-220V	22.0 Cu. Ft., Frost Proof	749.95	627.20

GENERAL ELECTRIC

Model	Description	Retail	Discount
TA 12 SR	11.5 Cu. Ft.	$259.95	$207.90

TWO DOOR AUTOMATIC DEFROST

Model	Description	Retail	Discount
TB12SR	11.8 Cu. Ft.	309.95	246.10
TB14SR	13.5 Cu. Ft.	329.95	265.35

TWO DOOR NO FROST

Model	Description	Retail	Discount
TBF14DR	14.2 Cu. Ft.	389.95	313.50
BF16DR	15.6 Cu. Ft.	429.95	340.45
TBF18ER	17.6 Cu. Ft.	399.95	318.15

AMANA*

BOTTOM MOUNTS

Model	Description	Retail	Discount
BC20N	20.1 Cu. Ft.	$659.95	$521.40

TOP MOUNTS

Model	Description	Retail	Discount
T16N	16.0 Cu. Ft.	$429.95	$345.40
TR16N	16.0 Cu. Ft.	459.95	372.90

REFRIGERATORS

TM18N	18.2 Cu. Ft.	479.95	TBF18SR	17.6 Cu. Ft.		337.15
TC18N	18.2 Cu. Ft.	529.95	TBF18DR	17.6 Cu. Ft.	459.95	365.20
TR20N	20.0 Cu. Ft.	569.95	TBF21DR	20.8 Cu. Ft.	499.95	399.00
TD20N	20.0 Cu. Ft.	619.95				
			SIDE BY SIDE			
SIDE-BY-SIDES			TFF18ER	18.4 Cu. Ft.	529.95	427.05
SR-17N	17.3 Cu. Ft.	$699.95	TFF19DR	18.8 Cu. Ft.	599.95	486.75
SR-19N	19.4 Cu. Ft.	719.95	TFF22DR	21.9 Cu. Ft.	699.95	569.80
SR-22N	22.3 Cu. Ft.	799.95	TFF24DR	23.8 Cu. Ft.	799.95	637.15
SR-25N	25.4 Cu. Ft.	849.95				
SD-19N	19.4 Cu. Ft.	779.95	**DISPENSER MODELS**			
SD1-22N	22.4 Cu. Ft.	1049.95	TBF21RR	20.6 Cu. Ft.	699.95	567.60
SD1-25N	25.5 Cu. Ft.	1099.95	TBF22RR	21.6 Cu. Ft.	979.95	777.70
			TFF24RR	23.6 Cu. Ft.	1099.95	859.65

*Fair Trade

Additional Charge for Color

FRIGIDAIRE

HOOVER

COMPACT CONVENTIONAL MODELS

D-43	4.3 Cu. Ft.	$179.95	$150.65
I-43	4.3 Cu. Ft.	194.95	159.60

R3001-1	2.9 Cu. Ft., Compact	$169.95	$127.45

HOTPOINT

CONVENTIONAL MODELS

D-100	10.0 Cu. Ft.	$259.95	$215.05
D-116	11.6 Cu. Ft.	279.95	232.95

SINGLE-DOOR MODELS

SSD10CR	Dial Defrost	$—	$170.50
SSD12CR	Dial Defrost	—	189.55

COMBINATION REFRIGERATORS AND FREEZERS

FCD-123T	12.3 Cu. Ft.	$299.95	$255.35
FCD-150T	15.0 Cu. Ft.	369.95	308.00
FPI-121T	12.1 Cu. Ft., Frost Proof	374.95	314.70

TWO DOOR MODELS

CTA12CR	Cycle Defrost	$—	$218.95

REFRIGERATORS

Model	Description		Retail	Discount
CTA14CR	Cycle Defrost		—	313.00
CTF14CR	No Frost		—	320.00
CTF14ER	No Frost		—	335.00
CTF16CR	No Frost		—	343.00
CTF16ER	No Frost		—	372.00
CTF18CR	No Frost		—	395.00
CTF18ER	No Frost		—	399.00
CTF21CR	No Frost		—	426.00
CTF21ER	No Frost		—	453.00
RT141R	14.0 Cu. Ft.		—	241.35
RT143R	14.0 Cu. Ft.		—	278.60
RT145R	14.0 Cu. Ft.		—	291.20
RT173R	17.1 Cu. Ft.		—	304.65
RT174R	17.2 Cu. Ft.		—	316.95
RT178R	17.2 Cu. Ft.		—	325.10
RT194R	19.2 Cu. Ft.		—	337.40
RT198R	19.2 Cu. Ft.		—	369.05
RS183R	17.5 Cu. Ft.		—	381.35
RS194R	19.0 Cu. Ft.		—	511.00
RS199R	19.0 Cu. Ft.		—	603.00
RS214R	21.0 Cu. Ft.		—	536.00
RS216R	21.0 Cu. Ft.		—	604.00
RS219R	21.0 Cu. Ft.		—	665.00
RS256R	25.0 Cu. Ft.		—	686.00
RS258R	25.0 Cu. Ft.		—	739.00

SIDE-BY-SIDE MODELS

Model		Retail	Discount
CSF19ER		$—	$454.70
CSF22ER		—	537.05
CSF22KR		—	614.90
CSF24KR		—	663.30

TAPPAN

28-INCH WIDTH MODELS
Model	Description	Retail	Discount
95-1204	12.2 Cu. Ft. Single Door W/Freezer	$—	$215.60

30-INCH WIDTH MODELS
Model	Description	Retail	Discount
95-1424	14.3 Cu. Ft., Auto. Defrost Refrig.	$—	$278.00
95-1544	15.0 Cu. Ft. Frost Free	—	337.70
95-1844	17.9 Cu. Ft. Frost Free	—	367.40
95-1864	18.0 Cu. Ft. Frost Free	—	392.70

31-INCH WIDTH MODELS
Model	Description	Retail	Discount
95-2164	21.4 Cu. Ft. Frost Free	$—	$434.50

WHIRLPOOL

Model	Description	Retail	Discount
EAL 12CT	12.4 Cu. Ft., Manual Defrost	$—	$216.15
EAL 14CT	14.0 Cu. Ft., Manual Defrost	—	246.40
EAT 12DT	12.0 Cu. Ft., Cycle Defrost	—	253.10
EAT 13DT	13.1 Cu. Ft., Cycle Defrost	—	269.90
EAT 14DT	14.1 Cu. Ft., Cycle Defrost	—	281.10
EAT 13JT	13.1 Cu. Ft., No Frost	—	295.70
EAT 15JT	15.2 Cu. Ft., No Frost	—	322.55
EAT 15JM	15.2 Cu. Ft., No Frost w/Ice Maker	—	368.50
EAT 15PK	15.1 Cu. Ft., No Frost	—	341.60
EAT 17GK	16.6 Cu. Ft., No Frost	329.00	299.05

CONSUMER GUIDE

REFRIGERATORS

95-2084	20.3 Cu. Ft. 3-Dr., Frost Free	—	518.10

33-INCH WIDTH MODELS
95-2284	22.0 Cu. Ft., 3-Dr., Frost Free	$—	$601.70

35½-INCH WIDTH MODELS
95-2484	24.0 Cu. Ft., 3-Dr., Frost Free	$—	$668.80
95-2494	24.0 Cu. Ft., 3-Dr., Frost Free	—	783.20

EAT 17SK	17.1 Cu. Ft., No Frost	—	341.60
EAT 17PT	17.2 Cu. Ft., No Frost	—	371.85
EAT 17PM	17.2 Cu. Ft., No Frost w/Ice Maker	—	417.75
EAT 19SK	19.3 Cu. Ft., No Frost	—	372.95
EAT 19PT	19.5 Cu. Ft., No Frost	—	403.20
EAT 19PM	19.5 Cu. Ft., No Frost w/Ice Maker	—	449.10

SIDE-BY-SIDE CONNOISSEUR TWINS
EAD 19GT	19.1 Cu. Ft.	$449.00	$404.30
EAD 19SK	19.1 Cu. Ft.	—	459.20
EAD 19PT	19.0 Cu. Ft.	—	493.90
EAD 19PM	19.0 Cu. Ft. w/Ice Maker	—	539.85
EAD 22PM	22.2 Cu. Ft. w/Ice Maker	—	608.15
EAD 25PM	25.1 Cu. Ft. w/Ice Maker	—	747.05

Additional charge for colors

WESTINGHOUSE

RC131R	12.5 Cu. Ft.	$—	$219.00
RT122R	12.0 Cu. Ft.		249.00

Additional charge for colors

Prices are accurate at time of printing; subject to manufacturer's change.

FREEZERS

FREEZERS

THE FIRST thing to determine before purchasing a freezer in 1975 is whether you really need one. What you will have to evaluate is your reason for wanting one. If you are contemplating the purchase of a freezer because you want the convenience of being able to buy in bulk, and thus eliminate the need for frequent shopping trips, or if you have discovered the joys of home growing and home freezing and need extra freezer space, then you will be satisfied with owning a freezer. But if you want a freezer because you think that it will be an economical investment in the long run, you are making a mistake.

It is true that you can save money by buying seasonal foods in large quantities when their prices are lowest, and you can save money by freezing and storing your own vegetables, homegrown or bought in season, and you can save money by buying large quantities of items when stores offer specials on them. But all of those savings dissipate when you consider the cost of depreciation, maintenance, and electrical consumption of the freezer and the cost of packaging materials.

A freezer ranges in price from about $175 for a compact chest-type to about $460 for a large upright. A freezer should last about 15 years. Divide the purchase price (including sales tax) by 15 and you know how much it will cost per year just to buy the unit. Add to that the cost of operating a freezer: A 15-cubic-foot freezer uses about 18 kilowatt hours a year. At 3 cents a kwhr, that comes to $54. In addition, foods to be stored in a freezer must be wrapped in a special moisture-proof

FREEZERS

material. Meats, for example, will not stay fresh in the wrapping that the supermarket uses. There are several types of wrapping materials to choose from—plastic bags, heavy paper—and they are all expensive. All this information is not to discourage you from buying a freezer, but to assure you that owning a freezer is not economical. But it is a convenience. It is up to you to decide that the convenience is worth the money it will cost you.

Size

ONCE YOU have determined that you want to buy a freezer, you must decide what size you should buy. Some of that consideration will depend on the amount of space you are willing to devote to a freezer. Measure the height, width, and depth of the area you have chosen for its location. Make sure there is access to an electrical outlet to which no other appliances are connected.

Your next consideration is how much capacity you need. To discover the best capacity for you, you must take into consideration the size of your family and the size of your refrigerator freezer. Also to be taken into consideration is your planned use for the freezer. If you plan to buy whole sides of beef or store lots of food, you should probably consider a 16- to 20-cubic-foot model. If you simply want storage for little extras —extra frozen vegetables, bread— a 10- to 12-cubic foot freezer will probably be adequate. If you are already able to store much of your needs in your refrigerator freezer, you do not need a large-capacity freezer. Plan your needed capacity carefully. More often than not, people buy freezers that are too large for their needs, so they are normally half empty. But to run at best efficiency, a freezer should be kept full.

Style

FREEZERS are available in two styles: upright and chest-type. Some of your decision about what style to buy will depend on the amount of space you have available; some will depend on a comparison of the advantages and disadvantages of each type.

The original home freezers were chest-type freezers. These are the least expensive freezers to buy, and they hold more food than a comparable-size upright. However, the food is harder to get at than is food stored in an upright. To retrieve a package of hamburger, you may have to move around several items to find it, and if it is at the bottom, you will have to bend deep into the freezer to get it. Manufacturers have tried to alleviate this problem by including wire mesh baskets with the unit. These baskets fit across the freezer and are handy for storing the most-often needed foods. Because the freezer is horizontal, instead of vertical, it takes a great deal of floor space and, therefore, you probably will not want to keep it in the kitchen. Most chest-type freezers are kept in basements or garages—which is not very handy for everyday use.

Upright freezers look like refrigerators and do not take up any more

FREEZERS

floor space than refrigerators do. Some studies have shown that uprights are slightly less efficient than chest-types because when opened more cool air escapes. However, CONSUMER GUIDE Magazine has found that the difference is negligible—not worth basing a choice on. Upright freezers usually have three or four fixed shelves as well as storage space in the door. The coolant that keeps the freezer cold and freezes your food runs in coils attached to these shelves. Some freezers also have an adjustable shelf. But this one is not connected to coolant coils so it should be used only to store food that is already frozen. It is as easy to get at the food in an upright freezer as it is to get at food in a refrigerator. You may still have to move items around to get at what you want, but you will not have to hang from your heels to get something from the bottom. If you live in an apartment and do not have a basement or garage, or if you simply want the convenience having the freezer in the kitchen you will probably be happiest with an upright model. On the other hand, if your kitchen is short on work space, a chest-type model can serve several functions for you: extra freezer storage and extra counter area.

Another factor that may help you decide which model to buy is defrosting. All chest-type freezers require manual defrosting. Most upright freezers also require manual defrosting, but almost every manufacturer offers one or several deluxe models that have automatic defrosting. CONSUMER GUIDE Magazine does not recommend automatic defrosting because of its exorbitant cost: The self-defrosting feature adds approximately $50 to the cost of a freezer, but, worse than that, it adds from $25 to $50 a year to your electric bill. Considering that a freezer has to be defrosted only once a year, that is too high a premium to pay. Granted that defrosting is an unpleasant job, we doubt that you would be willing to pay someone $28 to $53 to do it for you. If you would, then CONSUMER GUIDE Magazine suggests you do just that: buy a manual-defrosting freezer and hire someone to defrost it for you once a year. You will not be saving any money, but you will not be wasting electrical energy either. If you do buy a manual-defrost model, just make certain that it has a water drain in the bottom of the freezer compartment. During defrosting, the water from the melted frost drains through the hole and collects in a pan underneath, which is then emptied. Admiral offers a built-in water drain on some chest-type units. The unit connects to a water pipe which drains the water away—no emptying of a pan. However, this unit cannot be installed by simply plugging it into an electrical outlet the way others can.

Features

FREEZER manufacturers do not offer the array of luxury features that are offered for all other major appliances—a situation for which CONSUMER GUIDE Magazine is thankful. However, there are several basic features that you might find useful.

Lock. If your freezer will be located in the garage or in an area accessible to a curious child—or burglars—a lock is a necessity. All

FREEZERS

chest-type models used to include locks, but no more. Some manufacturers have located the lock on the side of their models. If so, make certain the freezer will be located in a spot where the lock will be accessible.

Light. Most upright freezers are lighted, as are refrigerators, but manufacturers are eliminating this feature from their less expensive models. If your freezer will be located in a well-lighted area, you do not need a light.

Signal light. This useful feature warns you when the current is off. If your freezer is accidentally unplugged, this is the only way you will know about it before it is too late. If the problem is more serious than a fallen-out plug—like a severe power failure—do not panic. Keep the door of the freezer closed to keep the cold air in. The food will not thaw for 12 to 20 hours under those conditions. If the freezer will be out of operation for a longer period of time, pack it with dry ice to protect the food. However, if at least 12 hours elapse, check the food before leaving it in the freezer when it turns on again. Any food that has discolored or looks strange should be thrown away.

Temperature control. A freezer should maintain a temperature of 0 degrees. If it does not—if it is too warm or too cold—a temperature control will give you the ability to adjust the freezer properly.

Warranty

BESIDES the parts and labor repair warranty that is available with a freezer, you should be concerned with a special kind of warranty that is often offered with freezers—a food spoilage warranty. Actually, this is an insurance policy, and damages are normally paid by an insurance company. Before payment is made, you must take a careful inventory of the spoiled food, have it notorized, and submit a formal claim. There are also a number of other conditions to these policies, which you should inquire about. Often the policy covers only one year, but there are some notable exceptions: General Electric carries a three-year food spoilage warranty, and Whirlpool offers a five-year warranty. The most common limit of payment is $200.

FREEZERS

BEST BUYS
FREEZERS

FREEZERS ARE judged on the basis of price in relation to soundness of construction, performance, warranty, and manufacturer's reputation. The following freezers are judged to offer the best values in light of these other considerations.

CHEST

Frigidaire CF-083 is an excellent economy model for apartments or small areas. The vinyl-clad lid can double as a countertop. This is an 8.3 cubic-foot model that features a sliding basket for holding small items. A dial allows you to control the freezer temperature, and a lock at the front of the unit insures security and safety. Missing is a power-on light which is only available on Frigidaire's larger chest freezers. But more important, there is no drain, which can make defrosting an especially troublesome chore. Defrost drains normally are not found on chests this small.
SPECIFICATIONS: Capacity (cubic feet), *8.3;* Height, *34 11/16'';* Width, *35 1/8'';* Depth, *23 1/4'';* Basket; Dividers, *1;* Temperature Control; Power-On Indicator; Door Lock.
Suggested Retail Price: $269.95   Low Price: $221.75

General Electric CB-20DR is for people who need loads of freezer space. This model has a 20.3 cubic-foot capacity. There are two sliding baskets, an up-front lock, adjustable temperature control, and a light to signal that the power is on. A plug at the bottom of the front of the freezer is an easy-to-get-at drain for defrosting.
SPECIFICATIONS: Capacity (cubic feet), *20.3;* Height, *35'';* Width, *57'';* Depth, *31'';* Basket, *2;* Dividers, *1;* Defrost Drain; Temperature Control; Power-On Indicator; Door Lock.
Suggested Retail Price: $379.95   Low Price: $319.50

Hotpoint FH15CR is a 14.8 cubic-foot chest that features a counterbalanced lid. This means that the lid does not have to be held up with your hand while you are looking for food in the freezer. There is one basket for holding small items, a built-in lock in front, and a temperature control. Like its brother, General Electric, Hotpoint chests beginning with this size have a front drain for easier defrosting.
SPECIFICATIONS: Capacity (cubic feet), *14.8;* Height, *35 7/8'';* Depth *32'';* Length, *46 1/2'';* Basket; Defrost Drain; Temperature Control; Power-On Indicator; Door Lock.
Suggested Retail Price: Not Available.   Low Price: $230.45

FREEZERS

UPRIGHT

Frigidaire UF-128 *is a compact upright freezer. Although it is only 28 inches wide, it has 12.8 cubic-feet of space, enough for most people's needs. Three of the four shelves are made of cooling coils with wire grates soldered over. The fourth shelf and the four shelves in the door have no special cooling properties and should be used to store foods that are already frozen. There is no power-on light, but there is a temperature control dial and a door lock. A stow-away drain hose aids in defrosting.*
SPECIFICATIONS: Capacity (cubic feet), *12.8;* Height, *59 1/8";* Width, *28";* Depth, *29 5/8";* Defrost, *manual;* Freezer Shelves, *4;* Door Shelves, *3;* Shelf Capacity (square feet), *13.2;* Temperature Control; Door Lock.
Suggested Retail Price: $289.95   Low Price: $247.50

General Electric CAF-16CR *is a self-defrosting model. Although CONSUMER GUIDE Magazine does not recommend frost-free freezers because of their waste of electrical energy, this is a good unit for people who are more interested in convenience than in ecology or economy. This is a 15.8 cubic-foot model. The cooling coils are not in the freezer cabinet; they are on the back of the cabinet. Because the shelves do not have to be attached to these coils (as they are on the manual defrost models), all of the shelves are adjustable. There is a lock in the door and a power-on light – features you would expect on this deluxe of a model.*
SPECIFICATIONS: Capacity (cubic feet), *15.8;* Height, *64";* Width, *30 1/2";* Depth, *30 11/16";* Defrost, *frost-free;* Freezer Shelves, *4;* Door Shelves, *4;* Shelf Capacity (square feet), *18.0;* Temperature Control; Door Lock.
Suggested Retail Price: $399.95   Low Price: $321.70

Kelvinator UDM160f *is a 16 cubic-foot manual-defrost model. Most noteworthy about this unit are its deep, high-capacity door shelves. Most freezers have rather shallow shelves. A defrost drain in the bottom of the unit makes defrosting less of a problem. Other features are an adjustable temperature control and an interior light.*
SPECIFICATIONS: Capacity (cubic feet), *16.0;* Height, *61 7/8";* Width, *32 1/8";* Depth, *27 7/8";* Defrost, *manual;* Freezer Shelves, *3;* Door Shelves, *5;* Shelf Capacity (square feet), *16.46;* Temperature Control.
Suggested Retail Price: $369.95   Low Price: $279.95

Westinghouse FU188R *has all the features you would want on an upright: drain to facilitate defrosting, door lock, power-on light, deep door shelves, interior light, and temperature control. This model is only $15 more than the economy version (Model FU182R) which lacks interior light, lock, and power-on light. These three features are certainly worth $15.*
SPECIFICATIONS: Capacity (cubic feet), *18.0;* Height, *64 9/16";* Width, *30";* Depth, *30 3/4";* Defrost, *manual;* Freezer Shelves, *4;* Door Shelves, *5;* Shelf Capacity (square feet), *18.6;* Temperature Control; Door Lock.
Suggested Retail Price: Not Available.   Low Price: $302.

FREEZERS

1975 Freezer Prices

ADMIRAL

	Retail	Discount
UPRIGHT MODELS		
F1053 10.1 Cu. Ft.	$—	$234.00
F1354 13.2 Cu. Ft.	—	254.00
NF1355 13.2 Cu. Ft. w/Auto Frost Con.	—	304.00
F1656 15.7 Cu. Ft.	—	289.00
NF1657 15.8 Cu. Ft. w/Auto Frost Con.	—	339.00
F2056 20.2 Cu. Ft.	—	354.00
NF2057 20.0 Cu. Ft. w/Auto Frost Con.	—	424.00
CHEST MODELS		
CF856 8.2 Cu. Ft.	$—	$244.00
CF1556 15.3 Cu. Ft.	—	299.00
CF2054 20.3 Cu. Ft.	—	319.00
CF2057 20.3 Cu. Ft.	—	334.00
CF2558 25.4 Cu. Ft.	—	369.00

AMANA *

	Retail	Discount
DEEPFREEZE CHEST FREEZERS		
C-7 7.2 Cu. Ft.	$199.95	$174.70
C-9 9.1 Cu. Ft.	229.95	191.50
C-11F 11.0 Cu. Ft.	279.95	239.70
C-15F 15.0 Cu. Ft.	339.95	276.65

GENERAL ELECTRIC

	Retail	Discount
CF-253 25.3 Cu. Ft.	449.95	360.65
UPRIGHT (RIGHT HAND)		
CA 12 CR 11.6 Cu. Ft.	$279.95	$225.40
CA 15 DR 14.8 Cu. Ft.	329.95	263.20
CA 21 DR 21.1 Cu. Ft.	429.95	346.65
CAF 16 CR 15.7 Cu. Ft.	399.95	321.70

HOTPOINT

	Retail	Discount
UPRIGHT CYCLE DEFROST		
FV10AR	$225.95	$183.70
FV12AR	254.95	202.95
FV15CR	297.95	239.80
FV21CR	399.95	316.25
UPRIGHT-NO FROST		
FVF16CR	$378.95	$299.20
CHEST		
FH6AR	$228.95	$180.10
FH15CR	—	230.45
FH20CR	—	272.80
FH25CR	—	314.05

316 CONSUMER GUIDE

C 19F	19.0 Cu. Ft.	379.95	310.25
C-23F	23.0 Cu. Ft.	439.95	348.30
C-28F	28.0 Cu. Ft.	479.95	381.90

UPRIGHT FREEZERS

U-13K	13.5 Cu. Ft.	$309.95	$258.70
U-18K	18.4 Cu. Ft.	409.95	344.95
U-23K	23.2 Cu. Ft.	479.95	393.10
UF-12K	12.2 Cu. Ft.	369.95	313.60
UF-16K	15.6 Cu. Ft.	459.95	387.50
UF-22K	21.9 Cu. Ft.	559.95	456.95

Fair Trade

FRIGIDAIRE

UPRIGHT FOOD FREEZERS

UF-128	12.8 Cu. Ft.	$289.95	$247.50
UF-160	16.0 Cu. Ft.	344.95	288.95
UF-191	19.1 Cu. Ft.	409.95	338.25
UF-211	21.1 Cu. Ft.	439.95	360.65

UPRIGHT FROST-PROOF FOOD FREEZERS

UFP-157	15.7 Cu. Ft.	$419.95	$339.35
UFP-187	18.7 Cu. Ft.	459.95	370.70

CHEST FOOD FREEZERS

CF-053	5.3 Cu. Ft.	$234.95	$196.00
CF-083	8.3 Cu. Ft.	269.95	221.75
CF-103	10.3 Cu. Ft.	289.95	235.20
CF-153	15.3 Cu. Ft.	329.95	268.80
CF-203	20.3 Cu. Ft.	389.95	313.60

WESTINGHOUSE

UPRIGHT MODELS

FU133R	13.1 Cu. Ft.	—	$247.00
FU182R	18.0 Cu. Ft.	—	291.00
FU188R	18.0 Cu. Ft.	—	302.00
FU208R	20.1 Cu. Ft.	—	357.00
FU178R	17.1 Cu. Ft.	—	390.00

CHEST MODELS

FC153P	15.3 Cu. Ft.	—	$270.00
FC158P	15.3 Cu. Ft.	—	281.00
FC208P	20.3 Cu. Ft.	—	345.00
FC258P	25.3 Cu. Ft.	—	390.00

WHIRLPOOL

VERTICAL FREEZERS

EAV 12DW	12.0 Cu. Ft., Deluxe	—	$235.20
EAV 16X	15.8 Cu. Ft., Custom, Textured Door	—	285.60
EAV 20FW	20.0 Cu. Ft., Supreme	—	344.95
EAV 15PW	15.3 Cu. Ft., Custom	—	$319.20
EAV 20M	19.6 Cu. Ft., W/Textured Steel Door	—	376.30

CHEST FREEZERS

EAH 15CW	15.1 Cu. Ft., Custom	—	263.20
EAH 17FW	17.3 Cu. Ft., Supreme	—	287.85
EAH 22FW	22.3 Cu. Ft., Supreme	—	324.80
EAH 27FW	26.9 Cu. Ft., Supreme	—	359.50

Prices are accurate at time of printing; subject to manufacturer's change.

AIR CONDITIONERS

1975 AIR CONDITIONERS

CAN YOU THINK of anything that revives body and soul so quickly as a breath of cool, dry air on a hot, humid day? Sticky, wilted, and cross, you find sweet relief coming home to serenely cool, air-conditioned rooms...unless, of course, you have made the wrong choice and have an air conditioner too small for the room you are cooling, or one too large for the space you have, or one that does not cool or work because your wiring is inadequate. These are the common mistakes people make, thus, the resultant complaints.

You will find air conditioners to fit all windows and installations problems. There are units for double hung windows, casement windows, slider windows, and through-the-wall designs. Some new small units, like the Welbilt Model 4725, are quite versatile: They can be installed in either casement, sliding and conventional sash windows.

Air conditioner prices range from just under $100 for small-capacity units with a minimum of features, to as high as more than $500 for a top-of-the-line high-capacity model with a variety of special features. CONSUMER GUIDE Magazine recommends that you shop for the proper capacity first, then find the model with the features you need and can afford in that capacity range. Above all, buy quality—proper size, durability, noise control, good filtering systems and circulation

AIR CONDITIONERS

system—in whatever capacity and price range you choose. Do not wait for a heat wave before you decide to make the purchase, or you may find that the dealer does not have the model you want or need. If you live in the northern climate, the best time to buy an air conditioner is in January, when demand is lowest and your bargaining power is greatest.

Capacity

THE BASIC function of an air conditioner is to remove the heat from a room, and all the features you are looking for must combine and work together to perform this function to the fullest. An air conditioner performs essentially five functions: it removes heat to provide cool; it dehumidifies by removing moisture; it cleans by removing moisture; it cleans by removing impurities through its filtering system; it ventilates or expels stale air; and it circulates the air. Comparing an air conditioner with an ordinary room fan, keep in mind that a fan simply circulates the air, whatever its condition—cool, hot, moist, dirty, etc. With an air conditioner, the air is circulated through cooling coils time after time and becomes colder and colder until it reaches a preset comfort temperature. From that point on the thermostat keeps the temperature at this constant level.

True comfort comes from a unit that has the proper capacity for the room in which it will be used, so determining capacity will be your most important decision. A too-small unit will work constantly, but will never succeed in keeping the room comfortably cool, especially during extreme hot spells. A too-large unit, on the other hand, will cause uneven cold spots. Capacity is measured in British Thermal Units (BTU's). A BTU is a measurement of the amount of energy needed to cool one pound of water one degree Fahrenheit.

The following are only very general estimates to give you an idea of what the various BTU capacities mean to you and what you should choose according to your needs:

• A unit with 4000 to 8000 BTU/hr capacity (portable series) will cool a small to medium relatively inactive room. Units with this capacity are always 115 volts, which allows for easy installation without special wiring. If you buy a unit that operates on 115 volts and 7 1/2 or less amps, you may be able to install it by simply plugging it into your present household circuit. If you do this, you must make certain that the lamps and appliances already connected to that circuit, and which you are likely to use at the same time the air conditioner is in use, do not exceed 869 watts total.

• A 7000 to 10,000 BTU/hr capacity unit (medium size) will cool a large, active room or two closely related rooms. These units are available in both 115- and 230-volt models. Some local codes require a separate, single-outlet circuit for the larger 115- or 120-volt models using more than 7 1/2 amps, and in some cities the code prohibits using a room air conditioner with any 115- or 120-volt circuit.

• A unit with 9000 to 24,000 BTU/hr capacity (larger series) will cool

CONSUMER GUIDE

AIR CONDITIONERS

two, three, or even four rooms if they are situated so that the air can flow from one to another. There is an overlap in the 12,000- to 14,000-BTU range where both 115- and 230-volt designs are available. If you already have 230-volt 14,000-BTU unit, it is less expensive than a 115-volt model of the same capacity.

- A 25,000 to 36,000 BTU/hr unit (extra-large series), designed primarily to cool large living areas, may be able to cool a six-room house, providing extra fans are used to circulate the air through all the rooms and that the air conditioner is located in an area where one room does not get the brunt of the cooling. These extra large units are always 230 volts.

Equally important to room size in determining capacity are the room exposure, insulation, number of windows and doors, length and height of walls, types of walls and ceilings, roof and floor construction, number of occupants, electrical and gas appliances in the area, and outdoor climate. To determine accurately the capacity of air conditioner you need, a Cooling Load Estimate Form for Room Air Conditioners is available at no cost from the Association of Home Appliance Manufacturers at 20 N. Wacker Dr., Chicago, Ill. 60606.

Energy Efficiency

THE MOST important recent design trend in room air conditioners is towards more efficient models. These high-efficiency units conserve energy which results in lower operating costs. Unfortunately, to obtain high efficiency and the resulting energy savings, units require larger coils and high-performance compressors and fan motors—all of which raise the retail price of the units. However, a low-efficiency unit, which appears to be a bargain in the purchase price, will be a luxury in the operation.

Most manufacturers are stating the energy efficiency ratio (EER) right on the units or on a tag. If the EER is not stated, you can figure it out yourself by dividing the BTU rating by the wattage. The EER figure is a measurement of how much cooling a unit gives for each dollar spent in electricity. The higher the EER number, the more efficient the unit.

Available Features

Multiple Fan Speeds. A fan in the air conditioner blows cool air into the room to circulate it. High fan speeds are used for fast circulation and quick cooling. They produce higher operating costs and more fan noise so it is a good idea to reserve the high speed only for those times when you want fast cooling. Lower fan speeds are used to maintain quiet, comfortable cooling. Most air conditioners have two fan speeds. Economy models may have only one. Deluxe or top-of-the-line models may have more than two, such as Fedders' 9000-BTU model which has three. On some solid-state units you may find dials that offer an infinite range of fan speeds. CONSUMER GUIDE Magazine has found that a two-speed unit is the most satisfactory.

AIR CONDITIONERS

Thermostatic Control. Although the fan runs continuously, the compressor turns on and off to regulate the temperature of the air. This system causes the most economical performance and is on most middle- and top-of-the-line models.

Automatic Control. This is usually available only on middle- to top-of-the-line models. It regulates the fan speed to give you the right amount of cool air to maintain the preset degree of comfort.

Air Direction Controls. Movable louvers or other devices that let you control the direction of the cool air are fairly standard. There are many versions. Most allow you to direct the air up, to the right and left, straight ahead, or in combinations. Other air conditioners, like the Gibson Air Sweep, actually change the air direction automatically through moving louvers or by an oscillating device in the unit itself. While air direction control is definitely a must feature, the automatic version is pure luxury.

Permanent Washable Filters. The filter cleans the air as it moves through the air conditioner. All units now have a permanent filter that you can vacuum or remove and wash when it gets dirty. Many of these filters are chemically treated to make them more effective. The filter should be easily accessible for inspection or removing. If you have to go to the bother of removing screws to get at the filter, you probably will not get at it often enough.

Sound Control. An air conditioner is composed of many noise-producing parts (as anyone with an older or inexpensively made model well knows). This noise is reduced and absorbed in today's air conditioners in many ways: insulation of the cabinet; cushion or suspension mounting of the noise producing parts, such as compressor and fan; and front-panel baffles which bend air to minimize sound. There are also air-conditioner models made by companies like Addison and Comfort-Aire that are grooved in the center. When the unit is mounted in the window, the window slides into the groove leaving the sound-producing parts outside and only the part that expels cool air and takes in warm air inside.

Special Decorating Elements. A panel that hides controls is useful if you have children with curious fingers. Flush-window design should be considered if it is important to you to be able to hide the unit behind the curtains when it is not in use. Do not spend more than is absolutely necessary on cabinetry. Instead, spend your money where it will do the most good—on the inside of the air conditioner.

Installation. Many of the lightweight, smaller-capacity, through-the-window models come equipped with an installation kit. For example, Emerson's units have built-in side panels that pull out to make the unit fit flush with the sides of the window. Installation kits are available on other units for all types of windows: casement, double hung, and sliding. Larger capacity models generally need to be installed by an expert.

AIR CONDITIONERS

BEST BUYS
AIR CONDITIONERS

ONE OF the most important considerations in CONSUMER GUIDE Magazine's evaluation of air conditioners is the energy efficiency ratio. The following units are judged to be efficient in operation while having the other attributes necessary to a quality appliance: good construction, reliability, and convenience of operation.

Admiral 81FY7 is part of the "Super Princess" series. This economy model combines high efficiency (9.1 EER) with the minimum of features necessary to make it convenient to use. There are two fan speeds, an adjustable thermostat, and an exhaust and fresh-air intake.
SPECIFICATIONS: BTU, 7,700; Volts, 115; Amps, 7.5; Watts, 850; Moisture Removal (Pints/Hr.), 1.8,; Fan Speeds, 2; CFM Air Delivery, 270; Energy Efficiency Ratio, 9.1; Weight, 109 lbs; Height, 14 1/4"; Width, 23"; Depth, 20"; Maximum Window Width, 40 1/2."
Suggested Retail Price: $319.95   Low Price: $279.95

Amana 614-2N is a high-capacity, high-efficiency unit. It is a 14,000-BTU model with an energy efficiency ratio of 10.3. There are three fan speeds, and adjustable thermostat, and an exhaust and fresh air intake system. The unit can be used on a fan-only position to circulate the air in the room without cooling. An extra plus is that, in spite of its power, this is a comparitively quiet unit.
SPECIFICATIONS: BTU, 14,200; Volts, 115; Amps, 12.0; Watts, 1380; Moisture Removal (Pints/Hr.), 3.7; Fan Speeds, 4; CFM Air Delivery, 400; Energy Efficiency Ratio, 10.3; Weight, 225 lbs; Height, 19 1/2"; Width, 27"; Depth, 29 3/8"; Maximum Window Width, 48"; Installation, window.
Suggested Retail Price: Not Available   Low Price: $406.00

Carrier FJ1121A is part of the Weathermaker 400 series. This is an 11,200 BTU model with an energy efficiency ratio of 8.1. There is a two-speed fan and adjustable thermostat, but the best feature about this unit is its easy mounting. For installing in a window, there are corrogated panels that pull out of each side of the unit to fill the window space to a maximum of 44 inches.
SPECIFICATIONS: BTU, 11,200; Volts, 115; Amps, 12.0; Watts, 1380; Moisture Removal (Pints/Hr.), 2.5; Fan Speeds, 2; Energy Efficiency Ratio, 8.1; Weight, 145 lbs.; Height, 18 5/8"; Width, 24 7/8"; Depth, 26 1/2"; Maximum Window Width, 44"; Installation, through wall or window.
Suggested Retail Price: $359.95   Low Price: $289.95

AIR CONDITIONERS

Chrysler Air-Temp M14-2WH-NL *has a 14,000 BTU/hr cooling capacity and an energy efficiency ratio of 10.2. The controls, which are concealed behind a panel, include a three-speed fan and an adjustable thermostat.*
SPECIFICATIONS: BTU, *14,000;* Volts, *115;* Amps, *120;* Watts, *1370;* Moisture Removal (Pints/Hr.), *3.8;* Fan Speeds, *3;* CFM Air Delivery, *405;* Energy Efficiency Ratio, *10.2;* Weight, *185 lbs;* Height, *18";* Width, *26 1/2";* Depth, *29 1/8";* Installation, *window.*
Suggested Retail Price: $429.95   Low Price: $379.00

Emerson 14EDIE *is part of the Quiet Kool Dynamic series. Like the Carrier model, this one has a built-in installation feature, corrugated sides, to fit the unit into a double-hung window. There is a three-speed fan, adjustable thermostat, and an attractive wood-grain front panel. The air filter slides out for easy cleaning.*
SPECIFICATIONS: BTU, *13,600;* Volts, *115;* Amps, *12.0;* Watts, *1,380;* Moisture Removal (Pints/Hr.), *4.1;* Fan Speeds, *3;* CFM Air Delivery, *450;* Energy Efficiency Ratio, *9.9;* Weight, *179 lbs.;* Height, *17 1/4";* Width, *26 1/2";* Depth, *27 5/8";* Maximum Window Width, *42";* Installation, *through wall or window.*
Suggested Retail Price: $454.95   Low Price: $399.95

Friedrich Quietmaster SL19B30 *has a five-speed fan and six-way air flow control. It ranges from 19,100 BTU's at the fastest setting to 18.500 at the slowest. The EER ranges from 9.3 to 9.0–quite efficient for a unit this size. The fan can be used without the compressor, on a fan-only setting, to circulate air in the room. This fine-quality unit is meant for people who have large and active areas to cool.*
SPECIFICATIONS: BTU, *19,100;* Volts, *230;* Amps, *9.4;* Watts, *2050;* Moisture Removal (Pints/Hr.), *3.8;* Fan Speeds. *5;* CFM Air Delivery, *650;* Energy Efficiency Ratio, *9.3;* Weight, *240 lbs.;* Height, *20 1/8";* Width, *28";* Depth, *32 5/8";* Maximum Window Width, *42 ";* Installation, *window.*
Suggested Retail Price: $609.95   Low Price: Not Available

General Electric AGDE910FA *is a super-economy unit. At 10,000 BTU's it has an energy efficiency ratio of 11.9. There is a two-speed fan, adjustable thermostat, fan-only selection, and exhaust and ventilation system. The front panel tilts down to reveal the washable filter. The controls are hidden behind a wood-grain panel. The Model AGDE910FA is part of the Superthrust series.*
SPECIFICATIONS: BTU, *10,000;* Volts, *115;* Amps, *7.5;* Watts, *840;* Moisture Removal (Pints/Hr.), *2.2;* Fan Speeds, *3;* CFM Air Delivery, *4.90;* Energy Efficiency Ratio, *11.9;* Weight, *153 lbs;* Height, *18";* Width, *26";* Depth, *31 3/8";* Maximum Window Width, *40;* Installation, *through wall or window.*
Suggested Retail Price: $449.95   Low Price: $379.95

Westinghouse ACO57S8D *is a compact 5000 BTU. It has an energy efficiency rating of 8.0, the most efficient compact in the Westinghouse line. The controls, a two-speed fan, 11-position thermostat, and vent and exhaust control, are hidden behind a wood-grain panel. The*

AIR CONDITIONERS

air directional louvres can be adjusted in two directions.
SPECIFICATIONS: BTU, *5,000;* Volts, *115;* Amps, *5.5;* Watts, *625;* Moisture Removal (Pints/Hr.), *1.6;* Fan Speeds, *2;* CFM Air Dolivery, *150;* Energy Efficiency Ratio, *8.0;* Weight, *60 lbs.* Height, *12 7/16";* Width, *19 1/4";* Depth, *17 1/4";* Maximum Window Width, *40";* Installation, *window.*
Suggested Retail Price: Not Available   Low Price: $175.40

Westinghouse AK104S1V *is a 10,000 BTU model designed to fit into sliding or casement windows. The shape of the unit is vertical instead of horizontal. An installation kit, included with the air conditioner, has a sliding panel that fills the top of the window area when the air conditioner is installed. There is a two-speed fan and adjustable thermostat. The only drawback is the efficiency. Although Westinghouse calls this a high-efficiency model, with an EER of 7.3 it is not as efficient as the other 10,000 BTU models we examined. However, if you have a problem-shaped window, this is a very fine unit to use in it.*
SPECIFICATIONS: BTU, *10,000;* Volts, *115;* Amps, *12.0;* Watts, *1375;* Moisture Removal (Pints/Hr.), *3.2;* Fan Speeds, *2;* CFM Air Delivery, *280;* Energy Efficiency Ratio, *7.3;* Weight, *96 lbs.;* Height, *19 1/4";* Width, *14 1/4";* Depth, *23 7/8";* Maximum Window Width, *36";* Installation, *slider/casement.*
Suggested Retail Price: Not Available   Low Price: $260.65

SPECIAL INFORMATION SERVICE
A Bonus for Readers of this CONSUMER GUIDE

CONSUMER GUIDE offers a special bonus to its readers who are interested in obtaining information as to where they can find the low prices on specific products listed in this guide. Simply fill out the form and mail. Please include 25 cents for postage and handling.

Please send me information on:

Product _____ Model Number _____

Manufacturer _____

Product _____ Model Number _____

Manufacturer _____

Your Name _____

Address _____

City _____ State _____ Zip Code _____

CONSUMER GUIDE Magazine
3323 West Main, Skokie, Illinois 60076

RANGES

1975 RANGES

FEW MANUFACTURERS have made any major technical changes in their 1975 ranges other than refinements in the innovations that were introduced in earlier years. However, major design and engineering changes are expected in the near future. That should not discourage you from buying a range in 1975, though, if you need one. No innovation is likely to come along that will make a 1975 range obsolete in the next few years. On the other hand, if you do not really need a range this year, you may want to hold off and see what these hinted-at changes are.

For the person who is in the market for a range in 1975, a trip to any appliance store will quickly show you that ranges are available in a wide assortment of shapes, styles, and colors. In making your final decision as to which one to buy, you will have to consider the space you have available, your cooking habits, and the type of fuel you have available to you.

Gas or Electric

THE FIRST decision you will have to make is between a gas or electric range. The major factor to consider is which type of fuel is already accessible to your kitchen. If you had an electric range before, and there is no gas line feeding to your kitchen, you will have that added expense of bringing in a gas line if you decide to buy a gas range. On the other hand, if you do not already have 240-volt wiring, which is

RANGES

needed for an electric range, the rewiring cost necessary to install an electric range could be quite high. Most modern homes are wired with 240-volt wiring to accommodate modern major appliances. In such a situation it is quite likely that both gas and electric fuel are both available to your kitchen. If that is the case, you will find that the cost of gas and electric ranges are the same, so your decision will have to be based on weighing other pros and cons.

If the decision is to be based on economy, then gas should be your choice. A gas range is less expensive to operate than an electric range. On the other hand, an electric range uses its electrical fuel more economically than a gas range uses its gas fuel. Of the electricitiy needed to operate an electric range, 75 percent is converted to heat. A gas range converts only 40 percent of its gas to heat. Still a gas range uses less gas than an electric range uses electricity.

But before you choose on the basis of economy alone, you should consider your cooking habits. What types of food do you prepare most often? Do you prefer top-of-range cooking over oven cooking? Do you prefer roasting and broiling over other methods? In the past, gas ranges have been decidedly preferable for top-burner cooking because of the ease of regulating burner temperatures. Gas appliance manufacturers were quick to point out that gas burners do not have to warm up and that they cool immediately. Electric range manufacturers have worked hard to overcome that weakness in the operation of their ranges and have almost overcome it. Almost all electric ranges now offer infinite heat control instead of the four or five heat settings that were previously available. Only General Electric still manufactures ranges with push-button controls marked high, medium-high, medium, and medium-low, and low. All modern electric ranges have improved burner coils that heat up quickly and can bring a pot of water to boiling as quickly as any gas range can. They still take some time to cool off, though, and can be a hazard if you accidentally touch them right after use. However, you will also burn yourself if you touch the metal burner grate on a gas range right after use. It takes a good deal of time for this to cool off too.

If you do the bulk of your cooking in the oven, you will find that the oven of a gas range produces a lot of extra heat which escapes into the room. This is why, incidentally, a gas oven is so inefficient in its use of fuel. The extra heat can be a special problem if your heating or air-conditioning thermostat is anywhere near the kitchen. In the winter, the thermostat will sense that the house is warm and will turn the furnace blower off so the rest of the house is too cold. In the summer, the thermostat will sense that the house is warm and will keep the air conditioner blower going, making the rest of the house uncomfortably cool and boosting your cooling costs. If you do not have air conditioning, the extra heat in the summer will be just plain uncomfortable and can make cooking unpleasant.

If you are interested in broiling foods, an electric range does the best job. The idea behind broiling is to apply heat to the food quickly and evenly. An electric range supplies heat faster than gas ranges do. Furthermore, it is more convenient to broil in an electric range. The

RANGES

broiling coils are at the roof of the oven, so broiling is done at waist height, on the top shelf of the oven. The broiling in gas ranges is done in a narrow compartment beneath the oven, at floor level. This means uncomfortable deep bending to tend to the food. Waist-level broiling is available on some gas ranges, but it is an expensive feature.

Whichever you choose, gas or electric, your major concern should be safety. Gas is certainly a more dangerous fuel than electricity in that more injuries result from the misuse of gas fuel than from electric fuel. But both are potential dangers. If you are buying a gas range, look for a seal of approval from the Gas Appliance Manufacturers' Association and from the American Gas Association. The seal is in the shape of a blue star or blue flame. Both of these groups test the manufacturers' finished products to be certain that they are of sound construction and will not leak gas. If you are buying an electric range, look for the Underwriters Laboratories seal. Underwriters Laboratories concentrates on testing the safety of electrical appliances.

Smooth Top

IF YOU decide to buy an electric range, you will have a choice between ranges with conventional burner coils and those with smooth-top surfaces. The smooth-top range was an innovation introduced by Corning in 1966. The surface of the range is a smooth ceramic plate. The first smooth-top range was the "Counter That Cooks," a built-in cooktop. They then went on to offer smooth-top cooking in a free-standing range. The first Corning Counterange featured thermostatic controls for automatic surface cooking. The heat source is actually a heating unit positioned under the decorative smooth top. The major drawback of this design is that it must be used with special flat-bottomed pots and pans, which are supplied with the range. If not, the ceramic may overheat, and ceramic, at very high temperatures, gradually reverts to the characteristics of glass. If the ceramic surface cracks, it is an expensive repair.

The most recent improvement on the original Corning concept is a change in the heating elements. The new ones operate similarly to conventional electric top surface units. There is no danger of the ceramic over-heating; therefore, any reasonably flat pots and pans can be used. Even Corning has introduced models of this type into its line. They have not, however, discontinued the earlier version, which is perfectly safe if used properly.

Another problem with smooth-top ranges is that they are not as efficient as conventional electric ranges. The heat transfer from surface to pan is somewhat slower than with conventional electric ranges; although once the heat is transferred, cooking times do not vary. In addition, the ceramic surface takes time to cool down, and because of the counterlike appearance, the ceramic surface is more likely to be a hazard than still-hot conventional coils.

The major advantage of the smooth-top ranges is their supposed ease to clean. If food boils over or if there are spills, they can be simply wiped away; nothing can spill down into the range. For anyone who has

RANGES

had the unpleasant experience of cleaning up the mess left by boiled-over spaghetti sauce, this is an enticing feature. But CONSUMER GUIDE Magazine wants you to be aware of some of the difficulties in cleaning that arise with the smooth-top ranges and which are not advertised by the manufacturers. The ceramic is quite susceptible to stains from minerals in the water. Therefore, if you want to keep the ceramic top white, it is important that the ceramic and pot surfaces be completely dry and clean whenever used. Also, if the ceramic is not cleaned properly, it will become porous and will eventually become hard to clean and will stain. "Cleaning properly" often means using a special cleaning agent instead of your usual cleaning products.

CONSUMER GUIDE Magazine does not recommend smooth-top ranges—at least not yet. They are expensive, and they cause at least as much work as they save. We are waiting for a manufacturer to develop a ceramic that is easier to take care of than the present material is.

Special Ranges

THERE ARE at least two special ranges that you may run into in your shopping. CONSUMER GUIDE Magazine does not recommend either of them because of their exorbitant price-tags, but we describe them here because they may well portend what will be developing in the future of the world of ranges.

The first of these special models is Westinghouse's Cool Top II, a magnetic induction-heat smooth-top which is unlike any conventional range. It cooks foods without the use of surface heating elements. Heating takes place only within the cooking utensil itself—the pot or pan—by a process known as electro-magnetic induction. Magnetic energy is used to induce heat in the utensil. Because this range does not rely on conduction of heat from a cooking unit or burner to a utensil as conventional ranges do, the surface is always cool. If a unit is accidentally left on after a utensil is removed, power is automatically shut off. Cooking starts and stops faster because there is no waiting for the surface and the utensil to heat. The cookware used, of course, must be made of a magnetic material such as iron, stainless steel, or pans with a steel core. The unit costs $1500 and is produced in limited quantities.

The second of these special ranges is produced by Frigidaire. It is a more down-to-earth unit with an equally futuristic feature called "Touch-and-Cook." This also is a smooth-top range, but it adds a computerlike digital control panel. The controls are part of a completely flat panel and are activated by the touch of a finger. There are no knobs, no dials, no push buttons. Although a bargain compared to Westinghouse's new model, the Frigidaire is still out of best-buy range with its $900 price.

Oven Cleaning

THERE ARE three ways to clean an oven: by hand, with a self-cleaning

RANGES

oven, and with a continuous-cleaning oven. The range that requires you to clean the oven manually is the least expensive to buy and the most disagreeable to clean. Recognizing that people do not like cleaning ovens, General Electric developed a self-cleaning oven. The self-cleaning oven uses a pyrolitic process that incinerates oven soil and reduces it to a powdered ash that can be wiped up with a sponge. During the special cleaning cycle, the oven is heated to approximately 900 degrees for about 2 hours. On some units the temperature is higher and the time is shorter, and on others the temperature is lower and the time is longer. In either case, when the temperature reaches 500 degrees, an internal safety lock engages to prevent anyone from opening the door while the oven is cleaning. When the cycle is complete, the oven begins to cool. The safety lock disengages when the temperature again reaches 500 degrees, and you can then open the door. During the cleaning process, all surfaces of the oven are cleaned.

Although it would seem that operating a self-cleaning cycle would be expensive, in reality it is not. On an electric range the entire cleaning cycle uses only about 5 kilowatt hours. At 3 cents a kwhr, that comes to 15 cents. With a gas range, the cost would be half if the cost per therm. were the same as the cost per kwhr. So it is actually cheaper—and a lot safer—to use a self-cleaning oven than to clean an oven by hand with chemicals. The difference in cost comes in the purchase price. A self-cleaning range is approximately $50 to $100 more than a conventional range. A side benefit, though, is that self-cleaning ranges must have a great deal more insulation than conventional ranges because of the high heat that must be absorbed. This insulation makes the oven more efficient in normal use than others are.

To combat the high retail cost of the self-cleaning feature, manufacturers developed another cleaning process—a continuous-cleaning process. This is a catalytic system that utilizes porous panels which have been specially treated with a coating that assists in the oxidizing of oven soil every time the oven is turned on. No matter how much this cleaning system is touted by salespeople or by manufacturers, it simply is not as effective as the self-cleaning system. For one thing, not all of the surfaces are treated with the special agent, so not all surfaces will be cleaned. In addition, although it does do a tolerably good job on small, normal splatters, large spills can be a problem. They must be wiped up, and you cannot use abrasives. If you do, you may scratch the surface or remove the treatment. Caloric is quite open about the drawbacks of the continuous-clean ranges. On one of their sheets describing such a range, they say that the catalytic system "gradually reduces oven soil to a presentably clean appearance." Actually, the treated surfaces on continuous-clean ranges never look like they have been cleaned completely.

In spite of its high purchase price, CONSUMER GUIDE Magazine recommends the self-cleaning ovens for people who do not want to or do not have the time to clean ovens. The convenience—and the safety derived from not using chemicals—is worth the cost. However, if you do not mind cleaning the oven, you can save a lot of money by buying a

RANGES

conventional range. The continual-cleaning range is only for people who do not care if their oven is not thoroughly clean and do not mind not being able to make it so, even by hand.

Features

WHEN YOU are looking at the extra specialized features offered by so many manufacturers, keep one thing in mind. Most manufacturers' ranges are pretty much the same; they usually have the same ovens and same burners. The basic difference between a manufacturer's economy range and luxury range is the number of extra features added to the luxury range. The actual quality of the unit is probably no better. So do not buy more features than you need. You will be adding to the cost without adding to the quality.

Self-timing. The most common feature you will find is one that either turns on the oven or turns it off or does both automatically. Such a feature on an electric range can be set to turn the range on at a specified time and to turn it off at another specified time. Gas ranges will turn on automatically, but they will not turn off. Instead, after a set period of time, the oven automatically lowers to 140 degrees. If you will be home shortly, that is fine. Studies have shown that most people do not use this feature even if they have it. Either they find it too difficult to operate or they do not really trust it.

Automatic temperature sensing. Gas ranges often are available with one burner that is thermostatically controlled and self-adjusts. Often the thermostats on these burners are incorrectly adjusted. If so, there is no way to repair them; they must be replaced. This is another feature that is rarely used.

Rotisserie. Many manufacturers offer an option of a built-in rotisserie. If you like this type of cooking, this is a feature you may want to consider. However, make certain you will not be paying more for the rotisserie attachment than you would for a separate unit. You can compare prices by checking the rotisseries recommended in the Food Preparation Appliance section of this guide.

Roast meat probe. A probe which attaches to the body of the oven is stuck into the meat. As the meat cooks, the probe registers the meat's temperature and automatically turns the oven off when the meat reaches a predetermined doneness. The probe feature adds about $50 to the cost of a range, making it the most expensive meat thermometer on the market. A regular meat thermometer, with one or two checks of the oven by you does the same job. If you want a feature that allows you to have the oven turn on and off while you are away, then buy an electric range with a self-timing feature. At least that feature is more versatile than the probe.

Lighted and windowed oven. Instead of a solid metal oven door, many ranges have a window set in the oven door, and an oven light that can be switched on from the outside of the oven. This feature can eliminate the repeated oven door opening that causes loss of oven heat and inefficient operation.

RANGES

RANGES BEST BUYS

THE FOLLOWING gas and electric ranges are judged superior in terms of their ease and efficiency of operation, safety, standard and optional features, performance, and price. We rated "Best Buys" in both the basic and the luxurious models on the market.

GAS RANGES

Caloric RLL 302 is a conventional 30-inch range with the broiler in a drawer beneath the oven section. This unit requires manual cleaning, but a continuous cleaning kit (treated oven liners) is available as an option. This is the most basic unit available, with no extra features–not even a timer or electrical outlet.
SPECIFICATIONS: Height, 36 9/16"; Width, 36"; Depth, 26 1/2"; Burners, 4; Ovens, 1. FEATURES: Type, free-standing; Type Cleaning, manual.
Suggested Retail Price: Not Available   Low Price: $175.30

Caloric RSM 699 is a luxurious unit with an eye-level second oven and a waist-high broiler. There is no need to do deep knee bends when broiling a steak on this range. Every feature imaginable is on this unit: self-cleaning oven, timer, electrical outlet, automatic meat probe, rotisserie and thermostatically controlled "burner with a brain." This is more range than most people will ever need, but is just right for the person who wants the ultimate in gas range capabilities.
SPECIFICATIONS: Height, 71 3/4"; Width, 36"; Depth, 26 1/2"; Burners, 4; Ovens, 2. FEATURES: Type, free-standing, eye-level; Type Cleaning, self-cleaning; Timed Cooking; Appliance Outlet; Waist High Broiler.
Suggested Retail Price: $804.95   Low Price: $643.30

Hardwick K9331 has many of the luxury features normally found only on self-cleaning ovens. There is a timed-cooking feature, waist-high broiling, "Burner with a Brain," and a special feature–a glass warming shelf that stands high above the burners. This has a continuous cleaning oven, which is not as effective as self-cleaning, but is adequate if you are not concerned about having a super-clean oven.
SPECIFICATIONS: Height, 53 3/4"; Width, 30"; Depth, 24 3/4"; Burners, 4; Ovens, 1. FEATURES: Type, free-standing; Type Cleaning, cont. clean; Timed Cooking.
Suggested Retail Price: $623.50   Low Price: $560.00

RANGES
Special Ranges

THERE ARE at least two special ranges that you may run into in your shopping. CONSUMER GUIDE Magazine does not recommend either of them because of their exorbitant price tags, but we describe them here because they may well portend what will be developing in the future of the world of ranges.

Roper 1394 *is a self-cleaning model with a waist-high broiler. This quality unit features a fluorescent panel light, timed oven, and controls at the front of the cook area for easy and safe access. The entire cooktop lifts up or off for easy cleaning.*
SPECIFICATIONS: Height, *46 7/8";* Width, *29 7/8";* Depth, *26 3/4";* Burners, *4;* Ovens, *1.* FEATURES: Type, *free-standing;* Type Cleaning, *self-cleaning;* Timed Cooking; Appliance Outlet.
Suggested Retail Price: $459.95   Low Price: $367.95

Electric Ranges

General Electric J380 *is a 30-inch self-cleaning range with the operating instructions printed right on the control panel where they are always handy. The oven has a window in the door and a light which can be activated by a switch on the outside of the door. The Model J390 is the exact same unit but adds the luxury features of an automatic meat thermometer and automatic rotisserie.*
Model J380
SPECIFICATIONS: Height, *47 3/4";* Width, *29 7/8";* Depth, *27 1/2";* Burners, *4;* Ovens, *1.* FEATURES: Type, *free-standing;* Type Cleaning, *self-cleaning;* Timed Cooking; Appliance Outlet.
Suggested Retail Price: $549.95   Low Price: $442.00
Model J390
Suggested Retail Price: $649.95   Low Price: 515.00

Whirlpool RYE3650 *is a continuous cleaning unit, for people who do not mind their oven not being the cleanest one in town. This 30-inch four-burner unit has the basic features of timed oven and electrical outlet. The outlet can also be set on the timer if you want to start your coffee when you get up in the morning without going into the kitchen. There is also an oven light and window. An optional accessory that is available is an automatic rotisserie.*
SPECIFICATIONS: Height, *41 1/2";* Width, *30";* Depth, *25";* Burners, *4;* Ovens, *1.* FEATURES: Type, *free-standing;* Type Cleaning, *cont. clean;* Timed Cooking; Appliance Outlet.
Suggested Retail Price: Not Available   Low Price: $239.95

MICROWAVE OVENS

BY FAR, the most exciting innovation in cooking is the microwave oven. Amana calls it the greatest cooking discovery since fire. The popularity of microwave cooking has soared since the first super-expensive models were introduced some years ago. Part of the reason for the increased popularity is that the prices have come down considerably—at least 50 percent. And part of the reason is because there are more models to choose from. As more manufacturers enter the microwave field and competition becomes fiercer, it is the consumer who stands to gain. More competition means the development of more convenience features, more choice in capacity, and, best of all, lower prices. At the moment prices range from about $200 to $450. But as more consumers buy microwave ovens, and as manufacturers increase production, the economies of greater production should produce lower prices.

How It Works

IN CONVENTIONAL cooking systems, the air and moisture surrounding the food is heated up. This heat is then transmitted to the food, and the food gets cooked. With microwave cooking, the cooking process also depends on heat, but the heat is not transferred from the surrounding air or water. Instead, a magnetron tube produces microwaves, which are transmitted to the food. The microwaves cause the molecules of the food to vibrate very quickly and to bump into each other billions of times a second. This vibration and bumping causes friction, and friction causes heat. It is that heat which causes the food to cook. So it is only the food that gets hot, not the oven itself. Of course, the cooking utensil in which the food sits will also get hot, but that is from the heat that is transmitted by the hot food; it is not heat produced by the oven.

Advantages

THE MOST obvious advantage of microwave cooking is that it saves time: a hamburger can be cooked in 60 seconds (if you do not mind a gray hamburger), a hot dog in 20 seconds, and a baked potato in 4

MICROWAVE OVENS

minutes. What a boon to the career woman/homemaker! A microwave oven can mean the end of day after day of "instant" meals, like broiled meats, and can mean the introduction of roasts and stews to the weekday menu. Microwave cooking can simplify entertaining as cooking times of favorite recipes are cut in half.

The microwave oven is also a great help when it comes to defrosting meats—a steak can be defrosted in about 90 minutes instead of the full day it would normally take. However, there are some precautions to take when defrosting. Microwaves are absorbed better in water, and as water forms from the defrosting process it is possible for the food to begin cooking unevenly. It is important to turn the food to keep the defrosting and slight cooking process even.

Another advantage is that you do not cook in normal cooking utensils, but can cook right on a serving dish—or even on a paper plate. That means less clean-up afterward. Speaking of clean-up: Since the microwave oven itself does not get hot, spills and splatters cannot be baked on. So all spills can simply be sponged away.

In addition to the time-saving element and the work-saving element, there is the energy-saving element. Because the heat is applied directly to the food and not to the area surrounding the food, there is a more economical percentage of electricity that is actually converted into productive heat. A microwave oven does, however, use a greater surge of power in its operation. But this greater surge is balanced by the greatly decreased cooking times. So in actual wattage use—that element that is reflected on your electric bill—there is no difference between cooking with a microwave oven or a conventional oven.

Disadvantages

THE MOST controversial subject concerning microwave ovens is their safety. When the microwave units were still an innovation, it was discovered that there was a problem of radiation leakage, just as there was with color televisions. Safety requirements were increased, and now leakage is virtually unheard of. However, CONSUMER GUIDE Magazine would suggest that any unit be checked for leaks once it is two years old.

When talking of the dangers of microwaves, it is important to differentiate between ionizing and non-ionizing rays. Ionizing rays, like X-rays and Gamma rays, can cause molecules to break apart. These can be very dangerous. Non-ionizing radiation does not cause molecule change. Radio waves, visible light, and microwaves are examples of non-ionizing rays. Microwave oven manufacturers have claimed that microwaves would cause heat before causing any tissue damage, but experts have claimed that damage could be caused without heat being apparent. One researcher, Dr. Susan Korbel, contends that microwaves can cause serious behavioral changes, and that the microwave effects are cumulative. All of these fears have led the Federal Drug Administration (FDA) to rule that all microwave units manufactured after August 1974 must be constructed so that the oven will not operate if one of the

MICROWAVE OVENS

door interlocks fails and will not operate until the interlock is repaired. This is to prevent the danger of operating the unit with the door open.

In examining all available information regarding microwave radiation, CONSUMER GUIDE Magazine believes that the arguments against microwave ovens are based mainly on conjecture and supposition, while the arguments in favor of these products are based on use and performance data and medical history. By no means are we saying that there are no possible hazards associated with microwave ovens; we are saying that the information available at this time does not warrant an assumption that they are hazardous with respect to excess radiation.

In addition to the question of safety, which is more of a question than anything else, there are some disadvantages to using a microwave oven that are much more apparent. For one thing, in spite of what manufacturers recommend, microwave ovens do not work well on all foods. If you try to fry an egg in one, it will come out rather strange looking; onions do not saute very well; and some meats do not get tender enough (because of the short cooking time).

Manufacturers are trying to solve these problems. Several now offer optional browning skillets, which are preheated in the microwave oven before eggs or onions are cooked in them. And both Amana and Litton have devised means for slowing down the cooking time enough to tenderize some meats. Amana suggests cooking with the defrost cycle activated instead of the regular microwave cycle. The defrost cycle (offered only on their top-of-the-line model) causes the microwaves to be turned on and off intermittently, which would slow down the cooking time (but it would still be much faster than conventional oven cooking). Litton is introducing for 1975 several models with a Vari-Cook control. This gives you the ability to reduce the microwave power when you want to cook things slower.

There is also the problem of browning. If you are cooking something as large as a roast or anything large enough to remain in the microwave oven longer than 20 minutes, it will brown adequately to be attractive. But thin foods, like hamburgers and steaks, will cook too quickly to get brown. You can sear these foods separately before or after they cook, which means extra time and clean-up, or you can buy a microwave oven that has an extra browning feature.

We have already talked about the advantage of being able to cook with glass and ceramic utensils and even on paper plates, but there is a disadvantage connected with this too. Microwaves pass through materials like glass, ceramic, and paper, but they are blocked by and bounce off metal. Because of this particular property of microwaves, you cannot use metal cooking utensils. You cannot even use a plate that has metal decoration. Not being able to use metal is not much of a hardship when it comes to cooking utensils, but it also means that you cannot use a meat thermometer. For that reason, it is quite easy to overcook foods in a microwave oven. Only with a great deal of experience will you be able to judge when the food is done the way you like it.

Although CONSUMER GUIDE Magazine applauds the FDA ruling about the door interlock fail, it creates another disadvantage for mi-

MICROWAVE OVENS

crowave cooking. It is inconvenient to cook foods that have to be stirred or that need checking for doneness. Every time the oven door is open, the microwave oven turns off and you have to start the unit up again afterwards.

One last disadvantage is the interference which operation of the microwave ovens cause to television and radio reception. Some manufacturers claim that there is no interference, but do not believe it. CONSUMER GUIDE Magazine found that almost all units caused severe interference.

Features

MICROWAVE ovens are now available with a number of extra features. Unlike the features offered on other appliances, most of the microwaves' features really do add to their convenience—as well as to their cost.

Size. Microwave ovens are now available in a variety of sizes. Of course, the larger sizes cost the most money. Manufacturers make a great deal of noise about the exterior dimensions of their units, but there is a great deal of difference between the exterior and interior dimensions. And it is the interior dimensions that tell you how big a turkey you will be able to fit in. When you look at the interiors of microwave ovens, they will look unbelievably small, but do not be deceived into buying a bigger unit than you need. You do not need any extra space around the food that is placed in a microwave oven as you do in a conventional oven, so the oven does not have to be any bigger than the roast you will be putting into it.

Interlock. All microwave ovens have at least two interlock systems. Amana has three. Check the manufacturer's tag to make certain that the unit you are buying was made after August 1974 and that it incorporates the interlock fail system ordered by the Federal Drug Administration.

Door seals. There are three types of door seals available: contact seals, compressible metal gaskets, and choke seals. While CONSUMER GUIDE Magazine finds no evidence of one being superior to the others, we do feel that contact seals may be more susceptible to wear over long periods and must be kept free of dust and food to assure a good seal.

Browning systems. If you object to gray-looking meat and do not want the extra work of browning the food separately, most microwave ovens are available with a browning system, either as an optional feature or included in the price. There are two types: elements and special utensil accessories. The elements—which are on some Litton, Montgomery Ward, Sharp, and all Thermador models—are like the coils used in electric ovens or portable broilers. The other system uses an accessory made of a ceramic material containing special metal strips. These strips absorb heat, making the ceramic "dish" or "skillet" hot enough to brown the food. Litton and Amana were the first to offer these types of accessories. A slight disadvantage of the utensil system is that you must preheat the utensils for several minutes. They also

MICROWAVE OVENS

cause splattering, giving you more to clean up.

Automatic defrosting. With this feature, you can defrost foods without cooking them at the same time. Some ovens come with high-low power settings (Toshiba and Sears); low is for defrosting. Others have a special defrosting cycle which incorporates on-off cycling of the oven CONSUMER GUIDE Magazine finds automatic defrosting a good feature if you frequently need to defrost large items or want the convenience of not delaying dinner too long because you forgot to take the steaks out of the freezer.

Timers. There are a variety of timers available, ranging from 12 minutes to 60 minutes. Generally 35 minutes is sufficient. A necessary feature of any timer is that the first five minutes be carefully calibrated so that you can accurately time a small item for, say, 2½ minutes. A feature that is gaining popularity is dual timing. One timer handles very precise settings up to 5 mintutes. The other handles times from 5 minutes up. Two separate timers are not a necessity as long as the single timer is carefully marked, with plenty of distance between each mark, for the first 5 minutes.

Doors. The oven door on a microwave oven can either open down, like a conventional oven door, or to the side. The design you choose will depend on which is more convenient for the location you have planned for your microwave oven.

Warming drawer. Thermador now has a microwave oven with a warming drawer beneath the oven section. This is a total waste of space and money in CONSUMER GUIDE Magazine's eyes. To make room for the warming drawer, Thermador took two inches away from the interior height of the oven. Those two inches can make a lot of difference when you are trying to fit a turkey into the oven. You will be better off buying a microwave oven that gives you the most space for the money. If you want to keep something warm, put it in your conventional oven.

2450 or 915 MHz. The Federal Communication Commission has assigned two frequency bands to microwaves: 2450 megahertz and 915 megahertz. The 2450 MHz system has a shallower penetration, which is adequate for small and medium size amounts of food. Large foods need to be cooked with a 915 MHz system. The 915 MHz system is found on all large microwave ovens, but the majority of ovens on the market have the 2450 MHz system.

Warranties. As you might imagine, the most important element of a microwave oven is the magnetron tube. The tube accounts for roughly half the cost of the entire unit. If it needs to be replaced, it is a very costly repair. Most microwave manufacturers warranty the entire unit for one year and the tube for an extra year. Amana offers a five year warranty on the whole unit, including the magnetron tube. Check the warranty carefully. Do not buy a unit whose magnetron tube is not warrantied for at least two years.

CONSUMER GUIDE

MICROWAVE OVENS

BEST BUYS: MICROWAVE OVENS

BEST BUY ratings of microwave ovens are based on several characteristics: performance, size, and features in relation to cost. No real consideration was given to attractiveness as this is a matter of taste. Only you will be able to decide which are the most attractive units. Only table-top models are rated, but many of these models are available with conventional-range combinations and almost all can be built in.

Amana Radarange R-1J is a basic microwave oven with few frills. The unit weighs only 81 pounds which makes it fairly portable. There is a 15-minute timer, and the interior measures 8 x 15 1/2 x 13 – which is about average. The door opens to the side. To brown fast-cooking foods, Amana now offers an optional browning skillet which is made for them by Corning and costs about $15. Amana is one of the major names in microwave ovens; their fine reputation and their 5-year warranty make this an attractive unit.
Suggested Retail Price: $369.95   **Low Price: $309.10**

Frigidaire RCM3-37S is the exact same size as the Amana and is only 2 pounds heavier. The Frigidaire is suspiciously the same as the Amana unit, in fact. The only real difference is the timer and cabinet trim. The timer on the Frigidaire unit is a 13-minute timer. The first two minutes are calibrated into 15-second divisions. The cabinet on the Frigidaire has a woodgrain trim, making it possibly more attractive for family-room use. There is not a browning skillet available. The warranty protects the entire unit for one year and the magnetron tube for four.
Suggested Retail Price: $379.95   **Low Price: $332.65**

General Electric JET80 is slightly smaller than either the Amana or Frigidaire. The interior dimensions are 7 3/4 x 13 3/4 x 13 3/4. The door opens down, like a conventional oven. The timer extends to 25 minutes, with the first 5 minutes calibrated into 15-second divisions. The Jet 80, unlike G.E.'s other microwave ovens, is made in Japan, by Sharp, a respected manufacturer of microwave ovens.
Suggested Retail Price: $379.95   **Low Price: $299.95**

Litton Minutemaster 402 has an automatic defrosting feature. This allows you to defrost food without also cooking it. The timer extends to 28 minutes, the first few calibrated into 15-second units. At 70 pounds,

MICROWAVE OVENS

this is one of the most portable microwave ovens on the market.
Suggested Retail Price: $399 **Low Price: $339**

Litton Minutemaster 416 *is Litton's latest and most luxurious model. Every feature imaginable is on this unit. A digital timer can be set for 1 second or 60 minutes. There is a separate automatic defrosting feature and Litton's new feature, vari-cook. This is a dial that allows you to control the strength of microwaves entering the food – which allows for slower cooking. (Another way to slow down the cooking of food is to cook with the defrost feature as suggested by Amana whose Model RR-4D has such a feature). If you want the ultimate in microwaves, the Litton 416 is it.*
Suggested Retail Price: $469 **Low Price: $389**

Panasonic NE6700 *is for the person who wants microwave cooking at a moderate price. Even with its comparatively low price though, this Panasonic has some luxury features. There is an interior light, and there is a separate automatic defrost cycle. The timer extends to 30 minutes–which is more than adequate.*
Suggested Retail Price: $479.95 **Low Price: $449.95**

Westinghouse KM420M *has a 14-minute timer; the first 5 minutes are divided into 15-second calibrations. The door opens to the side. There are no extra features on this oven, making it just a good basic unit. At 81 pounds, it is quite portable–in fact, an optional cart is available.*
Suggested Retail Price: Not Available **Low Price: $340.55**

CALCULATORS

CALCULATORS

THE PRICES of electronic calculators may have bottomed out and will probably be increasing through 1975. The dramatic drop in prices in 1974 was primarily due to the intense competition among manufacturers for the consumer market. Price increases during '75 will reflect national inflation and the increased price of materials used in the calculator's construction.

With calculators, the number of features is the major determiner of price—floating decimals, number of digits in the display, battery only vs. AC and AC/battery operation, as well as the unit's range of capabilities—all affect the unit's price. Since all these features affect calculator quality, you should know what to look for in terms of what you need. Do not pay for features you will seldom, if ever, use.

Batteries are another important factor to consider. Calculators with rechargeable batteries are more expensive initially, but they are cheaper in the long run than calculators whose batteries must be thrown away and replaced when they die. It does take longer to recharge a battery than to replace one, but most rechargeables can be used on AC power while they are recharging.

The current low-price record-holder is the $16.95 Novus 650 Mathbox. It can add, subtract, multiply, and divide up to 9999.99. It is small enough to fit into your pocket easily, its display is easy to read, and you can get an AC adapter for it. One limitation of this inexpensive calculator—its six-digit display—is less of a problem than most people think, at least for home use. You may wish for a bigger capacity on

CALCULATORS

occasion—most calculators now are 8-digit models—but you rarely need that many digits. The Novus Mathbox uses standard 9-volt batteries, and is backed by a 90-day warranty on parts and labor. If you are looking for a functional and basic calculator at an almost unbelievable price, the Novus Mathbox may be the one for you.

Display

THE DISPLAY is the part of the calculator that shows you the numbers. Most calculators use self-illuminated displays. Those used in hand-held calculators are usually either LED (Light-Emitting Diode) or fluorescent types, whose battery drain is comparatively low; gas-discharge and incandescent types are more common on AC-operated desk calculators. To the consumer, the main points to look for are those which affect ease of viewing: size, color, line thickness, mounting angle, and angle of view.

Obviously, the bigger the display digits, the easier they are to read. Bigger digits, of course, necessitate larger calculators to hold them. Bigger digits also drain more power; the display generally consumes more power than the calculating circuitry itself. Some manufacturers mount small displays under magnifiers, but these magnifiers tend to reflect glare into the viewer's eyes. Others (though fewer now than previously) conserve power by using displays that consist of rows of LED dots rather than continuous LED bars; such displays are harder to read. Most displays glow red or orange, but some people find that the blue-green Digitron displays are more comfortable on the eyes.

Mounting of the display is quite important. A display that faces straight up from the calculator face may be easier to use when the calculator is hand-held, but harder to use when on a desk-top model. An angle display may be a bit hard to read in the hand, but easier when the calculator rests on a flat surface. At least two calculators have stands to hold them at an inclined angle: the Victor Mini, whose carrying-case cover becomes a stand; and the Rockwell Financier, which has a folding kickstand built in.

Display placement is a factor on the Casio Mini series (and on a few similar-looking models which we suspect are built by Casio for other companies). Casio Mini displays are to the left of the keyboard rather than above it, as in most other calculators. This position makes the display easier to read when on a desk (your hand on the keyboard does not get between your eye and the display), but almost impossible to hold and work one-handed.

A recent innovation in displays, the liquid crystal display (LCD for short) began appearing in 1974. LCD's, which are viewed by reflected or transmitted light, do not "wash out" in bright sunlight as self-illuminated displays do. Moreover, they use a lot less battery power. They are, however, more difficult to see in dim light, and many people find them hard to read in any kind of light and from almost any angle. LCD's also have a poor reputation for reliability. CONSUMER GUIDE Magazine does not recommend LCD calculators at this stage of their

CALCULATORS

development, except to those people to whom long battery life is of paramount importance.

Keyboard

KEYBOARD functions differ widely on calculators and account for many of the differences in cost, versatility, and ease of operation among them. Most of the mini-units have ten keys for the figures 0 to 9 and an additional four for the basic arithmetic functions. Nearly all the more expensive models have keys for decimals. Other common keys are labeled "C", "CE", and "K" standing for "Clear", "Clear Entry," and "Constant" (abbreviated "K" to avoid confusion with "Clear"). The clear function wipes out all the numbers entered in a calculation, allowing you to start over again at zero; the clear entry just takes off the last number and function keyed in, permitting you to correct a mistake in the lastest step of a calculation without erasing all the previous correct entries. Both keys serve useful, complementary purposes.

The constant function—which is the simplest form of memory—may be present even when there is no key for it. This function is handy if you have to multiply or divide by the same figure repeatedly, and is especially handy if the figure has many digits that you would rather not constantly repeat (3.1415962, for example).

Memory systems that are more complex and versatile than the simple constant memory are also available, often in calculators that are little more expensive than the constant-memory models. There are three basic types: the single—"M"—key memory, the full access memory, and the accumulator, with a few special types showing up on some more expensive machines. The accumulator (usually signified by a key marked "A" or "T") adds together all the totals in a series of calculations.

Scientific Calculators

SCIENTIFIC calculators or "electronic slide rules" as they are sometimes called, can now be had for as little as $69.95 or as much as $795. and up. Some calculators are advertised as "electronic slide rules" just because they have square root keys. Actually, the minimum that really qualifies a calculator for that designation would probably be a list of features like that found on the Sinclair scientific, which has logarithmic and trigonometric functions and displays its answers in scientific, exponential notation—but has no square root key at all.

Some scientific calculators, chiefly the Hewlett-Packard models, use neither the arithmetic nor the algebraic entry systems used in simpler units, but use the system of either Polish or Reverse Polish notation. One of the differences in this system is that machines equipped for its use employ an "Enter" key instead of a "plus" or "minus" key. Polish notation is a "math language" that requires a bit more time to master, but calculators that use it make very complex calculations more simply once the language is learned.

CALCULATORS

BEST BUYS
CALCULATORS

Casio-Mini Memory *has an 8-digit display but reads answers up to 16 digits. The eight most significant digits are displayed first–the others when a key is depressed. The display could be seen from almost any angle, but its location to the left of the keyboard made it inconvenient for hand-held use. Zeroes are half the size of the other digits. Keyboard features include percent key, C, and CE (here labeled AC and C, respectively), and accumulating memory (which could be made to hold an entry and stop accumulating when desired.*
Suggested Retail Price: 49.95

Panasonic JE-883 *is an eight-digit, four-function calculator which provides excellent display (blue-green fluorescent type) with mild glare problems. The minus sign appears as a small red light below the display, a mild disadvantage. Keys are well shaped and spaced, with short definite travel. C and CE keys are standard, with built-in constant function on multiplication and division only.*
Suggested Retail Price: $89.95

Sinclair Scientific, *the least expensive true slide-rule calculator, is comparable in cost with manual slide rules but capable of much greater accuracy in much shorter time. The Scientific's display shows five significant digits and two exponent digits, and numbers must be entered in exponential, scientific notation only (the decimal point automatically follows the first digit). Trigonometric operations are performed in radians only (a degree-to-radian conversion factor is printed on the case), and log calculations are handled to base 10 only, with manual conversion (again with a factor on the case) to base-e logs required; no keys for pi or e are included.*
Suggested Retail Price: $69.95

Texas Instruments SR-50, *scientific calculator, with 10-digit mantissa and 2-digit exponent, enjoys an excellent reputation among users. Its key functions are similar to the Kings-Point SC-40, but the SR-50 also has factorial (x), a key to calculate the xth root of y, and a key which adds the displayed number to the memory. While it recharges in about three hours, the unit gives only about four to six hours of operation without recharging.*
Suggested Retail Price: $149.95

CONSUMER GUIDE

GARBAGE DISPOSERS

1975 GARBAGE DISPOSERS

THE GARBAGE disposer is one of the most economical appliances on the market. Not only is it not overly expensive to purchase, but it is quite inexpensive to operate. Garbage disposers range in price from about $75 to $150 or more. Generally, the more expensive a garbage disposer is, the more effective it is in handling all kinds of food waste. CONSUMER GUIDE Magazine suggests purchasing a unit in the middle-of-the-line to top-of-the-line range. The lower price units will not prove to be a bargain in the long run because of problems of jamming and inability to effectively handle such items as corn cobs.

When shopping for a garbage disposer, your major choice will be between a batch-feed or continuous-feed unit. With a batch-feed model, about two quarts of waste can be loaded into the unit, then a cover is locked into place, and cold water is run in to activate the motor. To add more garbage, the cover must be unlocked and removed. This automatically stops the motor. The motor of a continuous-feed unit is activated with a switch (like a light switch) which is usually mounted on the wall above the sink. The cover need not be in place while the disposer operates, so food can be loaded into the unit continually. Continuous-feed units are generally less expensive to purchase than batch-feed units, but that difference is made up in the installation costs. It is more expensive to install a continuous-feed unit because of the added installation of the wall switch.

CONSUMER GUIDE Magazine recommends spending the extra money in the purchase price of a batch-feed unit. This type of disposer is infinitely more safe to operate than the other. With the unit covered during operation, there is no danger of a child's curious hand being mangled by the powerful grinding mechanism. We are also quite fearful of the injury that might occur if an adult, who is loading a continuous feed unit while it is in operation, should push his or her hand too far into the unit while stuffing the garbage in. Even industry experts agree that the batch-feed units are the safest.

If you are in an area that has low water pressure, you probably will not be happy with a garbage disposer's operation. Disposers need water pressure to activate them. And you may have special problems if you have a septic tank. It is possible to have a disposer with a septic tank; however, the tank must be from 20 to 25 percent larger than normal. If you already have a septic tank that is of normal size, the addition of the garbage disposer means that the septic tank will probably have to be pumped and cleaned more frequently than at present.

GARBAGE DISPOSERS

BEST BUYS

THE FOLLOWING garbage disposers are judged "Best Buys" because of their quality construction, reliabilty, effectiveness, and cost. Although CONSUMER GUIDE Magazine recommends only batch-feed disposers, because of their safe operation, we include here continuous-feed models also–for those people who are replacing a continuous-feed unit and want to replace it with the same type.

Frigidaire FDS-8 is a continuous-feed unit. This is Frigidaire's top model and features a precision-balanced flywheel, which makes it a more powerful unit. A quick-mount installation system makes this easy to install (not counting the power switch).
SPECIFICATIONS: Sink Drain Diameter, 3 1/2-4"; Motor H. P., 1/2. FEATURES: Type, *Continuous Feed;* Automatic Reverse; Sound Insulater; Quick Mount Installation.
Suggested Retail Price: $134.95   Low Price: $104.00

KitchenAid KWS-200 is a batch-feed model. It holds about 2 quarts of waste per load, and has an automatic reset in case of overload. The entire enclosure is insulated for quieter operation, although no disposer is particularly quiet.
SPECIFICATIONS: Motor H. P., 1/2. FEATURES: Type, *Batch Feed;* Shredding; Automatic Reverse; Sound Insulater; Safety Feature; Quick Mount Installation; Overload Reset Button.
Fair Trade Price: $159.00   Low Price: Not Available

Maytag FB20 is a batch-feed model. The lid which is locked into place to start the unit, can be flipped over and used as a drain or stopper. Unlike Maytag's less expensive batch-feed unit, this one has a sound shield to help control the noise of the grinding.
SPECIFICATIONS: Sink Drain Diameter, 3 11/32"; Motor H. P., 1/2. FEATURES: Type, *Batch Feed;* Shredding; Sound Insulater; Safety Feature; Overload Reset Button.
Suggested Retail Price: Not Available   Low Price: $119.00

Waste King ss 8000, a continuous-feed unit, is called the Super Hush. What makes this a relatively quiet unit is fiberglass insulation surrounding the entire unit. This unit also has one of the best warranties: 5 years on parts and a 20-year corrosion protection guarantee.
SPECIFICATIONS: Sink Drain Diameter, 3 1/2"; Motor H. P., 1/2. FEATURES: Type, *Continuous Feed;* Sound Insulater; Quick Mount Installation.
Suggested Retail Price: Not Available   Low Price: $112.20

PHOTOGRAPHIC EQUIPMENT

PHOTO EQUIPMENT 1975

FOR THE PAST decade or so, cameras have been getting simpler and simpler to use, until today they have almost reached the "point-and-shoot" stage. This simplification has been running across the entire photographic equipment spectrum and takes in still and movie cameras, slide and movie projectors, lenses, meters, screens, and a whole host of accessories. Nowadays, you have to really plunge into the low price category to hit a movie projector that does not provide you automatic threading. Cartridge loading is now available on everything from the GAF 136XF that retails for $15.95, to the Kodak Ektasound D140R movie camera which carries a $299.95 price tag. Slide projectors that focus the slide on the screen automatically are now commonplace. And single-lens reflexes in almost every price range are easy to handle, and capable of doing everything except self-load and click the shutter.

This simplification has been a matter of evolution, rather than of revolution. It has been happening at a steady pace for the past ten years, and while the photographic equipment industry is a technically innovative and changing field, it has reached a developmental plateau in the 1975 model year. To be sure, there will be new products and models introduced during the year, and obsolete machines will vanish from the photo dealer's showcase, but there is really nothing revolu-

PHOTOGRAPHIC EQUIPMENT

tionary on the dealer's shelves that changes the basic process of recording an image on film.

You learned it all back in your elementary science classes: A camera is essentially a black box with a pinhole in one end through which light and an image pass onto film inside. Not much has changed in this process over the years. All modern still cameras are simply manifestations of what has gone before — they are now compact, have a mechanical shutter and mechanical film advance, and a lens to help focus the scene to be photographed.

Yet, despite the lack of innovations, any well-equipped photo store in 1975 will have a wondrous maze of cameras, lenses, enlargers, projectors, and other gadgets which numb the senses and exhaust the bank accounts of even the most inveterate enthusiast. And while you might not find anything startlingly new, you will find something to fill your every need—something easy-to-use, and simple to handle.

Which piece of equipment you should buy, therefore, becomes a vital question. It takes expert advice to find your way through the labyrinth of the photographic equipment marketplace; and that is what the following CONSUMER GUIDE Magazine report provides.

Single-Lens Reflex

ASK ANY camera salesperson what format is sold the most and the answer will be the single-lens reflex. Because there is so much consumer interest in the SLR, it is hardly surprising that manufacturers invest a good deal of their resources—technical and promotional—in this format. There are several reasons for the popularity of the SLR.

Other types of still cameras have two lenses—one through which light reaches the screen and another through which the photographer views and composes his picture. As a result, what the photographer sees is not always precisely what the film will record.

With an SLR, you view the scene through the same lens used to photograph it. A mirror inside the body reflects the image to be photographed upward into a five-sided prism, or pentaprism. There, the reflected (and inverted) scene is turned right side up again and bounced instantly to a focusing and composing screen, which you see. When you depress the shutter button, the mirror springs out of the way, allowing the light to pass directly from the lens to the exposed film. This system offers the following major advantages to the serious photographer:

Accurate composition. In theory, an SLR should show you precisely what the lens sees, so you cannot blame the camera if you crop away the top of someone's head. In practice, however, few SLR's give you a full view of the field.

Interchangeable lenses. Because you can see what the lens sees, it becomes practical (also expensive) for you to use a large number of lenses with a single SLR body.

Accurate built-in metering. The construction of a single-lens reflex permits manufacturers to install light-metering cells in the body of the

PHOTOGRAPHIC EQUIPMENT

camera, behind the lens, where they measure only the light that comes through the lens.

The most recent—and most highly touted—development in metering is automatic exposure control. Until this development, most SLR's with behind-the-lens metering were semiautomatic, or match needle, cameras. With such a camera, the photographer sets either of the two exposure controls—the lens aperture or the shutter speed—then adjusts the other exposure control to align a pointer, needle, or some such visual indicator seen in the viewfinder. In an automatic camera, the photographer sets one of the two exposure controls and presses the shutter-release button. The camera automatically adjusts the other control according to the film and the light conditions.

Before you let any flickering interest in SLR's with automatic metering get the better of you, perhaps you should know that few of these automatic SLR's represent any progress in the technological realm.

One small bit of innovative business, however, is the trend toward removing the dials and needles in behind-the-lens cameras and replacing them with light displays. Such a camera, the Fujica ST-901, made its appearance at the Master Photo Dealers' and Finishers' Association show in Chicago in March 1974. The new Fujica has a meter readout play that resembles the numerical display of one of those popular hand calculators. CONSUMER GUIDE Magazine hopes that Fuji has thought this change through thoroughly rather than just trying to change things for the sake of being "up-to-date." We consider the meter display in the Fujica ST-801 to be the best in the photographic industry, and we would hate to see it abandoned for something less useful.

Wherever the SLR goes in the next several years, one thing is certain—prices will continue upward. The new model cameras, with added features, and the improved models of SLR's, with their redesigned metering and lens-mounting systems, viewfinders, and other parts, will all carry heftier prices in 1975.

Cartridge Cameras

THE CARTRIDGE-loading camera is enjoying great popularity today, especially among snapshooters who like a camera that is lightweight, easy to carry, and is quick to load and unload—you merely drop the cartridge into place when loading, and lift it out when finished.

Kodak introduced the first Instamatic still camera in the early 1960's, and even though the concept was greeted with a negative reaction from other manufacturers, Kodak's competitors fell into line. About two years ago, Kodak created a second, smaller format called the Pocket Instamatic. The title was appropriate for although the cartridge idea, shape, and form were retained, the camera was small enough to fit into a pocket.

The Kodak 126 format, the original Instamatic, quickly gained acceptance because of its attributes: the 126 camera and its film are close to the same size as many 35mm rangefinders, thus, both their transparencies can be shown in the same projector. Kodak's newest cartridge

PHOTOGRAPHIC EQUIPMENT

format, the 110 size, has proved to be most popular with photographers who prefer prints over slides. 110 slide film is available, and there is no question of quality. Indeed, CONSUMER GUIDE Magazine tests prove 110 slides are equal, and in many cases superior, to 35mm slides. However, the choice of 110 prints over slides is economic—pocket-size photography requires different slide projectors than do 126 and 35mm. We consider this to be 110's drawback. CONSUMER GUIDE Magazine objects to the need for owners of 35mm gear to purchase and store added equipment.

Cartridge cameras are the most sensible for casual photographers. Whether you are interested in 126 slide-film format or the 110 print-film format, consider both sizes and then decide which is the best for your needs.

Polaroid

IN 1973 and 1974, the big news in instant picture photography was Polaroid's SX-70, the most technologically advanced photographic instrument on the consumer market. It incorporated breakthroughs in a dozen areas—from optics to battery design—that made it one of the most ingenious products around. It seemed unlikely that Polaroid could make news again, but that is what happened in September 1974, when the company introduced two more cameras: a lower-priced SX-70, called SX-70 Model 2, which had a list price of $30 less than the original; and the Zip, Polaroid's lowest priced instant camera to date. Zip produces finished black-and-white pictures in 30 seconds and sells for $14.

For consumers who like the instant picture concept, these cameras are more attractive than ever. Model 2 is functionally identical to the SX-70. The differences are only in the appearance. The Model 2 has an ivory-colored plastic body and contrasting mahogany-colored acrylic fiber covering. The deluxe SX-70 camera has a brushed chrome body trimmed with top-grain cowhide.

Instant photography may be easier than ever (prints no longer have to be coated with the new Polaroid film), but it has drawbacks the consumer must consider. The cameras produce instant prints, but they normally are not of as fine quality as those produced with negative film. Also, Polaroid film, particularly the SX-70 film, is very expensive in comparison to negative film.

Movie Equipment Trends

THE PROGRESS in Super 8 movie equipment continues to make exciting news for film makers. The press has been filled with success stories about the use of 8mm equipment in television, in industry, in education, and in a variety of other areas that were previously considered the exclusive domain of 16mm. What makes these changes most exciting is that professional 8mm users are operating with standard, stock equipment.

PHOTOGRAPHIC EQUIPMENT

CONSUMER GUIDE Magazine photo experts have ascertained that stations are converting to Super 8—particularly in some midwestern and southwestern regions, where television stations with smaller viewing audiences put a premium on economy—so that news footage, commercials, and even TV features can be produced inexpensively, yet with the high quality that Super 8 can provide. Super 8's unique attributes and its stunning economy also are creating entirely new markets for movies. If you have ever contemplated movie making as a source of income, you can now entertain such thoughts more seriously in the context of the lower-cost 8mm equipment.

Even if you plan to film only your vacations and the kids playing in your backyard, you need no longer be classified as an "amateur." The advancement of Super 8 not only changes its user's "image"; it also makes the treasured personal experiences which are committed to film all the higher in quality and all the better in entertainment value.

Experienced home-movie makers know that very often the most interesting of shots take place in light levels that are too low for the movie camera to record. Capturing such nighttime shots as the Cub Pack roasting marshmallows in the campfire would have been impossible several years ago, but now such a shot can be made with XL (existing light) cameras. This new development in Super 8 means that when the sun goes down or filming goes indoors, XL cameras can continue working without the aid of cumbersome lighting equipment.

Another exciting new development in the Super 8 field during the past several years—for both professional and amateur—is the introduction of synchronized sound. There are three Super 8 sound systems available at this time—Bell & Howell's Filmosound 8, Optasound, and the Kodak Ektasound system. CONSUMER GUIDE Magazine believes that while Filmosound and Ektasound are best suited for the amateur home-movie maker, Optasound meets the advanced amateur's need for speed and simplicity and the professional's requirements for choice of equipment and capability for complete editing.

Now that home movies can talk and cameras can be used in ordinary light like the illumination from table lamps or campfires, we will see the continuing production of XL (existing light) cameras that can record sound. This growing sophistication in movie equipment is also reflected in visible trends in the projector field. The first has been toward the use of rear projection screens and toward styles that look like tape recorders and television sets. Another is the continuing introduction of machines that play back magnetic and/or optical sound tracks which are used in the new synchronized sound movies.

Darkroom Equipment

PHOTOGRAPHY is more than taking pictures. In fact, many hobbyists consider darkroom work the heart of photographic creativity. In the darkroom you can translate your intentions when you snapped the shutter onto a finished photograph every bit as good as the print you get from a photofinishing plant. To some beginning darkroom enthusiasts,

PHOTOGRAPHIC EQUIPMENT

the initial investment in equipment seems forbidding. There are enlargers, in fact, that cost as much as $1000. You can also lavish many dollars more on the gadgets that make photographic processing easier or faster. Yet, you can also make enlargements that anyone would be proud of, and spend less than $150 for your equipment. Indeed, for about $50 you can buy all the equipment you need to develop your own film and to make contact prints, which are prints the size of the negatives.

You can start your experiment in darkroom work with a light-tight film-developing tank, a reel that accepts the size of film you use, a photographic thermometer, a watch, and the appropriate chemicals —film developer and fixer. You do not need a darkroom because you can wind the film onto the developing reel in a dark closet, drop the reel into the light-tight tank, and then carry out the other developing steps in ordinary room light. After some practice, this simple first step into processing will provide you with better quality black-and-white negatives than you usually get by sending your film to be professionally developed.

The next step is contact printing. For this you need a room you can black out or gain access to after dark. You also need four trays, running water, a print frame (or proofer), a photographic safelight (a yellow lamp or fixture with a yellow light), a white light with a switch that you can turn on for a second or so, paper developer, photographic fixer, a blotter for drying the prints, and photographic paper. The only necessary additional equipment you need to make enlargements is an enlarger. Enlarging does not really require any more space than does contact printing, though it requires a firm table or counter. You can use a print frame to hold enlarging paper, but most photographers use an enlarging easel. If you are on a tight budget, you can use two heavy rulers to hold the paper flat during exposure.

Briefly, the enlarger shines light through the negative to a lens. The lens projects an enlarged image of the negative onto the photographic paper. When the paper is developed and fixed, it is a lasting but enlarged facsimile of the scene that originally appeared on the negative. You develop and process enlarging paper the same way and with the same chemicals as you do contact paper. You can use enlarging paper for both jobs.

In addition to the basic tools mentioned, plus some sundries such as film clips, print tongs, stirring rods, and chamois or sponges to wipe the film, there are other devices that make darkroom work easier or more precise. There are special timers that tell you when the film is developed, and there are other timers that turn the printing or enlarging light on and off. Special focusing magnifiers help you focus your prints accurately. Print meters tell you how much exposure to give the prints. Special washers for film and for prints relieve you of the tedious chore of agitating your materials during washing. Print driers, some of them completely automatic, likewise help with the housekeeping. Nevertheless, you can get started with just the basics.

PHOTOGRAPHIC EQUIPMENT

Electronic Flash Units

SINCE THE earliest days of photography, flash has been an integral part of the picture-taking process. At first, a tray of highly dangerous powder was ignited to produce a flash of light. The powder method gave way to the flashbulb, and it was this convenient little "package of light" that gave indoor picture-taking its greatest boost. As artificial-light photography became more and more popular, the bulb itself became obsolete and was superceded by a permanent flashbulb known as the "electronic flash unit."

Since the beginning, the trend in the manufacture of electronic flash has been toward smaller units, more powerful flashing, and, during the last ten years, more automatic operation. In the fashion typical of this highly competitive industry, one manufacturer's technical improvement is seized upon by the competition, and within a year all the major firms have incorporated the new idea into their own products. This, in turn, leads to still greater advancement, more emulation, and a bewildering array of products to buy. The photo enthusiast benefits in the long run.

Flash units can be categorized according to battery types. All electronic flash units are powered by batteries. There are two general battery types—common replaceable batteries, similar to those used in flashlights and radios, and built-in rechargeable batteries usually of the nickel-cadmium type. Furthermore, many flash units with either type of battery also work on standard household A.C. power. Replaceable battery units generally produce a greater number of flashes than do rechargeable ones, and they have a relatively short recycling time (the period between flashes). Although nickel-cadmium cells do not pose these problems, neither do they provide as many flashes during the span of their charge. Longer recycling periods are generally also required with the rechargeable cells.

All flash units, regardless of their type of power source, can be further divided into manual and automatic classifications. Manual units require that the user calculate his or her own exposure setting by dividing the film guide number by the distance of the subject. Automatic models eliminate this calculation, requiring only one setting. All automatic units also have manual operation, should the subject be outside the limits of the automatic operation.

The newest advance in automatic flash is a system of saving energy, known popularly as "thyristorization." Units equipped with this system make use of the total amount of power supplied by the batteries. Thyristorized units divert the excess power back into the unit's main capacitor, to be used again. As a result, the number of flashes is increased and the recycling times are reduced.

Slide Projectors

SLIDE PROJECTORS are behaving better these days. Manufacturers have quieted down the units' fans, dulled their appetite for electricity and lightbulbs, reduced the bulk, and made the machinery run

PHOTOGRAPHIC EQUIPMENT

smoother. One of the newest trends in slide projectors is the use of the tungsten-halogen lamp (also known as the "quartz lamp," abbreviated to "Q" in some model designations) which manages to cast off more light for a longer period of time, while consuming the same or less electricity.

Another trend is Kodak's loss of domination of the slide projector business through its Carousel models. Keystone's latest models are at least fraternal, if not identical, twins to the Carousel. Added to that, the Bell & Howell slide cube concept hit Kodak right in its Carousel's weakest aspects. Carousel trays are expensive and bulky; the slide cube is cheap by comparison and takes up only a fraction of the volume.

The alternative offered by Kodak—and by almost everybody else vying for business against the Bell & Howell slide cube—is the stack loader. The stack loader takes a stack or deck of slides—up to 40 in number if they are standard cardboard-mounted slides—and automatically projects them as you have stacked them (a few projectors revert to semiautomatic status with the stack loader in place). A step up from just stacking the slides into the stack loader is the Kodak slide clip. This is a spring-loaded holder that securely clamps as many as 36 slides until you are ready to deposit them into the stack loader. Then you release them by applying pressure between your thumb and forefinger.

For the family with lots of slides, and modest means, the stack loader or the slide cube are essential in an automatic slide projector. The round tray is essential for the salesperson or the lecturer and is awfully handy for the carefully selected group of slides you want to keep out of harm's way; but many slides are snapshots, or less, that do not need to be enshrined in a relatively expensive dispenser.

Automatic focus is a feature you may like for your slide projector. Honeywell has pioneered a successful automatic focus feature, which has been incorporated into at least the top-of-the-line models by nearly every manufacturer. On many units, the feature is quiet enough, damped enough, and quick enough to correct meandering focus without calling attention to itself. It should be pointed out that the automatic focus does not actually focus the projector. You focus the projector; the automatic focus refocuses it.

Slide projectors have something in common with automobiles: a creeping tendency to become overladen with features. No reversal of this trend appears to be in sight. Features sell merchandise and prop up profits. Thus, most slide projectors have advanced far beyond the basics. The only essentials are a light source, a lens, and a frame to hold a single slide at a time. But few consumers would want such a Spartan machine.

When you purchase a slide projector, you will probably find much more than just the basics in any full-powered model from a brand name manufacturer that provides a strong warranty, service backup, and long-term replacement parts policy. If you want all that, then you will have to take a certain amount of automation; at least, automatic slide loading, along with the deal.

PHOTOGRAPHIC EQUIPMENT

PHOTO EQUIPMENT BEST BUYS

CONSUMER GUIDE Magazine *evaluates still cameras, movie cameras and projectors, enlargers, electronic flash units, and slide projectors on the basis of quality of lenses, sturdiness, ease of handling, and other features that are needed for flexibility and durability in use.*

SINGLE-LENS REFLEX CAMERAS

Bell & Howell FD35 *is a relatively new SLR, made by the company that formerly distributed Canon products in the United States. The Bell & Howell FD35 is identical in most respects to the Canon TLb, which we rate a "Best Buy." The one significant difference between the two is that the FD35 has a hot shoe, the TLb has an accessory shoe. If the FD35 can be found at a price comparable to the TLb, then it too merits a "Best-Buy" rating.*
(50mm f/1.8 lens)
Suggested Retail Price: $335.00   **Low Price: $220.00**

Canon F-1 *is a professional-type 35mm SLR. A top-of-the-Canon line model, it features open-aperture, and behind the lens metering. Despite some minor flaws, the F-1's quality is high throughout. The controls function with incredible smoothness, and its finish is excellent. Even at its relatively high price, value will be obtained for the money.*
(50mm f/1.4 lens)
Suggested Retail Price lens): $744.00   **Low Price: $528.44**

Canon TLb *is a good, inexpensive, solid camera with an FD series lenses. The TLb is a machine to grow with and possibly to grow beyond. No doubt Canon hopes that the TLb owner will eventually trade up to the FTb or the F-1. While the TLb is limited in top shutter speed (1/500 of a second) and has not a single frill, it is cheap to buy, affords open-aperture metering, and handles well.*
(50mm f/1.8 lens)
Suggested Retail Price: $325.00   **Low Price: $230.75**

Fujica ST-801 *although similar in many respects to the ST-701, meters at full aperture and has a wider metering range and a brighter viewfinder image. Fuji has managed to put all this capability into a body that*

PHOTOGRAPHIC EQUIPMENT

is only a little higher and no deeper, longer, or heavier than the ST-701. CONSUMER GUIDE Magazine finds the ST-801 to be quite a nice package. In our judgment, it offers good value for its price.
(55mm f/1.8 lens)
Suggested Retail Price: $380.00   Low Price: $285.00

Hanimex Praktica LTL is a simple, well-designed, smooth, accurate 35mm SLR camera, with a stop-down metering system, dim screen, and limited and off-center field of view. At a discount, the LTL might make a good buy for someone with a large collection of Praktica-threaded lenses or for a newcomer to the serious pursuit of photography.
(Oreston 50mm f/1.8 lens)
Suggested Retail Price: $289.95   Low Price: $194.25

Konica Autoreflex T3 is a rarity—a mechanically operated shutter-priority (SP) automatic with a truly comfortable shutter-button feel. The shutter has click-stopped speed settings from "B" through 1/1000. In the T3's price range you can choose among a wide variety of conventional machines. But if you decide that you really must have an automatic, this one should be seriously considered.
(50mm f/1.7 lens)
Suggested Retail Price: $459.95   Low Price: $337.70

Minolta SR-T100 has a clean and open layout. What is more, it has good viewfinder brightness, good film-speed range, ability to mount any automatic Rokkor lens, built-in battery checking, and a two-year warranty. Its disadvantages include peculiar rapid-advance operation, limited metering range, and lack of a 1/1000 top speed. Although we are not too enthusiastic about the machine at its recommended list price, we feel that it would be a "Best Buy" when offered at a substantial discount.
(50mm f/2.0 lens)
Suggested Retail Price: $315   Low Price: $207.90

Nikon F is a legend in its own time. It is a well-made, dependable, but peculiar camera that is best suited for the serious photographer or the working pro, who can get the most out of it and is experienced enough not to be discouraged by its heavy weight or other idiosyncrasies. In CONSUMER GUIDE Magazine's judgment, it provides solid value for its price.
(50mm f/1.4 lens)
Suggested Retail Price: $571   Low Price: $408.25

Nikon F2 is truly a professional machine, designed for people who earn their livings with cameras. Accordingly, it carries a rather high purchase price. Without reservation, CONSUMER GUIDE Magazine recommends the F2 to anyone who really needs the excellent solidity, performance, and ability that this camera offers. But it is perhaps too

PHOTOGRAPHIC EQUIPMENT

much machine for any but the most affluent and advanced amateurs.
(Photomic DP-1 Finder and 50mm f/1.4)
Suggested Retail Price: $815   **Low Price: $582.70**

Olympus OM-1 *has super-quietness, which the designers credit to air damping of the mirror, four ball-bearing trains in the shutter, a lightweight curtain drum, and large shock absorbers for the shutter. This is a camera worthy of careful consideration by amateur or professional because of its small size, light weight, and smooth handling.*
(50mm f/1.4 lens)
Suggested Retail Price: $524.95   **Low Price: $346.45**

MOVIE CAMERAS

Argus/Cosina 755XL *is one of the better-conceived XL units. It has no visual focusing but the 755XL has a large number of features for an XL such as power-zoom lens, backlight and spotlight compensation, and two speeds.*
Suggested Retail Price: $269.95   **Low Price: $178.20**

Beaulieu 4008 M3 *is a more satisfactory camera than the 4008 ZM2. While the M3 is capable of manual zooming only, the camera is unique in many ways and most of its features are valuable and effective. It handles nicely, is easy to use, and it produces excellent results in almost all models. It is Beaulieu's most workable Super 8 to date.*
Suggested Retail Price: $849   **Low Price: $636.75**

Kodak XL55, XL33, and XL10, *all work well, but CONSUMER GUIDE Magazine considers the XL55 to be the best of the group. It offers the greatest flexibility from an optical standpoint and is simple to use handheld. Consider it even if you are budget-minded. We feel that its extra versatility and flexibility is worth the increased investment. If budget considerations must figure prominently in your selection, we suggest that you consider the XL10, the lowest-priced member of the group.*
Suggested Retail Prices: XL10: $114.50, XL33: $119.50, XL55: $234.50
Low Prices: XL10: $86.15, XL33: $88.00, XL55: $175.40

Nikon R-10 Super *is a surpriser: Nikon chose to exclude an Instant Slow-Motion button. Even without this standard feature, the R-10, with its extensive variety of features and capabilities and its superb balance, is one of the most versatile cameras on the market. It is able to produce beautiful, intriguing, and, in some cases, unique footage.*
Suggested Retail Price: $995   **Low Price: $711.40**

MOVIE PROJECTORS

DeJur Insta-Valometer *is a multispeed projector, capable of running at*

PHOTOGRAPHIC EQUIPMENT

slow speeds. It is not a "suave" machine; in fact, it is rather brash and noisy. But it does its job well. It is a projector for people who want performance without "status appeal."
Suggested Retail Price: $220   **Low Price: $160.60**

Elmo ST-1200 *is one of the truly fine Super 8 sound projectors currently on the market. Its efficient design gives careful consideration to the often-overlooked aspect of inspection and cleaning of the film gate, threading path, and other internal components that can quickly get dirty and cause damage to the film. Its sound-recording system enables you to mix two sound sources simultaneously without accessories, while its accessory mixer gives you a total of five sources that can be recorded at once. Its monitor circuit lets you hear, balance, and evaluate your various sound sources both before and during the actual recording. Image quality was excellent in every regard. CONSUMER GUIDE Magazine believes that the ST-1200 will be a welcome device for all filmers who require high-quality equipment that is ruggedly built, and unusually versatile.*
Suggested Retail Price: $589.95   **Low Price: $389.35**

Kodak Moviedeck 475 *is a versatile machine with many features, and it produces an excellent screen image. It has four speeds and an automatic rewind control. On the negative side of the 475, the concealed film path could present problems and it takes a little extra effort to keep the machine clean.*
Suggested Retail Price: $224.50   **Low Price: $164.20**

ENLARGERS

Bogen T-35 *cannot be faulted on its appearance, economy, or compactness. Nevertheless, we feel that its limited baseboard magnification, lack of heat-absorbing glass, and inability to handle the larger format negatives are disadvantages.*
(50mm f/3.5 lens)
Suggested Retail Price: $79.95   **Low Price: $59.95**

Bogen 22A Special *bears a strong family resemblance to the attractive Bogen T-35, but CONSUMER GUIDE Magazine finds the 22A more versatile and convenient to use. The most salient difference is that the Bogen 22A Special can enlarge full-frame 2-1/4 x 2-1/4 inch negatives. With the Bogen 22A Special you can make borderless prints on 11 x 14-inch paper. The 22A's column stands 28 inches high, and the unit weighs 11 pounds.*
Suggested Retail Price: $112.50   **Low Price: $79.50**

Meopta Axomat II *is an excellent enlarger for a person chiefly interested in 35mm black-and-white prints. It is a well-made piece of equipment that can be taken apart easily for storage. It will make an 11 x 15 inch enlargement from a 35mm negative or do a 70 percent*

PHOTOGRAPHIC EQUIPMENT

miniaturizing job. It stands 37-3/4 inches high (storing height is 31 inches) and weighs 15-1/2 pounds.
(50mm f/4.5 lens)
Suggested Retail Price: $129.95   **Low Price: $79.50**

Meopta Opemus III *is a larger version of the Axomat II. It features excellent craftsmanship and finish and is attractive at its price for making black-and-white enlargements of 2-1/4 x 2-1/4 inch film. CONSUMER GUIDE Magazine believes it will also do a creditable job with smaller formats, though the Axomat II is recommended for the 35mm enthusiast. The Opemus III takes apart easily, packs neatly and is a good unit for the temporary or cramped darkroom. The Opemus has a maximum height of 39 inches (storing height: 30 inches) and weighs 20-1/4 pounds.*
(50mm f/4.5 lens)
Suggested Retail Price: $149.95   **Low Price: $89.95**

Super Chromega D Dichroic *enlarger represents the ultimate Omega effort in the diffusion color series. The Super Chromega D features dichroic color filters, interchangeable slide-in light multipliers, digital filtration readout, instant white-light focusing, a single lamp of high illumination, and a filtration range from 0 to 150 CC.*
Suggested Retail Price: $965.95   **Low Price: $750**

ELECTRONIC FLASH UNITS

Bauer E16 *truly qualifies as a portable flash; it will fit inside just about any pocket. It is the smallest and the only non-automatic model on CONSUMER GUIDE Magazine's "Best Buy" list. It is also the smallest flash gun on the market that has a built-in, rechargeable, nickel-cadmium battery. The E16 is meant for simplicity, and it works only with cameras equipped with a hot shoe (a live electrical contact). Thus, there is no synchronization cord. Though convenient, its performance is hampered by a long recharging time—14 hours. CONSUMER GUIDE Magazine considers its capacity of 40 flashes from such a charge, however, to be quite satisfactory. Initial recycling time is 8 seconds. After 10 flashes it is 10 seconds, and it increases to 20 seconds after 30 flashes.*
Suggested Retail Price: $59.95   **Low Price: $44.50**

Beseler 935A *is the best among the units resulting from the combined efforts of Beseler and Toshiba to bring electronics to photography. It is a compact, medium-size automatic unit that provides a choice of apertures and working distances. Minimum working distance is a noteworthy six inches, making this unit ideal for close-up shooting of such subjects as flowers, stamps, coins, etc. With f/2.8 the auto operation reaches to 16 feet, and with f/2 it extends to 22 feet – one of the longest distance ranges among units of this size. Other convenience features include a long A.C. cord and a detachable nine inch synchronization*

PHOTOGRAPHIC EQUIPMENT

cord. A full recharge of eight hours provides 60 flashes; a partial recharge of one hour will power 10 flashes. Its charge indicator lamp goes out when the battery has been fully rejuvenated.
Suggested Retail Price: $74.95   **Low Price: $54.55**

Braun F 18LS *is manufactured by a company which has always directed its efforts toward the professional market, but with the decision to enter the amateur field, the company developed a full line of flash units. The best, in CONSUMER GUIDE Magazine's opinion, is the F 18LS–a single-aperture automatic model with a rechargeable nickel-cadmium battery. This unit is compact and easy to use, but its inordinately long 15-hour recharging time represents a blunder in design. Fortunately, its 6-1/2 foot A.C. cord provides an emergency option when the battery runs out of its customary 60 flashes. For the first 15 flashes, the Braun recycles in 8 to 9 seconds. After 35 flashes, that interval doubles, and it reaches 30 seconds at 50 flashes. In addition to hot shoe operation, the F 18LS has a remarkably long 11 inch synchronization cord that provides a great measure of flexibility in picture taking.*
Suggested Retail Price: $84.95   **Low Price: $55.20**

Honeywell Auto/Strobonar 110 *is the result of Honeywell's efforts to automate its highly successful miniature, manual, disposable model 100 flash unit. The Auto/Strobonar 110 is merely the same external unit with provision for auto operation. Two penlight (AA-size) batteries provide the power for more than 200 flashes. The 110 is mainly a flash for family-type pictures taken in a moderate-size room. Using the recommended alkaline batteries the unit's first recycling period is about 10 seconds. A 12-inch synchronization cord, long by any standards, seems almost out of keeping with the mini nature of the 110. Nevertheless it affords flexibility of operation.*
Suggested Retail Price: $54.95   **Low Price: $40.30**

Honeywell Auto/Strobonar 360 *gives more performance for its size than its larger counterparts within the full line of Honeywell flash guns. The 360 is the smallest Auto/Strobonar with triple-aperture capability. More importantly, it incorporates most of the more desirable features in automatic flash. Its rechargeable nickel-cadmium batteries need only three hours for a complete rejuvenation. Its 12-1/2 inch synchronization cord can be detached for hot shoe operation or can be positively locked in place by a unique spring-loaded catch. There is no A.C. operation with this unit, presumably because Honeywell reasons that a quick recharge of the battery supplies enough energy for a few needed shots. The rapid recharging system generates 5 flashes after just 5 minutes and 15 flashes after 20 minutes. With a full charge, the first recycling times are in the 7 second range. This interval is consistent up to about 30 flashes, after which it rises to about 10 seconds.*
Suggested Retail Price: $99.95   **Low Price: $66.00**

Honeywell Auto/Strobonar 470 *has been upgraded for thyristoriza-*

PHOTOGRAPHIC EQUIPMENT

tion. The new Auto/Strobonar 470 is a copy of the 460 except for the required internal circuitry. Retained are such desirable features as a rechargeable battery with three hour rapid recharging plus partial recharging, triple automatic aperture selection, hot shoe provision, a locking screw for secure mounting on camera, and a detachable 14-inch synchronization cord with a long contact for secure connection to the unit itself. Based on the requirements of thyristorized shooting procedure, the 470 provides 500 flashes at recycling times of less than one second when used exclusively at a two-foot subject distance. From a medium subject distance of about ten feet, the number of flashes lowers to near 175 — but at the still awe-inspiring recycling time of less than one second.
Suggested Retail Price: $149.95   **Low Price: $95.70**

Rollei E19BC has smooth and fast operation, and is intended primarily for close-up photography rather than for general group and portrait shooting. Its automatic working distance covers between 16 inches and 11-1/2 feet. Power is supplied by four penlight (AA-size) batteries, good for about 200 flashes. For the first 50 flashes, an 8-second recycling period is needed. This increases to 12 seconds and then up to the 15 to 20 second level after 100 flashes. To keep the E19BC as small and efficient as possible, Rollei has not provided for A.C. operation.
Suggested Retail Price: $59.95   **Low Price: $24.95**

Vivitar 202 is the smallest automatic model in the "200 Series." It is a single-aperture unit that operates on four replaceable penlight (AA) batteries. Specifications indicate that the manufacturer decided to sacrifice power for the sake of rapid, efficient operation. Other examples: a hot shoe operation option and a foot-long detachable synchronization cord for flexibility during shooting. The 202 is a good example of the advantages (more and quicker flashes) and disadvantages (less power) of the replaceable battery unit as compared to the built-in battery type. Most striking of the 202's performance are the 450 flashes possible from a set of alkaline batteries. Initial recycling of 4 seconds is noteworthy. This brief interval continues for 20 flashes, rises to 6 seconds at 50 flashes, to 8 seconds at 100, 10 at 200, and no more than 15 seconds at 400 flashes.
Suggested Retail Price: $34.95   **Low Price: $25.85**

Vivitar 271 is the oldest flash unit on CONSUMER GUIDE Magazine's list. This unit is the middle product of a three-member line of double-aperture, nickel-cadmium automatic flash guns. Though not the most powerful of the trio, it has the most worthwhile options: a rapid one-hour recharging period, which is enough to generate more than 75 flashes; five minutes of charging provides power for 5 to 10 flashes. Other features include an indicator light to signal the duration of the recharge period, a swiveling foot for mounting the unit either horizontally or vertically, a locking screw for secure mounting, a calculator dial that lights up whenever the unit is turned on, and the provision for A.C.

PHOTOGRAPHIC EQUIPMENT

operation. One feature CONSUMER GUIDE Magazine would like to see remedied is the unit's rather short (6 inch) attached synchronization cord. The cord's short length and the fact that it is not detachable somewhat limits the photographer's capacity to move around for special shooting techniques (especially during manual operation).
Suggested Retail Price: $79.95   **Low Price: $59.95**

Vivitar 292 is one of the most complete flash units available today. The thyristorized 292 combines the best of two methods, with interchangeable and rechargeable nickel-cadmium batteries. This permits carrying around a spare, fully-charged, replacement battery. The 292 offers a triple choice of automatic apertures, a charging signal light, and a three-position swiveling mount with a locking switch. Optional accessories, in addition to the extra batteries, include an attachment for the reflector, for use with wide-angle lenses, and a remote-controlled sensor eye that permits bounce-flash shooting. Recharging time is a rapid one hour, resulting in 50 flashes per charge when the thyristor circuit is not in operation. A partial 20-minute charge provides an equal number (20) of flashes. During a normal 50 charge performance, the 292's recycling starts at 8 seconds and builds to 15 about halfway through its life. Thyristorized flashing depends on the distance at which the unit is used. At its closest (2 feet), almost 700 flashes can be obtained with almost immediate recycling; at a middle distance of about 10 feet, it permits 350 flashes at 2 second intervals.
Suggested Retail Price: $159.95   **Low Price: $104.95**

SLIDE PROJECTORS

GAF 2660 does what it is intended to do: projects slides well. It is a simple slide projector at the economy end of the GAF line. Its lines are simple and clean. Operation is semi-automatic, requiring a push-pull movement. A transparent lens cover has little effect on sharpness. Though neither especially cool nor noiseless, we found both these features adequate. The projector comes with a 400-watt lamp and a self-contained carrying case.
Suggested Retail Price: $79.95   **Low Price: $48.35**

Kodak Carousel 600 is a good slide projector that is as tough as nails and the last of the Carousel projectors to employ an ordinary projection lamp. It uses tools and dies that predate Kodak's more expensive projectors, but it remains in the line because it can be priced competitively. It has Kodak's Carousel device. CONSUMER GUIDE Magazine considers this an excellent value at the price.
Suggested Retail Price: $74.50   **Low Price: $61.10**

1975 Photographic Equipment Prices

AIREQUIPT

		Retail	Discount
2000 SERIES DUAL 8 PROJECTORS			
2500Z	F/1.5 Zoom Lens, Auto Rewind	$149.95	$110.00
2400Z	F/1.5 Zoom Lens, 2-way Rewind	139.95	102.65
2300Z	F/1.5 Zoom Lens, 2-way Rewind	124.95	91.65
2200	F/1.6 Anastigmatic Lens	104.95	77.00
2100Z	F/1.5 Zoom Lens	94.95	69.65
2100	F/1.6 Anastigmatic Lens	84.95	62.30
600 SERIES SLIDE PROJECTORS			
670Z	Zoom—Electronic Focus, 2-1/2", 5" f/3.5	$199.50	$132.00
670	Electronic Focus, 4" f/3.5 Lens	149.50	99.00
660	Electronic Focus 4" f/3.5 Lens	122.50	81.00
635	Remote Control Forward, Reverse, Focus	94.95	62.00
625	Semi-Automatic Operation, 4" f/3.5 Lens	59.95	41.00

ALPA

ALPA CUSTOMBUILT 35mm SLR CAMERAS
ALPA 11e, CHROME
W/Alpa Xenon 50mm f/1.9 Automatic.. $649.00 $486.75

		Retail	Discount
355X	Magicube Camera Outfit, Electronic Shutter	39.95	24.00
ARGUS SUPER 8 MOVIE OUTFITS			
5394	Super 8 Kit, 817 Camera, 848B Proj	$159.95	$111.95
5434	Kit, 831XL Camera, 849B Projector	227.95	150.50
5453	Kit, 809 Camera, 849B Dual Proj	119.95	79.15
5831	Kit, 831XL Low Light Camera	142.95	94.35
817CS	Super 8 Electric Eye Camera Package	73.75	51.60
818EG	2X Zoom Elec. Eye Camera w/ EK 160 Capabilities, Case	89.95	63.00
5535	Kit, 735 Super 8 Camera, 880Z Dual Projector, Light	439.95	308.00
5755	Kit, 755XL Low Light Camera, 890Z Dual Projector	469.95	310.20
ARGUS SUPER 8 MOVIE CAMERAS			
7310M	Same as 7310 w/Macro Lens	519.95	343.20
755XL	Argus/Cosina 3X Elec. Power Zoom, Low Light, f/1.2 Lens, Black	269.95	178.20
817	Electric Eye Movie Camera	59.95	41.95
817E	Electric Eye Movie Camera w/EK 160 Capabilities	54.95	38.50
818E	2X Zoom Electric Eye Movie Camera w/EK 160 Capabilities	74.95	52.50
831XL	Low Light Movie Camera	129.95	85.80

PHOTOGRAPHIC EQUIPMENT

W/Alpa Macro-Switar 50mm f/1.9	849.00	636.75
All-in-One Apochromat Automatic	549.00	411.75

ALPA 11e 1
W/Alpa Xenon 50mm f/1.9 Automatic	$799.00	$599.25
W/Alpa Macro-Switar 50mm f/1.9		
All-in-One Apochromat Automatic	999.00	749.25
W/o Lens	699.00	524.25

ALPA 11f, W/O METER
W/o Lens	$629.00	$471.75

ALPA 10d, CHROME
W/Alpa Xenon 50mm f/1.9 Automatic	$499.00	$374.25
W/Alpa Macro-Switar 50mm f/1.9		
All-in-One Apochromat Automatic	699.00	524.25
W/o Lens	399.00	299.25

ARGUS

ARGUS INSTANT LOAD/STILL CAMERAS
110K	Pocket Carefree Camera Outfit	$29.95	$21.00
5140	Pocket Carefree Camera/Pocket Electronic Flash Outfit	57.35	40.70
C40X	Pocket Electronic Camera Outfit	69.95	46.15
5470	Pocket Electronic Camera/Pocket Electronic Flash Outfit	89.95	59.35
126X	Magicube Camera Outfit	15.95	10.50

ARGUS DUAL EIGHT PROJECTORS
849B	848B Design w/Reel Storage	$74.95	$49.50
849Z	Same as 849B w/Zoom Lens	79.95	52.80
880Z	Argus Dual 8 Projector	149.95	105.00
890Z	Dual 8 Dualmaster w/Slow Motion	179.95	118.75
892Z	Similar to 880Z w/Zoom Lens	189.95	125.40

BAUER

CAMERAS
14-390	C-Royal 10E w/Lens Hood, Eye Cup, Remote Control	$829.95	$663.95
14-395	C-Royal 10E Macro w/Lens Hood, Eye Cup, Remote Control	879.95	677.55
14-380	C-Royal 8E Macro w/Lens Hood, Eye Cup, Remote Control	829.95	663.95
14-910	Leather Pouch for C-Royal 10E or C-Royal 8E Macro	42.50	34.00
14-340	C-4 Super 8 Camera	227.50	182.00
14-350	C-6 Super 8 Camera	339.95	271.95
14-360	C-8 Super 8 Camera	414.95	331.95
14-320	C5 XL w/Lenshood, Eye Cup, Strap, Remote Control	469.50	375.60
14-912	Pouch for C-4, C-6, C-8, C5 XL	25.50	20.40
14-300	Star XL Super 8mm Camera	149.95	119.95
14-310	Top Star XL w/8-20mm f/1.2 Power Zoom Lens	199.95	153.95
14-914	Pouch for Star XL	19.95	15.95

Prices are accurate at time of printing; subject to manufacturer's change.

PHOTOGRAPHIC EQUIPMENT

BELL & HOWELL

		Retail	Discount
SUPER 8 MOVIE CAMERAS			
491F	Zoom Camera w/Focus-Matic	$94.95	$69.30
492F	Power Zoom Camera w/Focus-Matic	109.95	79.20
493F	3 to 1 Power Zoom w/Auto Focus-Matic	124.95	89.10
670P	Low-Light f/1.3 Manual Zoom 671/XL Camera w/Focus Matic	124.95	89.10
671G	Low-Light f/1.3 Zoom 671/XL Camera w/Focus-Matic	194.95	135.30
673G	Low-Light f/1.3 Power Zoom 673 XL Camera w/Focus-Matic	234.95	180.90
1216A	6 to 1 Power Zoom w/Focus-Matic	259.95	200.15
SUPER 8 MOVIE PROJECTORS			
357B	Autoload Projector	$94.95	$69.30
357Z	Autoload Zoom Projector	109.95	78.10
489Z	Super 8 Magnetic Sound Projector w/Automatic Threading	349.95	248.60
1615	Compatible Projector w/1" f/1.6 Lens	109.95	78.10
1615Z	Compatible Projector w/18-30mm f/1.6 Zoom Lens	124.95	88.00
1620A	Compatible Projector w/Through-the-System Rewind	134.95	91.30
1620Z	Compatible Projector w/Through-the-System Rewind	149.95	102.30
1623A	Compatible Multi-Motion Projector w/Through the System Rewind	159.95	110.00

		Retail	Discount
FD 35 SINGLE LENS REFLEX CAMERA			
2026	W/50mm f/1.4 Lens, Case	$400.00	$264.00
2025	W/50mm f/1.8 Lens, Case	335.00	220.00

BOLEX

		Retail	Discount
SUPER 8 CAMERAS			
1018	525 XL	$239.50	$176.00
1017	480 Macrozoom	449.50	330.40
1014	450	324.50	238.50
1008	160 Macrozoom	330.00	242.00
1005	250	258.50	190.00
1003	233S Compact	136.00	99.00
1001	350 Macro Compact	289.50	220.00
SUPER 8 PROJECTORS			
Multimatic			
2400	w/f/1.1 17-34mm Zoom Lens	$319.50	$235.00
2404	w/f/1.1 23mm Lens	299.50	225.00
2402	w/f/1.3 12-30mm Zoom Lens	289.50	220.00
2406	w/f/1.3 20mm Lens	269.50	203.00
2340	18-3 w/f/1.3 15-30mm Zoom Lens	219.50	161.35
2342	18-3 Dual w/f/1.2 12.5-25mm Zoom Lens	249.50	183.40
2370	18-5L Super — w/f/1.3 15-27mm Zoom Lens	239.50	176.00

CONSUMER GUIDE

PHOTOGRAPHIC EQUIPMENT

1623Z	Compatible Multi-Motion Zoom Projector w/Through-the-System Rewind	179.95	124.30
1623XLZ	Model 1623Z for 50-60 Hz	199.95	143.00
1640A	Double Feature Compatible Inst. Proj.	159.95	110.00
1641A	Same as 1623Z w/Stop Motion, Slow Motion	189.95	132.95

SUPER 8 OUTFITS

K4141KT	W/491F Camera, 1615 Projector	$229.95	$149.60
K6303KR	W/670P Camera, 357Z Projector	249.95	162.80
K4203KP	W/492F Camera, 357Z Projector	259.95	165.00
K4343KP	W/493F Camera, 1620Z Projector	309.95	200.20
K6244KS	W/672G Camera, 1623Z Projector	424.95	277.20

SLIDE CUBE PROJECTORS

9770L	With Remote Control, Top Cover	$119.95	$77.00

SILENT MODELS

984A	W/Scan/Search. Accepts 2-1/2" Lens.	$94.95	$69.80
985	W/Control Panel, f/3.5 Lens	99.95	70.40
986	W/Remote Control, f/2.8 Lens	139.95	94.60
987A	W/Remote Control	129.95	90.20
987H	Same with Handle	139.95	102.85
991A	W/Remote Control, Auto Focus, 4" f/3.5 Lens	169.95	116.60
991Z	Same with 3-1/2 to 4-1/2" f/3.5 Zoom Lens	194.95	143.30
992	W/Remote Control, Auto Focus, 4" f/2.8 Lens, Slide Previewer	184.95	126.00
992D	Deluxe 992 model, Rosewood/Vinyl Storage Top	199.95	146.95

2380	SM8 Sound — w/f/1.3 12-30mm Zoom Lens	649.50	477.40
2470	SP80 Sound	424.50	312.00

H-16 EBM (ELECTRIC DRIVE) CAMERAS

1751	Body Only	$1,477.70	$1,086.10
1750	Compl. w/o 400' Mag. Lens	1,900.00	1,396.50
1754	Same as No. 1750 w/Vario Switar 100 POE Zoom Lens	3,170.00	2,329.95
1753	Compl. w/400' Mag., POE 100 Zoom Lens	3,602.00	2,647.45
1755	Compl. w/400' Mag. & Vario Switar POE No. 82	3,536.00	2,598.95

H-16 (SPRING WOUND) CAMERAS

1810	H-16 SBM w/o VF, Bayonet Mount.	$1,075.00	$790.10
1116	H-16 Rex 5 Complete, Rx-Turret	1,150.00	845.25
1117	H-16 Rex 5 w/o VF, Rx-Turret	1,110.00	815.85
1690	H-16 M-5 Complete, Single C Mount	570.00	418.95
1691	H-16 M-5 w/o Viewfinder, Single C Mount	530.00	389.55
1800	H-16 SB w/o VF, Bayonet Mount	720.00	528.00

BRAUN/NIZO

SUPER 8 CAMERAS

Nizo S-800 Camera w/Schneider Variogon 7-80mm.	$845.00	$603.90
Nizo S-560 Camera w/Schneider Variogon 7-56mm.	695.00	497.20
Nizo S-480 Camera w/Schneider Variogon 8-48mm.	595.00	425.70

Prices are accurate at time of printing; subject to manufacturer's change.

PHOTOGRAPHIC EQUIPMENT

CANON

SUPER 8MM MOVIE CAMERAS

		Retail	Discount
3-31101-21	AZ318M w/10-30 mm f/1.8 Lens, Case	$178.00	$126.38
3-30711-21	AZ518SV w/9.5-47.5mm f/1.8 Lens, Case	368.00	261.28
3-30811-32	AZ814 Electronic w/7.5-60mm f/1.4 Lens, Remote Switch 60, Case	560.00	397.60
3-31201-24	AZ1014 Electronic w/7-70mm f/1.4 Lens, Hood, Remote Switch	875.00	621.25
3-30501-21	Zoom DS-8 w/7.5-60mm f/1.4 Lens, Case	1,300.00	923.00

SUPER 8MM CINE PROJECTORS

		Retail	Discount
4-10486-21	Cine Projector S-400	$199.00	$141.29
4-10500-20	Cine Projector T-1	800.00	568.00

35MM SLR CAMERAS
CANON F-1

		Retail	Discount
1-20711-48	W/FD 50mm f/1.8 SC Lens	$634.00	$450.14
1-20711-39	W/FD 50mm f/1.8 SC Lens, & Hood, Case	679.00	482.09
1-20711-46	W/FD 50mm f/1.4 SSC Lens	699.00	496.29
1-20711-47	W/FD 50mm f/1.4 SSC Lens, & Hood, Case	744.00	528.24
1-20711-44	W/FD 55mm f/1.2 SSC Lens	799.00	567.29
1-20711-45	W/FD 55mm f/1.2 SSC Lens, & Hood, Case	844.00	599.24
1-20711-41	Body Only	514.00	364.94

CANON EX AUTO

		Retail	Discount
1-20821-23	W/EX 50mm f/1.8 Lens, Case	305.00	216.55

CANON EF

		Retail	Discount
1-21311-28	W/FD 50mm f/1.8 SC Lens	580.00	411.80
1-21311-29	W/FD 50mm f/1.8 SC Lens, Case	612.00	434.52
1-21311-26	W/FD 50mm f/1.4 SSC Lens	645.00	457.95
1-21311-27	W/FD 50mm f/1.4 SSC Lens, Case	677.00	480.67
1-21311-24	W/FD 55mm f/1.2 SSC Lens	745.00	528.95
1-21311-25	W/FD 55mm f/1.2 SSC Lens, Case	777.00	551.67

RANGEFINDER AUTOMATIC CAMERAS

		Retail	Discount
1-30821-21	Canonet 28 Camera w/40mm f/2.8 Lens, Case	$127.00	$90.17
1-31901-21	Canodate E Camera w/40mm f/2.8 Lens, Case	207.00	146.97
1-30831-31	Canonet G-III 17 w/40mm f/1.7 Lens, Case	187.00	132.77
1-30832-31	Canonet G-III 17 w/40mm f/1.7 Lens, Case, Black	205.00	136.40

CINEMA BEAULIEU

SUPER 8 CAMERA

		Retail	Discount
	5008S Single System Sound, 6-80mm f/1.2 Powerzoom lens	$1,488.00	$1,033.75

PHOTOGRAPHIC EQUIPMENT

1-207T1-21	High Speed Motor Drive Camera	2,120.00	1,505.20
CANON FTb			
1-20398-28	W/FD 50mm f/1.8 SC Lens	406.00	288.26
1-20398-29	W/FD 50mm f/1.8 SC Lens, Case	430.00	305.30
1-20398-26	W/FD 50mm f/1.4 SSC Lens	471.00	334.41
1-20398-27	W/FD 50mm f/1.4 SSC Lens, Case	495.00	351.45
1-20398-24	W/FD 50mm f/1.2 SSC Lens	571.00	405.41
1-20398-25	W/FD 55mm f/1.2 SSC Lens, Case	595.00	422.45
1-20398-21	Body Only	286.00	203.06
1-20399-28	W/FD 50mm f/1.8 SC Lens, Black	416.00	295.36
1-20399-29	W/FD 50mm f/1.8 SC Lens, Case, Black	440.00	312.40
1-20399-26	W/FD 50mm f/1.4 SSC Lens, Black	481.00	341.51
1-20399-27	W/FD 50mm f/1.4 SSC Lens, Case, Black	505.00	358.55
1-20399-24	W/FD 55mm f/1.2 SSC Lens, Black	581.00	412.51
1-20399-25	W/FD 55mm f/1.2 SSC Lens, Case, Black	605.00	429.55
1-20399-21	Body Only, Black	296.00	210.16
CANON TLb			
1-20397-38	W/FD 50mm f/1.8 SC Lens	301.00	213.71
1-20397-39	W/FD 50mm f/1.8 SC Lens, Case	325.00	230.75
10-466	4008ZM2 Auto Electronic w/Beaulieu Optivaron Super-Wide Angle 6-66mm (11:1) Motorized Zoom Lens f/1.8	$999.00	$749.25
10-465	4008ZM2 Reflex Control, Body Only	649.50	487.15
10-470	4008ZM3	849.00	636.75

EUMIG

MOVIE CAMERAS

11-048	Mini-3 Servofocus Super 8 Reflex Camera	$129.95	$90.95
11-049	Mini-3 Servofocus Display Including Case & Pistol Grip	149.95	104.95
23-077	Underwater Housing for Mini-3	60.00	42.00
16-047	Case for Mini-3 Camera	9.95	6.95
11-054	Mini-5 Super 8 Reflex Camera w/ f/1.9 8-40mm Macro Zoom Lens	279.95	185.00
11-055	Mini-5 Display Including Case & Pistol Grip	299.95	209.95
23-100	Underwater Housing for Mini-5	79.95	55.95
16-078	Case for Mini-5 Camera	11.95	8.35
11-130	Viennette 3 Super 8 Camera	159.95	112.00
11-150	Viennette 5 Super 8 Camera Including Macro-Attachment	259.95	159.00
11-180	Macro-Viennette 8 Super 8 Camera Incl. Title Set, All Attach. & Macro Lens	399.95	242.00
16-155	Case for all Viennette Cameras	25.00	17.50

Prices are accurate at time of printing; subject to manufacturer's change.

CONSUMER GUIDE

PHOTOGRAPHIC EQUIPMENT

PROJECTORS

		Retail	Discount
12-610	Mark-610-D, f/1.6 15-30mm Zoom Lens, Dual 8 Projector.	$219.95	$153.15
20-520	Deluxe Case for All Eumig Silent Projectors.	22.95	16.05
13-802	Mark-S-802, f/1.6 17-30mm Zoom Lens, Super 8 Sound Proj.	289.95	191.35
13-807	Mark-S-807, f/1.6 17-30mm Zoom Lens, Super 8 Sound Projector	399.95	263.95
13-810	Mark-S-810D, f/1.3 15-30mm Zoom Lens, Dual 8 Sound Projector.	499.95	329.95
13-811	Mark-S-810D Deluxe, f/1.0 18-28mm Zoom Lens, Dual 8 Sound Projector	560.00	369.60
14-713	Fairchild-Eumig 711R-Deluxe Model	475.00	366.00
14-711	Fairchild-Eumig 711-Economy Model	395.00	304.50

FUJI

FUJICA SINGLE-8 MOVIE CAMERAS

		Retail	Discount
ZP003	P-300 Camera w/Pouch Case.	$124.95	$93.70
ZZ450	Z-450 Camera w/Lenshood, Eyecup, Strap, Case.	279.50	209.60
ZZ600	Z-600 Camera w/Lenshood, Eyecup, Strap, Case.	379.50	284.60
ZZ800	Z-800 Camera w/Lenshood, Eyecup, Strap, Case.	479.50	359.60

		Retail	Discount
T9014	Chrome, w/50mm f/1.4 Lens, Battery, Eyecup, Strap.	595.00	446.25
T9114	Black, w/50mm f/1.4 Lens, Battery, Eyecup, Strap.	605.00	453.75
TC901	Chrome Body Only, w/Battery.	425.00	318.75
TB901	Black Body Only, w/Battery.	435.00	326.25
R9010	Hard Case	25.00	18.75

FUJICA ST-801 SINGLE LENS REFLEX CAMERAS

		Retail	Discount
T8018	Chrome, w/55mm f/1.8 Lens, Battery, Eyecup, Strap.	$380.00	$285.00
T8118	Black, w/55mm f/1.8 Lens, Battery, Eyecup, Strap.	390.00	292.50
T8014	Chrome, w/50mm f/1.4 Lens, Battery, Eyecup, Strap.	430.00	322.50
T8114	Black, w/50mm f/1.4 Lens, Battery, Eyecup, Strap.	440.00	330.00
TC801	Chrome Body Only, w/Battery, Eyecup, Strap.	260.00	195.00
TB801	Black Body Only, w/Battery, Eyecup, Strap.	270.00	202.50
R8010	Hard Case (Also fits ST-701)	22.50	16.85

FUJICA ST-701 SINGLE LENS REFLEX CAMERAS

		Retail	Discount
T7018	Chrome, w/55mm f/1.8 Lens, Battery, Eyecup, Strap.	$299.50	$224.60
T7118	Black, w/55mm f/1.8 Lens, Battery, Eyecup, Strap.	309.50	232.10

368 CONSUMER GUIDE

PHOTOGRAPHIC EQUIPMENT

FUJICASCOPE SINGLE-8 PROJECTORS, AND ACCESSORIES
ZM200	M-20 Single/Super 8 Self-threading, w/Zoom Lens	$135.00	$101.25
ZM330	M-33 Dual Self-threading, w/Zoom Lens	179.95	134.95
ZM900	M-90 Dual Self-threading, w/Halogen Lamp	329.95	247.45
ZM910	Wide/Tele Reversible Lens for MG-90	14.95	11.20
ZM911	Sync Box MG for MG-90	74.95	56.20

FUJICASCOPE SINGLE-8 SOUND PROJECTORS
ZM100	SH-1 Sound Projector w/Halogen Lamp	$444.50	$333.35
ZM110	Zoom Converter	11.95	8.95

FUJICA SINGLE-8, PULS-SYNC SYSTEM
ZM700	Fujicascope MX-70 Dual Projector for Puls-Sync Sound Movies	$489.95	$367.45
ZM701	Puls-Sync Kit, Corder, Controller, Pulse-Generator, Microphone, Connecting Cords for Z-800, MX-70	499.95	374.95
ZM702	Microphone Adapter, use w/T Grip	24.95	18.70
ZM703	Puls-Sync Box for Puls-Sync Kit, MX-70	179.95	134.95
ZM910	Wide/Tele Reversible Lens for MX-70	14.95	11.20

FUJICA ST-901 SINGLE LENS REFLEX CAMERAS
T9018	Chrome, w/55mm f/1.8 Lens, Battery, Eyecup, Strap	$545.00	$408.75
T9118	Black, w/55mm f/1.8 Lens, Battery, Eyecup, Strap	555.00	416.25
T7014	Chrome, w/50mm f/1.4 Lens, Battery, Eyecup, Strap	349.50	262.10
T7114	Black, w/50mm f/1.4 Lens, Battery, Eyecup, Strap	359.50	269.60
R7010	Semi-Soft Case	18.50	13.85

FUJICA COMPACT CAMERAS
VG100	GE Camera w/Soft Case, Batteries, Strap	$115.00	$86.25
VG101	GER Camera w/Hard Case, Batteries, Strap	135.00	101.25

GAF

GAF SUPER 8 MOVIE CAMERAS
XL 112 Super 8		$134.95	$94.45
XL 128 Super 8		199.95	126.40
SC/100 Movie Camera		64.50	41.15
SC/102 Movie Camera		89.50	58.60
ST/202 Movie Camera		104.50	73.00
ST/302 Movie Camera		124.50	87.00
ST/602 Movie Camera w/Recharger		224.50	157.00
ST/802 Movie Camera w/Recharger		279.50	193.15
ST/1002 Movie Camera w/Recharger		349.50	245.00

GAF SUPER 8 SOUND MOVIE CAMERAS
SS250XL	Available Light Zoom	$299.50	$219.50
SS605	6 to 1 Zoom	359.50	268.50
SS805	8 to 1 Zoom	399.50	289.00

Prices are accurate at time of printing: subject to manufacturer's change.

PHOTOGRAPHIC EQUIPMENT

		Retail	Discount
7071	Motor Drive Unit, Pistol Grip Batteries & Charger	470.00	336.05

KODAK

STILL CAMERAS
Kodak Instamatic Cameras

		Retail	Discount
A10RE	Pocket Instamatic 10 Camera Outfit	$24.95	$18.75
A10E	Pocket Instamatic 10 Camera	22.95	17.70
A20RE	Pocket Instamatic 20 Color Outfit	34.95	24.35
A20E	Pocket Instamatic 20 Camera	32.95	22.95
A30RAE	Pocket Instamatic 30 Color Outfit	54.95	38.25
A30AE	Pocket Instamatic 30 Camera	52.95	36.95
A40RE	Pocket Instamatic 40 Color Outfit	69.95	51.00
A40E	Pocket Instamatic 40 Camera	67.95	50.00
A50RE	Pocket Instamatic 50 Color Outfit	114.95	84.00
A50E	Pocket Instamatic 50 Camera	112.95	83.00
A60RE	Pocket Instamatic 60 Color Outfit	139.95	103.00
A60E	Pocket Instamatic 60 Camera	137.95	102.00
A1002	Instamatic Reflex Camera, w/f/1.9 Lens	224.50	156.00
A1011	Instamatic Reflex Camera w/o Lens, Black	153.00	107.10
AX-15R	Instamatic X-15 Color Outfit	18.95	15.85
AX-15	Instamatic X-15 Camera	16.95	14.85
AX-35	Instamatic X-35 Camera	47.95	40.75
AX-35R	Instamatic X-35 Color Outfit	49.95	42.45

GAF DUAL 8 MOVIE PROJECTORS

	Retail	Discount
2388 Dual 8 Projector	$89.95	$57.45
2388Z Dual 8 Projector	99.95	62.45
2488 Dual 8 Projector	109.95	72.90
2588Z Dual 8 Projector	129.95	83.60
2688Z Dual 8 Projector	144.95	95.00
2788Z Dual 8 Projector	159.95	106.65

MOVIE OUTFITS

	Retail	Discount
GAF Memories in Movies Outfit	$149.50	$77.40
1223 Movie Outfit	200.90	116.15
XL 1123 Movie Outfit	239.85	167.90
XL 1283Z Movie Outfit	314.85	220.40

INSTANT LOADING POCKET AND XF CAMERAS

	Retail	Discount
200XF Camera	$21.95	$15.35
200XF Color Outfit	23.95	16.75
440 Pocket Camera Outfit	51.95	37.50
440 Pocket Camera	49.95	35.50
220 Pocket Camera Outfit	31.95	20.20
220 Pocket Camera	28.95	20.65
76XF Camera	15.95	9.35
76XF Camera Outfit	17.95	10.85
660 Pocket Camera Outfit	129.50	90.65
660 Pocket Camera	114.50	80.15
880 Pocket Camera Outfit w/Strobe	144.50	101.15
880 Pocket Camera	129.50	90.65

PHOTOGRAPHIC EQUIPMENT

GAF STILL CAMERA — 35MM

Memo 35EE		$94.95
Memo 35EE Color Outfit-Electronic Strobe		119.95
L-ES SLR w/Case		419.50
L-CM SLR with 50mm f/2 Lens, Case		239.50
L-CS SLR with 55mm f/1.7 Lens, Case		269.50

SLIDE PROJECTORS

2660 Slide Projector		$79.95
2670 Slide Projector		99.95
2680 Slide Projector		119.95
2690 Slide Projector		154.95

HONEYWELL

PENTAX CAMERAS

7186	Pentax ES II w/50mm f/1.4	649.50	468.00
	SMCT Lens		
7187	Pentax ES II w/55mm f/1.8	599.50	432.00
	SMCT Lens		
7188	Pentax ES II Body Only	489.50	352.80
7191	Pentax Spotmatic F w/55mm f/1.8	379.00	272.88
	Lens, Chrome		
7193	Pentax Spotmatic F w/50mm f/1.4	429.00	309.00
	Lens, Chrome		
7179	Body, Chrome	269.00	193.70

PENTAX SPOTMATIC MOTOR DRIVE CAMERA & ACCESSORIES

7012	Pentax Motor Drive Unit Only	$368.00	$263.12
7013	Pistol Grip	52.00	37.60

STILL PROJECTORS AND VIEWERS

Kodak Carousel 100 Projector — Manual Focus

B100	W/Ektar 2-1/2 inch f/2.8 Lens	$79.50	$59.75
B100Z	W/Ektar Zoom Lens 2 to 3 inch f/2.8	109.50	82.50

Kodak Pocket Carousel 200 Projector — Remote Focus

B200	W/Ektar 2-1/2 inch f/2.8 Lens	$139.50	$97.85
B200Z	W/Ektar Zoom Lens, 2 to 3 inch f/2.8	169.50	116.95

Kodak Pocket Carousel 300 Projector — Automatic Focus

B300	W/Ektar 2-1/2 inch f/2.8 Lens	$189.50	$131.85
B300Z	W/Ektar Zoom Lens, 2 to 3 inch f/2.8	219.50	151.75

Kodak Carousel 600 Projector

B610Z	W/Zoom Lens, 102-152mm f/3.5	$104.50	$81.25
B611	W/o Lens	57.00	48.15
B614	W/Ektanar C f/2.8 Lens	74.50	61.10
B615	W/Ektanar-C f/2.8 Lens	74.50	61.10

Kodak Carousel 600K Projector

B614K	W/Ektanar C 4-inch f/2.8 Lens	$89.50	$71.60
B615K	W/Ektanar C 5-inch f/2.8 Lens	89.50	71.60
B610KZ	W/Ektanar C Zoom Lens, 4 to 6 inch f/3.5	119.50	91.70

Kodak Carousel 600H Projector

B604	W/Ektanar C 4-inch f/2.8 Lens	$89.50	$67.10
B605	W/Ektanar C 5-inch f/2.8 Lens	89.50	67.10
B600Z	W/Ektanar C Zoom Lens, 4 to 6-inch f/3.5	119.50	88.70
B601	W/o Lens	72.00	55.60

Kodak Carousel 650H Projector

B654	W/Ektanar C 4-inch f/2.8 Lens	$114.50	$80.15

Prices are accurate at time of printing; subject to manufacturer's change.

PHOTOGRAPHIC EQUIPMENT

Code	Description	Retail	Discount
	W/Ektanar C 5-inch f/2.8 Lens	114.50	80.15
BC655			
BC650Z	W/Ektanar C Zoom Lens, 4 to 6-inch	144.50	101.00
BC651	W/o Lens	97.00	68.50
Kodak Carousel 750H Projector			
BC754	W/Ektanar C 4-inch f/2.8 Lens	$144.50	$101.15
BC755	W/Ektanar C 5-inch f/2.8 Lens	144.50	101.15
BC750Z	W/Ektanar C Zoom Lens, 4 to 6-inch	174.50	121.55
BC751	f/3.5	127.00	89.00
	W/o Lens		
Kodak Carousel 760H Projector			
BC764	W/Ektanar C 4-inch f/2.8 Lens	$174.50	$122.15
BC765	W/Ektanar C 5-inch f/2.8 Lens	174.50	122.15
BC760Z	W/Ektanar C Zoom Lens, 4 to 6-inch	204.50	142.45
BC761	f/3.5	157.00	109.40
	W/o Lens		
Kodak Carousel 840H Custom Projector			
BC844	W/Ektanar C 4-inch f/2.8 Lens	$207.50	$145.25
BC845	W/Ektanar C 5-inch f/2.8 Lens	207.50	145.25
BC840Z	W/Ektanar C Zoom Lens, 4 to 6-inch	237.50	166.25
BC841	f/3.5	190.00	133.00
	W/o Lens		
Kodak Carousel 850H-K Projector			
BC854K	W/Ektanar C 4-inch f/2.8 Lens	$252.50	$185.15
BC855K	W/Ektanar C 5-inch f/2.8 Lens	252.50	185.15
BC850KZ	W/Ektanar Zoom Lens, 4-6 inch	282.50	207.15
Kodak Carousel 850H Projector			
BC854H	W8Ektanar C 4-inch f/2.8 Lens	$199.50	$133.00

Code	Description	Retail	Discount
D30RA	M30A Movie Outfit	108.50	80.00
XL MOVIE CAMERAS			
XL10	Kodak XL10 Movie Camera	$114.50	$86.15
XL33	Kodak XL33 Movie Camera	119.50	88.00
XL33R	Kodak XL33 Movie Outfit	124.95	92.00
XL55	Kodak XL55 Movie Camera	234.50	175.40
XL55R	Kodak XL55 Movie Outfit	239.95	179.60
XL320	Kodak XL320 Movie Camera	99.50	69.65
XL320R	Kodak XL320R Movie Outfit	106.50	74.55
XL330	Kodak XL330 Movie Camera	117.50	82.25
XL330R	Kodak XL330R Movie Outfit	124.50	87.15
XL340	Kodak XL340 Movie Camera	182.50	127.75
XL340R	Kodak XL340R Movie Outfit	189.50	132.65
XL350	Kodak XL350 Movie Camera	209.50	146.65
XL350R	Kodak XL350R Movie Outfit	216.50	151.55
XL360	Kodak XL360 Movie Camera	232.50	162.75
XL360R	Kodak XL360R Movie Outfit	239.50	167.65
16MM MOVIE CAMERAS			
98	Cine-Kodak K-100 Turret w/25mm f/1.9 Lens, 25mm Viewfinder Lens	$725.00	$543.70
92	Cine-Kodak K-100 Turret w/o Lens, Viewfinder	540.00	405.00
EKTASOUND MOVIE CAMERAS			
D130	130 Movie Camera	$189.50	$142.50
D130R	130 Movie Camera Outfit	199.95	144.77
D140	140 Movie Camera	289.50	222.90
D140R	140 Movie Camera Outfit	299.95	230.95

372   CONSUMER GUIDE

PHOTOGRAPHIC EQUIPMENT

Model	Description	Price 1	Price 2
BC855H	W/Ektanar C 5-inch f/2.8 Lens	199.50	398.50
BC850ZH	W/Ektanar C Zoom Lens, 4 to 6-inch f/3.5	229.50	409.95
BC851H	W/o Lens	182.00	

Kodak Carousel Custom 850H Projector
W/Automatic Focus

Model	Description	Price 1	Price 2
BC854	W/Ektanar 4-inch f/2.8 Lens	$232.50	$234.50
BC855	W/Ektanar 5-inch f/2.8 Lens	232.50	264.50
BC850	W/Ektanar Zoom Lens, 4 to 6-inch f/3.5	262.50	299.50
BC854	W/o Lens	215.00	329.50

Kodak Carousel Custom 850H-K Projector

Model	Description	Price 1	Price 2
BC854K	W/Ektanar C 4-inch f/2.8 Lens	$252.50	
BC855K	W/Ektanar C 5-inch f/2.8 Lens	252.50	
BC850KZ	W/Ektanar C 4 to 6-inch f/3.5 Zoom Lens	282.50	

Kodak Carousel Custom 860H Projector

Model	Description	Price 1
BC864	W/Ektanar 4-inch f/2.8 Lens	$254.50
BC865	W/Ektanar C 5-inch f/2.8 Lens	254.50
BC860Z	W/Ektanar C Zoom ENS, 4 to 6-inch f/3.5	284.50
BC861	W/o Lens	237.00

INSTAMATIC MOVIE CAMERAS

D22A	M22A Movie Camera	$34.50
D22RA	M22A Movie Outfit	38.50
D24A	M24A Movie Camera	49.50
D24RA	M24A Movie Outfit	53.50
D28A	M28A Movie Camera	84.50
D28RA	M28A Movie Outfit	88.50
D30A	M30A Movie Camera	104.50

Model	Description	Price 1	Price 2
D160	160 Movie Camera	133.00	306.85
D160R	160 Movie Camera Outfit	153.00	315.65

EKTASOUND MOVIE PROJECTORS

Model	Description	Price 1	Price 2
D235	235 w/22mm f/1.5 Lens	$161.95	$163.35
D235Z	235Z w/15-30mm f/1.3 Zoom Lens	161.95	184.25
D245	245 w/Record Capability, 22mm f/1.5 Lens	182.85	208.65
D245Z	245Z w/Record Capability, 15-30mm f/1.3 Zoom Lens	149.75	229.55

INSTAMATIC MOVIE PROJECTORS

Model	Description	Price 1	Price 2
M10	M10 w/22mm f/1.5 Lens	$112.50	$83.00
D67	M67 w/22mm f/1.5 Lens, Dual Format	114.50	84.00
D67K	M67-K w/f/1.5 Lens, Dual Format	118.00	87.00
D67Z	M67 w/f/1.5 Zoom Lens, Dual Format	134.50	99.00
D70A	M70 w/f/1.5 22mm Lens	149.50	110.00
D70Z	M70 w/f/1.5 Zoom Lens	169.50	125.00
D77	M77 w/f/1.5 Lens, Dual Format	129.50	96.00
D77Z	M77 w/f/1.5 Zoom Lens, Dual Format	149.50	110.00
D80A	M80 w/22mm f/1.5 Lens, Dual Format	164.50	121.00
D80Z	M80 w/f/1.5 Zoom Lens, Dual Format	184.50	136.00
D85	M85 w/22mm f/1.5 Lens, Dual Format	139.50	103.00
D85Z	M85 w/f/1.5 Zoom Lens, Dual Format	159.50	117.00
D95	M95 w/22mm f/1.5 Lens, Dual Format	179.50	132.00
D95B	M95 w/22mm f/1.0 Lens, Dual Format	194.50	143.00
D95Z	M95 w/f/1.5 Zoom Lens, Dual Format	199.50	147.00
D105	M105 w/22mm f/1.5 Lens, Cassette Load	139.50	103.00
D105Z	M105 w/f/1.5 Zoom Lens, Cassette Load	159.50	117.00
D105K	M105-K for 50/60 Hz AC, w/22mm f/1.5 Lens	149.50	110.00

Prices are accurate at time of printing; subject to manufacturer's change.

PHOTOGRAPHIC EQUIPMENT

		Retail	Discount
D105KZ	M105-K 50/60 Hz AC, w/f/1.5 Zoom Lens	169.50	125.00
D105P	M105-P w/20mm f/1.3 Lens	189.50	139.00

KODAK MOVIEDECK PROJECTORS

		Retail	Discount
D425	425 Projector w/22mm, f/1.8 Lens	$99.50	$76.95
D425Z	Same as above w/Zoom Lens	124.50	94.35
D435	435 Projector, 22mm, f/1.8 Lens, Automatic Rewind, 3 Projection selections	124.50	93.65
D435Z	Same as above w/Zoom Lens	149.50	111.10
D445	445 Projector 22mm f/1.5 Lens 5 Projection selections, Auto, Rewind, Fast Forward	149.50	109.35
D445Z	Same as above w/Zoom Lens	169.50	123.30
D455	455 Projector, 22mm, f/1.5 Lens, Viewing Screen, plus features above	174.50	127.65
D455Z	Same as above w/Zoom Lens	194.50	141.55
D465	465 Projector, 22mm f/1.5 Lens, 7 Projection selections, plus features above	199.50	145.95
D465Z	Same as above w/Zoom Lens	219.50	159.85
D475	475 Projector, 22mm, f/1.5 Lens, 9 Projection selections, Room-Light Lamp Outlet plus features above	224.50	164.20
D475Z	Same as above w/Zoom Lens	244.50	178.15

LEICA

		Retail	Discount

LEICA M5 CAMERAS

		Retail	Discount
10,501	Leica M5 w/o Lens, Chrome	$852.00	
10,502	Leica M5 w/Lens, Black	852.00	
10,503	Leica M5 w/50mm Summicron f/2 Lens, Chrome	1,182.00	
10,504	Leica M5 w/50mm Summilux f/1.4 Lens, Chrome	1,320.00	
10,505	Leica M5 w/50mm Summicron f/2 Lens, Black	1,182.00	
10,506	Leica M5 w/50mm Summilux f/1.4 Lens, Black	1,320.00	

LEICA CL CAMERA

		Retail	Discount
10,700	Leica CL Body w/Strap, Lens Cover	$315.00	
11,542	Leica CL Body w/40mm f/2.0 Lens	597.00	

LEICAFLEX CAMERAS

		Retail	Discount
10,011	Leicaflex SL, w/o Lens	$885.00	
10,012	Leicaflex SL w/o Lens, Black	885.00	
10,228	Leicaflex SL, w/50mm Summicron R f/2 Lens	1,197.00	

PHOTOGRAPHIC EQUIPMENT

KONICA

KONICA SINGLE LENS REFLEX CAMERAS
Autoreflex T3, Chrome

702-327	W/50mm f/1.7 Lens	$459.95 $337.70
702-324	W/50mm f/1.4 Lens	509.95 373.95
702-322	W/57mm f/1.2 Lens	599.95 440.00
702-301	Body Only w/Body Cap, Hot Shoe, Strap, Pad	360.00 264.00
702-447	W/50mm f/1.7 Lens	469.95 344.65
702-444	W/50mm f/1.4 Lens	519.95 381.30
702-442	W/57mm f/1.2 Lens	609.95 447.30
702-311	Body Only w/Body Cap, Hot Shoe, Strap, Pad	370.00 271.35

Autoreflex T3, Black

702-567	W/50mm f/1.7 Lens	$479.95 $352.00
702-564	W/50mm f/1.4 Lens	529.95 388.65
702-562	W/57mm f/1.2 Lens	619.95 454.30
702-302	Body Only w/Body Cap, Hot Shoe, Strap, Pad	380.00 278.65
702-687	W/50mm f/1.7 Lens	489.95 359.30
702-684	W/50mm f/1.4 Lens	539.95 395.95
702-682	W/57mm f/1.2 Lens	629.95 461.95
702-312	Body Only w/Body Cap, Hot Shoe, Strap, Pad	390.00 286.00

MAMIYA

MAMIYA C PROFESSIONAL CAMERAS

60015	Mamiya C220 Body	$193.00 $140.50
61030	Mamiya C220 w/80mm f/2.8 Lens	350.00 254.80
	Mamiya C330 Body	331.00 240.95
	Mamiya C330 w/80mm f/2.8 Lens	488.00 355.25
61031	Mamiya C330 Body, Black	358.00 260.60

MAMIYA/SEKOR

MAMIYA/SEKOR AUTO XTL 35mm CAMERAS

12-2760	W/Automatic 55mm f/1.8 Lens, No Case	$369.95 $264.50
12-2793	W/Automatic 55mm f/1.4 Lens, No Case	399.95 285.95
12-2829	Body Only (Without Lens), Chrome	279.95 200.15
12-2852	Body Only (Without Lens), Black	289.95 207.30

MAMIYA/SEKOR PRO AUTO XTL 35mm CAMERA (BLACK BODY)

12-2818	W/Automatic 55mm f/1.4 Lens, No Case	$409.95 $293.10
12-2911	Hard Eveready Case w/Hinged Back	29.50 19.50

MAMIYA/SEKOR 1000 DSX 35mm CAMERAS

12-1372	W/Automatic 55mm f/2.4 Lens & Case	$359.00 $270.00
12-1316	W/Automatic 55mm f/1.8 Lens & Case	339.00 220.00
12-1383	Body Only (Without Lens)	229.95 165.00
12-7053	Right Angle Viewfinder	49.50 33.00

Prices are accurate at time of printing; subject to manufacturer's change.

CONSUMER GUIDE

PHOTOGRAPHIC EQUIPMENT

		Retail	Discount
MAMIYA/SEKOR 500 DSX 35mm CAMERA			
12-1268	W/Automatic 50mm f/2.0 Lens & Case	$260.00	$179.50
12-1235	Body Only (Without Lens)	169.95	121.50
MAMIYA/SEKOR 528 TL 35mm CAMERA			
12-1718	W/48 f/2.8 Lens & Case	$169.95	$116.50
12-2623	Vivitar Telephoto & Wide Angle Lens Set/Case	24.00	15.85
MAMIYA/SEKOR 1000 DSX 35mm CAMERA			
	W/55mm, f/1.8	$329.95	$249.75

MINOLTA

		Retail	Discount
35MM SR CAMERAS			
049-900	SR-T100 w/MC 50mm f/2.0 w/o Case	$290.00	$191.50
049-908	SR-T100 w/MC 50mm f/2.0 w/Case	315.00	207.90
049-928	SR-T100 Action Pack Outfit	450.00	297.00
050-200	SR-T101 w/MC 50mm f/1.7 w/o Case	350.00	231.00
050-600	SR-T101 w/MC 50mm f/1.4 w/o Case	395.00	260.70
050-300	SR-T101 w/MC 58mm f/1.2 w/o Case	465.00	306.90
050-204	SR-T101 w/MC 50mm f/1.7 w/Case	375.00	247.50
050-604	SR-T101 w/MC 50mm f/1.4 w/Case	420.00	277.20
050-304	SR-T101 w/MC 58mm f/1.2 w/Case	493.00	325.40
098-200	SR-T101 w/MC 50mm f/1.7 Lens w/o Case, Black	360.00	237.60
098-600	SR-T101 w/MC 50mm f/1.4 Lens w/o Case, Black	405.00	267.30

		Retail	Discount
	XK Camera, AE Head, 50mm f/1.4 Lens w/o Case	795.00	524.70
MINOLTA 35MM XK CAMERAS			
062-221	W f/1.7 lens, AE Finder, w/o case	$753.00	$599.00
062-621	W f/1.4 lens, AE Finder, w/o case	798.00	639.00
062-321	W f/1.2 lens, AE Finder, w/o case	873.00	699.00
062-500	Body only	409.00	329.00
35MM CAMERAS			
195-008	Hi-Matic E Camera w/Case (FD:49mm)	$185.00	$122.10
195-028	Hi-Matic E Electroflash Kit	220.00	145.20
195-208	Hi-Matic E Camera w/Case, Black	165.00	109.00
6195-110	Case Only for Hi-Matic E	15.00	10.00
6195-417	Lens Shade for Hi-Matic E	7.00	5.50
6198-110	Case Only for Hi-Matic, 7S	15.00	10.00
6151-417	Lens Shade for Hi-Matic 7S	7.00	5.00
168-106	Hi-Matic F Camera w/Case (FD:46mm)	125.00	82.50
168-116	Hi-Matic F Electroflash Kit	150.00	99.00
6168-110	Case Only for Hi-Matic F	12.00	8.00
110 POCKET CAMERAS			
252	Autopak 50 w/Electronically Timed Shutter, Strap	$65.00	$42.90
251	Autopak 70 w/Electrically Controlled Shutter, Close-up Capability	80.00	52.80
6521-210	Pouch Case for Autopak	7.00	5.00
16MM COMPACT CAMERA			
220-057	16 QT Electroflash Kit	$115.00	$75.90

CONSUMER GUIDE

PHOTOGRAPHIC EQUIPMENT

Code	Description	Price	Price
098-300	SR-T101 w/MC 58mm f/1.2 Lens	475.00	313.50
098-204	w/o Case, Black		
	SR-T101 w/MC 50mm f/1.7 Lens	385.00	254.10
098-604	SR-T101 w/MC 50mm f/1.4 Lens	430.00	283.80
098-304	w/Case, Black		
	SR-T101 w/MC 58mm f/1.2 Lens	503.00	332.00
050-500	SR-T101 Camera, Body Only	240.00	158.40
098-500	SR-T101 Camera, Body Only, Black	250.00	165.00
064-200	SR-T102 w/MC 50mm f/1.7 w/o Case	400.00	264.00
064-600	SR-T102 w/MC 50mm f/1.4 w/o Case	445.00	293.70
064-300	SR-T102 w/MC 58mm f/1.2 w/o Case	515.00	339.90
064-204	SR-T102 w/MC 50mm f/1.7 w/Case	425.00	280.50
064-604	SR-T102 w/MC 50mm f/1.4 w/Case	470.00	310.20
064-304	SR-T102 w/MC 58mm f/1.2 w/Case	543.00	358.40
065-201	SR-T102 w/MC 50mm f/1.7 Lens		
	w/o Case, Black	427.00	281.80
065-601	SR-T102 w/MC 50mm f/1.4 Lens		
	w/o Case, Black	472.00	311.50
065-301	SR-T102 w/MC 58mm f/1.2 Lens		
	w/o Case, Black	547.00	361.00
065-205	SR-T102 w/MC 50mm f/1.7 Lens	452.00	298.30
065-605	SR-T102 w/MC 50mm f/1.4 Lens		
	w/Case, Black	497.00	328.00
065-305	SR-T102 w/MC 58mm f/1.2 Lens		
	w/Case, Black	575.00	379.50
064-500	SR-T102 Camera, Body Only	290.00	191.40
065-500	SR-T102 Camera, Body Only, Black	312.00	205.90

No. 126 INSTANT LOAD STILL CAMERAS

Code	Description	Price	Price
412	Autopak 600X Camera	$70.00	$46.20
412-006	Autopak 600X Funpak Outfit	80.00	52.80
6410-210	Pouch Case for 400X	6.00	4.00
6402-210	Pouch Case for 600X	7.00	5.00

SUPER 8 MOVIE CAMERA

Code	Description	Price	Price
384-010	XL-400 (FD: 46mm)	$280.00	$184.80
393-010	XL-250 (FD: 46mm)	220.00	145.20
329	Autopak 8-D4 (FD: 52mm)	210.00	138.60
386	Autopak 8-D6 (FD: 52mm)	300.00	198.00

35MM SLIDE PROJECTORS

Code	Description	Price	Price
365-400	Autopak AFT Auto Focus w/Timer	$170.00	$113.00
365-300	Autopak AF Auto Focus Projector	130.00	86.00

MIRANDA

Black Finish:

Code	Description	Price	Price
10-220	Auto Sensorex EE w/f/1.4 Lens, Case	437.40	312.75
10-225	Auto Sensorex EE w/50mm f/1.4		
	"E" Lens	417.45	298.45
10-230	Auto Sensorex EE w/f/1.8 Lens, Case	392.50	280.65
10-235	Auto Sensorex EE w/50mm f/1.8		
	"E" Lens	372.55	266.35
10-240	Auto Sensorex EE w/o Lens	302.50	216.30
10-205	Sensorex II w/f/1.4 Auto Lens	392.50	280.65
10-206	Sensorex II w/f/1.4 Lens, Case	372.55	266.35
10-207	Sensorex II w/f/1.8 Auto Lens	352.50	252.05

Prices are accurate at time of printing; subject to manufacturer's change.

CONSUMER GUIDE

PHOTOGRAPHIC EQUIPMENT

		Retail	Discount
10-208	Sensorex II w/f/1.8 Lens	332.55	237.75
10-209	Sensorex II w/o Lens	262.50	187.70
SENSORET			
10-190	Sensoret w/Pouch	$129.95	$92.40
10-195	Sensoret w/Pouch, EF-1 Flash	149.95	106.70
CAMERA CASES			
10-510	Deluxe Leather Case for Sensorex	19.95	13.95
17-980	Miranda Camera Kit Case	34.50	24.15

NIKON

NIKON F CAMERAS
		Retail	Discount
1505	Black, Body Only	375.00	268.10
	Black, w/50mm f/2	499.50	357.15
	Black, w/50mm f/1.4	591.00	422.55
	Black, w/55mm f/1.2	672.50	480.85
Nikon with Motor Drive			
1565	Chrome w/F36 Motor & Battery Pack	897.00	641.35
1566	Black w/F36 Motor & Battery Pack	917.00	655.65
1567	Chrome w/F36 Motor & Cord Type Pack	819.00	585.60
1568	Black w/F36 Motor & Cord Type Pack	839.00	599.90
1569	Black w/F250 inc. 2 Cassettes	1,242.50	888.40
Nikkormat EL			
1826	Black, Body Only	478.00	341.75
	Black, w/50mm f/2	602.50	430.80
	Black, w/50mm f/1.4	694.00	496.20

NIKON MOVIE CAMERAS & ACCESSORIES
		Retail	Discount
3202	Nikon R-8 Super	$799.50	$571.65
3212	Extreme Close-Up Lens EC-1	54.00	38.60
3213	Slide Copying Adapter ES-1	32.50	23.25
3214	Microscope Adapter EM-1	32.50	23.25

OLYMPUS

OLYMPUS OM-1 SLR CAMERA (CHROME)
		Retail	Discount
16-0061	W/50mm f/1.8 Lens, Case	$464.95	$306.85
16-0175	W/50mm f/1.4 Lens, Case	524.95	346.45
16-0290	W/55mm f/1.2 Lens, Case	634.95	419.05
16-0407	Body Only	329.95	217.75

OLYMPUS OM-1 SLR (BLACK)
		Retail	Discount
16-0119	W/50mm f/1.8 Lens, Case	$489.95	323.35
16-0234	W/50mm f/1.4 Lens, Case	549.95	362.95
16-0359	W/55mm f/1.2 Lens, Case	659.95	435.55
16-0441	Body Only	354.95	234.25

OLYMPUS 35 EC2 CAMERA (CHROME) GIFT KIT
		Retail	Discount
18-4506	Complete Kit	$129.95	$92.90

OLYMPUS 35 ECR CAMERA (CHROME) GIFT KIT
		Retail	Discount
18-4403	Complete Kit	$144.95	$104.00

OLYMPUS 35 RC CAMERA (CHROME) GIFT KIT
		Retail	Discount
18-4300	Complete Kit	$159.95	$114.35

PHOTOGRAPHIC EQUIPMENT

Nikon Photomic FTN
	Black, w/55mm f/1.2	775.50	554.50

1553	Black, Body Only	494.00	353.20
	Black, w/50mm f/2	618.50	442.20
	Black, w/50mm f/1.4	710.00	507.65
	Black, w/55mm f/1.2	791.50	565.90

Nikon Photomic FTN with Motor Drive
1560	Chrome w/Cordless F36 Motor	1,016.00	726.45
1561	Black w/Cordless F36 Motor	1,036.00	740.75
1562	Chrome w/F36 Motor & Cord		
	Type Pack	938.00	670.65
1563	Black w/F36 Motor & Cord		
	Type Pack	958.00	684.95
1564	Black w/F250 inc. 2 Cassettes	1,361.50	973.45

Nikkormat FTN
1825	Black, Body Only	285.00	203.75
	Black, w/50mm f/2	409.50	292.80
	Black, w/50mm f/1.4	501.00	358.20
	Black, w/55mm f/1.2	582.50	416.50

Nikon F2
1605	Black, Body Only	490.00	350.35
	Black, w/50mm f/2	614.50	439.35
	Black, w/50mm f/1.4	706.00	504.80
	Black, w/55mm f/1.2	787.50	563.00

Nikon F2 Photomic
1653	Black, Body Only	619.50	442.95
	Black, w/50mm f/2	744.00	531.95
	Black, w/50mm f/1.4	835.50	597.40
	Black, w/55mm f/1.2	917.00	655.65

Prices are accurate at time of printing; subject to manufacturer's change.

PETRI

CAMERAS
	FT-EE w/f/1.8, Case, Chrome	$299.95	$200.95
	FT-EE w/f/1.4, Case, Black	314.95	207.85
	FT II w/f/1.8, Case	289.95	195.80
	FT II w/f/1.8, Case	249.95	166.10
	FT II w/f/1.8, Case, Black	259.95	169.40
	FT II w/f/1.4, Case, Black	299.95	202.40
	FT X w/f/1.8, Case, Chrome	229.95	151.75

POLAROID

POLAROID LAND CAMERAS
2000	Zip Land Camera	$13.95	$10.25
440	Polaroid Automatic 440 Land Camera	109.95	80.80
432	Polaroid Automatic 430 Land Camera	89.95	66.10
419	Polaroid Automatic 420 Land Camera	64.95	47.75
260	Square Shooter 2	24.95	21.00
008	The Colorpack	39.95	31.00
490	Focused Flash for 400 Series	10.95	7.50
070	Camera System	194.95	139.40
071	SX-70 Land Camera Model 2	149.95	107.20
1950	Professional Land Camera	199.95	145.20
622	The Minute Maker Kit	35.95	26.40

PHOTOGRAPHIC EQUIPMENT

RICOH

		Retail	Discount
110 POCKET CAMERA			
2300	Rocohmatic 110X Pocket Deluxe	109.95	$72.60
2301	Case for 110X	3.95	2.65
AUTO TLS EE CAMERAS			
2090	Auto TLS EE Black w/50mm f/1.4	$429.95	$283.80
2091	Auto TLS EE Black w/50mm f/1.7	389.95	257.40
2092	Case for TLS EE	21.50	14.20
TLS 401 35mm SLR CAMERA			
2045	Chrome w/f/2.0	$349.95	$231.00
SINGLEX 35mm SLR CAMERAS			
2041	W/f/1.4 w/Case, Black	$349.95	$231.00
2051	W/f/1.7 w/Case, Black	319.95	211.20
2040	W/f/1.4 w/Case, Chrome	329.95	217.80
2050	W/f/1.7 w/Case, Chrome	299.95	198.00
2055	W/f/2.0, Chrome	269.95	178.20
2060	W/f/2.8 w/Case, Chrome	224.95	148.50
2066	Body Only w/Case, Black	219.95	145.20
2067	Body Only w/Case, Chrome	199.95	132.00
35mm CAMERA			
2560	500G 35mm Range Finder f/2.8 w/Case	$114.95	$75.90
	800 EES Range Finder f/2.8, Case	159.95	105.55
MOVIE CAMERA			
2603	Super 8 Model 800Z	$329.95	$217.80
2604	Deluxe Carry Case for 800Z	24.00	15.85

		Retail	Discount
80050	Super DM, Body Only, w/CC Finder	406.50	325.20
80060	Super DM, Body Only, w/Penta-Prism	364.50	291.60
80105	IC-1 w/50mm f/2.0	319.50	255.60
80105	IC-1, Body Only	244.50	195.60
80400	Eveready Case for Super DM	22.50	18.40
80410	Case for Supreme I & II	32.50	26.40
80420	Case for IC-1 w/50mm	19.50	16.00

YASHICA

		Retail	Discount
35MM CAMERAS			
	Electro-35GTN w/Grip/Tripod	$195.00	$128.70
	Electro-35GSN Kit	295.00	194.70
	Electro-35GSN w/Case	165.00	96.55
	Electro-35C w/Case	165.00	96.55
	Electro-35FC w/40mm f/2.8 Lens, Chrome	160.00	118.00
SUPER 8 MOVIE CAMERAS			
	Super 40K w/Accessories	$175.00	$130.45
	Super 8 LD-6 w/Accessories	370.00	244.20
	Electro 8 Macro w/Accessories	240.00	175.65
	LD-8 w/Remote Control, Man. Zoom Lever, Batteries	430.00	283.80
	YXL-1.1 w/Accessories	125.00	82.50
SINGLE LENS REFLEX CAMERAS			
	Electro AX f/1.7	$460.00	$331.75
	Electro AX f/1.4	510.00	336.05
	Electro AX f/1.2	600.00	427.65
	TL-X Body Only, Chrome	250.00	178.50

PHOTOGRAPHIC EQUIPMENT

SAWYER'S

SLIDE PROJECTORS
6017	Rotomatic 747AQZ	$212.95
6012	Rotomatic 747AQ	179.95
6007	Rotomatic 737AQ	162.50
6004	Rotomatic 727AQ	147.50
6001	Rotomatic 717A	129.50
6248	570AF Grand Prix	127.95
6249	570R Grand Prix	99.95
6250	570M Grand Prix	69.95

Rotomatic 747AQZ $149.10
Rotomatic 747AQ 126.00
Rotomatic 737AQ 114.10
Rotomatic 727AQ 103.60
Rotomatic 717A 91.00
570AF Grand Prix 89.60
570R Grand Prix 70.00
570M Grand Prix 49.00

DUAL VOLTAGE SLIDE PROJECTOR
| 6241 | Rotomatic 700 AI, Same as 717A w/Auto Timer, Int'l. Dual Voltage | $139.50 | $97.65 |

TOPCON

TOPCON CAMERAS
80000	Supreme I: Super DM w/CC Finder, 50mm f/1.4 Lenshood, Auto Winder	$791.00	$632.80
80004	Supreme II: Super DM w/CC Finder, 50mm f/1.8 Lenshood, Auto Winder	687.00	549.60
80010	Super DM w/CC Finder, 50mm f/1.4, Lenshood	664.50	531.60
80020	Super DM w/Penta-Prism, 50mm f/1.8, Lenshood	518.50	414.80

TL-Electro X ITS w/f/1.2 Lens, Case, Black 470.00 310.20
TL-Electro X ITS w/f/1.4 Lens, Case, Black 390.00 257.40
TL-Electro X ITS w/f/1.7 Lens, Case, Black 350.00 231.00
TL-Electro X w/f/1.2 Lens, Case, Chrome 460.00 303.60
TL-Electro X w/f/1.4 Lens, Case, Chrome 380.00 250.80
TL-Electro X w/f/1.7 Lens, Case, Chrome 340.00 224.40
TL-Electro w/f/2.0 Lens, Case 260.00 160.90
TL-Electro w/f/1.9 Lens, Case 280.00 186.00

TWIN LENS REFLEX CAMERAS
	Mat 124G w/Case	$195.00	$128.70
	YD w/Case	120.00	86.00

ELECTRO ULTRAMINIATURE CAMERAS
	Atoron Kit	$115.00	$72.25
	Atoron Electro Kit	190.00	140.80
	Close-Up Lens Set	30.00	21.00
	Filter Set (Y2, 80B, ND×4)	16.50	10.50
	Enl. Lens 21mm f/3.5	75.00	51.55
	Atoron Electro T Kit	215.00	157.80

INSTANT LOADING STILL CAMERA
	Palmatic-20, 110 Size Cartridge Loading	$28.00	$19.60
	Electro-100 w/MS-110 Elec. Flash Unit	95.00	71.15
	Electro-100 Kit w/Extender	75.00	49.50

Prices are accurate at time of printing; subject to manufacturer's change.

CONSUMER GUIDE

INDEX

A

AIR CONDITIONERS	318-321
Best Buys	322-324
American Motors	26-31
Appliances (See item, e.g. Dishwashers, Freezers, etc.)	
AUTOMOBILES	10-20
Best Buys	21-23
How to Buy	24-25
Prices & Accessories	26-107
American Motors	26-31
Gremlin	26-27
Hornet	26-29
Matador	26,29-31
Buick	30-37
Apollo	31-32
Century	30-35
Electra	30,34-37
Estate Wagon	30,34-37
Le Sabre	30,34-37
Regal	30,32-35
Riviera	30,34-37
Skyhawk	31-33
Cadillac	37-39
Chevrolet	39-53
Bel Air	39-41
Bel Air Wagon	40-42
Blazer	50-53
Camaro	42-43
Caprice Classic	39-41
Caprice Estate Wagon	40-42
Chevelle Malibu	42-45
Chevelle Malibu Wagon	44-46
Corvette	46-47
Impala	39-41
Impala Wagon	40-42
Monte Carlo	46-47
Monza	49-50
Nova	47-49
Vega	50-51
Chrysler	52-57
Cordoba	54-56
Imperial Le Baron	56-57
Newport	52-55
New Yorker	52-55
Town & Country	52-55
Dodge	56-65
Charger	62-63
Coronet	58-62
Crestwood	59-62
Dart	63-65
Monaco	56-59
Ford	66-77
Elite	73-75
Granada	70-71
LTD	66-68
Maverick	68-69
Mustang II	68-70
Pinto	71-73
Thunderbird	72-73
Torino	74-76
Lincoln	76-78
Continental	76-77
Mark IV	76-78
Mercury	78-85
Comet	80-81
Cougar	82-83
Montego	82-85
Marquis	78-80
Monarch	80-82
Oldsmobile	84-89
Custom Cruiser	87-89
Cutlass	84-89
Delta 88	87-89
Ninety-Eight	88-89
Omega	84-87
Starfire	84-87
Toronado	88-89
Vista Cruiser	84-87
Plymouth	89-97
Custom	92-95
Duster	95-97
Fury	89-93
Gran Fury	92-95
Road Runner	90-93
Scamp	95-97
Suburban	89-93
Valiant	95-97
Pontiac	98-107
Astre	104-106
Bonneville	98-100
Catalina	98-100
Firebird	100-101
Grand Ville	98-100
Grand Am	102-105
Grand Prix	100-103
Le Mans	102-105

382   CONSUMER GUIDE

INDEX

Safari	98-100
Ventura	106-107

B

Blenders	220-222
Broilers	222-223
Buick	30-37

C

Cadillac	37-39
CALCULATORS	**340-342**
Best Buys	343
Can Openers	223-224
Cassette Tape Recorders	122
Cartridge Cameras	348-349
Cartridges—Stereo	111-112
Cartridge Tape Recorders	122-123
Catalytic Converters	11-12
Chevrolet	39-53
Chrysler	52-57
Coffeemakers	224-225
Compact Audio Systems	113-114
Compact Cars	14-15
Compact Cars, Sporty	15
Corn Poppers	225
Crock Pots	229-230
Curler/Stylers	199-200

D

Darkroom Equipment	350-351
Detanglers	200
DISHWASHERS	**286-291**
Best Buys	292-293
Prices	294-295
Frigidaire	294
General Electric	294-295
KitchenAid	294-295
Maytag	294
Waste King	294-295
Whirlpool	295
DISPOSERS	**344**
Best Buys	345
Dodge	56-65
Dryers, Clothes (See Washers & Dryers)	

E

Electric Appliances (See item, e.g. Can Openers, Corn Poppers)
Electronic Flash Units	352

F

FLOOR CARE APPLIANCES	**255-258**
Best Buys	259-263
Prices	264-267
Bissell	264
Eureka	264-265
Hoover	264-265
Premier	265-266
Regina	266-267
Shop-Vac	266
Sunbeam	266-267
Floor Polishers	258
FOOD PREPARATION APPLIANCES	**218-232**
Best Buys	233-239
Prices	240-254
Black Angus	240-241
Dazey	240-241
Dominion	240-242
Farberware	242-243
General Electric	242-244
Grandinetti	244-245
Hamilton Beach	244-245
Hoover/Nesco	244-245
KitchenAid	245
National Presto	246
Norelco	247
Oster	246-247
Panasonic	246-248
Proctor-Silex	248-249
Rival	248-249
Ronson	249-250
Salton	250-251
Sunbeam	250-252
Toastmaster	252-253
Waring	253-254
West Bend	254
Ford	66-67
Four Channel Sound	123-124
FREEZERS	**310-313**
Best Buys	314-315
Prices	316-317
Admiral	316
Amana	316-317
Frigidaire	316-317
General Electric	316
Hotpoint	316
Westinghouse	317
Whirlpool	317
Frypans	226-227

G

Griddles	227-228

H

Hair Curler/Stylers	199-200
Hair Dryers, Bonnet	198-199
Hair Dryers, Hand-Held	197-198
Hair Dryers, Hard-Top	198-199
Hair Dryers, Pistol-Grip	196-197
Hair Setters, Roller	199
Headphones	114-115
HI-FI COMPONENTS	**108-115**
Best Buys	116-119
Prices (includes Tape Recorders)	
Acoustic Research	130
ADC	130
Advent	131
Akai	130-131
Altec	131-132
Bang & Olufsen	132-133

INDEX

Benjamin Elac/Miracord	133
Bose	133
Bozak	132
BSR	132-133
Dokorder	133
Dynaco	133-135
Empire	134-135
Fisher	135-136
Garrard	136-137
Harman-Kardon	136-137
Infinity Systems	136
Janszen	136-137
JBL	137-138
Jensen	138
JVC	138-139
Kenwood	139-141
KLH	140-141
Koss	141
Marantz	142-143
Panasonic	142-143
Panasonic/Technics	144-145
Phase Linear	145
Philips	144-145
Pickering	144
Pioneer	144-147
Rectilinear	147
Revox	146-147
Sansui	147-149
Scott	148-149
Sherwood	148-149
Shure	149-151
Sony	150-152
Sony/Superscope	152-153
Soundcraftsmen	152-153
Stanton	153-154
Superscope	154-155
Tandberg	154-155
Teac	154-156
Thorens	156
United Audio	156-157
Wollensak	156-157
Yamaha	156-157
Hot Lather Dispensers	202

I

Intermediate Cars	16
Irons	203

K

Knives, Electric	226

L

Lincoln	76-78
Luxury Cars	18-19

M

Makeup Mirrors, Lighted	200
Massagers	202
Mercury	78-85
MICROWAVE OVENS	333
Best Buys	336
Mini-Compact Cars	13
Mixers	228-229
Movie Equipment	349-350

O

Oldsmobile	84-89
Open-Reel Tape Machines	121

P

PERSONAL CARE APPLIANCES	195-216
Best Buys	204-207
Prices	208-216
Dazey	208
Dominion	209-210
General Electric	209-210
Grandinetti	209-210
Hamilton Beach	210
Hoover	210-211
Norelco	210-211
Northern	210-211
Oster	211-213
Panasonic	213
Proctor Silex	212-213
Remington	212-213
Ronson	213-214
Schick	214-215
Sunbeam	214-216
Toastmaster	216
Personal Luxury Cars	18
PHOTOGRAPHIC EQUIPMENT	346-353
Best Buys	354-361
Prices	362-381
Airequipt	362
Alpa	362-363
Argus	362-363
Bauer	363
Bell & Howell	364-365
Bolex	364-365
Braun/Nizo	365
Canon	366-367
Cinema Beaulieu	366-367
Eumig	367-368
Fuji	368-369
GAF	369-371
Honeywell	370-371
Kodak	370-374
Konica	375
Leica	374
Mamiya	375
Mamiya/Sekor	375-376
Minolta	376-377
Miranda	377-378
Nikon	378-379
Olympus	378
Petri	379
Polaroid	379
Ricoh	380
Sawyer's	281
Topcon	380-381
Yashica	380-381
Plymouth	89-97

384 CONSUMER GUIDE

INDEX

Polaroid	349
Pontiac	98-107

R

RADIOS	180-184
Best Buys	185-187
Prices	188-194
Admiral	188
General Electric	188-189
JVC	189
Panasonic	190-191
RCA	190-191
Sanyo	191-192
Sony	192-193
Zenith	192-194
RANGES	325-330
Best Buys	331-322
Receivers—Stereo	112-113
REFRIGERATORS	296-302
Best Buys	303-305
Prices	306-309
Admiral	306
Amana	306-307
Frigidaire	306-307
General Electric	306-307
Hoover	307
Hotpoint	307-308
Tappan	308-309
Westinghouse	308-309
Whirlpool	308-309
Rug Shampooers	258

S

Saunas, Facial	201
Shavers, Ladies'	201
Shavers, Men's	201
Single-Lens Reflex Cameras	347-348
Slide Projectors	352-353
Slow Cookers	229-230
Speakers—Stereo	113
Specialty Appliances	230-231
Sport Cars, High-Priced	20
Sport Cars, Low-Priced	19-20
Standard Cars	16-18
Stereo Components (See Hi-Fi Components & Tape Recorders)	
Subcompact Cars	14

T

TAPE RECORDERS	120-126
Best Buys	127-129
Prices (See Hi-Fi Components)	
TELEVISIONS	158-164
Best Buys	165-167
Prices	168-178
Admiral	168-169
General Electric	168-170
JVC	170
Magnavox	170-171
Motorola Quasar	171-172
Panasonic	172-173
Philco-Ford	172-173
RCA	173-175
Sanyo	174-175
Sony	174-175
Sylvania	175-176
Zenith	176-178
Toaster Ovens	231
Toasters	231-232
Toothbrushes, Automatic	202
TRASH COMPACTORS	217
Turntables—Stereo	110-111

W

Waffle Bakers	232
WASHERS & DRYERS	268-276
Best Buys	277-279
Prices	280-285
Frigidaire	280-281
General Electric	280-281
Hoover	280
Hotpoint	280-281
Maytag	281-283
Panasonic	283
Speed Queen	282-283
Westinghouse	283-284
Whirlpool	284-285
Water Pulsating Devices	202